Techniques for Fostering Collaboration in Online Learning Communities:

Theoretical and Practical Perspectives

Francesca Pozzi
Institute for Educational Technology – National Research Council (CNR), Italy

Donatella Persico
Institute for Educational Technology – National Research Council (CNR), Italy

Information Science REFERENCE

INFORMATION SCIENCE REFERENCE

Hershey · New York

Director of Editorial Content:	Kristin Klinger
Director of Book Publications:	Julia Mosemann
Acquisitions Editor:	Lindsay Johnston
Development Editor:	Dave DeRicco
Publishing Assistant:	Casey Conapitski
Typesetter:	Casey Conapitski
Production Editor:	Jamie Snavely
Cover Design:	Lisa Tosheff

Published in the United States of America by
Information Science Reference (an imprint of IGI Global)
701 E. Chocolate Avenue
Hershey PA 17033
Tel: 717-533-8845
Fax: 717-533-8661
E-mail: cust@igi-global.com
Web site: http://www.igi-global.com

Library of Congress Cataloging-in-Publication Data

Techniques for fostering collaboration in online learning communities : theoretical and practical perspectives / Francesca Pozzi and Donatella Persico, editors.
p. cm.
Includes bibliographical references and index.
Summary: "This book provides a focused assessment of the peculiarities of online collaborative learning processes by looking at the strategies, methods, and techniques used to support and enhance debate and exchange among peers"--Provided by publisher.
ISBN 978-1-61692-898-8 (hardcover) -- ISBN 978-1-61692-900-8 (e-book) 1. Internet in education. 2. Web-based instruction. 3. Interactive multimedia. 4. Distance education--Computer-assisted instruction. 5. Professional learning communities. 6. Instructional systems--Design. I. Pozzi, Francesca, 1972- II. Persico, Donatella, 1957-
LB1044.87.T43 2010
371.33'44678--dc22

British Cataloguing in Publication Data
A Cataloguing in Publication record for this book is available from the British Library.

Editorial Advisory Board

List of Reviewers

Georgia Lazakidou, *University of Piraeus, Greece*
Sharman Lichtenstein, *Deakin University, Australia*
Beatrice Ligorio, *University of Bari, Italy*
Lisa Lobry DeBruyn, *University of New England, Australia*
Ronald Lombard, *Chatham University, Pittsburgh, USA*
Feldia F. Loperfido, *University of Bari, Italy*
Stefania Manca, *Institute for Educational Technology – CNR, Italy*
Davide Parmigiani, *University of Genova, Italy*
Simeon Retalis, *University of Piraeus, Greece*
Miky Ronen, *Holon Institute of Technology, Israel*
Derek Rowntree, *The Open University, UK (recently retired)*
Luigi Sarti, *Institute for Educational Technology – CNR, Italy*
Paola F. Spadaro, *University of Bari, Italy*
Angela Sugliano, *University of Genova, Italy*
Manuel Delfino, *Institute for Educational Technology – CNR, Italy*
Guglielmo Trentin, *Institute for Educational Technology – CNR, Italy*
Michele Oh, *Institute for Educational Technology – CNR, Italy*

Table of Contents

Detailed Table of Contents

This chapter advocates the idea that the structuring techniques generally used to support students in online collaborative activities can be described in terms of three main dimensions, that we call the "three Ts": Task, Teams and Time. The chapter presents an explorative study, aiming to investigate the differences between the behavior of three groups of students performing activities based on three techniques which differ as to the levels of structuredness of Task, Teams and Time. While the first group was not given instructions on how to structure the work, the second group was given some hints about the need to use some kind of structure and the third group had precise instructions as to how to proceed along the Task, Teams and Time dimensions. The chapter presents the authors' reflections about the effects of these techniques based on qualitative analysis of students' reactions to the way the three activities were structured.

Collaborative learning is used as a key principle in several approaches for designing virtual learning environments. This is due to the fact that collaboration seems to foster individual knowledge acquisition, improve knowledge application, and increase social competencies. But collaborative learning is not always successful. Virtual learning places great and varied demands on collaboration, which means that learners often do not know how to collaborate adequately. In such cases, it is necessary to provide support. This chapter focuses specifically on two structuring methods, namely collaboration scripts and content schemes. To gain further insight into the topic, we will first describe the technical aspects of virtual collaborative learning. In the second section, we will depict the learning processes and outcomes of collaboration. Thirdly, we will discuss the theory and research on the structuring methods. The chapter ends with conclusions and practical implications.

This chapter focuses on the facilitation of collaborative problem solving by the method of content schemes. Content schemes are content-specific pre-structures of learners' collaboration facilities that apply representational effects for the purpose of facilitation. They support learners to focus on particular issues of a problem solving process. The chapter presents results from two studies in the context of collaborative problem solving using videoconferencing. The first study compared learning facilitated by a content scheme and learning without facilitation; the second study compared the content scheme facilitation with facilitation by an enhanced version of this content scheme. This enhanced version focused learners on providing evidence for their claims. Results show that while the content scheme itself had a big influence on learning outcomes, the enhanced version had a rather small impact compared to the regular version. This result raises the issue about the complexity of facilitation methods. Complex facilitation may be too sophisticated for providing benefits to learning processes.

The aim of this study is to examine means of fostering videoconference-based collaborative learning, by focussing on three issues: (1) to induce collaborative learners to write a co-construct, applying (in addition to their shared knowledge) their unshared knowledge, which tends to be neglected, according to the social-psychological research paradigm of information pooling; (2) to activate these learners in their dialogues to exchange unshared knowledge possessed by one learning partner, so that it becomes shared knowledge possessed by both partners (knowledge transfer); (3) to try out, as an instructional support measure, scripted, content-specific visualisation, combining a content scheme with an interaction script. An experiment was conducted with 30 learning dyads, divided into three conditions of videoconference-based learning with application sharing: without instructional support, with content-specific visualisation, and with scripted content-specific visualisation. As expected, the scripted content-specific visualisation led to a higher transfer of previously unshared knowledge to shared knowledge. But, contrary to expectation, the scripted content-specific visualisation did not induce the learning partners to apply more unshared knowledge in writing their co-construct. Instead, in all three experimental conditions, learners brought significantly more shared knowledge into the co-construct than would have been expected from the distribution of shared and unshared knowledge measured before collaboration.

We claim that the potentialities of the socio-constructivist framework can be fully exploited when a blended approach is introduced. Our blended model does not only mix offline and online contexts but it also combines several pedagogical theories and techniques (Progressive Inquiry Model, Jigsaw, Reciprocal Teaching, Collaborative Communities, and Dialogical Knowledge). The particular mix we propose generates a specific pedagogy through which a set of blended activities is designed. Some analyses conducted on blended courses for higher education and professional development where blended activities were tested are briefly discussed. These analyses concern: (a) the students' participation in blended context, (b) their expectations about the blended course and their perception about the processes of collaborative knowledge building, (c) the impact on students of role-taking, which is one of the blended activities included into the blended course. Results show that our blended approach has an impact on how students interact and talk in groups. At the end of the course, students display a collaborative discourse strategy mainly based on: (a) completing each other's sentence, (b) complex trajectories of participation, (c) changes of the perception of the self and of the group and (d) the effects of role-playing.

Entering a learning system based on CSCL models may be a challenging experience. Beginner users are required to accomplish several tasks for the first time, such as learning to communicate by written discourse in an asynchronous manner, as well as becoming familiar with communication technologies and with the learning system. In order to support their initial steps several measures, which focus mainly on socialization with peers and instructors/tutors and familiarization with the learning system, may be adopted. The focus of this chapter is to present a model and some related strategies to support students' initial socialization and familiarization in web-based learning environments. Such strategies have been developed and implemented by the authors over several years of experience as designers and instructors in graduate and post-graduate courses in Italy.

Most units of learning are being offered flexibly, either using distance education or online facilities, and often with asynchronous computer-mediated communication or online discussions. The use of asynchronous computer-mediated communication is believed to offer students the opportunity to communicate independently of time and place, and to ask questions, state opinions and offer advice when transferring interactive learning activities to an online environment. This chapter uses an action research framework to examine the quantity and nature of student engagement in a problem-based learning activity as a consequence of placing face-to-face instruction on and practice in problem-based learning prior to using asynchronous computer-mediated communication. The effectiveness of early placement of a 4-day residential component to improve student collaboration in the online problem-based learning activity was tested against six years (2001-2006) of electronically-archived online discussions in a 13-week, under- or post-graduate tertiary-level natural science unit.

This chapter provides a retrospective review of the utility and effectiveness of case study analyses to engage and support students in online collaborative learning within teacher education coursework. Specifically, the interrelationship among factors related to the instructor, the student, the tasks, and the on-line learning environments are examined resulting in suggestions for designing, implementing, and researching case study learning activities that foster and enhance collaboration in online teacher education course work.

This chapter offers an in-depth narrative of how one instructor in an online environment used the four lenses of critical reflection introduced by Brookfield (1995) – (1) self, (2) student reactions, (3) colleagues' perceptions, and (4) instructional theory – to adapt the use of Web 2.0 tools that have been found to be effective in promoting collaboration and constructivist learning. These tools can provide educators with the opportunity to examine collaboration and learning from multiple perspectives, while also serving as a way to rethink preconceived notions of how power is distributed in the classroom (Brookfield, 1995). In this chapter we share how the four lenses were used to design web 2.0 activities based on the specific grouping techniques, with the aim to construct a rich online experience.

This is a review of an action research project dealing with the impact of a role playing activity in an online course. Two instructors of an online graduate course collected observable data based on response and participation levels of students in an online discussion setting. Subsequently, utilizing the same discussion topic, the instructors combined for a course delivery team teaching and role playing approach to the discussion. In the second course the instructors assumed the roles of John Dewey, Mao Tse-Tung, and Aristotle and exchanged responses and comments with each other and with students. A comparison of the levels of responses between the two approaches utilizing the same rubric allowed to measure the impact of role play and team teaching. A review of research related to team teaching and role playing as approaches to enhance discussions provides background to decision to utilize these two approaches to enhance the discussion process.

This chapter addresses several issues and challenges that one faces when carrying out a real collaborative learning experience following a blended learning design that includes a mixture of face-to-face and online collaborative learning processes. The paper presents an experience based on a blended course on "Collaborative Educational Systems". This scenario employed a variety of collaborative strategies, methods and tools to support and enhance debate and information exchange among peers in order to complete a specific task: writing an essay collaboratively. Carrying out this task entails a preliminary study and analysis of the subject matter, which are also performed in a collaborative manner. We describe the educational scenario in detail, including the structure of the activities, the rules the groups were asked to apply and the procedures the students had to follow to accomplish the task. We finally analyze and evaluate this learning experience with a critical point of view as regards the collaboration strategies adopted, the way students built their own strategies combining the ones presented in the course, and the collaborative learning process and product.

Designing effective CSCL processes is a complex task that can be supported by existing good practices formulated as pedagogical patterns. From a cultural historical activity theory (CHAT) perspective previous research has shown that patterns served as Mediating Artefacts (MA) helping practitioners to make informed decisions and choices, being much closer to the practitioners' mindsets than complex learning design models, such as IMS-LD. However, a new challenge arises when the starting design element corresponds to Open Educational Resources (OER), i.e. free resources of high quality that are typically employed for individual learning. Recent research reported in this chapter has aimed to ana-

Preface

"Last Sunday I took my child to a soccer tournament. He is 7 years old and this was his first 'real match'. I was on the terrace and was so excited to see him over there, standing in his green football strip, listening to his coach's last advice with such an impressive seriousness. A number of parents sat on the steps with me, they all watched their children with similar feelings. A few minutes after the start of the match – I noticed he and his team mates were playing rather "spontaneously": it was clear that they hadn't been taught any schemes yet, or rules, so they ran randomly up and down the field, without any coordination. It was funny for us to see such a cheerful confusion, and of course, in the end, they lost the match. The following match was between two different teams and, at first, I was watching them without great care; but – slowly - my attention was drawn by one of the teams playing: the players were lined up on the field like soldiers, their first movements scanned by precise schemes and perfectly coordinated. Still, as the opposing team started coming forward and the match lit up, they seemed unable to invent on the fly schemes to follow the game, as if they couldn't play outside the schemes they had been taught. In the end the team lost the match as well."

The above quote is Francesca Pozzi's account of her own personal experience. The editors of this book regard this anecdote as a good metaphor of the problems and questions the book addresses, applied to the field of online collaborative learning. These include the following: how can we can support a collaborative process, scaffolding it without constraining it? How can we balance rules and procedures with spontaneity and creativity? Many of us have experienced collaboration failures. Sometimes collaboration fails because people who are supposed to work together, hardly start to communicate with each other; sometimes because, even if group members are required to discuss and do so by zealously following given sets of rules, they do not really share or negotiate their ideas, but simply level their positions. The point is that collaboration isn't easy to trigger, neither is it always successful.

However, collaboration is widely recognized as a catalyst of learning and creativity and – as such – collaborative learning approaches have become more and more popular and are regarded as desirable in those contexts where it is possible to set up the basic conditions for its delivery: they are adopted and promoted by academic institutions, companies, teacher training colleges, professional associations and schools, with the aim of making learning more meaningful, deep, and effective in the long run.

Besides, the widespread use of computers and the Internet at home, in the workplace and at school, and their ability to support communication and information sharing, has encouraged the adoption of collaborative learning approaches even at a distance. Since the 90s, the research field of Computer Supported Collaborative Learning (CSCL) has been attracting increasing attention focusing on how technology can enhance collaborative learning by supporting not only interaction among peers and groups, but also knowledge sharing among the members of a community.

This book focuses on those CSCL contexts where school or university students work online, usually through a CMC (Computer Mediated Communication) platform, and are subdivided into groups; each group is engaged in tasks (discussing a topic, solving a problem, studying a case, etc.) with concrete outputs to produce, which act as catalysts of interaction, collaboration and – in the end – of both individual and group knowledge building. In these contexts, the process is intrinsically learner-centered, as the teacher (or tutor, as the person in charge of the overall process is usually referred to) acts as mediator and learning facilitator. For several years the role of the tutor in CSCL processes has been thoroughly investigated: the tutors responsibilities, the methods to cope with large and diverse communities, the dos and don'ts of their way of dealing with possible problems, such as flaming, lack of participation, lack of convergence, etc. Even the tutoring styles have been put under the lenses of the CSCL researchers. Of course, it stands to reason that the tutor approach should be tailored to the learners' community, its features, background, previous experience and thereof ability to self-regulate. However, one firm point coming out from both practice and research, is that tutoring a learning community is a time-consuming and labour intensive, yet crucial task.

It is for this reason that, after the first phase of exploration of the tutor's role, a wealth of energy has been put into trying to devise methodological approaches and technological tools capable of easing and, whenever possible, guiding the tutor's work. Without this type of results, however large the acceptance of the theoretical principles may be, the culture of CSCL cannot become mature and best practice in this field cannot become as widespread as desired.

With these objectives in mind, several studies focused on how to support collaboration by providing a structure to scaffold group interactions, often starting from methods, tools and results consolidated in face-to-face settings. However, it soon became clear that even the question "how can I choose the right structure for a particular CSCL context" is probably not the right question. As a matter of fact, although it is largely acknowledged that the collaborative process needs to be supported, there is no clear idea among practitioners, nor consensus among researchers, on the extent to which it is advisable to support and "structure" collaboration.

This book addresses the issue of how to support collaboration in online learning communities by using techniques for structuring the learning activities, including the problem of whether, and to what extent these scaffolding methods are useful. The aim is to move one step forward in the direction of identifying criteria to choose the right approach, in the assumption and awareness that there is no such thing as the "one size fits all" solution, but rather a range of possible approaches among which it is important that instructional designers and tutors are able to choose. With this aim in mind, the book draws together, for the first time to our knowledge, the results of scattered research, concerning the most common techniques that can be used to structure collaboration in these contexts. The research efforts made so far in this field are large but quite diversified and in many cases their different standpoints make them hardly comparable or synergic. Even the research methods in this field are usually rather diversified, ranging from case studies to experimental work, from investigation of the effectiveness of one technique in specific contexts, to studies aiming to present and validate new methods and tools. This diversity is also testified by the terminological labyrinth that must be confronted before trying to make sense of the large number of chapters in this area.

In the following, therefore, we will try to disentangle the variety of standpoints adopted and terms used, not only in this volume, but in general, within the CSCL research field.

One of the issues mostly debated among researchers pertains the kind of delivery approaches for collaborative activities: many advocate the use of "blended approaches" (careful orchestration of face-to-face and online activities), as opposed to "purely online approaches"; yet others focus on the technology used to support interactions among learners: here the choice is between textual communication, video-conferencing systems, and software – emerged more recently – based on the use of 3D graphics environments.

At a finer level of detail, CSCL researchers and designers also discuss the nature of the activities they propose to students: in order to foster collaboration and exchange among peers, it is quite common in CSCL contexts to choose among collaborative techniques or strategies, usually borrowed (and adapted) by face-to-face contexts, such as for example the Discussion, the Peer Review, the Role Play, the Jigsaw or the Case Study. The report of experiences based on one or more of these techniques and the discussion of the observed results, is rather common in CSCL literature.

Moreover, in an effort to share practice and experience, not only among designers and researchers, but also with tutors/teachers, collaborative strategies and techniques are frequently described through more or less formalized languages. In particular, in the last few years the terms "Design Patterns (DP)", "Collaborative Learning Flow Patterns (CLFP)" or "Pedagogical Patterns" – have been increasingly used by a number of researchers, to identify the description in natural language of collaborative techniques and strategies, proposed as reusable solutions of "recurrent problems". Similarly, the so-called "Teaching Routines" are problem-oriented descriptions of collaborative techniques, where the focus is much more the role of the teacher while orchestrating the activities, rather than the tasks students have to perform. Here it is useful to stress the fact that the "communication objects" cited so far (i.e. DPs, CLFPs, Pedagogical Patterns, Teaching Routines, etc.), are all intended to allow communication among researchers, designers and tutors, while they are not – at least in principle - meant to communicate the activities to students.

Conversely, what is actually given to students to guide them through the collaborative activities, is called "script". There are two types of scripts: "macro-scripts" and "(micro)-scripts". The former are instructions, usually expressed verbally, containing the specification of the task to be performed, the time schedule of the activity, the team composition and the mode of interaction to be followed by students. The latter, the so called "(micro) scripts", are very specific instructions given to students (usually automatically, by the computer) to prompt them at various steps of the task. This is quite an important thread of research and it is often intertwined with the development of adaptive systems aimed at supporting collaboration.

Finally, a recent direction undertaken by some groups of researchers looks into what they call "content schemes" as tools to further scaffold collaboration among students. The content schemes are schematic representations of a framework for the expected output of students work (a table to fill in, or a document structure for the students to follow, etc).

The brief overview of the terms provided above, is synthesized in Figure 1. Most of the terms it contains are dealt with in one or more chapters of this book. The Figure is provided, so that the readers can better orient themselves among the topics of the various chapters.

Bearing in mind this rough map of the terms used in this book, we can take a closer look at the contents of the chapters.

The first four chapters (1 to 4) can be ideally gathered in a unique set, as they all propose reflections on the impact different types of structure have on the learning process.

Figure 1.

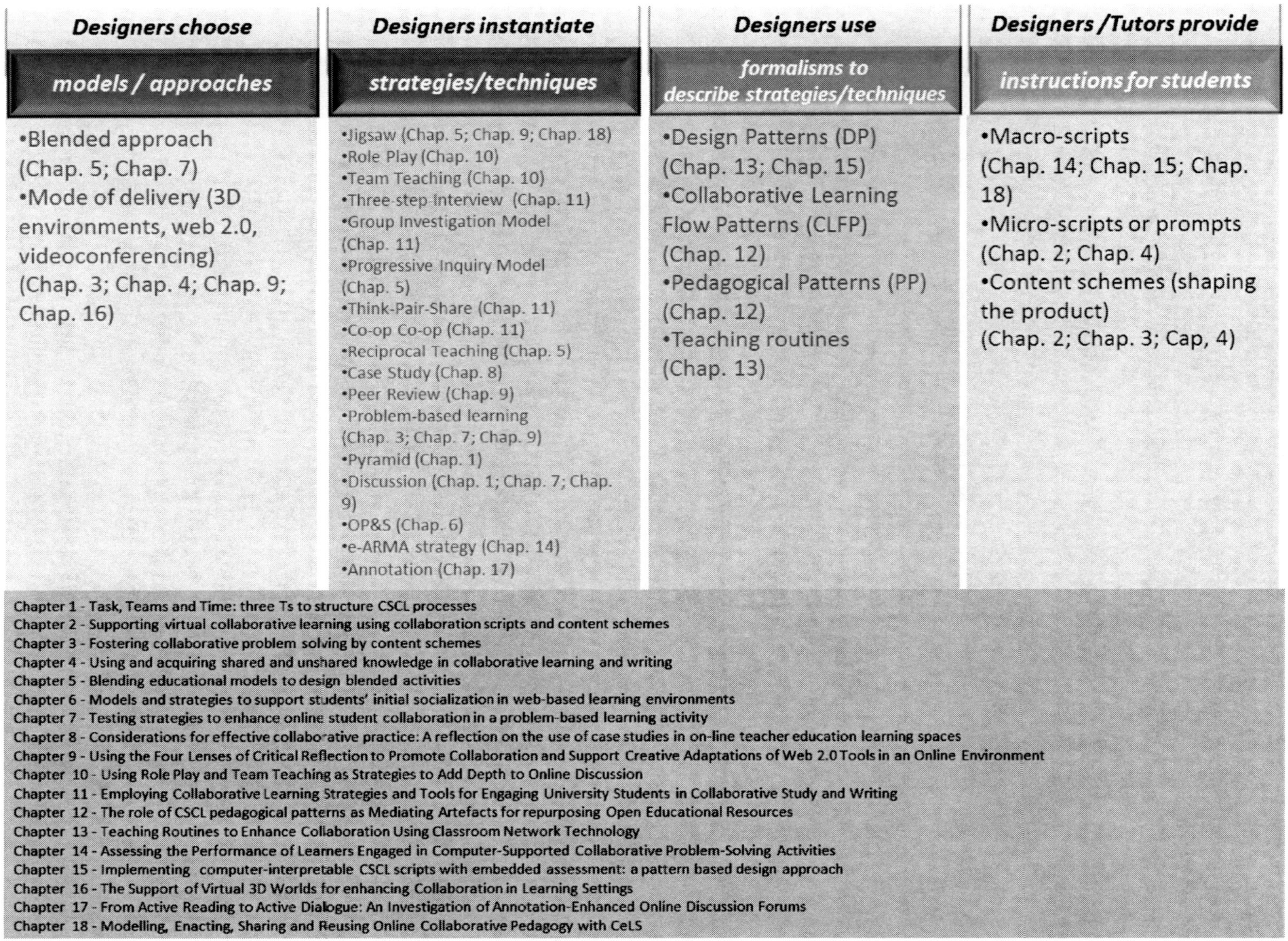
Designers choose
models / approaches
•Blended approach
(Chap. 5; Chap. 7)
•Mode of delivery (3D environments, web 2.0, videoconferencing)
(Chap. 3; Chap. 4; Chap. 9; Chap. 16)
Designers instantiate
strategies/techniques
•Jigsaw (Chap. 5; Chap. 9; Chap. 18)
•Role Play (Chap. 10)
•Team Teaching (Chap. 10)
•Three-step Interview (Chap. 11)
•Group Investigation Model (Chap. 11)
•Progressive Inquiry Model (Chap. 5)
•Think-Pair-Share (Chap. 11)
•Co-op Co-op (Chap. 11)
•Reciprocal Teaching (Chap. 5)
•Case Study (Chap. 8)
•Peer Review (Chap. 9)
•Problem-based learning (Chap. 3; Chap. 7; Chap. 9)
•Pyramid (Chap. 1)
•Discussion (Chap. 1; Chap. 7; Chap. 9)
•OP&S (Chap. 6)
•e-ARMA strategy (Chap. 14)
•Annotation (Chap. 17)
Designers use
formalisms to describe strategies/techniques
•Design Patterns (DP)
(Chap. 13; Chap. 15)
•Collaborative Learning Flow Patterns (CLFP)
(Chap. 12)
•Pedagogical Patterns (PP)
(Chap. 12)
•Teaching routines
(Chap. 13)
Designers /Tutors provide
instructions for students
•Macro-scripts
(Chap. 14; Chap. 15; Chap. 18)
•Micro-scripts or prompts
(Chap. 2; Chap. 4)
•Content schemes (shaping the product)
(Chap. 2; Chap. 3; Cap, 4)
Chapter 1 - Task, Teams and Time: three Ts to structure CSCL processes
Chapter 2 - Supporting virtual collaborative learning using collaboration scripts and content schemes
Chapter 3 - Fostering collaborative problem solving by content schemes
Chapter 4 - Using and acquiring shared and unshared knowledge in collaborative learning and writing
Chapter 5 - Blending educational models to design blended activities
Chapter 6 - Models and strategies to support students' initial socialization in web-based learning environments
Chapter 7 - Testing strategies to enhance online student collaboration in a problem-based learning activity
Chapter 8 - Considerations for effective collaborative practice: A reflection on the use of case studies in on-line teacher education learning spaces
Chapter 9 - Using the Four Lenses of Critical Reflection to Promote Collaboration and Support Creative Adaptations of Web 2.0 Tools in an Online Environment
Chapter 10 - Using Role Play and Team Teaching as Strategies to Add Depth to Online Discussion
Chapter 11 - Employing Collaborative Learning Strategies and Tools for Engaging University Students in Collaborative Study and Writing
Chapter 12 - The role of CSCL pedagogical patterns as Mediating Artefacts for repurposing Open Educational Resources
Chapter 13 - Teaching Routines to Enhance Collaboration Using Classroom Network Technology
Chapter 14 - Assessing the Performance of Learners Engaged in Computer-Supported Collaborative Problem-Solving Activities
Chapter 15 - Implementing computer-interpretable CSCL scripts with embedded assessment: a pattern based design approach
Chapter 16 - The Support of Virtual 3D Worlds for enhancing Collaboration in Learning Settings
Chapter 17 - From Active Reading to Active Dialogue: An Investigation of Annotation-Enhanced Online Discussion Forums
Chapter 18 - Modelling, Enacting, Sharing and Reusing Online Collaborative Pedagogy with CeLS

In particular, Pozzi and Persico (Chapter 1) claim that a structuring technique is not a mono-dimensional entity, but it is articulated into three main dimensions: Task, Teams and Time. Each technique tends to structure more heavily one of these dimensions, most often Task or Teams, rather rarely Time, but since these dimensions are not totally independent, the structure of the leading dimension often influences decisions on the other two. Of course, structuring techniques can be combined to better support the learning process on all three dimensions. The authors then report on the outcomes of an exploratory study where three groups of students carry out the same activity with support provided by different combinations of techniques along the three different dimensions.

Kopp and Mandl (Chapter 2) do not focus so much on how to structure strategies and techniques, as on how to structure instructions to be provided to students; in particular they discuss the use of collaboration scripts and content schemes as tools to scaffold collaboration. The chapter surveys a number of studies concerning the use of these tools and their effects on learning processes and learning outcomes, with the aim of providing the state of the art and identifying areas that deserve further research. The main conclusions are that, while these tools have proved effective in fostering content-specific cognitive processes and collaborative learning outcomes, there are at least two areas that need further investigation: the effects of these structuring methods on social processes and on individual learning outcomes. In addition, there is also a need for field studies that overcome the limits of present research, which is mostly based on experimental methods and therefore little suited to gain the insight we need into social processes and individual knowledge acquisition.

In the same vein, Helling and Ertl (Chapter 3) investigate the use of content schemes to foster collaborative problem solving in video-conferencing systems. The authors describe two situations where different content schemes are used to facilitate a collaborative problem solving activity, aiming to understand the impact of different content schemes on the learners' problem solving process and on the quality of the learners' problem solution.

Finally, Hron, Cress and Neudert (Chapter 4) report on an experiment of video-conference based collaborative learning, where the effects of scripts and content-schemes are also investigated. The experiment involved 30 dyads of learners engaging in the production of a collaborative artifact, and the main effects investigated concerned the extent to which students brought their unshared knowledge into the co-construct and this knowledge was actually shared with their partners, based on the social-psychological research paradigm of information pooling. The study outcomes sustain the hypothesis that the dyads supported with scripted content-specific visualization achieved a higher transfer of knowledge than dyads who did not receive instructional support and dyads who received support though content specific visualization only.

The second and larger set of chapters (chapters 5 to 13) reports on real life experiences of use of approaches, techniques and strategies and discuss the resulting learning processes.

In particular, Ligorio, Loperfido, Sansone and Spadaro (Chapter 5) propose and discuss a blended model for online collaborative activities. The model is based on the idea that, in order to gain the most from the socio-constructivist theoretical framework, it is useful not only to blend online with face-to-face activities, but also to mix different pedagogical techniques. After presenting some of the most common techniques, the authors describe an example of a course based on such a blended approach. The activities of the course have been tested in real contexts on university students and in-service teachers and some preliminary results are discussed in the chapter. This allows the authors to draw a set of useful recommendations for those who want to implement the model in contexts different from the original one.

Manca and Vanin (Chapter 6) propose strategies specifically devoted to support students' initial socialization in web-based learning environments. After discussing the role of socialization in learning processes, the authors concentrate on the importance of supporting learners' first steps within a learning environment and present a three-step guidance model named "Orienting, Preparing and Supporting" (OP&S). The application of the model can be concretized in guidance programs as a set of specific online and/or face-to-face activities that allow users to familiarize with technology, tools, resources and virtual places and to socialize with each other. The authors finally provide two different real-life examples where the OP&S model was implemented and propose their reflections on the model itself.

Lobry de Bruyn (Chapter 7) reports on prospects and problems usually faced in asynchronous Computer Mediated Communication (CMC) contexts and addresses the problem of identifying strategies to reduce the difficulties in using asynchronous CMC, especially in the context of problem-based learning within online environments. To this aim, the author presents an experience of online problem-based learning and investigates the impact caused by the early placement of a face-to-face meeting, held at the very beginning of the online activity. The chapter presents the results of content analysis of online discussions, supporting the inclusion of face-to-face teaching in online learning as a way to enhance online student collaboration in a problem-based learning activity.

The subsequent chapter, by McGhie-Richmond and Winter (Chapter 8), focuses on the use of case studies in on-line teacher education. Taking inspiration from an online collaborative project carried out in a Canadian Faculty of Education over two academic years, the authors provide a rationale for using online case studies to support student collaboration and the development of communities of practice, shedding light on both student and instructor factors that can contribute to successful online collaborative work. Finally, they provide an overview of the main challenges inherent in online collaborative work relative to case study analyses.

González-Acquaro and Preskill (Chapter 9) report on an experience, where the use of web 2.0 tools has been proposed in conjunction with some collaborative techniques (Jigsaw, Peer Review, and others), in an online environment. During the experience, the four lenses of critical reflection introduced by Brookfield were used to design web 2.0 activities based on specific grouping techniques; the same lenses are also used by the authors in the chapter to propose their critical reflections on the overall experience.

The use of role play and team teaching as strategies to add depth to online discussion, is presented and discussed in the chapter by Lombard and Biglan (Chapter 10). In particular, the authors, after presenting the rationale behind the decision to adopt these techniques within an online graduate course, propose and comment data based on response and participation levels of students in two real experiences, the former based on a traditional discussion, the latter based on a discussion where the instructors assumed roles and discussed with students by playing these roles.

Daradoumis and Kordaki (Chapter 11) describe an experience where a number of collaborative strategies were at the same time object of study and method to be used by students to perform a collaborative activity. During this activity students are required to write an essay collaboratively and to elaborate a new collaborative strategy by combining some of those that were the object of study. The description of the activity is enriched with methodological and technological considerations on the overall learning experience and – more specifically - on the strategies proposed, on the way students built their own strategies combining the ones presented during the activity, and finally on the collaborative learning process and product.

Conole, McAndrew and Dimitriadis (Chapter 12) look at CSCL Pedagogical Patterns not only as strategies to support collaboration, but also – from an unusual perspective - as tools to repurpose existing

Open Educational Resources (OER) for collaborative learning. The idea presented in the chapter takes inspiration from a set of workshops held with educational technology experts, where it was shown that a small set of patterns drawn from a CSCL pattern language together with other Mediating Artefacts (such as visual representations of Learning Designs) may be inspirational and effective in repurposing existing OER.

Last of this second group of chapters, Haydel DeBarger, Penuel, Harris and Schank (Chapter 13) report on an experience based on the use of Teaching Routines to support ICT-based collaborative learning activities in the classroom. In particular, the activities object of the chapter are all based on the Group Scribbles classroom network technology. The authors reflect on the main implementation challenges on the basis of the Routines already designed for middle school Earth science.

The next set of chapters, consisting of two items (Chapter 14 and Chapter 15), focuses on the issue of how to evaluate and assess online experiences based on collaborative activities.

In particular, Retalis, Petropoulou and Lazakidou (Chapter 14) propose a framework to assess the performance of learners engaged in a collaborative activity based on a CSCL strategy and related script. The framework can be used with different CSCL scripts and is aimed at enabling the teacher to analyse the quality of students' product and performance, thanks to a list of specific criteria. The chapter then illustrates an exploratory experience carried out by the authors, where some of the indicators of the framework were adapted and used to assess a specific CSCL strategy (eARMA). The preliminary results of such experience are then presented, and they indicate the model as an effective way to support teachers in performing assessment of script-based collaborative activities.

Villasclaras-Fernández, Asensio-Pérez, Hernández-Leo, Dimitriadis, de la Fuente-Valentín and Martínez-Monés (Chapter 15) propose a CSCL script, based on a Design Pattern, which incorporates not only learning stages, but also steps specifically devoted to the assessment of the collaborative learning process itself. The chapter describes a case study conducted by the authors, which covers the whole lifecycle of the CSCL script with embedded assessment activities: starting from the design of the script, and ending with its implementation and instantiation. The case study shows the feasibility of this approach, and provides information about the requirements of CSCL script authoring tools to employ assessment and learning design patterns to support non-expert designers in those tasks.

The last set (Chapters 16 to 18) is oriented towards the study of the type of technology used: Gütl (Chapter 16) presents two experiences of collaboration carried out within 3D learning environments. In particular, after introducing collaborative learning in general and collaborative virtual environments, his first case study reports on the preliminary results obtained by observing university students working together in small groups within Second Life; the second study, instead, gives an overview of the preliminary results obtained by students working within an ad hoc 3D world enabling hands-on experiences. Overall findings suggest that such learning environments' advantages are a promising thread to be further explored. On the negative side, there are usability issues that may limit their impact in the short term.

Xin, Glass, Feenberg, Bures and Abrami (Chapter 17) describe "Marginalia", a software add-on to Moodle, allowing the use of the annotation technique as a way to support active dialogue and group knowledge building within a forum. After presenting the dynamics of online discussion and providing an overview of the most common problems one may face when using a traditional forum, the authors describe how Marginalia can overcome such problems. The article concludes with an analysis of two trial classes employing Marginalia, which highlights that a number of uses of this technique are possible, some of which rather unexpected.

Finally, Ronen and Kohen-Vacs (Chapter 18) illustrate "CeLS", a web-based environment allowing teachers to create and share CSCL activities based on collaborative scripts. After presenting the overall CeLS approach, two common examples that demonstrate the use of CeLS for designing and enacting CSCL scripts are presented. A focus is then proposed on two specific functionalities offered by the environment: the CeLS "shared document editing" and "grouping by inputs". In the end the authors describe how a teacher could use the environment and illustrate its main potential and challenges.

Francesca Pozzi
Institute for Educational Technology - National Research Council (CNR), Italy

Donatella Persico
Institute for Educational Technology - National Research Council (CNR), Italy

Acknowledgment

We would like to thank a number of people who have encouraged and actively supported us in this editorial work: first of all, the members of the Editorial Advisory Board, the Reviewers, and the Authors of the chapters, for the care, reliability and hindsight with which they have contributed to this book; the staff of IGI Global, for their timely and professional help in all the phases of the book production, and Roger Tilley, of World English, who has revised our halting English for several years now (and must be fed up with Educational Technology articles!).

Our special thanks also go to all of our colleagues of the Istituto per le Tecnologie Didattiche and, in particular, to Giovanna Caviglione, for her tireless effort in making the book bibliographical references coherent and accurate, to Michela Ott, Luigi Sarti, Guglielmo Trentin, Stefania Manca, and Manuela Delfino for the many conversations that clarified our thinking and for the friendship and professional collaboration that provided the ideal humus for organizing our ideas around this book, to the Institute director, Rosa Bottino, for her encouragement and, last but not least, to Giuliana Dettori, who graciously allowed us to take advantage of her great experience in book editing.

Finally, our gratitude goes to our husbands, Massimiliano and Beppe, and our children, Riccardo, Matteo and Silvia, for their patience and forbearance (and also for their gentle, occasional reminders of their existence!) whilst we have spent so many hours working on this book.

We hope the end result does not let all of these people down, and of course the readers, too!

Francesca Pozzi
Institute for Educational Technology of the Italian National Research Council, Italy

Donatella Persico
Institute for Educational Technology of the Italian National Research Council, Italy

Chapter 1
Task, Teams and Time: Three Ts to Structure CSCL Processes

Donatella Persico
Istituto per le Tecnologie Didattiche - CNR, Italy

Francesca Pozzi
Istituto per le Tecnologie Didattiche - CNR, Italy

ABSTRACT

This chapter advocates the idea that the structuring techniques generally used to support students in online collaborative activities can be described in terms of three main dimensions, that we call the "three Ts": Task, Teams and Time. The chapter presents an explorative study, aiming to investigate the differences between the behavior of three groups of students performing activities based on three techniques which differ as to the levels of structuredness of Task, Teams and Time. While the first group was not given instructions on how to structure the work, the second group was given some hints about the need to use some kind of structure and the third group had precise instructions as to how to proceed along the Task, Teams and Time dimensions. The chapter presents the authors' reflections about the effects of these techniques based on qualitative analysis of students' reactions to the way the three activities were structured.

INTRODUCTION

According to Kanuka & Anderson (1999) "while not all instructional methods translate well to technology-mediated learning, most do - and some work even better online than in face-to-face learning environments". Despite this assumption, which was stated more than 10 years ago, there is still a lot of research around what kind of activities and strategies work in online environments and how they can be organized to better foster the collaborative process.

As a matter of fact, the types of learning activities that can be proposed to students in CSCL contexts are rather diversified, and range from open ended, unstructured discussions to highly structured tasks, with pre-defined learning objectives and a common artifact to be collaboratively produced by students as an output of their activity.

DOI: 10.4018/978-1-61692-898-8.ch001

The debate about how it is possible to support students' collaboration has focused, among others, on whether, to what extent and under what circumstances structuring the interactions among students enhances the effectiveness of the collaborative process (Demetriadis, Dimitriadis, & Fisher, 2009; Dillenbourg, 1999). While some studies support the claim that an excess of freedom in the way collaborative tasks are proposed may fail to engage all team members in productive interactions (Hewitt, 2005; Bell, 2004, Liu & Tsai, 2008; all cited in Demetriadis et al., 2009), others maintain that there is a danger also in exceeding in scaffolding students, that is "over-scripting" collaborative learning activities (Dillenbourg, 2002; Dillenbourg, 2004). According to these authors, too much guidance may hinder learners' creativity, flexibility and ability to self-regulate, therefore jeopardizing the co-construction of knowledge and ultimately causing a loss of effectiveness of the learning process (Dillenbourg & Jermann, 2007).

Very likely, the point is to strike a balance between the two extremes. Thus, it seems that choosing how and to what extent a collaborative activity should be structured is a crucial decision of the instructional designer. This choice should be made on the basis of the features of the target population, the objectives of the learning event, and the requirements of the context where the event is to take place (Palloff & Pratt, 1999; The cognition and Technology Group at Vanderbilt, 1991).

In the following, we will further elaborate on the meaning of the expression "degree of structuredness" to conclude that, in our opinion, the structure of an activity is probably not to be intended as a single dimension on which we can impose a metric, rather it is obtained through the interplay of at least three different dimensions through which the instructional designer may, or may not, provide guidance for the learners. These are what we call the "3Ts" of the structure of collaborative activities: namely "Task", "Teams" and "Time", the three dimensions along which support is usually provided. Persico and Pozzi (2010) provide arguments to support this claim and analyse a number of structuring techniques to show how the three Ts may serve their description in quite a complete manner.

In this chapter we focus on two particular structuring techniques, namely the Discussion and the Pyramid, describing them in terms of the three Ts, to introduce a study based on a real life experience where these techniques were used. In the reported experience three groups of students were proposed to carry out a collaborative learning activity, with different support provided along the three dimensions. Finally, the chapter proposes a discussion of the learning dynamics that emerged in the three groups mostly based on qualitative data about learners' opinions.

THE 3 Ts OF THE ACTIVITY STRUCTURE

Kanuka & Anderson (1999) discuss some frequently used techniques for fostering collaborative learning processes and define them in terms of "prescribed procedures and behaviours to be enacted by students". Strategies and techniques, which are usually selected by the instructional designer at a macro-design level, allow one to organize and scaffold collaborative activities (that is, structure them) and so to help students in reaching the learning objectives.

More recently, many researchers (Dillenbourg, 2002; Dillenbourg & Hong, 2008; Dillenbourg & Jerman, 2007; Kollar, Fisher, & Hesse, 2006; Weinberger, Ertl, Fisher, & Mandl, 2004; Fisher, Kollar, Mandl, & Haake, 2007) have investigated the concept of CSCL script, which is a specification at macro or micro-design level of how learners should go about the collaborative online activity. While our structuring techniques are very close to what Dillenbourg and Hong (2008) call macro-scripts, the micro-scripts are generally implemented through interaction prompts that help students to formulate their contributions to the discussion in well argumented ways (Weinberger & Fisher, 2006).

Collaboration strategies and techniques (or CSCL macro-scripts) and CSCL micro-scripts are therefore complementary ways to support students while they learn collaboratively: the former are more general, concerning a suggested procedure that can be then managed and tuned on-the-fly by either the tutor or the students; the latter is more specific and provides step-by-step hints and/or prompts about the way students should interact.

Building on these researchers' work, we argue that – generally speaking – Task, Teams and Time can be considered the characterizing elements of online collaborative activities and all structuring techniques focus on these dimensions to scaffold students' activities.

Thus a collaborative technique may be seen as the resultant of: a Task to be accomplished by students which usually envisages the production of a final output, the Teams which students should be aggregated in to accomplish the Task and their mode(s) of interactions, and the Time schedule proposed to students to carry out the activity.

The first T, the Task, is usually defined based on the learning objectives and the contents to be addressed. This is the dimension that usually leads the choices concerning instructional design to the greatest extent. The Task may be defined very thoroughly or there may be various degrees of freedom to its interpretation, execution and accomplishment. For example, the aspects learners are expected to investigate, the contents to be learnt, the learning materials to be used, and even the nature of the output (if any), can be decided by the instructional designer or be left, to some extent, to the learners choice. In some cases, learners are provided with "content schemes" (Helling & Ertl, 2011), that are a kind of low level structure shaping the Task and/or its output to channel students efforts and therefore focus the learners attention on specific aspects of the learning domain.

The second T, Teams, has to do with the social structure needed to accomplish the Task (Kerr & Bruun, 1983). Very often the reins of Teams definition are left in the hands of the designers and/or the tutors, provided they have a good knowledge of the individuals involved in the process: the group composition may be calibrated to foster learning dynamics, for example by diversifying competences, attitudes or opinions, levels of experience. On the contrary, on some other occasions, learners are left free to autonomously form their own groups, possibly on the basis of suggested criteria.

The third T, Time, has to do with the decomposition in phases of the activity to be performed and its schedule. As for the other two dimensions, one may take decisions for the learners or leave them free to choose the learning pace. While designers and tutors usually know the Task and its challenges better and are therefore better judges of the Time needed to carry it out, students know more about their commitments and more in general their preferences.

So, the degree of support given through a structuring technique may be very high along one dimension and lower on the others. For example, the same activity may be highly structured in terms of Time, in that the tutor clearly states when the activity should start and end, and indicates deadlines for each subtask, but quite unstructured in terms of Teams, if learners are free to choose the groups they want to work with. Of course, it may be the other way round, with a strictly defined social structure and a flexible schedule, leaving the learners a large amount of autonomy as for learning pace.

In principle these 3 dimensions are rather independent, but in practice they aren't. For example, in some cases, the aggregation in Teams and subteams may vary along the Time dimension because the collaborative technique requires different aggregations at different phases of the learning activity. This happens for example during a Jigsaw (Aronson, Bleney, Stephin, Sikes, & Snapp, 1978; Bloker, 2005), where the Time and Teams dimensions are very strictly intertwined. Similarly, the Case Study (Winter and McGhie-Richmond, 2005; Persico & Pozzi, 2010) concentrates on the Task and the other two dimensions are usually structured in accordance with the Task needs.

Besides using one single structuring technique at a time, it is not infrequent to combine different techniques in one activity; in particular this typically happens with techniques that focus on the Task dimension, which may be combined with others that rule the Teams dimension. Examples of this are the Case Study, which is often combined with the Jigsaw or the Role Play, or the Discussion, which can be used in conjunction with the Pyramid or the Role Play.

Furthermore, it is worthwhile mentioning the fact that – especially in formal educational settings – there are often some contextual constraints influencing the choices concerning the two components of Time and Teams, at least at the highest level (Delfino & Persico, 2007; Palloff & Pratt, 1999). This is because courses usually have a given audience and set duration and all the design choices must fit in with the general specifications of the whole course. Most often, the designer only defines the number and the duration of the phases composing the course within the given Time. As for Teams, the situation is similar: within a course, participants are usually pre-determined and some of their characteristics, such as their number and composition, can hardly be controlled either by the course designer, or by the tutors. That said, it is true that within a given student cohort sub-groups can be created, either by the tutor or autonomously by students, always with the aim of fostering debate, rich argumentation and hence learning.

One last consideration concerns the role of tutors in structuring the 3Ts: tutors are actually in charge of running the course and usually further customize (or adapt) the designers' choices acting at a micro-design level. Designers and tutors often work together, sometimes the same people cover the two roles, while in some cases there is a clear-cut distinction between the two. In any case, the tutor's work is in strict contact with the learners and this allows her/him to understand when there is a need for more guidance and support or when the learners are ready to be granted more freedom, therefore releasing some of the constraints imposed by the activity structure.

In conclusion, the 3 Ts together allow us to describe a collaborative technique, and more specifically the activity structure, in quite a complete manner (Persico & Pozzi, 2010).

Starting from these initial considerations, in the following we describe the Discussion and the Pyramid in the light of the Task, Teams, and Time dimensions. We have chosen these two examples of technique because in the subsequent section the focus is on an experience where these two techniques have been combined, and some preliminary results of the experience are presented and discussed.

THE 3 Ts IN PRACTICE

As already mentioned in the previous section, the collaborative techniques are usually chosen by the designer and adapted to the educational setting prior to the educational event, taking into consideration various variables, such as course objectives and content, characteristics of target group and context constraints. They also meet precise teaching needs (and often also methods/practices), in just the same way as in face-to-face settings (Persico, Pozzi, & Sarti, 2008).

The Discussion

The Discussion is, in principle, the most flexible technique of all as it does not impose almost any constraint on Task, Teams and Time.

However, there are different possible ways a Discussion can be organized. In particular, open-ended Discussions tend to be very little constraining, with participants being free to choose what to focus on and how to conclude the interaction process.

Another, rather frequent, type of Discussion comprises two phases: during the first phase the Task consists of individual study of some learning materials, while the second phase consists of a collaborative activity, where students are asked to carry out a joint task, based on what they studied during the first phase. Typical Tasks for this second phase entail harvesting information, organizing information (e.g. listing items according to some kind of priority), or solving a problem.

If a final output is foreseen, this can take the form chosen by learners during the Discussion itself, or - as already mentioned – its production can be guided and its structure pre-determined thanks to some kind of scheme.

The Task is usually the leading dimension in the Discussion, while choices regarding Teams and Time are made according to the need of accomplishing the given Task.

Concerning Teams, when participants have to produce an artifact, small groups (2-6 people) are a favorite choice, to avoid divergence of the flow of discourse, while open-ended Discussions, such as brainstorming, where divergent thinking is an asset, generally work better with relatively large groups (20-25 people). As for constraints concerning Time, these are mostly used to force the groups to reach some conclusions in a sensible spell.

An example of use of this technique will be provided later in this paper.

The Pyramid

This structuring technique lends itself quite well to situations or problems where there is no one right solution, but rather the problem solution is best reached by improving progressively an initial, sub-optimal hypothesis, possibly mediating among several possibilities or ideas.

The Pyramid (Kiared, Rezek, & Frasson, 2006) consists of splitting a large group into a number of smaller teams, each of which is supposed to draft a first solution to the given problem. Then the Teams have to join to form larger groups, which will compare the solutions and work out a better one, merging the original ones or choosing the best ideas from each. The subsequent phases consist of reiterating the process, by joining the groups and merging the solutions until all the participants work all together to elaborate the final solution. There are usually at least two phases in the Pyramid, often three or four, rarely more than five. The Teams dimension leads the process, while the Task is usually one that is best carried out by gradually improving one or more possible solutions taking ideas from various sources. The Time dimension follows from the need to rearrange the Teams, providing a schedule for the various phases, urging the Teams to work in parallel and synchronize themselves before they join together with one or more other Teams.

In online learning, usually the discussion forums structure mirrors the Teams' structure, which can effectively be represented by a pyramid, whose vertex is the larger group, working in one forum all together, while at the bases are the various Teams working each in a separate forum or conference.

An example of use of the Pyramid will be provided later in this paper.

Description of the Experience

In the following we present an explorative study carried out in a quasi-experimental setting, aiming to investigate differences between the behavior of three groups of students performing an activity based on three different structuring techniques. Specifically, while in order to carry out the proposed activity the first group was not given instructions on how to structure the work, so students had to decide on their own how to do it (pure Discussion), the second group was given some hints about the need to use some kind of structure (guided Discussion), while the third group had precise instructions as to how to proceed (Discussion combined with Pyramid).

The analysis of students' reactions to the 3 differently structured activities allows some interesting reflections about the effectiveness of using these techniques in online collaborative environments.

In the following the context of the study is presented and some preliminary results of the experience are reported.

Context

Within a university course for student teachers on the topic "E-learning for adults", run in 2010 by the University of Genoa – Faculty of Education, one module was specifically devoted to the use of collaborative techniques in CSCL environments.

The module envisaged a face-to-face 3-hour lesson, where the topic was introduced, followed by a 2-week online session (asynchronous), during which the students were requested to carry out a collaborative activity.

The main goal of the online activity was to make students familiarize with the most common online collaborative techniques through an experiential approach, that is, have them use the techniques so that they could personally experience their main characteristics. This approach is coherent with the ideas of situated cognition and constructivist collaborative learning (Brown, Collins, & Duguid, 1989; Garrison & Anderson, 2003; Scardamalia & Bereiter, 1994).

In order to achieve this goal, within the experiment the class - composed of 16 students (all females) –was split into 3 groups:

- Group A: 5 people;
- Group B: 5 people;
- Group C: 6 people.

During the face-to-face lesson all the students confirmed they were quite familiar with the CMC system they were going to use for the online activity, but none of them had previous experience of structured online collaboration, while some had experience of the use of collaborative techniques in face-to-face contexts.

The CMC system used by the students to interact during the experiment is called "AulaWeb", a customization of Moodle made by the University of Genoa for its students.

The three groups were moderated by the same tutor, who was also the one who introduced the topic during the face-to-face lesson.

Learning Activities

During the online activity, each group was proposed the "NASA game", a popular collaborative game where group members are presented a situation and asked to collaboratively solve a problem (see Table 1).

The problem consisted of pretending to be astronauts who survived a shuttle crash on the moon, and having to agree on the way to sort a list of objects - starting from an unordered list - to be used to safely arrive at the closest lunar module. Due to the impossibility for the astronauts to bring all the objects with them, they have to sort the objects according to importance for survival.

While this was the mission of all the three groups, the structure of the three activities was different; in particular:

- Group A had to carry out the Task through a simple, unstructured Discussion (see Table 2);
- Group B had to carry out the Task through a "guided Discussion", where before starting to debate, students were advised to negotiate internal rules and procedures (see Table 3);
- Group C had to carry out the Task through a highly structured Discussion, by following a Pyramid approach (see Table 4). In addition, this group was provided with a content scheme aimed to further guide

Table 1. Launching message addressed to the three groups

> *Good morning everybody!*
> *Welcome to this activity, dealing with structuring techniques for online collaborative learning.*
> *The aims of this activity are:*
> - *Experiment first-hand what it is like to collaborate online;*
> - *Try out one specific collaborative technique;*
> - *Reflect on the main features of several different collaborative techniques;*
> - *Identify strengths and weaknesses of different collaborative techniques.*
>
> ***Task***
> *You will have to face a problematic situation, that you should tackle together with your team mates. In the attached file you will find the problem description: download it and read it carefully.*
>
> ***Teams***
> *You will work in three different teams: the team members are listed at the end of this message. Each group will use a different collaborative technique. When you are done with this message, go to your group and follow your instructions. When all three groups have worked out their solution, we'll meet again in this area to draw some conclusions and reflect on work done by the three groups and on the differences between the adopted techniques.*
>
> ***Timing***
> *Phase 1 – from March 5th to March 16th – collaborative problem solving, each group with one technique.*
> *Phase 2 – from March 16th to March 19th – all together – conclusive reflections*
> *Detailed instruction concerning the composition of the three teams are provided here.*
> *Enjoy your work!*
> *F.P*

Table 2. Instructions for Group A

> *Welcome Group A!*
> *Have you read the problem description attached to my previous document? YES? Then we can start!*
> *Attached to this message you will find a list of 15 objects. Your team should produce a new list where the same objects are sorted by importance. Your group should not follow any specific rule: your only constraint is that you should find an agreement on the new list by the 16th of March.*
> *If you need help, I'll be here to support you.*
> *Have a good and fruitful discussion!*
> *F.P.*

Table 3. Instructions for Group B

> *Welcome Group B!*
> *Have you read the problem description attached to my previous document? YES? Then we can start!*
> *Attached to this message you will find a list of 15 objects. Your team should produce a new list where the same objects are sorted by importance.*
> *To do so, I advise you to start by choosing a strategy, that is, agree among yourselves how to proceed, choose the rules you intend to follow (for example, choose your own deadlines, who is to do what, etc); as soon as you have decided the strategy, you can start the discussion that will lead you to the problem solution.*
> *Be careful, though, you have time till March 16th to produce your list, so the strategy definition phase should not take too long!*
> *If you need help, I'll be here to support you.*
> *Have a good and fruitful discussion!*
> *F.P.*

group interactions while producing their output, which was the final list of objects. The content scheme was a table with two columns, the first column was initialized with the random list while the second column was to be filled in with the sorted list.

At the end of the activity, each group was asked to publish the result of their work and the three ordered lists were compared with one available on the web. The latter list was provided to students by clarifying that this was not the only possible solution, and that, provided that the argumenta-

Table 4. Instructions for Group C

> *Welcome Group C!*
> *Have you read the problem description attached to my previous document? YES? Then we can start!*
> *Attached to this message you will find a list of 15 objects. Your team should produce a new list where the same objects are sorted by importance.*
> *To do so, you should proceed as follows:*
> *1. Step 1 – work individually to fill in the attached table and post it in this area by March 9th.*
> *2. Step 2 – work in two groups of three: MP with A and J., while A. will work with V and MG. Each group will discuss the tables produced individually and will merge them in a shared one which is to be posted here by March 13th.*
> *3. Step 3 – you should all join one group of six and merge the two tables produced as a result of step 2 to produce one final table that should be posted here by March 16th.*
> *About the timing: given that you will be working through three steps, you'll need to log in on this platform quite frequently (at least once every two days) otherwise you might jeopardize the subsequent steps!*
> *If you need help, I'll be here to support you.*
> *Have a good and fruitful discussion!*
> *F.P.*

tions were correct, a number of solutions were possible. The aim of proposing the NASA game, though, was not the production of a "right list", but rather the focus was on the collaborative process.

Results

In our experiment, at the very end of the activity each student was required to comment on the activity just concluded, and to reflect on the main characteristics of the three approaches, as well as to highlight the main differences between them. In this section we report on the preliminary results obtained from the analysis of students' reactions to the proposed activity.

First of all, it is worthwhile mentioning the fact that all 3 groups were able to accomplish the Task in time and produced a shared list.

By looking at the interaction processes, it appears that the more the technique was structured, the highest was the number of messages exchanged (see Table 5). The intervention of the tutor was rather limited in all the three groups.

By analysing the students' messages on the performed activity (all the 16 students commented the activity as required by the tutor), all the students showed great enthusiasm about it and the majority of them expressed satisfaction about their group and the way it worked (see Table 6 for students' comments). For each comment, we have indicated the initial(s) of the student who made the comment and her group.

When considering the 3 different approaches proposed, students acknowledged that all 3 were functional to the task accomplishment, and recognized that the most structured approach (Discussion combined with Pyramid) led to a higher number of messages, but this – according to students – is simply due to the very nature of the approach and does not necessarily imply a better or a deeper negotiation process.

Table 5. Total number of messages per group

	Total messages sent by tutor	*Total messages sent by students*	*Mean messages per student*	*Standard deviation*	*TOTAL MESSAGES (tutor + students)*
Group A	3	53	10.6	4.83	56
Group B	2	64	12.8	2.86	66
Group C	4	102	17	4.05	106

Table 6. Comments by students of Group A, B and C

"The activity was really interesting, absorbing and fascinating... It looked like we really were in space... My impression is that all the groups have worked fruitfully; working together and having a harmonious climate in which to share opinions and "lists", is always something good." (F., Group A) *"I liked this activity very much. Each time I came back home, I was always curious to see if anyone had written on the forum; reading new reflections could lead us to new questions... It has been a stimulating experience..."* (V., Group A). *"As far as my impressions on this activity are concerned, I got on very well with my group and I found the task really funny! The climate was serene and friendly and we worked peacefully."* (C., Group B) *"In my opinion working in group is always a fabulous experience because you can capture interesting aspects, you can share, you can discuss.... I felt very comfortable."* (C., Group B) *"My considerations about this group work are more than positive.... I am quite satisfied with the collaborating climate we developed in a very natural way and with the effort each of us devoted to the work."* (E., Group B) *"First of all I want to say that I got on very well with my group. We developed a positive debate and a pleasant collaborative climate."* (V., Group B) *"I liked working in a group because I found it stimulating and fruitful to our aim. We discussed a lot and shared opinions; reaching an agreement was always possible, but rather "elaborated"."* (A., Group C). *"First of all, I'd like to say that I enjoyed this activity very much. It was not the first time I reflected on online collaborative activities, but in this case personally experimenting and evaluating a collaborative technique and comparing it with others, was funny and rather "focused" on our aim and course."* (MP., Group C)

Table 7 contains the main comments of the students grouped, for the sake of analysis, in six categories: the advantages and disadvantages of the three techniques.

Table 7 provides a rough idea of the participants' opinions about how the group work evolved in each of the three groups. Students were allowed to comment not only on their group's work, but also on the way the other groups had worked, because they had access to all the discussion areas and many of them actually took the opportunity to cast more than a glance at the other groups' activity.

The comments about Group A reveal that the lack of structure was perceived as a lack of coordination which probably caused people to contribute at different levels. The impression of the student R. (Group B) who pointed out that there were rather different degrees of contribution during the activity, is somehow confirmed by the standard deviation obtained by this group (see Table 5), which is quite high and suggests that in this group the differences between numbers of messages sent were rather high. On the other hand, this technique – according to 4 students – allows great freedom of expression and leads to a high degree of group cohesion.

At the other extreme, in Group C the choice was made to combine the Task structure offered by a Discussion (plus content scheme), with a Teams based structuring technique, the Pyramid. This was perceived to impose perhaps too strong constraints on the group work, especially in terms of Time; as a matter of fact, the Pyramid, although only in three phases, imposes a strict observance of the schedule. Although this technique seems to have produced the highest amount of participation, at least in quantitative terms (mean messages per student = 17; standard deviation = 4.05, see Table 5), many students claimed that the time schedule was too strict and difficult to meet; they reported that the workload was quite heavy and this negatively influenced interactions and, according to some, even entailed a lower quality of the output. It appears that the cons of this type of structure are more, and more significant, than those pointed out for the others. As for the content schema provided, it is interesting to note that 2 students regard it as useful, although one pointed out that sharing a file as an attachment to messages is not a good idea, from a practical point of view, probably due to the effort needed to keep track of versions. Indeed, it is likely that the use of a different method for sharing the content schema (such as a wiki) would have turned out more efficient. Among the pros, 3

Table 7. Main comments on the activity

Group / Approach	*Pros*	*Cons*
Group A – Pure Discussion	– Leave people free to express their opinions (L., Group A; J., Group C; V., Group A) – Easy task (V., group A) – Low effort required (N., group A) – Best output produced (Ale., group C) – Better for explaining and deepening positions and motivations (C., Group B) – Rule free means freedom to exchange few messages (L, Group A) – Leads to high group cohesion (J., Group C)	– Delayed replies (V., Group A) – Different levels of contribution to the work (R., Group B) – Difficult to adopt this technique with non-cohesive or numerous groups (R., Group B) – Missing coordinator/mediator in case of conflicts (L., Group A) – Lack of coordination entails little awareness of deadlines (V., Group A)
Group B – Guided Discussion	– Spontaneously converged towards Pyramid (R., Group B; Ale, Group C, G., Group C; C., Group B; L., Group A) – Best output produced (R., Group B; G., Group C; L., Group A) – It allows people to express themselves freely but with some limits (C., Group B) – Spontaneous choice of roles (C., Group B) – Spontaneous choice to create a content scheme (E., Group B)	– Risk of "losing the way", though this did not happen (C., Group B) – Rules have not really been defined; only deadlines have been discussed (E., Group B) – Less cohesion (J., Group C)
Group C – Discussion + Pyramid	– Very structured, gradual approach to collaboration (G., Group C) – Gradual approach, useful for those who are not familiar with collaboration (J., Group C) – Gradual approach to discussion (Ali., Group C) – More performing (N., Group A) – More messages entails more debate (R., Group B) – Usefulness of the content scheme (R., Group B) – Useful to summarize the situation through the content scheme (Ale, Group C) – Clear mission and clear pre-defined phases (Ale, Group C) – Many messages but all meaningful (Ale, Group C) – Organization has lead to best results (V., Group B) – Requires a wide discussion and many compromises (J., Group C)	– Strict time schedule (G., Group C; Ali., Group C; J., Group C; MP., Group C; V., Group C) – Difficult to meet intermediate deadlines (Ale., Group C; Ali., Group C) – The third phase was the most difficult (Ale., Group C; Ali., Group C) – Hard task (V., Group A) – Great effort required (J., Group C) – More messages, but less satisfactory output produced (L., Group A) – Sometimes compromises may lead to worse outputs (MP., Group C) – Use of attached files not so effective (L., Group A) – Difficult to start a new discussion again every phase (J., Group C) – The structure is important, but it may influence communication too much (J., Group C) – Difficult to manage – other techniques may allow a more "colloquial climate" (MP., Group C)

students pointed out how the structuring technique made the convergence more gradual, which can be helpful especially for inexperienced participants.

In between the two extremes (pure Discussion or grouping Pyramid), group B provided itself with a Teams structure and negotiated steps and Time to accomplish the Task. 5 students observed that the group spontaneously chose a structure very similar to a light version of the Pyramid (perhaps by imitation of group C); besides 1 student noted that the group provided itself with a sort of content scheme, while another student pointed out that the group was able to autonomously negotiate internal roles. 3 students judge the final list produced by group B the best of the three. As far as the cons mentioned by students for this technique, these are really few and mainly concern the risk for the group to lose the way and to be unable to really negotiate internal rules. This might suggest that between the two alternatives of providing a strong or a weak structure for students' activity, the best solution might be that of empowering students and making them participate as much as possible in the choices of how to proceed, therefore favoring the self regulation of the community of learners.

DISCUSSION AND CONCLUSION

In this chapter, after presenting the 3Ts – Task, Teams and Time - as three dimensions able to capture activity structuredness in CSCL contexts, two particular collaborative techniques have been put under the lens, namely the Discussion and the Pyramid. The two techniques are characterized by their being respectively focused on a different T: the Discussion is usually mainly determined by its Task, while the Teams and Time dimensions are usually of minor importance, the Pyramid is strongly characterized by the Teams component, while the other two dimensions play a minor role. Due to this diversity, the two techniques can be quite easily combined.

The chapter, then, illustrates an experience where three groups engaged in the same online collaborative activity were proposed three different structures: ranging from a pure Discussion, which is the least structured, passing through an enhanced, guided Discussion, coming to a Discussion (with content scheme) combined with a Pyramid, which is structured on both Task and Teams.

Up to now a qualitative analysis has been conducted on the final comments sent by students, where they express their impressions and opinions concerning the techniques, their main pros and cons. This chapter presents the data gathered from such analysis. At the moment we are also conducting the content analysis of the messages exchanged by the students during the online activity (De Wever, Shellens, Valcke, & Van Keer, 2006; Persico, Pozzi, & Sarti, 2009; Rourke, Anderson, Garrison, & Archer, 2001; Schrire, 2006), so our next step will be to elaborate on these new data, possibly comparing them with the students' reactions analyzed here.

From this preliminary analysis, it seems that the technique mostly appreciated by students is the enhanced, guided Discussion, which allowed them to make spontaneous choices, without being overwhelmed with pre-determined rules and without running the risk of losing the way.

No doubt the mission of Group B was a bit blurred, with low structured Teams and Time dimensions, while the Task dimension was made a little more complex by the input provided by the tutor to structure collaboration before starting to cope with the list; however, students' behavior proved that, whenever a group is sufficiently at ease with technology and online communication, a good way to strike a balance between no structure at all and a structure imposed by the designers, is to leave the last word on how to structure their own collaboration to the group members themselves, relying on their ability to self-regulate as far as Time and Teams are concerned. Group B actually did more than that: despite the fact that this was not explicitly required, students of this group even attempted to structure the Task, by deciding to use a content scheme.

It is worthwhile stressing the fact that none of the students of Group B was expert in online collaboration, but this did not prevent them from finding the group's own way. It is true, though, that the group has taken inspiration from the procedures followed by Group C, so maybe the fact of having a model they could follow (but not directly imposed upon them) helped the students of Group B to internalize some useful procedures and make the most of them.

As far as the pure Discussion is concerned, designers should reflect on the fact that the element of free expression was very much appreciated by most of the students and the fact that the Time component was scarcely structured was perceived as a positive element, able to make the activity light and easy to follow.

As far as the Discussion combined with the Pyramid is concerned, comments from this experience highlight that the designers should be careful to choose it only when the total amount of Time is enough for everything to fit in without making the group work too stressful. The gradual approach to discussion and agreement was perceived by many students as a positive element, and this has certainly to do with their being not really familiar with online collaboration.

In conclusion, we claim that there is no such thing as one "right way of structuring an activity", but that a careful tuning of Task, Teams and Time to determine the structure of an online activity, can and should be done.

In order to give a further contribution to this research field, our future efforts will be oriented to study the three Ts separately, by setting up experiments, where possible, to isolate each of the dimensions at a time, so to see whether and how the learning process is impacted by the single Ts in any way. This may turn out to be a difficult task due to the fact that the three Ts are not, in practice, really independent variables. A further direction of research might explore ways to make learners participate in some of the design decisions in terms of the three Ts.

REFERENCES

Aronson, E., Blaney, N., Stephin, C., Sikes, J., & Snapp, M. (1978). *The jigsaw classroom*. Beverly Hills, CA: Sage Publishing Company.

Bell, P. (2004). Promoting students' argument construction and collaborative debate in the classroom. In Linn, M. C., Davis, E. A., & Bell, P. (Eds.), *Internet Environments for Science Education* (pp. 114–144). Mahwah, NJ: Erlbaum.

Blocher, J. M. (2005). Increasing learner interaction: using jigsaw online. *Educational Media International*, *42*(3), 269–278. doi:10.1080/09523980500161486

Brown, J. S., Collins, A., & Duguid, P. (1989). Situated cognition and the culture of learning. *Educational Researcher*, *18*(1), 32–42.

De Wever, B., Shellens, T., Valcke, M., & Van Keer, H. (2006). Content analysis schemes to analyze transcripts of online asynchronous discussion groups: A review. *Computers & Education*, *46*(1), 6–28. doi:10.1016/j.compedu.2005.04.005

Delfino, M., & Persico, D. (2007). Online or face-to-face? Experimenting different techniques in initial teacher training. *Journal of Computer Assisted Learning*, *23*(5), 351–365. doi:10.1111/j.1365-2729.2007.00220.x

Demetriadis, S., Dimitriadis, Y., & Fischer, F. (2009). Introduction to the SFC-2009 Workshop. In: *Proceedings of the workshop "Scripted vs. free collaboration: alternatives and paths for adaptable and flexible CS scripted collaboration"*, Rhodes, June 2009. Retrieved April 10, 2010, from http://mlab.csd.auth.gr/cscl2009/SFC-files/SFC-2009-WorkshopProceedings.pdf

Dillenbourg, P. (Ed.). (1999). *Collaborative Learning: Cognitive and Computational Approaches*. Oxford, UK: Pergamon Press.

Dillenbourg, P. (2002). Over-scripting CSCL: The risks of blending collaborative learning with instructional design. In P. A. Kirschner (Ed.), *Three worlds of CSCL. Can we support CSCL* (pp. 61-91). Heerlen: Open Universiteit Nederland.

Dillenbourg, P. (2004). Split where interaction should happen - A model for designing CSCL scripts. In *Proceedings of the "Special Interest Meeting 2004 of EARLI SIG 6 and SIG 7"*, Tuebingen, 2004. Retrieved April 10, 2010, from http://www.iwm-kmrc.de/workshops/SIM2004/pdf_files/Dillenbourg.pdf

Dillenbourg, P., & Hong, F. (2008). The Mechanics of Macro Scripts. *International Journal of Computer-Supported Collaborative Learning*, *3*(1), 5–23. doi:10.1007/s11412-007-9033-1

Dillenbourg, P., & Jermann, P. (2007). Designing interactive scripts. In Fischer, F., Kollar, I., Mandl, H., & Haake, J. (Eds.), *Scripting computer-supported collaborative learning: Cognitive, computational and educational perspectives* (pp. 276–301). New York: Springer. doi:10.1007/978-0-387-36949-5_16

Fischer, F., Kollar, I., Mandl, H., & Haake, J. M. (Eds.). (2007). *Scripting computer-supported collaborative learning – cognitive, computational, and educational perspectives*. New York: Springer. doi:10.1007/978-0-387-36949-5

Garrison, R., & Anderson, T. (2003). *E-learning in the 21st century. A framework for research and practice*. London, UK and New York: Routledge Falmer. doi:10.4324/9780203166093

Helling, K., & Ertl, B. (2011, this book). Fostering collaborative problem solving by content schemes. In F. Pozzi & D. Persico (Eds.), *Techniques for fostering collaboration in online learning communities: Theoretical and Practical Perspectives*. Hershey, PA and New York, NY: IGI Global.

Hewitt, J. (2005). Toward an understanding of how threads die in asynchronous computer conferences. *Journal of the Learning Sciences*, *7*(4), 567–589. doi:10.1207/s15327809jls1404_4

Kanuka, H., & Anderson, T. (1999). Using Constructivism in Technology-Mediated Learning: Constructing Order out of the Chaos in the Literature. *Radical Pedagogy*, *1*(2).

Kerr, N. L., & Bruun, S. E. (1983). Dispensability of member effort and group motivation losses: free rider effects. *Journal of Personality and Social Psychology*, *44*, 78–94. doi:10.1037/0022-3514.44.1.78

Kiared, S. A., Razek, M. A., & Frasson, C. (2006). The Pyramid Collaborative Filtering Method: Toward an Efficient E-Course, *Proc. of Intelligent Tutoring Systems 8th International Conference (IST 2006)*, Jhongli, Taiwan, (LNCS 4053, pp. 248-257).

Kollar, I., Fischer, F., & Hesse, F. W. (2006). Computer-supported collaboration scripts - a conceptual analysis. *Educational Psychology Review*, *18*(2), 159–185. doi:10.1007/s10648-006-9007-2

Liu, C., & Tsai, C. (2008). An analysis of peer interaction patterns as discoursed by on-line small group problem-solving activity. *Computers & Education*, *50*(3), 627–639. doi:10.1016/j.compedu.2006.07.002

Palloff, R. M., & Pratt, K. (1999). *Building learning communities in cyberspace*. San Francisco, CA: Jossey-Bass Publishers.

Persico, D., & Pozzi, F. (2010). The three T's of the structure of online collaborative activities. In H. Uzunboylu (ed), *Innovation and Creativity in Education, Procedia - Social and Behavioral Sciences*, 2(2), 2610-2615. Retrieved April 10, 2010, from http://www.sciencedirect.com/science/journal/18770428

Persico, D., Pozzi, F., & Sarti, L. (2008). Fostering collaboration in CSCL. In A. Cartelli & M. Palma (Eds.), *Encyclopedia of Information and Communication Technology,* vol. I, (pp. 335-340). Information Science Reference, Hershey, PA-New York, NY: IGI Global.

Persico, D., Pozzi, F., & Sarti, L. (2009). A model for monitoring and evaluating CSCL. In Juan, A. A., Daradoumis, T., Xhafa, F., Caballe, S., & Faulin, J. (Eds.), *Monitoring and Assessment in Online Collaborative Environments: Emergent Computational Technologies for E-learning Support. Hershey, PA-New York*. NY: IGI Global.

Rourke, L., Anderson, T., Garrison, R., & Archer, W. (2001). Methodological Issues in the Content Analysis of Computer Conference Transcripts. *International Journal of Artificial Intelligence in Education*, *12*(1), 8–22.

Scardamalia, M., & Bereiter, C. (1994). Computer support for knowledge-building communities. *Journal of the Learning Sciences*, *3*(3), 265–283. doi:10.1207/s15327809jls0303_3

Schrire, S. (2006). Knowledge building in asynchronous discussion groups: Going beyond quantitative analysis. *Computers & Education*, *46*(1), 49–70. doi:10.1016/j.compedu.2005.04.006

The Cognition and Technology Group at Vanderbilt. (1991). Some thoughts about constructivism and instructional design. *Educational Technology*, *31*(10), 16–18.

Weinberger, A., Ertl, B., Fisher, F., & Mandl, H. (2004). *Cooperation scripts for learning via web-based discussion boards and videoconferencing, EARLI SIM 2004*, Retrieved April 10, 2010, from http://www.cs.uu.nl/docs/vakken/b3elg/literatuur_files/weinberg.pdf

Weinberger, A., & Fischer, F. (2006). A framework to analyze argumentative knowledge construction in computer-supported collaborative learning. *Computers & Education*, *46*(1), 71–95. doi:10.1016/j.compedu.2005.04.003

Winter, E. C., & McGhie-Richmond, D. (2005). Using computer conferencing and case studies to enable collaboration between expert and novice teachers. *Journal of Computer Assisted Learning*, *21*(2), 118–129. doi:10.1111/j.1365-2729.2005.00119.x

Wu, D., & Hiltz, S. R. (2004). Predicting learning from asynchronous online discussions. *Journal of Asynchronous Learning Networks*, 8(2). Retrieved April 10, 2010, from http://www2.hawaii.edu/~pusal/predicting_asyn_learning.pdf

KEY TERMS AND DEFINITIONS

Computer-Supported Collaborative Learning (CSCL): Field of study aimed at understanding how people learn together through the use of computers. It investigates both scenarios where learners are far apart and collaborate online and others where the learners interact face-to-face while the computer provides a learning environment or at least a number of tools. CSCL is rooted into socio-constructivist learning theories.

Structuring Technique: A consolidated strategy, usually chosen by the instructional designer and used by the tutor to scaffold and provide a suitable organisation to students learning activities. Common examples of collaborative structuring techniques are the jigsaw, the peer review, the role play, the case study, the discussion and the pyramid.

CSCL Scripts: Instructions, given to students, to guide them through the collaborative activities in CSCL contexts. CSCL scripts aim to implement specific structuring techniques. There are two types of scripts: "macro-scripts" and "micro-scripts". The former are instructions, usually expressed verbally, containing the specification of the task to be performed, the time schedule of the activity, the team composition and the mode of interaction to be followed by students. The latter are lower level instructions given to students (usually automatically, by the computer) to prompt them at various steps of the task. The prefix "micro" is often dropped and the term script is generally used to identify the micro-scripts.

Chapter 2
Supporting Virtual Collaborative Learning Using Collaboration Scripts and Content Schemes

Birgitta Kopp
Ludwig-Maximilians University, Germany

Heinz Mandl
Ludwig-Maximilians University, Germany

ABSTRACT

Collaborative learning is used as a key principle in several approaches for designing virtual learning environments (e.g. CTGV, 2000). This is due to the fact that collaboration seems to foster individual knowledge acquisition (Lou, Abrami, Spence, Poulsen, Chambers, & d'Apollonia, 1996), improve knowledge application (De Corte, 2003), and increase social competencies. But collaborative learning is not always successful (Salomon & Globerson, 1989). Virtual learning places great and varied demands on collaboration, which means that learners often do not know how to collaborate adequately. In such cases, it is necessary to provide support. This chapter focuses specifically on two structuring methods, namely collaboration scripts and content schemes. To gain further insight into the topic, the authors will first describe the technical aspects of virtual collaborative learning. In the second section, the authors will depict the learning processes and outcomes of collaboration. Thirdly, they will discuss the theory and research on the structuring methods. The chapter ends with conclusions and practical implications.

INTRODUCTION

Virtual collaborative learning is being used increasingly in different contexts: in schools, in universities, in higher or in further education. This is due to the fact that collaborative learning has several benefits, e. g. fostering individual knowledge acquisition (Lou et al., 1996), supporting knowledge application (De Corte, 2003), and encouraging the acquisition of social competencies. But collaborative learning is not successful in itself (Salomon & Globerson, 1989). There are some pre-conditions necessary for ensuring that collaborative learning will have a positive effect. In addition, virtual learning places even more demands on learners, who must handle both the technique as well as the physical absence of the collaborating partners. They must learn how

DOI: 10.4018/978-1-61692-898-8.ch002

virtual learning is connected to different ways of collaboration. In virtual collaboration, interaction occurs mainly through written forms. This specifically results in four main problems.

Firstly, the coordination must be more explicit in virtual collaboration to result in effective collaboration and a joint group solution (Ellis, Gibbs, & Rein, 1991). Especially in asynchronous scenarios, it may take more time for learners to respond to their group members' contributions (McGrath, 1990). Secondly, social presence is different in computer-supported learning environments. As such environments involve less communication channels than face-to-face learning scenarios (e. g. mimic, viewing direction, voice, clothing-styles, etc.), it is necessary to express missing nonverbal cues in different ways, such as using emoticons to create social presence (Gunawardena & Zittle, 1997). Thirdly, access to the information and knowledge of the collaboration partners is mediated and limited by the computer, which makes the development of transactive memory (Moreland, 2000) more difficult (Krauss & Fussell, 1990). Transactive memory is defined as meta-knowledge about the knowledge and information of the individual group members (Clark & Carlson, 1982; Wegner, Giuliano & Hertel, 1985). Transactive memory is only developed when groups communicate for the purpose of exchanging and sharing information (Hinsz, Tindale, & Vollrath, 1997). A fourth problem concerns the lack of references for individual contributions as there are time delays in replying to entries as well as insufficient references to the content (McGrath, 1990). Virtual communication lacks the non-verbal and para-verbal signs which regulate face-to-face communication. Therefore, there are a large number of messages which do not make reference to the preceding message (Friedman & McCullough, 1992).

Therefore, it is necessary to provide support in the form of structuring. There are two main ways of structuring the communication: collaboration scripts and content schemes. Collaboration scripts structure the collaboration process by giving learners different tasks or sub-tasks. Content schemes focus learners on content-specific aspects which are relevant for the task solution by structuring the task. The task is generally structured through the computer interface. Each of these methods has a different effect on learning processes and learning outcomes.

This chapter provides an introduction to the characteristics of virtual collaborative learning. These consist of learning outcomes, the technical aspects of virtual learning and the collaborative learning processes. In the second part, we will show two different ways of supporting virtual collaborative learning: collaboration scripts and content schemes. Thirdly, we will describe the direction of future research. The chapter ends with conclusions and further implications.

VIRTUAL COLLABORATIVE LEARNING

Collaborative learning is defined as "a situation in which two or more people learn or attempt to learn something together" (Dillenbourg, 1999, p.2). In virtual collaborative learning, collaborative learning is mediated by the computer. This means that learners only interact with the help of the computer. The main technical differentiation of collaborative learning which is supported by computers concerns synchronicity. This specifically involves learners collaborating synchronously while sitting simultaneously in different places in front of a computer or asynchronously, when learners are collaborating not at different points in time.

Synchronous communication often takes place with a chat or a videoconferencing tool. In this learning scenario, learners have a permanent connection to one another throughout the learning process via a shared application on their screen. They communicate either by typing statements or sentences when using computer chat or by speaking into a microphone during videoconferencing (see Ertl, Fischer, & Mandl, 2006). Such scenarios enable frequent learner interaction. When the computer provides asynchronous communication, learners often communicate through discussion boards in the learning environment. Discussion boards allow learners to express themselves by typing statements into the computer interface (Kopp, Schnurer, & Mandl, 2009). As the communication is asynchronous, there is no immediate reply to each learner's entry, but the learner can proceed at his/her own pace. The written messages are permanent and usually allow for later access as well as for editing and improving.

To gain further insights into virtual collaborative learning, we would like to focus on learning outcomes and key learning processes.

Learning Outcomes

The learning outcome of virtual collaborative learning is a key indicator of the success of collaborative learning. There are a lot of different ways of differentiating and defining learning outcome. Furthermore, in collaborative learning, there are two main methods of assessing the benefits of a collaborative learning scenario: either individually on the learner level or collaboratively on a group level.

Regarding individual learning outcomes, De Jong and Ferguson-Hessler (1996) distinguish between four kinds of learning outcomes: declarative knowledge (knowledge about objects, facts, and rules), procedural knowledge (knowledge which could be transferred in action), situative knowledge (knowledge about typical situations in a domain) and strategic knowledge (knowledge about relevant and adequate strategies for defining a task solution). Beyond this differentiation, the focus is often on the application of knowledge in subsequent situations, (Kopp, Ertl, & Mandl, 2006) as well as on learning transfer. These kinds of learning outcomes measure the sustainability of the acquired knowledge which is a main indicator of the performance and effectiveness of the group.

In assessing learning outcomes on a group level, Hertz-Lazarowitz, Kirkus and Miller (1992) suggest that the product of the collaboration process, e. g. a final collaborative problem solution, should be considered "group knowledge" to evaluate the quality of the collaborative knowledge construction. According to Salomon and Perkins (1998), it is important to analyze both individual and collaborative learning outcomes when investigating collaborative learning.

Especially in the context of learning with the computer, Salomon (1992) distinguishes between learning with and learning of the computer. This distinction refers to the aspect that learning environments could promote activities which are necessary during collaboration (learning *with*) and those which are relevant after collaboration respectively which could be used in another collaborative setting (learning *of*). Learning with the computer describes changes during working with the computer. Furthermore, computer-supported collaborative learning could foster competences or abilities learners could use and apply in other settings which are effects of learning with the computer (learning *of*). Such results from interacting with the computer are often more lasting changes.

Learning Processes

To gain further insights into learning processes we specifically differentiate between content-specific cognitive and social learning processes.

Content-specific cognitive learning processes specifically include discussions and the exchange of knowledge as well as argumentation and the consideration of different perspectives.

Discussions and the exchange of knowledge is a key aspect of collaboration. Only when knowledge is exchanged and disseminated among all group members can collaboration take place (Kopp & Mandl, 2006). In this context, the kind of knowledge being disseminated is the most important factor. Often group members only disseminate knowledge that is shared between all group members and do not disseminate knowledge that is unshared. This phenomenon is described in the information pooling paradigm (Stasser & Titus, 1985; Wittenbaum & Stasser, 1996). This paradigm describes the fact that group members often refer only to shared information, whereas they do not articulate the unshared information that only one group member has exclusive access to. But especially this last aspect – the dissemination of unshared information – is the main advantage of collaboration: that the group is able to perform better than individuals if they were working alone. During collaboration, the discussion should take place in two steps. In the first step, group members collect all the shared and unshared information which is relevant to defining a task solution (Dennis & Valacich, 1999). As soon as all group members have access to all information, they are able to discuss it. The discussion includes the exchange of different opinions as well as the evaluation of and reflection on information – important activities for gaining a deeper understanding of the task (Paechter, 2003). It was assumed that virtual learning environments could compensate for the effect of only disseminating shared information, but studies showed no difference when compared to face-to-face collaboration (Hollingshead, 1996).

Argumentation and considering different perspectives is another key activity in collaboration. Collaboration can profit from the different opinions and points of view of every group member. But this is only the case when group members adequately justify their points of view. In this respect, argumentation is defined as "a verbal and social activity of reason aimed at increasing (or decreasing) the acceptability of a controversial standpoint for the listener or reader, by putting forward a constellation of propositions intended to justify (or refute) the standpoint before a rational judge" (Van Eemeren, Grootendorst, & Henkeman, 1996, p.5). Especially in scientific discussions, arguing is necessary to explore diverse perspectives in collaborative task-solving by confronting cognitions and their foundations (Andriessen, Baker, & Suthers, 2003). Often these different perspectives are comprised of different knowledge, information and opinions which are necessary for solving an interdependent task collaboratively (Jonassen, 2000).

Content-specific cognitive learning processes are important for individual and collaborative knowledge acquisition and knowledge application. When discussing and exchanging different knowledge, learners become involved in the subject matter and therefore link their pre-knowledge with the new knowledge more deeply. In addition to knowledge acquisition, the application of knowledge is especially necessary when arguing and considering different perspectives which are used for defining a task solution. When engaging in such activities, knowledge application is fostered not only on a collaborative, but also on an individual level.

Social processes are key elements in collaboration. They are related to the interaction of the group members and are a pre-condition for effective collaboration. Even though, "collaborative learning" is the "royal road" to knowledge acquisition (e.g. Kreijins, Kirschner, & Jochems, 2003), grouping two or more people together is neither a guarantee that they will be able to collaborate, nor that they will be able to learn. There are four main aspects which are relevant in the context of social processes: constructive confrontations and conflict regulation, goal orientation and group's motivation, social influence processes, and the individuals' involvement in group activities and responsibility during group work.

Constructive confrontations among group members and conflict regulation is mainly based on social competences which include the ability to monitor progress through the tasks, the skill to manage competition and conflict, and the ability to modify and use different viewpoints as well as the willingness to provide mutual support (Cohen,

1994). Furthermore, it is also important that group members have the ability to take different points of view into account, to resolve conflicts and to come to a final solution which is satisfactory to all parties involved. In this context, it is necessary for group members to try to solve conflicts based on incompatible points of view in epistemic ways. This means that group members pay attention to the issue and elaborate on the different elements in depth, thus generating alternative and original solutions. Such conflict regulation also showed positive effects on argumentation (Schwarz, Neuman, & Biezuner, 2000).

Group goal orientation and motivation is a second key social aspect that is relevant for collaboration. Theories and research about group goal orientation (Dweck & Elliot, 1983; Elliot & Mc Gregor, 2001) showed positive and negative effects of pursuing a goal in learning contexts. Goals have been divided into mastery/learning goals and performance goals. It appears that holding mastery goals encourages persistence in terms of effort, self-regulated learning and open-mindedness since the goal is not to perform but rather to profit as much as possible from learning opportunities. Effects of performance goals are more complex. Holding "performance-avoidance" goals (trying to avoid failure) are negatively related to achievement and results in negative emotions and cognitions, low persistence in effort, and withdrawal. Holding "performance-approach" goals (seeking for good performance and success) is related to high achievement when intermediate feedbacks are positive, but is related to negative emotions and withdrawal in cases of ongoing negative feedback (Elliot & McGregor, 2001; Harackiewicz, Barron, Pintrich, Elliot, & Trash, 2002).

Social influence processes are highly relevant for collaboration, because they influence how groups search for and handle information and how group solutions are generated. Research on socio-cognitive conflicts showed that interaction with peers is more helpful for acquiring more advanced cognitive skills than interaction with experts, adults or teachers (Doise & Mugny, 1984). Moreover, minority influence is more likely to promote deeper scrutiny of information (Moscovici, 1980), creative and divergent thinking (Nemeth, 1986), knowledge transfer and generalization of learning (Quiamzade & Mugny, 2001). Conversely, one-directional, vertical knowledge transmission from an expert may encourage convergent thinking, the restriction of attention to elements already present in the cognitive field (Butera & Buchs, 2005), the confirmatory bias in formal reasoning (Butera & Buchs, 2005), and the tendency to protect one's own point of view rather than considering alternatives (Tomasetto, Mucchi-Faina, Alparone, & Pagliaro, 2009). Often it is not easy for learners to represent the minority in a group, because they are put under pressure to hold the same position as the majority.

Participation and responsibility in group work is another key aspect for successful virtual collaboration. It is necessary for all participants to engage in the group activity, put forward their points of view, and be encouraged to sustain their claims even if they are the minority in the group. The most common pitfalls in all forms of group collaboration are social loafing and free riding. Social loafing is when participants exert less effort in the group work than they would do in individual work (Latane, Williams, & Harkins, 1979). Free riding is when one or more learners do little or no work, thereby contributing almost nothing to the group's task (Kerr & Bruun, 1983).

Both social processes and content-specific cognitive processes are highly important to individual and collaborative knowledge acquisition and application. While active participation and taking responsibility in the group work are preconditions for every kind of effective collaboration with respect to learning outcomes, research on social influence processes with socio-cognitive conflicts as well as on constructive conflict regulation show how these activities influence performance. Conflicts are especially important in the context of collaborative learning. Conflicts stimulate increased knowledge acquisition and knowledge application when they are resolved in a constructive way such that every learner is satisfied with the conflict resolution.

STRUCTURING VIRTUAL COLLABORATION WITH COLLABORATION SCRIPTS AND CONTENT SCHEMES

As virtual collaboration is more demanding than face-to-face collaboration, it is necessary to provide support. One main technique is to structure the collaboration using collaboration scripts and content schemes. In the following section, we firstly define collaboration scripts and their different forms as well as their effects on collaboration processes and learning outcomes. In the second part, we will explain the same for content schemes.

Collaboration Scripts

The term script has been adapted from cognitive psychology that uses the term to describe individual memory structures (Schank, & Abelson, 1977). Originally used by Schank and Abelson (1977), a script is an internal memory structure of a "sequence of actions that define a well-known situation" (p.41), e. g. the restaurant script that involves getting seated, looking at the menu, ordering food, eating, and then paying (King, 2007). Such a script guides individuals through the roles and steps they have to follow and how they have to perform them in a specific social situation.

In educational settings, especially in computer-supported collaborative learning, this term is being used increasingly in the last few years (see Fischer, Kollar, Mandl, & Haake, 2007). In this context, the meaning of scripts is somewhat different. In contrast to the cognitive perspective in which a script is a "fairly static internal memory with a narrowly constrained set of actions and roles" (King, 2007, p.16), scripts in educational psychology are used to sequence and support the interaction of learning groups. In this context, Kollar, Fischer, and Hesse (2006) define collaboration scripts "as an instructional means that provides collaborators with instructions for task-related interactions, that can be represented in different ways, and that can be directed at specific learning objectives. These objectives can be reached by introducing different kinds and sequences of activities, which are implicitly or explicitly clustered according to collaboration roles. Scripted activities can be broken down into individual acts that together form a larger activity, and scripts can vary with respect to how much structure they provide" (p.162-163). Furthermore, collaboration scripts "mainly structure collaborative learning by assigning specific activities to learners" (Ertl, Kopp, & Mandl, 2007, p.216). These activities or roles are generally content-independent.

Collaboration scripts are widely used in scripted cooperation (Dansereau, 1988; O'Donnell & King, 1999) or cooperative teaching (O'Donnell & Dansereau, 2000). In scripted cooperation, the group consists of two learners with the roles of recaller and listener. Both learners have to fulfill specific activities in their roles. First, both partners read the material and take notes. Then the recaller summarizes the main ideas of the material orally, while the listener checks for errors and omissions. The listener provides feedback on errors or distortions when the recaller has finished summarizing. Then, both partners elaborate on the material they have read by adding details, generating examples, etc. (King, 2007). This example shows that scripts guide learners in their collaborative process by assigning specific activities to the learners which are mainly content-independent, but tailored to the task at hand, e.g. learning a theory or solving a problem. For the most part, collaboration scripts sequence collaboration in specific phases. In each phase, learners have to fulfill certain tasks which should foster cognitive and social activities. In research, collaboration scripts have been most frequently investigated with respect to their influence on content-specific cognitive activities which include, amongst other things, discussions and exchange of knowledge, argumentation and the consideration of different perspectives.

Concerning discussions and the exchange of knowledge, a study by Reiserer (2002) showed that collaboration scripts increased the dissemination of content-related information and decreased coordination-specific activities. Because the collaboration script provided a framework for how to collaborate, learners with the collaboration script disseminated more theoretical concepts and asked their collaborating partners for relevant information more frequently. This is a main indicator of sharing relevant knowledge and information. A study by Weinberger (2003) supports this finding. In his study, learners with the collaboration script were engaged more often in epistemic activities than in off-task activities. Härder (2003) used a script to structure the interaction of groups that were asked to solve a criminal case. In this script, learners were given tasks such as pooling or exchanging information. Results showed that learners with the script drew more inferences between individual pieces of information than learners without the script. Again, the collaboration script showed learners how to collaborate and highlighted the aspects they should focus on in collaboration. In this way, learners increased their knowledge-sharing activities.

In examining the impact of collaboration scripts on argumentation and considering different perspectives, a study by Stegmann (2008) implemented a structure in the virtual learning environment that defined the order of an argumentation sequence. This sequence was comprised of argument, counter-argument and reply. Results showed that in the learning discourse, the learners generated more complete argumentation sequences. With respect to the learning outcome, they gained factual and applicable knowledge through argumentation sequences (Stegmann, Weinberger, Fischer, & Mandl, 2004). In another study, an interdisciplinary team comprised of a medical student and a psychotherapy student had to solve a complex problem together by considering the perspective of the other person. The collaboration script included e.g. individual and collaborative phases, in which learners had to complete specific tasks which were relevant for solving the problem (Rummel & Spada, 2007). Learners received the script during a learning phase before they had to use the knowledge they had learned about collaboration with the script. They then collaborated with one another during the application phase. Results showed that learners with the script outperformed learners without the script in the collaborative processes and in the learning outcome. Therefore, the authors suggest that the collaboration script is able "to trigger learning about collaboration" (Rummel & Spada, 2007, p.51).

Effects of collaboration scripts on social processes in virtual collaborative learning have scarcely been the subject of investigation. There has been research in face-to-face settings, such as the Jigsaw method (Aronson, Blaney, Stephan, Sikes, & Snapp, 1978), which has shown positive effects on pro-social activities, such as conflict regulation (reduction of social conflicts and competition), and social influence processes (reduction of status-differences) in the classroom. A field study on virtual collaboration yielded different results. In this study, all groups were supported by a collaboration script using group rules, a rotating moderator and feedback (Kopp & Mandl, 2008). The learners' evaluation data regarding group goal orientation, constructive confrontations among group members, and taking responsibility in group work shows differences between the groups over time. Even though the two groups initially evaluated their collaboration very positively due to the structuring methods, their evaluation became more negative over time. This was mainly based on the groups' ineffective task-solving strategies (Kopp & Mandl, 2008).

Even though there is almost no research on the impact of collaboration scripts on social processes, there is a theoretical assumption that they have a positive influence on collaborative learning. With the specific help of collaboration scripts, learners may focus their attention more on social processes which are very helpful and functional for collaboration. Providing every learner with specific sub-tasks or information which is necessary for solving the task may increase constructive confrontations without competition and improve the learner's ability to modify and use different viewpoints. In this context, socio-cognitive conflicts are handled in a functional way. As learners are depending on each other's knowledge when giving different information, balanced participation and taking responsibility for the task solution could be improved. Furthermore, with collaboration strategies, learners may become motivated in such a way that they want to profit from collaborative learning as much as possible with respect to mastery goals.

When we look at the learning outcome, there is no consistent evidence regarding the positive effects of collaboration scripts on learning success. Positive effects on collaborative learning outcome regarding the application of knowledge were shown in two studies. In the first study by Baker and Lund (1997), learners were asked to draw a circuit in the learning environment C-Chene. Learners with the collaboration script showed more task-related and reflexive contributions than learners without the collaboration script. In the second study, learners who had to solve cases together were also better at applying theoretical concepts on case information when supported with collaboration script (Weinberger, Reiserer, Ertl, Fischer, & Mandl, 2003). The study by Rummel and Spada (2005) revealed positive effects on individual learning outcome regarding the acquisition of declarative and strategic knowledge. In this study, two students were asked to solve cases in an interdisciplinary team consisting of a medical student and a psychology student. The collaboration script showed alternating individual and collaborative phases and respective sub-tasks before the collaboration started. Learners with the script achieved better individual results in a test on topic-specific (declarative knowledge) and non topic-specific knowledge (strategic knowledge on collaboration) (Rummel, Ertl, Härder, & Spada, 2003). In addition, a study by Hron, Hesse, Reinhard and Picard (1997) showed the positive effect of a collaboration script on the collaborative and individual learning outcomes with respect to the application of knowledge. In this study, learners had to correct the inaccuracies in a structural diagram of a biological system. The collaboration script was realized as a strict procedure in which learners needed to confirm the collaborating partner's activity before carrying out a modification.

Content Schemes

Content schemes focus specifically on activities which are relevant for the collaborative task solution. They are based on the concept of mental schemata (Brewer & Nakamura, 1984) which are defined as "an inactive organization of past reactions, or of past experiences, which must always be supposed to be operating in any well-adapted organic response" (Bartlett, 1932, p.201). This definition is based on the assumption that individuals process all objects, situations, occasions and activities such that their components are cognitively represented as a coherent concept. Therefore, it is necessary that the relationships between the individual knowledge units are specified (Anderson & Pearson, 1984). Based on this definition schemata are the cognitive structures and processes that human knowledge and expertise is based on (Brewer & Nakamura, 1984).

Although content schemes were originally found in cognitive psychology, they are being increasingly used as an instructional tool in computer-supported collaborative learning. Based on the definition above, such content schemes include an expert meta-structure of important dimensions of the content in which the main components of the content are represented (Brooks & Dansereau, 1983). This means that the content is structured on a meta-level to show the relationship between the individual components of the content (Lambiotte, Skaggs, & Dansereau, 1993). Often the meta-structure of content schemes provides a placeholder for important dimensions of the content (Ertl et al., 2007). They make key components of the content salient so that learners are able to focus either on missing or existing parts of the content (Suthers, 2001; Suthers & Hundhausen, 2001). This representation of specific concepts can guide and focus learners in their task-solving process because it modifies the representational context of the task by "changing learners' subjective representation of the task and influencing their ability to solve the task" (Ertl et al., 2007, p.217). Thus, the task-solving process is positively influenced (Zhang & Norman, 1994).

In virtual learning contexts, content schemes are used less frequently than collaboration scripts. They are frequently presented as tables or matrixes and displayed permanently on the computer screen during the learning situation (Ertl et al., 2007). In a study by Kopp and Mandl (2007), learners received a table with the most important aspects of Attribution Theory on a meta-level (see Table 1, first and second line). With help of this meta-structure, learners were asked to complete the blank cells according to their knowledge on Attribution Theory as well as using the case information provided. Attribution Theory is used to explain and justify specific phenomena, such as a student's performance in school. The learner's task was to analyze the case of a student whose performance in Math had declined. To gain insight into the attribution patterns of the student, information regarding consensus and consistency were of main importance.

Content schemes especially focus on the supporting of content-specific cognitive activities, e. g. discussion and the exchange of knowledge or argumentation and the consideration of different perspectives. Furthermore, content schemes foster collaborative learning outcomes.

When we look at the impact of content schemes on learning processes, we can see positive overall effects. Concerning discussion and the exchange of knowledge and information pooling, studies showed that content schemes encourage learners to focus on the relevant information which is activated through representing the main components of the content. In a study on the peer-teaching of a psychological theory, Reiserer, Ertl and Mandl (2002) found that learners in the tutor role focused their teaching activities on all relevant aspects of the theory in a balanced way when they were supported with a content scheme, but only on one particular aspect when they were not supported. This effect could be shown in measuring the knowledge the tutees had acquired through the teaching phase according to the different theoretical aspects. Learners in the tutor role shared more information and were more thorough when they were supported with a content scheme than when they were not (Reiserer et al., 2002). This result was also found in a study by Weinberger and colleagues (Weinberger, Stegmann, Fischer, & Mandl, 2007) in which learners with a content scheme focused more on adequate knowledge concepts than on off-topic discourse. Content schemes have a kind of stimulative nature which

Table 1. Example of a content scheme (Kopp & Mandl, 2007)

Cause	**Information regarding**		**Attribution according to**	
	Consensus	Consistency	Kelley	Heider
Laziness	Low because he is the only one in class who is lazy	High because he has been lazy for a year now	Person	Internal, variable

focuses learners on relevant content-specific aspects they potentially would not have considered without support.

There is also research which shows a positive impact of content schemes on argumentation and the consideration of different perspectives. A study by Kopp and Mandl (2007) in which students had to solve a complex task together showed that content schemes support argumentation in two ways. First of all, in the learning discourse, learners not only stated claims, but justified their statements with adequate evidence. Secondly, they reacted more transactively to one another. They referred to the statements of their collaborating partners and put forward counter-arguments, evaluations, reflections or integrations. Such contributions imply that students had to take into account the points of view of their collaborating partner; a task that necessitates deep elaborative and evaluative cognitive processes.

The impact of content schemes on social processes has not yet been investigated. This is mainly due to the fact that content schemes are theoretically based on assumptions used in cognitive psychology. In recent years, these concepts of individual learning were adapted to collaborative learning and effectively used regarding learning outcome. However, in the context of social processes in collaboration, no concrete effects could be theoretically assumed.

Research mainly shows positive results of content schemes on learning outcome with respect to collaborative learning. In this context, the main improvements were seen in the application of knowledge. For example, in a peer-teaching study by Ertl, Reiserer and Mandl (2002), learners who had to learn and teach pedagogical theories and therefore acquire declarative and strategic knowledge were supported by a content scheme presented as table with four cells. Learners with such a scheme focused more on all four relevant elements of the theory – theory, evidence, pedagogical consequences, own evaluation – than learners without a content scheme. Even though the collaboration was more effective, the content scheme had no significant effect on individual knowledge acquisition. Almost same results are described in a study of Fischer, Bruhn, Gräsel and Mandl (2000). In this study, learners were given the task of evaluating teaching scenarios with help of specific pedagogical theories, thus applying their acquired knowledge. Learners with the content scheme related theoretical concepts to case information more often than learners without the content scheme. Again, there was no effect on the individual learning outcome. Groups supported by a content scheme collaboratively applied their knowledge better in developing case solutions in a study of Fischer and colleagues (Fischer, Bruhn, Gräsel, & Mandl, 2002) than groups without a content scheme. The study by Kopp and Mandl (2007) mentioned above showed positive effects of the content scheme on the collaborative as well as on the individual learning outcome in the ability of learners to apply their knowledge. Learners with the content scheme justified their case solutions more frequently with adequate theoretical concepts and case information both collaboratively and individually than learners without the content scheme.

SUMMARY AND FUTURE RESEARCH DIRECTIONS

When analyzing the two structuring methods provided by collaboration scripts and content schemes for supporting virtual collaborative learning, we can conclude that they mainly support learning processes and collaborative learning outcomes.

Upon closer examination of learning processes, research has only investigated content-specific cognitive activities, while social processes have not been analyzed to any level of detail. In these studies, collaboration scripts supported discussions and the exchange of knowledge as well as argumentation and helped learners consider different perspectives. It is assumed that collaboration scripts focus learners on specific sub-tasks and activities which are relevant for collaborative learning. In this context, collaboration scripts had the expected effects on learning processes. Several areas have not yet been the subject of investigation, such as the effects on social processes such as constructive confrontations and conflict regulation, group goal orientation and motivation, social influence processes or participation and taking responsibility. There is only one field study which has evaluated the interaction between goal orientation, task completion, group cohesion, and taking responsibility. However, with this data, no conclusions could be drawn regarding the effect of the collaboration script itself as there were no control groups.

Content schemes also had positive effects on content-specific cognitive activities in virtual collaborative learning. Content schemes focus learners' attention on relevant aspects of the collaborative task using a meta-structure of the content often represented as a table in the computer interface. On this basis, learners are able to engage in activities which are important to the success of the collaboration. Again, there is no research regarding the effects of content schemes on social processes. Even though content schemes are mainly designed to foster content-specific activities, it would be of interest to research whether they also support social processes.

When we look at the learning outcome, both collaboration scripts and content schemes generally improve the quality of collaborative task solutions. As long as structuring methods are available for the learners in the collaboration phase, they are used in the intended way such that the quality of the collaborative task solution improves. Thus, collaboration scripts and content schemes support the collaborative learning phase, but do not promote the internalization of the structuring methods (King, 2007). Only a few studies have also indicated the positive effects of the structuring methods on the individual learning outcome. In this context, it would be of interest to discover under which conditions the structuring methods affect not only the collaborative learning outcome, but also the individual learning outcome.

In summary, there are three main aspects which must be investigated in future research. First, the effects of collaboration scripts and content schemes on social processes must be analyzed in more detail. Second, the effects of the structuring methods on individual learning outcomes must be examined in more detail to gain deeper insights into how collaboration scripts and content schemes function. The main question revolves around how collaboration scripts and content schemes must be designed so that learners internalize the structures and are able to apply and transfer them to later situations (King, 2007; Kolodner, 2007). A third aspect concerns the kind of studies. To date, there have mainly been experimental studies with ad hoc groups created solely for testing collaboration scripts and content schemes. What is missing in research are field studies with groups who interact over a longer period of time. Especially when investigating social processes, field studies are necessary to gain further insights into the effects of structuring methods.

CONCLUSION AND PRACTICAL IMPLICATIONS

This chapter described two techniques for fostering virtual collaborative learning: collaboration scripts and content schemes. To gain further insight into the effectiveness of both support methods, we introduced two main indicators for successful collaborative learning, namely learning processes and learning outcomes. The second part showed the effects of collaboration scripts and content schemes on learning processes and learning outcomes. Research has shown that both support methods foster content-specific cognitive processes and collaborative learning outcome. The effects of collaboration scripts and content schemes on social processes have not yet been investigated through research. Furthermore, the specific effects on individual knowledge acquisition and application have not been explicitly clarified.

Using collaboration scripts and content schemes is generally a good way to increase the effectiveness of collaborative learning – at least during collaboration itself. Accordingly, learning processes and the collaborative task solutions are of higher quality when these supporting techniques are used. Therefore, for teachers using virtual collaborative learning in their classes, it is recommended that they implement such techniques in order to reduce the problems which are related to the specifics of virtual collaboration, e.g. coordination problems or the development of a transactive memory. As collaboration scripts specify the interaction with phases and sub-tasks, coordination may be much easier for learners when using such scripts. Furthermore, because content schemes provide a meta-structure for the content, is seems to be less difficult to develop transactive knowledge or memory which is based on meta-knowledge about the knowledge of the collaborative learners. Even though these two positive effects of collaboration scripts and content schemes have not yet been evidenced through research, it seems clear that the positive outcomes of the two structuring techniques are indeed based on such mechanisms.

REFERENCES

Anderson, R. C., & Pearson, P. D. (1984). A schema-theoretic view of basic processes in reading comprehension. In Pearson, P. D. (Ed.), *Handbook of reading research* (pp. 255–291). New York: Longman.

Andriessen, J., Baker, M., & Suthers, D. (2003). Argumentation, computer support, and the educational context of confronting cognition. In Andriessen, J., Baker, M., & Suthers, D. (Eds.), *Arguing to learn: Confronting cognitions in computer-supported collaborative learning environments* (pp. 1–25). Dordrecht, The Netherlands: Kluwer.

Aronson, E., Blaney, N., Stephan, C., Sikes, J., & Snapp, M. (1978). *The jigsaw classroom*. Beverly Hills, CA: Sage.

Baker, M., & Lund, K. (1997). Prompting reflective interactions in a CSCL environment. *Journal of Computer Assisted Learning, 13*(3), 175–193. doi:10.1046/j.1365-2729.1997.00019.x

Bartlett, F. C. (1932). *Remembering: An experimental and social study*. Cambridge, UK: Cambridge University Press.

Brewer, W. F., & Nakamura, G. V. (1984). The nature and functions of schemas. Center for the Study of Reading, Technical Report Bo. 325. In Wyer, R. S., & Krull, T. K. (Eds.), *Handbook of social cognition* (*Vol. 1*, pp. 119–160). Mahwah, NJ: Lawrence Erlbaum.

Brooks, L. W., & Dansereau, D. F. (1983). Effects of structural schema training and text organization on expository prose processing. *Journal of Educational Psychology, 75*(6), 811–820. doi:10.1037/0022-0663.75.6.811

Butera, F., & Buchs, C. (2005). Reasoning together: From focusing to decentering. In Girotto, V., & Johnson-Laird, P. N. (Eds.), *The shape of reason* (pp. 193–203). Hove, UK: Psychology Press.

Clark, H. H., & Carlson, T. B. (1982). Speech acts and hearer's beliefs. In Smith, N. V. (Ed.), *Mutual knowledge* (pp. 1–36). New York, NY: Academic Press.

Cognition and Technology Group at Vanderbilt. (2000). Adventures in anchored instruction: Lessons from beyond the ivory tower. In Glaser, R. (Ed.), *Advances in instructional psychology: Educational design and cognitive science* (pp. 35–99). Mahwah, NJ: Erlbaum.

Cohen, E. G. (1994). Restructuring the classroom: Conditions for productive small groups. *Review of Educational Research, 64*(1), 1–35.

Dansereau, D. F. (1988). Cooperative learning strategies. In Weinstein, C. E., Goetz, E. T., & Alexander, P. A. (Eds.), *Learning and study strategies: Issues in assessment, instruction, and evaluation* (pp. 103–120). New York: Academic Press.

De Corte, E. (2003). Designing learning environments. In Verschaffel, L., Entwistle, N., & Merrienboer, J. J. G. v. (Eds.), *Powerful learning environments: Unravelling basic components and dimensions* (pp. 21–33). Amsterdam, The Netherlands: Pergamon.

De Jong, T., & Ferguson-Hessler, M. G. M. (1996). Types and qualities of knowledge. *Educational Psychologist, 31*(2), 105–113. doi:10.1207/s15326985ep3102_2

Dennis, A. R., & Valacich, J. S. (1999). Rethinking media richness: towards a theory of media synchronicity. In *Proceedings of the 32nd Annual Hawaii International Conference on Systems Sciences* (pp.1-10).Los Alamitos, CA: IEEE Press

Dillenbourg, P. (1999). What do you mean by 'collaborative learning. In Dillenbourg, P. (Ed.), *Collaborative learning: Cognitive and computational approaches* (pp. 1–19). Oxford, UK: Elsevier.

Doise, W., & Mugny, G. (1984). *Social Processes in Children's Learning*. Cambridge, UK: University Press.

Dweck, C. S., & Elliot, E. S. (1983). Achievement motivation. In Mussen, P., & Hetherington, E. M. (Eds.), *Handbook of child psychology* (pp. 643–691). New York: Wiley.

Elliot, A. J., & McGregor, H. (2001). A 2x2 achievement goal framework. *Journal of Personality and Social Psychology, 80*(3), 501–519. doi:10.1037/0022-3514.80.3.501

Ellis, C. A., Gibbs, S. J., & Rein, G. L. (1991). Groupware: Some issues and experiences. *Communications of the ACM, 34*(1), 35–58. doi:10.1145/99977.99987

Ertl, B., Fischer, F., & Mandl, H. (2006). Conceptual and socio-cognitive support for collaborative learning in videoconferencing environments. *Computers & Education, 47*(3), 298–315. doi:10.1016/j.compedu.2004.11.001

Ertl, B., Kopp, B., & Mandl, H. (2007). Supporting collaborative learning in videoconferencing using collaboration scripts and content schemes. In Fischer, F., Kollar, I., Mandl, H., & Haake, J. M. (Eds.), *Scripting computer-supported communication of knowledge – cognitive, computational and educational perspectives* (pp. 213–236). Berlin Heidelberg, Germany: Springer.

Ertl, B., Reiserer, M., & Mandl, H. (2002). Kooperatives Lernen in Videokonferenzen. *Unterrichtswissenschaft, 30*(4), 339–356.

Fischer, F., Bruhn, J., Gräsel, C., & Mandl, H. (2000). Kooperatives Lernen mit Videokonferenzen: Gemeinsame Wissenskonstruktion und individueller Lernerfolg. *Kognitionswissenschaft, 9*(1), 5–16. doi:10.1007/s001970000028

Fischer, F., Bruhn, J., Gräsel, C., & Mandl, H. (2002). Fostering collaborative knowledge construction with visualization tools. *Learning and Instruction, 12*(2), 213–232. doi:10.1016/S0959-4752(01)00005-6

Fischer, F., Kollar, I., Mandl, H., & Haake, J. M. (2007). *Scripting computer-supported communication of knowledge–Cognitive, computational, and educational perspectives*. New York: Springer.

Friedman, L. B., & McCullough, J. (1992). Computer conferencing as a support mechanism for teacher-researches in rural high school. In Waggoner, M. D. (Ed.), *Empowerment networks: Computer conferencing in education* (pp. 139–156). Englwood Cliffs, NJ: Prentice Hall.

Gunawardena, D. N., & Zittle, F. (1997). Social presence as predictor of satisfaction within a computer mediated conferencing environment. *American Journal of Distance Education, 11*(3), 8–25. doi:10.1080/08923649709526970

Harackiewicz, J. M., Barron, K. E., Pintrich, P. R., & Elliot, A. J., Thrash, Tm. M. (2002). Revision of achievement goal theory: Necessary and Illuminating. *Journal of Educational Psychology, 94*(3), 638–645. doi:10.1037/0022-0663.94.3.638

Härder, J. (2003). *Wissenskommunikation mit Desktop-Videokonferenzsystemen: Strukturierungsangebote für den Wissensaustausch und gemeinsame Inferenzen.* Unpublished dissertation, Albert-Ludwigs-Universität, Freiburg, Germany.

Hertz-Lazarowitz, R., Kirkus, V. B., & Miller, N. (1992). Implications of current research on cooperative interaction for classroom application. In Hertz-Lazarowitz, R. (Ed.), *Interaction in cooperative groups: The theoretical anatomy of group learning* (pp. 253–280). New York: Cambridge University Press.

Hinsz, V. B., Tindale, R. S., & Vollrath, D. A. (1997). The emerging conceptualization of groups as information processors. *Psychological Bulletin, 121*(1), 43–64. doi:10.1037/0033-2909.121.1.43

Hollingshead, A. B. (1996). Information suppression and status persistence in group decision making. The effects of communication media. *Human Communication Research, 23*(2), 193–219. doi:10.1111/j.1468-2958.1996.tb00392.x

Hron, A., Hesse, F.-W., Reinhard, P., & Picard, E. (1997). Strukturierte Kooperation beim computerunterstützten kollaborativen Lernen. *Unterrichtswissenschaft, 25*(1), 56–69.

Jonassen, D. H. (2000). Toward a design theory of problem solving. *Educational Technology Research and Development, 48*(4), 63–85. doi:10.1007/BF02300500

Kerr, N. L., & Bruun, S. (1983). The dispensability of member effort and group motivation losses: Free rider effects. *Personality and Social Psychology Bulletin, 44*(1), 78–94. doi:10.1037/0022-3514.44.1.78

King, A. (2007). Scripting collaborative learning processes: a cognitive perspective. In Fischer, F., Kollar, I., Mandl, H., & Haake, J. M. (Eds.), *Scripting computer-supported communication of knowledge – cognitive, computational and educational perspectives* (pp. 13–37). Berlin Heidelberg, Germany: Springer.

Kollar, I., Fischer, F., & Hesse, F. W. (2006). Collaboration scripts - A conceptual analysis. *Educational Psychology Review, 18*(2), 159–185. doi:10.1007/s10648-006-9007-2

Kolodner, J. L. (2007). The roles of scripts in promoting collaborative discourse in learning by design. In Fischer, F., Kollar, I., Mandl, H., & Haake, J. M. (Eds.), *Scripting computer-supported communication of knowledge – cognitive, computational and educational perspectives* (pp. 237–262). Berlin Heidelberg, Germany: Springer.

Kopp, B., Ertl, B., & Mandl, H. (2006). Wissensschema und Skript - Förderung der Anwendung von Theoriewissen auf die Aufgabenbearbeitung in Videokonferenzen. *Zeitschrift für Entwicklungspsychologie und Pädagogische Psychologie, 38*(3), 132–138. doi:10.1026/0049-8637.38.3.132

Kopp, B., & Mandl, H. (2006). Gemeinsame Wissenskonstruktion. In Bierhoff, H.-W., & Frey, D. (Eds.), *Handbuch der Sozialpsychologie und Kommunikationspsychologie* (pp. 504–509). Göttingen, Germany: Hogrefe.

Kopp, B., & Mandl, H. (2007). Fostering Argumentation with Script and Content Scheme in Videoconferencing. In: C. Chinn, G. Erkens, & S. Puntambekar (Eds.), *Proceedings of Mice, Minds and Society – The Computer Supported Collaborative Learning Conference, 8* (pp. 382-392), New Jersey: International Society of the Learning Sciences.

Kopp, B., & Mandl, H. (2008). *Collaborative online learning: A heterogeneous phenomenon.* Paper presented at the Conference on Knowledge Construction in E-Learning Context. (pp.23-29). Aachen University: Sun SITE Central Europe, RWTH. Retrieved April, 13, 2010, from http://ftp.informatik.rwth-aachen.de/ Publications/CEUR-WS/Vol-398/S1_KoppEtAl.pdf

Kopp, B., Schnurer, K., & Mandl, H. (2009). Collaborative learning in virtual seminars: Analyzing learning processes and learning outcomes. In C. O'Malley, D. Suthers, P. Reimann & A. Dimitracopoulou (Eds.), *Proceedings of Computer Supported Collaborative Learning Practices – CSCL 2009 Conference*. (pp.151-160). New Jersey: International Society of the Learning Sciences.

Krauss, R. M., & Fussell, S. R. (1990). Mutual knowledge and communicative effectiveness. In Galegher, J., Kraut, R. E., & Egido, C. (Eds.), *Intellectual teamwork: Social and technological foundations of cooperative work* (pp. 111–145). Hillsdale, NJ: Lawrence Erlbaum Associates.

Kreijins, K., Kirschner, P. A., & Jochems, W. (2003). Identifying the pitfalls for social interaction in computer-supported collaborative learning environments: a review of research. *Computers in Human Behavior, 19*(3), 335–353. doi:10.1016/S0747-5632(02)00057-2

Lambiotte, J. G., Skaggs, L. P., & Dansereau, D. F. (1993). Learning from lectures: effects of knowledge maps and cooperative review strategies. *Applied Cognitive Psychology, 7*(6), 483–497. doi:10.1002/acp.2350070604

Latané, B., Williams, K., & Harkins, S. (1979). Many hands make light the work: The causes and consequences of social loafing. *Journal of Personality and Social Psychology, 37*(6), 822–832. doi:10.1037/0022-3514.37.6.822

Lou, Y., Abrami, P. C., Spence, J. C., Poulsen, C., Chambers, B., & d'Apollonia, S. (1996). Within-Class Grouping: A Meta-Analysis. *Review of Educational Research, 66*(4), 423–458.

McGrath, J. E. (1990). Time matters in groups. In Galegher, J., Kraut, R. E., & Egido, C. (Eds.), *Intellectual teamwork: Social and technological foundations of cooperative work* (pp. 23–61). Hillsdale, NJ: Lawrence Erlbaum Associates.

Moreland, R. L. (2000). Transactive memory: learning who knows what in work groups and organizations. In Thompson, L., Messik, D., & Levine, J. (Eds.), *Shared Cognition in Organizations: The Management of Knowledge* (pp. 3–31). Hillsdale, NJ: Lawrence Erlbaum.

Moscovici, S. (1980). Toward a theory of conversion behavior. In L. Berkowitz /Ed.) [New York: Academic Press]. *Advances in Experimental Social Psychology, 13*, 209–239. doi:10.1016/S0065-2601(08)60133-1

Nemeth, C. J. (1986). Differential contributions of majority and minority influence. *Psychological Review, 93*(11), 23–32. doi:10.1037/0033-295X.93.1.23

O'Donnell, A. M., & Dansereau, D. F. (2000). Interactive effects of prior knowledge and material format on cooperative teaching. *Journal of Experimental Education, 68*(2), 101–118. doi:10.1080/00220970009598497

O'Donnell, A. M., & King, A. (Eds.). (1999). *Cognitive perspectives on peer learning*. Mahwah, NJ: Lawrence Erlbaum.

Paechter, M. (2003). *Wissenskommunikation, Kooperation und Lernen in virtuellen Gruppen. Lengerich*. Germany: Pabst Publisher.

Quiamzade, A., & Mugny, G. (2001). Social influence dynamics in aptitude tasks. *Social Psychology of Education*, *4*, 311–334. doi:10.1023/A:1011388821962

Reiserer, M. (2002). *Peer-Teaching in Videokonferenzen. Effekte niedrig- und hochstrukturierter Kooperationsskripte auf Lernprozess und Lernerfolg*. Unpublished Dissertation, Ludwig-Maximilians-Universität München, München, Germany.

Reiserer, M., Ertl, B., & Mandl, H. (2002). Fostering collaborative knowledge construction in desktop videoconferencing. Effects of content schemes and cooperation scripts in peer-teaching settings. In Stahl, G. (Ed.), *Computer support for collaborative learning: Foundations for a CSCL community – CSCL 2002* (pp. 379–388). Hillsdale, NJ: Lawrence Erlbaum.

Rummel, N., Ertl, B., Härder, J., & Spada, H. (2003). Supporting collaborative learning and problem-solving in desktop-videoconferencing settings. *International Journal of Educational Policy, Research, and Practice*, *4*(1), 83–115.

Rummel, N., & Spada, H. (2005). Learning to collaborate: An instructional approach to promoting collaborative problem solving in computer-mediated settings. *Journal of the Learning Sciences*, *14*(2), 201–241. doi:10.1207/s15327809jls1402_2

Rummel, N., & Spada, H. (2007). Can people learn computer-mediated collaboration by following a script? In Fischer, F., Kollar, I., Mandl, H., & Haake, J. M. (Eds.), *Scripting Computer-Supported Collaborative Learning* (pp. 39–55). New York: Springer. doi:10.1007/978-0-387-36949-5_3

Salomon, G. (1992). Effects with and of computers and the study of computer-based learning environments. In De Corte, E., Linn, M. C., Mandl, H., & Verschaffel, L. (Eds.), *Computer-based learning environments and problem solving* (pp. 249–263). Berlin Heidelberg, Germany: Springer.

Salomon, G., & Globerson, T. (1989). When teams do not function the way they ought to. *International Journal of Educational Research*, *13*(1), 89–99. doi:10.1016/0883-0355(89)90018-9

Salomon, G., & Perkins, D. N. (1998). Individual and social aspects of learning. *Review of Research in Education*, *23*(1), 1–24. doi:10.3102/0091732X023001001

Schank, R. C., & Abelson, R. P. (1977). *Scripts, plans, goals and understanding*. Hillsdale, NJ: Lawrence Erlbaum.

Schwarz, B. B., Neuman, Y., & Biezuner, S. (2000). Two wrongs may make a right: If they argue together! *Cognition and Instruction*, *18*(4), 461–494. doi:10.1207/S1532690XCI1804_2

Stasser, G., & Titus, W. (1985). Pooling of unshared information in group decision making: Biased information sampling during discussion. *Journal of Personality and Social Psychology*, *48*(6), 1467–1478. doi:10.1037/0022-3514.48.6.1467

Stegmann, K. (2008). *Argumentative Knowledge Construction. Analysing and Facilitating Discursive Processes, Cognitive Processes, and Knowledge Acquisition During Collaborative Argumentation in Online Discussions*. Dissertation, Ludwig-Maximilians-University.

Stegmann, K., Weinberger, A., Fischer, F., & Mandl, H. (2004). Scripting argumentative knowledge construction in computer-supported learning environments. In *Proceedings of the EARLI SIG 2004*. (pp.320-330). Retrieved April, 13, 2010, from http://www.iwm-kmrc.de/workshops / SIM2004/?go=prog

Suthers, D. (2001). Towards a systematic study of representational guidance for collaborative learning discourse. *Journal of Universal Computer Science*, *7*(3), 254–277.

Suthers, D., & Hundhausen, C. D. (2001). Learning by constructing collaborative representations: An empirical comparison of three alternatives. In P. Dillenbourg, A. Eurelings, & K. Hakkarainen (Eds.), *Proceedings of the First European Conference on Computer-Supported Collaborative Learning (euroCSCL)* (pp. 577-584). Maastricht, The Netherlands: McLuhan Institute.

Tomasetto, C., Mucchi-Faina, A., Alparone, F. R., & Pagliaro, S. (2009). Differential effects of majority and minority influence on argumentation strategies. *Social Influence*, *4*(1), 33–45. doi:10.1080/15534510802257510

Van Eemeren, F. H., Grootendorst, R., & Henkemans, F. S. (1996). *Fundamentals of argumentation theory - A handbook of historical backgrounds and contemporary developments*. Mahawah, NJ: Lawrence Erlbaum.

Wegner, D. M., Giuliano, T., & Hertel, P. T. (1985). Cognitive interdependence in close relationships. In Ickes, W. J. (Ed.), *Compatible and incompatible relationships* (pp. 253–276). New York: Springer.

Weinberger, A. (2003). *Scripts for computer-supported collaborative learning*. Dissertation, Ludwig-Maximilians-University Munich, Germany. Retrieved April, 13, 2010 from http://hal.archives-ouvertes.fr/docs/00/ 19/01/71/PDF/Weinberger_2003.pdf

Weinberger, A., Reiserer, M., Ertl, B., Fischer, F., & Mandl, H. (2003). Facilitating collaborative knowledge construction in computer-mediated learning with structuring tools. In Bromme, R., Hesse, F., & Spada, H. (Eds.), *Barriers and biases in net based communication. Norwell: Kluwer.*

Weinberger, A., Stegmann, K., Fischer, F., & Mandl, H. (2007). Scripting argumentative knowledge construction in computer-supported learning environments. In Fischer, F., Kollar, I., Mandl, H., & Haake, J. M. (Eds.), *Scripting Computer-Supported Collaborative Learning* (pp. 191–211). New York: Springer. doi:10.1007/978-0-387-36949-5_12

Wittenbaum, G. M., & Stasser, G. (1996). Management of information in small groups. In Nye, J. L., & Brower, A. M. (Eds.), *What's social about social cognition? Research on socially shared cognition in small groups* (pp. 3–28). Thousand Oaks, CA: Sage Publications.

Zhang, J., & Norman, D. A. (1994). Representations in distributed cognitive tasks. *Cognitive Science*, *18*(1), 87–122. doi:10.1207/s15516709cog1801_3

KEY TERMS AND DEFINITIONS

Collaboration Script: In educational psychology and computer-supported collaborative learning, the term collaboration script is used to sequence and support the interaction of learning groups. Collaboration script is defined "as an instructional means that provides collaborators with instructions for task-related interactions, that can be represented in different ways, and that can be directed at specific learning objectives. These objectives can be reached by introducing different kinds and sequences of activities, which are implicitly or explicitly clustered according to collaboration roles. Scripted activities can be broken down into individual acts that together form a larger activity, and scripts can vary with respect to how much structure they provide" (Kollar, Fischer, & Hesse, 2006, p. 162-163).

Content Scheme: Content schemes as an instructional tool in computer-supported collaborative learning include an expert meta-structure of important dimensions of the content in which the main components of the content are represented (Brooks, & Dansereau, 1983). They make key components of the content salient so that learners are able to focus either on missing or existing parts of the content (Suthers, 2001; Suthers & Hundhausen, 2001). This representation of specific concepts can guide and focus learners in their task-solving process because it modifies the representational context of the task by "changing learners' subjective representation of the task and influencing their ability to solve the task" (Ertl et al., 2007, p. 217).

Chapter 3
Fostering Collaborative Problem Solving by Content Schemes

Kathrin Helling
Bundeswehr University of München, Germany

Bernhard Ertl
Bundeswehr University of München, Germany

ABSTRACT

This chapter focuses on the facilitation of collaborative problem solving by the method of content schemes. Content schemes are content-specific pre-structures of learners' collaboration facilities that apply representational effects for the purpose of facilitation. They support learners to focus on particular issues of a problem solving process. The chapter presents results from two studies in the context of collaborative problem solving using videoconferencing. The first study compared learning facilitated by a content scheme and learning without facilitation; the second study compared the content scheme facilitation with facilitation by an enhanced version of this content scheme. This enhanced version focused learners on providing evidence for their claims. Results show that while the content scheme itself had a big influence on learning outcomes, the enhanced version had a rather small impact compared to the regular version. This result raises the issue about the complexity of facilitation methods. Complex facilitation may be too sophisticated for providing benefits to learning processes.

INTRODUCTION

Collaborative problem solving is estimated to be beneficial for learning processes and outcomes. Learners usually work collaboratively on case material in collaborative problem solving scenarios and this case material usually comprises of theory concepts and evidence (case information). By combining theoretical concepts with evidence from the case material, learners experience theory application. This approach allows them to reach a deeper understanding of the learning material (see Renkl, Mandl, & Gruber, 1996). Furthermore, learners share their perspectives on the case material within the collaborative setting and these different perspectives support them to apply their knowledge to different contexts outside the learning environment. In this context, Gijbels, Dochy,

DOI: 10.4018/978-1-61692-898-8.ch003

van den Bossche, and Segers (2005) call problem based learning one of the major developments of educational research, recently— mainly because problem based learning environments provide an active use of knowledge (DeCorte, 2003) with the goal to facilitate the transfer of the knowledge acquired and to avoid the acquisition of inert knowledge (see Renkl, Mandl &, Gruber 1996). Therefore, problem-based learning environments usually apply the principles of situated learning (see Lave & Wenger, 1991). Besides, literature on problem-based learning relies on different theoretical frameworks (see DeCorte, 1996; Glaser, Raghavan & Baxter, 1992), which commonly agree on an organised domain-specific knowledge base (or Joint Problem Space, according to Baker, Hansen, Joiner & Traum, 1999; Roschelle & Teasley, 1995) and meta-cognitive (often strategic) functions that operate on that knowledge (see Gijbels et al. 2005). With respect to the domain-specific knowledge base, Sugrue (1995) defines learners' knowledge structure as consisting of concepts, principles and links from concepts and principles to conditions and procedures for the application of knowledge. Considering strategic functions, he states the importance of planning and monitoring the problem solving process (see also Gijbels et al. 2005). Furthermore, learners have to negotiate shared meanings to establish a common knowledge base for collaboration. Thereby they engage in clarifying processes that are often referred to as 'grounding in communication' (see Clark & Brennan, 1991; Dillenbourg &Traum, 2006).

To sum up, processes of computer-supported collaborative problem solving can be characterised by three aspects (see Ertl, Kopp, & Mandl, 2006): *clarifying*, *strategic*, and *content-specific*.

Clarifying aspects of problem solving refer to several kinds of activities (e.g. discussion, actions, and gestures). Learners perform them in order to negotiate a "common ground" (Clark & Brennan, 1991) — a basis for their problem solving. By this, learners come to a common understanding of the task and create the Joint Problem Space (Baker et al., 1999; Roschelle & Teasley, 1995), which defines the central terms of a problem and brings the learners perspectives down to a common denominator.

The planning of the problem solving *strategy* and its evaluation is an important strategic aspect of collaborative problem solving processes. According to Bruhn (2000) it is necessary in collaborative learning where learners have to agree on their course of actions (e.g. timing and sequencing).

The *content-specific* work on the task is considered relevant for effective collaboration due to the presumed correlation between the quantity and quality of content-related communication and learning outcomes (Cohen & Lotan, 1995). According to Weinberger (2003) such work activities are social interactions (e.g. externalisation and elicitation of content) and epistemic activities (e.g. the definition, elaboration and argumentation of new content). Through successful engagement in these interactions learners work on a shared product or outcome, the collaborative problem solution, which can be seen as shared mental artefact (see Bereiter, 2002).

Collaborative Problem Solving in Videoconferencing

Collaborative problem solving in videoconferencing implicates some peculiarities for the learners because they do not share physical space. In a videoconferencing scenario, learners are spatially dispersed but they can communicate in spoken words by a microphone and speakers. Furthermore, they can see the head and chest of their learning partners by video transmission (see Finn, Sellen, & Wilbur, 1997). The videoconferencing environment usually provides a shared application for working on the collaborative problem solution. This shared application is a shared work space on the computer screens of the learners. It enables them to take mutual notes and work on the same document collaboratively (see e.g. Ertl, 2003;

Fischer, Bruhn, Gräsel, & Mandl, 2002; Ertl, Fischer, & Mandl, 2006). All learners can see and modify this document and thereby every learner has the chance to participate in the process of constructing the collaborative problem solution. The spatial dispersion of learners may require extended coordination of the synchronous work on the document provided in the shared work space, which could result in increased verbal efforts (e.g. Acker & Levitt, 1987; O'Connaill, Whittaker, & Wilbur, 1993). For example, learners cannot point out aspects of the document to each other by using a finger and they may have to use the mouse pointer or describe the meant location verbally. Therefore, learners may invest more efforts in processes of clarifying communication and grounding (Clark & Brennan, 1991) for referring to particular elements of their shared artefact. Thus, the videoconferencing scenario could increase learners' need for grounding in communication.

In summary, learners' collaborative problem solving comprises of several activities like the content-specific application of theoretical concepts on problems and strategic processes for planning and monitoring the application of knowledge, and clarifying processes to resolve possible misunderstandings. These activities result in a shared mental artefact, the collaborative problem solution. Besides the advantages of problem-based learning, learning environments for collaborative problem solving contain some challenges for learners, and learners may sometimes not have the strategic skills necessary for developing a collaborative problem solution. Furthermore, the scenario of videoconferencing could provide further constraints and affordances for the learners. The following section will consider the issue of how instructional support could facilitate learners' collaborative problem solving with respect to its process and outcomes.

FACILITATING COLLABORATIVE PROBLEM SOLVING IN VIDEOCONFERENCING

Facilitation of collaborative problem solving can aim at different aspects of the learning process. Therefore, facilitation may introduce different facilitation methods. The main focus lies on strategies for fostering the collaborative problem solving process, which are often implemented by structuring tools. "Structuring tools aim at facilitating processes of collaborative knowledge construction by guiding interaction with constraints and affordances of the learning environment, by suggesting a structure to learners' collaboration or by providing support regarding the learning contents" (Weinberger, Reiserer, Ertl, Fischer & Mandl, 2003, p. 4). Some structuring tools aim at resolving issues of group phenomena and missing collaboration skills by the application of scripts for collaboration (see e.g. Ertl, Fischer, & Mandl, 2006; Fischer, Kollar, Mandl, & Haake, 2007; Rummel & Spada, 2005; Weinberger, 2003; Weinberger, Ertl, Fischer, & Mandl, 2005) or trainings for collaboration (see Rummel & Spada, 2005). Other structuring tools aim at content-specific facilitation, by providing content strategies and visualisation of content aspects. These can be implemented in a learning environment by methods like mapping (Fischer et al., 2002) or content schemes (Ertl, Fischer, & Mandl, 2006). The introduction of content-specific structuring tools to the learners can be realized by pre-structuring the shared artefact or the shared application in videoconferencing. In the context of this chapter, we will illustrate and analyze the facilitation method of the content scheme in detail.

Content Schemes

Content schemes use the mechanisms of task representation. They provide and modify the representational context of a task by visualising a structure or strategy. This structure often works as a template by providing placeholders for important dimensions or aspects of the content, e.g. a tabular pre-structure. Zhang and Norman (1994) postulate that such a modified representational context of a task may also change learners' subjective representation of this task. Ertl, Fischer, and Mandl (2006) discuss that the modified context may also introduce an implicit strategy for solving a task. Both, the modified subjective representation as well as the introduced strategy, may facilitate learners' ability to solve the task. An additional aspect of content schemes is the salience of contents (see Suthers & Hundhausen, 2003). The contents entered by learners in the scheme remain salient during the collaboration process. Furthermore, the template effect of a content scheme supports the salience of content dimensions: even if learners do not enter anything at all in the pre-structured table they can see which content dimensions are relevant for the specific problem solving process. Due to these aspects of salience, Suthers and Hundhausen (2001) postulate the concept of "representational guidance". Its implementation allows to guide learners and to focus their learning activities, particularly on contents which would have been neglected without the availability of a content scheme (see Ertl, Fischer, & Mandl, 2006; Ertl, Kopp, & Mandl, 2008). Consequently, representational guidance can be an important mechanism for providing learners with a strategy for collaborative problem solving.

Many studies provide evidence for the effects of content schemes in the context of individual learning settings (see Brooks & Dansereau, 1983; Kotovsky & Fallside, 1989; Kotovsky, Hayes & Simon, 1985; Larkin, 1989; Zhang & Norman, 1994; Zhang, 1997). During the last decade, their beneficial effects were further supported by their use to facilitate computer-supported collaborative problem solving (see e.g. Ertl, Fischer, & Mandl, 2006; Ertl et al., 2008; Fischer et al., 2002; Suthers & Hundhausen, 2001). Fischer et al. (2002) investigated the effects of structural visualisation and were able to show beneficial effects of the content scheme on the collaboration process and outcomes. Suthers and Hundhausen (2001) also reported similar effects with respect to tabular content schemes. Fischer, Bruhn, Gräsel, and Mandl (2000) and Bruhn (2000) discovered that content schemes changed collaboration processes in videoconferencing with respect to knowledge convergence, but without affecting the outcomes. The studies of Ertl, Fischer, and Mandl (2006) and Ertl et al. (2008) show the particular effect of content schemes on guiding learners and focusing their attention to specific contents.

Based on this background, this chapter will provide insights into facilitating collaborative problem solving in a computer supported audio-visual learning environment (videoconferencing). It has a focus on facilitation by a content-related pre-structuring of the collaboration processes: a *content scheme* to facilitate learners' task-specific strategies. The chapter presents different types of content schemes for the learners, which were analyzed in two empirical studies with regard to their influence on the actual *processes of collaborative problem solving* and the *quality of collaborative problem solutions*.

RESEARCH QUESTIONS

The chapter investigates how different types of content schemes can be used for collaborative problem-solving. As collaborative problem solving relies strongly on linking theoretical concepts with evidence provided by case material (see e.g. Kuhn, Weinstock, & Flaton, 1994; Sodian, Zaitchik & Carey, 1991; Suthers & Hundhausen, 2003), it is obvious that learners need to thoroughly examine evidence to receive the full benefits of collaborative problem-solving. However, such an examination of case materials is not always done by learners to an appropriate extent. The research described in this chapter has a focus on two aspects: the first study analysis in how far content schemes can facilitate collaborative problem solving (in general); the second study has a particular focus on the issue of evidence use, in particular the provision of case information. It investigates how content schemes can be improved to supports learners to consider more evidence from the case material in their collaborative problem solutions. This chapter has a focus on how content schemes can facilitate *processes* and *outcomes* of collaborative problem solving in video conferencing. The content schemes of both studies are compared with respect to their impact on the processes and outcomes, which is reflected in the following research questions:

Research question 1: In how far do different types of content schemes have an effect on learners' problem solving processes?

Research question 2: In how far do different types of content schemes have an effect on the quality of learners' collaborative problem solution?

METHOD

Learning Scenario

The focus of the two studies was on the effects of content schemes on collaborative problem solving in videoconferencing. In both studies, the problem solving approach was implemented in the learning scenario by giving the learners the role of school psychologists who worked on a case of a pupil's problems in school. In particular, they had to deal with the pupil's problems in mathematics, taking into account the three perspectives of the pupil's teacher, his mother, and the pupil himself. They received a case framework, which contained the background story and case information specific to the three particular perspectives. The learners had to make a collaborative analysis of the case in order to find possible causes for the pupils' problems according to the attribution theory. All three perspectives comprised of different case information (evidence) which was distributed among the three learners. This resource distribution was implemented differently in both studies. In the first study, the three different perspectives had a minor extent of shared evidence, which resulted in a lower task difficulty. In the second study, there was no shared evidence and therefore the task difficulty was higher.

The experimental sessions comprised of two learning activities. At first, in an individual learning activity (25-30 minutes) learners had to read a text about the attribution theory of Kelley (1973) and Heider (1958) with the aim to familiarise with the main concepts of this theory. Secondly, in a collaborative learning activity (40-50 minutes) groups of three learners had to solve the case of the pupil's problems at school together. Therefore, it was necessary to extract and compile evidence of the three different perspectives from the case framework and to classify it according to the attribution theory. All learners were instructed to exchange their knowledge about evidence of their respective perspective. During the collaboration process, learners were connected via a desktop videoconferencing system that included an audio- and video-connection. A shared application – in particular a joint word processing document – was available on the computers of all three learners (it could be edited by each of them) to support their collaborative problem solution.

Participants and Design

Both studies applied the same learning scenario but provided facilitation to a different extent. The experimental design of study 1 compared a control condition with a content scheme treatment (general focus). In this study, 78 undergraduate students of educational science took part (26 triads, see Table 1). In study 2, the general content scheme applied in study 1 was compared to a content scheme with enhancements for introducing evidence in the process of collaborative problem solving (evidence focus). In that study, 60 students of

Table 1. Design of the two studies

Content Scheme			
	without	with	enhanced
Study 1 (general)	13 triads	13 triads	--------
Study 2 (evidence)	--------	10 triads	10 triads

education science and psychology took part (20 triads, see Table 1). As Table 1 indicates, both studies had the general content scheme in common and compared it with another treatment. In both studies, the participants, some framing conditions, and the instruction with respect to the application of evidence were slightly different, and thus they will be analyzed separately in the following.

Realisation of the Treatment and Use of the Content Scheme

Applying the content scheme aimed at fostering collaboration domain-specifically by visualising important dimensions of the content. Thereby, the content schemes focused learners' attention on the different aspects important for analysing attribution patterns. In both studies, learner triads with the support measure of the *content scheme* or *enhanced content scheme* received it during the collaborative problem solving activity. Both types of the content scheme were made available to the learners via the shared application of the videoconferencing setting. Learners without content scheme worked with a shared application which was not pre-structured. In turns, all three learners had the possibility to insert information in the shared application – either in the pre-structured tables of the content schemes or in the unstructured document.

In the *content scheme*, the causes for the pupil's problems in mathematics were the starting point for the collaborative problem solving process. Learners had to identify the different causes provided in the case materials of the three different perspectives of the pupil, teacher and mother. The next category comprised of the theoretical concepts of the attribution theory: consensus and consistency. Regarding this category, learners had to identify the respective information from the case information and determine whether the particular instance had a high or low value. Based on these determinations, the learners had to find the corresponding attribution patterns according to the theoretical work of Kelley and Heider (see Table 2).

The *enhanced content scheme* had basically the same structure as the content scheme but was designed with two additional rows to support learners' differentiation between theory and evidence (see Figure 1). Thus, the enhancement provided different layers for each cause, one for theory (dark grey) and the other one for evidence (light grey).

Both types of the content schemes did not give an explicit strategy to the learners but rather vi-

Table 2. Content scheme with exemplary case information and attribution

Causes	Case Information		Attribution Pattern	
	Consistency	Consensus	by Kelly	by Heider
Subject of Mathematics	High, all pupils have difficulties in Math in 8th grade	High, difficulties during complete duration of 8th grade	object	External Stable

Figure 1. Enhanced content scheme with exemplary case information and attribution

	Causes	Case information		Attribution pattern	
		Consistency	Consensus	Kelly	Heider
Theory		High	High	Object	External Stable
Evidence	Subject of Mathematics	all pupils have difficulties in Math in 8th grade	difficulties during complete duration of 8th grade		
Theory					
Evidence					
Theory					
Evidence					

sualized the important aspects of finding causes, connecting them with evidence information about consensus and consistency and finally determining the attribution pattern.

Dependent Variables

The study analyzed the problem solving processes and the quality of the collaborative problem solution for evaluating the effectiveness of the treatments.

Analysis of the Problem Solving Process

For the problem solving process analysis, the spoken discourse of the learner groups was transcribed and segmented into turns. Each turn was coded according to a fixed coding scheme (see Table 4; Ertl, Kopp & Mandl, 2006). The coding scheme provided three main categories: (1) content-specific negotiation, (2) strategic negotiation, and (3) clarifying negotiation (grounding). Besides this, the coding scheme provided also a category for off task and sub-categories. These last two categories are of minor importance for the analysis performed in this chapter and therefore the focus will be on the three main categories in the following.

A turn was coded as content-specific negotiation, if learners dealt with evidence or theoretical concepts in order to construct the collaborative problem solution. The category of strategic negotiation comprised of activities of discussing a strategy for problem solving, planning subsequent steps and evaluating the current progress or quality of the collaborative problem solution. Clarifying negotiation aimed at reaching a shared understanding among learners. It was directed to establish grounding in communication (see Clark

Table 4. Coding scheme for learners' problem solving processes

Category	Turn
Content-specific	E.g.: "In the 8th grade, all pupils have problems with math."; "Do you have some information about consensus?"
Strategic	E.g.: "We should summarise, somehow."; "Should we go ahead with another cause?"
Clarifying	E.g.: "I can't understand you."; "Jasmine took the perspective of the pupil's mother."

& Brennan, 1991), to resolve problems in understanding the specific perspectives represented by each learner, and to deal with challenges in handling the learning environment from a technical perspective. In both studies, two different raters analyzed 10% of the discourses to ensure objectivity. The inter-rater reliability of the coding scheme was good (study 1: κ =.88; study 2; κ =.94).

Analysis of the Quality of Collaborative Problem Solution (Outcome)

For measuring the quality of collaborative problem solution, the status of the joint problem solution was analyzed at the end of the collaboration process. The joint problem solution was created by the learners during their collaboration process: learners noted the results of the case solution in the shared application. Correctly identified evidence, correct determinations of consensus and consistency and correct attributions were marked and summed up to a score. The maximum score was 200 (100 points for the correct identification of all evidence, 100 points for correct identification and application of all theoretical concepts). The closer the score of a learners' problem solution was to the maximum, the higher was its overall quality. To ensure objectivity of the analyzes, two raters coded 10% of the tests. In both studies, the inter-rater reliability of coding was good (study 1: r=.87; study 2: r=.87).

RESULTS

Problem Solving Processes

The first research question considered the effect of the content schemes on learners' problem solving processes. In study 1 (general), the proportion of learners' turns in the three categories of content-specific negotiation, strategic negotiation and clarifying negotiation showed little difference between the treatment with content scheme and the treatment without support (control treatment). In both treatments, the majority of turns was related to the content of the problem solution. Learners in the treatment without content scheme uttered 83% of content-specific talk, and learners supported with content scheme produced 86% content-specific turns. The strategic planning of the problem solving process was second: 14% of the turns made by learners in the treatment without content scheme, and 13% of the turns of learners in the treatment with content scheme were related to the strategic planning of the collaborative problem solution. Clarifying negotiation had the smallest share of the discussions in both treatments (without content scheme: 3%, with content scheme: 1%). Descriptively, learners with content scheme used less strategic and less clarifying negotiation than learners in the control group. This enabled learners with content scheme to work more content-specifically.

In study 2 (evidence), the number of learners' turns in the three process categories again showed little difference between the two treatments. The majority of turns comprised of content-specific negotiation (with content scheme: 90%; with enhanced content scheme: 87%). The second most frequent turns in both treatments were related to clarifying negotiation. Learners in the treatment with content scheme produced 7% clarifying turns, and learners who were supported with the enhanced content scheme used 8% of their discourse for clarifying. Strategic planning of the problem solution was used to the least extent in both treatments of study 2 (evidence). The discourse of triads in the content scheme treatment comprised of 3% strategic talk, and learners supported with the enhanced content scheme dedicated 5% of their discussions to strategic planning. Comparing the treatment of the content scheme with the treatment of the enhanced content scheme, the frequencies of clarifying and strategic negotiation increased for learners who received support by the enhanced content scheme. In consequence, learners in the treatment with enhanced content scheme had a minor proportion of content-specific negotiation.

Even if both studies are not directly comparable, we can see differences with respect to the effects of the pre-structuring provided in each of them. In study 1 (general), the structure provided by the content scheme reduced strategic and clarifying talk, and therefore enabled learners to focus more on content- specific negotiation. Yet, the opposite happened in study 2 (evidence): the additional structure, which was provided by the enhanced content scheme increased the learners' need to engage in strategic and clarifying talk and therefore reduced their content-specific negotiation. Furthermore, we can see that learners of study 2 (evidence) had a higher proportion of content-specific talk, needed much more clarifying, but were less engaged in strategic talk than learners of study 1 (general). These observations may have been caused by differences in the instruction given to learners in both studies. In study 2 (evidence), the instructions focused learners more on evidence and the distribution of resources. As learners of study 2 (evidence) had no shared evidence, they may have needed to invest more clarifying activities (grounding) to establish a shared knowledge base.

Quality of Collaborative Problem Solution (Outcome)

The second research question focused on the effect of the content schemes on the learners' collaborative problem solution. Figure 2 presents the values of the quality of collaborative problem solution for study 1 (general) for the categories of theory and evidence. Learners in the treatment with content scheme achieved a higher quality in their collaborative problem solution than learners in the treatment without content scheme. Especially, the results for the identification of theoretical concepts improved dramatically for learners using the content scheme. Furthermore, these learners also identified on average 25% more evidence than learners without content scheme.

Figure 3 presents the results regarding the quality of collaborative problem solution of study 2 (evidence). The data shows that learners in the treatment with enhanced content scheme scored slightly better than learners who were supported with the general type of the content scheme. This result relates to both categories, theory as well as evidence.

The comparison of these outcomes reveals some differences in the effect of the content-specific facilitation method. In study 1 (general), a great impact of the content scheme was re-

Figure 2. Study 1 (general) Average quality of problem solution with and without content scheme, by theory and evidence (0-100 points each)

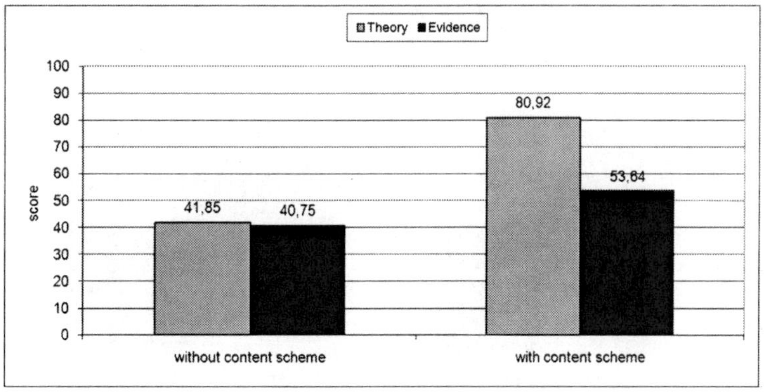

ported: the quality of the theory concepts identified by learners almost doubled and a huge gain in evidence identification was observed. Such an impact could not be reported for the enhanced content scheme in study 2 (evidence). It just provided marginal gains in theory as well as in evidence identification by learners. This may be obvious for the category of theory, as the enhanced content scheme did not provide more facilitation for this category than the general content scheme. However, the results for the category of evidence raise the question why the enhanced content scheme did not show any greater effect. Comparing the outcomes of both studies, the higher task difficulty of study 2 is reflected in the theory scores of the general content scheme condition of both studies, which dropped from 81 to 56 points. However, the outcomes show also a reduction in the difference between theory and evidence. In study 2, learners identified a higher proportion of evidence in both treatments as compared to the theory identified in the content scheme treatment of study 1.

SUMMARY AND DISCUSSION

The aim of this chapter was to describe how content schemes may influence problem solving processes and outcomes. Therefore, we presented two studies: study 1 (general) compared the effect of a *content scheme* with a control treatment in which learners did not get content-specific support; study 2 (evidence) investigated effects of an *enhanced content scheme* for dealing with evidence in problem solving. The general content scheme treatment used the same facilitation method for both studies and could therefore serve as baseline for the comparison of the two studies. The results showed differences between both studies with respect to problem solving processes and to learning outcomes. We attribute these differences to the increased task difficulty of study 2 (evidence), which resulted from a different distribution of evidence in the case material of learners. Furthermore, the specific focus on evidence in the instructions provided for learners in study 2 (evidence) might have influenced the problem solving processes and outcomes. Considering these two limitations for our discussion, we can emphasize the following findings:

In study 1 (general), the content scheme affected descriptively the collaborative problem solving by reducing the proportion of learners' strategic planning and their need for clarifying negotiation. By this result, we presume that the content scheme introduced an implicit strategy to the collaboration process, which enabled learners

Figure 3. Study 2 (evidence) Average quality of problem solution with content scheme and enhanced content scheme, by theory and evidence (0-100 points each)

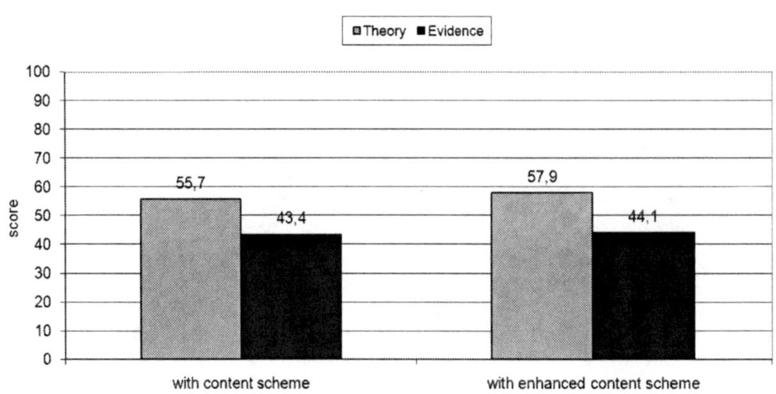

to work more content-specifically. Thereby, the content scheme may have substituted learners strategic actions (see also Ertl, Kopp, & Mandl, 2006). Furthermore, the content scheme provided learners with a clear gain in the quality of learning outcomes – with respect to theory as well as with respect to evidence. This result underlines research results which show that content-specific pre-structuring can be an important facilitation method in collaborative settings and strengthens the findings of earlier research with respect to the instructional value of representational guidance (see e.g. Ertl, Fischer, & Mandl, 2006; Suthers & Hundhausen, 2003).

Study 2 (evidence) aimed at improving the general content scheme with an evidence-specific enhancement. Yet, this treatment did not meet the expectations with regard to its effectiveness. Based on our theoretical assumptions, there are three possible explanations for the results. First of all, the effect of representational guidance and salience may be limited by the complexity of the content scheme. According to Suthers and Hundhausens (2003) the concept of salience works with a clear indication of missing items to learners through the provision of representational guidance. However, this effect may decrease with a growing complexity of the intervention: each field in the provided pre-structured template may receive proportionally less attention from the learners. A second explanation postulates an interaction of the complexity of an intervention with the learner's experiences (see Dobson, 1999). Dobson discussed that a beneficial tool needs to correspond with the learners' abilities. If the tool was too powerful, it may have exceeded the learners' skills to use it and therefore learners may not take the full benefits of it. Third, one may consider that the amount of evidence provided by the learners was relatively high (about 75% of the theory concepts). It may be the case that the enhanced content scheme introduced a deductive strategy to substantiate theory claims by evidence, instead of an inductive approach. This would mean that learners started the problem solution with naming theory concepts and then searched for evidence which fits to the theory, instead of identifying existing evidence first and classifying it by theory concepts—and for such a strategy the proportion of identified evidence (75%) may already be a ceiling effect.

IMPLICATIONS AND FUTURE RESEARCH

This chapter provided insights in the strengths and limitations of content schemes for facilitation of collaborative problem solving. It would be of further interest to see how the specific processes of content-specific, clarifying and strategic negotiation correlate with the outcomes, and if particular processes can predict outcomes in a certain way. However, for a comparison of these aspects the frames of both studies were too different. The learning setting as well as the intervention had an effect on the problem solving processes, and the results for this research question would hardly be interpretable. The differences in the clarifying, strategic and content-specific problem solving processes of both studies (see "Results: Problem Solving Processes") are an indicator for these effects. Ertl, Kopp, and Mandl (2006) as well as Helling (2006) identified strategic activities as an important predictor for collaborative outcomes (see also Gijbels et al., 2005). Yet, in the context of studying the facilitation of problem solving strategies this issue would need a more differentiated analysis than would be possible in the scope of this chapter.

Furthermore, the issue of the interaction of content schemes and videoconferencing should be analyzed in more detail. The shared work space may receive much more of learners' attention in virtual settings than in physically co-present settings due to the fact that it is the main interaction channel of learners in such settings. Issues in this context were further explored by Ertl, Kopp, and Mandl (2006). In their study, they analyzed how far learners' discussions were related to the creation of the shared external representation. Furthermore, the Fischer et al. (2002) study compared learning processes and outcomes in a videoconferencing condition with a face-to-face condition. Both studies were able to show peculiarities of content-specific support in videoconferencing. Further research may investigate the effects of such support in the three different settings videoconferencing, face-to-face with computer support, and face-to-face without computer support to gather in deep insights of the effects of content schemes.

This chapter presented the method of content scheme, which relies on the concept of representational guidance, for facilitation of collaborative problem solving on a content-specific level. Other methods, like collaboration scripts, focus on pre-structuring the interaction of learners in collaborative settings. Collaboration scripts aim at the instructional introduction of beneficial collaboration strategies and prevention of undesired group effects. Studies have shown that the combination of scripts and schemes provides best effects for collaboration outcomes (see e.g. Ertl, Fischer, & Mandl, 2006). Scripting research nowadays deals with flexible scripting which relates to generic scripts for different purposes (see e.g. Dillenbourg & Jermann, 2007; Haake & Pfister, 2007). Further research in the context of content schemes should also focus on the issue of flexibility. In this context, future content scheme approaches should consider how schemes interact with a learner's prior knowledge. Ertl, Kopp, and Mandl (2005) could show that the facilitation by content schemes was able to balance out differences in the learners' prior knowledge (see also Ertl, 2009; Ertl & Mandl, 2006). This opens the chance for the flexible provision of particular content schemes adapted to different prior knowledge levels that can particularly facilitate learners on lower competence levels.

CONCLUSION

In this chapter, we analyzed and compared collaborative learning processes and outcomes of two different content scheme treatments and a control condition from two studies. By this procedure, we were able to show the impact of two content schemes on problem solving processes and outcomes of learners in a videoconference setting. The general content scheme showed a facilitating effect for the content-specific work on the task by providing an implicit strategy for problem solving and it improved the learning outcomes by focusing learners' attention on the relevant theory concepts and evidence required for a high quality problem solution. The enhanced content scheme was subject to certain limitations with regard to its facilitating effect: its complexity increased the learners' need for clarifying negotiation, and it reduced the salience of theory and evidence dimensions by splitting the learners' attention between both aspects. Also, the enhanced content scheme implied a rather deductive strategy which may have prevented learners from starting the problem solving process with the identification of existing evidence, followed by the application of theory concepts on this evidence.

From both studies, we can draw implications for the implementation of content schemes in educational practice. First of all, content schemes are a powerful means to support collaborative problem solving. The application of content schemes in collaborative problem solving in videoconferencing makes important aspects of the problem solving salient during the collaboration process. This could enable learners to build an implicit strategy for problem solving (see Ertl, Fischer, & Mandl, 2006). However, the impact of the tool is limited. If content schemes get more and more complex, their supportive effect may be limited to a particular level. Additionally, influences from the learning setting and task presentation, as well as the combination of the content scheme approach with scripting approaches, should be considered for the purpose of facilitating learners' collaborative problem solving processes and outcomes.

ACKNOWLEDGMENT

This research was funded by Deutsche Forschungsgemeinschaft (DFG), project number MA 978/13-3 and MA 978/13-4. We would particularly like to thank Prof. Dr. Heinz Mandl and Dr. Birgitta Kopp who were strongly engaged in the design and implementation of the projects and the respective studies.

REFERENCES

Acker, S. R., & Levitt, S. R. (1987). Designing videoconference facilities for improved eye contact. *Journal of Broadcasting & Electronic Media, 31*(2), 181–191.

Baker, M., Hansen, T., Joiner, R., & Traum, D. (1999). The role of grounding in collaborative learning tasks. In Dillenbourg, P. (Ed.), *Collaborative Learning: Computational and Cognitive Approaches* (pp. 31–63). Oxford, UK: Elsevier Science.

Bereiter, C. (2002). *Education and mind in the knowledge age*. Mahwah, NJ: Erlbaum.

Brooks, L. W., & Dansereau, D. F. (1983). Effects of structural schema training and text organization on expository prose processing. *Journal of Educational Psychology, 75*(6), 811–820. doi:10.1037/0022-0663.75.6.811

Bruhn, J. (2000). *Förderung des kooperativen Lernens über Computernetze. Prozess und Lernerfolg beim dyadischen Lernen mit Desktop-Videokonferenzen*. Frankfurt am Main, Germany: Peter Lang.

Clark, H. H., & Brennan, S. E. (1991). Grounding in communication. In Resnick, L. B. (Ed.), *Perspectives on socially shared cognition* (pp. 127–149). Washington, DC: American Psychological Association. doi:10.1037/10096-006

Cohen, E. G., & Lotan, R. A. (1995). Producing equal-status interaction in the heterogeneous classroom. *American Educational Research Journal, 32*(1), 99–120.

De Corte, E. (1996). Learning theory and instructional science. In Reimann, P., & Spada, E. (Eds.), *Learning in humans and machines* (pp. 97–109). Oxford, UK: Elsevier.

De Corte, E. (2003). Designing learning environments that foster the productive use of acquired knowledge and skills. In De Corte, E., Verschaffel, L., Entwistle, N., & Merrienboer, J. J. G. v. (Eds.), *Powerful learning environments: Unravelling basic components and dimensions* (pp. 21–33). Amsterdam, The Netherlands: Pergamon.

Dillenbourg, P., & Jermann, P. (2007). Designing integrative scripts. In Fischer, F., Kollar, I., Mandl, H., & Haake, J. M. (Eds.), *Scripting computer-supported collaborative learning. Cognitive, computational and educational perspectives*. Dordrecht, The Netherlands: Springer. doi:10.1007/978-0-387-36949-5_16

Dillenbourg, P., & Traum, D. (2006). Sharing solutions: Persistence and grounding in multimodal collaborative problem solving. *Journal of the Learning Sciences, 15*(1), 121–151. doi:10.1207/s15327809jls1501_9

Dobson, M. (1999). Information enforcement and learning with interactive graphical systems. *Learning and Instruction, 9*(4), 365–390. doi:10.1016/S0959-4752(98)00052-8

Ertl, B. (2003). *Kooperatives Lernen in Videokonferenzen. Förderung von individuellem und gemeinsamem Lernerfolg durch external repräsentierte Strukturangebote [Cooperative learning in videoconferencing. Support of individual and cooperative learning outcomes by representational aids].* [Dissertation, Ludwig-Maximilians-Universität München]. Retrieved April 8, 2010 from http://edoc.ub.uni-muenchen.de/archive/ 00001227/01/Ertl_Bernhard_M.pdf

Ertl, B. (2009). Conceptual and procedural knowledge construction in computer supported collaborative learning. In C. O'Malley, D. Suthers, P. Reimann & A. Dimitracopoulou (Eds.), *Proceedings of the CSCL2009 conference Computer supported collaborative learning practices.* (pp. 137-141). Retrieved April 8, 20101 from http://www.isls.org/: International Society of the Learning Sciences (ISLS).

Ertl, B., Fischer, F., & Mandl, H. (2006). Conceptual and socio-cognitive support for collaborative learning in videoconferencing environments. *Computers & Education, 47*(3), 298–315. doi:10.1016/j.compedu.2004.11.001

Ertl, B., Kopp, B., & Mandl, H. (2005). Effects of an individual's prior knowledge on collaborative knowledge construction and individual learning outcomes in videoconferencing. In Koschmann, T., Chan, T.-W., & Suthers, D. D. (Eds.), *Computer supported collaborative learning 2005: the next 10 years!* (pp. 145–154). Mahwah, NJ: Lawrence Erlbaum Associates.

Ertl, B., Kopp, B., & Mandl, H. (2006). Fostering collaborative knowledge construction in case-based learning in videoconferencing. *Journal of Educational Computing Research, 35*(4), 377–397. doi:10.2190/A0LP-482N-0063-J480

Ertl, B., Kopp, B., & Mandl, H. (2008). Supporting learning using external representations. *Computers & Education, 51*(4), 1599–1608. doi:10.1016/j.compedu.2008.03.001

Ertl, B., & Mandl, H. (2006). Effects of individual's prior knowledge on collaborative knowledge construction and individual learning outcomes in videoconferencing. In S. A. Barab, K. E. Hay & D. T. Hickey (Eds.), *Proceedings of Making a difference: the 7th International Conference of the Learning Sciences (ICLS): Vol. 1*, (pp.161-167). Mahwah, NJ: International Society of the Learning Sciences/ Lawrence Erlbaum.

Finn, K. E., Sellen, A. J., & Wilbur, S. B. (Eds.). (1997). *Video-mediated communication.* Mahwah, NJ: Lawrence Erlbaum.

Fischer, F., Bruhn, J., Gräsel, C., & Mandl, H. (2000). Kooperatives Lernen mit Videokonferenzen: Gemeinsame Wissenskonstruktion und individueller Lernerfolg. *Kognitionswissenschaft, 9*(1), 5–16. doi:10.1007/s001970000028

Fischer, F., Bruhn, J., Gräsel, C., & Mandl, H. (2002). Fostering collaborative knowledge construction with visualization tools. *Learning and Instruction, 12*(2), 213–232. doi:10.1016/S0959-4752(01)00005-6

Fischer, F., Kollar, I., Mandl, H., & Haake, J. M. (Eds.). (2007). *Scripting computer-supported communication of knowledge - Cognitive, computational, and educational perspectives.* Berlin, Heidelberg: Springer.

Gijbels, D., Dochy, F., van den Bossche, P., & Segers, M. (2005). Effects of problem-based learning: A meta-analysis from the angle of the assessment. *Review of Educational Research, 75*(1), 27–61. doi:10.3102/00346543075001027

Glaser, J., Raghavan, K., & Baxter, G. P. (1992). *Cognitive theory as the basis for design of innovative assessment: Design characteristics of science assessments* (No. CSE Tech. Rep. No. 349). Los Angeles, CA: University of California, National Center for Research on Evaluation, Standards, and Student Testing.

Haake, J. M., & Pfister, H. R. (2007). Flexible scripting in net-based learning groups. In Fischer, F., Mandl, H., Haake, J. M., & Kollar, I. (Eds.), *Scripting computer-supported communication of knowledge - Cognitive, computational, and educational perspectives*. Berlin, Heidelberg: Springer.

Heider, F. (1958). *The psychology of interpersonal relations*. New York, NY: Wiley. doi:10.1037/10628-000

Helling, K. (2006). *Einfluss von Wissensschema und Ressourcenverteilung auf die Erstellung einer gemeinsamen externalen Repräsentation und den kooperativen Lernerfolg in Videokonferenzen. Aspekte der Bearbeitung und Koordination*. Unpublished Magister Thesis, Ludwig-Maximilians-Universität München.

Kelley, H. H. (1973). The processes of causal attribution. *The American Psychologist, 28*, 107–128. doi:10.1037/h0034225

Kotovsky, K., & Fallside, D. (1989). Representation and transfer in problem solving. In Klahr, D., & Kotovsky, K. (Eds.), *Complex information processing: The impact of Herbert A. Simon* (pp. 69–108). Hillsdale, NJ: Lawrence Erlbaum.

Kotovsky, K., Hayes, J. R., & Simon, H. A. (1985). Why are some problems hard? Evidence from Tower of Hanoi. *Cognitive Psychology, 17*(2), 248–294. doi:10.1016/0010-0285(85)90009-X

Kuhn, D., Weinstock, M., & Flaton, R. (1994). Historical reasoning as theory-evidence coordination. In Carretero, M., & Voss, J. F. (Eds.), *Cognitive and Instructional Processes in History and the Social Sciences* (pp. 377–401). Hillsdale, NJ: Lawrence Erlbaum Associates.

Larkin, J. H. (1989). Display-based problem solving. In Klahr, D., & Kotovsky, K. (Eds.), *Complex information processing: The impact of Herbert A. Simon* (pp. 319–341). Hillsdale, NJ: Lawrence Erlbaum.

Lave, J., & Wenger, E. (1991). *Situated learning: Legitimate peripheral participation*. New York: Cambridge University Press.

O'Connaill, B., Whittaker, S., & Wilbur, S. (1993). Conversations over video conferences: An evaluation of the spoken aspects of video-mediated communication. *Human-Computer Interaction, 8*(4), 389–428. doi:10.1207/s15327051hci0804_4

Renkl, A., Mandl, H., & Gruber, H. (1996). Inert knowledge: Analyzes and remedies. *Educational Psychologist, 31*(2), 115–121. doi:10.1207/s15326985ep3102_3

Roschelle, J., & Teasley, S. D. (1995). The construction of shared knowledge in collaborative problem solving. In O'Malley, C. (Ed.), *Computer Supported Collaborative Learning* (pp. 69–97). Berlin, Heidelberg: Springer.

Rummel, N., & Spada, H. (2005). Learning to collaborate: An instructional approach to promoting collaborative problem solving in computer-mediated settings. *Journal of the Learning Sciences, 14*(2), 201–241. doi:10.1207/s15327809jls1402_2

Sodian, B., Zaitchik, D., & Carey, S. (1991). Young children's differentiation of hypothetical beliefs from evidence. *Child Development, 62*(4), 753–766. doi:10.2307/1131175

Sugrue, B. (1995). A theory-based framework for assessing domain-specific problem solving ability. *Educational Measurement: Issues and Practice, 14*(3), 29–36. doi:10.1111/j.1745-3992.1995.tb00865.x

Suthers, D. D., & Hundhausen, C. D. (2001). Learning by constructing collaborative representations: An empirical comparison of three alternatives. In P. Dillenbourg, A. Eurelings & K. Hakkarainen (Eds.), *Proceedings of the First European Conference on Computer-Supported Collaborative Learning (euroCSCL)* (pp. 577-584). Maastricht, The Netherlands: McLuhan Institute.

Suthers, D. D., & Hundhausen, C. D. (2003). An experimental study of the effects of representational guidance on collaborative learning processes. *Journal of the Learning Sciences*, *12*(2), 183–218. doi:10.1207/S15327809JLS1202_2

Weinberger, A. (2003). *Scripts for computer-supported collaborative learning*. München, Germany: Unpublished Inaugural-Dissertation, Ludwig-Maximilians-Universität.

Weinberger, A., Ertl, B., Fischer, F., & Mandl, H. (2005). Epistemic and social scripts in computer-supported collaborative learning. *Instructional Science*, *33*(1), 1–30. doi:10.1007/s11251-004-2322-4

Weinberger, A., Reiserer, M., Ertl, B., Fischer, F., & Mandl, H. (2003). *Faciliating collaborative knowledge construction in computer-mediated learning with structuring tools*. Retrieved 08.09.2009, from http://epub.ub.uni-muenchen.de /archive/00000266/

Zhang, J. (1997). The nature of external representations in problem solving. *Cognitive Science*, *21*(2), 179–217. doi:10.1207/s15516709cog2102_3

Zhang, J., & Norman, D. A. (1994). Representations in distributed cognitive tasks. *Cognitive Science*, *18*(1), 87–122. doi:10.1207/s15516709cog1801_3

KEY TERMS AND DEFINITIONS

Application Sharing: Mechanism that allows collaboration partners to work with the same application on the same document simultaneously.

Content Scheme: A content-specific representation of the structure of a particular topic.

Collaboration: Tight working together with a strong commitment of collaboration partners.

Collaborative Learning: Method of learning by which a group of learners collaborate to achieve improved learning results.

External Representation: A material display of knowledge and information which may include facts but also procedures and structures.

Instructional Design: The didactical rationale for a learning scenario which includes instructional elements as well as the application of tools.

Learning Case: Description of a real-world scenario, which helps learners to apply their knowledge.

Mental Artefact: Immaterial product, which collaboration partners construct during the process of collaboration.

Shared Problem Space: The shared knowledge of collaboration partners which is necessary to solve a problem collaboratively.

Videoconferencing: Users use webcams and headsets to have a face to face conversation via internet. Videoconferencing is often combined with the use of a shared application to enable users to work collaboratively with the same software tool.

Chapter 4
Using and Acquiring Shared and Unshared Knowledge in Collaborative Learning and Writing

Aemilian Hron
Knowledge Media Research Center (KMRC), Germany

Ulrike Cress
Knowledge Media Research Center (KMRC), Germany

Sieglinde Neudert
Knowledge Media Research Center (KMRC), Germany

ABSTRACT

The aim of this study is to examine means of fostering videoconference-based collaborative learning, by focussing on three issues: (1) to induce collaborative learners to write a co-construct, applying (in addition to their shared knowledge) their unshared knowledge, which tends to be neglected, according to the social-psychological research paradigm of information pooling; (2) to activate these learners in their dialogues to exchange unshared knowledge possessed by one learning partner, so that it becomes shared knowledge possessed by both partners (knowledge transfer); (3) to try out, as an instructional support measure, scripted, content-specific visualisation, combining a content scheme with an interaction script. An experiment was conducted with 30 learning dyads, divided into three conditions of videoconference-based learning with application sharing: without instructional support, with content-specific visualisation, and with scripted content-specific visualisation. As expected, the scripted content-specific visualisation led to a higher transfer of previously unshared knowledge to shared knowledge. But, contrary to expectation, the scripted content-specific visualisation did not induce the learning partners to apply more unshared knowledge in writing their co-construct. Instead, in all three experimental conditions, learners brought significantly more shared knowledge into the co-construct than would have been expected from the distribution of shared and unshared knowledge measured before collaboration.

DOI: 10.4018/978-1-61692-898-8.ch004

INTRODUCTION

People who are involved in collaborative settings often have the task of building knowledge by collaboratively writing a text on some subject matter (Scardamalia & Bereiter, 2006; Weinberger, Stegmann, & Fischer, 2007). In the context of learning, the desired learning outcomes of such a task are twofold (Cress, 2008): The learners should acquire knowledge (individual learning outcome), and the group should produce a high-quality external artefact (collaborative learning outcome). Concerning the *collaborative learning outcome,* it is crucial that the learners contribute as much as possible of their task-specific prior knowledge to the process of discussing and creating their joint product. In this respect, the social effect of information pooling (Stasser & Titus, 1985) suggests that learners prefer to contribute knowledge which they all own (shared knowledge), and neglect knowledge that is only owned by one or a few of them (unshared knowledge). Concerning the *individual learning outcome,* a significant aspect is to what extent learners enrich their existing knowledge by acquiring knowledge from each other. This means that learners adopt previously unshared knowledge from others, and in this way make it shared knowledge (interpersonal knowledge transfer). In the present study, an instructional support measure was applied to foster these processes. The support measure was designed to encourage learning dyads to introduce both shared and unshared knowledge into their collaborative problem solving process. To investigate the effect of information pooling and the transfer of knowledge in collaborative learning, the study is based on a quantitative methodology as applied by Jeong and Chi (1999, 2007). Knowledge was measured in a propositional way, and shared knowledge was taken for granted if the learning partners possessed knowledge on the very same concept.

THEORETICAL BACKGROUND

Shared and Unshared Knowledge as Input into the Process of Collaborative Learning

The issue of instructional support, inducing collaborative learners to introduce as much task-specific knowledge as possible into the collaboration process (their shared and unshared knowledge), has been investigated only insufficiently so far. Several social-psychological studies do, however, deal with the role of shared and unshared knowledge which group members bring into their collaboration. They show mainly positive effects of shared knowledge, as far as problem solving in working groups is concerned (e.g., Weisband, 2002). Regarding the use of both shared and unshared knowledge in collaboration, the social-psychological research paradigm of "information pooling" (Stasser & Titus, 1985) appears to be relevant. One phenomenon that has been very well examined in this field is the stable effect of preferring shared information in a group decision process. It has been demonstrated repeatedly that shared information in group decisions is clearly preferred, while unshared information tends to be neglected (Larson, Christensen, Franz, & Abbott, 1998; Wittenbaum & Stasser, 1996). This effect has been referred to as the "collective information sampling bias" (Wittenbaum, Hubbell, & Zuckerman, 1999). It occurs both ways, so to speak: when making statements in a discussion, and when taking information from others repeatedly in the course of this discussion. This effect has also been observed in computer-based groups communicating synchronously (e.g., Dennis, 1996). Wittenbaum and Stasser (1996) explain this effect by assuming that a preference for shared information simplifies mutual reference and communication in groups by establishing some common ground (Clark & Brennan, 1991). We may assume that the process of knowledge exchange is fundamental for reaching a common knowledge base for decisions within a group. But if this knowledge exchange is incomplete, in favour of shared knowledge, this may have negative consequences on the quality of a group decision. Regarding collaborative learning, this finding suggests that collaborative problem solving may also be impaired, because shared knowledge is preferred and unshared knowledge is neglected. So for learning tasks of this type, as described above, this is an effect that might have to be expected.

In the field of collaborative learning, studies on knowledge input into the process of collaboration have, so far, focused on shared knowledge, while unshared knowledge has not explicitly been considered. Thalemann and Strube (2004) investigated the significance of shared knowledge in net-based collaborative problem solving on the basis of the information pooling paradigm. Their study did not, however, go into the aspect of instructional support for applying shared/unshared knowledge. Rather, the type and amount of prior shared knowledge that each learner of a learning dyad had available was varied, as an independent variable, in several experimental conditions. As a result, the task solutions were better if the collaborating partners had some knowledge in common, than if they had no shared knowledge at all. So the study demonstrated the assumed positive effect of shared knowledge on collaborative problem solving. Fischer and Mandl (2005) investigated sharing of knowledge resources in learning dyads which were given instructional support in various forms. Subjects were working together on an educational problem in two different collaboration conditions (videoconferencing vs. face to face). Instructional support was given through two types of graphical representation tools (content-specific vs. content-independent). Knowledge resources that were meant to be used for problem solving were supplied at the beginning of collaboration, and these included, among other resources, some case information and theoretical concepts concerning the problem. Results showed a strong convergence of the learning partners during the collaboration process, as far as their use of the knowledge resources was concerned. Using the content-specific graphical representation tool - in contrast to the content-unspecific tool -, learners converged within a narrower scope of knowledge resources, and these were more appropriate for solving the problem.

The studies mentioned above demonstrate that shared knowledge, as input into the process of collaborative learning, has a positive effect on joint problem solving. But the aspect of unshared knowledge has not been dealt with explicitly. As far as collaborative tasks are concerned, we assume in the present study that both shared and unshared task-specific knowledge will be relevant. So we have provided collaborative support measures that were designed to encourage learning dyads to introduce both their shared and unshared knowledge into their collaborative problem solving.

Shared and Unshared Knowledge as Outcomes of Collaborative Learning

A further research topic of the present study deals with shared knowledge as an outcome of collaborative learning, and a special focus here is on shared knowledge that was previously unshared. Can we expect the acquisition of shared knowledge as a result of collaboration, and is this beneficial to the result of individual learning? In most studies on collaborative learning, it is more or less explicitly accepted that collaborative learning leads to a development of shared knowledge (e.g., Pfister, Wesner, Holmer, & Steinmetz, 1999; Van Boxtel, van der Linden, Roelofs, & Erkens, 2002). Often, the jointly constructed products of learning partners are seen as evidence that they have shared knowledge, without examining (explicitly) to what extent they have really shared this knowledge (e.g., Wang, Laffey, & Poole, 2001). So far, only a few studies have addressed the issue of shared knowledge as a direct outcome of collaborative learning.

Hatano and Inagaki (1991) examined to what extent students developed shared comprehension in the course of group discussions, each with more than twenty students. As a result of qualitative analyses it became evident that, after discussions, knowledge differed considerably, not only among students belonging to different groups, but also among students who had been in the same group. Hatano and Inagaki suggested that this was caused by the students' non-uniform representations and by their different ways of comprehension, making knowledge acquisition an idiosyncratic process, unique to the single learner. But other qualitative studies on shared knowledge as an outcome of collaborative learning came to completely different conclusions. Roschelle and Teasley (1995) analyzed the dialogues between collaborative learners working on a physics problem. The dialogue analysis was based on conversational structures (such as narration, questions, and socially-distributed productions), as they have been documented in Conversational Analysis and Pragmatics (e.g., Goodwin & Heritage, 1990) as effective means for achieving convergent meanings. Roschelle and Teasley found evidence for theses structures in the dialogues, and concluded that the learners had, in fact, achieved shared knowledge. Roschelle (1996) focused on the learners' mutual construction of understanding, while explaining physical phenomena on a theoretical basis. An analysis of their dialogues showed that in the course of conversational interaction the collaborative learners approximated in their cognitive and communicative processes. Roschelle interpreted these findings as evidence for the acquisition of shared knowledge.

A few studies have addressed the issue of shared knowledge as an outcome of collaborative learning by using quantitative methods. Jeong and Chi (1999, 2007), in a collaborative face-to-face scenario, examined the development of shared knowledge by a quantitative pre-post-test design, with the collaborative learning followed by individual testing. Shared knowledge was taken for granted if the two learning partners had knowledge on the very same concepts. Results showed that learners shared more knowledge after collaboration; however, this increase was modest. It could be attributed to collaborative interaction, rather than to environmental input (e.g., shared learning texts). Analysis revealed that learning partners who were more interactive acquired more shared knowledge than less interactive partners. Collaborative dialogues and learning artefacts, like drawings, also indicated that shared knowledge was acquired during collaboration. Thalemann and Strube (2004), in addition to demonstrating that shared knowledge is a facilitator for collaborative problem solving (see above), also found that participants acquired shared knowledge during collaboration, and that this was mostly correct knowledge. The study of Fischer and Mandl (2005), additionally to investigating the joint use of knowledge resources (see above), explored the extent to which learners under different experimental conditions shared knowledge as an outcome of collaborative learning. They found that the relation of shared knowledge to unshared knowledge was less than 1 to 5. The different experimental conditions did not influence this result.

Altogether, research results on shared knowledge as an outcome of collaborative learning are inconsistent. But we consider it reasonable to expect shared knowledge, though to a lesser extent than one would assume, as a result of learning. Concerning this issue, hardly any research has yet been carried out on the question as to whether previously unshared knowledge, was finally transferred and used by a learning partner, therefore becoming shared knowledge.

Instructional Support Measures

We applied two instructional support measures for collaborative learning to a videoconference setting with application sharing: a content-specific visualisation and, in addition, a scripted content-specific visualisation. The scripted support combined content-specific visualisation with a coordinating collaboration script that instructed the learners to engage in interactions which are known to be conducive for learning (Fischer & Mandl, 2005).

A content-specific visualisation represents the central characteristics and structures of the learning material. The effects of such external representations have, so far, mainly been studied within the context of individual problem solving (e.g., Cox & Brna, 1995). Supporting collaborative learning by using a content-specific external representation, also referred to as content scheme (Ertl, Kopp, & Mandl, 2007), means that through the representation, collaborative learners are provided with the context for a task. They are also provided with placeholders for important dimensions of content, in order to focus their discourse on important topics in the course of collaborative knowledge construction. Suthers (2001) refers to this measure as representational guidance. It has often been shown that external representation and visualisation could improve learning in collaborative settings (Roschelle, 1996; Suthers, 2001). In videoconference-based collaborative settings, results are heterogeneous. Fischer, Bruhn, Gräsel, and Mandl (2000) found that content schemes modified collaborative learning processes in videoconferencing, but did not seem to affect collaborative or individual learning outcomes. In three studies in their laboratory, Ertl, Fischer, and Mandl (2006) report differing results in fostering collaborative videoconferencing by content-specific support. In their first study, there were no effects on learning outcomes, in the second study, there were some effects on collaborative learning outcomes, and in the third study, there were some effects on both individual and collaborative learning outcomes. In the second and third study, content-specific support was combined with a collaboration script that structured collaborative problem solving, leading to an interaction effect of the two combined measures. Ertl, Fischer, and Mandl (2006) explained the inconsistent findings with the interplay between their particular support measures and the respective collaborative task types, and they regarded further research as necessary.

Concerning the issue of shared knowledge, the study of Fischer and Mandl (2005, see above) on fostering collaborative learning by content-specific visualisation tools in videoconferencing is the only one that goes into this matter. In that study, the visualisation tools had positive effects on the joint use of knowledge resources, but did not facilitate the construction of shared knowledge. In the light of their findings, Fischer and Mandl suggest, as a potentially effective instructional measure, a scripted visualisation, that is, a shared graphical representation with a coordinating collaboration script (see also Ertl et al., 2006). Such a combined scaffold could benefit from the possibly positive effects of scripting collaborative interactions (e.g., Hron, Hesse, Cress, & Giovis, 2000; Rummel & Spada 2007; Weinberger, Ertl, Fischer, & Mandl, 2005). In the present study, we apply two instructional support measures: content-specific visualisation and a combination of content-specific visualisation with a coordinating collaboration script. Especially the scripted support measure should encourage collaborators to bring their shared/unshared knowledge into the collaboration process, and to exchange unshared knowledge in order to acquire shared knowledge as an outcome of this process.

METHOD

Participants

Sixty students, aged between 21 and 29, took part in the investigation. They were students of various disciplines at the University of Tübingen. Students of physics were not allowed to take part in order to eliminate a possible effect of pre-knowledge. The participants were randomly assigned to each of the three experimental conditions of the study. For each of these conditions, ten same-sex two-person groups were formed, altogether 17 female learning dyads and 13 male learning dyads. Same-sex groups were preferred to exclude possible distortions in communication because of specific gender patterns (Yates, 1997), which might have led to unequal participation or dominance of one partner.

Material

The material consisted of a multimedia learning program, a writing task, a blank flow chart and a computer screen for communication and accomplishing the collaborative writing task. The multimedia learning program on solar astronomy comprised seven chapters. In the experiment, the chapter dealing with the birth of stars and their evolution was used. The material to be learned was primarily presented by means of audio commentaries, accompanied by animations and videos. The writing task was the following: The participants had to describe the development process of a star, from its birth to its death. The content-specific visualisation was given on paper as a blank flow chart, consisting of unlabeled boxes and rhombs, ordered according to the development stages of a star.

The videoconference was established by means of three networked workstations with 19" monitors and VCON ViGO (video over IP) with two ViGO Towers (desktop cameras, audio encoders, and integrated loudspeakers). At each of the two conference places there was a workstation and a ViGO Tower. The third workstation served to control the course of the conference. The application sharing was accomplished by Microsoft NetMeeting. The network (100 Mbit/s) caused a slight audio delay which, however, did not disturb the communication.

Experimental Design and Procedure

The experimental session with a learning dyad covered four phases (see Figure 1). After learning with the multimedia learning program (phase 1), the individual writing task in phase 2 served to measure the shared and unshared knowledge which each learner possessed prior to the videoconference. During the videoconference (phase 3), the learners worked collaboratively on the writing task. For doing this, they could draw on their individually written texts from phase 2. The text which the dyads produced in the videoconference was considered as their co-construct, and it served as a measure for their collaborative learning outcome. The individual writing task following the videoconference (phase 4) served to measure the individual learning outcome.

There were three experimental conditions: "*without instructional support*", "*with content-specific visualisation*", and "*with scripted content-specific visualisation*". Under each condition, the learners sat in separate rooms in front of a computer screen for working on the individual writing task and the collaborative writing task. The computer screen was the same in each condition; but

Figure 1. Phases of the experimental session

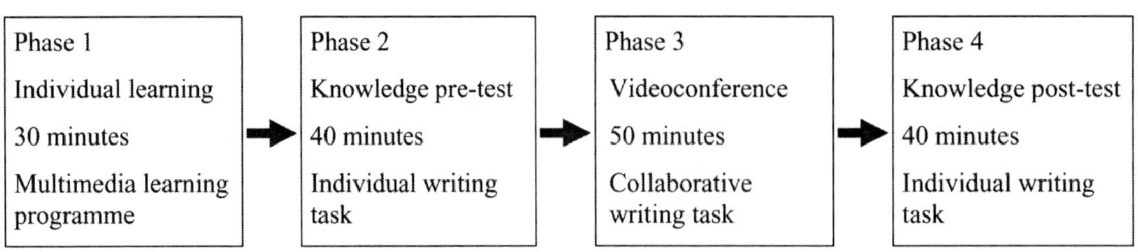

under the condition *with scripted content-specific visualisation* a collaboration script (see Figure 2) was visible in the upper part of the screen. Under each condition, a learner could see the video picture of his / her learning partner, and a shared workspace was provided. Both learners could write in a joint editing window, but only one learner at a time. The right to write had to be passed on to the other learner (relay control; Noël & Robert, 2004). Moreover, the shared workspace also included the private windows of the learners with their individual texts they had produced during phase 2. That means that these texts were visible for both. In order to make a learner's text completely visible for both partners, they had to scroll the window. A learner could only scroll his/her own window, making it necessary for the learners to make request. The learners could not add text from their private windows to the joint editing window by "copy and paste". In the conditions *without instructional support* and *with content-specific visualisation*, passing the editing work on was totally dependent upon the disposition of the learners. In the condition *with scripted content-specific visualisation*, the editing work and turn-taking were regulated by the collaboration script.

Under the conditions *with content-specific visualisation* and *with scripted content-specific visualisation*, each learner received a sheet of paper with a flow chart, visualizing the development stages of a star, a topic which they had learned from their multimedia learning program. But the labels denoting the boxes and rhombs were missing. The learners were instructed to insert these labels before jointly writing the text about the development of a star. In case that they did not agree on a label, they were advised to proceed and deal with this problem later in the course of their following text production. Moreover, the learners were instructed to stick to the structure visualized by the flow chart while co-constructing their text. The flow chart was permanently available during the videoconference. Under the condition *with scripted content-specific visualisation*, a collaboration script was shown on the computer screen for each stage of the development of a star, corresponding to a box of the flow chart. The script, located in the upper part of the screen (see Figure 2), was designed to make the learners work on the task in a stepwise, successive fashion, and to intensify their discussion and knowledge exchange. The respective development stage of a star which was meant to be discussed at any given time was indicated by the

Figure 2. Computer screen under the condition "with scripted content-specific visualisation"; collaboration script on the right (original German text translated to English)

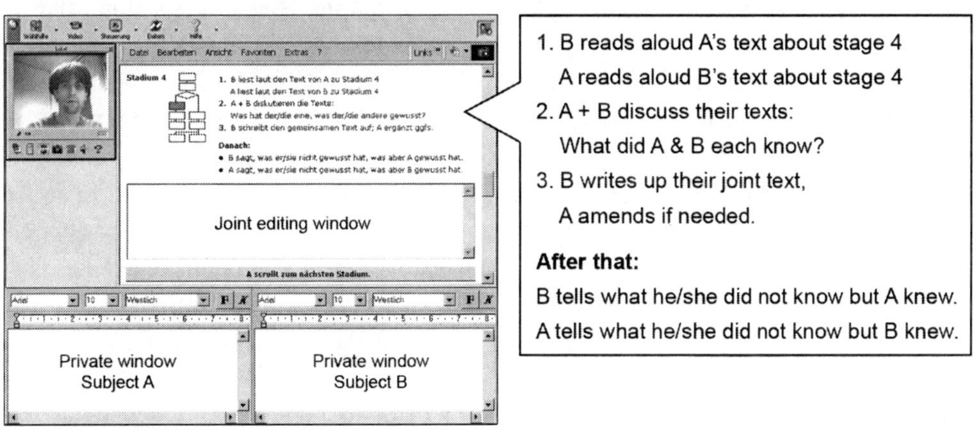

stage number and the corresponding element in the flow chart was highlighted on the screen; the flow chart on the screen was placed beside the collaboration script and was the same as the paper version. The collaboration script regulated the learners′ interaction by guiding them through five steps (Figure 2, see text on the right): Three steps dealt with discussing and jointly writing a text by changing activity roles, and encouraging the learners to introduce their shared/unshared knowledge into this process; two subsequent steps were meant to induce the learners to reflect on their unshared knowledge, likewise by changing activity roles. Figure 2 depicts the screen displaying stage 4 for working on the problem. At this stage, B has to write and A has to scroll to the next stage.

At the beginning of the experiment, the learners were familiarized with operating the shared workspace, and during this process they practiced handing over the permission to write. They were instructed to pay attention to the texts in both private windows. Moreover, the learners with *scripted content-specific visualisation* were introduced to working with the collaboration script.

Expectations

The following Expectation 1 refers to the collaborative learning outcome, Expectation 2 to the individual learning outcome.

Expectation 1: The three experimental conditions have different potency in inducing learners to bring their unshared knowledge into the co-construct. We especially expect that the co-constructs of the dyads working with *scripted content-specific visualisation* show a higher ratio of unshared knowledge to total knowledge (i.e., shared knowledge plus unshared knowledge) than the co-constructs of the dyads working without instructional support. In the condition with only *content-specific visualisation* it is not advisable to have this same expectation, bearing in mind the results of previous research. Since some caution is called for here, we treat this issue in an exploratory way. The expected effect here is that the co-constructs in the three conditions differ in their comprehensiveness, with the result that the dyads with *scripted content-specific visualisation* have a more complete collaborative learning outcome than the dyads without instructional support.

Expectation 2: We expect that the three experimental conditions differ in the extent to which they induce interpersonal knowledge transfer. Such interpersonal knowledge transfer has taken place whenever a learner did not know an item after the individual learning phase, this item was brought into the co-construct by the learning partner in the collaboration phase, and afterwards the learner did know it in the knowledge post-test as an item of shared knowledge. We expect that the dyads working with *scripted content-specific visualisation* show a larger knowledge transfer than the dyads without instructional support. Again, in the condition with only *content-specific visualisation* we consider such an expectation to be inadvisable, but treat this issue with caution in an exploratory way. The expected effect should lead to respective differences among the experimental conditions, regarding the extent of knowledge finally shared.

Dependent Variables

The texts were analyzed with a coding template, which differentiated among 126 knowledge pieces (KPs) into which the spoken text from the multimedia program had been subdivided. Each KP corresponded roughly to a proposition, for example, "the sun is a star", that was stated in the text. According to this coding template, 30 co-constructed texts from the videoconference (phase 3) and 60 individual texts written thereafter (phase 4) were coded. Moreover, to measure pre-knowledge, 60 individual texts from phase 2 were coded. For a reliability check, a second coder coded 20 randomly chosen texts. A Cohen's Kappa =.74 resulted. With respect to expectations 1 and 2, the analysis of the texts served to measure the quantity and portion of unshared and shared KPs in the texts.

RESULTS

Preliminaries

To test Expectation 1, each KP that was part of a dyad's co-construct was coded as a shared KP (if it was known by both learning partners in the knowledge pre-test in phase 2) or as an unshared KP (if it was known by only one learner in the knowledge pre-test in phase 2). Based on this coding, for each co-construct the ratio of unshared knowledge to the total knowledge involved in the co-construct was computed and compared across the experimental conditions. In this process the dyad constituted the unit of analysis. The collaborative learning outcome was measured by the comprehensiveness of the co-construct, which is described by the number of KPs being part of the co-constructs. To test Expectation 2, the number of transferred KPs was counted for each dyad. These were items which only one of the learners knew in the knowledge pre-test, which were then part of the co-construct, and which in the knowledge post-test were also known to the other learner, or, in other words, which had became part of the knowledge finally shared. Additionally, for each dyad the amount of the knowledge finally shared was calculated in the knowledge post-test. Across the three experimental conditions, there were no differences in the prior knowledge (both unshared and shared knowledge) of the subjects, measured by the knowledge pre-test (phase 2).

The learning dyads working *with scripted content-specific visualisation* were not able to complete the task in the given time of 50 minutes. This was due to the collaboration script, which demanded from the learners that they mutually read their texts, discuss their texts and exchange knowledge. To get comparable results for the three experimental conditions, only the first 95 KPs (or respective developmental stages of the stars), for which there were data for each dyad, were taken into account for the analysis. Two dyads did not follow the ideal typical sequence for working through the task that had been suggested by the content-specific visualisation, but skipped or neglected some stages of the development of a star.

Collaborative Learning Outcome

For testing Expectation 1, an ANOVA was calculated with the three experimental conditions as independent variables, and the ratio of previously unshared to total knowledge in the co-construct as dependent variable. Contrary to expectation, this analysis revealed no statistically significant differences between the conditions ($F (2, 27) =.331; p >.05$), showing that the collaborative learning outcome was not affected by scripted content-specific visualisation. There was also no effect in the condition with only *content-specific visualisation*. In the co-constructs, there was no greater amount of unshared knowledge in relation to total knowledge. Moreover, we also found no differences in the total number of KPs in the co-construct across the three experimental conditions ($F (2, 27) =.15; p >.05$).

Instead, in accordance with the "collective information sampling bias" (Wittenbaum et al., 1999), we found that in all three experimental conditions people brought statistically significant more shared knowledge into the co-construct than would have been expected from the distribution of shared and unshared knowledge in the knowledge pre-test. A two-factorial ANOVA with the within-factor *time* (knowledge pre-test vs. co-construct) and the between-factor *condition* revealed a statistically significant effect of *time* ($F (1, 27) = 26.84; p <.001; eta^2 =.50$). In the knowledge pre-test, the mean portion of shared knowledge to total knowledge was 25.3% and in the co-construct it was 29.8%.

Individual Learning Outcome

Concerning Expectation 2, the knowledge transfer under the three conditions was compared with a one-factorial ANOVA. This analysis revealed statistically significant differences among the conditions ($F (2, 27) = 5.64$; $p <.05$; $eta^2 =.30$). Table 1 shows the transferred knowledge that in the end became part of the learners′ shared knowledge.

Additional Scheffé post hoc tests were calculated to decide which of the paired differences among the three conditions was responsible for the statistically significant result. It revealed that the significance was due to the difference between the conditions *without instructional support* and *with scripted content-specific visualisation*.

Apart from these differences, with respect to the amount of the knowledge finally shared, we also found statistically significant differences between the experimental conditions in the knowledge post-test ($F (2, 27) = 3.65$; $p <.05$; $eta^2 =.21$), as shown in Table 2. Additional Scheffé post hoc tests show that the statistically significant result was due to the difference between the conditions *without instructional support* and *with scripted content-specific visualisation*.

DISCUSSION

The present study deals with specific measures to foster collaborative learning through application sharing by dyads who communicate through a videoconference. A special focus of the study was on the shared and unshared knowledge of the learning partners that was assumed to be relevant for working on the learning task. According to the social-psychological paradigm of information pooling (Stasser & Titus, 1985), we expected shared knowledge to have a higher chance of being applied in the interaction phase, and unshared knowledge a higher chance of being neglected. To encourage collaborative learning, we applied content-specific visualisation as an instructional support measure, and under one of the experimental conditions this was combined with a coordinating collaboration script. Such a combined instructional support measure was expected to induce the learners to intensify their discourse. As a result, we expected the learners – in addition to their shared knowledge – also to bring their unshared knowledge into the joint problem solving process, to create a more comprehensive co-construct (as the outcome of their collaborative learning). Moreover, we expected an intensive knowledge exchange between the learners that would lead to a transfer of unshared knowledge between the learning partners, which would result in a greater extent of shared knowledge in the end.

The current state of research is insufficient, as far as the relevance of shared and unshared knowledge and its relationship to collaborative learning is concerned. Accordingly, there are hardly any research findings about knowledge exchange between collaborative learners, or a possible knowledge transfer as a result of such an exchange, which would turn unshared knowledge into shared knowledge. Likewise, there are hardly any reported experiences with an instructional support measure that combines content-specific visualisation or a content scheme with a collabora-

Table 1. Mean and standard deviation of knowledge transfer: Number of KPs that were at first unshared knowledge (in the knowledge pre-test) but then were transferred to the learning partner and became also his/her knowledge (reflected in the knowledge post-test)

Experimental condition	*M*	*SD*	*n*
Without instructional support	5.40a	2.066	10
With content-specific visualisation	7.50	2.415	10
With scripted content-specific visualisation	9.70b	3.802	10
p <.05. Means with different letters significantly differ with Scheffé post hoc.			

tion script (Ertl et al., 2006). For all these reasons, we were cautious in formulating our expectations. We had clear expectations only with regard to our combined support measure, that is, scripted content-specific visualisation. Here we expected effects on exchange and transfer of knowledge because of the detailed collaboration script in conjunction with visualisation. We considered possible effects in the condition *with only content-specific visualisation* in an exploratory manner.

Our expectations were fulfilled differently. While Expectation 1, regarding unshared knowledge brought into the co-construct (the collaborative learning outcome), did not come true, Expectation 2, regarding the interpersonal knowledge transfer (the individual learning outcome), turned out to be valid. Scripted content-specific visualisation led to a higher transfer of unshared knowledge, which was then shared by the respective learning partners, fulfilling Expectation 2. This knowledge, proved in the knowledge pre-test to be unshared, was then brought into the co-construct by one learner, and finally proved to be possessed by both learners in the final knowledge post-test. In our opinion, it was the interaction between content-specific visualisation and the coordinating collaboration script that has led to this result. The collaboration script in conjunction with visualisation clearly structured the problem solving process, and this encouraged the learners to have an intensive knowledge exchange within the single steps for working on the task (development stages of a star). The learners were explicitly requested to exchange their knowledge, and, in particular, to exchange their *unshared* knowledge. This process resulted in shared knowledge that was more comprehensive than previously.

Under the condition *with scripted content-specific visualisation*, the learners needed more time to accomplish the joint task than under the two other experimental conditions. This means that an extended time for working on the topic is an essential element of the support measure, and this may also be true for many other collaborative support measures (cf. Dillenbourg, 1999). Though a confounding effect (with implications for the learning outcome) may be possible in our investigation, we believe that the intensive knowledge exchange induced by the support measure was the cause of the knowledge transfer that we were able to observe.

With regard to Expectation 1 (concerning the collaborative learning outcome), in the co-constructs there was no greater amount of unshared knowledge in relation to total knowledge. This was true under the condition *with only content-specific visualisation* as well as under the condition *with scripted content-specific visualisation*. Quite the contrary, we found that under all three experimental conditions people brought statistically significant more shared knowledge into the co-construct than would have been expected from the distribution of shared and unshared knowledge, as indicated by the pre-test. This result has to be interpreted as a social effect of information pooling (Stasser & Titus, 1985), which evidently prevailed under all three experimental conditions. This preference for shared knowledge, and

Table 2. Mean and standard deviation of the amount of the finally shared knowledge in the knowledge post-test

Experimental condition	*M*	*SD*	*n*
Without instructional support	10.20a	4.826	10
With content-specific visualisation	14.30	5.832	10
With scripted content-specific visualisation	16.50b	5.169	10
p <.05 Means with different letters significantly differ with Scheffé post hoc.			

neglect of unshared knowledge, turned out to be without consequence for the knowledge transfer that occurred, due to the combined instructional support measure (scripted content-specific visualisation). This measure requested the learners firstly to write down their joint text regarding the development stage of a star, and after that to exchange the knowledge they did not share. Thus, the subsequent exchange of unshared knowledge had an effect on the knowledge transfer (turning unshared knowledge to shared knowledge), but was independent from and had no effect on writing the co-construct.

In our study, we found that collaborative learners developed shared knowledge, but, despite instructional support measures, the amount of shared knowledge was rather small. We found a mean relation of transferred (or shared) knowledge to unshared knowledge of one to four. This relation corresponds approximately with the results of Jeong and Chi (1999, 2007) and Fischer and Mandl (2005), who found a relation of shared knowledge to unshared knowledge that was one fifth or less. More research on this topic will be necessary to further clarify the essentials of collaborative learning. Moreover, some other basic issues should also be investigated in more depth. Studies should further clarify the relation of collaborative knowledge building and individual learning (Moskaliuk, Kimmerle, & Cress, 2008). Future studies should also investigate to what extent the collective information sampling bias might impede collaborative learning, and how instructional support measures could remedy such a possibly detrimental effect. Further investigations are also needed into the suitability of instructional support measures, especially combined with content-specific and interaction related measures. The present study could only touch on these issues, and the results indicate the need for further research.

REFERENCES

Clark, H. H., & Brennan, S. E. (1991). Grounding in communication. In Resnick, L. B., Levine, J. M., & Teasley, S. D. (Eds.), *Perspectives on socially shared cognition* (pp. 127–149). Washington, DC: American Psychological Association. doi:10.1037/10096-006

Cox, R., & Brna, P. (1995). Supporting the use of external representations in problem solving: The need for flexible learning environments. *Journal of Artificial Intelligence in Education*, *6*(2-3), 239–302.

Cress, U. (2008). The need for considering multilevel analysis in CSCL research. An appeal for the use of more advanced statistical methods. *International Journal of Computer-Supported Collaborative Learning*, *3*(1), 69–84. doi:10.1007/s11412-007-9032-2

Dennis, A. R. (1996). Information exchange and use in small group decision making. *Small Group Research*, *27*(4), 532–550. doi:10.1177/1046496496274003

Dillenbourg, P. (1999). What do you mean by collaborative learning? In Dillenbourg, P. (Ed.), *Collaborative-learning: Cognitive and computational approaches* (pp. 1–19). Oxford, UK: Elsevier.

Ertl, B., Fischer, F., & Mandl, H. (2006). Conceptual and socio-cognitive support for collaborative learning in videoconferencing environments. *Computers & Education*, *47*(3), 289–315. doi:10.1016/j.compedu.2004.11.001

Ertl, B., Kopp, B., & Mandl, H. (2007). Supporting collaborative learning in videoconferencing using collaboration scripts and content schemes. In Fischer, F., Kollar, I., Mandl, H., & Haake, J. M. (Eds.), *Scripting computer-supported communication of knowledge – cognitive, computational and educational perspectives* (pp. 212–236). Berlin, Heidelberg: Springer.

Fischer, F., Bruhn, J., Gräsel, C., & Mandl, H. (2000). Kooperatives Lernen mit Videokonferenzen: Gemeinsame Wissenskonstruktion und individueller Lernerfolg [Cooperative learning with video-conferencing systems: Collaborative knowledge construction and individual learning outcomes]. *Kognitionswissenschaft*, *9*(1), 5–16. doi:10.1007/s001970000028

Fischer, F., & Mandl, H. (2005). Knowledge convergence in computer-supported collaborative learning - the role of external representation tools. *Journal of the Learning Sciences*, *14*(3), 405–441. doi:10.1207/s15327809jls1403_3

Goodwin, C., & Heritage, J. (1990). Conversation analysis. *Annual Review of Anthropology*, *19*, 283–307. doi:10.1146/annurev.an.19.100190.001435

Hatano, G., & Inagaki, K. (1991). Sharing cognition through collective comprehension activity. In Resnick, L. B., Levine, J. M., & Teasley, S. D. (Eds.), *Perspectives on socially shared cognition* (pp. 331–348). Washington, DC: American Psychological Association. doi:10.1037/10096-014

Hron, A., Hesse, F. W., Cress, U., & Giovis, C. (2000). Implicit and explicit dialogue structuring in virtual learning groups. *The British Journal of Educational Psychology*, *70*(1), 53–64. doi:10.1348/000709900157967

Jeong, H., & Chi, M. T. H. (1999, April). *Constructing shared knowledge during collaboration and learning.* Paper presented at the AERA Annual Meeting, Montreal, Canada.

Jeong, H., & Chi, M. T. H. (2007). Knowledge convergence and collaborative learning. *Instructional Science*, *35*(4), 287–315. doi:10.1007/s11251-006-9008-z

Larson, J. R. Jr, Christensen, C., Franz, T. M., & Abbott, A. S. (1998). Diagnosing groups: The pooling, management, and impact of shared and unshared case information in team-based medical decision making. *Journal of Personality and Social Psychology*, *75*(1), 93–108. doi:10.1037/0022-3514.75.1.93

Moskaliuk, J., Kimmerle, J., & Cress, U. (2008). Learning and knowledge building with Wikis: The impact of incongruity between people's knowledge and a Wiki's information. In G. Kanselaar, V. Jonker, P.A. Kirschner, & F.J. Prins (Eds.), *International perspectives in the learning sciences: Cre8ing a learning world*, (Vol. 2 pp. 99-106). *Proceedings of the 8th International Conference for the Learning Sciences – ICLS 2008*. Utrecht, The Netherlands: International Society of the Learning Sciences, Inc.

Noël, S., & Robert, J.-M. (2004). Empirical study on collaborative writing: what do co-authors do, use, and like? *Computer Supported Cooperative Work*, *13*(1), 63–89. doi:10.1023/B:COSU.0000014876.96003.be

Pfister, H.-R., Wessner, M., Holmer, T., & Steinmetz, R. (1999). Negotiating about shared knowledge in a cooperative learning environment. In C. Hoadley, & J. Roschelle (Eds.), *Computer Support for Collaborative Learning* (pp. 454-457). *Proceedings of the CSCL '99 Conference*. Palo Alto, CA: Stanford University.

Roschelle, J. (1996). Learning by collaborating: Convergent conceptual change. In Koschmann, T. (Ed.), *CSCL: Theory and practice of an emerging paradigm* (pp. 209–248). Mahwah, NJ: Lawrence Erlbaum.

Roschelle, J., & Teasley, S. D. (1995). The construction of shared knowledge in collaborative problem solving. In O'Malley, C. (Ed.), *Computer supported collaborative learning* (pp. 69–97). Berlin, Heidelberg: Springer.

Rummel, N., & Spada, H. (2007). Can people learn computer-mediated collaboration by following a script? In Fischer, F., Kollar, I., Mandl, H., & Haake, J. (Eds.), *Scripting computer-supported collaborative learning: Cognitive, computational and educational perspectives* (pp. 39–55). New York: Springer. doi:10.1007/978-0-387-36949-5_3

Scardamalia, M., & Bereiter, C. (2006). Knowledge building: Theory, pedagogy, and technology. In Sawyer, K. (Ed.), *Cambridge handbook of the learning sciences* (pp. 97–118). New York: Cambridge University Press.

Stasser, G., & Titus, W. (1985). Pooling of unshared information in group decision making: Biased information sampling during discussion. *Journal of Personality and Social Psychology*, *48*(6), 1467–1478. doi:10.1037/0022-3514.48.6.1467

Suthers, D. D. (2001). Towards a systematic study of representational guidance for collaborative learning discourse. *Journal of Universal Computer Science*, *7*(3), 254–277.

Thalemann, S., & Strube, G. (2004). Shared knowledge in collaborative problem solving: Acquisition and effects. In K. Forbus, D. Gentner, & T. Regier (Eds.), *Proceedings of the 26th Annual Conference of the Cognitive Science Society* (pp. 1333-1338). Mahwah, NJ: Erlbaum. Retrieved April 6, 2010, from http://www.cogsci.northwestern.edu/cogsci2004/papers/paper317.pdf

Van Boxtel, C., van der Linden, J., Roelofs, E., & Erkens, G. (2002). Collaborative concept mapping: Provoking and supporting meaningful discourse. *Theory into Practice*, *41*(1), 40–46. doi:10.1207/s15430421tip4101_7

Wang, M., Laffey, J., & Poole, M. J. (2001). The construction of shared knowledge in an internet-based shared environment for expeditions (iExpeditions). *International Journal of Educational Technology, 2*, 1-16. Retrieved April 6, 2010, from http://www.ed.uiuc.edu/ijet/v2n2 / v2n2feature.html

Weinberger, A., Ertl, B., Fischer, F., & Mandl, H. (2005). Epistemic and social scripts in computer-supported collaborative learning. *Instructional Science*, *33*(1), 1–30. doi:10.1007/s11251-004-2322-4

Weinberger, A., Stegmann, K., & Fischer, F. (2007). Knowledge convergence in collaborative learning: Concepts and assessment. *Learning and Instruction*, *17*(4), 416–426. doi:10.1016/j.learninstruc.2007.03.007

Weisband, S. (2002). Maintaining awareness in distributed team collaboration: Implications for leadership and performance. In Hinds, P., & Kiesler, S. (Eds.), *Distributed work* (pp. 311–333). Cambridge, MA: MIT Press.

Wittenbaum, G. M., Hubbell, A. P., & Zuckerman, C. (1999). Mutual enhancement: Toward an understanding of the collective preference for shared information. *Journal of Personality and Social Psychology*, *77*(5), 967–978. doi:10.1037/0022-3514.77.5.967

Wittenbaum, G. M., & Stasser, G. (1996). Management of information in small groups. In Nye, J. L., & Brower, A. M. (Eds.), *What's social about social cognition? Research on socially shared cognition in small groups* (pp. 3–28). Thousand Oaks, CA: Sage Publications.

Yates, S. J. (1997). Gender, identity and CMC. *Journal of Computer Assisted Learning*, *13*(4), 281–290. doi:10.1046/j.1365-2729.1997.00031.x

KEY TERMS AND DEFINITIONS

Content-Specific Visualisation: Instructional support measure that represents the central characteristics and structures of the learning material.

Information Pooling: Social psychological effect that suggests peer learners to prefer contributing knowledge which they all own (shared knowledge), and neglect knowledge that is only owned by one or a few of them (unshared knowledge). (Stasser & Titus, 1985)

Scripted Content-Specific Visualisation: Instructional support measure that combines a content-specific visualisation with a coordinating collaboration script.

Chapter 5
Blending Educational Models to Design Blended Activities

M. Beatrice Ligorio
University of Bari, Italy

F. Feldia Loperfido
University of Bari, Italy

Nadia Sansone
University of Bari, Italy

Paola F. Spadaro
University of Bari, Italy

ABSTRACT

The authors claim that the potentialities of the socio-constructivist framework can be fully exploited when a blended approach is introduced. Our blended model does not only mix offline and online contexts but it also combines several pedagogical theories and techniques (Progressive Inquiry Model, Jigsaw, Reciprocal Teaching, Collaborative Communities, and Dialogical Knowledge). The particular mix the authors propose generates a specific pedagogy through which a set of blended activities is designed. Some analyses conducted on blended courses for higher education and professional development where blended activities were tested are briefly discussed. These analyses concern: (a) the students' participation in blended context, (b) their expectations about the blended course and their perception about the processes of collaborative knowledge building, (c) the impact on students of role-taking, which is one of the blended activities included into the blended course. Results show that our blended approach has an impact on how students interact and talk in groups. At the end of the course, students display a collaborative discourse strategy mainly based on: (a) completing each other's sentence, (b) complex trajectories of participation, (c) changes of the perception of the self and of the group and (d) the effects of role-playing.

DOI: 10.4018/978-1-61692-898-8.ch005

INTRODUCTION

E-learning discloses all its potentialities when it is carefully designed and theoretically grounded. The socio-constructivist framework is particularly useful in designing e-learning courses based on a vision of learning as collaborative knowledge building (Brown & Campione, 1990; Dillenbourg, 2002; Koschmann, 1996; Scardamalia & Bereiter, 1994). We claim that the potentialities of the socio-constructivist framework can be fully exploited when a blended approach is introduced. Blended learning implies integration of technology based and face-to-face activities (Alvarez, 2005; Bonk & Graham, 2006), but also mixing different pedagogical models, alternating individual study to group activity, and requiring the students to elaborate a variety of tasks and end-products (Ligorio & Annese, in press).

In fact, making available a wide array of tools, proposing different tasks and activities, and presenting the information in various formats means fostering a complex and rich learning process (Human-Vogel & Bouwer, 2005). The combination of offline and online needs to be carefully designed to avoid a replication of the activities or an unfair use of one of them. Rather what starts in one context should be finalized in the other, developing a positive loop. New stimuli and inputs should be produced, feeding new activities that may take place in either one or the other context.

Meetings in presence between students and teachers are important moments for many reasons-for instance, to support interpersonal relationships; to offer a space and time to solve ambiguities and to clarify aspects that may be obscure online; to support decision making and responsibility taking; and to deliver certain types of information. At the same time, online students and teachers can perform activities difficult to be organized in presence because of lack of time and – often – lack of space, such as writing and reading and discussions based on the readings.

In this chapter, we propose an architecture of blended learning for higher education where online and offline are reciprocally enriched and collaborative learning is supported. Details of how this combination is designed will be given in the following paragraphs.

BACKGROUND

A few researchers have revealed limitations and failures of online learning. Ackerman and his colleagues (Ackerman, 2009; Ackerman & Goldsmith, 2008) discovered a lower achievement of students when reading digital materials instead of printed ones. Kurtz and Amichai-Hamburger (2008) reported a sense of loneliness perceived when physical contact with teacher and peers is lacking. Finally, Shemla and Nachmias (2007) revealed that students lack sufficient skills to deploy in an educationally relevant way when learning with online technologies. The blended approach seems to be able to exploit the potentiality of online learning and to overcome some of these problems. However, blending online and offline contexts is not sufficient per se; instead, specifically designed pedagogical models are needed to achieve effective blended courses.

When designing theories for blended learning, specific problems may arise. For instance, time management requires particular attention and the educational material used for a course needs to be selected and organized in a proper way. At the same time, lecturing cannot be delivered without taking into consideration what happens online. Finally, since each of the devices available online (chat, forum, shared whiteboard, etc.) sustain specific type of interaction, each of them should be used for proper objectives.

In our opinion, a new pedagogy is needed to support efficient blended courses. Such pedagogy should be crafted by mixing already existing models proven to be efficient with appropriate adaptations of these models to consider both offline and online contexts. In the following paragraphs, we will report on a few models we used as inspiration. These models are mostly based on a constructivist vision of learning, stressing the fundamental role of social interaction on effective learning. Then, a specific blended course will be described designed upon this pedagogy.

Progressive Inquiry Model (PIM)

The Progressive Inquiry Model (PIM) designed by Hakkarainen, Lipponen and Järvelä (2002) suggests considering learning as an inquiry process starting from general and broad questions - called "research questions"- and proceeding towards critical and scientific thinking. In this model, students are spurred to finalize their learning to realize a common and shared objective. This principle helps students to collaborate in order to reach a status beyond individual achievements.

The PIM is composed of a few phases organized as a spiral. Some of these phases take place online, others offline. This model assigns to the discussion a relevant role in the learning process. By discussing, students can refine their ideas, create a collective meaning, and gather different points of view about the learning contents and materials.

When applied to a blended course, the PIM offers a tidy sequence of activities, some of them organized mainly in presence; others take place mainly online and some Internet features, such as web-forum and data base, are particuarly useful.

Jigsaw

Jigsaw is the name of a model (Aronson & Patnoe, 1997) aimed at creating a collaborative climate based on the elaboration of collective learning achievements.

In a Jigsaw classroom, a topic is divided into sub-parts and students are divided into as many groups as the sub-parts. Each group, composed of 5 to 7 students, is in charge of becoming "expert" on the sub-part assigned. Later, groups are recomposed and formed by experts from the initial groups; each member of a new group is now responsible for teaching the sub-part studied in their original group to the other members. In this way, students can master the entire topic by learning the information offered by their peers in the new group.

Jigsaw offers a model for grouping students to enhance the learning processes based on collaboration. When applied to blended courses, it fosters the organization of online groups. In fact, students can be easily grouped and re-grouped virtually. Furthermore, the exchange of information, the reciprocal commenting on each other work, and the construction of collective products are fostered by many tools available in the Internet.

Reciprocal Teaching

Reciprocal Teaching (RT) (Palincsar & Brown, 1984) was originally designed to teach students how to make sense of what they read. This model assumes that making sense of texts is essentially negotiated within a community; therefore, students discuss what they read in their group with their peers and the teacher. RT is segmented into four sub-activities: (a) summarizing: the group summarizes what was just read; (b) questioning: posing good questions is an activity that implies the selection of relevant information from the text as well as the ability to recognize what is eventually lacking in the text; (c) clarifying: students are forced to discuss about their own incomprehension by reporting unclear points; (d) predicting: students are required to predict how the text will continue. By doing so, the interconnection between the various parts of the text should be recognized and they can see how what has been read is useful to anticipate what is to follow in the text.

This set of activities is first lead by the teacher. Later, each student in turn replaces the teacher in leading the discussion. When introduced in blended courses, RT develops academic skills such as critical reading and comprehension of the digital materials. The digital environment can be used to practice collaborative reading by comparing ideas and opinions about the reading with their peers.

Collaborative Communities

Collaborative learning occurs in special groups called communities. This means special attention should be given to group work and to balance individual responsibilities with a sense of collective belonging and shared enterprise. A few concepts outlined by the models of the Community of Practice (CoP) (Wenger, 1998) and the Community of Learners (CoL) (Brown & Campione, 1990) are particularly useful.

CoP is a model originally designed to analyze professional contexts and later extended to any learning context. According to this model, learning happens when people can participate in cultural practices, crucial for the community; therefore, learning is closely related to: (a) a growing sense of personal engagement into the practice; (b) a common objective; and, (c) a set of constantly negotiated procedures, routines, and languages.

CoL, instead, are specifically designed for schools. Students are considered as active learners, able to increase, deepen, and evaluate their own knowledge. Each student is, at the same time, a learner and a teacher when s/he becomes an expert on a specific part of the learning content. In this sense, within CoL activities are based on the exchange of roles, self-evaluation, active searching of sources, and metacognition.

Swapping roles, in particular, is a crucial aspect of this model. First of all, the number of possible roles is expanded. A CoL is not composed only of teachers and student; instead, there are also roles based upon members' expertise or designed in terms of the activities undertaken. For instance, when a student has a certain skill, then a role can be designed based upon that skill. Similarly, when there is a task to be performed then a role based on the responsibility for that activity can be set. Having many roles, each member of the community can experience them and try out the interaction styles connected to them.

The organization into groups is essential in a CoL. Groups are an ideal place to test the roles, discuss, and compare ideas and information. The groups regularly meet and update each other about their progress through the so-called "cross-talk" meetings meant as moments for groups to reciprocally challenge each other about the activities under development. Students, in fact, during the "cross-talk", reciprocally ask critical questions and offer stimuli for new directions.

In blended courses, community-based models are useful in many ways. First of all, specific practices can be built. For instance, providing the opportunity to repeat activities over time with the same structure allows progressive appropriation of the virtual space; at the same time, the sense of community is fostered. Secondly, individual participation is sustained by assigning individual responsibilities, for example by distributing specific interdependent roles to each student. Role taking, in fact, promotes the sense of belonging, enabling the virtual space to become a place where students negotiate their common learning goals. Finally, self- and dynamic assessment – for instance by maintaining individual e-portfolios - makes students aware of the specific learning strategies requested by a blended course.

Dialogical Knowledge Building

Socio-constructivism prefers the definition of knowledge building over the more common term "learning". As Scardamalia and Bereiter (2007) point out, learning is often referred to individual's achievements, whereas knowledge building contains a clear attempt to improve collective learning. Such a result is only possible through a guided and structured interaction between peers and expert guidance. To enrich this perspective, discussions and interactions between many points of view is considered as crucial. The interactive moments should not be aimed at converging toward a pre-fixed definition or idea; on the contrary, the multiplicity of perspectives should be maintained. When many points of view are confronted, argued, mixed and integrated, then knowledge building implies a dialogical management between many positions, each of them provided by a "voice", in the bakhtinian sense (Bakhtin, 1981). This means that no attempt is made to converge toward a unique and common point of view; rather, new knowledge is possible when all the positions and voices are considered and reciprocally enriched (Roth, 2009). The concepts of voicing and dialogicality are very relevant as theoretical underpinnings for the blended course, in particular when synchronous (chat) and asynchronous (forum) discussions are offered.

In the following paragraphs, we will describe the model we propose for a blended course designed for higher education. This model is rooted in a pedagogical model gained by mixing the models described above. The practical description of our course is based upon a few experiences at a higher level, with university students and in-service teachers.

SETTING UP THE CONTEXT

The model we propose requires a radical reorganization of the context. We recommend a four-step strategy to set it up.

The first step is to group the students. As we know (Blumenfeld, Marx, Soloway, & Krajcik, 1996; Dillenbourg, 1999), small groups are the engine of collaborative learning. In fact, small groups support active learners and foster individual responsibility for achieving common goals and joint enterprise (Wenger, 1998). Considering the recommended group size is about six to eight individuals, the number of groups to be formed depends on the total number of students attending the course (i.e., when there are 17 students then two subgroups can be formed; one of 8 members and another one of 9).

The second step concerns the organization of the course into units. The number of units composing the course depends on the time available and on the general aims of the course. The teacher is usually in charge of organizing the content and the sequence of the units, although there should be space for flexibility and negotiation with the students in order to take into account their pre-existing knowledge and interests. We recommend giving the students an overview of the units, the rationale of their sequence, each unit's goals, and the goals of the whole course. Furthermore, we propose considering a final unit devoted to the preparation of a collective product; for instance, a list of important points about the course or an instrument such as a grid to guide observational activities. In any case, the preparation of such products is a way to force the students to go back to all the units and discover the links between them. The sense of fragmentation that units can induce should be overcome and students should be able to transform the knowledge acquired into a practical tool.

The third step concerns outlining an agenda to schedule the face-to-face meetings. This agenda depends upon the possibilities and constraints of the course and the participants, but at least one meeting per week is recommended. Changes in the agenda are possible and they do not jeopardize the course as long as the changes are notified in advance.

In between the face-to-face meetings, students are required to perform a set of online activities, hosted on a platform. The fourth step comprises a specific training to familiarize students with the virtual place. Usually one week is enough for participants to master the basic skills to navigate and communicate through the Internet. During the time allocated to explore the platform, students could open personal folders where they can talk about themselves and up-load visual and/or audio materials they consider as representative of their interests and inclinations. By doing so, they are exploring all the options and tools available on the platform.

THE PLATFORM

The platform used for our courses is called Synergeia (www.euro-cscl.org/site/itcole). Synergeia - a free platform developed during a European project - provides many tools able to support knowledge building and critical, reflective thinking. It also allows students to share documents and ideas. Synergeia was designed with the explicit aim if to operationalizing many of the features collaborative knowledge building should have.

Synergeia's main tool is the discussion forum. Three types of discussion forums are possible within the platform: informal, problem-oriented, and knowledge building-oriented. Depending on the type of forum selected, different labels for notes are available. These labels refer to thinking types, which are scaffolds meant explicitly for knowledge building. In fact, before entering a note, writers are required to choose a specific thinking type for their note and therefore are forced to reflect upon the contribution of to the existing discussion (Am I proposing a working theory? Is my note deepening the knowledge already built? Am I stating a problem?). The thinking type selected for a note is displayed together with the subject and the author. Synergeia offers other interesting tools supporting critical and creative thinking. For instance, Map tool is a graphics tool that combines a chat and a shared white-board. Students can work with it synchronously to construct concept maps. The chat window allows coordination of the task and discussion about the drawing of maps. To build the maps, students can use tools such as simple shapes (triangles, squares, and circles), arrows and text.

Many tools are also available to check and supervise students' activities within the platform, as well as the history of each document posted on Synergeia. Footprints, stars, and glasses are icons representing tools containing information about all the objects stored in Synergeia: who created, read, deleted or edited them. Furthermore, a tool is available for queries about each individual student either within each single folder or within the whole course. Finally, a daily report is released by Synergeia's server, which contains all the activities occurring within the online course.

THE BLENDED ACTIVITIES

Our peculiar idea of blended learning integrates online and offline activities inspired by the models described above. Online and offline contexts are strictly interwoven although some of the activities are mainly taking place face to face and others are mainly happening online. In the following description, we will illustrate each activity and the specific pedagogical principles guiding it.

We will first describe how the mainly-offline activities are structured; right after, we will report about the activities taking place mainly online. These activities were designed and tested on university students and in-service teachers, but we believe with the due adjustments they could be introduced also into high and secondary schools as well as professional training.

Activities Mainly Offline

Generally, the offline encounters take place once a week with about two hours allotted for each meeting. During the meetings, participants have no access to computers. Two types of meetings are planned: (1) *standard* meetings, and (2) *discussion* meetings.

The *standard* meetings are considered as the starting point for the unit and are anchored to the teacher's lecture. During the first *standard* meeting, the teacher presents the course and describes the activities. The following *standard* meetings are started by students selected to participate within a specific role called "critical friend". (An explanation about this will come later in the paragraph about role-taking). The critical friend compares and integrates the products of the various groups commenting upon the work done by other groups. By doing so, a sense of a common goal is kept. Right after, the teacher lectures for about 30-40 minutes. The lecture ends with the definition of a research question arising from the lecture. Such a research question guides the activities for the upcoming unit. The *standard* meetings are concluded with a collective discussion about the activities to be performed and by assigning individual reading and roles.

The *discussion* meetings are considered a consolidation of the work previously performed, with two types of discussion taking place: group discussion, during which the group members compare their points of view on the same topic; and plenary discussion, involving all the students. Basically, the orchestration of small group discussions and plenary discussions mirrors the structure of the online discussions. In fact, inter- and intra-group discussions occur online too. From an educational point of view, the discussion meetings allow students to accomplish many of the recommendations constructivism offers. Students can improve their collaborative strategies by following-up and finalising the discussions occurring online. Metacognition is also advanced by letting the students reflect upon the interactive processes involving the groups. Furthermore, the dialogical dimension can be maintained because of the encounter between many voices and perspectives.

In the following table, the structure of the face-to-face meetings is reported; for each activity, the pedagogical reference into which the activity is grounded is mentioned in addition to the aim of each activity.

All together the structure of the face-to-face meetings represents a routine in CoL's terms in addition to practice in CoP's terms. In both perspectives, the aim is to support a progressive appropriation of the way of discussing, thinking and building knowledge collaboratively and critically.

Activities Mainly Online

In between the face-to-face meetings, students are required to perform a set of activities taking place mainly online. These activities are described below:

1. Reading and writing. Each participant is required to read individually the educational material the teacher assigns to him/her. To perform this task, a few days are usually allotted. This assignment is given at each unit; therefore, each student is required to read a number of documents similar to the number of units composing the course. Later, students have to write a short critical review about that material. To write such a review, the teacher offers the following precise indications: (a) reporting the main issues of the document read, (b) outlining the contribution to the research question of the unit, (c) giving a personal opinion, and (d) from the second unit on, comparing the paper with the previously read materials either by the same student or other students.

The critical reviews are posted in a virtual folder and all the group members have to read and comment on them. The reviews represent the starting-point for the online discussions in each group, but they also support cross-group discussions around the same materials. In fact, the same material is read by one student in each group. Therefore, the number of students reading the same material depends on the number of groups composed. For instance, if in a course there are three groups, there will be three students reading the same material and they will confront and discuss the particular reading and their reviews on it. This activity leads, therefore, to a twofold level of discussion: an intergroup discussion about the same materials and a group discussion around all the materials of the unit. Students enter the group discussion with two "voices": their own personal view and that of the author of the material read avoiding naïve and rhetorical discussions.

Furthermore, for each unit, the teacher reads and corrects two to three reviews for each group so that, by the end of the course, each student will have at least two commented reviews. The students are required to read and discuss in group the teacher's comments even when they do not concern their own review in order to improve the students' writing skills. The reviews are aimed at enhancing the students' ability to acquire their own critical self-assessment.

This activity is rooted both in an adapted Jigsaw model and in the RT. In fact, students cover a piece of the unit with their individual readings and by posting and reciprocally reading the reviews they cover the content of whole the unit. The discussion around a research question is clearly inspired by the PIM. Reading many papers and being encouraged to express personal points of view assures the dialogical nature of the discussion. In fact, many voices are involved in this activity—specifically, the students' voice, both as an individual and as part of a group, the experts of the material read, and finally the voice of the teacher.

2. Discussing. Many types of discussions are possible online: informal, organizational

Table 1. Structure of the mainly face-to-face meetings

Standard meetings (about 10 in total)	Start-up: 30-40 minutes for critical friends report Pedagogical references: cross-talk and CoP Aim: critical review and monitoring of the activity performed
	a) Teacher Lecturing: 30-40 minutes on basic concepts and relevant issues about the new unit Pedagogical references: CoL Aim: give new information b) Negotiation of a research question for the unit Pedagogical reference: Progressive Inquiry model Aim: support and guide the group discussions
	a) Close-down: 30-40 minutes' collective discussion about the organisation of online activities (roles, timing and specific contextual matters) Pedagogical principle: CoL Aim: support active learning and self monitoring b) The teacher assigns individual reading material Pedagogical references: CoP Aim: support active learning and give the basis for the group discussion
Discussion meetings (more or less 3 in total)	Group Discussion: 30-40 minutes Pedagogical reference: CoL Aim: consolidation of the activities performed
	Plenary Discussion: 30-40 minutes All the groups compare their work Pedagogical references: Cross-talk, Jigsaw, CoP Aim: build the sense of a common enterprise
	a) Teacher Lecturing: 30-40 minutes Pedagogical references: CoL Aim: give new information b) The teacher assigns individual reading material Pedagogical references: Individual responsibility CoP Aim: support active learning and give the basis for the group discussion

and unit-specific. Informal and organizational discussions are possible throughout the course as students are allowed to open up new discussion forums whenever they like. These spaces represent interesting opportunities for students to express their thoughts and feelings about their participation in the course. They are important spaces because various matters are addressed and solved and, above all, a sense of community is built. While informal and organizational discussion forums are freely organized by the students, the unit-specific discussions are guided by the PIM. In fact, in the first place students try to answer the research question by contributing with concepts and ideas taken from the educational material read and from the review written by the colleagues. In the second place, students define some practical indicators useful to construct an observational grid that they will use at the end of the course to perform observational activities. The definition of the practical indicators is a way to make theories concrete. This phase is carried out through a plenary discussion between all the groups. Moving from small group discussion to cross-group discussion is considered an important aspect for collaborative learning and community building. Comparison between groups develops mechanisms of discrimination and cooperation, both driving to an identification process useful to activate psychosocial dynamics of group building. The plenary discussion is also a way to conduct the crosstalk described by the CoL model.

3. Searching for new materials. Students are encouraged to search for new material to better address the unit and to post it online accompanied by a short justification. The justification contains information about author and/or website credibility, why the material should be considered relevant for the unit, and how it can contribute to the inquiry on the unit's research question. Students appreciate this practice and increasingly select interesting educational material. This activity has a twofold aim: it supports the students' sensation of being active, by contributing to the selection of educational materials; at the same time, students can reflect on the criteria for recognizing valuable information obtained on the Internet.

4. Building collaborative products. Before moving to a new unit, participants are required to collaboratively build three products: a written synthesis, a conceptual map, and a checklist.

The synthesis describes how the group worked during the unit-specific discussion. The teacher provides a guideline about this product which includes the following points: (a) the text should be no longer than 500 words, (b) it should describe if and how the PIM was applied during the discussion, (c) it should scrutinize how the thinking types were used. The synthesis production clearly aims to sustain reflective thinking and to provide inputs to improve the reasoning and inquiry process for the next unit.

The conceptual map can be designed by using the Synergeia tool called Maptool. Maptool makes it possible to build maps by chatting in a synchronous mode. The map should contain the main ideas born from the discussion and the final research answer given by the group. The Maptool activity is useful for improving learning through the recognition of primary concepts of knowledge and the relationships between them (Novak, 1977; Novak & Gowin, 1984). The chat logs and the final maps are stored in a folder and students can discuss and comment on them. In this way, reflection is fostered on the process of building a concept map and on the differences between composing a text and a map. Offering the possibility to work with maps and to interact synchronously is a way to allow students to try different formats and communication modes. Different modalities of participation are, therefore, fostered as recommended by the CoP model.

The checklist is sketched out during each unit, but it is definitively achieved in the final one, when students collect all the indicators they defined during the previous units. In order to create a better final product, they re-examine units that were unclear or not fully exploited. The checklist can be considered the common enterprise, gained through mutual engagement of students who work on a shared repertoire (Wenger, 1998).

Each group produces a synthesis, a map, and a checklist at the end of each unit. All the groups completely devoted to this task build the final common checklist collectively during the last unit. Having end products incarnating the group work means externalizing the culture of the group. Texts, maps, and lists are products upon which the groups can reflect to analyze and assess the work done. Once external to the group, these products easily became artifacts triggering new ideas and new knowledge building. This is the principle that Bruner (1996) calls externalization.

5. Role-taking. In our model, a number of roles are proposed and all of them are aimed at shaping active students. In fact, ideally, each student should always play a role; in this way, the student can always have the responsibility of some task essential for the group and for the whole course. All roles are meant to interweave the process of learning with the acquisition of abilities and professional skills. The roles so far tested in our blended courses are:

(a) E-tutor, focusing on group management and supporting group discussion;
(b) Critical friend, designed to promote cross-group collaboration by reading and commenting on the activities and products of a different group;
(c) Responsible for a collaborative product (unit indicators, unit synthesis, map, final checklist), having the responsibility to guide the activities necessary to finalize the product and to describe it during the face-to-face meetings;
(d) Responsible for taking notes and/or video clips from face-to-face meetings and uploading them online. Students covering this role should be sensitive to the needs of the students not able to attend the class. At the same time, they contribute to the improvement of the metacognitive understanding of what happens in class.

The whole set of roles is meant to support positive social interaction, knowledge building, and a sense of students challenging themselves. In fact, students find themselves acting in ways they would not normally do, so they experience new ways of being. Role-playing has an impact on self-representation, broadens the space of the "possible selves" (Markus & Nurius, 1986), and enriches the identity trajectory. Different situations, triggered by the roles, make salient different aspects of the self and produce new identity positioning (Hermans, 2004). Specific discussions about the roles, about how students feel when playing them and how to improve their efficacy, are available throughout the course. These discussion forums are presented as crucial moments for the knowledge building process.

6. *E-portfolio and self-assessment.* In order to support self-evaluation and meta-cognitive reflection about the activities performed, students are required to construct a personal folder and complete a sheet of self-assessment. The folders are considered as a place to upload material about themselves and their own participation in the course. They are called e-portfolios and are used at different moments of the course—at the start-up of the course where students are required to post their expectations and the goals they would like to achieve, and at the end of each unit, where students are required to fill in self-assessment sheets and to select their best products of the unit. At the end of the course, they report their assessment about the course and their own learning; they also compare their self-assessment with their initial expectations.

The self-evaluation sheet is composed of several questions, through which students describe how the activities performed (reviewing, role-taking, online and offline discussions, conceptual maps, indicators and checklist, etc.) contributed to their learning in terms of both content and skills. Self-assessment stimulates students' metacognitive processes and reflection on their own abilities and skills; moreover, it supports the development of critical self-evaluation. At the end of the course, the teacher takes into account the progress in filling in the self-evaluation sheets. In, fact, self-direct learning and metacognition are relevant for the knowledge building process.

Table 2 presents a synopsis of the activities performed mainly online with the annotation of the pedagogical references and their aims.

The set of activities proposed with our model is designed mainly to support active learners and collaborative knowledge building. In fact, individual learning (by reading and writing) is the starting point for subsequent collaborative activities such as discussing and preparing group products. Indeed, the complex architecture of this blended course allows, at the same time, individual work, work within small groups, and large groups activity.

Research Results

From a research point of view, our method allows the collection of a huge amount of data. Online and offline discussions and the material produced by the students can be analyzed according to different perspectives and approaches. Below we illustrate some analyses already conducted both on university courses and courses for in-service professional development of teachers.

Collaborative Talking

The effects of blended collaboration on learning can be detected by looking at the discussion strategy used by the group. A few focus group

Table 2. Structure of the mainly online activities

Reading and writing	Individual reading of the material assigned Individual writing of a short review following the teacher directions Cross-group discussion involving students reading the same material Collective discussion about the teachers' comments on the review Pedagogical references: Jigsaw, RT, dialogical perspective; PIM Aim: develop academic skills in reading and writing
Discussing	Group discussion about the research question Pedagogical references: PIM and dialogical perspective Aim: express ideas (both personal and based on the readings) and compare
Searching new materials	Students search for new material relevant for the unit Pedagogical references: CoL and CoP Aim: recognize scientific material
Building collaborative products	Written synthesis of how the group discussed Conceptual map about the main ideas discussed and the answer to the research question elaborated by the group Checklist about how to see in practice the discussed ideas Pedagogical references: PIM; collaborative knowledge building and externalization Aim: academic skills and practical skills about e-learning (the content of the course)
Role-taking	E-tutor, critical friend, responsible of the collaborative products, responsible for taking notes and/or video clips from face-to-face meetings and up-loading them online. Pedagogical references: scaffolding, CoL, CoP, self development and positioning Aim: support active learning and responsibilities taking
E-portfolio and self-assessment.	Opening and maintaining a personal folder Filling in a self-assessment sheet Pedagogical references: self-assessment and metacognition Aim: improve skills to self-assess expectations, activities, collaboration

discussions were analyzed to understand how collaborative learning and knowledge building were perceived by the students. The analyses additionally focused on how collaborative and knowledge building eventually changed as a consequence of students' exposure to a blended course designed with our model. During the focus groups at the end of the course, students were required to report how they felt about the course and how they thought it could be improved. The qualitative analysis was focused on the argumentative strategies used by students during the discussion. Results showed that students mastered more strategies of argumentation based on a complex collaborative construction of meaning than strategies based on simple reciprocity (Cucchiara, Spadaro, & Ligorio, 2008). For example, the students mostly re-elaborated other students' sentences (in 26% of turns) and completed each other's sentences (in 26% of turns, see Table 3 - Excerpt n. 1). They also showed a tendency to progressively and collectively build the discourse, showing collective thinking and a shared understanding of the topic under discussion (Schegloff, 1987). Some reciprocal reparations were also used (in 9% of turns).

Participation

Socio-constructivism redefines learning in terms of participation. A Social Network Analysis was also performed to examine how participation evolved during a blended course, by comparing face-to-face and online discussions on the same topic and by analyzing discussions occurring at different moments (at the starting of the course, half way, and at the end). Results show that being exposed to online and offline contexts allow students to experience different kinds of participation in the group. In particular, students appear to adapt their style of interaction to the communication environment; therefore specific participation trajectories were generated. For example, some students who were peripheral during the face-to-face discussion seem to be more central in the online discussion, becoming active and perfectly integrated into the community's participation network. There were also participants who followed stable participation trajectories, activating the same strategies in different interaction contexts. For example, some members maintain the same popularity in both offline and online discussions and they remain always crucial reference points for the whole community.

Also identity positionings (Hermans, 2004) changed according to the communication context: when online, the positionings were based on individual dimensions; when offline, the collective dimensions seem to be more relevant. In the online context, the internal individual positioning is central (0.87 of centrality degree, max=1), in fact, several discursive markers reveal students' private ideas or feelings that emphasize the subjectivity of each single participant ("My curiosity is awakened by reflection on these differences..."; Clelia, online forum). In contrast, in the offline context, the internal collective positioning becomes central (1.00): students display many discursive markers about their sense of belonging to the community, such as the use of collective pronouns, especially "we" ("Now sometimes we meet in chat too, and we use our Skype..."; Francesca, focus group) (Ligorio, Annese, Spadaro, & Traetta, 2008).

Table 3. Excerpt 1. Example of completing each other sentences

168 G: yes, at the end each role was//
169 F: //moved forward
170 G: //yes, at the beginning we interpreted it eh eh (hhh) in our manner and later we evolved in it
171 F: well, we have tried to evolve it

Perception of the Self and of the Group during the Course

Some focus group discussions were conducted and analyzed with a twofold aim: (1) to sustain students' meta-cognitive processes and reflection about the course; (2) to explore the initial expectations about the course and understand students' opinions of it at the end. Thus, we conducted two focus groups at the start of the course—one focusing on offline (during a lesson) and the other online (via chat) activity—and two at the end (one offline and one via chat). These discussions were analyzed through discourse analysis. The concepts of chronotope and polyphony (Bakhtin, 1981) were used as methodological tools to understand the students' discourses. We found:

1. In the initial discussions, students interpreted the course through a comparison with the other courses attended before (past chronotopes) and through a "group voice", a "we" useful to handle the novelty (see Table 4 - Excerpt n. 2: "our way of studying"). They interpreted the course like a new chronotope to be faced through the support of the group. In this sense, the polyphony is constituted by the only voice of the group.
2. In the final discussions, the "we" was no longer a tool to handle the novelty, but rather the group became the place to learn. There was a transformation in the perception of the group; that is, students believed the group activities supported both individual and collective learning. This detachment from the group as a tool to understand a new reality is confirmed by the students' re-appropriation of their "voice" even when reporting a group collective position. Chronotopes are now referred to the "here and now" of the course and the learning is perceived as strongly situated (see Table 5 - Excerpt n. 3).
3. In the online discussions, students were in great need of defining their identity to mark their presence. They often tried to assign specific features to each participants (i.e. color, character's side) so as to be able to properly attribute each utterance to the right speaker.

Role-Play

We also performed an analysis of how the various proposed roles were played by the participants and how they were perceived. The participation styles change over time—students moved from individual positions toward more social positions. This movement is quite complex and it is sensitive to many dimensions, such as the specific role played, the topic under discussion, and the general evolution of the group they belong to (Ligorio,

Table 4. Excerpt n. 2. Other courses, other times

L: I think our way of studying slightly varies depending on what we study even in the university context. I mean one course may need more synthesis, often it depends on the books, how they are written.

Table 5. Excerpt n. 3. Learning in groups

L: therefore we knew whom to talk to and whom to ask certain questions... roles inside the group were created or rather read **M**: no, actually for me it has also been the same but the approach it has been very different. At the beginning, in my opinion, the difference between the first -let's say group- and the second group was... also at the beginning, we were more confused, we needed to interact more and we did it continuously. However, at the end I think I understood how it worked: we acquired competencies (more or less) on the tools and on how to move around on the platform, we interacted much less, wherease during the first unit we interacted about anything, we did not do it the end.

Annese, Spadaro, & Traetta, 2008). In another study (Spadaro, Sansone, & Ligorio, 2009), we compared two blended courses with the aim of verifying the impact of the two roles (the e-tutor and the student responsible of the collaborative writing task) in terms of participation and preference for one of these two roles. Results show that both roles were perceived as useful to foster participation and to improve communication and collaboration skills. Participants prefer one or the other role based on specific motivations. 27.7% of the respondents preferred a role on the basis of intrinsic features attributed to it; 34% of the participants explained that the role was tuned with their personal attitudes; 23.4% of participants preferred a certain role because it developed their individual skills and promoted a more active participation in the course; 14.9% liked a role because they found it useful to acquire new social and collaborative skills.

Through the quantitative analysis of participation, we found that when students assumed the role of tutor their participation increased—sometimes it even doubled. We also performed a qualitative analysis by means of a specific category system (5 categories: supportive, emotional, didactic, collaborative, organizational) on the notes posted by the students while performing the role of tutor. The analysis revealed that the students not only increased their participation quantitatively, but they adopted a supportive interaction style (see Table 6 - Excerpt n. 4).

Such a style had not been used before taking on this role and, to a certain extent, was maintained also after the role was abandoned.

However, it was found that the roles were differently perceived depending on the type of students. For instance, in-service teachers preferred roles and activities closer to their routine practices, such as being responsible for a written product. In fact, both this role and activity resembles the learning activities to which they were accustomed. University students, on the other hand, preferred roles perceived as depending on their personal attitudes (Spadaro, Sansone, & Ligorio, 2009).

Recommendations and Criticalities

A few preconditions are necessary to implement our model:

1. The context should afford an alternation of face-to-face and online encounters;
2. There should be a real intention to exploit the potentialities of technology supporting online interactions;
3. The teacher should master the general educational principles about e-learning and collaborative models;
4. There should be at least one trained online tutor available to support the teacher during the course;
5. An online platform should be available.

On the other hand, it is not strictly required for students to have high technology skills. In fact, under the technical point of view, students are just required to up-load and down-load, to open new folders, to contribute to web-forum and to participate in the creation of a map by using a shared board. Furthermore, through recording and note-taking during the face-to-face meetings posted online, students not able to attend the class

Table 6. Excerpt n. 4. Supportive style

L: Good job! I think you explained the central topic very well; probably you could tell us where you found the additional information you gave us. However, you've been great!

can be easily be updated about what happened during the meetings.

The main weak point of our model is its complexity. Students pointed out this aspect in their feedback of the various courses in which they participated. Teachers too often experienced an overload of work to start, monitor, scaffold and assess the different activities. A way to overcome this problem is to consider this model as a wide proposal within which the specific course can be cut out. This means that a teacher can decide to select certain activities and leave out others, depending on the needs and constraints of the specific course, such as number of students participating, student's pre-knowledge and skills, time allotted, and tools available. A teacher could, for instance, dedicate most of the time and efforts to model only a few roles leaving out the others. The same applies to the activities; not all of them have to be implemented. In this view, our model works as a matrix from which many different courses can be generated. Furthermore, a course could start with a few activities and roles and gradually new activities and roles can be introduced.

FUTURE RESEARCH DIRECTIONS

The blended approach seems to be very appealing for both higher education and professional development. The model proposed here should illustrate that it is not enough to mix online and offline instructional practices to obtain a successful blend. Much more reflection is needed about the tools used and how to organize the setting. Most importantly, a profound reconsideration is needed of the theoretical models and frameworks already existing. Actually, it could be the case that introducing our blended model, some theoretical principles and ideas could find new vigor and new occasions to be deeper understood. Our explicit attempt is to clearly show how each activity we propose (both online and offline) is theoretically grounded. However, the most important aspect we want to underline is that although it is possible to distinguish between activities mainly occurring online or offline, all of them are possible only if space and time is allotted for them in both contexts. It is our intention, in the future, to better understand the interplay of these contexts by looking more in depth into students' interactions and how much each context influences the other.

CONCLUSION

The blended model we present here was tested in various courses with different types of students (university courses, in-service teachers). In either case, we found that this complex architecture affects students' learning strategies. Students always felt encouraged to move from rote learning toward learning through collaboration and discussion. They were also forced to keep a certain pace all through the course so they had to be always active and felt a growing responsibility for their group.

In general, the innovation introduced with this model was appreciated and understood; students recognized that they improved critical thinking and discussion strategies, but these skills seemed to remain confined to the course attended and they were not transferred to other courses. This result calls for reflection on how strong and thorough are the learning models students have and how difficult it is to change them. Innovation needs a long exposure and a change of mentality and attitude that obviously cannot be reached through one course only.

REFERENCES

Ackerman, R. (2009). The Subjective Feelings of Comprehension and Remembering Accompanying Text Learning On-Screen. In Y. Eshet-Alkalai, A. Caspi, S. Eden, N. Geri, & Y. Yair (Eds.), *Proceedings of the Chais conference on instructional technologies research 2009. Vol. 4 Learning in the technological era*, (pp. 1-7) Raanana, Israel: The Open University of Israel.

Ackerman, R., & Goldsmith, M. (2008). Learning directly from screen? Oh-no, I must print it! Metacognitive analysis of digitally presented text learning. In Eshet, Y., Caspi, A., & Geri, N. (Eds.), *Learning in the technological era* (*Vol. 3*, pp. 1–7). Raanana, Israel: Open University of Israel.

Alvarez, S. (2005). Blended learning solutions. In B. Hoffman (Ed.), *Encyclopedia of Educational Technology*. Retrieved March 20, 2010, from http://edweb.sdsu.edu/eet/

Aronson, E., & Patnoe, S. (1997). *The jigsaw classroom: Building cooperation in the classroom* (2nd ed.). New York: Longman.

Bakhtin, M. (1981). *The Dialogic Imagination*. Austin, TX: University of Texas Press.

Blumenfeld, P. C., Marx, R. W., Soloway, E., & Krajcik, J. (1996). Learning with Peers: From small group cooperation to collaborative communities. *Educational Researcher*, *25*(8), 37–40.

Bonk, C. J., & Graham, C. R. (Eds.). (2006). *The Handbook of Blended Learning: Global Perspectives, Local Designs*. San Francisco, CA: Pfeiffer.

Brown, A. L., & Campione, J. C. (1990). Communities of learning and thinking: Or a context by any other name. [Basel,CH: Karger.]. *Contributions to Human Development*, *21*, 108–125.

Bruner, J. (1996). *The Culture of Education*. Cambridge, MA: Harvard University Press.

Cucchiara, S., Spadaro, P. F., & Ligorio, M. B. (2008). Identità e comunità in contesti collaborativi: un'esperienza blended universitaria [Identity and community in collaborative contexts: a blended university experience]. *Qwerty*, *1*, 23–48.

Dillenbourg, P. (1999). What do you mean by collaborative learning? In Dillenbourg, P. (Ed.), *Collaborative-learning: Cognitive and Computational Approaches* (pp. 1–19). Oxford: Elsevier.

Dillenbourg, P. (2002). Over-scripting CSCL: The risks of blending collaborative learning with instructional design. In P. A. Kirschner (Ed), *Three worlds of CSCL. Can we support CSCL?* (pp. 61-91). Heerlen, Nederland: Open Universiteit Nederland.

Hakkarainen, K., Lipponen, L., & Järvela, S. (2002). Epistemology of inquiry and computer-supported collaborative learning. In Koshmann, T. D. (Eds.), *CSCL 2: Carrying Forward the Conversation* (pp. 129–156). Mahwah, N.J.: Laurence Erlbaum Associates.

Hermans, H. (2004). Mediated identity in the emerging digital age: A dialogical perspective. *Identity: An international Journal of theory and research, 4*(4), 297-405.

Human-Vogel, S., & Bouwer, C. (2005). Creating a complex learning environment for mediation of knowledge construction in diverse educational settings. *South African Journal of Education*, *25*(4), 229–238.

Koschmann, T. (1996). Paradigm shifts and instructional technology. In Koschmann, T. (Ed.), *CSCL: Theory and practice of an emerging paradigm* (pp. 1–23). Mahwah, NJ: LEA.

Kurtz, G., & Amichai-Hamburger, Y. (2008). *Psychosocial well-being and attitudes toward e-learning*. Paper presented at the 3rd Chais Conference, Raanana, Israel.

Ligorio, M. B., & Annese, A. (in press). Blended activity design approach: A method for innovating e-learning communities in higher education. In Blachnio, A., Przepiorka, A., & Rowinski, T. (Eds.), *Internet in Psychology Research*. Warsaw: Cardinal Stefan Wyszynski University Press.

Ligorio, M. B., Annese, S., Spadaro, P. F., & Traetta, M. (2008). Building intersubjectivity and identity in on-line communities. In B. M. Varisco (Ed.), *Psychological, pedagogical and sociological models for learning and assessment in virtual communities of practice* (pp. 57- 91). Milano, IT: Polimetrica.

Markus, H., & Nurius, P. (1986). Possible selves. *The American Psychologist, 41*(9), 954–969. doi:10.1037/0003-066X.41.9.954

Novak, J. D. (1977). *A theory of education*. Ithaca, NY: Cornell University Press.

Novak, J. D., & Gowin, D. B. (1984). *Learning how to learn*. New York and Cambridge, UK: Cambridge University Press.

Palincsar, A. S., & Brown, A. L. (1984). Reciprocal teaching of comprehension-fostering and comprehension-monitoring activities. *Cognition and Instruction, 1*(2), 117–175. doi:10.1207/s1532690xci0102_1

Roth, W. M. (2009). *Dialogism: A Bakhtinian Perspective on Science and Learning*. Rotterdam: Sense Publisher.

Scardamalia, M., & Bereiter, C. (1994). Computer Support for Knowledge-Building Communities. *Journal of the Learning Sciences, 3*(3), 256–283. doi:10.1207/s15327809jls0303_3

Scardamalia, M., & Bereiter, C. (2007). Fostering communities of learners and knowledge building: An interrupted dialogue. In Campione, J. C., Metz, K. E., & Palincsar, A. S. (Eds.), *Children's learning in the laboratory and in the classroom: Essays in honor of Ann Brown* (pp. 197–212). Mahwah, NJ: Erlbaum.

Shemla, A., & Nachmias, R. (2007). Current State of Web-Supported Courses at Tel-Aviv University. *International Journal on E-Learning, 6*(2), 235–246.

Spadaro, P. F., Sansone, N., & Ligorio, M. B. (2009). Role-taking for Knowledge Building in a Blended Learning course. *Journal of e-Learning and Knowledge Society, 5*(3), 11-21.

Wenger, E. (1998). *Communities of Practice. Learning, Meaning and Identity*. Cambridge, UK: Cambridge University Press.

ADDITIONAL READING

Bershin, J. (2004). *The blended book of learning*. San Francisco: Pfeiffer.

Blumenfeld, P. C., Marx, R. W., Soloway, E., & Krajcik, J. (1996). Learning with Peers: From small group cooperation to collaborative communities. *Educational Researcher, 25*(8), 37–40.

Dernt, M., & Motschnig-Pitrik, R. (2005). The role of structure, patterns, and people in blended learning. *The Internet and Higher Education, 8*(2), 111–130. doi:10.1016/j.iheduc.2005.03.002

Dziuban, C. D., Moskal, P. D., & Hartman, J. (2005). Higher education, blended learning, and the generations: Knowledge is power: No more. In Bourne, J. R., & Moore, J. C. (Eds.), *Elements of Quality Online Education: Engaging Communities* (pp. 85–100). Needham, MA: Sloan-C.

Garrison, D. R., & Kanuka, H. (2004). Blended learning: Uncovering its transformative potential in higher education. *The Internet and Higher Education, 7*(2), 95–105. doi:10.1016/j.iheduc.2004.02.001

Garrison, D. R., & Vaughan, N. (2008). *Blended learning in higher education*. San Francisco, CA: Jossey-Bass.

Ligorio, M. B., & Veermans, M. (2005). Perspectives and patterns in developing and implementing international web-based Collaborative Learning Environments. *Computers & Education, 45*(3), 271–275. doi:10.1016/j.compedu.2005.04.007

Murphy, E. (2004). Recognizing and promoting collaboration in an online asynchronous discussion. *British Journal of Educational Technology*, *35*(4), 421–431. doi:10.1111/j.0007-1013.2004.00401.x

O'Donnell, A. M., Hmelo-Silver, C., & Erkens, G. (2005). *Collaborative learning, reasoning, and technology*. Mahwah, NJ: Lawrence Erlbaum.

Rovai, A. P., Ponton, M. K., & Baker, J. D. (2008). *Distance learning in higher education: A programmatic approach to planning, design, instruction, evaluation, and accreditation*. New York: Teachers College Press.

Singh, H. (2003). Building Effective Blended Learning Programs. *Educational Technology*, *43*(6), 51–54.

So, H.-J., & Brush, T. A. (2008). Student perceptions of collaborative learning, social presence and satisfaction in a blended learning environment: Relationships and critical factors. *Computers & Education*, *51*(1), 318–336. doi:10.1016/j.compedu.2007.05.009

KEY TERMS AND DEFINITIONS

Blended: A combination of offline and online together with a combination of educational models and activities.

Focus Group: Small-group discussions, where all the participants can contribute with the scope to gather in-depth information and views on a specific topic.

Jigsaw: A technique to create a collaborative climate based on the elaboration of collective learning achievements.

Progressive Inquiry: A model considering learning as an inquiry process supporting critical and scientific thinking.

Reciprocal Teaching: A technique to teach students how to make sense of what they read.

Group Discussion: Both web-based and face-to-face discussion.

Routine: A set of activities repeated over time.

Role-Taking: Roles designed upon educational principles sustaining students' active learning.

Chapter 6
Models and Strategies to Support Students' Initial Socialization in Web-Based Learning Environments

Stefania Manca
Institute for Educational Technology - CNR, Italy

Luca Vanin
University of Milano-Bicocca, Italy

ABSTRACT

Entering a learning system based on CSCL models may be a challenging experience. Beginner users are required to accomplish several tasks for the first time, such as learning to communicate by written discourse in an asynchronous manner, as well as becoming familiar with communication technologies and with the learning system. In order to support their initial steps several measures, which focus mainly on socialization with peers and instructors/tutors and familiarization with the learning system, may be adopted. The focus of this chapter is to present a model and some related strategies to support students' initial socialization and familiarization in web-based learning environments. Such strategies have been developed and implemented by the authors over several years of experience as designers and instructors in graduate and post-graduate courses in Italy.

INTRODUCTION

In today's experience, the growth and the gradual evolution of digital learning environments still presents many critical issues. In the context of online learning communities that are based on the principles of CSCL, for instance, one of the most crucial phases is when students enter the learning system. The reason why this phase is so critical is twofold. First, for most students it is their first online learning experience and they have to face several new problems, including learning to communicate by written discourse in an asynchronous manner, becoming familiar with communication technologies and with the learning system (Piskurich, 2003). Second, team learning and collaboration always involves a deepening

DOI: 10.4018/978-1-61692-898-8.ch006

process of participation in a group, and it is closely connected to that of construction of group identity. Being part of a group or a community means, most of all, building a common and shared identity with the other members, as well as developing an active, self-sustaining participation (based also on criticism, conflict and means of conflict resolution) (Herring, 2004). Indeed, participation especially implies the reorganization of individual identities and the construction of a collective and shared identity within the group (Wenger, 1998).

Numerous studies, from the student side (e.g. Booker & Rebman, 2005; Trekles Milligan & Buckenmeyer, 2008) and from the hiring decision-makers' perspective (Adams, 2008), have analyzed the factors implied in the acceptability of e-learning. Drop-out risk has been one of the most important issues tackled by distance learning literature. Among the various factors the following are undoubtedly the most recurrent: individual background, intrinsic and/or extrinsic motivation, academic integration, social integration, and technological environment (Jun, 2005). Other reasons have been explored (Araque, Roldan, & Salguero, 2009) and different methods to measure drop-out have been adopted (Lykourentzou, Giannoukos, Nikolopoulos, Mpardis, & Loumos, 2009). What emerges is that participants should be intrinsically motivated to complete their online studies with success and satisfaction (Bishop, 2007).

One of the most successful measures to complete an online program successfully seems a robust sense of community (Conrad, 2005; Dawson, 2006) and a good level of social presence (Rourke, Anderson, Garrison, & Archer, 2001; Caspi & Blau, 2008). In these terms, one points out the importance of an orientation process that is able to facilitate not only access to the educational system, but above all entry into the peer group (i.e. in the community of learners), integration in the learning environment and socialization with all the subjects involved (teaching staff, support staff, peer group, etc.). Therefore, these activities set themselves the objective of reducing the initial difficulties for what concerns the initial knowledge and the skills required and aims at reducing any possible gaps with regard to the technical and interactive aspects (e.g. use of the platform, online interaction, use of tools).

The aim of this study is to present a model and some associated strategies able to facilitate the introduction of students in an online learning environment as part of their educational program. The ideas that will be presented have emerged as a result of the experience of the authors as designers and instructors in their long term involvement in graduate and post-graduate courses in Italy. The main purposes of the chapter are to present the three-step model named "Orienting, Preparing, and Supporting" (hence OP&S) and some solutions suitable to help learners taking their first steps in a CSCL environment based on the massive use of CMC. Two examples based on the implementation of the model will be provided to make the theoretical principals of the model explicit.

THE ROLE OF SOCIALIZATION IN LEARNING PROCESSES

The social, relational, and affective dynamics of learning are receiving more and more attention in the study of learning processes. Researchers and practitioners have acknowledged that a well-established social dimension is the prerequisite for collaborative learning and group-based work, especially within those approaches that are more sensitive to socio-constructivist provisions (e.g. Garrison & Anderson, 2003).

Social presence has been defined as "the ability of participants in a community of inquiry to project themselves socially and emotionally, as 'real' people (i.e., their full personality), through the medium of communication being used" (Garrison, Anderson, & Archer, 1999, p. 94). The literature has shown how social presence seems to support cognitive objectives as it encourages and supports meaningful critical thinking processes in a community of learners: affective objectives that result in appealing, engaging, and rewarding group interactions may lead to an increase in socio-academic and institutional integration and results (Rourke, Anderson, Garrison, & Archer, 2001). Moreover, a good level of social presence may be a predictor of satisfaction and perceived learning (Gunawardena & Zittle, 1997; Richardson & Swan, 2003) and an indicator of success and quality of the learning experience (Swan & Shih, 2005; So & Brush, 2008).

From this point of view, socialization becomes a strategic choice to facilitate participation in CSCL environments. Socialization strategies reflect the use of ICT to satisfy individuals' social needs (e.g. online societies and game-playing) and may enhance learning more effectively, since learners are more familiar with the norms and approaches in e-learning environments (e.g. they might obtain better response from an instructor by using emoticons because they animate a conversation) (Wan, Wang, & Haggerty, 2008).

The literature also highlights how socialization, defined as the process through which the teacher–student interaction activates the exploratory learning behavior, advances internal working models and mostly intrinsic motivation (Yli-Luoma & Naeve, 2006). Thus, the main purpose of socialization is not only to facilitate an entry level of participation, but also to foster cognitive processes and deep learning (Kanuka, Rourke, & Laflamme, 2007; Offir, Lev, & Bezalel, 2008).

A crucial role, in this sense, is played by tutors and moderators, who may facilitate interaction, participation and cognitive presence through engaging questions, focused discussion, challenging ideas, etc., as measures through which learners may create meaning and receive a confirmation of their understanding (Anderson, Rourke, Garrison, & Archer, 2001; Garrison & Cleveland-Innes, 2005).

PREPARING AND SUPPORTING E-LEARNERS AND EDUCATIONAL SETTING

Several studies have been published about how to facilitate e-learners access and how to prepare a learning setting suitable to their needs. One of the main distinctions has been made between novice vs. expert users (Lazonder, Biemans, & Wopereis, 2000) and represents a central matter in driving *newbies* into the community. Brown (2001) explains the amount of time and the cognitive resources invested by users in familiarizing with the *technology*, the *teaching method*, the *contents* and the *social aspects* of the community in which they are involved. Novices invest much more time and resources to get acquainted with the technological tools and less to socialize within the community, while expert users usually invert this relationship investing more time and energies in the socialization process. The amount of resources at one's disposal, in these terms, depends on different levels of expertise and on previous experience carried out in CSCL environments. This aspect must be taken into consideration when designing CSCL environments and during the phases of socialization and community building.

From the tool/environment perspective, great attention should also be paid to the design of human vs. technical aspects, in order to facilitate a perceived usefulness and the interaction among learners. Designing the teaching/learning environment means using projects and activities that ask users to participate in the sharing of ideas and knowledge building (Johnson, Hornikb, & Salas, 2008).

Design has a relevant role both for the general educational process, and for the pedagogical perspective (Bereiter, Scardamalia, Alexander, & Winne, 2006; Blythe, 2001; Gao, Baylor, & Shen, 2005). The choice of the pedagogical model directly influences the usage that users are expected to make of the CSCL environment, the amount of psychological resources invested in the learning program and, consequently, the general success of the program.

Applying a rational user- and learning-centered design allows instructional designers to clarify expectations (by the educational staff and by the learners), to select manageable and suitable contents, to structure appropriate activities (collaborative or individual, before and during the course) and to carry out assessment congruent with the intended goals (Garrison & Cleveland-Innes, 2005).

However, an effective design of the learning environment, of software and online tools, is not considered sufficient to grant successful CSCL processes, provided that human elements are important as well (Spitzer, 2002). Preparing users means offering them specific meta-training courses (Piskurich & Piskurich, 2003), providing definite knowledge, technical and interactive skills through online documentation. Several solutions may be adopted to achieve this purpose. First of all, a previous selection of potential e-learners (Guglielmino & Guglielmino, 2003; Redding, 2003) allows designers and educational staff to define and recognize the students' profile in two directions: one to understand learners' needs and to explain to them the educational requirements and, second, to recognize potential gaps between students' profile and educational requirements (by a design perspective).

Some studies adopted the approach of classroom pre-courses concentrated on technical skills, either in presence or at a distance (Bozarth, Chapman, & LaMonica, 2004; Perrine & Spain, 2008; Piskurich & Piskurich, 2003). This solution aims to provide instruments to fill the gap mentioned above.

A third range of solutions concerns the support offered during the process (Edwards & Fintan, 2001; Frieden, 1999; Gao, Baylor, & Shen, 2005; Lee, 2001). Learners need continuous support for problems such as information and documentation retrieval, technical access to the CSCL environment, usage of the interactive tools, etc. This kind of support could be part of the preparation phase as a meta-training program (Vanin, Castelli, Pepe, & Addimando, 2008; Vanin & Castelli, 2010).

A THEORETICAL MODEL TO ORIENT NEWBIES

Here we present a three-step guidance model named "Orienting, Preparing and Supporting" (OP&S) that might be useful to lead the design process. As a matter of fact, informative guidance and preliminary orientation seem to be the first steps to introduce students to the educational environment and to facilitate socialization among learners and familiarization with the tools.

Model Phases

The first phase of the model, named *Orienting,* refers to all the solutions that provide potential learners with a general informative guidance about the course, the program, the usage of CSCL environments and the technical tools. In CSCL systems the focus at the beginning of the program is centered on overcoming the gap between organizational and didactical aspects (web-based course characteristics, differences from traditional courses, main learning tools) and students' characteristics (requirements for admission, self-regulation, self-management and readiness/willingness to interact with other students). Orienting means providing information in terms of "what does the University ask of students" (basic hardware, software, technical equipment, general requirements, rules, and expected results and issues), "what opportunities are offered to students" (professional development programs, post-graduate programs, career opportunities) and "how the whole system works" (role of technology, interaction, usage of CSCL environments, etc.).

In this direction an important usage of information is to communicate what Pan and Scarbrough

(1999) define as the principal components of a knowledge system: the *infrastructure*, the *infostructure* and the *infoculture*. Infrastructure is the "strong" element of the organization, composed of the hardware and the software of the communication platform, the network of physical and communicational contacts between members. Infostructure includes all the formal rules which govern the exchange of information between the actors of the organization and produces a specific code, used by the actors to understand, exchange ideas and give sense to cultural metaphors and common language. Third, and probably the most important in educational contexts, infoculture is the culturally based code that organizations have developed to fit in their specific social and cultural environment.

The second phase, *Preparing*, regards what may be called "meta-training", that is the sum of organizational and educational solutions aimed at providing users with the knowledge and the skills required to participate successfully on the course (see also Castelli, Vanin, & Brambilla, 2006). This phase is often neglected in e-learning programs, even though this could be a main cause of drop-out, and describes the Preparing phase as potential fulfillment of the gap between users' profile and requirements coming from the educational system. The main purpose of this phase is to reduce the resistance to technology, to facilitate users' access to CSCL environments and to provide users with all the basic knowledge and technical skills required during the educational program. This purpose can be achieved either by distance activities or courses in presence.

The third and last phase, *Supporting*, includes solutions aimed at offering motivational, relational and technical assistance to students as long as the learner's permanence in the educational process lasts.

Model Implementation

Since different needs and distinct approaches to give informative support and guidance correspond to different levels of access to the educational system, this model may be implemented as the representation of a progressive passage through different organizational actions or "symbolic rooms" (Castelli, Vanin, & Brambilla, 2006), in which any step aims to offer deeper and more complete preparation and training. Several operative levels, with a huge range of tools, activities and degree of guidance, may be identified (in Figure 1 a possible development of the OP&S model is illustrated, with different sub-activities and aims).

Considering *Room 1* as a space in some way external compared to the educational system, the first problem that arises regards orientation (*Orienting* phase) of the potential subscribers. The objective of this first passage is to offer a complete, informative orienting phase so as to make the

Figure 1. The "Orienting, Preparing and Supporting" model

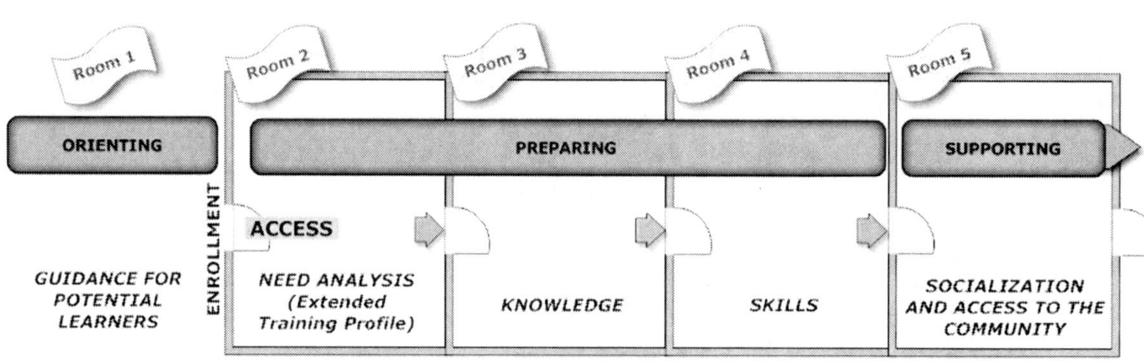

initial choice of whether to enrol or not on the educational system and to be able to assess any possible similar offers of other educational systems. Should one be dealing with a module within a wider path, Room 1 supplies general indications about the contents of the course, any possible prerequisites required, and all the informative material relative to the objectives, the teaching program, the tools used, and the different means of learning and teaching.

Having concluded the enrolment procedure, the learners enter *Room 2*, in which the *Preparing* phase begins, i.e. a set of activites that aims at supplying the participants with the knowledge and skills necessary to tackle the teaching program. Room 2 therefore concentrates on an analysis of the participants' needs, by means of an analysis of the *Extended Training Profile* (Vanin, Castelli, & Brambilla, 2007), in terms of socio-anagraphic, training, professional and experience profile for what concerns participation on previous training courses based on CSCL. With this information, the educational system is able to arrange the subsequent preparation steps for learners, with the objective of eliminating any possible existing gaps between the student's profile and the requests of the educational system.

Therefore, the following Rooms 3 and 4 have the objective of supplying participants with all the basic knowledge (*Room 3*) and skills (*Room 4*) necessary to handle the learning program. The operation may take place in two ways at least. On the one hand, the learning system may be limited to supplying a syllabus of the knowledge and skills required, leaving the necessary time to the students to fill any possible gaps between their own profile and the requirements from the course. On the other, a more complete and responsible and in many ways more effective approach, envisages that the learning system prearranges tools, materials, formative pathways (both at a distance and in presence) to tackle such gaps, inviting all the participants to take part.

Room 3 concentrates on the starting knowledge required, on the acquisition of the specific, basic vocabulary and on possession of the elementary notions useful to handle the successive learning contents. As an example, in this case one might deal with the technical lexicon (linked with the interactive tools used in the formative process), or of the general and elementary notions useful for successive in-depth study (for instance, the main branches of a subject, the historical or conceptual development of the teaching that will be delivered, or even the theoretical coordinates to correctly collocate the successive teaching). Room 3 may require the reading of guides and specific documentation, navigation of multimedial resources, the tracing of information on the net, etc., and concentrates mainly on contents.

Having concluded this phase, Room 4 concentrates on the skills required to tackle the learning process. The objective of this phase of *Preparing* is to supply students with the cognitive skills (e.g. how to move within the resources and tools, how to tackle individual study, how to organize the skills acquired), technical skills (usage of the CSCL, use of the resources and tools online), interactive skills (how to relate to the other participants, what rules to respect in the exchange of information, what tools to use for which types of communication) and problem solving skills (where to find the information necessary to solve any possible problems, who to contact on the teaching staff, how to tackle any possible problematical situations). As illustrated in the picture, Room 4 concentrates its efforts mainly on the process, identifying any possible problematical areas that might arise during the training course. This activity can take on different shapes, e.g. standard frontal lectures, surfing in online resources, treasure hunts on the Internet, metaphorical activities for socialization and self introduction. With Room 4 one can consider the process of Preparing learners concluded. Now they are able to recognize the theoretical, conceptual and terminological coordinates necessary to tackle the course contents and have the technical skills required to interact with the other subjects involved in the learning process.

In *Room 5* (*Supporting* phase), therefore, learners can face entry into the community (if existing) and in any case begin to move along the learning process: it is only at this time that learners enter fully into the generally understood learning system. From this moment on, the technical staff on the one hand, and the community of learners, on the other, will supply the support necessary to tackle every successive pedagogical and didactic device.

The advantages of such an approach are quite evident. In first place, the progressiveness of Rooms 2, 3 and 4 welcomes learners in a soft way, bringing about positive behavior with regard to the very same learning system: reduction of the gap between the student profile and the requirements of the learning system takes place through gradual acquisition of knowledge and skills before the same are even made necessary. For instance, learners become able to use interactive tools before they really have to use them for the purposes of the learning process.

In second place, the above described system of rooms envisages an active role for the participant but triggers what Lave and Wenger (1991) define as *legitimate peripheral participation*, that is "a particular mode of engagement of a learner who participates in the actual practice of an expert, but only to a limited degree and with limited responsibility" (p. 14): with a minor effect of stress, the participant may gradually experiment with different degrees of use of the CSCL and the interactive tools, without the tension due to the reaching of a result.

Finally, the socialization phase takes place as a result of a process of familiarization with the learning system, with the interactive tools and with the other subjects involved. Thanks to the previous rooms, the participant is now able to move among the different technical solutions proposed, (s)he has the theoretical and terminological knowledge necessary and, consequently, may concentrate on the learning system and on the interaction with the other participants and the teaching staff.

As will be seen in the next paragraph, there are different tools and activities to handle this gradual passage by means of *guidance programs*, i.e. programs suitably designed to offer activities and tools to reach the specific results of each phase of the system of orientation by rooms.

GUIDANCE PROGRAMS

The theoretical model presented above can be applied to different CSCL educational and professional contexts. In the design phase, the OP&S model's steps can be developed in different ways, depending on the learners' initial levels of knowledge and skill, their educational background, and didactical purposes.

The application of the described model can be concretized in guidance programs as a set of specific online and/or face-to-face activities that aim to familiarize users with technology, tools, resources and virtual places, and to socialize with the other learners.

As a set of structured activities with an explicit educational purpose, the programs can be made by a specific activity that aims to familiarize users with technology, or by an informative tour among all tools, resources and virtual places, or by a welcome activity that aims to present users to each other, or by a mixture of different paths.

By a methodological perspective, guidance programs can be structured, semi-structured or unstructured. *Structured* means that an activity can follow just one direction, i.e. an article reading on a specific topic and an online assessment. *Semi-structured* activities define a specific flow but do not provide further indication on how goals can be achieved. *Non-structured* activities do not provide a defined schema and leave users completely free.

On the other hand, for what concerns content and process of the program, instructional designers have to take into consideration two important dimensions while developing guidance programs: the core activity and the roles.

The Core Activity

The guidance program may focus on *content*, for instance by managing programs about the basic knowledge required to approach the educational course; on *process*, coping with the requests from the educational system, the way to use the CSCL environment or the technological tools, etc.; or on *socialization*, through ways by which participants introduce themselves to the rest of the community. These three dimensions do not rule out one another since a guidance program can be focused on one or all the three dimensions.

Content-based activities aim to provide focus on educational content and can be improved as pre-training activities with the purpose of providing learners with specific knowledge, in terms of preliminary definition, basic exploration of the subject, introductory rudiments. This activity, in online education, may take the form of content exploration, group seminars or discussion groups, comparison of different perspectives among users and online article discussion, "treasure hunts", searches on the Web, etc.

Process-based activities are focused on learning and interactive processes and aim to familiarize users with knowledge building and sharing processes, discussion techniques, interaction attitudes, etc. Several CSCL studies focus on debate-based learning and peer negotiation through some techniques and scripts that are usually content-independent and work as scaffolds to activities. Some examples are Discussion, Peer Review, Role Play, Jigsaw, Case Study, etc. For instance, in the Jigsaw technique:

the content to be addressed is segmented into sub-items and each learner is assigned the task to study in detail his/her sub-item. To do so, all the students who should become "experts" of a specific sub-item, join together in the so called "expert group", with the aim of discussing the main points of their segment and rehearsing a presentation. At the end of this phase, expert groups are loosened and new groups are formed, called "jigsaw groups". Within his/her new jigsaw group, each learner is asked to report his/her segment to the others, so that at the end all the groups gain a complete overview of the content. (Pozzi, 2009, p. 670)

Socialization-based activities are very frequent in the first stages of educational and learning programs. The main purpose of this kind of guidance activity is to help users to get acquainted with each other and to encourage them to write their first posts as well as to familiarize with the technological tools (i.e. the CSCL environment). This kind of activity does not focus on specific content and is often limited to a brief self-introduction in the forum: after registration, users are asked to introduce themselves to the community, providing some information about previous study, work experience, expectations about the course, etc.

Among the resources tutors and instructors have at their disposal to facilitate initial interaction and socialization among students, there is the activation of metaphors. Metaphor is a linguistic artefact that may facilitate the expression of emotions and the representation of the affective domain in web-based learning environments. Studies in this field show that this feature may be effective in giving substance and concreteness to the immateriality of the web, and in expressing and representing affective domain in a written-discourse based learning environment for adult learners (De Simone, Lou, & Schmid, 2001; Delfino & Manca, 2007; Manca & Delfino, 2007). Indeed metaphors and figurative language may be seen as linguistic tools to conceptualize the learning environment in an original manner and, at the same time, to communicate emotions and social presence in a creative way through text.

The Roles

Since one of the main purposes of the approach described here is to facilitate the path that brings learners to socialization and integration in the online group of peers, guidance programs give great relevance to the community life cycle and to different roles assumed by users in the community. Kim (2000) distinguishes four levels of online community users: *visitors* (outsiders without a persistent identity in the community), *novices* (new members who need to be introduced into the community), *regular* users (established members that are comfortably participating in the community activities), *leaders* (expert users, volunteers and staff) and *elders* (long-time oldbies/expert users who share their knowledge and transmit culture, history and values of the community).

In CSCL environments, and generally in educational programs, this taxonomy could be more complex (see Figure 2). First of all "visitors" can be expanded into two sub-categories: *potential* users (who are interested in the educational program, search for information but are not yet enrolled on the course) and *peripheral* users (who have already subscribed to the educational program and are ready for guidance programs). Second, *newbies* could be described as users who are attending guidance programs, while *beginners* are users who have successfully completed the guidance program and are attending the educational course tout court. Between newbies and beginners we can define a socialization bridge, the boundary of the community that states who is out and in of the group of learners. Third, in the educational context the "leaders" category refers to both elders and staff. *Expert* users are also older users, who have gained a lot of experience in using CSCL environments, and may be considered as an important resource in guidance programs, thus offering support in community building. Guidance programs also define the roles taken by moderators, tutors, teachers and technical staff in determining what users are expected to do in the CSCL environment.

Applying the OP&S model, these categories take on a different perspective. The Orienting phase, indeed, is central in welcoming potential students and to give them all the informative guidance in the previous passage. This phase ends after potential users have become regular participants, first as peripheral users, then as newbies. The main difference in these two levels is that peripheral users are those who have only terminated the submission phase in terms of administrative practices, while newbies are those who

Figure 2. Access and users' life cycle in CSCL environment, adapted from (Kim, 2000)

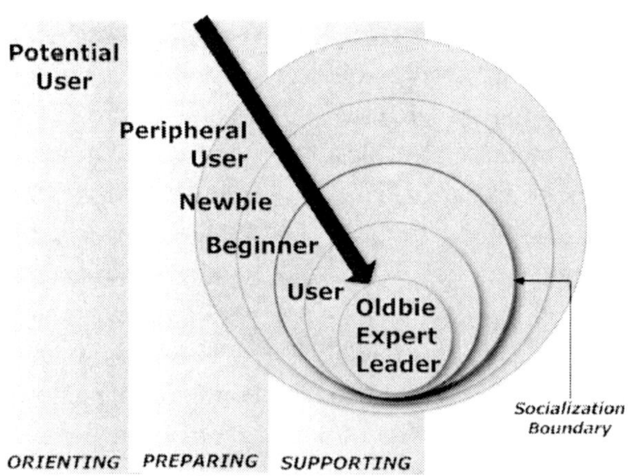

start the educational process. This "social boundary" determines the difference between the administrative perspective (potential and peripheral students) and the educational and community perspective (i.e. all the remaining user levels).

The examples described below derive from two different blended learning contexts, in which a guidance program was implemented following the OP&S model. In spite of differences about course typology (post graduate vs. graduate), length (12 weeks vs. one year) and kind of content-based activities (group vs. individual activities), the two learning contexts had the typology of familiarization phase in common, both based on the activation of a metaphor.

The Genoa Case

The context was a 12-week post-graduate course addressed to student teachers of the Post-graduate School for Secondary School-teaching of the University of Genoa, held in the 2004/2005 academic year (see Delfino & Persico, 2007 for further details). The course adopted the blended approach combining five face-to-face lessons and 12 weeks of online activities delivered at a distance via a computer conferencing system (FirstClass™). The group of participants was composed of 95 student teachers and 7 tutors. Among the students 77 were female and 18 were male. Their mean age was 31.3 years (SD = 5.3).

The aim of the course was to bring participants to a good degree of mastery of the educational use of ICT. Face-to-face sessions were devoted to lay the bases for both a better understanding of the subject (from a theoretical point of view) and an effective participation in online activity (from a practical point of view). The course plan and structure were characterized by experiential learning, and the activities required collaboration among participants, peer-reviewing and cooperative production of artefacts.

Online instructional activities were arranged in a number of phases, and the environment was organized in different areas of interaction, comprising some familiarization and socialization facilities, and a metacognitive area to encourage reflection. The interactions were based on conversations that took place in the online conferences aimed at making students debate specific topics in order to collaboratively achieve the given tasks. For all activities the whole cohort of students was arranged into subgroups under the guidance of experienced tutors.

The application of a guidance program based on the three-step model was possible only partially. As for the *Orienting phase*, since the course was a mandatory one (and no alternative choice was possible), students were however provided with general information about the course (type of activities, their length, etc.).

As far as the *Preparing phase* is concerned, an initial survey, whose aim was to obtain information about students' digital literacy level, their expectations and their previous knowledge about the course topic, was carried out before the course started. At the first face-to-face meeting, students were provided with information about the course organization, the deadlines to meet, the assessment criteria and the online learning environment.

As far as the *Supporting phase* is concerned, given the blended nature of the course, a combination of online and face-to-face activities devoted to foster a higher level of socialization and sense of togetherness among participants was chosen. In order to promote harmony among participants, particular attention was devoted to the design of the social component, acting in parallel on both online and face-to-face modalities. The measures taken to foster social presence were deemed particularly important due to the high number of participants and to the fact that, although they shared parts of the study curriculum, only some of them had met face-to-face before the course.

Online sessions devoted to familiarization with the platform and socialization within the community of participants were metaphorized, in order to increase the sense of belonging to the community, to provide a framework for role distribution, identity creation and awareness of one's responsibility (Manca & Delfino, 2007). The metaphor of navigation was proposed and thus the course was described as a sea-voyage in which each participant-sailor was supposed to choose a boat (Caravel, Cruise liner, Fishing-boat, Motorboat, Sailing boat, Steamboat, Submarine). Afterwards, each group of sailors had three weeks to negotiate and decide on a name for their boat, a motto and a symbol.

Furthermore, all participants were provided with a common Cafè area, where all non-course related discussion took place. At the same time during face-to-face sessions an attempt was made to guarantee the continuity with the online activities acting on participants' identity, recognisability and participation. For example, to allow participants to identify the colleagues they were interacting with online, they were given personal badges bearing their names and were invited to seat in the classroom close to their online team-mates.

The Milan Case

The context was a three-year Distance Degree in Psychology at the University of Milan Bicocca – Psychology Faculty (Ex Nettuno Consortium) held in the 2008/2009 academic year. The group of participants was composed of 70 first year students and 5 tutors (expert students coming from the second and the third year). The students were 51 females and 19 males, with a mean age of 34.7 (SD = 6.4). All the online activities took place in a PhP Bulletin Board (http://www.phpbb.com/), a popular sequential web forum.

The experience described here represents only a part of the educational process activated within the undergraduate course, which lasts three years indicatively and means the passing of 44 exams, delivered by blended learning means: preparation and in-depth study at a distance and exams in presence.

The application of a guidance program on the basis of the model proposed here followed the following phases.

As for the *Orienting phase*, on the site of the Faculty already from the spring an informative guide is arranged on the undergraduate course and an informative questionnaire to record the first level of Extended Training Profile. In this way it is possible to make a forecast of the average profile of the students who might enrol on the undergraduate course starting from the month of September. This phase also extends beyond immatriculation, supplying at the time of enrolment a first guide with certain additional indications and the request to subscribe to a mailing list.

For what relates to the *Preparing phase*, in the guide sent to those enrolled a complete questionnaire is also included, that is able to reveal the Extended Training Profile of those enrolled. On the basis of the results the program of the successive phases is better defined and adapted. By means of the sending of a second guide, that is more detailed and in-depth than the previous one, documents, online resources and interactive materials are indicated which go deeper into certain aspects of the learning system, supply the basic lexicon (especially for what concerns the technical aspects and tools) and offer a complete panorama of the learning structure, contents dealt with in the following passages, etc. Some weeks after the sending of the documentation on knowledge, three typologies of activity are arranged. The first regards the exploration of the CSCL environment from the point of view of the tools, leaving learners the possibility of freely exploring them and becoming acquainted with the different functions. Second, users participate on a short presentation in presence, during which educational staff present a complete panoramic tour of the educational system and reply to all the questions coming from the first and second phases.

For what concerns socialisation activities, during the meeting in presence, users are invited to register on a web forum and, as soon as possible, to write a short self-presentation, to explore the CSCL environment and to report doubts and questions. This activity is completely non-structured and aimed at encouraging users to write their first post, independently of the content.

Finally, an activity based on a metaphor is activated able to complete this exploration with a massive use of the interactive tools and to start to socialize with the others enrolled on the same year of course. In this phase, the students interact only with their peers enrolled on the same year of course and only later do they come into contact with the community in the widest sense. Like sailors, distance students browse in a world of online resources (learning objects, documents, tools, etc.). In the first step of activities students have to choose a boat (symbolized by a specific thread or a conference area) just replying to a tutor's posting or creating a new one. In the second step, collaborating with tutors and the other students that chose the same boat, they have to find a name and an evocative phrase for the boat. This simple three-week activity aims to familiarize users with online tools, preparing them for the following online educational activities, as well as socializing with the community of participants.

Finally, as far as the *Supporting phase* is concerned, having terminated the welcoming activity and entered the community of students, a double type of support is offered: on the one hand, through a help desk from the staff, FAQ and guides to the use of the tools and, on the other, through the support offered by the more expert students.

CONCLUSION

The aim of this contribution is to provide a view about possible strategies that may be adopted to encourage participation during the early stages in a CSCL environment, through the design of several activities and guidance programs.

At present most of the literature is narrowed to theoretical models or general guidelines to orient students in CSCL environments, while fewer studies have been published about case studies and concrete solutions. Our chapter has presented a three-step model, "Orienting, Preparing and Supporting", whose aim is to gradually provide users with the necessary skills to participate successfully in a CSCL course. Through the three phases, participants are progressively equipped with a general informative guidance about the course, the program, the usage of CSCL environments and the technical tools; with a meta-training program able to facilitate users' access to CSCL environments and to provide them with all the basic knowledge and technical skills required during the educational program; with activities aimed at offering motivational, relational and technical assistance during the whole educational experience.

Therefore the model presented is collocated at the start of the educational process, as a fundamental passage through different initiatives able to gradually insert the participants in the educational process and supply them all the basic knowledge and skills necessary to tackle the various objectives and tasks envisaged. The main advantage of this approach lies in the opportunity of distinguishing between two different tasks: on the one hand, learning how to move along the learning path (which tools to use, how to interact with the other participants, what knowledge to ripen in order to tackle the contents of the course, etc.), while, on the other, concentrate on the main activities of the course itself.

The first result in the OP&S model is reached before the educational process itself, while the second is reached, even by means of the socialization itself between the course participants, only when the learners can concentrate exclusively on such a task. Otherwise said, in the most widespread practice participants on an online course learn how to use the interactive tools by acting in the educational process. In the model proposed by us, instead, these operations are separated, an ample space is given to familiarization with interactive tools and the CSCL environment and, only in a second moment, does one allow access to the peer group, the contents, and the formative process *tout court*.

This approach allows learners to concentrate step by step on two different objectives: first learn how to move in the learning environment and, then, act directly. Socialization, in this sense, represents a real and true educational tool and becomes one of the intermediate results of the process, not a simple instrumental variable: the learner comes into contact with the group only after having acquired (from the theoretical and practical point of view) the fundamental principles of this interaction and having understood its fundamental role in the field of the educational process.

An implementation of the model, through the description of some possible activities (on content, relation and process) to carry out during the three phases, has also been presented. Special focus has been placed on the social dimension of learning and the role played by the community. One of the most important purposes of the model described is exactly to facilitate entry into the community, toward the construction of a collective and shared identity. From this perspective, different levels of participation at various steps of being part of the community and how to move through the different levels of participation have been highlighted.

Further studies should be carried out to compare our model with alternative proposals and solutions. First of all, we are aware that additional orienting activities should be identified, as well as meta-training programs capable of levelling initial differences in terms of technological skills and methodological tools. Moreover, monitoring and assessment of this kind of program, both at intermediate steps and after completion, would allow one to evaluate their effectiveness in terms of achieved results.

REFERENCES

Adams, J. (2008). Understanding the factors limiting the acceptability on online courses and degrees. *International Journal on E-Learning*, *7*(4), 573–587.

Anderson, T., Rourke, L., Garrison, D. R., & Archer, W. (2001). Assessing teaching presence in a computer conferencing context. *Journal of Asynchronous Learning Networks*, *5*(2), 1–17.

Araque, F., Roldan, C., & Salguero, R. (2009). Factors influencing university drop out rates. *Computers & Education*, *53*(3), 563–574. doi:10.1016/j.compedu.2009.03.013

Bereiter, C., Scardamalia, M., Alexander, P. A., & Winne, P. H. (2006). Education for the Knowledge Age: Design-Centered Models of Teaching and Instruction. In Alexander, P. A., & Winne, P. H. (Eds.), *Handbook of educational psychology* (pp. 695–713). Mahwah, NJ: Lawrence Erlbaum Associates.

Bishop, J. (2007). Increasing participation in online communities: A framework for human-computer interaction. *Computers in Human Behavior*, *23*(4), 1881–1893. doi:10.1016/j.chb.2005.11.004

Blythe, S. (2001). Designing online courses: user-centered practices. *Computers and Composition*, *18*(4), 329–346. doi:10.1016/S8755-4615(01)00066-4

Booker, Q. E., & Rebman, C. M. Jr. (2005). E-student retention: factors affecting customer loyalty for online program success. *Issues in Information Systems*, *6*(1), 183–189.

Bozarth, J., Chapman, D. D., & LaMonica, L. (2004). Preparing for Distance Learning: Designing an Online Student Orientation Course. *Journal of Educational Technology & Society*, *7*(1), 87–106.

Brown, R. E. (2001). The process of community-building in distance learning classes. *Journal of Asynchronous Learning Networks*, *5*(2), 18–35.

Caspi, A., & Blau, I. (2008). Social presence in online discussion groups: testing three conceptions and their relations to perceived learning. *Social Psychology of Education*, *11*(3), 323–346. doi:10.1007/s11218-008-9054-2

Castelli, S., Vanin, L., & Brambilla, M. (2006). Il modello di orientamento "a stanze". Analisi dei bisogni e formazione universitaria a distanza. *Tecnologie Didattiche*, *39*, 57–66.

Conrad, D. (2005). Building and Maintaining Community in Cohort-Based Online Learning. *Journal of Distance Education*, *20*(1), 1–20.

Dawson, S. (2006). A study of the relationship between student communication interaction and sense of community. *The Internet and Higher Education*, *9*(3), 153–162. doi:10.1016/j.iheduc.2006.06.007

De Simone, C., Lou, Y., & Schmid, R. F. (2001). Meaningful and interactive distance learning supported by the use of metaphor and synthesizing activities. *Journal of Distance Education*, *16*(1), 85–101.

Delfino, M., & Manca, S. (2007). The expression of social presence through the use of figurative language in a web-based learning environment. *Computers in Human Behavior*, *23*(5), 2190–2211. doi:10.1016/j.chb.2006.03.001

Delfino, M., & Persico, D. (2007). Online or face-to-face? Experimenting with different techniques in teacher training. *Journal of Computer Assisted Learning*, *23*(5), 351–365. doi:10.1111/j.1365-2729.2007.00220.x

Edwards, M. A., & Fintan, C. (2001). Supporting the Collaborative Learning of Practical Skills with Computer-mediated Communications Technology. *Journal of Educational Technology & Society*, *4*(1), 80–92.

Frieden, S. (1999). Support Services for Distance Education. *Journal of Educational Technology & Society*, *2*(3), 48–54.

Gao, H., Baylor, A. L., & Shen, E. (2005). Designer Support for Online Collaboration and Knowledge Construction. *Journal of Educational Technology & Society*, *8*(1), 69–79.

Garrison, D. R., & Anderson, T. (2003). *E-learning in the 21st century: A framework for research and practice*. London, UK: RoutledgeFalmer. doi:10.4324/9780203166093

Garrison, D. R., Anderson, T., & Archer, W. (1999). Critical inquiry in a text-based environment: Computer conferencing in higher education. *The Internet and Higher Education*, *2*(2/3), 87–105. doi:10.1016/S1096-7516(00)00016-6

Garrison, D. R., & Cleveland-Innes, M. (2005). Facilitating Cognitive Presence in Online Learning: Interaction is not Enough. *American Journal of Distance Education*, *19*(3), 133–148. doi:10.1207/s15389286ajde1903_2

Guglielmino, L. M., & Guglielmino, P. J. (2003). Identifying Learners. Who are ready for E-Learning and supporting their success. In G. M. Piskurich (Ed.), *Preparing Learners for E-Learning* (pp. 19-33). San Francisco, CA: Pfeiffer (John Wiley & Sons, Inc.).

Gunawardena, C. N., & Zittle, F. (1997). Social presence as a predictor of satisfaction within a computer mediated conferencing environment. *American Journal of Distance Education*, *11*(3), 8–25. doi:10.1080/08923649709526970

Herring, S. C. (2004). Computer-mediated discourse analysis. An approach to researching online behavior. In Barab, S. A., Kling, R., & Gray, J. H. (Eds.), *Designing for virtual communities in the service of learning* (pp. 338–376). Cambridge, MA: Cambridge University Press.

Johnson, R. D., Hornikb, S., & Salas, E. (2008). An empirical examination of factors contributing to the creation of successful e-learning environments. *International Journal of Human-Computer Studies, 66*(5), 356–369. doi:10.1016/j.ijhcs.2007.11.003

Jun, J. (2005). Understanding E-dropout. *International Journal on E-Learning, 4*(2), 229–240.

Kanuka, H., Rourke, L., & Laflamme, E. (2007). The Influence of Instructional Methods on the Quality of Online Discussion. *British Journal of Educational Technology, 38*(2), 260–271. doi:10.1111/j.1467-8535.2006.00620.x

Kim, A. J. (2000). *Community Building on the Web: Secret Strategies for Successful Online Communities*. Berkeley, CA: Peachpit Press.

Lave, J., & Wenger, E. (1991). *Situated learning: Legitimate peripheral participation*. Cambridge, MA: Cambridge University Press.

Lazonder, A. W., Biemans, H. J. A., & Wopereis, I. G. J. H. (2000). Differences between Novice and Experienced Users in Searching Information on The World Wide Web. *Journal of the American Society for Information Science American Society for Information Science, 51*(6), 576–581.doi:10.1002/(SICI)1097-4571(2000)51:6<576::AID-ASI9>3.0.CO;2-7

Lee, J. (2001). Instructional Support for Distance Education and Faculty Motivation, Commitment, Satisfaction. *British Journal of Educational Technology, 32*(2), 153–160. doi:10.1111/1467-8535.00186

Lykourentzou, I., Giannoukos, I., Nikolopoulos, V., Mpardis, G., & Loumos, V. (2009). Dropout prediction in e-learning courses through the combination of machine learning techniques. *Computers & Education, 53*(3), 950–965. doi:10.1016/j.compedu.2009.05.010

Manca, S., & Delfino, M. (2007). Learners' representation of their affective domain through figurative language in a web-based learning environment. *Distance Education, 28*(1), 25–43. doi:10.1080/01587910701305293

Offir, B., Lev, Y., & Bezalel, R. (2008). Surface and deep learning processes in distance education: Synchronous versus asynchronous systems. *Computers & Education, 51*(3), 1172–1182. doi:10.1016/j.compedu.2007.10.009

Pan, S. L., & Scarbrough, H. (1999). Knowledge management in Practice: An Exploratory Case Study. *Technology Analysis and Strategic Management, 11*(3), 359–374. doi:10.1080/095373299107401

Perrine, R. M., & Spain, J. W. (2008). Impact of a Pre-Semester College Orientation Program: Hidden Benefits? *Journal of College Student Retention: Research. Theory into Practice, 10*(2), 155–169.

Piskurich, G. M. (Ed.). (2003). *Preparing Learners for E-Learning*. San Francisco, CA: Pfeiffer (John Wiley & Sons, Inc.).

Piskurich, G. M., & Piskurich, J. F. (2003). Utilizing a classroom approach to prepare learners for E-Learning. In G. M. Piskurich (Ed.), *Preparing Learners for E-Learning* (pp. 45-72). San Francisco, CA: Pfeiffer (John Wiley & Sons, Inc.).

Pozzi, F. (2009). Using collaborative techniques in virtual learning communities. *EC-TEL2009 -. Lecture Notes in Computer Science, 5794*, 670–675. doi:10.1007/978-3-642-04636-0_66

Redding, T. R. (2003). Preparing Your Learners for My E-Learning. An E-Learning Vendor's Point of View. In G. M. Piskurich (Ed.), *Preparing Learners for E-Learning* (pp. 155-168). San Francisco, CA: Pfeiffer (John Wiley & Sons, Inc.).

Richardson, J. C., & Swan, K. (2003). Examining Social Presence in Online Courses in Relation to Students' Perceived Learning and Satisfaction. *Journal of Asynchronous Learning Networks*, *7*(1), 68–88.

Rourke, L., Anderson, T., Garrison, D. R., & Archer, W. (2001). Assessing social presence in asynchronous text-based computer conferencing. *Journal of Distance Education*, *14*(3), 51–70.

So, H.-J., & Brush, T. A. (2008). Student perceptions of collaborative learning, social presence and satisfaction in a blended learning environment: Relationships and critical factors. *Computers & Education*, *51*(1), 318–336. doi:10.1016/j.compedu.2007.05.009

Spitzer, D. R. (2002). Don't Forget the High-Touch with the High-Tech in Distance Learning. In Rossett, A. (Ed.), *The ASTD E-Learning Handbook* (pp. 164–174). New York: McGraw-Hill.

Swan, K., & Shih, L. F. (2005). On the nature and development of social presence in online course discussions. *Journal of Asynchronous Learning Networks*, *9*(3), 115–136.

Trekles Milligan, A., & Buckenmeyer, J. A. (2008). Assessing students for online learning. *International Journal on E-Learning*, *7*(3), 449–461.

Vanin, L., & Castelli, S. (2010). Informarsi, informare, formare. Il caso Nettuno in Bicocca. *Giornale Italiano di Psicologia dell'Orientamento, 11*(1), 48-61.

Vanin, L., Castelli, S., & Brambilla, M. (2007). Il profilo formativo allargato: un ruolo strategico nella formazione a distanza. In P. G. Rossi (Ed.), *Progettare e-Learning: processi, materiali, connettività, interoperabilità e strategie* (pp. 504-515). Macerata: EUM.

Vanin, L., Castelli, S., Pepe, A., & Addimando, L. (2008). Orienting, preparing and supporting. An academic guidance model to orient distance student. In Cartelli, A., & Palma, M. (Eds.), *Encyclopedia of ICT* (pp. 1–9). Hershey, PA: Idea Group Inc.

Wan, Z., Wang, Y., & Haggerty, N. (2008). Why people benefit from e-learning differently: The effects of psychological processes on e-learning outcomes. *Information & Management*, *45*(8), 513–521. doi:10.1016/j.im.2008.08.003

Wenger, E. (1998). *Communities of practice. Learning, meaning, and identity*. Cambridge, MA: Cambridge University Press.

Yli-Luoma, P. V. J., & Naeve, A. (2006). Towards a semantic e-learning theory by using a modelling approach. *British Journal of Educational Technology*, *37*(3), 445–459. doi:10.1111/j.1467-8535.2006.00615.x

KEY TERMS AND DEFINITIONS

Socialization: The process through which learners in a distance education environment get acquainted with peers and instructors/tutors by means of a set of facilities planned to build a sense of community and social presence.

Familiarization: The process through which learners in a distance education environment become familiar with the learning systems and its technological and methodological tools.

The OP&S Model: A theoretical model to design and implement online systems to give students information and support. The first phase of the model, named *Orienting*, refers to all the solutions that provide potential learners with a general informative guidance about the course, the program, the usage of CSCL environments and the technical tools. The second phase, *Preparing*, regards what may be called "meta-training", that is the sum of organizational and educational solutions aimed at providing users with the knowledge and the skills required to participate successfully on the course. Then, the last phase, *Supporting*, includes solutions aimed at offering motivational, relational and technical assistance to students during the whole educational course year.

Guidance Program: A set of specific online and/or face-to-face activities that aim to familiarize users with technology, tools, resources and virtual places, and to socialize with the other learners.

Meta-Training: A preliminary process that starts before the educational process and aims to give students all the basic knowledge and skill to cope with the requirements stated by the program or the course.

Chapter 7
Testing Strategies to Enhance Online Student Collaboration in a Problem-Based Learning Activity

Lisa A. Lobry de Bruyn
University of New England, Australia

ABSTRACT

Most units of learning are being offered flexibly, either using distance education or online facilities, and often with asynchronous computer-mediated communication or online discussions. The use of asynchronous computer-mediated communication is believed to offer students the opportunity to communicate independently of time and place, and to ask questions, state opinions and offer advice when transferring interactive learning activities to an online environment. This chapter uses an action research framework to examine the quantity and nature of student engagement in a problem-based learning activity as a consequence of placing face-to-face instruction on and practice in problem-based learning prior to using asynchronous computer-mediated communication. The effectiveness of early placement of a 4-day residential component to improve student collaboration in the online problem-based learning activity was tested against six years (2001-2006) of electronically-archived online discussions in a 13-week, under- or post-graduate tertiary-level natural science unit.

INTRODUCTION

Combining online delivery with problem-based learning activities requires opportunities for students to interact with each other and develop a range of skills and competencies (personal, people and professional) in conjunction with the knowledge base so they can confidently enter the workplace. Problem-based learning activities (Barrows & Tamblyn, 1980; Barrows, 1985; 1988; 2002; Bjorck, 2002) using a case study approach to problem-solving and self-directed research, delivered online, is a learning approach that can supports knowledge acquisition to actively engage students in the learning process, and enable students to develop and strengthen their competencies in the areas of information literacy, communication, self-directed learning, and solv-

DOI: 10.4018/978-1-61692-898-8.ch007

ing 'real-world' problems (Boud & Feletti, 1997). Furthermore, online delivery of problem-based learning activities offers those students learning at a distance, and often in isolation, the opportunity to communicate asynchronously with other students; and to work collaboratively with others to: brainstorm, analyse and redefine the issues in relation to the problem-based learning activity as well as engage in social interaction. Nevertheless, there remains some uncertainty among students about online learning, as shown by reported higher attrition rates (Carr, 2000), and lower levels of course satisfaction (Sikora & Carroll, 2002) in online courses. Educators too express concern about how well problem-based learning activities and online delivery can be combined to create a learning environment that motivates students to engage in positive social interaction and learning as well as achieve the desired learning outcomes (Vonderwell & Zachariah, 2005, Rourke & Kanuka, 2007; Rovai, 2007). Hara and Kling (2000; 2001) suggest that students undertaking online courses experience " ... confusion, anxiety, and frustration due to perceived lack of prompt or clear feedback from the instructor, and from ambiguous instructions on the course Web site and in e-mail messages from the instructor" (p.68). Rovai and Jordan (2004) interpreted this finding as suggesting deficiencies in online courses were related more to poor design of online discourse and inappropriate pedagogy used by instructors who have limited knowledge and skills in designing and facilitating learning activities, and creating a sense of community through online discussions in online courses.

Communication amongst peers is an integral part of creating an interactive learning environment (including facilitating learning and creating a sense of community amongst learners). The research presented here focused on the capacity of asynchronous computer-mediated communication to support collaborative learning amongst students within the context of a problem-based learning scenario delivered online to off-campus students, with a compulsory face-to-face teaching component (residential school). This chapter specifically tests whether early timing of face-to-face teaching (*small group learning experience*) in a problem-based learning activity can enhance collaborative online discussions of a problem-based learning activity by comparing it with the *collective learning experience*. This chapter also explores the variation in group functioning and whether it is possible to determine the characteristics of a functional learning group. The change in timing of face-to-face instruction in the problem-based learning activity to before the commencement of the teaching period provided the instructor with an opportunity to evaluate three changes in the teaching approach. Firstly, the formation of small peer student groups for subsequent communication on Discussion Boards that had already met each other at the residential school. Secondly, those same students had, in a classroom situation, practiced the problem-based learning activity, and used the structured learning guide. Thirdly, the students met, and were taught by the instructor at the residential school and became familiar with instructor expectations and style of teaching prior to the semester starting. None of these changes to the teaching approach were possible, prior to 2004, as the timing of the residential school was fixed at eight weeks into the semester, and student groupings, especially small peer groups, for online discussions could not be created as students still had not confirmed their attendance at the residential school.

BACKGROUND: PROSPECTS AND PROBLEMS FOR ONLINE COMMUNICATION IN A LEARNING ACTIVITY

The literature review focuses specifically on the benefits of and difficulties in using asynchronous computer-mediated communication to provide an interactive learning environment, one which facilitates learning and creates a sense of community amongst learners, in the context of the delivery and exploration of an interactive problem-based learning activity in an online environment. Normally in a classroom environment the various steps of problem-solving process are conducted face-to-face in small groups: introducing one's self, setting ground rules, acknowledging prior learning, identifying contributions to group learning, identifying learning needs and activities, and finally working through the problem-solving process. Ideally, when the problem-solving process is transferred to an online environment, asynchronous computer-mediated communication allows students to communicate independently of time and place, and even allows small groups to be created to communicate questions, opinions and advice. The use of threaded online discussions that allow asynchronous communication was considered advantageous when the times at which students will want to access the online discussion is unpredictable. Threading allows students to trace and keep track of conversational chains, as each note has a subject label, and is organised in a hierarchical structure that only includes those messages that are related. Unrelated threads are kept separate, and this allows students to pursue multiple avenues of thought without becoming confused (Hewitt, 2001).

The literature examining the use of asynchronous computer-mediated communication for supporting online learning activities cites a number of advantages (Harasim, Hiltz, Teles, & Turoff, 1998; Hewitt, 2001; Mason & Kaye, 1989; 1990). These include:

- Connectivity and accessibility. There is increased group interaction since the discussions are open and not limited to face-to-face meeting times. Also, the collective knowledge of the class and external online resources are more accessible to students (Eastmond, 1994).
- Equitable communication between students is encouraged as there is no need for 'turn taking' (Graddol, 1989) and ideally everyone can be 'heard', including those more reticent students, without being intimidated by more vocal students.
- Student reflection is also fostered through messages being preserved electronically; messages can be revisited and reread; and students having "time for reflection before they commit their ideas to public scrutiny" Mason & Kaye, 1990, pp.15-38). In addition, student reflection is encouraged by providing thinking and extra time to process information (Rovai & Jordan, 2004).
- Student conversations using asynchronous computer-mediated communication are boundless in time and space which promotes greater student interaction. Also, because time and location are not restricting communication, the instructor can expect all students to contribute to discussions.

Online communication facilities offer the promise of increased student interactivity, flexibility and accessibility, and improved learning. Yet many difficulties, such as higher student attrition rates and lower levels of student satisfaction, may be encountered when solely relying on using asynchronous computer-mediated communication (Harasim et al., 1998; Light & Light, 1999; Carr, 2000; Guzdial & Turns, 2000). These originate from the lack of student initiative in discussions, limited critical discourse on learning issues by students (Kanuka, Rourke, & Laflamme, 2007; Rourke & Kanuka, 2007), and student preference for 'face-to-face' learning. Such factors which contribute to the difficulties when using synchronous computer-mediated communication include:

- Technical difficulties associated with access to or use of computer software or hardware or interface characteristics of the learning management system or discussion board (Yip, 2002; Vonderwell & Zachariah, 2005). However, over time these issues are becoming less common.

- Communication anxiety, accentuated when student/instructor responses are not immediate, and feedback is not specific or timely (Hara & Kling, 2001). Also, students who are new to the online environment, may be reluctant to join in the conversation in case they say something silly, out of place, or poorly presented; and, because messages can often not be edited or erased, students are concerned about the permanency of an ill-conceived message, and how it will be perceived by other students/instructor. Equally, the domination in some online conversations by a small number of students may alienate those students less confident of their contributions (Mason & Lockwood, 1994).
- Lack of social presence, because the medium does not allow for social cues, especially those which are non-verbal and which, if available, would lead to greater immediacy, and hence more intense, affective and immediate interactions between student-student and teacher-student (Rourke, Anderson, Garrison, & Archer, 1999; Garrison, Anderson, & Archer, 2001; Stacey, 2002). The lack of social presence has sometimes been attributed to the lack of feedback or teacher immediacy given to students on their postings and "there is little to no gratification for the time spent composing a message" or "Without feedback, one can never be sure that someone has ever read the message." (Rovai, 2007, p.82).
- Limited student interaction, either because the learning environment is not designed or facilitated to provide students with motivation to interact, such as class sizes being too small or too large or online discussions lacking structure and guidance concerning instructor' expectations (MacKnight, 2000; Rovai, 2007). In addition, student interaction may be low as it does not rely on confidence or attention-getting skills, or because of low student confidence in what they may want to say, either is not important or not contributing anything new to the discussion (Guzdial & Turns, 2000).
- The lack of support for convergent processes (e.g., analysing and synthesising) (Hewitt, 2001) with the majority of student contributions in online discussions classified as exploratory in nature i.e. brainstorming, and as such does not represent critical thinking (Garrison et al., 2001; Kanuka et al., 2007).
- Time management is often necessary as the time spent online can easily exceed the time spent in face-to-face classes, since online discussions are boundless (in relation to time and location) and are typically always open (Rourke & Kanuka, 2007).
- Information overload can occur due to the amount of information, and the additional information to which students are guided by links to other material, thus overwhelming students to the point of torpor (Lobry de Bruyn & Prior, 2001).
- Misconceptions can occur when students receive no clear feedback to indicate whether their point is clear, and this situation is further compounded by "learner reluctance to push peer thinking and understanding" (Hewitt, 2003, pp.31-45).
- Traditional roles are often maintained, "the student speaks, the teacher answers, confirms, approves and reinforces" (Henri, 1995, p.158, quoted in Light & Light, 1999).

In conclusion, despite the range of issues canvassed above there is little empirical evidence to demonstrate the benefits of or identify strategies to reduce the difficulties in using asynchronous computer-mediated communication, especially in the context of the delivery and exploration of a problem-based learning activity in an online environment. Wheeler, Kelly and Gale (2005, p.135) "speculated" on the reasons for students' criticism that online discussions "prohibited rather than liberated discussions" as including the following:

- lack of familiarity or confidence of use,
- the permanency of the message archive,
- asynchronous aspects meaning that there would be no instantaneous response,
- time disparity in use with some students accessing before others.

If discussion facilities are to be used in problem-based learning then these issues should be considered in the design of the learning environment (Wheeler et al., 2005). The following research and its findings hopes to demonstrate, through an action research framework, the strategy of timing face-to-face instruction and guidance early in the unit of learning in a problem-based learning activity has value. With subsequent online student interaction resulting in enhanced online discussions and greater student engagement in the learning activity and with each other.

RESEARCH CONTEXT: DESCRIPTION OF THE PROBLEM-BASED LEARNING ACTIVITY OVER 2001-2006

The online problem-based learning activity in *Land Assessment for Sustainable Use* with off-campus students was applied in the following way in both learning experiences. Situation statements or scenarios were introduced to the students online every 4 weeks during the semester via the unit home page. The situation statements were structured around the unit content which focuses on identification of, causes of and solutions to land degradation problems, and the concepts and practices involved in land capability assessment and land use planning. The situation statements were based on realistic scenarios, where the natural resource management problems were complex, interrelated and several symptoms could relate to different land degradation issues. Also information sources are based on the 'real-world' situation, in that, the information required to resolve the situation is: imperfect, variable in quality and coverage and needed to be assessed by the student for its worth, relevance and credibility. The student was expected to locate their learning resources, and information literacy was a learning outcome that was assessed in the individual written response to the question/s at the end of the situation statement. Before the commencement of the learning activity students were directed to online introductory notes on problem-based learning. These notes included information about the learning approach, how it differed from more traditional forms of teaching and learning, and how it would be delivered and executed in the unit of learning. The problem-based learning activity was completed around three separate situation statements or scenarios, part 1 and 2 (contributing 30% to the unit grade) were submitted together two thirds through the semester (week 9), while part 3 (contributing 30% to the unit grade) was submitted at the end of the semester (week 13).

The learning outcomes of the online, problem-based learning activity were to create the opportunity for individual students to:

- review and think critically about the information on the content areas in question;
- demonstrate that they can access up-to-date, relevant and informative information about the content areas in question;
- interpret and interrogate information they have collected and form their own opinion, and follow-up questions in relation to the content area in question;

- deliver a written response that demonstrates a high degree of synthesis and analysis of the relevant content area;
- within the written response supply evidence that demonstrates that they have understood the content area and have critically evaluated information used in the written response (i.e., they are able to judge its level of reliability and worth);
- produce a written response that can be easily read and understood by a wide audience;
- reflect on learning arising from the process of composing the written answer.

Assessment of student performance was based on the above learning outcomes and built into a criterion-referenced framework using a marking schedule. The structured learning guide (Lobry de Bruyn, 2002; 2004) was designed to offer students an approach to solving the situation and developing skills in problem-solving and independent research skills as well as a time-frame for completion for the learning activity. The structured learning guide was particularly useful for scaffolding students unfamiliar with the approach and providing students with clear directions as to when their involvement in online discussions was required and explaining the nature of the activity. For instance, students would need to be able to formulate and communicate questions in response to the situation statements as well as respond to questions posted by students on the online discussions at designated times during the semester. Students made use of the technology by participating in online discussions using WebCT, over two weeks for each scenario of the problem-based learning activity, except for the scenario examined face-to-face at the residential school. Student participation in online discussions was focused on the problem-solving part of the problem-based learning activity, as well as engaging in self-directed learning (i.e., reading and research) either using the online teaching material or material obtained independently via the Internet. Instructor involvement in online discussions was timely and strategic, with feedback on each completed scenario of the problem-based learning activity. Instructor responses would be posted to the student groups weekly in the online discussions and there would be discretionary responses to individual messages, especially if the student group response was deemed inadequate. On Discussion Boards, a week after students were introduced to the scenario or situation statement as 'meet the situation', and in response to student questions, the instructor posted a rejoinder on the Discussion Board that 'fleshed out' the answers to most of the student questions communicated over the previous week arranged in a conversational reply. Hence, students should have been confident that their messages were read by the instructor and their questions considered, and responded to in the rejoinder. As a preface to the rejoinder, all the student questions were collated and tabulated indicating their nature, frequency and number of students participating. To contextualise the information supplied in the rejoinder, students were encouraged by the instructor in online Discussion Boards to conduct further self-directed research and reading.

RESEARCH APPROACH: STUDENT GROUPS AND DATA ANALYSIS

As already mentioned, the unit of learning is a tertiary-level unit - *Land Assessment for Sustainable Use* -offered at under- and post-graduate level taught to a mixed degree, dual-mode (on- and off-campus) student cohort, and utilises learning resources delivered both in hard copy and online. All students participating in this research were learning off-campus, undertaking the problem-based learning activity, described in the previous section, online. In addition, the students had to attend a compulsory residential school, either eight weeks into the semester (2001-2003) or before the semester commenced (2004-2006). Characteristically an off-campus student is mature-age, employed, and mostly undertaking the unit at undergraduate or graduate diploma level with a small proportion at Master level. The numbers of students involved in the study are detailed in Table 1, and studied the unit of learning from 2001 to 2006, in distinct cohorts. The data reported here was electronically-archived from online discussions over a 13-week period over six years (2001-2006), and averaged over two three year periods (2001-2003, 2004-2006) termed the *collective learning experience* (potentially 60 enrolled students in one group) and *small group learning experience* (potentially 6 enrolled students per group) respectively. These two types of learning experiences vary in the timing of compulsory face-to-face instruction on and practice in the problem-based learning activity conducted during a 4-day residential school in the unit of learning, and hence the ability to form small peer groups that have met face to face **before** communicating online, with the same group composition (*small group learning experience*). In the *collective learning experience* the students were only able to communicate online in the brainstorming phase of the problem-based learning activity as one large group, and had already experienced two parts of the learning activity before meeting face to face at the residential school. Both learning experiences use the same blended delivery, instruction and learning activities (online, and face-to-face), as well as the same core learning materials. The small peer groups used during the residential school for class activities consisted of 5 to 6 people, and were composed by the facilitator keeping in mind considerations such as geographic proximity to each other, prior learning and experience, mix of degree type, gender balance and career aspirations.

The introduction outlines the rationale for the movement of the face-to-face residential component which allowed students to meet, work in small groups, practice and experience problem-based learning face-to-face before being required to interact in online discussions around the next part or scenario of the problem-based learning activity (*small group learning experience*). Using an action research framework this research evaluated the level and nature of student engagement in asynchronous computer-mediated communication as a consequence of adjusting the position of the 4-day face-to-face residential component in the online problem-based learning activity to before the commencement of the unit of learning (*small group learning experience*), rather than eight weeks into the unit (*collective learning experience*). Through content analysis of student and instructor messages on Discussion Boards under the conditions mentioned earlier this chapter evaluates student engagement in the problem-based learning activity, and with each other by specifically examining: student participation, the level of concentration on problem-solving in the learning activity, the degree of convergent processes (i.e., degree of analysis, synthesis, and summarising) and level of social presence.

The methodology for the content analysis is explained in greater detail in Lobry de Bruyn (2004), and definition of content analysis terms is supported by references and footnotes accompanying Tables 3, 4, 5, 6, 7 and 8, including the author's modifications of schemes to include more specific behaviours or actions. The analysis presented here involved examining student participation in online discussions (Table 1 and Table 2), and content analysis of individual student messages for the presence of text that could be coded using the following content analysis schemes. The scheme developed by Orrill (2002) was used to code student messages (only once) to examine the level of concentration on problem solving in the learning activity (Table 3 and Table 4), and Hewitt's scheme (2001) was used to quantify the level of convergence and interactivity occurring in student messages (Table 5 and Table 6), while the content analysis schemes by Stacey (2002) and Rourke, Anderson, Garrison, and Archer (1999) were used for defining and measuring social presence (Table 7 and Table 8). The data for the variables used are presented as: student participation (percentage), student output (number per student), composition of messages under defined categories (percentage) and percentage change between the two learning experiences (*collective* and *small group*) (Table 1 to Table 7), and types of learning groups (*functional* and *non-functional*) (Table 2 to Table 8). To allow direct comparisons between learning experiences and types of learning groups the data were defined number per student or as a percentage. The unit of analysis was an individual posting. Therefore this research identifies the presence of defined categories (once), and a student posting could be coded several times under different categories, but not the frequency of categories within a posting. There was also selective use in the findings of direct, sometimes abridged, quotes from Discussions Boards to highlight pervasive themes and provide examples of findings. Also, data were statistically analysed to identify any significant differences in amount and nature of student communications on Discussion Boards as a consequence of group size combined with early scaffolding of student learning (*collective experience* versus *small group experience*). The data were examined to ascertain the influence of student cohort variation from year to year, and the influence this might have on the type of group learning (*functional* versus *non-functional*). Each learning group was classified as functional if it had more than 2 threads per student, and non-functional with less than 2 threads per student, which means that students in functional groups were engaging with the learning activity and with each other as peers, as shown by the student output. Depending on the nature of the data distribution one-way ANOVA or non-parametric one-way ANOVA were used to examine the influence of the preceding variables (*collective experience* versus *small group experience*, *functional* versus *non-functional*).

Table 1. Assessment of student messages in online Discussion Boards over 13 weeks comparing collective learning experience (mean number = 32 students per group, 2001-2003) with small group learning experience (mean number = 4.2 students per group, 2004-2006). (Total number of enrolled off-campus student in unit of learning; $n_{2001} = 63$, $n_{2002} = 65$, $n_{2003} = 60$, $n_{2004} = 23$, $n_{2005} = 22$, $n_{2006} = 19$)

Learning Experience	collective 2001-03 mean	small group 2004-06 mean	% change between experience
	no	no	%
Messages (mean total)	85.7	34.1	-59
Threads (per student)	1.4	3.8	166
Branches (per student)	1.2	4.4	259
Ratio of Branches to Threads (%)	86	116	35
Student messages (per student)	2.2	6.3	188
Instructor messages (mean total)	15.3	8.1	-47
Student repeat messages (per student)	1.2	5.3	339
Total no of students per group	32	4.2	-84
Participation rate (%)	51	85.5	68
off-campus students in unit of learning	62.7	21.3	-66

RESEARCH RESULTS AND DISCUSSION

Tables 1 to Table 7 compare quantity and nature of student messages under a *collective learning experience* (mean number = 32 students in one group, 2001-2003) and *small group learning experience* (mean number = 4 students per group, 2004-2006) in online Discussion Boards over 13 weeks in a unit of learning revolving around a three part (scenario) problem-based learning activity. While Tables 2 to 8 compare quantity and nature of student messages emanating from *functional learning groups* (mean number = 5 students in one group, 2004, 2006) and *non-functional learning groups* (mean number = 11 students per group, 2001-2006), irrespective of their *learning experience* in online Discussion Boards. The discussion will explore both aspects under student participation, student engagement with the problem-based learning activity and under social presence student engagement with each other.

Student Participation in Online Discussions

In the *small group learning experience*, there was a dramatic increase in the number of student messages (up by 188%), and student repeat messages (up by 339%), compared with students conducting the same learning activities as a *collective* without having met face-to-face prior to undertaking the online problem-based learning activity (Table 1). Participation rates by students in the *small group learning experience* in online Discussion Boards remained high (85.5% mean over three years), while the proportion of students participating in the learning activity as a collective hovered around 51% of the off-campus student cohort for three years, and in 2003 was only 40% (Table 1).

Table 2. Assessment of student messages in online Discussion Boards over 13 weeks comparing functional learning groups (mean number = 5 students per group, 2004, 2006) with non-functional learning groups (mean number = 11 students per group, 2001-2006). (Total number of enrolled off-campus student in unit of learning; $n_{2001} = 63$, $n_{2002} = 65$, $n_{2003} = 60$, $n_{2004} = 23$, $n_{2005} = 22$, $n_{2006} = 19$*)*

Learning Groups	Functional # 2004/06 mean	Non functional # 2001-06 mean	% change between groups
	no	no	%
Messages (mean total)	58	38	53
Threads (per student)	2.6	1.0	154
Branches (per student)	5.2	0.5	1033
Ratio of Branches to Threads (%)	164	61	35
Student messages (per student)	10.2	2.4	323
Instructor messages (mean total)	8.9	9.8	-9
Student repeat messages (per student)	7.3	0.5	1230
Total no of students per group	5	11	-59
Participation rate (%)	85	62	25
off-campus students in unit of learning	21	42	-50

Functional Groups are defined where the average output per student is 2 threads, Non-functional Groups are defined where the average output per student is less than 2 threads.

Table 3. Degree of content related to problem solving identified in student messages in online Discussion Boards over 13 weeks comparing collective learning experience (mean number = 32 students in one group, 2001-2003) with small group learning experience (mean number = 4.2 students per group, 2004-2006), using Orrill's (2002) content analysis scheme (total enrolled off-campus student numbers in unit of learning; $n_{2001} = 63$, $n_{2002} = 65$, $n_{2003} = 60$, $n_{2004} = 23$, $n_{2005} = 22$, $n_{2006} = 19$) * $p < 0.01$, ** $p < 0.001$ *comparison between collective and small group learning experience*

Learning Experience	collective			small group		
Years	2001-03			2004-06		% change between experience
Content Analysis #	Student Output	% of mean total messages		Student Output	% of mean total messages	Student Output
	Mean	n = 86		Mean	n = 34	
Problem solving only	0.5	18		0.6	7	25
Task only	0.6	22		1.7	25	194
Other only	0.3	11		0.5	5	81
Problem-solving and task aspects	0.5	20		2.6*	47	395
Problem-solving and other aspects	0.3	10		0.5	4	78
Task and other aspects	0.3	10		0.6	10	134
Task, Problem-solving and other aspects	0.3	10		0.2	3	-24
Grand total	2.6			6.7		

Definition of content analysis terms:

Problem Solving: Notes focused on presenting the student's thinking, asking a question related to the content of the problem or otherwise engaged the students in thinking about the problem.

Task: Notes were related to the logistics of the assignment task such as verify layout, due dates, length of written component of assignment. Lobry de Bruyn also included directions provided by students to research information e.g. Internet addresses and web sites, and arrangements being made for sharing research tasks or compiling list of questions or meeting on- or offline.

Other: Notes did not focus on problem or the unit.

In the *collective learning experience* low student participation on Discussion Boards could have been as a result of the high proportion (49% over three years) of restricted internet access either at work (12%) or limited opportunity to access the internet (37%), since access to the internet was only after work hours at home.

However, the *small group learning experience* had similar levels of restricted or limited internet access with 51% of the student cohort only able to access the internet after work hours at home, and 6% with restricted access at work, yet there was a 68% increase in student participation in Discussion Boards. This finding may reflect the reduced number of messages per group, due to smaller group size in the *small group learning experience,* hence requiring less time to read than the *collective learning experience* (as pointed out by the above quote), and therefore easier for students to undertake, and maintain concentration on the learning activity. Another possible reason for high levels of student activity under the *small group learning experience*, is that when students were placed in a small group of four to six people having met face-to-face, communication anxiety is decreased, and student concern over not contributing anything new to the discussion is reduced (Guzdial & Turns, 2000). In addition, individual student concern over not contributing anything new to the discussion is reduced when

*Table 4. Degree of content related to problem solving identified in student messages in online Discussion Boards over 13 weeks comparing functional learning groups (mean number = 5 students in one group, 2004, 2006) with non-functional learning groups (mean number = 11 students per group, 2001-2006), using Orrill's (2002) content analysis scheme (total enrolled off-campus student numbers in unit of learning; $n_{2001} = 63$, $n_{2002} = 65$, $n_{2003} = 60$, $n_{2004} = 23$, $n_{2005} = 22$, $n_{2006} = 19$) * $p < 0.01$, ** $p < 0.001$ comparison between functional and non-functional learning groups*

Learning Groups	Functional			Non-functional		% change between groups
Years	2004/2006			2001-06		
Content Analysis #	Student Output	% of mean total messages		Student Output	% of mean total messages	Student Output
	Mean	n = 58		Mean	n = 38	
Problem solving only	1.0	6.5		0.3	8.6	245
Task only	2.8	28.6		0.8**	22.6	237
Other only	1.1	9.2		0.1	4.4	731
Problem-solving and task aspects	3.1	31.7		1.9	47.4	65
Problem-solving and other aspects	0.9	5.2		0.2	4.7	452
Task and other aspects	1.1	14		0.3**	8.9	252
Task, Problem-solving and other aspects	0.4	4.9		0.1	3.4	328
Grand total	10.5			3.7		183

Definition of content analysis terms: as for Table 3

the average group size is four students (*small group learning* experience) in comparison to 32 students (*collective learning* experience). Students in the *collective learning experience* (potentially 60 enrolled students in one group) were much more reticent than the *group learning experience* (potentially 6 enrolled students per group) to post messages if they thought they would be repeating or duplicating what other students had already said and did not wish to be perceived as failing to contribute anything new to the online discussions, for example, "sorry for the repetition of many questions…" (Message 23, July 26, 2002, 8.11am), "Hopefully not too repetitive." (Message 31, July 28, 2002, 5.05pm) "I hope this is not repeating too much of what has already been said…" (Message 33, July 28, 2002, 9.56pm) or having read the questions felt what they would have added is already represented by other student questions:

In addition, all students in the *small group learning experience* had met the instructor at the residential school and probably felt they could relate more easily to instructor postings. Even though, instructor participation in *small group learning experience* was less frequent than in the *collective learning experience*, the nature of the messages presented greater moderation or modelling of behaviours (offering advice, collating and responding to student questions), that could have contributed to higher student participation rates.

Student motivation to become involved in Discussion Boards was considered to be self-rewarding or intrinsic, as it was linked directly to learning outcomes, and provided significant assistance to the problem-solving aspects of the learning activity (Lobry de Bruyn, 2002), and hence should improve the students' abilities to comprehend and complete the problem-based

Table 5. Nature of student engagement in online Discussion Boards over 13 weeks comparing collective learning experience (mean number = 32 students per group, 2001-2003) with small group learning experience (mean number = 4.2 students per group, 2004-2006), using Hewitt's (2001) analysis of thread type. (Total enrolled off-campus student numbers in unit of learning; $n_{2001} = 63$*,* $n_{2002} = 65$*,* $n_{2003} = 60$*,* $n_{2004} = 23$*,* $n_{2005} = 22$*,* $n_{2006} = 19$*) ** $p < 0.01$*, *** $p < 0.001$ *comparison between collective and small group learning experience*

Learning Experience	collective			small group		% change between experience
Year	2001-03			2004-06		
Thread type#	Student Output	% of mean total messages		Student Output	% of mean total messages	Student Output
	Mean	n = 86		Mean	n = 34	
Stand-alone	1.0	38		2.3	44	135
Add-on	1.5	58		3.4	43	122
Multiple	0.6	23		2.3*	28	283
Convergent	0.0	0		0.0	0.1	-

Definition of Thread type:

Stand-alone: Notes that introduce new ideas to the conference and do not build on previous lines of inquiry. Typically, a stand-alone note is one that begins a new thread.

Add-on: A note that builds on the ideas of one other note in the conference. Typically, notes in which one person responds to an idea that someone else has introduced.

Multiple: Notes that make a reference to two or more previous notes, but not in a way that would be considered an attempt at convergence.

Convergent: A note that discusses some of the ideas expressed in two or more other notes in the conference.

Table 6. Nature of student engagement in online Discussion Boards over 13 weeks comparing functional learning groups (mean number = 5 students per group, 2004, 2006) with non-functional learning groups (mean number = 4.2 students per group, 2004-2006), using Hewitt's (2001) analysis of thread type. (Total enrolled off-campus student numbers in unit of learning; $n_{2001} = 63$*,* $n_{2002} = 65$*,* $n_{2003} = 60$*,* $n_{2004} = 23$*,* $n_{2005} = 22$*,* $n_{2006} = 19$*) ** $p < 0.01$*, *** $p < 0.001$ *comparison between functional and non-functional learning groups*

Learning Group	Functional			Non-functional		% change between groups
Year	2004/2006			2001-06		
Thread type#	Student Output	% of mean total messages		Student Output	% of mean total messages	Student Output
	Mean	n = 58		Mean	n = 38	
Stand-alone	2.6	28		1.9	50	38
Add-on	6.4	58		1.4**	40	343
Multiple	4.1	33		0.9*	23	358
Convergent	0.1	0.3		0.0	0	-

Definition of Thread type: as for Table 5

*Table 7. Level of social presence, cognitive and system responses identified in student messages in online Discussion Boards over 13 weeks comparing collective learning experience (mean number = 32 students per group, 2001-2003) with small group learning experience (mean number = 4.2 students per group, 2004-2006) responses, using Stacey (2002), and Rourke et al. (1999) content analysis schemes (total enrolled off-campus student numbers in unit of learning; n_{2001} = 63, n_{2002} = 65, n_{2003} = 60, n_{2004} = 23, n_{2005} = 22, n_{2006} = 19) * $p < 0.01$, ** $p < 0.001$ comparison between collective and small group learning experience*

Learning Experience	collective			small group		
Year	2001-03			2004-06		% change between experience
Content analysis #	Student Output	% of mean total messages		Student Output	% of mean total messages	Student Output
	Mean	n = 86		Mean	n = 34	
Interactive responses	1.4	54		3.8	50	176
Affective responses	0.5	18		1.3	18	172
Cohesive responses	1.8	67		4.7*	74	175
Total Social presence	3.6			9.7		175
Cognitive responses	2.4	90		5.8*	92	149
System responses	0.3	11		0.2	2.6	-17
Grand total	112			61.5		

Definition of content analysis terms:

Interactive: Includes complimenting, expressing appreciation or agreement, asking unsolicited questions, referring to others' messages, quoting from others' messages and continuing a thread. Lobry de Bruyn also included apologising.

Affective: Includes expressing emotion, feeling or mood, use of humour and self-disclosure.

Cohesive: Includes addressing or referring to other students by name, and/or the group as we, us, our, group, and salutations.

Cognitive: Includes discussion and commentary on the unit content.

System: Includes discussion related to the software or access issues.

learning activity. Nevertheless, the intrinsic motivation for students to complete and do well in the learning activity does not necessarily rely on them posting messages (i.e. participation), especially if a critical mass of students were contributing, but could also accrue to those students who, although silent, access the Discussion Board, and read messages.

This student behaviour has been labelled as social 'loafing' or 'lurking' (Nonnecke & Preece, 2003). Lurking or social loafing would have been more likely in the *collective learning experience* rather than *small group learning experience* as the former had larger numbers of students contributing, and could 'afford' students not posting messages – "and any of you silent types who may be listening?" (Message 474, August 12, 2005, 7.58pm). Also, 'lurking' was more likely to be tolerated or unnoticed in a *collective learning experience* rather than in a *small group learning experience* of online discussions. Reason being that in a small and familiar group – *small group learning experience* - if several people chose not to contribute the discussion would have collapsed or left too much responsibility for compiling and listing questions to one or two individuals. In addition, in the *small group learning experience* of communicating online it would be more difficult to remain anonymous as all members had met face-to-face, and consequently 'lurking' would

Table 8. Level of social presence, cognitive and system responses identified in student messages in online Discussion Boards over 13 weeks comparing functional learning groups (mean number = 32 students in one group, 2001-2003) with non-functional learning groups (mean number = 4.2 students per group, 2004-2006), using Stacey (2002), and Rourke et al. (1999) content analysis schemes (total enrolled off-campus student numbers in unit of learning; $n_{2001} = 63$, $n_{2002} = 65$, $n_{2003} = 60$, $n_{2004} = 23$, $n_{2005} = 22$, $n_{2006} = 19$*)* * $p < 0.01$, ** $p < 0.001$, *** $p < 0.0001$ *comparison between functional and non-functional learning groups*

Learning Groups	Functional			Non-func-tional		% change between groups
Years	2004/2006			2001-06		
Content analysis #	Student Output	% of mean total messages		Student Output	% of mean total messages	Student Output
	Mean	n = 58		Mean	n = 38	
Interactive responses	7.0	64		1.6***	44	329
Affective responses	2.2	21		0.6*	16	277
Cohesive responses	7.5	76		2.7***	71	178
Total Social presence	16.8			4.9***		240
Cognitive responses	8.7	86		3.6***	95	140
System responses	0.5	3.5		0.1	4.3	255
Grand total						

Definition of content analysis terms: as for Table 7

have been less socially acceptable. Also, the person engaging in such behaviour could have been easily identified. Hence, the tipping point for group functionality is lower in the *small group learning experience* because if two to three individuals are unable or unwilling to participate the whole learning group is affected, but in the *collective learning experience*, even if half the students did not contribute it is not as noticeable, even to those that were contributing (Table 2).

Since student participation in online Discussion Boards was confined to a two week period per scenario low participation by some students seemed to be a result of poor time management and missing the 'window' of opportunity for participating in online discussions e.g., "Boy if you don't get in quick most of the obvious questions I would have asked area already posed" (Message 21, July 25, 2002, 3.39pm). Poor skills in time management or lack of time is expressed by students across all group learning experiences, but especially in those groups that did not function well (Table 2), and upon closer examination of the content of student messages, the most likely reasons for not contributing to online discussions were technical, and 'life getting in the way' or in other words 'competing demands' for time, and study not necessarily being the first priority. Evidence for this was taken from the following quotes:

Nature of Student Engagement in Online Discussions

In Table 3 the level of student focus on problem-solving is explored using Orrill's (2002) content analysis scheme. The amount of student output from *small group learning experience* was consistently higher in all categories, but significantly more under 'Problem-solving and task aspects' with 395% increase compared with per student output from a *collective learning experience* ($p < 0.0036$, F 12.2). In the *small group learning experience* there is greater sharing of responsibilities and evidence of co-operation such as making arrangements to meet online, compile questions, allocate tasks and post them to the instructor. For example:

Overall in the *small group learning experience* there was a 27% increase in messages being coded as 'Problem-solving and task aspects' (47%) compared with 20% when the students were working in the *collective learning experience* of a problem-based learning activity (Table 3). Examining the actual content of student messages it does seem that in a small group students were less distracted by 'Other' issues (down 6%), unrelated to the learning activity, and required less scaffolding of their learning in "how to" engage in online discussions as evidenced by fewer postings by the instructor explaining the nature of the learning activity. For students in the *collective learning* experience the use of the structured learning guide had yet to be explained to them, and the approach seems to require more face-to-face explanation, and they were communicating online in Discussion Boards as individuals rather than as a learning group. For example, in the *collective learning experience* of problem-based learning there were more student postings wanting guidance in how to undertake the learning activity, and a greater need for instructor immediacy, as shown by the following exchange:

Examining functional groups and non-functional learning groups the significant differences were that functional learning groups had a higher student output under 'task only' ($p < 0.004$, F 12), and 'task and other aspects' ($p < 0.002$, F 14.4) when compared with non-functional learning groups, while none of the other categories were significantly different between learning groups (Table 4). As discussed in detail later under social presence, those in the *small group learning experience* of problem-based learning activity, were able to offer each other guidance, advice and support in undertaking the learning activity. For example in functional learning groups there was more evidence of peer support in guiding other students through the problem-based learning activity:

Members of a functional learning group offered a degree of gentle persuasion or 'cajoling' to get other group members involved ("Can you let me know if I'm heading in the right directions?" Message 776, September 4, 2006, 4.10pm). For instance, instead of instructor prompting to motivate students to participate it was more likely to come from peers in the *small group learning experience* of online discussions as demonstrated by the following quotes:

Two ways of examining students' engagement in monitoring their own understanding was to examine their disposition toward summarising and to examine the rationales they provided to explain choices or decisions they had made. The results using the first method indicated that by placing students in the *small group learning experience* and scaffolding their learning before they undertake online discussions it led to a substantial increase in individual student output with a 283% increase in Multiple notes, and 122% increase in Add-on notes, and 135% increase in Stand-alone notes compared with those students using Discussion Boards as a large, unscaffolded *collective learning experience* (Table 5). Those notes that were categorised as Multiple were undertaking one or several of the following activities: compiling questions, negotiating tasks amongst the student group, such as arranging times for all students in a group to be active online, directing other students to resources either online or on the Internet (web addresses), explaining to other students land management practices and their impacts, and adding questions to the group's existing list. Nevertheless, examining the relative percentage composition of notes revealed no significant difference, even though the proportion of Add-on notes in the *small group learning experience* was down by 15% from the *collective learning experience*, while the proportion of Stand-alone notes in the *small group learning experience* increased by 6% from the earlier *collective learning experience* when students were not scaffolded before embarking in online discussions of the problem-based learning activity (Table 5). The increase in Stand-alone notes in the *small group learning experience* was largely attributed to students more willing to offer their opinion on the situation statement and greater contribution by students to compiling a list of questions for other students to read, and amend. Despite, the significant improvement in student use of Discussions Boards in the *small group learning experience*, the proportion of Multiple notes ($p < 0.01$, F 7.56) was only 5% higher compared with the *collective learning experience* of the learning activity, reflecting only a slight increase in references to other students' messages, and still no considerable convergence of notes was observed (Table 5).

An example of a posting that would be considered Multiple note is shown below:

However, if the data is examined on the basis of group functionality then a clearer picture emerges with functional learning groups having significantly more Multiple notes ($p < 0.05$, F 4.86, proportion of total messages up by 10%), and Add-on notes ($p < 0.005$, F 11.2, proportion of total messages up by 18%), and a 22% decline in the proportion of total messages categorised as Stand-alone notes compared with non-functional learning groups, regardless of group experience (Table 6).

In Hewitt's (2001) analysis of student use of threaded online discussions virtually all messages could be characterised as Add-on notes with few people attempting to tie together ideas from different sources. Hewitt (2001) made the point that the 'reply' convention of asynchronous computer-mediated communication software prompts students to respond to a single note without considering the overall discussion (thread). Often, it seems students reply to a thread and leave the subject label (thread) intact, even though the content of the message may have drifted away from the original purpose. It was also likely that students do not read earlier messages to grasp how the discussion has evolved. Students in posting messages on Discussion Boards were more likely to refer to the most immediate thread (Hewitt, 2003), but some groups kept a thread 'alive' for extended periods of time, and this behaviour was more common in *small group learning experience*. Evidence for this behaviour was provided by examining student messages, in the problem-based learning activity and analysing the branches to thread ratio (Table 1). Comparing the *collective* and *small group learning experience* it shows that those students discussing the situation statement in small groups were more likely to continue the thread as shown by the higher ratio of branches to thread (Table 1). Further support is given for extended student interaction when functional learning groups (all from the *small group learning* experience) are separated from non-functional learning groups and the ratio of branches to threads increases by 48% (Table 2).

The second method, examining the use of rationale allows one to establish the level of student mastery as well as whether the students were working collaboratively by explaining their position to others (Hewitt, 2001). A posting was considered to use rationale if there was any opinion or evidence offered (Orrill, 2002). It was concluded that there was limited evidence of student use of rationale, and student rationale was only supplied after instructor prompting. However, this finding was more a reflection of the learning activity and the prescribed use of Discussions Boards which was restricted to the exploratory phase of learning – brainstorming, prioritising and listing questions and identifying learning resources – whereas the use of rationale was expected, and assessed in the individually written response to the problem-based situation statement, which was submitted during the semester.

Level of Social Presence in Online Discussions

Table 7 compares the level of social presence exhibited when communicating online in the *collective learning experience* (mean number = 32) compared with the *small group learning experience* (mean number = 4). Overall (for both experiences, *collective* and *small group learning experience*) the majority of messages were coded as cognitive (mean 91%, related to content of the unit). While around 70% of the messages had some form of cohesive response, 52% of the messages were interactive and only 18% of the messages recorded the presence of affective responses (Table 7). The per student output of social presence in online Discussion Boards is far higher in the *small group learning experience* with a 175% increase in student messages being categorized as containing some form of social presence (Table 7). In particular, cohesive responses in *small group learning experience* were coded in 74% of all messages compared with the *collective learning experience* (67% of all messages) which indicates that the *small group learning experience* can build a stronger sense of connection between individual members, and there was a two-fold significant increase ($p < 0.007$, F 9.97) in student output compared with the *collective learning experience* (Table 7).

When learning groups did not function well those learning groups recorded significantly less interactive responses (44% of messages contained an interactive response compared to functional learning groups where interactive responses were much higher at 64% of messages) (Table 8). Also, in non-functional learning groups the per student output in all social presence categories was two to three fold lower than functional learning groups and statistically significant in all instances (Table 8). In general, those messages coded as having interactive responses were often students agreeing with each other or apologizing for not contributing to the online discussions earlier or for sounding too repetitive. Other examples of interactive responses, where students complimented each other or praised the learning experience (all from the *collective learning experience*):

Of the functional learning groups, two particular groups in the *small group learning experience*, 2004 (group 5) and 2006 (group 1), recorded higher than average proportion of messages coded as containing interactive responses at 74% and 73% respectively, hence creating a virtuous circle. In these situations the following were typical interactive responses from students in a *small group learning experience* indicated gratitude, provision of peer support and motivation from other students to group members when they were asked unsolicited questions around the content, for example by explaining soil pH readings and land management practices:

The proportion of affective responses were the same in both learning experiences (*collective* and *small group*), and were lower than all other social presence categories, at 18% (Table 7), but the nature of the affective responses varied between the two learning experiences as students in the *collective experience* were combining two activities, one to introduce themselves and the other to formulate questions for part one of the problem-based learning activity, while in the *small group learning experience* the introduction of students to each other had already occurred during the residential school in a face-to-face session. In the *small group learning experience*, most of the affective responses were coded as 'self-disclosure' where students were either introducing themselves or lamenting their lack of prior knowledge on the topic, but on the other hand hopeful of learning more:

In *collective learning experience* the nature of the majority of affective responses were humor-related or more personal revelations with other group members exchanging details on holidays or experiences outside the learning activity, and few were related to feelings of inadequacy regarding the learning activity compared with the *collective learning experience*. Another type of affective response, although infrequently used, were emoticons such as "I think I answered my own question ;-)" (Message 681, August 13, 2006, 12.23pm), "I can't find the attachment either:)" (Message 237, August 19, 2003).

Hara, Bonk and Angeli (2000) found that 27% of units (in this case paragraphs) consisted of some form of social cues. These were categorized as self-introduction, expression of feeling, greeting, closure, jokes, the use of symbolic icons and compliments to others. Examining the content of the students' messages in this research for social presence, it was found that evidence of social presence was mostly restricted to opening and closing remarks and was rarely recorded throughout the body of the student posting. However, the density of social presence in this research has yet to be calculated and will require quantifying the frequency of coded units per posting, not merely establishing their presence per posting. Where social presence has been examined quantitatively, as Rourke et al. (1999) have done, with a social presence density figure that yields a unit of incidents per 1,000 words, the figures can be quite small. In their study, Rourke et al. (1999) recorded 33 incidents per 1,000 words. This is because social presence may consist of cohesive responses (e.g., salutations) that if used, would be expected to only appear at the beginning and/or end (once or twice) in a student message.

SUMMARY OF RECOMMENDATIONS

Hara et al. (2000) in their study of asynchronous online discussions suggest, as Henri argues, that "research in computer conferencing content is usually restricted to the gathering of quantitative data on participation" (1992, p. 122):

> Clearly, the next step in understanding computer conferencing and Web-based course delivery is to investigate not just the quality and types of electronic social interaction patterns, but also the impact on student course performance and long term retention of course material.

They also recommend (Hara et al., 2000), as this research would support, combining quantitative analysis, weekly conference activity graphs, and qualitative analysis to avoid simplistic interpretations of online discussions based solely on participation rates. Throughout their study (Hara et al., 2000) they were aware of the need to triangulate the interpretation of participant messages, and conduct additional interviews and retrospective reports such as student evaluation of their own dialogue transcripts, however impractical that might be, to validate the researchers' interpretation of students' discourse.

The main finding was that unless students are supported in the learning activity and in online discussions through face-to-face teaching early in the unit of learning and in small learning groups then student participation was predictably low, of unequal and of varying nature, as shown by those students placed in a *collective learning experience* (mean student number in unit over three years = 63), but also in those groups that were not functioning (mean student number in group over three years = 11). To improve the level of student engagement in online discussions there needs to be greater instructor immediacy and explicit linking of the purpose of online discussions to student outcomes or learning objectives, specifically of the assessment task. These improvements were largely achieved by timing the face-to-face component of this unit of learning to allow for more appropriate timing of scaffolding on and instruction in problem-based learning and use of online discussions in the learning activity. Some 20 years ago, Harasim (1986) identified face-to-face sessions as a "critical factor" in the successful design and facilitation of a "computer learning environment" with greater active participation, improvement in group dynamic and sense of connectivity, and increased student confidence. With early placement of the residential component of the online unit to before the beginning of the semester, it allowed for greater guidance and practice for students unfamiliar with problem-based learning, online instruction, and the purpose and outcomes of student participation in online discussions. In addition, it provided groups with the opportunity (not always taken up) to establish group connections, and establish ground rules for online discussions before they returned to their respective homes. Face-to-face teaching prior to online discussion also led to improvements in instructor immediacy, greater focus on the learning activity, and higher levels of social presence, especially social cohesion between group members and there was evidence of co-operation and sharing of tasks. Although online delivery of learning activities is favoured for reasons of flexibility and 'ease of access' there are still sound pedagogical reasons, as demonstrated here, to retain a face-to-face component in the delivery of online learning to scaffold student learning and create a better sense of a learning community, as also supported by Rovai and Jordan (2004).

Student Participation and Viable Group Size

Instructing students on how to approach problem-based learning, when studying off-campus, was more demanding than first anticipated, especially when face-to-face instruction and practice in problem-based learning occurred eight weeks into the semester by which time students were to have already completed two scenarios of the problem-based learning activity using asynchronous computer-mediated communication. The obvious problem for the instructor was the difficulty in monitoring and facilitating student communication as a *collective learning experience* where potentially there could have been 60 students online. There is a critical group size (Rovai, 2002) in online discussions with evidence that too few members generate little discussion and too many generate a sense of being overwhelmed (Rice, 1994). Rovai suggests eight to ten people as a minimal critical mass for encouraging good interaction, while 20 to 30 people in a single group was the most students a single instructor can facilitate easily (Rovai, 2002). The findings of the work reported here would suggest that if all members were active then a group of four people can generate meaningful discourse, but often any fewer members, especially if not active is not a viable group size. Equally, too many members in a group can lead to lower levels of participation and increased likelihood of 'lurking' behaviour. Larger groups also allow for the reality of attrition or group members inability to contribute due to other commitments. Even though, students in the *small group learning experience* had very similar levels of Internet access compared with *collective learning experience* students, once they were placed in small groups with people they had met face-to-face, they were more inclined to participate (with a three year average of 85.5%), and this can be largely attributed to group size being the appropriate size (four to five active participants) to motivate and encourage all members to contribute, and reduce individual communication anxiety. Nevertheless there were also groups that did not function well in the *small group learning experience*, and in some cases student attrition or lack of commitment to the online discussions meant that some groups fell below the critical size to have a meaningful discussion, and this could happen more easily in the small group learning experience. Sutherland, Marcus and Jessup (2005) suggested that to maintain focus on the learning activity and to encourage students to use online discussions it was best to limit discussion groups to five students and this would lead to greater individual participation (Webb, 1989; 1992), and "reduce the number of postings as well as the time required to read postings thus making it easier to follow threads in the discussion" (Sutherland et al., 2005, p.556).

Learning Design Considerations

A number of suggestions for improving the use of asynchronous computer-mediated communication as a means of facilitating student inquiry and problem-solving, and potentially improving level of convergence in online discussions were made by Hewitt (2001). His suggestions included: appointing a moderator to summarise the discussion (preferably a student so other students could develop a deeper understanding of the problem solving processes and the ways in which ideas may interrelate); assigning tasks that require group synthesis; using a linear discussion format and finally, augmenting asynchronous computer-mediated communication with synchronous technologies (such as video conferencing) to make group coordination and negotiating group consensus easier. McLean (1999) also suggested separating the substantive content from "meta-communication" of the knowledge building process to avoid cluttering the work space with messages about due dates and deliverables rather than concentrating on the problems and issues under discussion. For subsequent years the online discussions have been solely reserved for the learning activity. Kanuka et al. (2007) would also suggest, from empirical research, that cognitive presence or critical discourse was highest in those online learning activities that were well structured, provided clearly defined roles and responsibilities for students and overtly provoked students to confront each others' opinions such as Webquest and debates.

The present design of online discussions, using small peer groups with face-to-face instruction prior to interacting in online discussions conforms to a number of design and facilitation principles outlined by Rovai (2007) that will increase student participation and engagement in the problem-based learning activity, and hence achieve the desired learning outcomes (outlined earlier). These are:

- Authentic topics (see description of the problem-based learning activity),
- Viable group size (see above),
- Structured learning design.

Discussions were structured with the use of a structured learning approach so that students clearly understand what was expected of them in the learning activity (Lobry de Bruyn, 2002). The structured learning guide, and situation statements which recommend activities and timeframes, should support all students, but especially those who have difficulty organising their time or who are unfamiliar with the learning approach, which requires independent learning, and indicate the appropriate time and effort needed for the learning activity and to achieve the desired learning outcomes.

From the perspective of the research reported here the use of asynchronous computer-mediated communication and degree of convergence could be improved by further integrating student participation with assessment and learning outcomes, such as designing tasks that require students to demonstrate synthesis and summarising skills. Rovai (2003; 2004; 2007) strongly suggests extrinsic motivation is provided by grading students' online participation in discussions, and these criteria should be clearly communicating to students through a Discussion Rubric (that quantifies and describes best practice in online discussions), so that instructor expectations regarding student involvement in online discussions are unambiguous. Vonderwell and Zachariah (2005) observed that when students were assigned specific roles in online discussions they maintained online presence and participated more frequently than the rest of the group members, while all of the students reported that student tasks and assessment criteria for the discussions influenced their participation. However, the mechanisms by which student interaction and messages on the online discussions will be assessed needs to be carefully crafted to avoid an unwieldy, non-authentic and cumbersome assessment process for students and instructors alike.

Social Presence in an Online Community

Stacey (2002) emphasized the role of the instructor in modeling social presence factors and monitoring and moderating online Discussion Board interactions to foster a secure and collaborative learning environment that facilitates and builds social presence. Instructor intervention is particularly useful when group size falls below a viable size, and discussion groups may have to be amalgamated to ensure continued online discussions. The experiences of this research would concur with these findings and suggest further that the future success of combining online communication facilities with problem-based learning activities is only ensured by enthusiastic and committed instructors who are prepared to monitor their teaching and to share their successes and failures (learning experiences) with candor and openness. Ongoing preparedness to experiment and reflect on teaching practice is required, and to create greater group identity and ownership the instructor has given groups the opportunity to name their group. So far, those groups who quickly decided on a group name have maintained a good level of group participation, and those groups who either could not agree on a name or who had only partial group consensus on a name are less engaged and active in the online discussions.

CONCLUSION

Kukolja Taradi, Taradi, Radic and Pokrajac (2005) reported that using problem-based learning with Web technology positively impacts on student learning outcomes as shown by more involvement with peers, and better results in assessment tasks. Akkoyunlu and Yilmaz Soylu (2006) found through interviews with 64 students, that with those students who were high achievers, and participated in forums then their views on blended learning, and in particular online learning were more positive, then those who were low achievers and did not participate in forums. Nevertheless, most of the students still preferred the face-to-face learning environment, especially in conjunction with online learning, and face-to-face interaction was integral in supporting those unfamiliar with online learning (Akkoyunlu & Yilmaz Soylu, 2006). The strength of blended learning is that it provides a means to ensure learners are supported and facilitated through self-directed learning activities (Bonk et al., 2002). Certainly the data presented here from the content analysis of online discussions supports the inclusion of face-to-face teaching in online learning. By offering students choice and flexibility in the learning activities, well thought out learning design, improved scaffolding of student learning through face-to-face instruction in and practice of the problem-based learning activity, and the opportunity to form small peer groups for online discussions was potentially a more fulfilling and robust form of learning.

REFERENCES

Akkoyunlu, B., & Yilmaz Soylu, M. (2006). A study on student's views on blended learning environment. *Turkish Online Journal of Distance Education, 7*(3), art.3.

Barrows, H. S. (1985). *How to design a problem-based curriculum for the preclinical years*. New York: Springer.

Barrows, H. S. (1988). *The tutorial process*. Springfield, Ill: Southern Illinois Press.

Barrows, H. S. (2002). Is it truly possible to have such a thing as dPBL? *Distance Education, 23*(1), 119–122. doi:10.1080/01587910220124026

Barrows, H. S., & Tamblyn, R. M. (1980). *Problem-based learning: An approach to medical education*. New York: Springer.

Björck, U. (2002). Distributed problem-based learning in social economy – key issues in students' mastery of a structured method of education. *Distance Education, 23*(1), 85–103. doi:10.1080/0158791022012399I

Bonk, C., Olson, T., Wisher, R., & Orvis, K. (2002). Learning from focus groups: An examination of blended learning. *Journal of Distance Education, 17*(3), 97–118.

Boud, D., & Feletti, G. (1997). *The challenge of problem-based learning*. London, UK: Kogan Page.

Carr, S. (2000). As distance education comes of age, the challenge is keeping the students. *The Chronicle of Higher Education, 46*, A39–A41.

Eastmond, D. V. (1994). Adult distance study through computer conferencing. *Distance Education, 15*(1), 128–152. doi:10.1080/0158791940150109

Garrison, D. R., Anderson, T., & Archer, W. (2001). Critical thinking, cognitive presence, and computer conferencing in distance education. *American Journal of Distance Education, 15*(1), 7–23. doi:10.1080/08923640109527071

Graddol, D. (1989). Some CMC discourse properties and their educational significance. In Mason, R., & Kaye, A. (Eds.), *Mindweave: Communication, computers and distance education* (pp. 236–241). New York: Pergamon Press.

Graham, C. R. (2006). Blended learning systems: definition, current trends and future directions. In Bonk, C. J., & Graham, C. R. (Eds.), *Handbook of blended learning: Global perspectives, local designs* (pp. 3–21). CA: Pfeiffer.

Guzdial, M., & Turns, J. (2000). Effective discussion through a computer-mediated anchored forum. *Journal of the Learning Sciences, 9*(4), 437–469. doi:10.1207/S15327809JLS0904_3

Hara, N., Bonk, C. J., & Angeli, C. (2000). Content analysis of online discussion in an applied educational psychology course. *Instructional Science, 28*(2), 115–152. doi:10.1023/A:1003764722829

Hara, N., & Kling, R. (2000). Students' distress with a Web-based distance education course: an ethnographic study of participants' experiences. *Information Communication and Society, 3*(4), 557–579. doi:10.1080/13691180010002297

Hara, N., & Kling, R. (2001). Student distress in web-based distance education. *EDUCAUSE Quarterly, 24*(3), 68–69.

Harasim, L. (1986). Educational applications of computer conferencing. *Journal of Distance Education, 1*(1), 59–70.

Harasim, L., Hiltz, S. R., Teles, L., & Turoff, M. (1998). *Learning networks: A field guide to teaching and learning online*. Cambridge, MA: MIT Press.

Henri, F. (1992). Computer conferencing and content analysis. In Kaye, A. R. (Ed.), *Collaborative Learning Through Computer Conferencing: The Najaden Papers* (pp. 115–136). New York: Springer.

Hewitt, J. (2001). Beyond threaded discourse. *International Journal of Educational Telecommunications, 7*(3), 207–221.

Hewitt, J. (2003). How habitual online practices affect the development of asynchronous discussion threads. *Journal of Educational Computing Research, 28*(1), 31–45. doi:10.2190/PMG8-A05J-CUH1-DK14

Kanuka, H., Rourke, L., & Laflamme, E. (2007). The influence of instructional methods on the quality of online discussion. *British Journal of Educational Technology, 38*(2), 260–271. doi:10.1111/j.1467-8535.2006.00620.x

Kukolja Taradi, S., Taradi, M., Radic, K., & Pokrajac, N. (2005). Blending problem-based learning with Web technology positively impacts student learning outcomes in acid-base physiology. *Advances in Physiology Education, 29*, 35–39. doi:10.1152/advan.00026.2004

Light, P., & Light, V. (1999). Analysing asynchronous learning interactions: Computer-mediated communication in a conventional undergraduate setting. In Littleton, K., & Light, P. (Eds.), *Learning with computers: Analysing productive interaction* (pp. 162–178). New York, NY: Routledge.

Lobry de Bruyn, L. (2002). *Description of Problem Based Learning in Natural Resource Management.* Retrieved March 21, 2007, from http://www.learningdesigns.uow.edu.au/exemplars/info/LD28/index.html.

Lobry de Bruyn, L. A. (2004). Monitoring online communication: can the development of convergence and social presence indicate an interactive learning environment? *Distance Education, 25*(1), 67–81. doi:10.1080/0158791042000212468

Lobry de Bruyn, L. A., & Prior, J. C. (2001). Changing student learning focus in natural resource management education – Problems (and some solutions) with using problem-based learning. In L. Richardson, & J. Lidstone (Eds), *Proceedings of the Joint International Conference Flexible learning for a flexible society. ASET/HERDSA 2000* (pp. 441-451). Toowoomba, Queensland Australia: ASET/HERDSA.

MacKnight, C. B. (2000). Teaching critical thinking through online discussion. *EDUCAUSE Quarterly, 23*(4), 38–41.

Mason, R., & Kaye, A. (Eds.). (1989). *Mindweave: Communication, computers and distance education*. New York: Pergamon Press.

Mason, R., & Kaye, A. (1990). Towards a new paradigm for distance education. In Harasim, L. (Ed.), *Online education: Perspectives on a new environment* (pp. 15–38). New York: Praeger.

Mason, R., & Lockwood, F. (1994). *Using communications media in open and flexible learning*. London: Kogan Page.

McLean, R. S. (1999). Meta-communication widgets for knowledge building in distance education. In C. Hoadley, & J. Roschelle (Eds.), Proceedings of the *Computer Support for Collaborative Learning (CSCL) Conference* (383-390), Mahwah, NJ: Lawrence Erlbaum Associates.

Nonnecke, B., & Preece, J. (2003). Silent participants: Getting to know lurkers better. In Leug, C., & Fisher, D. (Eds.), *From usenet to CoWebs: Interacting with social information spaces* (pp. 110–132). Amsterdam, The Netherlands: Springer-Verlag.

Orrill, C. H. (2002). Supporting online PBL: Design considerations for supporting distributed problem solving. *Distance Education, 23*(1), 41–57. doi:10.1080/01587910220123973

Rice, R. (1994). Network analysis and computer-mediated communication systems. In Galaskiewka, S. W. J. (Ed.), *Advances in social network analysis* (pp. 167–203). Newbury Park, CA: Sage.

Rourke, L., Anderson, T., Garrison, D. R., & Archer, W. (1999). Assessing social presence in asynchronous text-based computer conferencing. *Canadian Journal of Distance Education, 14*(2), 50–71.

Rourke, L., & Kanuka, H. (2007). Barriers to online critical discourse. *International Journal of Computer-Supported Collaborative Learning, 2*(1), 105–126. doi:10.1007/s11412-007-9007-3

Rovai, A. (2007). Facilitating online discussions effectively. *The Internet and Higher Education, 10*(1), 77–88. doi:10.1016/j.iheduc.2006.10.001

Rovai, A. P. (2002). Building sense of community at a distance. *International Review of Research in Open and Distance Learning*, *3*(1), 1–16.

Rovai, A. P. (2003). Strategies for grading online discussions: Effects on discussions and classroom community in Internet-based university courses. *Journal of Computing in Higher Education*, *15*(1), 89–107. doi:10.1007/BF02940854

Rovai, A. P. (2004). A constructivist approach to online college learning. *The Internet and Higher Education*, *7*(2), 79–93. doi:10.1016/j.iheduc.2003.10.002

Rovai, A. P., & Jordan, H. M. (2004). Blended learning and sense of community: A comparative analysis with traditional and fully online courses. *International Review of Research in Open and Distance Learning*, *5*(2).

Ryan, R. M., & Deci, E. L. (2000). Intrinsic and extrinsic motivation: classic definitions and new directions. *Contemporary Educational Psychology*, *25*(1), 54–67. doi:10.1006/ceps.1999.1020

Sikora, A. C., & Carroll, C. D. (2002). *Postsecondary education descriptive analysis reports (NCES 2003-154). US Department of Education, National Center for Education Statistics*. Washington, DC: US Government Printing Office.

Stacey, E. (2002). Social presence online: Networking learners at a distance. *Education and Information Technologies*, *7*(4), 287–294. doi:10.1023/A:1020901202588

Sutherland, L., Marcus, G., & Jessup, A. (2005). From face-to-face to blended learning: issues and challenges in redesigning a professional course. In Brew, A., & Asmar, C. (Eds.), *Higher Education in a changing world, Research and Development in Higher Education* (*Vol. 28*, pp. 551–558). Sydney, Australia: HERDSA.

Vonderwell, S., & Zachariah, S. (2005). Factors influencing participation in online learning. *Journal of Research on Technology in Education*, *38*(2), 213–230.

Webb, N. (1989). Peer interactions and learning in small groups. *International Journal of Educational Research*, *13*(1), 21–31. doi:10.1016/0883-0355(89)90014-1

Webb, N. (1992). Testing a theoretical model of student interactions and learning in small groups. In Hert-Lazarowitz, R., & Miller, N. (Eds.), *Interaction in co-operative groups: the theoretical anatomy of group learning* (pp. 102–119). London, UK: Cambridge University Press.

Wheeler, S., Kelly, P., & Gale, K. (2005). The influence of online problem-based learning on teachers' professional practice and identity. *ALT-J Research In Learning Technology*, *13*(2), 125–137.

Yip, W. (2002). Student's perceptions of the technological supports for problem-based learning. *Education and Information Technologies*, *7*(4), 303–312. doi:10.1023/A:1020957320335

KEY TERMS AND DEFINITIONS

Blended Learning: A blended learning system combines face-to-face instruction with computer-mediated instruction (Graham, 2006).

Information Overload: Difficulties a person can have in understanding an issue and making decisions because they are presented with too much information.

Intrinsic Motivation: To be motivated means to be moved to do something. Hence, intrinsic motivation is to undertake an activity for its inherent satisfaction rather than because of external pressures, prompts or rewards (Ryan & Deci, 2000).

Problem-Based Learning: The essence of problem-based learning is characterised by the adage "involve me and I understand". It is student-centred, actively engaging the learners in constructing new knowledge, and reflecting upon their understandings, as well as developing skills and attitudes that inform the learning process and outcomes. It is learning centered on a problem, a query or a puzzle that the learner wishes to solve. It is an approach to curriculum which is problem-centered rather than discipline-centered with a focus on an integrated curriculum structured by 'real world' problems.

Linear Discussion Format: Linear discussion format does not allow branching and all notes are simply stored in a single, chronological order. WebCT Discussions™ allows for threaded or unthreaded display of notes, with the latter being a linear discussion format.

Social Presence: Is the ability of learners to project themselves socially and affectively in a community of inquiry (Rourke et al., 1999).

Chapter 8
Considerations for Effective Collaborative Practice:
A Reflection on the use of Case Studies in On-Line Teacher Education Learning Spaces

Donna McGhie-Richmond
University of Victoria, Canada

Eileen Winter
Institute of Child Education & Psychology Europe, Ireland

ABSTRACT

This chapter provides a retrospective review of the utility and effectiveness of case study analyses to engage and support students in online collaborative learning within teacher education coursework. Specifically, the interrelationship among factors related to the instructor, the student, the tasks, and the on-line learning environments are examined resulting in suggestions for designing, implementing, and researching case study learning activities that foster and enhance collaboration in online teacher education course work.

INTRODUCTION AND CONTEXT OF THE STUDY

The authors take a retrospective look at an online collaborative project carried out in a Canadian Faculty of Education over two academic years, 2003-2004. The initial collaboration (Winter & McGhie-Richmond, 2005) represented the first online collaborative work for the two faculty members and the students enrolled in two graduate special education courses. In each year, a course in collaborative consultation comprised of 20 experienced elementary and secondary school practitioners was involved. They are referred to as 'experts'. The second group was a cohort of 20 pre-service student teachers from the Master of Teaching (MT) programme in the faculty undertaking their special education module. Their in-school experience was confined to the practice teaching sessions required by their programme. This group is referred to as 'novices'. In each of the two years, the instructors established small

DOI: 10.4018/978-1-61692-898-8.ch008

groups (4-5 participants per group) combining experts and novices from the two courses to undertake special education case studies. It is important to note that both courses consisted of 12 face to face weekly evening classes of 3 hours for a total of 36 hours. The collaborative case studies constituted the assignment for each course. The facility of working online was *in addition* to the regular scheduled classes. The instructors had maximum autonomy and flexibility in terms of coursework and assignments providing these met the course objectives and were consistent with the university's quality assurance requirements.

The project revolved around two major questions articulated by Ethell and McMeniman (2000, p. 87). The first, "How best to prepare individuals for the complex and multifaceted profession of teaching…"; the second, "How can the knowledge of expert classroom teachers be made available to student or novice teachers if such knowledge is, to a large degree, unarticulated, tacit in nature, and grounded in experience?" (p. 88). Research suggests that expert teachers' knowledge is superior to that of novice teachers in both content and pedagogy (Livingston & Borko, 1989; Bereiter & Scardamalia, 1992; Sternberg & Horvath, 1995). It is essential that this knowledge, often referred to as 'practical knowledge' (Carter, 1990; Eraut, 1994; Fenstermacher, 1994), be passed on to new teachers to avoid the situation where, "the wheels of teaching have to be reinvented by each new generation" (Brown & McIntyre, 1995, p. 14). This is particularly relevant in this project where accessing the expertise of the experienced practitioners in the collaborative online context was key. In the context of special education courses and the current climate of inclusion this would seem to have particular resonance. Closing the gap between theory and practice remains one of the greatest challenges in teacher education.

The instructors believed that having the two cohorts collaborate on special education case studies could provide opportunities for:

- pre-service student teachers to access the 'practical knowledge' of the more experienced and more expert practitioners;
- the experienced cohort to practice and to develop their collaborative consultation skills;
- a collaborative, shared experience centered on a 'real world' classroom situation and designed to stimulate and develop higher-level critical and analytical thinking skills.

The intention was that the case studies should challenge the students to interact with and apply theory to everyday classroom situations. The rationale was based on the assumption that the most meaningful and long lasting learning takes place when the learners are involved actively in the learning process. The problem solving involved in collaboration requires active participation, with individual preparation and contributions towards the solutions. In case studies, there are many potential solutions that depend on the work of group members and on the collective choices made regarding how to proceed in resolving the case.

Both instructors were aware that web-based learning had increased in recent years and is regarded generally as an effective teaching and learning medium (Gerhing, 1994; Golberg, 1997; McCollum, 1997). Sustained asynchronous communication allows learners, distant in both time and place, to collaborate effectively in the social construction of knowledge (Jonassen, Davidson, Collins, Campbell, & Haag, 1995; Hiltz & Wellman, 1997). Web Knowledge Forum (WebKF), a web based collaborative knowledge building application and system, facilitated the online collaborative work (WebKF, 2000). Adding a web based component required considerable instructor collaboration to ensure that the aims of the respective courses were met and that the case studies presented meaningful learning experiences for the distinctly different student cohorts. The cases were selected from Hutchinson (1999, p. xiv), who provides samples taken from Canadian inclusive classrooms. This was extremely important contextually since cases "should provoke discussion of some of the important issues facing Canadian teachers". A framework for the case analysis process in written format, guidelines for preparing and submitting the written final report (see Hutchinson, 1999, pp. 2-7), plus criteria for evaluating the completed case studies were established for the participants. These guidelines provided a logical structure for discussions, as it was essential to specify what was expected during the collaboration. On completion of the project, all group members were required to sign off on the final submission as verification of their personal contribution to the case study, their work as team members, and their agreement with the written outcomes of the task. Participants completed regular university required course evaluations at the end of the courses, and also provided evaluative feedback on the case study process by way of a Plus, Minus, Interesting (PMI) inventory (DeBono, 1994). This is an attention-directing device to help individuals to organize their thinking into what they found to be positive, negative or just interesting about the project as a whole. Student quotes, selected from these evaluations, are included to illustrate the emergent issues.

Both instructors were highly experienced in the area of collaboration, cooperative learning and in the use of special education case studies as learning tools. However, neither was particularly experienced in the online aspect of the undertaking. This chapter examines the issues that emerged in relation to the use of case studies in the collaborative online venture. The authors place a retrospective lens on the project, raise a number of questions emerging from the original work and discuss these with reference to the current literature on online learning and the diverse strategies now utilized in online collaboration and specifically the use of case studies. Among the issues explored are those relating to monitoring of individual and collective learning and accountability; the role of the instructor in the interactive process; establishing a 'social presence' online; the challenge of developing a community of practice with relatively unfamiliar participants; and the value or otherwise of a face-to-face component.

The questions that frame the analysis are:

1. What student-related factors influence online collaborative case study work and the development of a community of practice?
2. What is the role of the instructor in facilitating participation and collaboration in case study analysis in an online environment?
3. What are the challenges related to online collaborative work relative to case study analyses?
4. In what ways does online collaborative case study work contribute to the development of teacher communities of practice?

The outcomes of this chapter include:

- Rationale for using online case studies to support student collaboration and the development of communities of practice;
- Student factors that can contribute to successful online collaborative work;
- Instructor factors to be considered in designing, implementing, and supporting online collaborative work with students; and
- Challenges inherent in online collaborative work relative to case study analyses.

BACKGROUND

Four broad topics merge in this initiative: collaboration, collaborating online, communities of practice, and case studies. Each is defined and discussed as it relates to the project.

Collaboration

Collaboration refers to a process or style of working that enables participants to work together on academic tasks. Friend and Cook (2009, p. 7) define collaboration as,

...a style for direct interaction between at least two co-equal parties voluntarily engaged in shared decision-making as they work toward a common goal.

Dennen (2000) asserts that collaboration can be used to develop critical thinking skills and states, "Through collaboration and socialization, students must listen, articulate, clarify, and negotiate in their quest to create meaning" (p. 329). Konstanidis, Tsiatsos, and Pomportsis (2009, p. 280) describe collaborative learning as,

...a general term used for the description of educational practices based on the simultaneous cognitive and mental effort of multiple students or/and educators.

Knowledge is generated in collaborative learning environments primarily through the relationships and interactions among the participants. As Palloff and Pratt (1999, p. 160) assert, "The importance of collaboration in achieving learning outcomes hinges on the group's ability to work with and respond to each other".

A critical component of any collaboration is the discussion that occurs during the task since the purported benefits must be mediated by the exchanges and interactions among the participants (Pressley & McCormick, 1995). Collaboration provides multiple opportunities for discussion, argument, negotiation, and reflection (Agostinho, Lefoe & Hedberg, 1997). According to Harasim (1989, p. 51), the learners are "involved in constructing knowledge through a process of discussion and interaction with learning peers and experts". The instructor becomes a facilitator of the students' construction of knowledge (Hiltz & Benbunan-Fich, 1997).

Collaborating Online

Online learning makes use of the Internet to,

...access learning materials; to interact with the content, instructor, and other learners; and to obtain support during the learning process, in order to acquire knowledge, to construct personal meaning, and to grow from the learning experience. (Ally, 2004, p. 5)

A major advantage of the online environment is the ability to work together where it might otherwise be impossible due to factors of distance and time (Hiltz, 1994). Considerable research points to the effectiveness of online collaboration (Bouras, Giannaka, & Tsiatsos, 2008; Dillenbourg, Baker, Blaine, & O'Malley, 1996; Veerman & Veldhuis-Diermanse, 2001) to support student interaction and learning. Projects, such as case studies, that require interaction among participants may be particularly suited to online work (Kirschner, Strijbos, Kreijns, & Beers, 2004; Tutty & Klein, 2008).

One of the most important considerations in designing online learning environments is "catering for communication and interaction between the participating students and educators" (Konstanidis et al., 2009, p. 281). Discussion forums have the potential to level the playing field wherein teachers and learners become equal participants in the interaction (Alvarez-Torres, 2001) and are typically student, rather than teacher-centered (Bump, 1990; Chun, 1994; Sullivan & Pratt, 1996; Warschauer, Turbee, & Roberts, 1996; Williams, Tanner, & Jessop, 2007). Discussion activities in particular are known to support student learning (DeWert, Babinski, & Jones, 2003; Ellis, Goodyear, Prosser, & O'Hara, 2006; Guzdial, & Turns, 2000).

Communities of Practice (CoP)

Lave and Wenger (1991) coined the phrase 'communities of practice' to describe groups of practitioners who share work, responsibility and knowledge. According to Wenger (2006), communities of practice consist of groups of people who share a concern or a passion for something they do and learn how to do it better as they interact regularly. Grossman, Wineburg, and Woolworth (2001) apply the term to an informal network of practitioners working together and engaged in a process of collective learning.

The essential element of a community of practice is that responsibility for learning is shared. Indeed, shared responsibility for participating, decision-making, resources, and accountability for outcomes are also fundamental characteristics of collaboration (Friend & Cook, 2009). Through sharing knowledge and skills, groups are able to accomplish more and, according to diSessa and Minstrell (1998), this leads to deeper understanding of content and processes for the group members.

Hull and Saxon (2009, p. 637) assert, "Human nature is to desire community, and when activities are aimed at fostering co-construction of knowledge, individuals in a group will use opportunities such as common problem-solving in attempts to establish community". Case studies provide opportunities for co-constructing knowledge and developing a community of practice within an online learning environment.

Case Studies

The success of collaboration requires a genuine purpose or goal that is meaningful to the participants (Agostinho et al., 1997; Friend & Cook, 2009). Case studies provide this clearly defined purpose for collaboration by utilizing authentic, real world tasks that require analytical and critical thinking skills, and a knowledge of theory and current research. They allow instructors to present real or hypothetical situations that require group analysis, discussion, and the use of concepts to make recommendations aimed at achieving a preferred solution (Benbunan-Fich & Hiltz 1999; Grabinger & Dunlap, 2002). The participants combine their skills and knowledge to identify and analyze the issues presented to create and evaluate possible solutions and pathways to action.

Case studies are used extensively in pre-service teacher education course work (Reichelt, 2000). Sudzina (1999, p. vii) claims that they have, "captured the imagination of educators". They represent an opportunity to bring real world issues to pre-service teachers and have the potential to involve participants in "those slices of life that illustrate a myriad of dilemmas from moral issues to classroom management" (Sudzina, 1999, p. vii). They offer participants an opportunity to expand and extend teaching skills and problem-solving abilities while offering opportunities to examine their grasp of contemporary issues, their perceptions and their misconceptions of educational dilemmas (Sudzina, 1999). Cases can bridge the gap between theory and practice and are particularly instructive in pre-service teacher education. Grabinger and Dunlap (2002, p. 24) reason,

Realistic problems hold more relevance to students' needs and experiences because they can relate what they are learning to problems and goals that they see every day. Therefore it encourages students to take ownership of the situation and their own learning....because the situations students encounter during learning are authentic and reflect the true nature of problems in the real world, it develops deeper and richer...knowledge structures leading to a higher likelihood of transfer to novel situations. Finally, because complex problems require a team approach that provides natural opportunities for learners to test and refine their ideas and to help each other understand the content, it encourages collaboration and negotiation.

Case studies help participants to understand how educational theory applies to classrooms. According to Sudzina (1999, p. vii), "Students also report increased satisfaction with their grasp of issues and the range of strategies explored to cope with life in schools". Using cases requires participants to,

> *...go below the surface of a situation – to probe into the presenting problem or problems to understand the deeper or more pervasive events of the case in order to offer solutions. Case method eschews immediate responses, facile answers, and single solutions. (Silverman, Welty & Lyon, 1996, p. xxi)*

Learning through cases is essentially constructivist as it is both an active and an interactive learning process (Gideonse, 1999). In collaborating participants interact with each other, with the material, and are required to test their own understandings and perceptions related to the case. Through discussing the issues presented, participants strive to bridge the gap between 'knowing' and 'doing' (Barnes, Christensen & Hansen, 1994).

Benbunan-Fich and Hiltz (1999) propose four fundamental principles involved in using case studies in teaching. These include situational analysis, participant involvement, non-traditional roles for instructors, and the relationship between analysis and action. Learning occurs through the participants' involvement and the collaboration with peers demanded by the case study method (Harasim, 1990). Group case presentation is, according to Benbunan-Fich (1997, cited in Benbunan-Fich & Hiltz, 1999) more enriching. The teamwork involved requires individuals to externalize their thought processes, contribute and defend their analysis, and to take account of alternate and possibly challenging perspectives. This has the potential to increase both learning and self-esteem potentially resulting in more positive attitudes towards learning (Salomon & Globerson, 1989). The collective process aims to develop a deeper understanding of the issues than would be achieved by an individual working alone (Silverman, Welty & Lyon, 1996). Exposing participants to alternative and sometimes challenging points of view can increase understanding and motivate learning (Glasser & Bassok, 1989). As used in teacher education, case studies typically illustrate 'teacher in action' where theory meets practice and pedagogical issues need to be resolved.

The steps for case study analyses outlined by Hutchinson (1999) provide structure and guide students through the process thus supporting the co-construction of knowledge while potentially nurturing reflective practice. The ambiguity that is often inherent in cases can promote a range of interpretations from students who typically have different backgrounds and experiences.

ISSUES

The questions and issues arising from the review of the initial project are broadly related to student, instructor, and task considerations. A framework that poses and responds to key questions, by drawing upon the research literature, is used. It will become apparent that the issues are highly interrelated and interdependent. Moreover, the issues do not fall neatly into categories of student, instructor, and task-related issues as initially anticipated. Rather, they are complex and interrelated and in many ways defy tidy categorization. Invariably, issues related to the student, instructor, and the task are evident in each response. Student quotes that are derived from the evaluations and student feedback received at the end of the respective courses are used to illustrate the issues.

Q1: What student-related factors influence on-line collaborative case study work and the development of a community of practice?

Two significant, inter-related factors emerged in the project: communication and social presence.

Communication

Communication in online collaborative learning is computer-mediated and often asynchronous, imposing challenges to the collaborative learning process (Rourke, Anderson, Garrison, & Archer,

2001; Garrison, Anderson, & Archer, 2001). Mäkitalo, Weinberger, Häkkinen, Järvelä, and Fischer (2005, p. 604) contend, "due to the novelty and the complexity of its social context, online collaborative learning courses can be regarded as a highly uncertain form of communication, in which learners may need additional support to reduce uncertainty". Uncertainty can occur at two levels: (a) socio-emotional, in which participants do not receive immediate feedback on how others react to their messages, whether they agree or disagree with individual suggestions, and how they will organize their joint work; or (b) epistemic, in which participants may be uncertain about the quality of their contributions (Mäkitalo et al., 2005).

Palloff and Pratt (2005, p.10) argue "students and faculty alike need to interact and communicate frequently as collaborative work ensues. There needs to be a shared responsibility for learning". The asynchronous nature of online exchanges may be problematic in certain instances where rapid responses are required (Clift, Mullen, Levin, & Larson, 2001; Curtis & Lawson, 2001; Conrad, 2002; Winter & McGhie-Richmond, 2005). Curtis and Lawson (2001, p. 22) point out:

Online interactions differ in quite important ways from face-to-face discussion. Online interactions lack the non-verbal cues that are a component of face-to-face contact, and this may reduce the extent of the communication that occurs. Much online conversation occurs asynchronously, with substantial delays in receiving a reply. This may have both advantages and disadvantages for the participants. The lack of spontaneity associated with a seminar group gathered around the one table may be offset by the possibility of having greater time for reflection and generation of a considered response.

As noted by students in the project, the advantage of having the class 'in session' potentially at all times may be offset if participants expect, but do not receive instant responses and reactions.

I had a problem waiting for people to respond. I wanted to get on with it in my own time (expert)

It is quite difficult to really 'discuss' when we are not all there at the same time (novice)

The absence of body language and eye contact was an issue for some experienced teachers who may be more accustomed to pupil and colleague presence, ongoing eye contact and clear body language.

Using the web emphasizes how dependent I am on reading a person's voice, expression or body language.... I had to make assumptions about the tone in which a comment might have been written (expert).

Face-to-face meetings at the beginning of the courses in the second year facilitated the initial development of community that, in turn, supported online collaborative work. Conrad (2002) report similar experiences.

In a 5-year case study of the evolution of a training course for teachers from face-to-face to the introduction of online collaborative learning, researchers found the quality of student group discussion and the richness of the analyses of the learning task to be far superior when completed online (Delfino & Persico, 2007). This was attributed to a number of factors including the lack of time constraints, automatic written record of interactions that favour reflection, critical thinking and analysis, as well as evaluation analysis. Other researchers share similar findings (Francescato, Mebane, Porcelli, Attanasio, & Pulino, 2007; Garrison et al., 2001; Meyer, 2003). Harasim (1990) argues that the increased time involved in asynchronous communication allows for more in-depth reflection and formulation of comments and suggestions. The asynchronous structure gives more time to articulate responses fully and thoughtfully than would be the case in a face-to-face class where responses to the discussion are expected quickly.

Social Presence: Contributing to Sense of Community

Gonzalez, Burke, Santuzzi, and Bradley (2003, p. 631) suggest that the most important difference between face-to-face and distance collaboration is,

...the presence or salience of social context cues. Within more traditional group settings, face-to-face interactions contain non-verbal information about the other group members (e.g. appearance, status differences, and tone of voice) that help people to regulate their own behaviour in terms of the group norms....Computer-mediated environments differ from traditional group settings in the amount and type of social and emotional information that is conveyed during group interaction, and, as a result, are likely to show differences in the manifestation and role of social-motivational aspects of group performance in comparison to traditional groups.

An important aspect of creating a virtual community appears to be the disclosure of personal information in ways that demonstrate membership of a particular group; these disclosures serve to reinforce the students' collective identity (Williams, Tanner, & Jessop, 2007). Anderson (2004, p. 274) explains social presence as,

...the establishment of a supportive environment such that students feel the necessary degree of comfort and safety to express their ideas in a collaborative context. The absence of social presence leads to an inability to express disagreements, share viewpoints, explore differences, and accept support and confirmation from peers and teacher.

A number of researchers refer to the 'social presence' that can be lacking in an online environment and its significant contribution towards developing a sense of community; a community that is critical for learning (Delfino & Persico, 2007; Francescato et al., 2007; Rovai, 2002; Williams, Tanner, & Jessop, 2007) and is foundational to developing and sustaining a community of practice (Grossman et al., 2001).

In this project, participants were asked to introduce themselves by providing information about their teaching experiences with students with special needs, their experiences working with a variety of professionals (e.g., speech language pathologists, psychologists, special education consultants, etc.) on school teams, and their experience in working in an online environment. They were also asked to share more personal information such as hobbies and interests.

Rovai (2002) provides evidence of a significant relationship between classroom community and perceived cognitive learning. Online learners who have a strong sense of community and perceive greater cognitive learning feel less isolated and have greater satisfaction with their academic programs, possibly resulting in fewer dropouts. He argues,

Increasing feelings of community should not only help reduce feelings of isolation....but should also increase motivation to learn and make available a larger set of resources in the form of other learners who can be called upon to assist learning... Such outcomes can promote cognitive learning, as suggested by the positive significant relationship between sense of community and cognitive learning found in the present study. (p. 328)

Subsequently, Rovai (2007, p. 81) stresses,

We must foster strong community through the quality and not exclusively the quantity of interactions. Consequently, a sense of community must be carefully and skillfully nurtured by the online instructor for students to achieve the full benefits of community membership in meeting their educational goals.

Developing relations in online collaborative work can be challenging, calling for adjustments in interactions that enhance the effectiveness of group work and learning. Delfino and Persico (2007, p. 9) argue,

All participants, especially trainees who are new to the method need to learn how to relate to others online in order to limit the drawbacks of written asynchronous communication and exploit its advantages, such as the fact that message persistency favours reflection on content and allows flexibility in time.

Critically important is creating a favourable online atmosphere, which can be challenging when participants make negative and inflammatory remarks within exchanges. The social cues inherent in face-to-face interactions that support communication and collaborative work are absent in an online environment. Further, the public and lasting nature of the interaction may be an issue for some students, as seen in this project.

I have to put my ideas up for all to see, so I have to think carefully (novice)

Everything we discussed was there to see…a little intimidating….hard to find just the right words especially when I did not agree (novice)

It is quite possible that they [the novices] have valid comments or concerns but lack the confidence to commit those comments to the WebKF for all to see (expert)

There is some evidence that while face to face and online environments both support the development of friendships, those friendships that are formed in online groups last longer and lead to more varied exchanges (Francescato et al., 2007). Francescato et al. (2007) hypothesize that the particular challenge and effort inherent in developing relations on-line in the absence of non-verbal cues may contribute to the endurance of those relations.

The asynchronous nature of computer-mediated learning need not be a barrier to student communication and learning. However, establishing a social presence among students is critical to communication and impacts interaction and ultimately learning in important ways. Moreover, the permanence of communication exchanges appears to favour student discussion, reflection and learning.

Q2: What is the role of the instructor in facilitating participation and collaboration in case study analysis in an online environment?

The instructor's role is pivotal in designing the course and the specific learning tasks that facilitate participation and collaboration. These include encouraging the use of the online tools and supports, and supporting active participation among all students, encouraging higher order thinking skills and facilitating learning in online forums (Kreber, 2001; McLoughlin & Mynard, 2009). Instructors working online must be skilled at presenting a positive, professional persona while creating a safe and supportive environment in which students feel competent, confident to participate, and feel that their contributions are valued. Students need to know that the instructor is accessible publicly, within the discussion forum, and privately via telephone or email. In this project each class also met face-to-face on a weekly basis. The instructors were, therefore, physically as well as virtually accessible and had opportunities to develop a rapport with the groups prior to the online case study portion of the courses.

Online discussions are the vehicle for completing the case study assignment and for developing the collaborative group processes that ensure effective communication and positive learning outcomes (Pressley & McCormick, 1995). Ensuring and promoting effective online discussion and co-construction of knowledge among all students is a primary role of the instructor. Hansford and Wylie (2001) recognize the complexities of issues that impact the success of online discussions and collaborations, indicating that bulletin board discussion activities in particular, are often ill defined or lack any real purpose for the students involved. Moore (1993) illustrates the complexity of managing effective discussions that lead to high levels of understanding and learning by suggesting three types or levels of interactions that occur; interaction with the materials; the instructor; and with peers. Online, there is an additional aspect that includes the interaction of all parties with a computer interface (Hansen, 1996 cited in Curtis & Lawson, 2001, p. 23). Research indicates that online tasks requiring critical thought and responses that include an opinion appear to attract a higher level of student response (Williams et al., 2007). Case studies can facilitate interactions by providing a purpose for collaboration: one that is highly meaningful for learners and supports the co-construction of knowledge, and development of community (Paulsen, 1995).

There is evidence that certain conditions need to be present in order for higher-order thinking to occur in online discussion forums, suggesting that the initial instructor prompt or question may have a bearing on the nature of student postings. McLoughlin and Mynard (2009) investigated higher-order thinking processes in online discussion forums revealing that the majority of the postings could be classified as 'exploration' or 'integration'. Hull and Saxon (2007) examined differences in co-construction of knowledge as well as social interaction as a function of providing different instruction techniques in asynchronous online courses. They found that co-construction of knowledge and the extent to which participants engaged in negotiating meaning were related directly to the instructions given. Relatively simple alterations in instructions, such as increasing instructional statements and using open-ended questions, yielded a substantially enhanced learning outcome within online learning. They conclude,

Online methods of instruction can ... be utilized effectively but appear to depend upon how well the teacher/instructor can establish a line of questioning that supports inclusion and targeted discussion with questioning that requires participants to bring new information to the group that is relevant based upon consideration of what others have already suggested. This kind of mediating activity begins with the instructor, and must continue to be supported by the instructor throughout the discussion (p. 636).

Instructor supports such as providing guiding questions to groups as they work appear to have little impact on the amount of student learning, but does influence the way students interact within the group (United States Department of Education, 2009). Guzdial and Turns (2000, p. 441) define effective discussion as: (a) sustained; (b) having broad participation; and (c) focused on course topics. They contend that these three goals are,

...important stepping stones toward effective computer-supported collaborative learning. Although meeting these goals does not, in itself, mean that learning is going on (collaboratively or individually); the existence of these three conditions in a discussion forum is suggestive that learning may be occurring.

Hansford and Wylie (2001) contend that instructors 'scaffold' discussion among students rather than direct it. Further, discussions that are 'anchored' are known to be more effective than discussions that are not (Guzdial & Turns, 2000; Williams et al., 2007). The kinds of anchors or prompts used to stimulate responses influence interaction and learning (Guzdial & Turns, 2000). Guzdial and Turns (2000) suggest three characteristics for designing anchors: (a) anchors should invite discussion; (b) the anchor's lifetime needs to be sufficiently long; and (c) the anchor (and the discussion) should be tied to the curriculum. The case study analysis framework used in this project (see Hutchinson, 1999) provided effective anchors for the participants and a framework for effectively scaffolding student analysis and responses. These included defining the issues of the case, analyzing the data inherent in the case, generating possible solutions and criteria, evaluating alternative solutions; and developing implementation plans.

Q3: What are the challenges related to online collaborative work relative to case study analyses?

Two particular challenges emerged in the project and are discussed under roles and responsibilities, and assessment.

Roles and Responsibilities

Although this is a highly 'student related' factor, roles and responsibilities emerged as a significant challenge. Collaborative work, either face-to-face or online, requires students to undertake roles and responsibilities requisite for successful completion and learning. Group processes significantly influence online collaborative learning (Gonzalez et al., 2003; Kirschner et al., 2004; Strijbos, Martens, Jochems, & Broers, 2007). The research literature reveals that defining roles and responsibilities is important, but that it be allowed to emerge in the group (McGrath & Hollingshead, 1994; Palloff & Pratt, 1999; Winter & McGhie-Richmond, 2005). Developing group processes early on in collaborative work is important and rather than pre-assigning roles and responsibilities, Palloff and Pratt (1999) suggest that guidelines and procedures should be free flowing and generated by the participants. They also stress the importance of group development early on before moving into content, and that groups should meet in person if possible.

The feedback from year one of the project suggested that the students wanted to meet with their groups prior to commencing the case studies. Organizing the two classes on the same evening in year two and having the groups meet on the first evening of the course facilitated this by providing opportunities for face-to-face interaction and group organization, while ensuring that participants received the same information about the project and expectations. This also supported the potential of developing a successful 'community of practice'. Participants were encouraged to use WebKF as their main means of collaboration, but it was not compulsory to do so. Mutual engagement in the collaborative process is fundamental to developing a community of practice. Our project experience attests to the significant role that even one face-to-face meeting can have on group processes and interactions.

There is some evidence that pre-assigning roles can be effective in supporting group interaction, as well as the quality of work. In online, project-based work, groups that are assigned functional roles aimed at promoting organization and coordination of activities are more coordinated and focused on the task (Kirschner et al, 2004). The researchers hypothesize that functional roles can provide social affordance for developing group cohesion and a sense of responsibility, as well as stimulating social interaction among group members. In follow up research, Strijbos et al. (2007) studied the effect of prescribed function roles instruction, compared to no instruction, on group performance and collaboration. The results reveal that roles are likely to affect the perceived level of group efficiency. Functional roles also increased task coordination and reported collaboration progress. Role groups reported more frequently than non-role groups that the agreements they made about tasks and deadlines stimulated progress. Overall, the results suggest that functional roles stimulate coordination and overall group efficiency in collaborative project-based online courses. Further, collective efficacy may engender task cohesion in online collaboration in groups and task cohesion may in turn mediate the effect of collective efficacy on group functioning (Gonzalez et al., 2003).

Lack of adequate leadership has been cited as one of the factors responsible for computer conferencing failure (Kerr, 1986 cited in Mason, 1991). In the first year of this project a specific leadership role and its associated responsibilities was assigned to the 'expert', experienced teachers. It was anticipated that they would undertake these roles effectively, with little adverse impact on the collaborative processes. However, this imposed leadership role appeared to be somewhat detrimental to the development of a collaborative learning community. A lack of understanding of the leadership role of the experts arose as an issue within some groups. Some novices perceived that the experts interpreted their leadership role as one of delegating work to the novices as revealed in the following comment.

I felt the experts in our group exploited us; they delegated an awful lot of the work but failed to do any themselves (novice).

As for the experts, there was some acknowledgement of the challenge they experienced in understanding and negotiating their leadership role.

This experience made me aware that what I consider collaboration may not always be that unless I make a conscious effort not to take over (expert).

Perceptions and beliefs such as these can interfere with the collaborative case study process and ultimately interfere with the development of a community of practice.

When the group members negotiated their own roles and responsibilities in year two, collaboration improved. It may be that there was perceived to be more parity among the participants when groups negotiated their own roles and responsibilities. As Friend (2000, p131) asserts,

Professional collaboration is not about 'like'; it is about respect. It has intrinsic value to the extent that professionals who have high regard for and better understand one another are more likely to take the risks involved in working together.

Assessment

The kinds of assessments that are used to evaluate student contributions and learning play a significant role in motivating students, supporting online collaborative work, and encouraging learning. MacDonald (2003, p. 378) explored the role of assessment with respect to both processes and products of online collaborative study stating, "In light of the new emphasis on a skills agenda in Higher Education, not only must the assessment be appropriate to the subject content of the course, it must also have an important role in supporting course pedagogy". MacDonald's findings underline the role of assessment in ensuring online participation, and in supporting the practice and development of online collaborative learning. Proficiency in the tools and software environment speeds up online participation, however, students must also learn how to interact online with peers. Further, the extent to which these peer-to-peer interactions contribute to their learning and understanding will vary with proficiency in online interaction. Competence in teamwork, negotiation skills, group-decision-making, and task management are essential in online collaborative work. MacDonald argues, "all these stages in the development of competence in online collaboration may need to be reflected in the design of the assessment, and how this is done will depend on initial assumptions on the competence of students at the start of the course" (p. 378).

One of the most significant challenges associated with collaborative work in any context arises with respect to assessment and evaluation, where grading and marks are concerned. In this particular project, the assessment scheme was articulated very clearly to the students prior to embarking on the case studies. The basic principles of group learning such as: individual accountability, mutual support, team building, and positive interdependence were reviewed carefully with the students. Positive interdependence was emphasized as it "promotes a situation in which individuals work together in small groups to maximize the learning of all members, sharing their resources, providing mutual support, and celebrating their joint success" (Johnson, Johnson, & Holubec, 1998, 4:6).

Group and individual efforts were recognized with marks assigned as follows:

- A group assessment for the completed case study
- A individual self assessment focusing on one's personal contribution to the project;

- Peer assessment based on the in-class presentation of the case studies; and
- An individual mark given by the instructor based on the completed written case study.

While the instructors could track contributions on-line, individual accountability was further addressed by requiring all group members to sign off on the final case study submission as verification of their personal contribution to the study, their work as team members, and their agreement with the written outcomes of the task. There was also an emphasis on individual reflection on contributions and group processes as fundamental to the group and learning. In the course feedback, although not mentioned specifically by the students in relation to marks, there were some concerns expressed around the levels of participation. Some participants perceived that some members of their group did not contribute as much as others. This issue is common to group work, highlighting a challenge for instructors in designing and facilitating online collaboration.

Q4: In what ways can online collaborative case study work contribute to the development of teacher communities of practice?

Online collaborative case studies that focus on the dilemmas of teaching provide education students with opportunities to work together towards understanding and eventually resolving teaching dilemmas. Case studies support pre-service teachers in further understanding the classroom context in the absence of extensive experience. Case studies provide graduate-level teachers with opportunities to examine dilemmas that they may have experienced in their practice. Working jointly provides opportunities to share knowledge, perspectives, and experiences and to develop relationships resulting in a community of practice.

The foregoing discussion of issues and challenges reveals that the manner in which collaborative case study work is organized and supported can enhance or interfere with the development of a community of practice.

RECOMMENDATIONS

The issues that arose in the project are addressed by providing recommendations based largely on the initial experience, subsequent retrospection, and the literature that has been reviewed. The recommendations are framed, in general, by the questions addressed in this chapter.

A Community of Practice

The project was set within the framework of developing a community of practice where groups of teachers and teacher candidates share work, responsibility and knowledge. Online case studies provide a vehicle for shared focus and enable a community of practice to develop. Student related factors such as communication and social presence are critical components of developing a community of practice, as are aspects of the instructor role.

Communication in an online learning environment is paramount to establishing and maintaining collaborative relationships that contribute positively towards developing communities of practice. It is recommended that guidelines and rules for interactions and for the frequency of communication be articulated clearly at the beginning of projects. Adequate time needs to be provided for asynchronous online discussion. These steps can decrease the complexity and increase the certainty of communications, minimize the effects of asynchronous communication, and optimize time and productive collaborative work.

Establishing and developing a social presence online is critical. Students should share introductions that reveal both professional and personal experience and interests. These provide opportunities for the participants to connect. Guidelines ensure maximum and relevant information is shared that will support the development of social presence and reduce isolation. Information elicited can be tailored specifically to the course content, goals, and activities. Note that social presence continues to develop in the regular communications and interactions that occur throughout the course within the context of the learning activities as well as social chat features.

Instructors play a role in acknowledging and facilitating student connections by providing forums specifically for social-emotional interactions among students. The use of emoticons (e.g. ☺) and paralanguage (e.g., hmmm, 'Yup'), self-disclosure, humour, praise, invitations, greetings, acknowledgements social sharing, and personal advice are known to support social presence in online learning environments (Swan, 2003). Instructors should share and model these communication tools in interactions with the students.

Instructors play a prominent role in terms of accessibility and in facilitating student learning by prompting and responding to the communications that are occurring among the students. While instructors do not typically lead the discussion in online collaborative case study work, they are responsible for establishing the conditions under which collaborative work can occur. The steps inherent in case study analysis provide a framework for instructors to provide anchors or prompts that promote student discussion leading to higher order thinking and learning.

Rovai (2007) proposes a framework emphasizing the dual instructor roles of designer and facilitator. The framework emphasizes the role of the instructor as both a designer of the online learning environment and a facilitator of student interactions in online collaborative work. His suggestions address the issues of social presence; social-emotional, content and task-related discussions; and facilitating student-to-student interactions that will help build a community of practice among students. Our project experiences attest to the utility of Rovai's suggestions.

Challenges

During the course of the project some specific challenges arose. The most significant of these were related first, to roles and responsibilities in a collaborative venture and second, to the assessment of student work.

Online collaborative case study work requires explicating the role of team functions and communication at the outset of the work. It cannot be assumed that all participants will know how to work optimally and effectively on the case study, let alone within an online learning environment. It is recommended that specific guidance be provided that focuses on the nature and importance of collaborative team work, accountability, and how to collaborate effectively online. In reviewing the project over the two years, on balance, the recommendation in relation to roles and responsibilities is to allow these to be negotiated within each group at the start of the case study work. Spending time discussing the roles and responsibilities and individual accountability of team members is necessary to highlight and smooth this process for the participants. Accountability is fundamental to collaborative work and the relevancy of the task is also paramount. As Shepperd (1993) suggests, free riding or loafing can be reduced if participants find the case studies to be highly relevant, their contributions are clearly identified and they can see how their efforts contribute to the solutions.

Assessment is fundamental to student motivation, engagement, and learning. It is recommended that online collaborative case study work be closely connected to assessment. Clear assessment criteria tied to interaction processes as well as products of case analyses are recommended. Studies show that more students will participate in online collaborative activities if they are linked to assessment, and that such assignments may also have a positive effect on the quality and number of postings (MacDonald, 2003). Student assessment is traditionally focused on course content and is highly individualized; however, online collaborative case study work provides an ideal opportunity to develop collaborative processes and skills. It is recommended that instructors consider the products and processes of online collaborative case study work which involve both individual and group effort. It is recommended that this be reflected in the assessment with respect to the weighting of the evaluation. A portion of student evaluation should be allocated to assessment that focuses on the team collaborative process. In some respects an online learning environment is favourable to face-to-face collaboration for studying and developing collaborative processes. The written dialogue provides participants with opportunities to review and reflect on their postings and subsequent responses. Moreover, the written record provides evidence of the collaborative process that can be examined and reflected on as part of the assessment process. It is also important to consider that this type of assessment may require additional time and effort that needs to be acknowledged and accounted for.

The examination of the issues that arose in this project relative to current research reveals the prominence of student collaboration and the role it plays in developing knowledge and a community of practice as a pedagogical technique as well as a research focus.

FUTURE RESEARCH DIRECTIONS

MacDonald (2003, p. 378) asserts, "If we can acquire some understanding of how online collaboration takes place, then it becomes easier to plan ways of supporting students to achieve competence". Further research is needed to understand the complexity and utility of online collaborative case study work in teacher education programs. A primary area for attention is examining the quality of interactions among participants, including the instructor, in online collaborations and the effect on students' construction of knowledge and the development of communities of practice.

Rovai (2007) and others (see Garrison, Anderson, & Archer, 2000; Garrison & Anderson, 2003) call for further research examining the relationship between student learning and computer-based technologies used in online learning environments. The role of social factors and their impact on social construction of knowledge, and student learning outcomes are not well understood and models are needed. Rovai (2007) proposes a model for conceptualizing and researching online discussions. Two interrelated components are suggested: (a) course design to create a constructivist learning environment, and (b) the use of the design to facilitate online discussions. Rovai's model holds promise for conceptualizing online collaborative case study work in teacher education for the purposes of designing and implementing online course work, as well as researching the student, instructor, task, and technology factors that interact and contribute to effective online teacher education.

Delfino and Persico (2007) also call for further research investigating the development of relations online, particularly when and how patterns of social climate evolve and the factors that may contribute to insincerity and the consequent impact on group discussion.

Guzdial and Turns (2000) suggest developing theory related to discussion anchors, the prompts and cues that instructors use to encourage and support student interaction. They argue, "Such a theory would help an instructor with the task of integrating the tool into their classes because the creation of anchors is one task associated with integration" (p. 465). Hull and Saxon (2009) also call for research examining the role of instructor strategies that encourage and support dialogue among and higher level thinking skills within participants in online collaborative work.

There continues to be little research that explores the use of collaborative case study analysis in online teacher education programs. The ability to collaborate is an essential skill for all teachers, especially in today's inclusive classrooms. Case study analyses provide an authentic learning context described by one novice as,

...like working with real children...at last!

Collaborative case study analysis provides a rich methodology for developing a community of practice among educators. Conducting such analyses online provides opportunities to explicate and examine the collaborative processes among participants. In particular, further research is needed that explores the interactive patterns between novice and expert teachers and how instructors can facilitate interaction to optimize learning and community of practice. Moreover, online collaborative case studies provide instructors with opportunities to highlight and research collaboration as important and worthy of study in teacher education.

CONCLUSION

This chapter reviewed the utility and effectiveness of case study analyses to engage and support students in online collaborative learning within teacher education coursework. The use of case studies in teacher education is well established; doing them collaboratively online less so. Case studies provide a defined purpose and structure for collaboration by using authentic, real world tasks that involve analytical and critical thinking skills and a knowledge of theory and current research. Instructors present situations that require group analysis, discussion, and collaboration to reach satisfactory outcomes.

Our review suggests that the online collaboration in relation to the case studies can contribute to the development of communities of practice. In both years of the project, groups came together to share work, responsibility and knowledge as suggested by Lave and Wenger (1991). The groups engaged in problem solving, discussing issues and questions, seeking help, and sharing assets and resources. Although the 'communities' involved in this project came together for coursework purposes, there is significant potential for similar groups to come together online to discuss special education issues related to their day to day practice. As one participant stated,

This is the only time we have had any input on collaborating with other teachers....We should be doing this all the time....It is what we will be doing in schools. (novice)

Online learning is an effective option for the induction of new teachers and ongoing professional development with experienced practitioners. The student related issues such as asynchronous communication and establishing online social presence are not unfamiliar and may be overcome as participants become accustomed to the medium. The loss of face-to-face dialogue can be challenging and does require a change on the part of the participants and the instructor. However, as Fullan (1993, p. 24) points out "...change is a journey, not a blueprint". He contends that with any change comes uncertainty, learning, anxiety, difficulties, and fear of the unknown but with eventual success, "there are great highs, ecstatic feelings of accomplishment, and moments of great satisfaction and well being" (p. 25). Collaborating online may challenge some of the traditional assumptions about teaching where the learner has to be present physically. Even though the participants were at a distance, the project demonstrates, "The importance of collaboration in achieving learning outcomes hinges on the group's ability to work with and respond to each other" (Palloff & Pratt, 1999, p. 160).

As with any teaching and learning endeavour, the instructor's role is critical. This project required a significant shift from traditional face-to-face teaching, well established over many years, for the instructors. It was a sharp learning curve, one that continues to this day. In commenting on both teachers and learners, Naidu, Barrett and Olsen (2000, p. 121) suggest,

Learners shift from being passive receptacles to being active participants in the search for knowledge....they learn to acquire and use knowledge, and instructor-roles shift from dispensers of information to producers of environment which allow learners as much as is possible on given topics.

In conclusion, internet-based discussion forums are now common practice in many university classes (Guzdial & Turns, 2000). In our project the case studies enabled novice and more expert teachers to work together on real world tasks that required their skills and knowledge to complete. The online collaboration allowed the groups to 'meet', to share ideas and to work together towards an appropriate solution. It brought together novice and expert teachers for the purpose of developing their knowledge and skills in special education. There is, currently, a major focus on inclusion in schools worldwide and collaborations such as this can provide teachers with opportunities to access the knowledge of their colleagues in ways that will be beneficial for all.

Post-Script

In their current institutions, both authors continue to expand their work with online teaching. Their ongoing experiences validate the issues that have been discussed in this chapter. Each strives to ensure that all courses provide high quality online opportunities that maximize student participation and collaboration. The authors are 'guests' on each other's courses and interact asynchronously with the students some 7300 kilometers away and with an 8-hour time difference.

REFERENCES

Agostinho, S., Lefoe, G., & Hedberg, J. (1997). *Online collaboration for effective learning: A case study of a postgraduate university course.* Retrieved September 14, 2009, from http://ausweb.scu.edu.au/proceedings/agostinho/paper.html

Ally, M. (2004). Foundations of educational theory for online learning. In Anderson, T., & Elloumi, F. (Eds.), *Theory and practice of online learning* (pp. 3–31). Athabasca, AB: Athabasca University.

Alvarez-Torres, M. (2001). *On 'chatting' in the foreign language classroom.* Clearing House Item 00098655, 74(6), 313–316.

Anderson, T. (2004). Teaching in an online learning context. In T. Anderson & F. Elloumi, (Eds.). *Theory and practice of online learning.* Retrieved April 9, 2010, from http://www.cde.athabascau.ca/online_book/

Barnes, L., Christensen, R., & Hansen, A. (1994). *Teaching and the case method.* Boston, MA: Harvard Business School Press.

Benbunan-Fich, R., & Hiltz, S. R. (1999). Educational applications of CMCS: Solving case studies through asynchronous learning networks. *Journal of Computer Mediated Communication Studies, 4* (3) March 1999. Retrieved July 15, 2009, from http://jcmc.indiana.edu/vol4/issue3/benbunan-fich.html

Bereiter, C., & Scardamalia, M. (1992). Cognition and curriculum. In Jackson, P. (Ed.), *Handbook of research on curriculum* (pp. 517–542). New York: Macmillan.

Bouras, C., Giannaka, E., & Tsiatsos, T. (2008). Exploiting Virtual Environments to Support Collaborative E-Learning Communities. *International Journal of Web-Based Learning and Teaching Technologies, 3*(2), 122.

Brown, S., & McIntyre, D. (1995). *Making sense of teaching*. Buckingham, UK: Open University Press.

Bump, J. (1990). Radical changes in classroom discussion using network computers. *Computers and the Humanities*, *24*(1-2), 49–65. doi:10.1007/BF00115028

Carter, K. (1990). Teachers' knowledge and learning to teach. In Houston, W. R. (Ed.), *Handbook of research on teacher education* (pp. 291–310). New York, NY: Macmillan.

Chun, D. (1994). Using computer networking to facilitate the acquisition of interactive competence. *System*, *22*(1), 17–31. doi:10.1016/0346-251X(94)90037-X

Clift, R. T., Mullen, L., Levin, J., & Larson, A. (2001). Technologies in context: Implications for teacher education. *Teaching and Teacher Education*, *17*(1), 33–50. doi:10.1016/S0742-051X(00)00037-8

Conrad, D. (2002). Deep in the hearts of learners: Insights into the nature of online community. *Journal of Distance Education*, *17*(1), 1–19.

Curtis, D. D., & Lawson, M. J. (2001). Exploring collaborative online learning. *Journal of Asynchronous Learning Networks*, *5*(1), 21–34.

de Bono, E. (1994). *Parallel thinking: from Socratic thinking to de Bono thinking*. Middlesex, UK: Viking.

Delfino, M., & Persico, D. (2007). Online or face-to-face? Experimenting with different techniques in teacher training. *Journal of Computer Assisted Learning*, *23*, 351–365. doi:10.1111/j.1365-2729.2007.00220.x

Dennen, V. P. (2000). Task structuring for online problem based learning: A case study. *Journal of Educational Technology & Society*, *3*(3), 329–336.

DeWert, M. H., Babinski, L. M., & Jones, B. D. (2003). Safe passages: Providing online support to beginning teachers. *Journal of Teacher Education*, *54*(4), 311–320. doi:10.1177/0022487103255008

Dillenbourg, P., Baker, M., Blaye, A., & O'Malley, C. (1996). The evolution of research on collaborative learning. In Spada, E., & Reiman, P. (Eds.), *Learning in Humans and Machine: Towards an interdisciplinary learning science* (pp. 189–211). Oxford, UK: Elsevier.

diSessa, A., & Minstrell, J. (1998). Cultivating conceptual change with benchmark lessons. In Greeno, J., & Goldman, S. (Eds.), *Thinking practices in mathematics and science learning* (pp. 155–188). Hillsdale, NJ: Lawrence Erlbaum.

Ellis, R. A., Goodyear, P., Prosser, M., & O'Hara, A. (2006). How and what university students learn through online and face-to-face discussion: Conceptions, intentions, and approaches. *Journal of Computer Assisted Learning*, *22*, 244–256. doi:10.1111/j.1365-2729.2006.00173.x

Eraut, M. (1994). *Developing professional knowledge and competence*. London, UK: Falmer Press.

Ethell, R. G., & McMeniman, M. M. (2000). Unlocking the knowledge in action of an expert practitioner. *Journal of Teacher Education*, *51*, 87–101. doi:10.1177/002248710005100203

Fenstermacher, G. D. (1994). The knower and the known: The nature of knowledge in research on teaching. In Darling-Hammond, L. (Ed.), *Review of Research on Teaching* (*Vol. 20*, pp. 3–56). Washington, DC: American Educational Research Association.

Francescato, D., Mebane, M., Porcelli, R., Attanasio, C., & Pulino, M. (2007). Developing professional skills and social capital through computer-supported collaborative learning in university contexts. *International Journal of Human-Computer Studies*, *65*, 140–152. doi:10.1016/j.ijhcs.2006.09.002

Friend, M. (2000). Myths and misunderstandings about professional collaboration. *Remedial and Special Education, 21*(3), 130–132, 160. doi:10.1177/074193250002100301

Friend, M. & Cook, (2009). *Interactions: Collaboration skills for school professionals*. (6th ed.). Toronto, ON: Pearson Education.

Fullan, M. (1993). *Change forces: Probing the depths of educational reform*. London, UK: Falmer Press.

Garrison, D. R., & Anderson, T. (2003). [st *century: A framework for research and practice*. London, UK: Routledge Falmer.]. *E-learning*, ▪▪▪, 21.

Garrison, D. R., Anderson, T., & Archer, W. (2000). Critical inquiry in a text-based environment: Computer conferencing in higher education. *The Internet and Higher Education, 2*(2–3), 87–105.

Garrison, D. R., Anderson, T., & Archer, W. (2001). Critical thinking, cognitive presence, and computer conferencing in distance education. *American Journal of Distance Education, 15*(1), 7–23. doi:10.1080/08923640109527071

Gehring, G. (1994). A degree program offered entirely online: Does it work? In D. Foster and D. Jolly (Eds.), *Proceedings of the Third International Symposium on Telecommunication in Education* (pp. 104-106), November 10-13, Albuquerque, New Mexico.

Gideonse, H. D. (1999). What is a case? What distinguishes case instruction? In Sudzina, M. (Ed.), *Case study applications for teacher education* (pp. 1–7). Boston: Allyn & Bacon.

Glasser, R., & Bassok, M. (1989). Learning theory and the study of instruction. *Annual Review of Psychology, 40*, 631–666. doi:10.1146/annurev.ps.40.020189.003215

Golberg, M. (1997). CALOS: First results from an experiment in computer-aided learning for operating systems. In *Proceedings of the ACM's 28th SIGCSE Technical Symposium on Computer Science Education. SIGCSE, 29*(1), 48-52.

Gonzalez, M. G., Burke, M. J., Santuzzi, A. M., & Bradley, J. C. (2003). The impact of group process variables on the effectiveness of distance collaboration groups. *Computers in Human Behavior, 19*, 629–648. doi:10.1016/S0747-5632(02)00084-5

Grabinger, R. S., & Dunlap, J. C. (2002). Problem-based learning as an example of active learning and student engagement. *Lecture Notes in Computer Science Vol. 2457, Advances in Information Systems* (375-384). London, UK: Springer Verlag.

Grossman, P., Wineburg, S., & Woolworth, S. (2001). Toward a theory of teacher community. *Teachers College Record, 103*(6), 942-1012, Retrieved September 3, 2009, from http://www.tcrecord.org/Content.asp?ContentId=10833

Guzdial, M., & Turns, J. (2000). Effective discussion through a computer-mediated anchored forum. *Journal of the Learning Sciences, 9*(4), 437–469. doi:10.1207/S15327809JLS0904_3

Hansford, D., & Wylie, A. (2001). *Evaluating online collaborative learning: A case study in increasing student participation*. Retrieved July 21, 2009, from http://scs.une.edu.au/CF/Papers/pdf/Hansford.pdf

Harasim, L. (1989). Online education: A new domain. In Mason, R., & Kaye, T. (Eds.), *Mindweave: Computers, communications and distance education* (pp. 50–62). Oxford, UK: Pergamon Press.

Harasim, L. (Ed.). (1990). *Online education: Perspectives on a new medium*. New York, NY: Praeger-Greenwood.

Hiltz, S. R. (1994). *The virtual classroom: learning without limits via computer networks*. Norwood, NJ: Ablex Publishing Corporation.

Hiltz, S. R., & Benbunan-Fich, R. (1997). Supporting collaborative learning in asynchronous learning networks. Invited keynote address for the *Symposium on Virtual Learning Environments and the role of the Teacher.* Milton Keynes, England April 28th,1997. Retrieved July 12, 2009, from http://web.njit.edu/~hiltz/CPProject/unesco.htm

Hiltz, S. R., & Wellman, B. (1997). Asynchronous learning networks as a virtual classroom. *Communications of the ACM, 40*(9), 44–49. doi:10.1145/260750.260764

Hull, D. M., & Saxon, T. F. (2009). Negotiating of meaning and co-construction of knowledge: An experimental analysis of asynchronous online learning. *Computers & Education, 52*(3), 624–639. doi:10.1016/j.compedu.2008.11.005

Hutchinson, N. L. (1999). *Teaching exceptional children and adolescents: A Canadian casebook.* Scarborough, ON: Prentice Hall Allyn & Bacon Canada.

Johnson, D., Johnson, R., & Holubec, E. (1998). *Cooperation in the classroom.* Boston, MA: Allyn & Bacon.

Jonassen, D., Davidson, M., Collins, C., Campbell, J., & Haag, B. B. (1995). Constructivism and computer-mediated communication in distance education. *American Journal of Distance Education, 9*(2), 7–26. doi:10.1080/08923649509526885

Kirschner, P., Strijbos, J., Kreijns, K., & Beers, P. J. (2004). Designing electronic collaborative learning environments. *Educational Technology Research and Development, 52*(3), 47–66. doi:10.1007/BF02504675

Konstanidis, A., Tsiatsos, T., & Pomportsis, A. (2009). Collaborative virtual learning environments: Design and evaluation. *Multimedia Tools and Applications, 44*, 279–304. doi:10.1007/s11042-009-0289-5

Kreber, C. (2001). Learning experientially through case studies: A conceptual analysis. *Teaching in Higher Education, 6*(2), 217–228. doi:10.1080/13562510120045203

Lave, J., & Wenger, E. (1991). *Situated learning: Legitimate peripheral participation.* Cambridge, UK: Cambridge University Press.

Livingston, C., & Borko, H. (1989). Expert-novice differences in teaching: A cognitive analysis and implications for teacher education. *Journal of Teacher Education, 41*(1), 36–41. doi:10.1177/002248718904000407

Mäkitalo, K., Weinberger, A., Häkkinen, P., Järvelä, S., & Fischer, F. (2005). Epistemic cooperation scripts in online learning environments: Fostering learning by reducing uncertainty in discourse? *Computers in Human Behavior, 21*, 603–622. doi:10.1016/j.chb.2004.10.033

Mason, R. (1991). Moderating educational computer conferencing. *DEOSNEWS,* 1(19). Retrieved April 9, 2010, from http://www.emoderators.com/papers/mason.html

McCollum, K. (1997). A professor divides his class in two to test value of online instruction. *The Chronicle of Higher Education, 43*(24), A23.

McDonald, J. (2003). Assessing online collaborative learning: Process and product. *Computers & Education, 40*(4), 377–391. doi:10.1016/S0360-1315(02)00168-9

McGrath, J., & Hollingshead, A. (1994). *Groups Interacting With Technology.* Thousand Oaks, CA: Sage.

McLoughlin, D., & Mynard, J. (2009). An analysis of higher order thinking in online discussions. *Innovations in Education and Teaching International, 46*(2), 147–160. doi:10.1080/14703290902843778

Meyer, K. A. (2003). Face-to-face versus threaded discussions: The role of time and higher-order thinking. *Journal of Asynchronous Learning Networks*, *7*(3), 55–65.

Moore, M. (1993). Three types of interaction. In Harry, K., John, M., & Keegan, D. (Eds.), *Distance education: new perspectives*. London, UK: Routledge.

Naidu, S., Barrett, J., & Olson, P. (2000). Improving instructional effectiveness with computer-mediated communication. In Squires, D., Conole, D., & Jacobs, G. (Eds.), *The Changing Face of Learning Technology*. Cardiff, UK: University of Wales Press.

Palloff, R. M., & Pratt, K. (1999). *Building learning communities in cyberspace: Effective strategies for the online classroom*. San Francisco, CA: Jossey-Bass.

Palloff, R. M., & Pratt, K. (2005). *Collaborating online: Learning together in community*. San Francisco, CA: John Wiley & Sons, Inc.

Paulsen, M. F. (1995). *The Online Report on Pedagogical Techniques for Computer-mediated Communication*. Retrieved July 3, 2009, from http://www.nettskolen.com/forskning/19/cmcped.html

Pressley, M., & McCormick, C. B. (1995). *Advanced educational psychology for educators, researchers, and policymakers*. New York, NY: Harper Collins.

Reichelt, M. (2000). Case studies in L2 teacher education. *ELT Journal*, *54*(4), 346–353. doi:10.1093/elt/54.4.346

Rourke, L., Anderson, T., Garrison, D. R., & Archer, W. (2001). Methodological issues in the content analysis of computer transcripts. *International Journal of Artificial Intelligence in Education*, *12*(1), 8–22.

Rovai, A. P. (2002). Sense of community, perceived cognitive learning, and persistence in asynchronous learning networks. *The Internet and Higher Education*, *5*(4), 319–332. doi:10.1016/S1096-7516(02)00130-6

Rovai, A. P. (2007). Facilitating online discussions effectively. *The Internet and Higher Education*, *10*(1), 77–88. doi:10.1016/j.iheduc.2006.10.001

Salomon, G., & Globerson, T. (1989). When teams do not function the way they ought to. *The Journal of Educational Research*, *13*(1), 89–100. doi:10.1016/0883-0355(89)90018-9

Shepperd, J. A. (1993). Productivity loss in performance groups: A motivation analysis. *Psychological Bulletin*, *113*(1), 67–81. doi:10.1037/0033-2909.113.1.67

Silverman, R., Welty, W. M., & Lyon, S. (1996). *Case studies for teacher problem solving* (2nd ed.). New York: McGraw-Hill.

Sternberg, R. J., & Horvath, J. A. (1995). A prototype view of expert teaching. *Educational Researcher*, *24*(6), 9–17.

Strijbos, J., Martens, R. L., Jochems, W. M. G., & Broers, N. J. (2007). The effect of functional roles on perceived group efficiency during computer-supported collaborative learning: A matter of triangulation. *Computers in Human Behavior*, *23*(1), 353–380. doi:10.1016/j.chb.2004.10.016

Sudzina, M. (1999). *Case study applications for teacher education*. Boston, MA: Allyn & Bacon.

Sullivan, N., & Pratt, E. (1996). A comparative study of two ESL writing environments: A computer-assisted classroom and a traditional oral classroom. *System*, *29*(4), 491–501. doi:10.1016/S0346-251X(96)00044-9

Swan, K. (2003). Developing social presence in online course discussions. In Naidu, S. (Ed.), *Learning and teaching with technology: Principles and practices* (pp. 147–164). London, UK: Kogan Page.

Tutty, J. I., & Klein, J. D. (2008). Computer-mediated instruction: A comparison of online and face-to-face instruction. *Educational Technology Research and Development*, *56*(2), 101–124. doi:10.1007/s11423-007-9050-9

U.S. Department of Education. (2009). *Evaluation of evidence-based practices in online learning: A meta-analysis and review of online learning studies*. Washington, DC: Office of Planning, Evaluation, and Policy Development. Retrieved September 3, 2009, from http://www.ed.gov/about/offices/list/opepd/ppss/reports.html.

Veerman, A., & Veldhuis-Diermanse, E. (2001). Collaborative learning through computer-mediated communication in academic education. In P.Dillenbourg, A. Eurelings, & K. Hakkarainen(Eds.), *Proceedings of the 1st European conference on computer-supported collaborative learning. European perspectives on computer-supported collaborative learning* (pp.625-632). Maastricht, the Netherlands: University of Maastricht Press.

Warschauer, M., Turbee, L., & Roberts, B. (1996). Computer learning networks and student empowerment. *System*, *24*(1), 1–14. doi:10.1016/0346-251X(95)00049-P

WebKF (Web Knowledge Forum). (2000). *Information and demo at the World Wide Web*. Retrieved January 4, 2010, from http://www.knowledgeforum.com

Wenger, E. (2006). *Communities of practice: A brief introduction*. Retrieved August 15, 2009, from http://www.ewenger.com/theory/

Williams, A., Tanner, D., & Jessop, T. (2007). The creation of virtual communities in a primary initial teacher training programme. *Journal of Education for Teaching*, *33*(1), 71–82. doi:10.1080/02607470601098336

Winter, E., & McGhie-Richmond, D. (2005). Using computer conferencing and case studies to enable collaboration between experienced and novice teachers. *Journal of Computer Assisted Learning*, *21*, 118–129. doi:10.1111/j.1365-2729.2005.00119.x

ADDITIONAL READING

Conrad, R., & Donaldson, J. A. (2004). *Engaging the online learner: Activities and resources for creative instruction*. San Francisco, CA: Jossey-Bass Publishers.

KEY TERMS AND DEFINITIONS

Assessment: The process of measuring student knowledge, skills, and attitudes.

Asynchronous Communication: Communication that occurs by way of the computer where the sender and the receiver are engaged in the communication at different times, that is, not concurrently.

Case: Study: Real-world scenarios that present dilemmas commonly found in teacher education practice

Collaboration: A style or manner of interacting and communicating with people

Communities of Practice: The social learning and socio-cultural practices that emerge when people with shared goals work together to achieve those goals

Online Learning: Learning that takes place through interacting with materials and people by way of the computer

Chapter 9
Using the Four Lenses of Critical Reflection to Promote Collaboration and Support Creative Adaptations of Web 2.0 Tools in an Online Environment

Katia González-Acquaro
Wagner College, USA

Stephen Preskill
Wagner College, USA

ABSTRACT

This chapter offers an in-depth narrative of how one instructor in an online environment used the four lenses of critical reflection introduced by Brookfield (1995) – (1) self, (2) student reactions, (3) colleagues' perceptions, and (4) instructional theory – to adapt the use of Web 2.0 tools that have been found to be effective in promoting collaboration and constructivist learning. These tools can provide educators with the opportunity to examine collaboration and learning from multiple perspectives, while also serving as a way to rethink preconceived notions of how power is distributed in the classroom (Brookfield, 1995). In this chapter the authors share how the four lenses were used to design Web 2.0 activities based on the specific grouping techniques, with the aim to construct a rich online experience.

INTRODUCTION

The use of a theoretical framework in the development and implementation of learning activities for adult learners in a variety of classroom settings is not new. Concepts such as helping students become critical thinkers, collaborators, reflective practitioners are often mentioned in the literature (Brookfield, 1987; Mezirow, 1991) as essential for instructors to consider when thinking about instructional methods and materials that will increase students' opportunities to be "producers of knowledge" (Scardamalia & Bereiter, 2003, p.1307) and not just passive learners.

DOI: 10.4018/978-1-61692-898-8.ch009

The challenge becomes how to "get students on that trajectory… in which knowledge is socially constructed, and best supported through collaborations designed so that participants share knowledge and tackle projects that incorporate features of adult teamwork, real world content, and the use of varied information sources" (Scardamalia & Bereiter 2003,p. 1370).

Over ten years ago, Jonassen (1996) introduced the idea that computer applications should be seen as powerful "Mindtools" that can help learners become skilled at "scaffold[ing] different forms of reasoning about content" (Jonassen, Carr, & Yueh, 1998, p.24). Jonassen, et al. (1998) argued that by reframing computer technologies as Mindtools that represent a "constructivist view of technology," learners can become actively engaged in "interpreting the external world and reflecting on their interpretations" (p. 28). More recently, Jonassen, Howland, Marra, and Crismond (2008) explained that by seeing knowledge building as a social enterprise in which learners utilize instructional technologies as collaborative "construction tools," learners are then able to increase shared knowledge that takes full advantage of the multiple perspectives found in any diverse group. Getting learners to engage in shared knowledge in an online learning environment can often be a challenge. Yet without such engagement the education of learners is frequently shortchanged. As Brookfield and Preskill (2005) have noted, "without broad participation, students do not get the practice in expressing their ideas cogently, and the group lacks the diversity of opinions it needs" (p. 234). Building on this literature, the present chapter tells the story of one instructor's efforts to employ Brookfield's 4 critical lenses to better harness the power of Web 2.0 tools with her students and promote the sort of rich, collaborative class participation that can result in deeper, more meaningful learning. Drawing on data culled from instructor self-reflection, student feedback, peer dialogue, and scholarly literature, an online community emerged that students experienced as not only broadly participatory, but also both intellectually engaging and productively collaborative.

BACKGROUND

National trends indicate that distance-learning courses in higher education are rapidly proliferating (NCES, 2008). The increasing availability of information technology coupled with the various needs of traditional and non-traditional students are shaping the extent to which credit and non-credit distance learning courses are viable options (Lim, Kim, Chen, & Ryder, 2008). Definitions of what constitutes distance learning have also evolved. According to a report by NCES (2008) distance education is " …defined as a formal education process in which the student and instructor are not in the same place. Thus, instruction may be synchronous or asynchronous, and it may involve communication through the use of video, audio, or computer technologies, or by correspondence (which may include both written correspondence and the use of technology such as CD-ROM)" (p.1).

Faculty interested in incorporating distance learning opportunities into their classes are often challenged by limited knowledge of software usage and technical requirements, as well as lack of opportunities to clearly establish a connection between learning goals, and technological environments and tools utilized (Notar, Wilson, & Montgomery, 2005). The difficulties inherent in learning about the tools can often hinder the inclusion of best instructional practices and limit the development of materials that can foster critical thinking skills and classroom discourse and collaboration.

Jonassen (2006) explained how "concepts are the basis for meaning making and communication"…and how "communicating without concepts is impossible" (p. 177). But he also described how research on instructional technology has often focused on the attainment of these concepts and variables affecting concept learning but not necessarily how they are being formed and utilized. Jonassen (2006) argued concepts should not be learned in isolation, but must be connected to the real world problems that individuals actually grapple with, and that they should use those concepts to address those problems on both an individual and collective level. This interplay between concepts in the abstract and in everyday life enables a more "complex and problem-centered learning environment" (p. 179). When thinking about "concepts in use" (Jonassen, 2006, p. 179) and the benefits of collaborative practices, the idea of "collective cognitive responsibility" comes to mind (Scardamalia, 2002, p. 68). Scardamalia (2002) expressed how adult learners bring "distinctive roles and skills" to a learning environment and how "collective cognitive responsibility" requires learners to have the "responsibility for the success of a group effort…distributed across all members rather than being concentrated in the leader" (p. 68). Faculty members interested in facilitating classroom discourse and collective cognitive responsibility must recognize that there will be some decentering of their role as authority figures, thus leading to a redistribution of power in the learning environment, as they utilize Web 2.0 tools, data driven user centered web applications that facilitates online collaborative activities (O'Reilly, 2005), to enhance Computer Supported Collaborative Learning (CSCL). In some cases, this may mean that some students assume an inordinately large instructional role that must be monitored and adjusted to give all students an opportunity to be in the teaching role.

Some of the main challenges in the inclusion of Web 2.0 tools to enhance CSCL appear to be in areas that can assist faculty with transferable skills that can inform practice to enhance pedagogy. Finnegan (2006) expressed this dilemma while conducting research in the area of technology and higher education. He found that most results were not "generalizable" relevant only "for a particular course or program" and did not inform efforts to improve teaching in general (p. 144). "Used well, technology can assist institutions in providing student-centered, assessment driven courses; but it cannot replace effective teaching by qualified faculty" (p. 144).

Brookfield (1995) challenged educators to adopt a critically reflective perspective which requires them to examine how power in the classroom undermines equity and participation and obliges them to question assumptions that get in the way of productive learning. The excitement and availability of a plethora of online collaborative tools should always be utilized within the context of a reflective framework that will allow faculty to explore not only the value of a tool or strategy for a particular assignment but also how its usage affects the classroom environment and the "transformational" process of a faculty's pedagogy (Finnegan, 2006).

To aid instructors in the process of challenging certain pedagogical perspectives, Brookfield (1995) urges us to adopt multiple lenses. These lenses include listening to students' experiences, getting feedback from colleagues, consulting relevant literature, and interrogating our individual experiences as teachers and learners. Employing these lenses rigorously, our teaching becomes more democratic and we "create conditions under which all voices can be heard…and in which educational processes are seen to be open to genuine negotiation" (Brookfield, 1995, p.44).

Brookfield and Preskill (2005) have claimed that teachers who prize democratic discussion must adopt a critical stance toward their pedagogical practices which opens them up to a diversity of perspectives and encourages them to use techniques to increase participation and enhance learning. Prensky (2001) reinforces this point when he notes that because online learners bring an unusually varied set of styles and expectations to their classes, faculty are obligated to adapt to those styles and expectations with a broad array of pedagogical approaches.

There are proven collaborative techniques such as small group discussion, jigsaw, and peer review that are often utilized by faculty to elicit a more powerful and collaborative learning environment. The selection of sound pedagogical strategies coupled with careful consideration of materials, such as the usage of Web 2.0 tools, can contribute to achieving shared knowledge and a higher level of mutual understanding. One leading example of such tools are Google Docs, which can provide a powerful way to increase knowledge building and promote collaboration by encouraging users to create documents that can be accessed by others for revising and viewing (Van Horn, 2007). Rheingold (2006) has noted, "When we expose our decisions to others, and they reciprocate, the aggregation of our decisions creates a new resource" (¶ 2). Similar to Google Docs, wikis allow users to collaborate on creating web pages (Hazari, North, & Moreland, 2009). Both technologies have Mindtool properties in that they allow users to model knowledge promotion, edit documents collaboratively, and foster both informational accuracy and collective knowledge building. Jonassen, et al. (2008) write that these environments allow for a great deal of critical analysis as students "evaluate the ideas being co constructed" (p 107). Finally, blogs and podcasts are an important addition to the growing list of Mindtools that can be fruitfully employed by online instructors to promote collective knowledge building. In the case of blogs, as Williams and Jacobs (2004) have pointed out, there is a sense of community among bloggers that can be reproduced in the classroom that encourages a socially constructed "warehousing of captured knowledge" (p. 233). Podcasts, too, which are roughly equivalent to audio or video blogs, are not just useful enhancements to lessons, but can be employed even more potently to broaden learners' project-based learning (Jonassen, et al, 2008).

THE HEART OF THE MATTER: USING THE FOUR LENSES OF CRITICAL REFLECTION

Using Web 2.0 tools to promote meaningful and collaborative learning requires that the instructor have a framework to continuously monitor and improve the course environment. Brookfield's (995) "critical reflective process" in which instructors view the classroom through four lenses proved to be a robust approach to ensuring a quality learning environment, as this case study will demonstrate. This section of the chapter is organized according to the framework of the four lenses in which the instructor used the perspectives of self, students, colleagues, and the scholarly literature to examine, critique, and improve teaching.

The first lens of autobiography, or self, is explored through the instructor's journal reflections. The journal recorded all aspects of the class, but especially what the instructor felt as she participated in the class, how actively and engagingly the students seemed to be responding to the class's activities, and what it was like for her as a learner, as well as the instructor, to be part of this class. The second lens of student reactions was captured through frequent use of the Critical Incident Questionnaire (CIQ) developed by Brookfield (1995). Regularly, students were asked to respond anonymously to the following five questions: (1) When were you most engaged? (2) Most distanced? (3) Most affirmed? (4) Most surprised? and (5) Most puzzled or confused? Students also commented briefly on the usefulness of the tools and the instructor provided feedback on adaptations that were made based on their responses. These reactions were analyzed and shared with the class, and the instructor solicited suggestions for how the class should be changed or the tools further adapted. The third lens of colleagues was documented through a journal kept of regular conversations between the instructor and an online teaching expert, which included the expert's feedback, ideas, suggestions, and critiques. Finally, the fourth lens of the theoretical literature was utilized by the instructor of this chapter to bring a more critical, generalized, and scientific perspective to these specific teaching experiences.

A Case Study: Practitioner's Voice

When given the opportunity to develop and implement online courses for the summer the first author, who was also the instructor of the 4-week asynchronous online graduate education course that is the focus of this article, was ecstatic. She wanted to create courses that were engaging, in which students could collaborate with her, share ideas, examine real life situations, and carefully consider different points of view in the literature, while also using materials and strategies that her current and future teachers could take back to the field. Carefully considering the needs of adult learners has always guided her practice...what she refers to as "knowing who your audience is" and ongoing written and oral reflections have always been instrumental in decisions made about her courses. When she read Brookfield's (1995) *Becoming a Critically Reflective Teacher* the way practice was viewed through different lenses made perfect sense. Armed with Brookfield's critical lenses as her theoretical framework, she secured the assistance of an expert colleague in the area of technology and education to dialogue with, started to carefully search for readings related to the topic, and began her journal, excerpts of which are represented in this text in italics.

Even before the class began, students had many questions about what was expected of them. Additionally, their questions seemed to reflect a rather limiting and individualistic view of how an online class might be organized. Questions such as this one suggested a lockstep, assignment by assignment approach: "Dr. K, are the summer online classes going to be confined just to readings and questions to which I will respond?" Or questions like this one similarly reflected a highly regulated and linear organizational method: "Are online classes going to be a PowerPoint and a follow-up quiz?" As she listened to some of the questions being posed by students, she realized that many viewed online learning as a very independent endeavor, not necessarily a collaborative one, and she was intent on making sure that the experience that they had online was similar to the ones they experienced during face to face interactions.

The use of Brookfield's four lenses proved to be critical to the development and implementation of the activities that were selected for each week. The opportunity to view the classroom from all the different perspectives reflected aspects that would not have been anticipated ordinarily. She also noticed that Brookfield's lenses did not influence her in a linear way but that each lens had an impact on the other lenses cumulatively over time, making it hard to conclude which lens was having the greatest impact on her practice.

Special Note: The next section of this article is the narrative description of what happened on a week-by-week basis in this 4-week asynchronous online graduate education course in the area of curriculum theory and design. This online course was taught at a liberal arts college in New York. A total of 15 students were involved and one of the students registered for the online course was 40 years old and the rest were between the ages of 22 and 30 years old. The first author of this article, the sole instructor of the course, will narrate her experiences using the first person.

Week One

The focus for week one was to build a sense of community while also considering the structure of the sessions. Conversations with colleague P and a review of the literature indicated that students often experience feelings of "isolation" (Stewart, 2008) lack of "self-direction" (Hsu & Shieve, 2005) and confusion about technical tools. This disorientation is often mentioned as a challenge in distance education courses and that can easily contribute to increased "attrition rates" (Hyllegard, Deng, & Hunter, 2008). Thinking about Brookfield's (1995) words "Of all the methods available for changing how we teach, putting ourselves regularly in the role of the learner has the greatest long term effects" (p. 50), I realized that I only had a small window of opportunity to create a sense of community and clarity. It was thus critical to get to know the students, create an environment of open communication in which everyone's perspectives is valued to prevent students from dropping out of the course, owing to online disorientation, before getting a chance to learn about its potential benefits. Knowing that utilizing collaborative grouping techniques and infusing Web 2.0 tools to enhance the collaborations was a key to success, I was careful not to overwhelm students with my own excitement about the tools. I needed to carefully consider how to coordinate the introduction of each tool, while sustaining interaction between students.

Realizing how having a sense of community would probably be a key factor in being able to provide all learners with opportunities to feel comfortable discussing their overall learning experience, I chose to have students answer an open ended question about their interests to help them get to know one another. This sense of community and type of discussion has always worked during face to face classes but with an online environment only lasting four weeks and with a good amount of content needing to be covered, I had to make sure a connection was built from the beginning while also providing a way to model online interactions. I had recently returned from a professional gathering in which some participants lamented the "oversimplification" of some online discussions in which students are often asked to answer what some regard as trivial personal questions. With these experiences in mind, I inserted these reflections in my journal. *"Getting to Know you- Am I oversimplifying my first class session?- " There is so much content I need to cover in what really appears to be little time, but I want to get to know my students in order to tailor the class to meet their needs. The idea of discussions with "meaning" and the value of personal stories. I strongly believe that taking time during a class session to build community does not take from the overall learning experience but creates closeness within groups. What may seem as oversimplification of discussions to me it is a way to show students that in this class we value personal stories, hobbies, ideas, dreams everyone brings- plus this can help all of us when trying to make connections from theory to practice- "authentic connections". In my own experiences taking online classes, it was this connection that made me eagerly want to share perspectives, agree and disagree with peers and enter into healthy debates.*

This activity of posing an open-ended question helped me learn more about the students and was extremely helpful when creating collaborative groups that were not homogenous. As Reeves (2009) has noted, "The lack of personal relationships in the context of Web 2.0 is a problem because of the high level of trust needed between content contributors and users" (p. 87). Thus, one of the keys to successful online classes is maintaining close personal relationships with students. Without them, the trust needed to have frank and open conversations cannot be built. Furthermore, discussions with P, my reflective colleague, encouraged me to create that connection making sure students were able to feel my presence as the instructor and the value of their collective experiences and comments. This is further noted by Klobas and Haddow (2000) who have found that when learners share personal information with one another they are able to establish identities in online environments that are distinctive and powerfully human.

P and I also discussed the need to carefully consider how to introduce the different tools to be utilized. It was decided that technical tools would be better off explained session by session, bringing them into use gradually in the course to avoid feelings of confusion or the possibility of being overwhelmed. We also sought to take into account different learning styles and to ensure that instructions were written and also given in an audio/video format. By introducing the tools slowly, there was also more of an opportunity to practice using the tools and lessen feelings of helplessness prior to introducing the course content. In addition, P suggested scheduling ongoing live office hours via Chat to provide assistance as needed.

Because Moodle, the course management system of the college was being utilized, I wanted to make sure I was able to work with what was available while adding tools that could easily complement the structure already in place. I needed to consider the fact that many of the Web 2.0 tools were new for me as well and if something happened the technical support of the college could be accessed. When thinking about the selection of tools to utilize with grouping techniques, I came across an article in which the authors discussed computer attitudes and ability of pre service teachers infusing technology into their practice. Lambert and Cuper (2008) explained how "limited exposure to technology integration" (p. 387) or courses in which technology was not utilized for " critical thinking" or "problem solving skills" can negatively affect the perception of the value of the tool in the learning process (p. 387).

My autobiography as a learner and teacher highlighted the fact that I valued giving my students problem based activities to complete in a collaborative way. The literature corroborated the need to focus on problem based learning activities in which different perspectives must be taken into account. The use of collaborative grouping in problem solving activities can provide learners with the opportunity to "represent the problems they are solving in more than one way" while carefully considering the fact that "problem solving is too often proceduralized" (Jonassen, 2003, p. 364). The availability of Web 2.0 tools to create mental models for "multiple representations" is an important consideration since collaborative grouping can get different perspectives across "connecting the problem to domain understanding" (Jonassen, 2003, p. 367) while a Web 2.0 tool can aid learners in creating mental models that can help bring all the ideas together. P encouraged me to go ahead and use the forum for domain knowledge (to exchange ideas) and Web 2.0 tools such as Google Docs as a place for students to work specifically on the problem assigned. These were two separate tools – forum and Google Docs - that worked well individually and also combined. Peer review collaborative grouping technique using the Forum was a good way to help students respond to each other's perspectives about the concepts covered in class in a written form, while the addition of video podcasts provided an opportunity for students to have access to an "observational tool" to serve as a model of what was being highlighted during class. P suggested Google Docs as a way for students to complete the assignment because all students could organize their learning in one place, edit their work responding to each other's writing, while also giving the instructor an opportunity to see the history of the involvement of each member of the group. I started forum discussions by asking an open-ended question related to the materials being covered and by also asking students to respond to a comment made by a peer. Table 1 provides information about week 1. Although all of the grouping techniques and tools utilized were helpful, receiving specific comments from the students in the Critical Incident Questionnaire (Table 2) affirmed their value while helping me consider week 2 groupings, materials, and tools (Table 3).

Week Two

"I feel a bit worried about switching group members for this week's assignments. During week 1 everyone worked so well together in their groups...the midterm is approaching, but I do not want students to get too comfortable in their groups and perhaps miss out on the perspectives

of others. I know a jigsaw group has worked in my face-to-face classes but creating one online? Could that be a recipe for disaster in terms of stressing my students by changing the structure of the course?" As a facilitator for this learning environment, I started week two with a better sense of how students were feeling about the learning environment, tools and grouping techniques that were utilized during week one. As noted in my journal entry, however, I was a bit concerned about introducing a new technique and tools now that most had overcome their initial struggles and were finally feeling comfortable with the online format. Comments from students such as those below made me aware that students appreciated the use of the tools on their own and in combination with the grouping techniques, but that how they were introduced had to be carefully considered:

- " I think I got fully engaged once I learned how to use Google Docs, and realize how great communication is now that we can work together through the internet"
- " The group assignment was difficult, but I was eager to learn how this would be possible"
- " I was having some difficulties with using Moodle so intensely, I am coming along slowly and probably by the time I get it down the course may be over☺ "

One student, in response to actions that were most affirming or helpful said " When Dr. K can easily reply to a message of yours in a matter of a few minutes at anytime" was affirming but a comment made by one student "needing direct feedback" made me aware of the need to create additional opportunities for individual feedback. I noted in my journal *"I am happy students feel I am there for them.. but I need to make sure students can continue to rely on each other as a "learning community" for feedback in case I am not able to*

Table 1. Using the four lenses of critical thinking to plan week one

Focus for Week One: Building Community			
Self	**Student**	**Colleague**	**Theory**
What helped me feel connected as a learner during distance learning? • Clarity and flexible structure • Connection to members of the group • Collaboration=Healthy Debates • Understand how to use all the tools and requirements • Place to communicate with others and ask questions if needed Implications on how I teach: Emphasis on learners getting to know one another Discussion groups (small and large). Clear organization and structure of activities Problem Based Learning to Build Community (Engagement)	Anonymous way to provide feedback using CIQ	Technical tools: Should the technical tools be explained together or not? Detract from content? Overwhelm/Confuse students which can affect attrition rates? Tools/groupings Learning Styles: Audio, Video and Written descriptions Communication: "Live" virtual hours	Attrition rates a big concern Tools: Self-efficacy of students Isolation-Lack of Self-Direction Confusion Emphasis on tools and not pedagogy Multiple representations-problem solving-mental models
Design Decisions for Week One- What the lenses reflected back			
Collaborative Grouping Selection Peer Review (responding to writing from peers)		**Tools to be Utilized** Forum (discussion) Google Docs (Web 2.0) Video Podcasts (Web 2.0) Chats (live office hours) Reading Assignments (theory and practice)	

Table 2. Critical incident questionnaire (CIQ) results from week one

At what moment in class were you most engaged as a learner?
5 students mentioned the readings, video podcasts and project- Showing process, found concepts interesting. 5 students mentioned the forum- Giving and receiving feedback 5 students mentioned the Google Docs Group Project assignments- Believed working collaborative online was a positive experience, great communication with Google Docs, group project was difficult but eager to learn, helped interactions, made me check back often.
At what moment in class were you most distanced as a learner?
1 student did not feel distanced 1 student mentioned group project being challenging with work schedule. 1 student mentioned difficulty of finding time to complete all the readings 3 students mentioned when starting out, learning new aspects of technology-figuring out how to use different items. 3 students mentioned the first session 1 student mentioned the i-Tunes video 3 students mentioned Google Docs- feeling confused 1 student mentioned the immediate thought of doing a group project 1 student mentioned needing direct feedback.
What actions from anyone in the forums did you find most affirming or helpful?
4 students mentioned positive environment- Replies for peers, constructive criticism 3 students mentioned correspondence/responses and feedback from professor- Insight provided- positive feedback reassuring, shows she wants to be there as much as possible for students, fast replies 4 students mentioned forum- everyone being helpful about what to do next when confused, insightful, fast responses to questions, helpful to have disagreement about views/different perspectives. 2 students mentioned leadership displayed by other students- Being able to share knowledge with others less experienced with the topic 1 student mentioned everyone's actions to be most helpful- every individual showing different concepts to what we are working on. 1 student mentioned positive feedback in the introductions forum.
What event surprised you the most?
5 students mentioned Google Docs- Now feeling comfortable using tool, seeing the finished product and everyone's role in completing it, easiness of working as a group without meeting face to face. 1 student mentioned the different backgrounds and educational interest of the class- Felt that it made collaboration and class more interesting. 4 students mentioned being able to do group work online/receiving an assignment to do group work- The idea seemed impossible/all worked out. 2 students mentioned helpfulness of everyone in the class. 2 student mentioned nothing- Everything was straightforward. 1 student mentioned listening to professor's voice/audio file.
What actions from anyone in the forums did you find most puzzling or confusing?
1 student mentioned students using multiple email addresses for Google Docs assignment 9 students mentioned nothing – Clear, calm and friendly personalities 1 student mentioned speaking over the internet and not in person/impersonal 1 student mentioned miscommunication in forum- "simply because it is the first time a lot of people are using online resources for group work" 2 students mentioned responses in the forum- A discussion means different opinions 1 student mentioned Google Docs.
Response from students about the helpfulness of tools to help with the online learning environment
Forums, video podcasts and Google Docs received the highest rankings as a tool Chats received the lowest ranking as a tool
Adaptations that were made to the second week of classes based on feedback from the first week.
Due dates directions/time for group projects/forums and larger assignments changed from noon to 11:55 PM to accommodate schedules. Virtual office hours after work times. Forums questions only -due Mondays- remained due at noon because of the additional days to complete. Continued the use of video podcasts in additional sessions and collaborative activities combined with readings and forum discussions.

Table 3. Using the four lenses of critical rhinking- eeflecting on CIQs of week one to plan week two

<table>
<tr><th colspan="4">Focus for Week Two: Individual Accountability and Group Goals</th></tr>
<tr><th>Self</th><th>Student</th><th>Colleague</th><th>Theory</th></tr>
<tr><td>What helped me as a learner when responsible for sections of projects as well as group final outcomes?
• Availability of materials
• Space to organize
• Self regulation
Implications on how I teach:
Clear directions
Relevant materials-up to date
Provide purpose of activity
Individual responsibility toward group goals
Shared knowledge and "collective cognitive responsibility"</td><td>Anonymous way to provide feedback CIQ
Use of video podcasts and forums
Readings connected to activities
Challenge of students using multiple email addresses when using Google Docs
Due Dates
Virtual Office Hours After Work Times to Ask Questions
Need for "direct" individual feedback.
Web 2.0 tool appreciated –found useful for the learning process</td><td>Wikis allows users to collaborate and see who is contributing</td><td>Self regulation
Evaluation of individual and group contributions.
Editing/viewing capabilities</td></tr>
<tr><th colspan="4">Design Decisions- What the lenses reflected back</th></tr>
<tr><td colspan="2">Collaborative Grouping Selection
Jigsaw Method (engage with course materials- and one another)
Inclusion of individual assignments to complement group work and provide direct/individual feedback</td><td colspan="2">Tools to be Utilized
Forum (discussion)
Wiki (Web 2.0)
Video Podcasts (Web 2.0)
Chats (Live Office Hours)
Reading Assignments (theory and practice)</td></tr>
</table>

answer right away." The pacing of the introduction of these tools had to be closely monitored, while providing examples of how these tools and techniques could help their daily practice.

I chose to start session one of week two not only providing feedback to students about the CIQ results but also explaining the selection of the grouping techniques by describing their purpose and the rationale behind their selection. Adult learners especially need to see the connection between the techniques and tools they use and their daily lives.

Based on the results of the CIQ for week one, I kept the forum as a main place for discussion of the materials, video podcasts to show "process", while sustaining interest with readings and assignments that were current and collaborative in nature. Students mentioned feeling "most engaged during the forums where we had the chance to interact with classmates, particularly when we were introducing ourselves during the first class session. It was enjoyable to give and receive feedback from classmates during forum assignments." I felt that by always having certain pieces in place, students would feel a sense of comfort in the environment and perhaps be open to the new techniques and tools. The challenge mentioned by the student who worked late into the evening was taken into consideration by extending "live" office hours using the Chat forums of Google Mail (having afternoon and late evening office hours times) and by extending assignment due dates to 11:55 PM to allow students who work in the afternoon to complete assignments in a timely manner.

Using the lens of autobiography, I reflected on how it was helpful for the students to have opportunities to become an expert in a particular subject and then to have a forum to share ideas that built upon their initial knowledge. These types of activities were helpful in the self-regulation of study habits and readiness for presentations, a topic mentioned as a challenge in distance learning. As a teacher, creating opportunities for students to experience individual accountability toward the "collective cognitive responsibility" (Scardamalia, 2002, p. 68) is important and the jigsaw method was a great way to model this behavior. Here is how Brookfield and Preskill (1999) describe it: "Teachers and students begin by generating a short list they would like to study. Each student becomes an "expert" on one of these topics... in discussion with other students who are experts on the same topics...Once all members of each group have mastered their chosen subject, they form a second set of small groups containing one representative from each of the expert groups" (p. 141).

P suggested utilizing a wiki to complement the grouping technique because the students wanted to develop an online study guide for the midterm and he felt that this tool, while having similar properties to Google Docs (collaborative editing), was a more "open" environment (no need to invite people to join, more of an open resource) which was a perfect match to the collaborative technique of jigsaw. Just as others have found, I used wikis with some success to foster effective collaboration, strengthen community, and encourage students to participate in a group-based effort to construct understanding and create new knowledge

When reviewing the literature, one of the challenges of using a wiki was the "organic nature of

Table 4. Critical incident questionnaire (CIQ) results from week two

At what moment in class were you most engaged as a learner?
3 students mentioned the forums- Applying our reading to critical thinking responses, forums engaging, viewpoints 1 student mentioned reading the textbook 9 students mentioned the assignments 2 students mentioned the video podcasts- Pointing out some great points.
At what moment in class were you most distanced as a learner?
4 students did not feel distanced 6 student mentioned challenge of completing assignment 3 students mentioned the readings. 2 students mentioned feeling nervous about the upcoming midterm.
What actions from anyone in the forums did you find most affirming or helpful?
12 students mentioned feedback from peers- Assistance in helping finding solutions to an issue, quick responses, when members of the class respond to something I have written in the forum, whether to agree or disagree, everyone is helpful and interactive, affirming-pointing out skills that I had forgotten to mention, learning the materials different ways, constructive criticism. 3 students mentioned professor's feedback- constructive criticism, receiving detailed feedback on activity seeing the red marks on the documents helped me see what I can do to enhance activity, examples you provided helped me feel at ease in crating my own.
What event surprised you the most?
6 students mentioned jigsaw activity 3 students mentioned nothing surprised them 1 student mentioned quick responses received. 3 students mentioned individual activities helped understand the process. 2 students mentioned how well the group work turned out. Easiness of using the tool
What actions from anyone in the forums did you find most puzzling or confusing?
13 students mentioned nothing was puzzling of confusing 1 student mentioned how one group created their study guide 1 student mentioned the assignment
Response of students about the helpfulness of tools to help in the online learning environment.
Forums, video podcast and wikis received the highest rankings as a tool Chats received the lowest ranking as a tool.
Adaptations that were made to the third week of classes based on feedback from the second week.
Continuation of the use of collaborative tools, forums, and collaborative grouping assignments in which students could build upon individual knowledge by having different viewpoints

wikis which allows anyone to add anything, which can lead to a chaotic information space" (Ficther, 2005, p. 48). Taking this into consideration, I realized that the course management system provided opportunities for groups to be created in visible ways allowing each group to have a wiki of their own that they could edit while being able to view everyone else's. The final result was wikis that were well developed, clear, and a good resource for students. It was apparent that students in their groups gave pointers on how study guides should be developed and created, which could be taken as a sign that students were comfortable giving each other feedback on their work.

Responses to the second week of CIQ's indicated that students appreciated the assignments and use of a wiki to develop a study guide collaboratively while acknowledging the helpfulness of the structure. Students appeared to find the materials interactive and helpful to their understanding of the concepts (Table 4) and comments from the CIQ were considered when planning week 3 (Table 5).

Week Three

Results from week two of the CIQ's indicated that students appreciated working on an individual activity while also having the opportunity to collaborate and contribute to an assignment. When students are involved in problem based learning activities, they are being challenged to "seek solutions to real life problems" (Duch, Groh, & Allen 2001) while thinking "critically and analytically" (Duch et al., 2001) about their learning. In week three, a project based learning activity was introduced with group discussion as the collaborative technique in order for students to provide a representation of what has been learned while being able to integrate theoretical and practical information. "The core idea of project based learning is that real world problems capture students' interest and provoke serious thinking as the students acquire and apply new knowledge in a problem solving context" (David, 2008, p. 80). Utilizing the four lenses revealed that having the opportunity to learn by doing while having real world applications for projects could be an excel-

Table 5. Using the four lenses of critical thinking reflecting on CIQs of week two to plan week three

<table>
<tr><th colspan="4">Focus for Week Three. Learning by Doing</th></tr>
<tr><th>Self</th><th>Student</th><th>Colleague</th><th>Theory</th></tr>
<tr><td>What helped me as a learner when developing higher order thinking skills?
• Problem Based and Project Based Learning
Implications on how I teach:
Discussion instrumental
Need for connection to "authentic experiences"
Grouping considerations
Midterm needed?</td><td>Anonymous way to provide feedback CIQ
Value of individual contributions toward group's goals
Video Podcasts
Forums essential
Readings</td><td>Interactive/virtual tours for community resources (websites)- "Authentic experiences"
Video podcasts(observational tools)
Blogs</td><td>Project based learning supports higher order thinking skills
Authentic Experiences/Real Life Application
Discussion</td></tr>
<tr><th colspan="4">Design Decisions- What the lenses reflected back</th></tr>
<tr><td colspan="2">Collaborative Grouping Selection
Group Discussion (project based learning)</td><td colspan="2">Tools to be Utilized
Forum (discussion)
Blogs (Web 2.0)
Video Podcasts (Web 2.0)
Chats (live office hours)
Reading Assignments (theory and practice)
Websites</td></tr>
</table>

lent way for students in the class to demonstrate their ability to utilize higher order thinking skills. "Common characteristics associated with active learning include the use of higher level thinking and engagement of students in activities that encourage exploration and subsequent evaluation of their involvement" (Williams & Chinn, 2009, p.166). The use of discussion as a collaborative grouping technique was considered essential for this activity since "Developing students' capabilities to cooperate, communicate, and make decisions is a critical task" (Huo, 2007, p. 237).

P explained that the use of blogs and video podcasts to bring in more authentic real life applications toward the project could facilitate the engagement of the students toward the activity. Providing students with the opportunity to carefully examine local community resources and relevant materials through the use of readings, video podcasts, and blogs was seen as a way to create "intentional engagement" (Graffam, 2007) in order to immerse students in their work.

"I want students to have all these different resources in order to work on their projects and I know we do not have many more sessions left…time allocation is important" Realizing that this project based activity would tackle different dimensions of critical thinking, I decided to have students continue to work on it as the main assignment for week four while also having them complete the forums for discussion materials. Students were asked to examine local community resources and related information in order to be able to participate in the discussions. Since all CIQs had indicated up to that point how valuable video podcasts had been as observational tools to connect theoretical information to practice they were also included for this week. In conversations with P, we spoke about how with video podcasts there could be far fewer voices from the "outside" being heard because of the technical knowledge needed to create and distribute video podcasts. But by adding blogs, a relatively simpler self-publishing tool, students were exposed to a wider array of perspectives. "Blogging…offers a channel for more intimate communication" (Colgan, 2005, p.61) which is a great way for students to connect and feel more invested with the community as they are working on their projects in a critical way.

Up to this point, forums and assignments that were included in all sessions were carefully selected in order to provide students with the opportunity to demonstrate individual acquisition of skills while also participating in shared knowledge. *"The students are working so hard, collaborating, critically reflecting in the forums, the activities they are completing demonstrate their understanding of materials and growth…why am I including a midterm? I wonder if the concept of "purpose" –doing well on the midterm affected the development of well created study guides "* I struggled with this since I wanted to make sure students were completing the readings of all chapters but also realized how fast paced the course had been and the volume of materials and activities included had been extensive. Although students had truly worked hard infusing concepts learned to all of their assignments, a midterm provided a way to incorporate specific concepts I wanted to make sure all students had the opportunity to reflect upon. It appeared that having a purpose (the midterm), considered essential for adult learners, was instrumental in their overall engagement with the material when developing the study guides during week two. One student commented about the midterm "It was very challenging but I really enjoyed taking it. I guess it showed to myself how much I was getting out of the class" I wrote in my journal *"Although the forum provided opportunities for discussion of concepts from the readings the midterm provided students with another medium to demonstrate individual knowledge of materials covered up to this point…now I need to create a rubric for the final project based learning activity that will consider both individual and group contributions"*. The rubric for the final assignment carefully considered all the materials and included sections in which students were going to be able to demonstrate how the knowledge acquired affected their project development. For the final project assignment, all students had to complete the forums to discuss materials but were given the option of selecting an individual or group assignment. It is interesting to point out that only two students elected to complete the individual assignment, which signals how much students enjoyed the collaborative process with their peers.

Comments from the CIQ for week three indicated that students were engaged with the materials and valued the collaborations of peers and the instructor. Some students commented how "there has not been an opportunity to be distanced" while some were surprised by how much the study guide helped when they took the midterm this week with one student saying "how different it was to be sitting home taking a midterm, very relaxing with less pressure than being in a classroom." The use of video podcasts and blogs appeared to also contribute to the understanding of the readings and add to the discussions of the forums with a student expressing how "One member of my group really took the time to answer my ideas or thoughts, and encouraged me to follow through with my ideas" (Table 6).

Week Four

All students were finalizing the final projects and the forums for week four related to readings assigned for the week. It was interesting to see how many of the students were logging in daily, not just when sessions were posted, in order to participate in the discussions and the development of their final projects. We were also impressed by the leadership many students displayed in following up, organizing and taking the time to carefully re-examine items discussed in previous sessions when completing forums and assignments.

FUTURE RESEARCH DIRECTIONS AND CONCLUSION

Examining teaching practices through the use of a critical reflective stance can provide instructors with the opportunity to consider closely how their decisions about groupings and tools shape the learning environment for collaboration. Those decisions can either create barriers for students, which inhibit learning, or they can provide opportunities for all stakeholders to learn from different perspective while promoting higher order thinking skills.

One of the things learned in the process of teaching this course was that the instructor couldn't simply put forward a series of preconceived techniques for collaboration that had proven successful in the past. Each technique had to be subjected to critical reflection based on observations, assessments of student learning and feedback, as well as dialogues with a colleague and corroboration from theoretical literature. The selection of the techniques changed over time based on which techniques were most effective in fostering participation and supporting collaboration. For instance, jigsaw turned out to the especially useful for this group of students during the second week of class because the students had reached a stage where their collaborations could not go deeper without their assuming individual accountability for learning from a collaborative group. Jigsaw allowed the students to become experts on particular topics which gave them a new focus for their learning and a new basis for contributing to the reconfigured collaborative groups they were assigned to. This focus provided them with new motivation to work with their groups and afforded them a renewed sense of responsibility to complete their part of the overall task effectively. In fact, this whole process of learning to be individually accountable to the group helped the students see that their learning as individuals would stagnate without the diversity and expansiveness available in group-based collaborative environments.

Table 6. Critical incident questionnaire (CIQ) results from week three

At what moment in class were you most engaged as a learner?
5 students mentioned assignments 1 student mentioned the video podcasts 5 students mentioned the forums 1 student mentioned the readings 2 students mentioned midterm 1 student did not answer this question
At what moment in class were you most distanced as a learner?
6 students did not feel distanced- There has not been an opportunity to be distanced 4 student mentioned challenge of completing assignment 3 students mentioned chapters/textbook 2 student mentioned the forum
What actions from anyone in the forums did you find most affirming or helpful?
6 students mentioned the helpfulness of the study guide when taking the midterm- The use of one big review was very helpful because some students were able to find information and elaborate on things I did not understand from reading the text 2 students mentioned professor's feedback- Reading professor's feedback, Dr. K always answers quickly. 7 students mentioned forum- Response and encouragement to my ideas/thoughts, receiving thanks from group members for my work
What event surprised you the most?
1 student mentioned having options for the final activity 4 students mentioned taking a midterm online- Less pressure, structure of the exam, how long it took, interesting to see how it will be. 5 students mentioned the group work -surprises me every time! 1 student mentioned the experiential learning component- Really awesome! 3 students mentioned nothing 1 student mentioned how everything comes together
What actions from anyone in the forums did you find most puzzling or confusing?
12 students mentioned nothing was puzzling of confusing 1 student mentioned the assignment- The final project takes a while to comprehend 1 student mentioned getting confused by some many posts. 1 student mentioned a group member not contributing as much.
Response from students about the helpfulness of the tools to help with the online learning environment.
Forums, blogs and video podcasts received the highest rankings as a tool Chats received the lowest ranking as a tool 1 student added a separate comment about the readings saying " I really enjoyed the additional handout provided- It was very clear and it helped me in my forum post"
Adaptations that were made to the fourth week of classes based on feedback from the third week.
Continuation of the use of forums for discussion and collaborative tools for feedback.

How the different tools were selected and used was also subject to critical reflection on the part of the instructor. For instance, the instructor did not anticipate how creatively the students would make use of wikis to strengthen the social network of the class. The students took the initiative to use the wikis to share diverse areas of interest that not only enhanced the sense of "social presence," but also expanded the menu of topic areas to be collaboratively explored. The sharing of topics of interest that emerged from wikis led to some unexpected collaborations among students and became an important component of their final projects for the class.

For faculty interested in promoting democratic practices, it is important to articulate learning goals without making unwarranted assumptions about the ever changing needs of learners. The collaborative nature of the grouping situations that were considered for this course and the use of tools to enhance those collaborations were effective because students were not only informed as to why they were being utilized but also because they knew that their opinions and needs were valued and carefully considered in making course decisions. We are not saying that the power of the instructor can be completely erased from the experience, nor that it should be, but that the effects of the effort to draw students more deeply into curricular and course organization choices may require a strong tolerance for power sharing. Being open to adapting practices that may be so ingrained in us due to different experiences as learners and teachers is not an easy task. The use of Brookfield's critical lenses to consider grouping techniques and tools selected to enhance collaboration was by turns enlightening, frustrating, and often exhausting. But the value of avoiding the mistakes that can occur when we have an "uncritical stance of our practice" (Brookfield, 1995, p. 1), limiting the growth of our students and ourselves as learners and practitioners, makes the experience adopting of the critical lenses an extremely worthwhile one.

Utilizing the lenses of critical reflection was a powerful way to examine the dynamics of an effort to enhance collaboration and, in the end, was just one part of the overall learning experience. Tools on their own without considering grouping strategies become just that-tools. Grouping strategies without the right materials can become just a technique. The combination of tools, strategies, and understanding the needs of learners framed by a critical reflective framework can provide opportunities for all voices to be heard, for adults to "self- direct and regulate their learning" and for distance education experiences to become a "human experience" and not just a place to deposit information.

For future research in distance education we encourage the continuation of critically reflective practices using Brookfield's lenses as a framework encouraging faculty to adapt their pedagogy in the light of what they learn from the theoretical literature, the perspectives of colleagues, the actual experiences of students, and the insights that emerge from ongoing autobiographical reflection.

REFERENCES

Brookfield, S. (1987). *Developing critical thinkers: challenging adults to explore alternative ways of thinking and acting*. San Francisco, CA: Jossey- Bass.

Brookfield, S. (1995). *Becoming a critically reflective teacher*. San Francisco, CA: Jossey Bass.

Brookfield, S., & Preskill, S. (2005). *Discussion as a way of teaching*. San Francisco, CA: Jossey Bass.

Colgan, C. (2005). Computer blogs: Boon or bane? *Education Digest: Essential Readings Condensed for Quick Review*, *71*(4), 57–63.

David, J. (2008). What research says about project-based learning. *Educational Leadership*, *65*(5), 80–82.

Duch, B. J., Groh, S. E., & Allen, D. E. (2001). *The Power of Problem-Based Learning*. Sterling, VA: Stylus Publishing, LLC.

Fichter, D. (2005). Intranets, wikis, blikes, and collaborative working. *Online*, *29*(5), 47–50.

Finnegan, C. (2006). Technology: Revolutionizing or Transforming College? *Innovative Higher Education*, *31*(3), 143–145. doi:10.1007/s10755-006 9015-7

Graffam, B. (2007). Active learning in medical education: Strategies for beginning implementation. *Medical Teacher*, *29*(1), 38–42. doi:10.1080/01421590601176398

Hazari, S., North, A., & Moreland, D. (2009). Investigating pedagogical value of wiki technology. *Journal of Information Systems Education*, *20*(2), 187–198.

Hou, H., Chang, K., & Sung, Y. (2007). An analysis of peer assessment online discussions within a course that uses project-based learning. *Interactive Learning Environments*, *15*(3), 237–251. doi:10.1080/10494820701206974

Hsu, Y. C., & Shiue, Y. M. (2005). The effect of self-directed learning readiness on achievement comparing face-to-face and two-way distance learning instruction. *International Journal of Instructional Media, 32*(2), 143–155.

Hyllegard, D., Deng, H., & Hunter, C. (2008). Why do students leave online courses? Attrition in community colleges distance learning courses. *International Journal of Instructional Media, 35*(4), 429–243.

Jonassen, D. (2003). Using cognitive tools to represent problems. *Journal of Research on Technology in Education, 35*(3), 362–379.

Jonassen, D. (2006). On the role of concepts in learning and instructional design. *Educational Technology Research and Development, 54*(2), 177–196. doi:10.1007/s11423-006-8253-9

Jonassen, D., Carr, C., & Yueh, H. (1998). Computers as mindtools for engaging learners in critical thinking. *TechTrends, 43* (2), 24--32. Retrieved June 12, 2009, from http://www.siue.edu/education/techready/5_Software_Tutorials/5_AncillaryPages/Mindtools.pdf

Jonassen, D., Howland, J., Marra, R. M., & Crismond, D. (2008). *Meaningful learning with technology* (3rd ed.). Upper Saddle River, NJ: Pearson/Merrill Prentice Hall.

Jonassen, D. H. (1996). *Computers in the classroom: Mindtools for critical thinking*. Columbus, OH: Merrill/Prentice-Hall.

Klobas, J. E., & Haddow, G. (2000). Evaluating the impact of computer-supported international collaborative teamwork in business education. *International Journal of Educational Technology, 2*(1).

Lambert, J., & Cuper, Y. (2008). Technology, transfer, and teaching: The impact of a single technology course on preservice teachers' computer attitudes and ability. *Journal of Technology and Teacher Education, 16*(4), 395–410.

Lim, J., Kim, M., Chen, S., & Ryder, C. (2008). An empirical investigation of student achievement and satisfaction in different learning environments. *Journal of Instructional Psychology, 35*(2), 113–119.

Mezirow, J. (1991). *Transformative dimensions of adult learning*. San Francisco, CA: Jossey- Bass.

NCES - National Center for Education Statistics - U.S. Department of Education. (2008). *Distance Education at Degree-Granting Postsecondary Institutions: 2006-07*. Retrieved September 1, 2009, from http://nces.ed.gov/pubsearch/pubsinfo.asp?pubid=2009044

Notar, C., Wilson, K., & Montgomery, M. (2005). A distance learning model for teaching higher order thinking. *College Student Journal, 39*(1), 17.

O'Reilly, T. (2005). *What is Web 2.0?* Retrieved December 20, 2009, from http://oreilly.com/web2/archive/what-is-web-20.html

Prensky, M. (2001, October). "*Digital Natives, Digital Immigrants*" Retrieved September 10, 2009, from http://www.marcprensky.com/writing

Reeves, D. (2009). Three challenges of Web 2.0. *Educational Leadership, 66*(6), 87–89.

Rheingold, H. (2006, November 1), "*Social Bookmarking, Tagging, Music/Photo/Video Sharing*" Message posted. Retrieved April 9, 2010, from https://www.socialtext.net/medialiteracy/index.cgi?social_bookmarking_tagging_music_photo_video_sharing

Scardamalia, M. (2002). Collective cognitive responsibility for the advancement of knowledge. In B. Smith (Ed.) *Liberal education in a knowledge society*, 67-98. Chicago, ILL: Open Court.

Scardamalia, M., & Bereiter, C. (2003). Knowledge building. In *Encyclopedia of education* (2nd ed., pp. 1370–1373). New York, NY: Macmillan Reference.

Stewart, D. (2008). Classroom management in the online environment. *Journal of Online Learning and Teaching*, *4*(3), 371–375.

Van Horn, R. (2007). Web applications and google. *Phi Delta Kappan*, *88*(10), 727–792.

Williams, J., & Chinn, S. (2009). Using Web 2.0 to support the active learning experience. *Journal of Information Systems Education*, *20*(2), 165–174.

Williams, J., & Jacobs, J. (2004). Exploring the use of blogs as learning spaces in the higher education sector. *Australasian Journal of Educational Technology*, *20*(2), 232–237.

ADDITIONAL READING

Becker, H., & Lovitts, B. (2003). A Project-based Approach to Assessing Technology. In Haertel, G., & Means, B. (Eds.), *Evaluating educational technology: Effective research designs for improving learning*. New York, NY: Teachers College Press.

Freedman, T. (Ed.). (2006). *Coming of age: An introduction to the new worldwide web*. Ilford: Terry Freedman Ltd. Retrieved June 12, 2009, from http://terry-freedman.org.uk

Jonassen, D., & Hung, W. (2008). All Problems are not Equal: Implications for Problem-Based Learning. *The Interdisciplinary Journal of Problem-based Learning.*, *2*(2), 6–28.

Knowles, M. S. (1984). *The Adult Learner: A Neglected Species* (3rd ed.). Houston, TX: Gulf.

Lawless, K., & Pellegrino, J. W. (2007). Professional Development in Integrating Technology Into Teaching and Learning: Knowns, Unknowns, and Ways to Pursue Better Questions and Answers. *Review of Educational Research*, *77*(4), 575–614. doi:10.3102/0034654307309921

Lohnes, S., & Kinzer, C. (2007). Questioning Assumptions about Students' Expectations for Technology in College Classrooms. *Innovate 3*(5). Retrieved August 15, 2009, from http://www.innovateonline.info/index.php?view=article&id431

Uden, L., & Beaumont, C. (2006). *Technology & Problem-based Learning*. Hershey, PA: Information Science Publishing.

Vygotsky, L. S. (1978). *Mind and society: The development of higher mental processes*. Cambridge, MA: Harvard University Press.

Warnick, B. R., & Burbules, N. C. (2007). Media Comparison Studies: Problems and Possibilities. *Teachers College Record*, *109*(11), 2483–2510.

Wiggins, G., & McTighe, J. (2006). *Understanding by Design*. Upper Saddle River, NJ: Pearson Education.

KEY TERMS AND DEFINITIONS

Collaborative Grouping: A technique in which students of different abilities are grouped together to share different viewpoints.

Curriculum: A guideline for a course of study

Pedagogy: An approach to teaching and learning

Reflective Practices: Ongoing assessment of experiences and events in a learner's life.

Student Centered Learning: Focusing on the educational needs of students with different learning styles and needs.

Student Empowerment: Increasing the confidence of learners to take control of their learning experiences.

Web 2.0: Data driven user centered web applications that facilitates online collaborate activities.

Chapter 10
Using Role Play and Team Teaching as Strategies to Add Depth to Online Discussion

Ron Lombard
Chatham University, USA

Barbara Biglan
Chatham University, USA

ABSTRACT

This is a review of an action research project dealing with the impact of a role playing activity in an online course. Two instructors of an online graduate course collected observable data based on response and participation levels of students in an online discussion setting. Subsequently, utilizing the same discussion topic, the instructors combined for a course delivery team teaching and role playing approach to the discussion. In the second course the instructors assumed the roles of John Dewey, Mao Tse-Tung, and Aristotle and exchanged responses and comments with each other and with students. A comparison of the levels of responses between the two approaches utilizing the same rubric allowed to measure the impact of role play and team teaching. A review of research related to team teaching and role playing as approaches to enhance discussions provides background to decision to utilize these two approaches to enhance the discussion process.

INTRODUCTION

Teaching online courses presents challenges for the instructor in pursuit of creating an environment in which exchange of ideas and demonstrations of deep levels of understanding are displayed. The instructor must stimulate discussion between the instructor and the students and among the students. The instructor must also insure students attain a deep level of understanding without utilizing familiar teaching techniques that are only effective in a traditional setting. Finally, the instructor must create, maintain and evaluate the course and student knowledge levels in relation to course objectives. Achieving these goals calls for a major commitment of time, content knowledge, interactive discussions with students, and effective assessment and feed back for student work.

DOI: 10.4018/978-1-61692-898-8.ch010

The online instructor needs to meet course objectives through effective utilization of strategies and resources. Research has provided insights into the massive amount of time required for the construction and conducting of an effective online course (Hunt, 2009; Stagg-Peterson & Slotta, 2009). Reviewing of research related to online teaching points out an online approach can consume even more time and energy than teaching, face to face, in the classroom, as the instructor had to be perceived by students as being "right there" online with them, leading by example with time, energy, and commitment, or students' participation would quickly fade. The position that online courses can require more time and commitment than most face to face courses has been maintained since the early commitment to the creation of such a delivery system (Cavanaugh, 2005; Dunlap, 2005; Maddux, 2004). It is this understanding of the commitments of time and ongoing assessment that led to an exploration of the possibility of having a team of teachers present an activity in this course. Sharing the load, in terms of the role play in the discussion, could be accomplished by having two instructors take active roles in the discussions.

The beliefs of the instructors for a successful implementation and application of both strategies, team teaching and role playing during discussions, centers on the view that if students are to function adequately beyond the artificial classroom environment, they must realize that important issues are complex and open to numerous and often contradictory interpretations. They must come to terms with the paradoxical nature of knowledge. The opinions of experts are no more valid than the boundaries of their academic fields, their professional training, and their personal talents and biases (Yang, Newby, & Bill, 2005). College students need to understand that neither reason nor the scientific method provides us with absolute certainty, and that "Ultimate Truth" does not reside with any one discipline or individual. Initially, students will be surprised, disturbed, even frustrated by the unusual atmosphere of a team-taught class. Instructors must be aware of this potential reaction, and help their students adjust. Otherwise, students become totally confused and some might simply give up trying (Shafer, 2008).

Also conditions for conflict in the process of team teaching are abundant. Folger, Poole, and Stutman (2005) characterize such conflict in the context of the possibility of interferences with one individual's views or focus. The question arises as to course configuration, different instructors assuming leadership roles in differing modules of the course or a complete integration of subject and pedagogy (Shaprio & Dempsey, 2008). All of these are issues that need to be dealt with by the instructors for a successful implementation of their course.

This action research effort was to meet these challenges and it was made in the context of a course on education philosophies based on the use of a discussion board in a unique, interactive manner. Interactivity in an online course serves the purpose of maintaining student interest and forming a learning community involving both the students and instructors. The search for aspects that improve this interactive environment and online learning is worthy of exploration in the context of fostering the effectiveness of online instruction. Creating and providing instruction for these courses led to concerns related to the levels of interactivity in each course, the amount of time required for course construction, and the depth of understanding provided through course interactions.

The course instructor began to make an examination of changes that could be made in the course to enhance the discussion process to make it more effective. Two issues arose as to what strategies could be utilized in bringing about deep levels of understanding in regards to content and its application in various contexts. Issue one was the amount of time individual instructors spend dealing with all the aspects of online courses leading to an examination of the possibility of employing team teaching aspects to the discussion activities of the course. This led to a collaborative effort by two instructors to work on improvement of course activities. The goal for this team approach was to allow for a deeper level of discussion of content information presented in the course, by providing additional voices to the perspective of the discussion and allow adequate opportunities to respond to student comments asking students questions at the critical thinking level. Issue two was to provide the discussions with a level of higher relevance and allowing for an enhancement of perspective viewpoints. The approach reviewed to deal with this issue was the use of role play by the instructors to allow for an exchange of comments and responses between students and the instructors through the persona of the instructors' roles. Role play was viewed as an attempt to provide an opportunity for students to deal with application of content in real-life situations.

CONTEXT OF THE STUDY

The course is entitled "Perspectives on Education" and its major goal is to have students review various philosophies of education and the development of the American educational system. The format for the course was online with major emphasis placed on students carrying out assigned projects and taking an active role in online discussions. Content material is actively discussed throughout the course and students are asked to apply materials to present educational issues. The course is limited to fifteen students in consideration of the amount of discussion to be carried out by the instructor. In the first version of the online course the culminating activity for the course was a traditional discussion dealing with the philosophies of education in the context of reform and liberal, moderate, and conservative perspectives. The instructors found it difficult to obtain the expected levels of insight through the discussions in the context of the philosophies and the application to contemporary educational issues. Likewise, since it is a culminating activity, students seem to have become less inclined to take a highly active participatory part in the discussion and limited their comments to avoid conflict with the perspectives of other students. The discussion was conducted over a number of days and did provide the expected levels of insights from students.

Rationale for the Approach Chosen

The application of team teaching research data would deal with efforts to aid a single instructor in responding to the extensive time and effort requirements for an effective course. After the course had been presented for the first time, it was decided to review research that could aid in enhancing the discussion forum This review was aimed at finding ways to create and assess student understanding of course content that goes deeper than the level of knowledge, calling for students to display the ability to make connections and demonstrate applications of knowledge. The review of differing strategies to enhance the level of interaction through the discussion forum was connected to the efforts to enhance critical thinking levels and also increase student participation levels through creating a process that made the discussion materials more interesting and active.

The possible positive impact of utilizing team teaching as a strategy to enhance the delivery of the course was researched. While the concept of team teaching is not a new idea, its application for an online course is not a common practice. Team teaching results in a course that presents materials and discusses issues from a multi-perspective approach. The opportunities for individualized support and the modeling of instructor collegiality also aid in creating a community of learning (Vogler & Long, 2003). Research points to the implementation of a team teaching approach to create a learning environment that requires active participation of instructors and students (Salas,

2006). The application of a team approach shifts the focus from educational content to the design of activities that require interactivity since two instructors share the load (Piechura-Couture, Tichenor, Touchton, Maciasaac, & Heins, 2006).

Palloff and Pratt (2004) present the view that collaboration is the "heart and soul" of an online course (p.6). Two instructors modeling collaboration provides an opportunity for this process to be viewed and experienced by students. Palloff and Pratt (2004) further recognize that such collaboration provides the deeper level of understanding needed for real learning to take place (p.7). The team can benefit from the division of teaching responsibilities by dividing students, technical and socialization activities, and assessment responsibilities, while opportunities always exist for a cross-over or shifting of responsibilities. Such instructor teams must feel comfortable with the realization that each team member has unique and differing contributions for a course (Kain, 2006). Also an ongoing process to meet and discuss the progress of the course is of paramount importance if the activities and interactions are to be effective in meeting course objectives (Shibley, 2006).

In addition to the team teaching technique, the instructors decided to implement a role playing approach into the course. This decision was based on research dealing with capabilities of team teaching and role playing to enhance discussions through viewing multiple perspectives on education. Generating dialogue required for an effective online discussion board is difficult. Taking this process to another level involving role playing can be quite a large step for students and instructors. While it is convenient for students to log on and review comments in online courses, the responses are random and isolated bringing a feeling of disconnect to the dialogue process. Students also have a tendency to be nice to each other and make conscious efforts to not make comments that appear disagreeable. Instructor questions and comments should encourage students to provide clarity for positions and to challenge the positions of others. All participants build and construct new knowledge utilizing the elements of the discussion as building blocks for the process. One successful approach to obtain this goal is utilizing a role play situation and assigning specific roles for participants. When assuming a role- persona participants are not necessarily taking a personal stance, but rather are stating the position and reaction of a specific role, with the role's unique views and perspectives. This approach can take the discussion to a new level of enthusiasm and insight sparking a more robust discussion reflecting numerous perspectives (Murray, 2000).

Role play builds on participant interaction and can create social bonding for participants leading to maintenance of motivation levels. Reflection also increases since students do not sit passively allowing the instructor to provide all knowledge. Participants begin to communicate role perspectives and insights and to assume responsibility for their own learning (Bergin, Eckstein, Manns, & Wallingford, 2001). Role play is a useful technique in online courses because it affords more time for instructors to work individually with students. The instructor is actively involved in the role play and models behaviors for students. Feedback is provided in the context of the discussion topics and depth of understanding is enhanced by probing responses and questions by the instructor (Headly, 2005). Also important is the fact that role play allows for exposure to new perspectives allowing student's opportunities to exhibit depth of understanding difficult to reach in most classroom environments.

Role playing places participants in an environment, in which they are challenged emotionally to deal with discussion comments, in a free-form approach that they review before making logical response. This situation simulates real-life situations, where views and perspectives come quickly and can be emotionally charged. Both cognitive and affective domains are called upon to deal with proposing and defending positions within a social experience of the discussion (Fannon, 2005).

This approach follows many of the aspects of the Socratic method making the pedagogy strategy student centered and calling for critical review of discussion exchanges. Role playing provides an excellent environment in which to employ the approach of attempting to provide realism in terms of interaction (Nelson & Blenkin, 2007).

Research supports the importance of the instructor's role of mentor, coach, and facilitator. As mentor, the instructor models the construction of knowledge and the defense of beliefs. As a coach and facilitator the instructor provides prompts that invoke reflections and feedback that keeps motivation high (Murphy, Mahoney, Chen, Mendoza-Diaz, & Yang, 2005). A major goal of the instructor should be to encourage students toward deep levels of inquiry related to insights and observations expressed through discussions (Waltonen-Moore, Stuart, Newton, Oswald, &Varonis, 2006). The goal for the instructors in this scenario is to take an active part in the discussion requiring students to present a high level understanding of connections to varied educational philosophies.The application of critical thinking skills are central to the proposed activities for this course and allow for the use of reflective activities that in turn can be expressed in the context of real-life situations (Danchak, 2002; MacKnight, 2000; Raleigh, 2000). When course instructors review the content of student responses and interactions, they are providing an excellent picture of the depth of understanding (Matters, 2005).

Discussions will serve as a two way street with the student providing insights and observations and the instructor facilitating, by providing opportunities for in-depth investigation, and providing constructive feedback to students. This successful exchange facilitates the acquisition of higher-order thinking skills for the transferring and applying information to new situations (Wu & Hiltz, 2003). The discussion format expands knowledge and skills and reflects the opportunity for students to utilize discussion to obtain textual knowledge (Gambrell, 2004; Gaoyin & Tao, 2005). This result is based on the online discussion's student-centered approach, the intensity of student writing, on-demand interactions with other students and the instructor, and more personalized feedback to students (Kassop, 2003).

The discussion board serves as a replacement for face to face oral interaction in the creation of an online learning community and reveals various methodologies and structures that can lead to the creation of this community. The instructor assumes the role of facilitator in the electronic dialogue (Waltonen-Moore, Stuart, Newton, Oswald, & Varonis, 2006). Research, justifies the approach of team teaching, by expresses the assertion from online instructors that the creation, monitoring, and instruction of online courses require more time than traditional classes (Cavanaugh, 2005).

Recognizing the crucial role that dialogue and discussion play in the course, efforts were made to link the content with construction of social learning activities that initiate consolidation of the expansion of knowledge at a level of reflection. Bird (2007), based on the work of Fowler and Mayes (2000), proposes all three ingredients content, construction, consolidation should be included as a major portion of online courses. Content consists of the basic knowledge required of the course, knowledge construction involves the collaborative process of interacting within the discussion forum, and consolidation is the reflective activity of discussion participants, after they have had the opportunity to assess other participant perspectives.

The decision was made to incorporate the approaches of Fowler and Mayes (2000) since these approaches are directed toward reflection in the context of learning. This approach functions at both intellectual and affective levels allowing participants to explore their own experiences and knowledge in contrast to perspectives offered by the instructors. As proposed by Bird (2007), this pedagogical model has the following features: (1) it is a social constructivist approach, (2) it is an active, rather than passive, learning experience, (3) equal attention is given to the elements of content, construction, and consolidation, (4) an ongoing dialogue and discussion serve as the key learning processes. This effort at collaborative learning would allow for an ongoing assessment of student abilities to display understanding of connections of content. It would also allow participants to apply content knowledge to judgments of perspectives that differ from those of individual participants.

In deciding on the approach to be taken in course activities, one of the instructors involved in this study suggested the format of a socio-drama to spark discussion and elicit reactions from course participants. Such an approach had some appeal since the utilization of socio-drama has three primary aims: an improved understanding of a social situation, an increase in participants' knowledge about their own and other people's roles in relation to that situation, and an emotional release or catharsis as people express their feelings about the subject (Eckloff, 2006).

The course instructors reviewed materials dealing with the utilization of the online course discussion board to provide the communication for all course participants finding positive support for such an approach. In the area of training managers and business personnel, role playing scenarios were presented as one of the most promising training techniques (Bos & Shami, 2006; Sogunro, 2004). Further investigation centering on the effective use of role playing as a strategy for an online course (Ciardiello, 1993; Dickey, 2003; Dickey, 2005; Kuh & Hu, 2001; Tannenbaum, 1996; Lebaron & Miller, 2005; Pettenger & Young, 2008; Song, Hannafin, & Hill, 2007) reveal insights as to the positive aspects of this strategy, finding that role-playing activities offered opportunities for experiential learning and situated learning within a collaboration learning environment. Role play*ing* strategies identified goals and learning outcomes, and aligned them with four knowledge domains; factual, conceptual, procedural and metacognitive. Materials presented by the University of Illinois (Curriculum, Technology, & Education Reform (CTER), 2009), present views that the use of the role playing strategy in an online setting provides for the following:

- allows students to develop an understanding of others' perspectives;
- encourages students to work with others in analyzing situations and developing workable solutions;
- provides students an opportunity to apply concepts they have learned in a rich, realistic environment;
- gives students the chance to gain insights into interpersonal challenges they are likely to face in their careers and private lives;
- enables students to effectively contrast problem-solving methods by role playing a situation several times from diverse perspectives;
- offers a constructive channel through which feelings can be expressed and feedback processed.

Using role playing should be a priority if teachers value students' ability to examine perspectives other than their own. First and foremost, this technique allows students to be exposed to new ideas and perspectives from the role that they play in the activity. While they may not agree with them, the students can come to understand other perspectives. As a learning methodology, role-playing attempts to help students discover personal meanings within their social worlds and to resolve personal dilemmas with the aid of their social group. In the context of sustained student participation role playing is viewed as a strategy that ranks high in relation to attention, participation and motivation. The strategy also allows higher education learners to bring personal experience into the activity, enhancing levels of critical thinking (University of Florida – Center for Instructional Technology and training, 2007).

EVALUATION METHOD AND DATA FROM THE FORMER EXPERIENCE

Baseline data was collected in relation to obtained and expected levels of achievement of students in terms of participation levels, insights, applications of content, and willingness to express individual views. A review of past courses, prior to the implementation of the role play strategy in the discussion forum did not yield the levels of participation or depth of understanding as expected by the two online course instructors.

The two instructors worked together in the creation of a rubric that could be used to assess the expected levels of achievement for students to demonstrate a real depth of understanding. The rubric would be utilized as a means to review both the levels of student active participation and the depth of understanding displayed by students' reflections, replies, and comments as observed by the instructors. The review of the rubric would provide insights as to how well this particular activity was able to achieve the levels of understanding, sharing of differing perspectives, and applications to various educational issues. Instructor observations would be based on a review of an archived copy of discussions and comments on a BlackBoard discussion board.

The criteria for assessment indicators to be utilized by the instructors through the rubric consisted of instructor observations based on the insights, levels of participation, ability to discuss content information as it applies to contemporary education issues, and willingness to express independent views based on various perspectives and philosophies expressed by others in the discussion process. When this rubric was utilized to assess student ability to obtain expectations for the activity, it provided data demonstrating that some adaptation to the discussion process was needed to raise student levels of achievement in each of the assessment dimensions. The instructors viewed the results with the thought in mind that action research was needed to see if some other approach to this activity could enhance levels of student achievement.

The assessment rubric was based on the dimensions of the specific attributes and abilities the instructors sought from student participants. The dimensions being assessed were supported by observable demonstrations by students including increased insights, level of participation, content knowledge, and the ability of students to make connections between content knowledge and contemporary education issues. The dimension referring to "keeping to the topic" served as an assessment of students' ability to maintain a coherent flow of the discussion in a clear and concise manner. Special attention was paid to the assessment of students' willingness to express views that challenge others including instructors. The emphasis on this assessment required the instructors to take note of the students' efforts to maintain their individual views in reaction to perceptions and comments of the instructors and other students.

For each of the assessed dimensions found within the rubric, listed here are the indicators reviewed to determine the ability of the participants to reach the instructors' expected levels of achievement.

- Levels of participation – The level of participation by individual students should increase during the activity. The comparison of the rubrics before and after the implementation of the role playing into the discussion activity would provide insight into levels of increased participation.
- Content knowledge application – The level of content knowledge displayed by students should increase during the activity. The comparison of the rubrics would provide insight into the level of improvement.
- Connection of insights – Connections made between content knowledge in the context

of the discussion topics related to contemporary issues should increase during the activity. The measurement of improvement is based on the difference between the pre and post insights demonstrated during the role playing aspect of the activity.

- Maintaining topic centered comments and responses – The activity was to provide observable evidence that students remained on topic throughout the discussions. The evidence was a comparison of the rating on rubrics related to the discussion topic before and after the implementation of the role playing element.
- Expression of individual views – Students' willingness to express views that take into account differing perspectives on issues should increase during the activity. The assessment would involve reviewing examples of observable measures of the students' growth individuality in the context of self-reflection. The comparison of pre and post rubrics would serve as observable evidence.

The constructed rubric utilized to evaluate student levels of perception, willingness to provide individual comments and insights, and level of participation is presented in Table 1. The rankings three through one for each dimension provides a scale to measure the expectation levels for students in each dimension as viewed by the instructors. Table 1 provides a description of the scale used in the study.

Table 2 represents data collected before any aspects of the role play was introduced as a strategy. Specifically, it shows the number of students out of a total of fifteen who fell into ranking areas for each of the dimensions being assessed. A rank of three represents the expected level of student achievement. A rank of two or one indicates areas that need enhancement to reach the instructors' expectations. This table represents.

Based on the findings from the review of the assessment materials, the two instructors made the decision to carry out an action research on what actions could be taken to enhance student levels of achievement in the context of the instructor expectations. To enhance the depth of student understanding, the two instructors would combine their resources and carry out research to search

Table 1. Description of ranking for each dimension

Dimensions	Ranking=3	Ranking=2	Ranking=1
Level of Participation	Takes highly active role in discussion process	Displays adequate level of participation	Could increase level of participation
Content knowledge application	Displays excellent application of content knowledge in context of discussions	Displays adequate application of content knowledge in context of discussions	Displays inadequate application of content knowledge in context of discussions
Connection insights for content	Numerous excellent connections made between content areas to contemporary issues	Adequate but unclear connections made between content areas to contemporary issues	Limited connections made between content areas to contemporary issues
Responses and comments on topic	Student is consistent in keeping responses and comments on topic	In most cases students is able to keep responses and comments on topic	Student is inconsistent in keeping responses and comments on topic
Willingness to express individual views	Questioning of instructor-persona views and expression of individual views evident throughout discussions	In some cases questioning of instructor-persona views and expression of individual views are displayed	Little or no effort to express views demonstrating individual insight or express non-instructor supported positions through discussions

Table 2. Number of students per ranking

Ranking	3	2	1
Level of Participation	2	10	3
Content knowledge application	4	9	2
Connection insights for content	4	8	3
Responses and comments on topic	8	5	2
Willingness to express individual views	5	7	3

for an approach that could bring about this enhancement.

The two online instructors decided to enhance the depth of understanding exhibited by students in online classes through the employment of the strategies of team teaching and role play. An activity was planned to incorporate both strategies, with the instructors assuming specific roles on the discussion board and sharing responsibilities to enhance the level of dialogue. Students would be called upon to express views and perspectives related to education in response to comments made by the instructors in the context of the roles the instructors assumed. The instructors, in role persona, would make observational comments and respond to student directed questions. While in role, instructors would respond and reflect on current educational issues in the context of the role's historical period and educational environment. Comments between the instructors and with students would deal with differing educational philosophies and the role of education in culture. Students would be required to apply their own perspectives on education in response to comments and questions made by the role playing instructors. Reviewing the research literature would provide insights into the specific areas that the instructors planned to apply to the activity.

EXPERIMENTAL REVISION OF THE COURSE

The instructors searched for a discussion activity that would serve as a device to enhance levels of student participation and place emphasis on the application of knowledge and use of critical thinking skills related to content covered dealing with differing philosophies of education as presented in the classroom environment. A discussion between the instructors centered on a means by which participants would have the opportunity to ask questions related to educational philosophies, increasing their level of knowledge to the point at which they could challenge aspects of conflicting philosophies and offer individual insights reflecting their own attitudes and beliefs related to a broad philosophy of education. The instructors encouraged students to examine another philosophical perspective; modeling critical thinking strategies to display a deep level of understanding and connections between differing perspectives.

Based on the reviewed literature concerning efforts to enhance critical thinking the course instructors decided that both team teaching and the use of role play could provide an excellent approach to online teaching. The specific culminating activity selected for the course was the social interaction of a banquet in which the instructors would assume roles and interact with students. The students would utilize background information that had been provided through the course and maintain their role as students. The discussion environment was based on a program created by Steven Allen, in what many critics refer to as the ultimate talk show. The series was presented on the PBS network under the title of "Meeting of the Minds" in a typical chat-show format. The common element of each show was the interaction and discussion between the featured characters to create a deeper level of understanding of the characters, their actions, their historical circumstances, and their impact on history and society. Allen's creation of the Meeting of the

Minds series provided an active and entertaining forum that resulted in a deeper understanding of historical and contemporary problems and beliefs. The characters, interviewed and interacting with the program's host, assumed the persona of a historical character and maintained that character's historical perspective even in discussions based on contemporary issues.

The instructor team utilized the Meeting of the Minds format to deepen understandings of aspects of American education in the context of historical figures' reactions to contemporary aspects of education. To keep the interaction between characters fresh and active, the instructors decided that more than one voice in the discussion process would offer different perspectives on topics. Characters from different periods of history interacted together in the Meeting of the Minds, so the instructors decided to utilize educators from different eras in their role play. The instructors would assume the roles of these characters and interact with students in the persona of that role with posting under that character's name.

The course instructors decided that characters-role selection must detail insights of not only the character's life period and experience but also interactions with contemporary observations related to education.

The instructors reached consensus on the selection of a historical figure who would provide insight of the movement for equality in American education into the modern era and a historical figure who maintained classical beliefs in relation to education, but with increasing emphasis on the individual. The instructors selected John Dewey as the historical figure who personified these philosophies. Dewey's selection reflected the early twentieth century movement toward the value of the individual and a belief in the education of the whole child. The decision to select a character-role deeply representing a classical approach to education led to the e selection of Aristotle. Aristotle's selection reflected the classical belief that only a few members of society would benefit from classical education. An elitist viewpoint was emphasized in the philosophy of Aristotle. The planning of education not left to the masses but rather to the select few who have a classical background. His view point is firm in the belief that these elite individuals need to control education and educational thought. The role play between these two instructor character-roles and exchanges with student participants would simulate discussions related to the goals and motives of education to support the existing culture or to challenge and question aspects of cultural beliefs in face of changing times.

Further discussions between the instructors suggested the addition of a character reflecting the impact of rapid change on the social and political aspects of education. The concepts of evolution, revolution, and political and social development needed to be examined. A state controlled educational process with emphasis placed on sorting and placing large segments of the population into specific groups in the context of education displays the problems created by a revolutionary process to bring about social and economic change. The educational process is given the opportunity to bring about change in many areas of the society, but under the direct control and limitations of the state. This educational process also reflects the rising concerns of national control of education and potential for reform in contemporary America. While reform can be positive, is it a process that should be evolutionary or revolutionary in its approach to change? And what is the cost to the educational system when reform occurs? Mao was selected based on the impact on Chinese education brought about by China's "cultural revolution". The selection of Mao was also based on the knowledge of the fact that Mao's education included training as a classroom teacher. This feeling of relevance creates a discussion component that provides real learning opportunities and assessment of participant knowledge and application skills and a realization that one individual can have a major impact on a nation's educational processes.

In the presentation format for the activity, student participants are presented with copies of the rubric that will be utilized to assess student participation in the context of assessing levels of student understanding prior to the beginning of the activity. The rubric aids in keeping the discussions centered on topics that will call for students' to display their knowledge of the various philosophies of teaching and learning in the context of contemporary educational issues.

Also, prior to the activity, student participants in the discussions were provided with background information dealing with each of the character-roles being carried out by the instructors. Instructors began a discussion forum online by introducing themselves and providing information related to their experiences with education. This information aided students in asking questions and responding to comments in relation to the instructors' role playing. Students were expected to monitor any comments made between instructors, playing out their roles. This allowed students to ask questions and express their perceptions on aspects of education in the context of the information provided by the role-playing instructors, viewed through the lens of the rubric.

In particular, the rubric was utilized as means to review both the levels of student active participation and the depth of understanding displayed by students' reflections, replies, and comments as observed by the instructors. The review of the rubric provided insights as to how well this particular activity achieved the levels of understanding, sharing of differing perspectives, and applications to various educational issues. Instructor observations were based on an archived copy of discussions and comments on a BlackBoard discussion board.

The basic goal of the culminating activity is for students to demonstrate background knowledge related to various theories of learning and philosophies expressed by individuals with major impact on development of American educational philosophies. This activity was designed utilizing aspects of the discussion board and a team teaching approach. Another goal of the activity is the development in students of a deep level of understanding of the concepts of the course through discussion and interactivity with instructors and fellow students. The activity called for the collaboration of both instructors to assume roles employed in the online discussions with students. Students would assume the roles of invitees to meet with the personas of the instructors in a social setting, expressing comments and exchanging responses with the instructors.

The specific format of the instructors' activity making effective use of team teaching and role

Table 3. Online assignment for each student

Session 1 **Cocktail Hour Conversation – (This will run for period of two days)** On the discussion board each Guest introduces himself - When I was young, I had experience in education (or school) and that made me formulate my opinion on education *The honored guests you will be holding discussions with are:* *Aristotle* *John Dewey* *Mao Tse-Tung* *You will want to review some background about each to aid you in your conversations with them* (Background materials provided for students)
Instructions for interacting with guests in discussion The guests will ask for you to respond with early experiences with schooling that you have that led you to your present position on the teaching-learning process. Please respond to each guest but also respond to two of your classmates. This will continue over a three day period. You should check throughout the day in relation to responses to your comments from the guests and other students.

playing follows the social interaction of a banquet. First, the students are introduced to the Banquet Assignment through an invitation to the Banquet. They are then made aware of the expectations of the assignment. Table 3 reproduces the online assignment for each student.

Assumptions Related to Session One

Session one, Cocktail, is utilized as a transition activity to introduce characters and makes participants feel comfortable in taking part in this activity. Some students find exchanges with these characters difficult at first. A feeling prevails that one might say the wrong thing or express a thought that might be ridiculed by authority figures. Participants need time to suspend feelings of reality when conversing with characters. Small talk of a general nature is helpful during this session so participants can feel comfortable talking with others. When this feeling of comfort is achieved, the conversation will flow and exchanges allow participants to share their individual beliefs and perspectives. To increase the comfort level of the students the instructors must click the anonymous selection for posting and type in the name of the character they are portraying in the address section before they post a comment or observation.

Assumptions Related to Session Two

Now that introductions have been made and students feel comfortable with the process, a real discussion can take place between the guests and the students. By this time perspectives are out in the open and guests will relate some of their perspective to contemporary educational issues, attempting to draw as many students into the discussion as possible.

DISCUSSION OF RESULTS

The instructors, by reviewing and monitoring the feedback and exchanges between students and with each other, gained insight into the students' level of understanding in the context of educational issues and philosophies. This monitoring of student responses and comments were assessed by an instructor created rubric used to assess the pre-role playing strategy. The instructors reviewed all the discussion materials expressed by students, throughout the discussions, for observable indicators of improvement and growth.

The instructors also reviewed post-activity discussions and the pre-activity discussions in the context of the rubric to assess the impact of the addition of role playing to reach the goals of the activity set by the instructors.

Table 4 displays the number of students who fell into each scoring category under each of the dimensions.

The rubric utilized for assessment prior to and after implementation of the role playing facet of the course activity is presented in Table 4. The scores for students in each of the pre and post areas are in both cases determined by instructor observations in the context of the comments and responses provided by the students throughout the conversation. Both of the instructors carry out the assessment and totaling of student comments and responses. The same criteria are utilized in the review of the rubrics in the context of the instructors' observations.

An analysis of the two rubrics reveals that the implementation of the role playing aspect of the activity greatly enhanced the level of discussions. In particular, the levels of active participation in the discussion process increased along with willingness for students to express their individual views. These were two of the major goals for implementing role playing into the discussion activity. An overall review of the comparison of the rubrics presents a clear case for the use of role play to enhance student participation and provide

Table 4. Assessment results: number of students for each rank

Dimension assessed	Pre-role play rubric data			Dimension assessed	Implemented role play rubric data		
Ranking	**Rank 3**	**Rank 2**	**Rank 1**		**Rank 3**	**Rank2**	**Rank 1**
Level of Participation	2	10	3	Level of Participation	9	6	0
Content knowledge application	4	9	2	Content knowledge application	8	7	0
Connection insights for content	4	8	3	Connection insights for content	9	6	0
Responses and comments on topic	8	5	2	Responses and comments on topic	10	5	0
Willingness to express individual views	5	7	3	Willingness to express individual views	11	4	0

further enhancement in having students apply knowledge and insights to discussions.

CONCLUSION

Observations Session One

Both instructors noticed that students responses not only increased, but critical observations were observed at a level not displayed prior to role play implementation. Students appeared to be more focused and centered in relation to instructor expectations due to both clear objectives presented at the start of the activity and also to the direct discussion methods used in the activity. All in all, role play implementation was beginning to have a positive impact.

Observations Session Two

Most important, both instructors were pleased with the increase of students in terms of meaningful participation and demonstrating a depth of understanding, due to utilization of role playing. Discussions with students at the end of the course also revealed that many students felt the activity enhanced the level of understanding in the context of applying content information to specific educational perspectives.

While the sample group for the implementation of this role playing and team teaching activity was small it did yield insights and support to the assumption that the use of role play could enhance the levels and depth of discussions. Discussions with students at the completion of the activity made it clear that the utilization of the role playing aspect adds a great deal of real world relevance to application of content materials in the context of contemporary educational issues.

The comparison of the pre and post rubrics displays a substantial increase in all the facets of the dimensions listed as being required for demonstration of increased depth of understanding and enhancement of levels of participation. In most cases the students falling into the highest areas of expectation for each of the dimensions is doubled in number, with no students falling into the lowest level after the implementation of role playing into the discussion activity. The implementation of the use of two instructors to take part in a role playing activity was so successful that planning is taking place to expand the process to other areas of the course and into other courses that would benefit from expansion of the discussion process as an effective format for assessment.

REFERENCES

Bergin, J., Eckstein, J., & Manns, M. L., & Wallingford, E., (2001). Patterns for Gaining Different Perspectives. *A Part of the Pedagogical Patterns Project Pattern Language Version 0.6.* Retrieved March 20, 2010, from http://pedagogicalpatterns.org/current/gaindiffperspective.pdf

Bird, L. (2007). The 3 C's Design Model for Networked E-Learning: A tool for Novice Designers. *Innovations in Education and Teaching International*, *26*(3), 153–168. doi:10.1080/14703290701251231

Bos, N., Sadat, N., & Shami, S. (2006). Adapting a Face-to-Face *Role-Playing* Simulation for Online Play. *Educational Technology Research and Development*, *54*(5), 493–522. doi:10.1007/s11423-006-0130-z

Cavanaugh, J. (2005) Teaching Online – A Time Comparison. *Online Journal of Distance Learning Administration.* Retrieved March 20, 2010 from http://www.westga.edu/~distance/ojdla/spring81/cavanaugh81.htm

Curriculum, Technology, & Education Reform (CTER) (2009). *CTER online master of education program, University of Illinois at Urbana-Champaign,* retrieved March 20, 2010 from http://wik.ed.uiuc.edu/index.php/Role_playing

Danchak, M. M. (2002) Bringing Affective Behavior to e-Learning. *The Technology Source.* Retrieved March 20, 2010, from http://technologysource.org/article/bringing_affective_behavior_to_elearning/

Dickey, M. D. (2003). Teaching in 3D: Pedagogical affordances and constraints of 3D virtual worlds for synchronous distance learning. *Distance Education*, *24*(1), 105–122. doi:10.1080/01587910303047

Dickey, M. D. (2005). Three-dimensional virtual worlds and distance learning: two case studies of Active Worlds as a medium for distance education. *British Journal of Educational Technology*, *36*(3), 439–451. doi:10.1111/j.1467-8535.2005.00477.x

Dunlap, J. (2005). Workload Reduction in Online Courses: Getting Some Shuteye. *Performance Improvement*, *44*(5), 18–26. doi:10.1002/pfi.4140440507

Eckloff, M. (2006). Using sociodrama to improve communication and understanding. *et Cetera. 63,* (3), *259-270..*

Fannon, K. (2005). *'Needle-stick'- A Role-Play Simulation: Transformative Learning in Complex Dynamic Social Systems.* Retrieved March 20, 2010, from http://www.avetra.org.au/downloads/Vol2_1%20-%202003%20-%20Fannon.pdf

Fisher, B. (2009). *Role play as a teaching method in multi-stakeholder natural resource* 2006, Lao PDR. Retrieved March 20, 2010, from http://www.mekong.es.usyd.edu.au/projects/mli/initiatives_partners/roleplay_manual_ubu.pdf

Folger, J. P., Poole, M. S., & Stutman, R. K. (2005). *Working Through Conflict: Strategies for Relationships, Groups, and Organizations* (5th ed.). Boston: Pearson/Allyn and Bacon.

Fowler, C., & Mayes, J. (2000). Learning Relationships from Theory to design. In Squires, D., Conole, G., & Jacobs, G. (Eds.), *The Changing Face of Learning Technology* (pp. 39–50). Cardiff, UK: University of Wales Press.

Gambrell, L. (2004). Shifts in Conversations: Teacher-led, Peer-Led, and Computer-Mediated Discussions. *The Reading Teacher*, *58*(2), 212–216. doi:10.1598/RT.58.2.9

Headley, S. (2005). Five Role I Play in Online Courses. *Journal of Online Education, 2* (1). Retrieved March 20, 2010, from http://www.innovateonline.info/index.php?view=article&id=78

Hunt, J. (2009). Attitude is Everything. *Diverse Issues in Higher Education*, *26*(3), 19–25.

Kain, D. (2006). Choose Colleagues Before Friends for Teaching Teams. *Education Digest*, ▪▪▪, 53–57.

Kassop, M. (2003) Ten Ways Online Education Matches, or Surpasses, Face-to-Face Learning. *The Technology Source,* Retrieved March 20, 2010 from: http://technologysource.org/article/ten_ways_online_education_matches_or_surpasses_facetoface_learning/

Kuh, G. D., & Hu, S. (2001). The effects of student-faculty interaction in the 1990s. *The Review of Higher Education*, *24*(3), 309–332. doi:10.1353/rhe.2001.0005

Lebaron, J., & Miller, D. (2005). The Potential of Jigsaw Role Playing to Promote the Social Construction of Knowledge in an Online Graduate Education Course. *Teachers College Record*, *107*(8), 1652–1675. doi:10.1111/j.1467-9620.2005.00537.x

MacKnight, C. (2000). Teaching Critical Thinking through Online Discussions. *EDUCAUSE Quarterly*, *23*(4), 38–41.

Maddux, C. (2004). Developing *Online Courses:* Ten Myths. *Rural Special Education Quarterly*, *23*(2), 27–33.

Matters, G. (2005, June). *Designing Assessment Tasks for Deep Thinking.* Paper presented at the Twelfth Annual Conference of the Curriculum Corporation, Brisbane, Australia. Retrieved March 20, 2010, from http://cmslive.curriculum.edu.au/verve/_resources/Matters_edited.pdf

Murphy, K. L., Mahoney, S. E., Chen, C., Mendoza-Diaz, N. V., & Yang, X. (2005). A Constructivist Model of Mentoring, Coaching, and Facilitating Online Discussions. *Distance Education*, *26*(3), 341–367. doi:10.1080/01587910500291454

Murray, B. (2000). Reinventing Class Discussion Online. *Monitor on Psychology, 31*(4). Retrieved March 20, 2010, from http://www.apa.org/monitor/apr00/reinventing.html

Nelson, D., & Blenkin, C. (2007). The Power of Online Role-Play Simulations: Technology in Nursing Education. *International Journal of Nursing Education Scholarship, 4*(1). Retrieved March 20, 2010, from http://www.bepress.com/ijnes/vol4/iss1/art1

Palloff, R., & Pratt, K. (2004). *Collaborating Online: Learning Together in Community*. New York: Jossey-Bass.

Pettenger, M., & Young, N. (2008). Investigating the Impact of Role Play Simulations on Student Learning: An Assessment Model. In *Conference Papers - ISA's 49th, International Studies Association, 2008, Annual Convention, Bridging Multiple Divides.* Hilton San Francisco, San Francisco, CA, USA. Retrieved April 13, from http://www.allacademic.com/meta/p250818_index.html

Piechura-Couture, K., Tichenor, M., Touchton, D., Maciasaac, E., & Heins, H. D. (2006). Co-teaching: A model for education reform. *Principal Leadership*, *6*(9), 39–43.

Raleigh, D. (2000). Keys to Facilitating Successful Online Discussions. *Teaching with Technology Today, 7* (4). Retrieved March 20, 2010, from http://www.uwsa.edu/ttt/raleigh.htm

Salas, A. (2006). The Rosy Future of Distance Ed. *The Hispanic Outlook in Higher Education,* 33-38.

Shafer, I. (2008). *Team Teaching: Education for the Future. Dept of education and training / new south wales.* Retrieved March 20, 2010, from http://www.usao.edu/~facshaferi/teamteaching.htm.

Shapiro, E., & Dempsey, C. (2008). Conflict Resolution in Team Teaching a Case Study in Interdisciplinary Teaching. *College Teaching*, *56*(3), 157–162. doi:10.3200/CTCH.56.3.157-162

Shibley, I. (2006). Interdisciplinary Team Teaching: Negotiating Pedagogical Differences. *College Teaching, 54*(3), 271–275. doi:10.3200/CTCH.54.3.271-274

Sogunro, O. (2004). Efficacy of role-playing pedagogy in training leaders: some reflections. *Journal of Management Development, 23*(3/4), 335–339.

Song, L., Hannafin, M., & Hill, J. (2007). Reconciling Beliefs and Practices in Teaching and Learning. *Educational Technology Research and Development, 55*(1), 27–51. doi:10.1007/s11423-006-9013-6

Stagg, C., Peterson, S., & Slotta, J. (2009). Saying Yes to Online Learning: A First – Time Experience Teaching an Online Graduate Course in Literacy Education. *Literacy Research and Instruction, 48*(2), 120–137. doi:10.1080/19388070802226303

Tannenbaum, J. E. (1996). *Practical ideas on alternative assessment for ESL students.* Washington, DC. (ERIC Clearinghouse on Languages and Linguistics, ED395500).

University of Florida – Center for Instructional Technology and training (2007). *Role Play*. Retrieved March 20, 2010, from http://www.citt.ufl.edu/toolbox/toolbox_rolePlay.php

Vogler, K., & Long, E. (2003). Team Teaching Two Sections of the Same Undergraduate Course: a Case Study. *College Teaching, 51*(4), 122–127. doi:10.1080/87567550309596426

Waltonen-Moore, S., Stuart, D., Newton, E., Oswald, R., & Varonis, E. (2006). From Virtual Strangers to a Cohesive Online Learning Community: The Evolution of Online Group Development in a Professional Development Course. *Journal of Technology and Teacher Education, 14*(2), 287–312.

Wu, D., & Hiltz, S. (2003). *Online Discussions and Perceived Learning.* Paper presented at the Ninth Americas Conference on Information Systems. Retrieved March 20, 2010, from http://citeseerx.ist.psu.edu/viewdoc/download?doi=10.1.1.98.8584&rep=rep1&type=pdf

Yang, Y., Ting, C., Newby, T., & Bill, R. (2005). Using Socratic Questioning to Promote Critical Thinking Skills Through Asynchronous Discussion Forums in Distance Learning Environments. *American Journal of Distance Education, 19*(3), 163–181. doi:10.1207/s15389286ajde1903_4

ADDITIONAL READING

Al-Shamman, M. (2005). Assessing the learning experience in a business process re-engineering (BPR) course at the University of Bahrain. *Business Process Management Journal, 11*(1), 47–63. doi:10.1108/14637150510578728

Anderson, T. D., & Garrison, D. R. (1995). Critical Thinking in Distance Education: Developing Critical Communities in an Audio Teleconference Context. *Higher Education, 29*(2), 183–199. doi:10.1007/BF01383838

Anonymous,. (2005). Precor Shapes Up to a Change of Culture. *Human Resource Management International Digest, 13*(6), 24–27.

Balch, W. R. (1983, October). The use of role-playing in a classroom demonstration of client centered therapy. *Teaching of Psychology, 10*(3), 173–174. doi:10.1207/s15328023top1003_17

Beck, A. (2006). Adventures in *Team Teaching*: Integrating Communications into an Engineering Curriculum. *Teaching English in the Two-Year College, 34*(1), 59–70.

Caldwell, J., Dodd, K., & Wilkes, C. (2008). Developing a *team* mentoring model. *Nursing Standard, 23*(7), 35–38.

Chou, C. (2003). Interactivity and interactive functions in web-based learning systems: A technical framework for designers. *British Journal of Educational Technology*, *34*(3), 265–279. doi:10.1111/1467-8535.00326

Clark, M., Nguyen, H.T., & Bray, C[UNKNOWN ENTITY &!YearPlace;], & Levine. R.E. *Team-Based Learning in an Undergraduate Nursing Course*. *Journal of Nursing Education, 47*, (3), 111-118. doi:10.3928/01484834-20080301-02

Dennen, V. P., Darabi, A. A., & Smith, L. J. (2007). Instructor-learner interaction in online courses: The relative perceived importance of particular instructor actions on performance and satisfaction. *Distance Education*, *28*(1), 65–79. doi:10.1080/01587910701305319

Duncombe, S., & Heikkinen, M. H. (1988). Role-playing for different viewpoints. *College Teaching*, *36*(1), 3–5.

Fischer, J. (2002). Improving approaches to multicultural education: teaching empathy through role playing. *Multicultural Education*, *9*(4), 25–26.

Gaoyin, Q., & Tao, L. (2005). In-service Teachers and Computer Mediated Discussions. *Reading Horizons*, *46*(2), 115–133.

Hanawalt, A. (2005). The Empress of Online: Reflections of an Experienced Online Instructor. *International Alliance of Women in Music Journal*, Spring 2005, Retrieved March 20, 2010, from http://www.iawm.org/articles_html/hanawalt_online_teaching.html

Johnson-Curiskis, N. (2006). Online course planning. *Journal of Online Learning and Teaching, 2*(1). Retrieved March 20, 2010, from http://jolt.merlot.org/05014b.htm

Lin, M., Lake, V. E., & Rice, D. (2008). Teaching Anti-Bias Curriculum in Teacher Education Programs: what and How. *Teacher Education Quarterly*, *35*(2), 187–201.

Loertscher, D. (2008). Purposeful co-teaching: real cases and effective strategies. *Teacher Librarian*, *36*(2), 63–66.

MacKnight, C. B. (2000). Teaching Critical Thinking through Online Discussions. *EDUCAUSE Quarterly*, *23*(4), 38–41.

Maddrell, A. M. C. (1994). A Scheme for the Effective Use of Role Plays for an Emancipatory Geography. *Journal of Geography in Higher Education*, *18*(2), 155–162. doi:10.1080/03098269408709251

Mandernach, B., Gonzales, R., & Garrett, A. (2006). An examination of online instructor presence via threaded discussion participation. *Journal of Online Learning and Teaching, 2*(4). Retrieved March 20, 2010, from http://jolt.merlot.org/vol2no4/mandernach.htm

Mintz, S. (1996). Aristotelian virtue and *business* ethics education. *Journal of Business Ethics*, *15*(8), 827–839. doi:10.1007/BF00381851

Morris, L., Xu, H., & Finnegan, C. (2005). Roles of Faculty in Teaching Asynchronous Undergraduate Courses. *Journal of Asynchronous Learning*, *9*(1), 65–82.

Newberry, B. (2005). The use of bulletin boards for discussions in online learning. *International Journal of Instructional Technology and Distance Learning, 2*(11). Retrieved March 20, 2010, from http://www.itdl.org/Journal/Nov_05/article04.htm.

Nikendei, C., Kraus, B., Schrauth, M., Weyrich, P., Zipfel, S., Herzog, W., & Junger, J. (2007). Integration of role-playing into technical skills training: a randomized controlled trial. *Medical Teacher*, *29*(9/10), 956–966. doi:10.1080/01421590701601543

Olorunnisola, A. A., Ramasubramanian, S., Russill, C., & Dumas, J. (2004). Case Study Effectiveness in a Team-Teaching and General-Education Environment. *The Journal of General Education*, *52*(3), 175–198. doi:10.1353/jge.2004.0005

Oros, A. L. (2007). Let's Debate: Active Learning Encourages Student Participation and Critical Thinking. *Journal of Political Science Education*, *3*(3), 293–311. doi:10.1080/15512160701558273

Paretti, M. C. (2008). Teaching Communication in Capstone Design: The ***Role*** of the Instructor in Situated Learning. *Journal of Engineering Education.*, *97*(4), 491–504.

Parrot, A. (1987). Is Queen Victoria lecturing today? Teaching human sexuality using famous personalities. *Teaching Sociology*, *15*(3), 257–262. doi:10.2307/1318339

Penny, K. (2008). Syllabus Selection: Innovative Learning Activity. *The Journal of Nursing Education*, *47*(9), 435–437.

Sanchez, A., & Lopez, L. E. (1993). *Making Connections: An In-Depth Concept Teaching Technique.* Paper presented at a Meeting of the Center for Critical Thinking. (ERIC Accession No. ED375091).

Schrum, L., & Hong, S. (2002). Dimensions and strategies for online success: Voices from experienced educators. *Journal of Asynchronous Learning Networks*, *6*(1).

Shaw, C. M. (2004). Using Role-Play Scenarios in the IR Classroom: An Examination of Exercises on Peacekeeping Operations and Foreign Policy Decision Making. *International Studies Perspectives*, *5*(1), 1–22. doi:10.1111/j.1528-3577.2004.00151.x

Thilmany, J. (2009). Soft – Skill Prescription. *Mechanical Engineering (New York, N.Y.)*, *131*(4), 12–14.

Williams, V. C. (2006). Assuming Identities, Enhancing Understanding: Applying Active Learning Principles to Research Projects. *Journal of Political Science Education*, *2*(2), 171–186. doi:10.1080/15512160600669015

Wilson, B. M., Pollock, P. H., & Hamann, K. (2007). Does Active Learning Enhance Learner Outcomes? Evidence from Discussion Participation in Online Classes. *Journal of Political Science Education*, *3*(2), 131–142. doi:10.1080/15512160701338304

KEY TERMS AND DEFINITIONS

Action Research: Action research is a reflective process of progressive problem solving that can be applied to improving strategies for effective pedagogy through the implementation of new strategies and review of the strategies effectiveness. The basic format to be followed is to recognize a problem, research information related to that problem, create a plan to deal with the problem in an effective manner and implement the determined solution into an environment in which this solution can be observed in action. The final step is to assess the ability of the implemented solution to solve the original problem and provide suggestions that may further enhance the solution to meet its original purpose.

Deeper Understanding: Deeper understanding is the goal of having students demonstrate levels of understanding above the content knowledge level and display higher order thinking skills in the context of content materials. This needs to be expressed through student insights that allows for applications of content in varied and connected circumstances.

Online Learning: Online Learning calls for an approach for instructors to make themselves as present as possible in the online environment. The role of the instructors also becomes more of a coach or facilitator making student centered activities as important as possible.

Role Playing: Role playing is a strategy that provides opportunities for course participants to take part in activities that are projecting real life situations. Instructors assuming the personas of specific roles can create environments that call for critical thinking on the part of students taking part in role playing activities.

Rubric: A rubric can be defined as a scoring tool that lists the criteria for a piece of work or list the specific expectations for students in the context of their work. It assesses what counts or is given specific value. Rubrics can be utilized to assess projects or student work in the context of criteria that is difficult or impossible to score in terms of objective evidence. So a rubric is most useful when dealing with elements to be assessed that are subjective in nature or deal with attitudes or feelings.

Socio-Drama: Socio-drama centers on the importance of interactions and perspectives concerning itself with group issues. It is a group action method in which participants act out an agreed upon social situation spontaneously and discover alternative ways of dealing with problems and interactions. It concerns itself with those aspects of roles that we share with others and helps people to express their thoughts and feelings, solve problems, and clarify values.

Socratic Approach: The Socratic approach named after the philosopher Socrates, is a form of inquiry and debate between individuals with opposing viewpoints based on asking and answering questions to stimulate critical thinking and to illuminate ideas. This approach matches well the use of discussion boards for online courses since it is a dialectical method, often involving an oppositional discussion in which the defense of one point of view is pitted against the defense of another. The process is student-centered and provides an opportunity for students to demonstrate critical thinking skills and insights reflecting deep levels of understanding.

Team Teaching: Team teaching is an effort for more than one instructor to take part of the planning and presentation of the course allowing for a division of labor and sharing various perspectives in relation to materials covered in the course. To be successful it does call for a coordinated planning process for its implementation to be effective.

Chapter 11
Employing Collaborative Learning Strategies and Tools for Engaging University Students in Collaborative Study and Writing

Thanasis Daradoumis
Open University of Catalonia, Spain & University of the Aegean, Greece

Maria Kordaki
Patras Unversity, Greece

ABSTRACT

This chapter addresses several issues and challenges that one faces when carrying out a real collaborative learning experience following a blended learning design that includes a mixture of face-to-face and online collaborative learning processes. The chapter presents an experience based on a blended course on "Collaborative Educational Systems". This scenario employed a variety of collaborative strategies, methods and tools to support and enhance debate and information exchange among peers in order to complete a specific task: writing an essay collaboratively. Carrying out this task entails a preliminary study and analysis of the subject matter, which are also performed in a collaborative manner. The authors describe the educational scenario in detail, including the structure of the activities, the rules the groups were asked to apply and the procedures the students had to follow to accomplish the task. They finally analyze and evaluate this learning experience with a critical point of view as regards the collaboration strategies adopted, the way students built their own strategies combining the ones presented in the course, and the collaborative learning process and product.

DOI: 10.4018/978-1-61692-898-8.ch011

INTRODUCTION

Computer-Supported Collaborative Learning (CSCL) is one of the most influencing research paradigms dedicated to improve teaching and learning with the help of modern information and communication technology (Dillenbourg, 1999). Collaborative or group learning refers to instructional methods where students are encouraged to work together on learning tasks. Collaborating in small groups may constitute a powerful means for promoting and enhancing learning and social interaction. Recent studies of e-learning have pointed out that involving learners in collaborative learning activities could positively contribute to extending and deepening their learning experiences, test out new ideas, improve learning outcomes and increase learner satisfaction, at the same time decreasing the isolation that can occur in an e-learning setting (Palloff & Pratt, 2004). Furthermore, collaborative learning situations can provide a natural setting for demanding cognitive activities which can also trigger collaborative learning mechanisms such as knowledge articulation as well as sharing and distributing the cognitive load (Dillenbourg, 1999).

However, many teachers remain unsure of why, when, and how to integrate collaboration into their teaching practices in general as well as into their online classes (Panitz, 1997; Brufee, 1999). In addition, the effectiveness and success of a group of learners depends on a variety of issues during its lifecycle (Pipek & Wulf, 1999). Furthermore, during task realization, students learning via CSCL technology and methods need guidance and support in order to collaborate effectively and achieve their learning goals successfully. This fact is especially critical when it has to do with collaborative learning practices that are carried out over a long period of time, employing a blended learning approach (a traditional classroom with face-to-face interaction supplemented by online resources), and engaging students to work together to solve a complex real problem and participate in a variety of activities (Kiesler & Sproull, 1987; Dobson & McCracken, 1997; Cameron, Barrows, & Crooks, 1999; Thomas, 2000).

The essential role of appropriate tools to help teachers and students with their mindful and appropriate learning has been acknowledged by many researchers (Lloyd & Wilson, 2001; Babiuk, 2005). Such tools are essential in all types of education. Essentially, in web-based education and blended education, the existence of this kind of tools is crucial for the teachers' and students' more effective involvement (Koper & Tattersall, 2005).

This chapter reports a real collaborative learning experience that has been carried out following a blended learning design approach that includes a mixture of face-to-face and online collaborative learning processes employing a variety of collaborative strategies, methods and tools to support and enhance debate and information exchange among peers in order to complete a specific task. The task consisted in writing an essay collaboratively, which includes a preliminary study of the subject matter which is also performed in a collaborative manner.

In particular we present an educational scenario which is implemented in a real classroom of a fourth year undergraduate university course, called "Collaborative Educational Systems", which lasts a term (13 weeks). The scenario specifies a structure for the activities to be carried out, dictates the rules that learning groups should apply in order to collaborate and indicates the procedures to be followed by students to accomplish the task at hand. Given a pool of collaboration strategies, techniques and tools, students are encouraged to build their own strategy that fits better the dynamics and idiosyncrasy of their group. This results in developing self-regulated methods which foster collaboration and tackle the task more effectively. However, it also presents some risks and problems that we had to face during the collaborative process. We provide an extensive discussion of the issues involved in the design, management, monitoring, and evaluation of the learning processes that take place in the realization of this scenario.

In our study, we show the many benefits of a blended collaborative learning approach: increased classroom size, accessibility of material and flexibility, but also noted that motivation and technological ability are major factors in the success of a student in a blended environment. Our approach brings new expectations and requires changes in attitudes and reward structures for both the learners and the teachers, such as new roles, different pedagogic and learning methods, and technological and training supports that enable learners build up social structures, encourage learning and develop critical thinking skills.

The organization of the chapter is as follows. First, background issues are addressed in the field of collaborative blended learning which concern the design and application of collaborative learning scenarios, collaborative strategies, collaborative tools, etc. The subsequent section provides a detailed description of our case study, specifying the context of the collaborative learning experience. This context will be presented in terms of participants, course and task description. Then, we present our methodological approach that fosters collaborative study and writing in a blended learning environment. We describe the conceptual framework of our approach that includes the given tasks, the activities to be carried out, the collaborative strategies and tools employed, the specific contextual requirements for a strategy/tool to be adopted. The fifth Section proceeds to discuss the technological aspects that can better support collaboration. We try to give an answer to the question of what technical features are necessary to match the design of the collaborative learning scenario and make the use of the collaborative strategy chosen feasible and effective. The sixth Section then addresses monitoring and evaluation issues of the collaborative learning scenario. We discuss how to monitor, understand, and evaluate group learning as well as how to assess individual and group learning and how to evaluate both the learning process and product. The final two sections summarize the results of the empirical study and draw the conclusions and future directions of our research.

BACKGROUND

Our collaborative learning experience takes part in a blended learning environment that includes a mixture of face-to-face and online collaborative learning processes. Blended learning is an approach to learning and teaching which combines and aligns learning undertaken in face-to-face sessions with learning opportunities created online (Littlejohn & Pegler, 2006). The aim of blended learning is basically to join the best of classroom or face-to-face learning with the best of online learning. Recent research has started to focus on the aspect of collaboration in a blended learning environment, in which both benefits and drawbacks have been identified. On the one hand, the opportunities presented by an online collaborative activity are many and have been accounted in the literature (Browne, 2003; Macdonald, 2003; Pallof & Pratt, 2004; Roberts, 2005; Van Eijl & Pilot, 2003). On the other hand, several constraints of online collaboration are presented in five categories: perceptions, negative attitudes, skills, technology and reality (Nel & Wilkinson, 2006).

As regards *perceptions*, several students may have no prior experience with online collaboration, as it is in our case. Then, it is understandable that many of them may initially have various misconceptions. In our context, which is described in next section, our students had never carried out collaborative activities in an online environment, and had no clear idea about what it would require of them to be successful learners in this setting. They really did not expect that participation in an online learning mode would require them to play a more active role in their own and their fellow students' learning experiences (Masiello, Ramberg, & Lonka, 2005). Moreover, some students may perceive online activities to be more difficult and time-consuming than any face-to-face activity (Taylor, 2005), whereby others may believe that the course would be easier to pass (than a traditional face-to-face course) due to the inclusion of an online element (Springfield, 2005). From all this, it becomes apparent that many students perceive e-learning as "easy-learning." As a result of this misconception, as we will explain in Section 4, we had to make a plan for striving against students' belief that they did not need to attend the face-to-face sessions if some of the course content and activities were available online.

As concerns *negative attitudes*, according to Roberts (2005) it is fairly common for students to initially show resistance to the idea of working in groups. While some students' negativity might stem from prior experiences in similar situations, others might just not like group work (Taylor, 2005). In our case, some students had worked in pairs through contact meetings to carry out an assignment in previous courses, so they participated in some kind of informal, voluntary collaboration with a classmate they knew very well, so they were feeling confident and comfortable with collaboration. But in general, there are several students that probably do not like to be dependent on others and consequently prefer to work on their own. In our case, where they had been asked to form groups of four members in order to collaborate, it became apparent that some students were not very excited to live this experience. So, a special care had to be taken in order to overcome students' reluctance and anxiety to collaborate, as explained in Section 4.

When it comes to the requirement of specific *skills/knowledge*, most students are not usually aware that active participation behaviour (both synchronous and asynchronous), well-balanced contributions and role playing, self- and peer-evaluation, peer involvement and commitment, etc. are very important factors of online group success (Daradoumis, Martínez, & Xhafa, 2006). They therefore do not realise that they need different/additional skills and knowledge to successfully interact/operate in this environment (Muirhead, 2001; Masiello et al., 2005). Macdonald (2003) also warns that the extent to which students will collaborate and interact in the online environment is dependent on their level of competence. In our case, students had limited experience of real group work and hardly any experience with online interaction/ collaboration. In such cases, students are unlikely to possess the group/collaborative skills needed to successfully complete an online collaborative activity or participate in an online discussion (Browne, 2003; Macdonald, 2003; Roberts, 2005; Taylor, 2005). For this reason, specific collaboration strategies should be provided to the students that will allow them to structure their activities efficiently as well as apply effective rules and procedures to accomplish the task. These issues are also discussed in Section 4.

Technology is another important issue and means for supporting the whole enterprise. Several tools can be used to help both teachers and students engage into a real, fruitful and effective collaboration. The matter here is the type of tools that should be chosen, among a rich variety of existing collaborative tools, as well as the appropriate combination of them in order to provide an effective and costless support. Even though the use of technology is intended to enhance the student learning experience, this is certainly not always the case. Indeed, technology may cause negative results to those students who may be dominated by anxiety and confusion when trying to use new tools due to their inexperience or time constraints (Masiello et al. 2005). Students may be also reluctant of staying online on a steady basis or simply they do not realize the importance of being aware of the state of their shared workspaces or what their peers have recently done so that they can react on time and thus maintain a fluent and consistent group interaction. It therefore becomes apparent that students need both some initial guidance and continuous support in the use of the various collaborative e-learning tools (Pallof & Pratt, 2004; Masiello et al., 2005). Another problem that hinders the efficient use of technology is that some students do not have access to a personal computer and the Internet at home, which prevents them from participating during the evenings and over weekends (Browne, 2003). In Section 5, we try to provide solutions to these issues and suggest those technological tools, aspects and features that are necessary to best match the design of the collaborative learning scenario and support the collaboration more efficiently. For instance, since students were completely dependent on technology to carry out discussions aiming to support learners' collaborative knowledge construction (no face-to-face discussions were allowed), specific tools were chosen to facilitate asynchronous or synchronous discussion according to the collaborative task that had to be carried out.

Finally, *reality* is an important factor that one should always take into account. As Nel and Wilkinson (2006) mention, any teacher wants to create an ideal environment for online collaboration, but reality will (in most cases) prevent him/her from achieving an idyllic vision. Some students may encounter difficulties to find the most ideal group members; others might not even be prepared to collaborate in order to learn (Browne, 2003). Some students may be more demanding and active than others; other students may have difficulties to keep to deadlines (Masiello et al., 2005). Some consistent group members will prepare before participating in an online activity or discussion, or attending a face-to-face session, while other members will not do so. Another factor that plays an important role to the success of group work is the duration of the course. Courses, like ours, that last a whole term (13 to 15 weeks) may offer the teacher and the students a comfortable amount of time to prepare, design and implement an interesting long term collaborative learning scenario, but specific care should be taken so that students remain active and constantly engaged into their collaborative activities during the term, since it is easy that some students feel relaxed or get disconnected for some time, thus losing their rhythm or hindering the smooth realization of the agreed group plan and organization (Daradoumis & Xhafa, 2005).

All in all, the above issues dictate a careful and proper design and application of a collaborative learning scenario, which includes the use of appropriate activities and collaborative strategies, efficient rules and procedures, as well as suitable collaborative tools. Very similar considerations can be also found in Delfino and Persico (2007). Our approach will take all the above constraints into account and will deal with as many of the issues listed by trying to provide a most effective solution to the majority of them. All these important aspects are discussed in detail in the following sections.

THE CONTEXT OF THE COLLABORATIVE LEARNING EXPERIENCE

The educational scenario of our case study is a real classroom of a fourth year undergraduate university course, called "Collaborative Educational Systems", which spans over a term (a 13-week period). The size of the class is rather small: there were 18 enrolled students, from which 12 participated in the collaborative learning experience actively, whereas the rest of them decided not to be involved in the group work and preferred auditing the course and the experience. The main reason of the auditing choice is that these students were lacking confidence in participating into such a demanding practice, and they were not feeling sure about their real involvement and commitment toward collaboration. Evidently, these 6 students were not awarded any final grade and they had to repeat the course next term. However, the contact they had with the experience, even in a passive way, proved to be very beneficial since they saw that the venture was feasible, so any fears or hesitations they had about online collaboration were substantially reduced.

Case Study Description

The blended learning design of the course includes a three-hour face-to-face contact session per week. During this session, first some theoretical aspects of the course are exposed by the teacher, and then the focus of the lesson shifts to discuss the matters that concern the realization of the online collaborative learning practice. The general aim of the course is to introduce students to basic concepts of Collaborative Educational Systems, that is, to environments that promote and facilitate learning through collaboration. Then its specific goals are to let students become familiar with theoretical models and methodological approaches as well as with systems and tools that support collaborative learning. The challenge of the course is to engage students into this new field in a real and practical way and, most importantly, produce changes in attitudes and perceptions, define new roles, introduce different pedagogic and learning methods, and provide technological and training supports that enable learners build up social structures, encourage learning and develop knowledge and critical thinking skills.

To this end, the introductory face-to-face session is dedicated to inform students about the course design and requirements, and basically turn their focus of attention into the collaborative spirit of the course. Thus, students are asked to form groups of four members and an open discussion about the benefits and difficulties of online collaboration is organized, aiming at initiating students into this endeavour. Since students are in the last year of their studies, most of them know each other, so it is not difficult for them to take the initiative to create good synergies and groups. The role of the instructor here is to invigilate the group formation process and assure the creation of well-formed groups. In our case, three groups are created. As a consequence, the first objective of the course is accomplished.

Then, the main course requirement is explained. This is the online implementation of a collaborative practice, which spans all over the term and consists of the elaboration of specific tasks which are thoroughly explained to the students. The successful realization of the collaborative practice includes the following steps:

1. Given the big variety of collaboration strategies/methods that exist in literature (Kordaki, Siempos & Daradoumis, 2009), the instructor facilitates the students a list of twenty selected ones which are briefly presented in class. In particular, the instructor explains the steps of each strategy and the way it is used in a context-free situation.
2. Students are required to choose a small set of the above strategies (up to four) that best fit their individual characteristics, preferences and styles. Students are encouraged to search the literature in order to find more details about how the chosen strategies have been used in practice, and which are the benefits and limitations of their application in real collaborative settings. This will give them a clear idea of the goal, function and dynamics of each strategy.
3. Based on this knowledge and the tasks that should be accomplished, students are then asked to design and build a new collaboration strategy that best fits the dynamics and idiosyncrasy of their group, by combining ideas and techniques of the strategies they analyzed as well as applying their own ideas, and use this innovative collaborative approach to carry out all the phases/tasks of their collaborative practice (from studying a selected chapter to writing an essay about the chapter topic). This new strategy should clearly describe its goals and general function

and, most importantly, it should specify all the steps and actions that group members should take to accomplish the collaborative practice successfully.

4. To carry out the collaborative practice, each group should first choose a chapter of the course manuscript. Each chapter describes a specific topic on theoretical models, methodological approaches as well as systems and tools that support collaborative learning. As such, each group chooses a different topic to work on. This task engages students into an online synchronous discussion which gives group members the opportunity to experience a rather relaxed and informal interaction that allows them to perform a decision-making process and initiates them into a long-term collaborative endeavour.
5. Each group member should individually study the chapter. To check whether students understood the topic, the instructor creates a forum for each group with the aim to engage group members into asynchronous discussions. The asynchronous mode of discussion allows group members to reflect upon their peer responses, evaluate them and then compose a common answer which will be assessed by the instructor. This task may last between 7 and 10 days.
6. Specific tools are also supplied to students to support online collaboration. Each tool has a particular role and function and thus is used to support specific tasks of the collaborative practice.
7. Groups have to elaborate specific progress reports and present their on-going work every four weeks in the face-to-face sessions. This produces open discussions in the class among the students and the instructor as a moderator, which makes students reflect not only on their own work but also on the others' work and achievements.
8. The instructor sets up specific criteria for assessing both group and individual performance. We need to give both formative assessments (how are they doing?) and summative assessments (did they achieve learning and project goals?). We also need to assess both the individual and team contributions, including both the collaborative process and its individual and collective outcomes.

We explain this learning scenario in more detail in the following sections.

THE CONCEPTUAL AND METHODOLOGICAL FRAMEWORK OF OUR APPROACH

The basic components of the conceptual framework of our approach are presented in Figure 1.

The students and their online groups are situated in the center of the learning process. So, they will receive input from all possible components/sources that take part in the support of group work and which contribute to the successful realization of their collaborative practice.

First of all, the *instructor* participates in a double mode. He/she interacts with and supports the students both in the face-to-face sessions and in the online collaborative environments where groups deploy their work and learning. The instructor's role and function are important since he/she also contributes in a variety of ways. In particular, he/she:

- facilitates students the collaboration strategies they will use to build their own collaborative approach to accomplish their task;
- provides students the necessary and most appropriate tools to support their work;
- supplies all the necessary materials that provide the basis for students' work;.
- will specifies useful criteria for assessing individual and group work, following a formative and summative method.

Figure 1. The conceptual framework

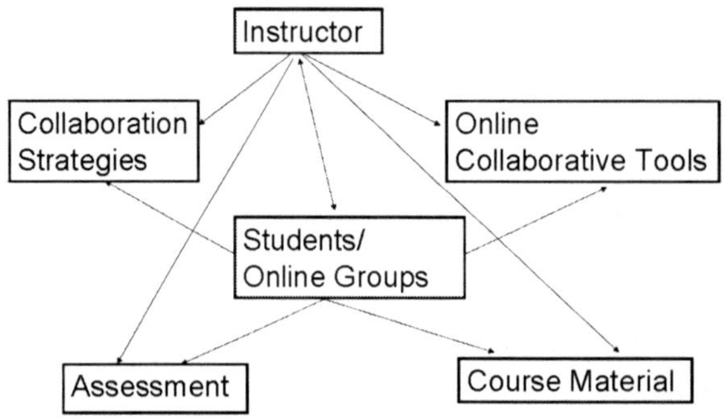

Moreover, each of the other sources contributes in its own particular way to the success of group work and individual performance.

More specifically, *collaboration strategies* are used to facilitate students' work, overcome the limitations and problems students face due to false perceptions and lack of experience in such settings, combat their fears and negative attitudes, help students acquire the specific skills/ knowledge they need, guide them in the best use and exploitation of the different online tools that support their work, and finally orientate them to adapt themselves to the reality and the true conditions of their situation in the best possible way.

To this end, the instructor provides the students with a set of twenty representative context-free collaboration strategies and asks the students to make the best use of them so that they build a full, flexible and effective collaborative context within their group which will lead them to a successful realization of their tasks. These strategies were selected as being representative of the achievement of diverse learning objectives. A detailed description of such strategies can be found in (Kordaki et al., 2009). The following are examples of these strategies, and the learning objectives they allow to achieve:

- *Brainstorming* (Osborn, 1963); focuses on the generation of a large number of ideas for the solution of a problem.
- *Student Teams Achievement Divisions* (STAD; Slavin, 1978); motivates students to encourage and help each other, while at the same time accelerates their achievements.
- *Jigsaw* (Aronson, Blaney, Sikes, Stephan, & Snapp, 1978); emphasizes interpersonal inter-dependence while allows groups to get to know a topic in depth, by making individuals become experts on a sub-topic and teach each other until the whole topic becomes familiar to all members of the group.
- *Group Investigation Method* (Sharan & Hertz-Lazarowitz, 1980); promotes the use of learning activities/problems that groups analyse in sub-problems, studied by each group member, discuss and draw conclusions and then perform a collaborative writing of reports which are assessed in discussion with teacher.
- *Co-op Co-op* (Kagan, 1985); enhances collaboration by means of discussion, open-ended problems and activities, problem decomposition into suitable individual tasks, and composition of the group solution through discussion.
- *Guided Reciprocal Peer Questioning* (Palincsar & Brown, 1984; Martin & Blanc, 1984; Kagan, 1992; 1994); encourages discussion and critical thinking through open-ended questions.

- *Three Step Interview* (Kagan, 1994); enhances team building and in-depth understanding of the topic that students deal with through their engagement into an interview and role-playing.
- *Think-Pair-Share* (Lyman, 1981); students have the time to think individually of an answer to a given question and then share their opinion with a peer (forming pairs); finally, each pair shares its common answer in a larger group of four or more members (it may include the whole class).
- *Paired Annotations* (Millis & Cottell, 1998); promotes cooperative learning through accountability and positive interdependence (students discuss key issues, exchange ideas and questions, look for differences, comment and prepare a common attitude and treatment of the subject matter).
- *Double entry journal* (Berthoff, 1981); gives students the ability to unfold their thoughts regarding a topic which help them concentrate on important terms and develop critical thinking and knowledge.

The most important contribution and innovation of our approach here is the way we suggest students to use these strategies. In particular, students should design a new collaborative strategy and use it to carry out their practice, following specific steps:

- Students should first study and analyze the existing collaborative strategies, understand their functioning and use (look for more information in literature, if necessary), and then choose a small set of them (up to four) that best fit their particular characteristics, preferences and styles as well as the specific tasks of the practice they have to carry out.
- Students get in their groups and exchange their ideas, preferences, goals, attitudes, perceptions, skills and knowledge, while they also take the tasks and the reality under which they will collaborate into account. Based on all these factors and their preferred individual collaborative strategies, students discuss and design a new common collaborative strategy for their group that combines ideas and issues of the existing strategies but can also contain personal ideas of the group members.
- Each group should thoroughly describe the functioning of their strategy in a document that will be handed over to the instructor who should evaluate and approve it. In particular, groups should provide the following information:
  - which are the existing strategies that the group has used as a basis for creating the new group's strategy;
  - justify clearly the reasons that guided the selection of the aforementioned strategies, and specify what type of actions of these strategies can be useful and contribute toward both the accomplishment of an effective collaboration (and consequently of the activity goals) and the composition of the new strategy;
  - state why the new strategy suits the idiosyncrasy, goals and preferences of the group, how it can help in the organization of the tasks that members will realize, and how it will support the structure and functioning of the group;
  - thoroughly describe the steps and actions which the new strategy consists of and the way they can be applied in the whole process of collaborative work, starting from the study of the selected chapter/topic to the realization of the new article. More specifically, each step of the new strategy will have to specify clearly and ex-

pressively the goals it sets: what each group member will do, that is, the tasks that a member will undertake to fulfill; how he/she will carry them out (e.g., through which tools, methods, etc); how he/she will collaborate with the rest of group members; and, which is the role that the various discussions (in forums and chats) play when they are performed within the group;
    - for each step of the new strategy, the students should state the existing strategy it came from (that is, in which idea or issue it relies on) or whether it is a member's new idea.
- The new collaboration strategy should then be applied for accomplishing the following tasks (in this case, the collaboration strategy urges students to interact with the *course materials* which are an important component/source of the collaborative learning experience):
    - Students should collaborate in their group to select and study a chapter from the course manuscript which contains 18 chapters. Each chapter refers to a specific topic, ranging from theoretical models and methodological approaches to systems and tools that support collaborative learning. Consequently, the choice of a chapter binds the students and their group to a particular topic which they have to study, understand and finally elaborate it further significantly, writing a new article/essay through collaborative writing, which incorporates new ideas, issues and trends.
    - Collaboration occurs from the beginning of the practice. During the initial phase, to support a more effective study and understanding of the chapter topic, group members participate in online asynchronous discussions, where each member sets at least one specific comprehension question to the other members. The instructor may also set questions to the whole group. This procedure allows group members to reflect upon their peer responses, evaluate them and then compose a common answer which will be assessed by the instructor. This task may last between 7 and 10 days.
    - At the end of the above process, each group prepares a presentation of its topic and exposes it in a face-to-face session. So all students of the class obtain some basic knowledge of several topics of the course book. After each presentation the instructor encourages discussion of the presented topic, by urging students to ask questions to the presenters.
    - Having obtained valuable knowledge and understanding of their topic, each group then starts a process of searching for new *materials* about the topic in the literature. After each member has identified and selected various new information about the topic, the group gets together to discuss, analyze and decide which information to keep and how to structure the new article. To support the realization of this difficult task through an effective collaboration a specific tool is used, the CMapTools, as explained in next section.
    - After the structure of the new article is clearly defined, each group should write it collaboratively, using a wiki, as explained in next section.

The next sections describe how technology can support collaboration in this scenario and how evaluation issues are addressed.

HOW TECHNOLOGY CAN SUPPORT COLLABORATION

Technology plays a key role in accomplishing this collaborative learning scenario successfully. At the same time technology may raise important obstacles and create problems to the students. We must find a way to balance the advantages of technology with its possible negative effects so that it finally results into a positive experience that will foster collaboration and enhance learning outcomes.

To select the most appropriate technologies to support each step of the experience effectively, we were guided by the specific tasks that groups had to carry out, as explained in the previous sections. Each task has its own needs and demands, so tools have to satisfy them in the best possible way, providing at the same time flexibility and ease of use; that is, they should not add any heavy workload either to the students or the instructor.

To this end, we used the Basic Support for Cooperative Work (BSCW) system, a groupware tool that enables mainly asynchronous collaboration over the web (Bentley et al., 1997). BSCW offers shared workspaces that groups can use to store, manage, jointly edit and share documents, realize threaded discussions, etc. This collaborative platform proved to be very useful to both students and the instructor since it offered the following functionalities.

- *Workspace structure and group organization*: BSCW gave the students the opportunity to create a unique online workspace, representing their group, where they could store the files, documents, information sources, etc. that they used during the realization of their practice. Each group could then define its own way to structure its workspace and represent the main interactions among its members as well as determine the most suitable organization of group tasks and activities (Figure 2).
- *Group calendar*: This functionality allowed groups to define a common calendar where they annotated the start and end date of the group learning tasks and other activities.
- *Task planning and realization*: All groups used this functionality to determine and organize the tasks that they had to carry out in order to achieve the goals of the collaborative practice. This included the assignment of specific members that were needed to accomplish a task, the explicit definition of the needs of each task, as well as the specification of the outputs produced by each task.
- *Asynchronous discussion forums*: As Figure 2 shows, several discussion forums have been created to achieve the various needs of the group. Each forum addressed a specific need and goal and proved to be very useful for the continuous and effective communication among group members.
- *Activity awareness*: An important feature of the BSCW platform is the awareness service that offers to all participants. BSCW sends a daily activity report to the e-mail address of all participants with all the activities and events that took place the previous day at the group workspace. In addition, it sets a special symbolic icon besides the workspace objects which denote that a change has occurred (e.g. a new object was created, an existing object has been read, modified, moved, erased, etc.). All the functionalities allow both the instructor and the group members to be aware of what is happening in the group workspace.

Another important tool that has been used in the collaborative practice is the *CmapTools*, a tool that is used to build concept maps collaboratively (Cañas et. al., 2004). This task proved to be a valuable middle step before the final task of writing the article/essay collaboratively. During

Figure 2. Extract from workspace structure and group organization

Group 3 — 17 items

est@, fil@, ist@, upc@

Nom	Mida	Creator	Data	Acció
Calendar of Group 3	0	atanasi	2009-10-09	
Conceptual map Includes the conceptual map created by means of the CmapTools and the corresponding chat carried out with this tool.	2	atanasi	2009-10-09	
Information sources Includes all the documents, articles, links, etc. related with the realization of the collaborative practice.	1	atanasi	2009-10-09	
Interviews	3	atanasi	2009-10-09	
Presentations Includes all partial presentations that took place during the realization of the collaborative practice	3	atanasi	2009-10-09	
Presentations (the last) The final presentations of the practice exposed at the last class of the semester.	2	atanasi	2009-10-09	
Reports Group's monthly reports about group work and functioning	3	atanasi	2009-10-09	
Summary of synchronous discussions Summary of all chats carried out by the group members during the realization of the collaborative practice	1	atanasi	2009-10-09	
Tasks Organization and description of group tasks	8	atanasi	2009-10-09	
Collaboration strategy Describes the details of the new collaboration strategy built by the group.	70.5 K	atanasi	2009-10-09	
Chapter/topic selection forum Contains all initial discussions that took place so that groups select the topic (chapter) that they should study and then extend collaborativelly.	6	atanasi	2009-10-09	
Collaboration strategy forum Group members disccuss the way to design a new collaboration strategy for their group work, based on existing collaboration strategies selected by each member, their group dynamics, goals, preferences, needs, etc.	6	atanasi	2009-10-09	
Conceptual map forum Contains group members' point of view regarding the type of concepts that might constitute the conceptual map that should be created by the group.	6	atanasi	2009-10-09	
Critical reflection forum Group members judge each other contributions, while they open small discussions about issues, problems and open questions that preoccupy group members.	6	atanasi	2009-10-09	
Final article forum Group members expose their ideas, opinions and questions and discuss the ways they will collaboratively write the new article in their wiki space.	4	atanasi	2009-10-09	
Group Forum This is the group's general forum for informal or general information exchange.	1	atanasi	2009-10-09	
Topic discussion forum (Duration=3days) Group members set questions to their peers related to the topic, so that to be	3	atanasi	2009-10-09	

this phase, each group collaborated closely, using also the chat functionality of the tool, to build the concept map of their article, by determining the main and secondary concepts that constituted their topic as well as the relationships between them. At the end of this process, the groups had managed to obtain a clear enough idea of the article map, so, it was easier for them to proceed to the next and final step of their work, that is to translate this concept map into text, structuring and expressing their ideas into an article form.

The final and also very important tool used by groups in this process was a wiki. Again this tool allowed groups to work collaboratively to share and write down their ideas in a multimedia fashion, combining different media: text, images, even video as additional, auxiliary means when need. The result of this effort was a well-written article easily accessible in the web.

MONITORING AND ASSESSING THE COLLABORATIVE LEARNING EXPERIENCE

One of the most difficult tasks of an online collaborative learning experience is the monitoring and assessment of group work (Daradoumis et al., 2006). The most important challenge is how to evaluate not only the final (and intermediate) products of collaboration but also the collaborative process itself. The approach adopted in this case study was to establish specific criteria (expectations) and then measure against them. This technique was found to be quite successful.

At a first stage, the awareness information offered by the BSCW platform allowed the instructor to monitor and assess the progress of each group and its members effectively, since he/she was able to have a clear enough picture of the individual and group contributions. Group members could also apply peer evaluation easily since they were aware of their peers work and were also able to react rapidly since they were receiving notifications of their peer contributions.

Most importantly, our approach points out the importance of aligning course goals and objectives with group activity and assessment. To this end, the instructor provides clear specifications of what he/she wants the students to come up with and explains why they are doing it. Students know that the instructor wants them to come up with something interesting and creative, and that further motivates them. Students were very excited about that, and tried to meet the established criteria as closely as possible.

As a consequence, *a Team Policies and Expectations Agreement* is proposed: it includes a list of expectations and policies created by the instructor for group work, and a form where students create their own team policies and expectations agreement. Students work together in their groups to create their own agreement which provides them with a clear picture of what is expected of them and what they can expect from their peers.

The criteria used to motivate, monitor and assess students' work are listed below, with a weight beside each criterion:

1. Design of a new collaboration strategy: 15%
2. Application of the collaboration strategy: 10%
3. Design and implementation of the various activities (tasks) of the collaborative practice, as well as of the discussions carried out on the BSCW platform and via other means: 15%
4. Collaborative planning and conceptualization of the group's new article by means of the CmapTools: 10%
5. Collaborative writing of the group's new article through the Wiki tool: 10%
6. *Group Processing form*: this is a form for students to fill in to evaluate the team's progress toward effective group functioning. This form is meant to provide formative feedback to the students and encourage them to reflect on how their team is working together. Both self- and peer-assessment reports were created every three weeks: 10%
7. Evaluation of quality of the final product (new article): 20%
8. Presentation of the partial and final work to the class: 10%

As regards the actual artifacts created by the three groups and their quality, we can say that one group reached an excellent work, whereas the other two, although they tried hard, produced rather moderate quality outputs. A major issue in the presented scenario was the "creation and application of a new strategy" (criteria 1 and 2). This is not a straightforward achievement. Besides, the analysis of the work done showed that the successful accomplishment of these two criteria was a very important factor that contributed to a more effective realization of the whole collaborative practice.

As an example, Table 1 shows an effective new strategy designed by one of the groups., This strategy successfully evolved during collaboration, several challenges were confronted by the students during the process, and all this endeavor contributed to accomplish the tasks and goals of the collaborative practice. The group chose the following four collaboration strategies to build their new strategy: *Group Investigation Method, Co-op Co-op, Think-Pair-Share*, and *Three Step Interview*. The selection of these strategies was mainly guided by the interests, idiosyncrasy and styles of the group members as well as the way they intended to achieve the learning goals of the collaborative practice. The subject they chose to deal with was "Virtual Collaborative Environments". To this end, they produced a list of the main tasks/phases that constituted the basic steps of the new collaboration strategy.

All the above steps provide an example of how our approach has been applied in a real situation, how collaboration evolved in a specific successful group and, in particular, how a group is able

Table 1. A new collaboration strategy built by a learning group

Interview between group members: This step is based on basic actions taken by the *Three-step Interview* method and its purpose was not only to allow the members to get to know each other better but also to be aware of each member's knowledge of the subject. The interviews were carried out by means of a chat tool.
Information search and collection: With this step, each member is assigned the task to look at the Web and the University Library for material related to the subject matter. Here, the group applies the reasoning dictated by the *Group Investigation Method*, according to which the selected material is judged by each member for its relation to the subject matter and is classified according to the domain structure.
Meditation about the content that the article should address: Based on the *Think-Pair-Share* method, each member sets a question so that the other members think about it, answer it and share their opinion with the others. In this way, several parallel asynchronous discussions take place (through the BSCW forums) aiming at meditating on the material found and making suggestions on the subtopics that their article should address.
Evaluation and determination of the specific and final subtopics of the article Following the *Think-Pair-Share* and *Group Investigation* methods, and based on the discussions of the previous step, each member writes reports arguing about the subtopics he/she thinks appropriate for the article and shares them with the rest of the team members. Each member evaluates the reports based on criteria such as the feasibility of the ideas and solutions proposed and a final group report is produced stating the decisions taken, the conclusions made and specifying the final subtopics of the subject matter.
New information collection/re-elaboration: Each member is assigned a specific subtopic to search, analyze and elaborate. Previous information found is re-elaborated, and new possible complementary pieces of information are added.
Presentation of the subtopics: This step is based on the *Co-op Co-op* method. Each member makes a presentation of the subtopic he/she was responsible for in front of the other members. This is supported by a PowerPoint presentation and lasts 15 minutes so that each member is sufficiently informed on each subtopic of the article. After each presentation the other members ask questions and further explanations.
Evaluation of the current situation: Based on the *Group Investigation Method*, at the end of all presentations, the group performs a discussion into a BSCW forum in order to evaluate the situation and draw the final conclusions. In this step, all members have the opportunity to be evaluated for the work done as well as to evaluate the others (each member can express his/her critical opinion about the presentation of the rest of the members). The group is now ready to pass to the two final stages of its collaborative work: the design and writing of the article.
Creation of the concept map of the article: During this phase, the group collaborates closely, using the CMapTools and its chat functionality, to build the concept map of the article. The group members determine the main and secondary concepts that constitute their topics as well as the relationships between them.
Writing the article: In this last phase, students collaborate to write the content of the article based on the concept map produced before and using a Wiki tool to elaborate and publish it in the Web.

to construct and apply a new collaboration strategy to achieve a given learning goal. All in all, this experience gave students the opportunity to develop several skills, both methodological and technological, as shown below.

More specifically, collaborative writing had the following effects:

- *Skills developed*: Critical thinking, brainstorming, negotiation, delegation of tasks, writing.
- *Technology support for student's work*: Ability to author and edit content collaboratively -- asynchronously and in real time; ability to maintain versions; ability to track changes and contributions.

Students Critiques (such as the ones emerged when group members view/read the work of their peers and provided constructive feedback) had the following effects:

- *Skills developed*: Productive criticism.
- *Technology support for student's work*: ability to upload work, ability to control access (viewing/editing), ability to comment, track participation.

Student Reflections occurred in the shared workspace of the group and the discussion forums, and had the following effects:

- *Skills developed*: reflection, exposure to different opinions.
- *Technology support for student's work*: ability to control access; ability to control rights (edit/view); attribution of comments to a person (non-anonymous).

Group Presentations allows students work to combine their different perspectives on a topic, research it, and create a presentation that reflects the groups' conclusions. It had the following effects:

- *Skills developed*: working in groups to develop consensus, presentation skills, delegation of tasks, encouraging accountability for assigned tasks.
- *Technology support for student's work*: a way to author and edit presentation content asynchronously and in real time; ability to narrate presentation with audio and video, if necessary; ability to store and maintain past versions; ability to control access rights (viewing/editing).

In any case, we need to improve further the experience and consolidate it, applying a number of methods and techniques, which we did not use in the way we wished. For instance, as regards the ways to use to prepare students for collaborative learning, we possibly need to:

- set up clearer rules about tasks that will be assigned as ''collaborative tasks";
- involve students themselves in creating the rules/policies for collaborative learning;
- give them clearer expectations, let them shape the project, assess often and clearly;
- prepare and train the instructor adequately;
- communicate that risk-taking is acceptable and normal;;
- get comfortable with trial and error and develop a high tolerance for experimentation;
- let students know that collaborative learning will provide both the teacher and themselves a way to innovate. Then, let them feel confident that they will receive teacher's support and monitoring all the way long;
- allow them to self define success.

As regards the strategies we can employ for fostering true collaborative learning, we possibly need to:

- Create authentic learning experiences that are real world, messy, with no clear path to decision, and invite learners to bring their knowledge, experiences, skills, etc. to the table and solve.

- Cast a spotlight on process and engage learners in critical self-reflection.
- Be creative when assembling a number of different elements that will be composed and lead to student's collaborative work/ projects.
- Reward true collaborative learning.

Certainly, different situations and challenges may appear in other cases (e.g., in less successful groups) which deserve a thorough study and analysis. Some of these issues are discussed in the following sections.

FUTURE RESEARCH DIRECTIONS

In the previous sections, we described the realization of a collaborative learning scenario that took place in a blended learning environment. We explained the complexity of such an endeavour in detail, and we suggested both methodological and technological solutions to support the whole process. Several other issues still need a broader and more effective answer, so our research continues along this line and focuses on several directions, such as:

- Describe the group dynamics that spring out from the application of a collaboration strategy.
- Analyze the tutor's role and how the tutor can anticipate and influence such dynamics.
- Discuss how technology can support the tutoring activity more effectively, especially monitoring and assessment issues.
- Provide a thorough analysis of the collaborative learning experience and interpret the results from a critical point of view.
- Propose improvements for a future implementation of the experience.
- Investigate whether the design and application of a new collaboration strategy by the group itself accomplishes more *social support* (McGrath, 1991) by the group members, that is:
  - improves and enhances the members' contribution to the achievement of mutual trust;
  - encourages members to provide more motivational and emotional support to their peers;
  - achieves a better participation and contribution to conflict resolution.
- Explore whether the proposed collaborative scenario achieves better *help services* (McGrath, 1991) by all participants in the collaborative process (both the instructor and group members), that is:
  - Help is timely;
  - Help is relevant to the student's needs;
  - Help is qualitative;
  - Help is understood by the student;
  - Help can be readily applied by the student.
- Investigate different ways to construct and use collaboration strategies and tools as well as effective ways to measure other factors that influence task performance, such as: cognitive empowerment (self-esteem, self-knowledge, self-efficacy in the domain of interest), locus of control, self-knowledge, ambition, general efficacy, motivation to action and community orientation, capacity for life-long learning, attitudes to information technology, and attitudes to collaborative work.
- Experiment how different technology can be used to enhance collaboration, since there are cases where the amount and nature of collaboration between partners has less to do with the availability of computer

software and more to do with the way the instructor designs and structures the collaborative practice (Kozma, 1999).

- Determine what metrics we can use to decide which tools are "pedagogically sound"; how would the students learn to use them; how we can integrate these tools better to support successful collaborative learning experiences; and, how we can scale up the use of these tools without significantly adding to the students' and the instructor's workload.
- Provide a more thorough analysis of the specific contextual requirements that one has to take into account for a strategy/tool to be adopted.
- Design a more systematic and effective monitoring and evaluation approach, guided by semi-automated tools, that gives the instructor the ability to define flexible and efficient methods to monitor, support and assess collaborative work and learning, and gives the students the opportunity to regulate their learning and participation in their group without any additional overhead (Persico, Pozzi, & Sarti, 2009).

CONCLUSION

This chapter provides a framework for structuring collaborative learning opportunities and selecting technologies to enhance learning outcomes in a blended learning environment. We presented the design and implementation of a new collaborative learning practice for incorporating cutting edge pedagogy into traditional curricula and classrooms. In particular, we proposed a novel methodological approach that fosters online collaborative study and writing. We innovated by encouraging and inspiring leaning groups to design themselves a new collaboration strategy that springs out of existing collaboration strategies, which fits better the idiosyncrasy and dynamics of the group, and use it to define, structure and carry out their collaboration in the best possible way.

Doing so, students assume a more responsible role for their actions, develop an active participation behavior, provide better and well-balanced contributions, and increase their involvement and commitment toward collaboration, joint learning and accomplishment of the common goal. In addition, the adoption and correct implementation of their new collaboration strategy allows them, on the one hand, to organize their groups and define their collaborative tasks and activities (such as discussions) in a more systematic, efficient and reliable way; and, on the other hand, to decide better about the way to employ the available tools.

After the end of the experience, students were asked, through a questionnaire and personal interviews, about their satisfaction with respect to both the group learning process and the acquisition of new knowledge and skills that may be used for teamwork in the real world. Students were generally satisfied for both criteria. Furthermore, when the practice has been completely assessed by the instructor, all of this work was put together, and a shared repository of information emerged; this brings a possibility that students might start building on one another's work.

Another achievement of our approach is *student reflection*. In particular, students managed to enrich their learning by engaging each other on the topic they found interesting or useful by drawing upon previous course work, opinion or life experience. Using the collaborative BSCW platform, students posted materials they thought would be of interest to one another. These materials grew over the course of the term as students provided new materials from which to learn. Many students really tried to find the most diverse information sources. Sometimes it was a group summary of a reading, sometimes notes from a lecture, sometimes a reaction to something in the popular press. When this happened, dialog emerged in the group and most members usually addressed the matter. Pedagogically, this was exciting because students posted things to learn from, and they learned about what they thought from responding to each other. The emphasis on writing and discussing forced all students to think and reflect on the topic and how it relates to both the course and what is going on in the research field. Finally, writing a report about group work and functioning every three weeks, allowed them to enter another reflexive process.

All in all, the experience proved to be positive and interesting for all participants. The issues referred above can certainly improve and make it more effective, producing more advantages and less overhead. More experimentation will show more interesting results, since we surely need more meaningful and effective collaborative learning experiences.

ACKNOWLEDGMENT

This work has been partially supported by the Spanish Ministry of Education project TIN2008-01288.

REFERENCES

Aronson, E., Blaney, N., Sikes, J., Stephan, G., & Snapp, M. (1978). *The JIGSAW classroom.* Beverly Hills, CA: Sage Publications.

Babiuk, G. (2005). A Full Bag of "Tech Tools" enhances the reflective process in Teacher Education. In C. Crawford et al. (Eds.), *Proceedings of the Society for Information Technology and Teacher Education International Conference 2005* (pp. 1873-1877). Chesapeake, VA: AACE.

Bentley, R., Appelt, W., Busbach, U., Hinrichs, E., Kerr, D., & Sikkel, S. (1997). Basic Support for Cooperative Work on the World Wide Web. *International Journal of Human-Computer Studies, 46*(6), 827–846. doi:10.1006/ijhc.1996.0108

Berthoff, A. E. (1981). *The making of meaning.* Portsmouth, NH: Heinemann Boynton/Cook Publishers.

Browne, E. (2003). Conversations in cyberspace: A study of online learning. *Open Learning, 18*(3), 245–259. doi:10.1080/0268051032000131017

Brufee, K. A. (1999). *Collaborative Learning: Higher Education Interdependence, the authority of knowledge.* Baltimore, MD: The John Hopkins University.

Cameron, T., Barrows, H. S., & Crooks, S. M. (1999). Distributed Problem-Based Learning at Southern Illinois University School of Medicine. In C. Hoadley & J. Roschelle (Eds.). *Computer Support for Collaborative Learning. Designing New Media for a New Millenium: Collaborative Technology for Learning, Education, and Training* (86-94), Palo Alto,CA: Stanford University.

Cañas, A. J., Hill, G., Carff, R., Suri, N., Lott, J., Eskridge, T., et al. (2004). CmapTools: A Knowledge Modeling and Sharing Environment. In A.J. Cañas, J.D. Novak, and F.M. González, (Eds.), *Proceedings of Concept Maps: Theory, Methodology, Technology, The First International Conference on Concept Mapping* (125-133). Pamplona, Spain: Universidad Pública de Navarra.

Daradoumis, T., Martínez, A., & Xhafa, F. (2006). A Layered Framework for Evaluating Online Collaborative Learning Interactions. *International Journal of Human-Computer Studies. Special Issue on ". Theoretical and Empirical Advances in Groupware Research, 64*(7), 622–635.

Daradoumis, T., & Xhafa, F. (2005). Problems and Opportunities of Learning together in a Virtual Learning Environment. In Roberts, T. S. (Ed.), *Computer-Supported Collaborative Learning in Higher Education* (pp. 218–233). Hershey, PA: Idea Group Press.

Delfino, M., & Persico, D. (2007). Online or face-to-face? Experimenting with different techniques in teacher training. *Journal of Computer Assisted Learning*, *23*(5), 351–365. doi:10.1111/j.1365-2729.2007.00220.x

Dillenbourg, P. (Ed.). (1999). *Collaborative Learning. Cognitive and Computational Approaches. Advances in Learning and Instruction Series*. New York: Elsevier Science Inc.

Dobson, M., & McCracken, J. (1997). Problem based learning: A means to evaluate multimedia courseware in science & technology in society. In T. Muldner & T. C. Reeves (Eds.), *Educational Multimedia/Hypermedia and Telecommunications.* Charlottesville, VA: Association for the Advancement of Computing in Education (AACE).

Kagan, S. (1985). Co-op Co-op: A flexible cooperative learning technique. In R. Slavin, S. Sharan, S. Kagan, R., Hertz-Lazarowitz, C. Webb and R. Schmuck (Eds.), *Learning to cooperate cooperating to learn*, (pp.437-452). New York: Plenum Press.

Kagan, S. (1992). *Cooperative learning* (7th ed.). San Juan Capistrano, CA: Resources for Teachers, Inc.

Kagan, S. (1994). *Cooperative learning*. San Clemente, CA: Kagan Publishing.

Kiesler, S., & Sproull, L. (1987). *Computing and change on campus*. New York: Cambridge University Press.

Koper, R., & Tattersall, C. (Eds.). (2005). *Learning Design: A handbook on modeling and delivering networked education and training*. Berlin, Germany: Springer.

Kordaki, M., Siempos, H., & Daradoumis, T. (2009). Collaborative learning design within open source e-learning systems: lessons learned from an empirical study. In Magoulas, G. (Ed.), *Submitted as a chapter in: E-Infrastructures and Technologies for Lifelong Learning: Next Generation Environments*. Hershey, PA: IGI Global.

Kozma, R. (1999). Students collaborating with computer models and physical experiments. In C. Hoadley & J. Roschelle (Eds.), *CSCL '99*. (314-322). Mahwah, NJ: Lawrence Erlbaum Associates

Littlejohn, A., & Pegler, C. (2006). *Preparing for Blended E-Learning: Understanding Blended and Online Learning*. London, UK: Routledge.

Lloyd, G., & Wilson, M. (2001). Offering Prospective Teachers Tools to Connect Theory and Practice: Hypermedia in Mathematics Teacher Education. [Norfolk, VA: AACE.]. *Journal of Technology and Teacher Education*, *9*(4), 497–518.

Lyman, F. (1981). The responsive classroom discussion. In Anderson, A. S. (Ed.), *Mainstreaming Digest*. College Park, MD: University of Maryland College of Education.

MacDonald, J. (2003). Assessing online collaborative learning: process and product. *Computers & Education*, *40*(4), 377–391. doi:10.1016/S0360-1315(02)00168-9

Martin, D. C., & Blanc, R. (1984). Improving Reading Comprehension through Reciprocal Questioning. Techniques. *Life Long Learning*, *7*(4), 29–31.

Masiello, I., Ramberg, R., & Lonka, K. (2005). Attitudes to the application of a web-based learning system in a Microbiology course. *Computers & Education*, *45*(2), 171–185. doi:10.1016/j.compedu.2004.07.001

McGrath, J. E. (1991). Time, Interaction and Performance (TIP). A Theory of Groups. *Small Group Research, 22*, 147–174. doi:10.1177/1046496491222001

Millis, B. J., & Cottell, P. G. (1998). *Cooperative Learning for Higher Education Faculty. ACE, Series on Higher Education*. Phoenix, AZ: Oryx Press.

Muirhead, B. (2001). Enhancing social interaction in computer-mediated distance education. *Ed at a Distance Journal, 15*(4). Retrieved April 8, 2010, from http://ifets.ieee.org/discussions/discuss_sept2000.html

Nel, L., & Wilkinson, A. (2006). Enhancing Collaborative Learning in a Blended Learning Environment: Applying a Process Planning Model Export. *Systemic Practice and Action Research, 19*(6), 553–576. doi:10.1007/s11213-006-9043-3

Osborn, A. F. (1963). *Applied imagination: Principles and procedures of creative problem solving* (Third Revised Edition). New York: Charles Scribner's Sons.

Palincsar, A. S., & Brown, A. L. (1984). Reciprocal Teaching of Comprehension-Fostering and Comprehension-Monitoring Activities. *Cognition and Instruction, 1*(2), 117–175. doi:10.1207/s1532690xci0102_1

Palloff, M. R., & Pratt, K. (2004). Learning together in Community: Collaboration Online. *Proceedings of the 20th Annual Conference on Distance Teaching and Learning*. Retrieved April 8, 2010, from http://www.uwex.edu/disted/conference/Resource_library/proceedings/04_1127.pdf

Panitz, T. (1997). Faculty and Student Resistance to Cooperative Learning. *Cooperative Learning and College Teaching, 7*(2).

Persico, D., Pozzi, F., & Sarti, L. (2009). Design Patterns for Monitoring and Evaluating CSCL Processes. *Computers in Human Behavior, 25*(5), 1020–1027. doi:10.1016/j.chb.2009.01.003

Pipek, V., & Wulf, W. (1999). A groupware's life. In Bødker, S., Kyng, M. and Schmidt, K. (eds.). *Proceedings of the 6th European Conference on Computer-Supported Cooperative Work*. (199-218), Dordrecht, The Netherlands: Kluwer Academic Publishers.

Roberts, T. S. (2005). Computer-supported collaborative learning in higher education: An introduction. In: Roberts, T. S. (ed). *Computer-supported collaborative learning in higher education* (1–18). Hershey, PA: Idea Group Publishing.

Sharan, S., & Hertz-Lazarowitz, R. (1980). A group-investigation method of cooperative learning in the classroom. In Sharan, P. Hare, C. Webb & R. Hertz-Lazarowitz (Eds.), *Cooperation in education*. Provo, Utah: Brigham Young University Press.

Slavin, R. E. (1978). Student teams and achievement divisions. *Journal of Research and Development in Education, 12*, 39–49.

Springfield, E. (2005). How to create an online course. *University of Michigan School of Nursing*. Retrieved April 8, 2010, from http://www.nursing.umich.edu/facultyresources/bestPractices/edTechText.doc

Taylor, V. (2005). Online group projects: Preparing the instructors to prepare the students. InRoberts, T. S. (ed). *Computer-supported collaborative learning in higher education* (19–50). Hershey, PA: Idea Group Publishing.

Thomas, R. (2000). Evaluating the Effectiveness of the Internet for the Delivery of an MBA programme. *Innovations in Education and Training International, 37*(2), 97–102.

Van Eijl, P., & Pilot, A. (2003). Using a virtual learning environment in collaborative learning: Criteria for success. *Educational Technology, 43*(2), 54–56.

KEY TERMS AND DEFINITIONS

Activity Awareness: In Computer-Supported Collaborative Learning (CSCL), activity awareness gives learners indications of what is happening and what has happened recently in collaborative activities in their group. It enables learners to be aware of the latest information created their peers and of the progress made as regards the tasks they share in their group space. In general, we define activity awareness to be the awareness of long term joint efforts directed at specific goals and objectives that promotes informed action and reaction. This extends most prior work in awareness that has focused on social (who is present?) or action (what is happening?) awareness. Instead, activity awareness focuses on the "why?" aspect to awareness. Important issues include awareness of the overall situation, social expectations and dependencies within a group, and shared task goals and status. Technology plays a vital role in the process of awareness creation, however one has to clarify in what ways communication technology affects awareness creation.

Blended Learning (Course): Blended Learning refers to a mixing of different learning environments. It can combine face-to-face instruction with computer mediated instruction. It also applies science or IT activities with the assistance of educational technologies using computer, cellular or iPhones, Satellite television channels, videoconferencing and other emerging electronic media. Learners and teachers work together to improve the quality of learning and teaching, the ultimate aim of blended learning being to provide realistic practical opportunities for learners and teachers to make learning independent, useful, sustainable and ever growing. In a blended course scenario, the teacher will have to decide which parts are online, which parts are offline. A basic example of this is a course of English as a second language where the instructor reaches the conclusion that all audio-based activities (listening comprehension, oral expression) will take place in the classroom where all text-based activities will take place online (reading comprehension, essays writing).

Collaboration Strategies/Methods: Collaborative strategies/methods are processes, behaviors and conversations that relate to collaboration between individuals. These methods specifically aim to increase the success of teams as they engage in collaborative problem solving. Many of the strategies involve assigning roles within each small group (such as recorder, participation encourager, summarizer) to ensure the positive interdependence of group participants and to enable students to practice different teamwork skills. Other strategies develop problem-solving abilities, understanding of complex relationships, and decision making in the face of uncertainty. These terms usually do not refer to loosely structured group work in which students are told simply to "work together" on a problem of assignment. Collaboration strategies are content-free, and thus can be used in a variety of contexts. Studies have shown that in well structured collaborative groups, students consistently learn many different subjects better, whereby they are able to organize their thoughts in a less threatening context than whole-class discussions, and then share their thoughts with the class.

Collaborative Learning Scenario: A collaborative learning scenario refers to methodologies and environments in which learners engage in a common task where each individual depends on and is accountable to each other. Often, such a scenario uses a variety of approaches in education that involve joint intellectual effort by students or students and teachers. It is commonly illustrated when groups of students work together to search for understanding, meaning, or solutions or to create an artifact or product of their learning. Collaborative learning activities can include collaborative writing, group projects, joint problem solving, debates, study teams and other activities. Finally, a collaborative learning scenario may include scripts that structure collaborative learning by creating roles and mediating interactions while allowing for flexibility in dialogue and activities.

Collaborative Educational Systems: A Collaborative Educational System is a specific environment that supports learners in both their individual and collaborative learning, thus giving birth to a new class of learners, e-learners, who can work and learn together irrespective of their geographical location. Such systems provide the capabilities to share information and exchange views in order to reach a common understanding. In general, in this context, collaborative learning refers to a collection of tools which learners can use to assist, or be assisted by others. Such tools include Virtual Classrooms (i.e. geographically distributed classrooms linked by audio-visual network connections), chat, discussion threads, application sharing (e.g. a colleague projects spreadsheet on another colleague's screen across a network link for the purpose of collaboration), among many others.

Computer-Supported Collaborative Learning (CSCL): Computer-supported collaborative learning (CSCL) is a method of supporting collaborative learning using computers and the Internet. It is related to Computer Supported Cooperative Work (CSCW) and cuts across research in psychology, computer science, and education. The technology allows individuals who are far apart to collaborate on-line. The use of these tools is increasing, however many teachers are still new to what tools are available on the Internet and how to use them effectively. CSCL is a method for bringing the benefits of collaborative learning and cooperative learning to users of distance or co-locative learning via networked computers, such as the courses offered via the Internet or in a digital classroom. The purpose of CSCL is to scaffold or support students in learning together effectively. CSCL supports the communication of ideas and information among learners, collaborative accessing of information and documents, and instructor and peer feedback on learning activities. CSCL also supports and facilitates group processes and group dynamics in ways that are not achievable by face-to-face communication (such as having learners label aspects of their communication).CSCL is a way of integrated teaching.

Educational Scenario: An educational scenario describes an educational activity, where the focus and starting point is a real life situation and not a theory. It refers to learning goals within a topic, and more specifically suggests learning activities, use of resources, and may also discuss the role of participating actors. For instance, in a scenario you first learn about water by visiting a river, not by reading a book. The scenario may be an idea that has already been developed and evaluated and found to be successful or a new idea that is being formed and prepared for implementation.

Group Dynamics: Group dynamics is the study of groups, and also a general term for group processes. Relevant to the fields of psychology, sociology, and communication studies, a group is two or more individuals who are connected to each other by social relationships. Because they interact and influence each other, groups develop a number of dynamic processes that separate them from a random collection of individuals. These processes include norms, roles, relations, development, need to belong, social influence, and effects on behaviour. The field of group dynamics is primarily concerned with small group behaviour. This term also refers to the understanding of the behaviour of people in groups, such as task groups, that are trying to solve a problem or make a decision. An individual with expertise in 'group process', such as a trained facilitator, can assist a group in accomplishing its objective by diagnosing how well the group is functioning as a problem-solving or decision-making entity and intervening to alter the group's operating behaviour.

Monitoring: Monitoring in CSCL means to observe the behaviour, communications, activities, or other changing information of individuals or groups. Monitoring may refer to several aspects, such as 'monitoring competence' or 'self-monitoring' can be described as awareness of what one knows. A high level of monitoring competence means one can make accurate assessments of one's skill or knowledge, while a low level means the opposite. Specific software can be used to track every student as they progress through a qualification, specifically checking behaviour and progress, quickly flagging up problematic issues such as low participation or a swift decline in progress, and thus enable a coordinator to intervene accordingly.

Chapter 12
The Role of CSCL Pedagogical Patterns as Mediating Artefacts for Repurposing Open Educational Resources

Gráinne Conole
The Open University, UK

Patrick McAndrew
The Open University, UK

Yannis Dimitriadis
University of Valladolid, Spain

ABSTRACT

Designing effective CSCL processes is a complex task that can be supported by existing good practices formulated as pedagogical patterns. From a cultural historical activity theory (CHAT) perspective previous research has shown that patterns served as Mediating Artefacts (MA) helping practitioners to make informed decisions and choices, being much closer to the practitioners' mindsets than complex learning design models, such as IMS-LD. However, a new challenge arises when the starting design element corresponds to Open Educational Resources (OER), i.e. free resources of high quality that are typically employed for individual learning. Recent research reported in this chapter has aimed to analyze the eventual contribution of CSCL patterns such as Collaborative Learning Flow Patterns (CLFP) in the repurposing process of existing OER for collaborative learning. Preliminary evidence coming from a set of workshops with educational technology experts shows that a small set of patterns drawn from a CSCL pattern language together with other MA, such as visual representations of Learning Designs, may be inspirational and effective in repurposing existing OER. Further research is under development that builds on the successful workshop format and involves practitioners in face-to-face and virtual workshops. This new set of experiences aims to analyze the effectiveness of the pedagogical patterns and other complementary MA in helping practitioners exploit the great potential of OER in the framework of the Open Learning Network (OLnet) project funded by The William and Flora Hewlett Foundation.

DOI: 10.4018/978-1-61692-898-8.ch012

INTRODUCTION

Technology-Enhanced Learning (TEL) reflects many flavors and modalities of pedagogies and techniques that match different needs or perceptions regarding the teaching/learning processes. For example, proposals and systems may focus on individual or collaborative learning, face-to-face or distance settings, project or problem-based scenarios, models based on transmission or participation, etc. On the other hand, an increasing number of Information and Communication Technologies (ICT) tools and educational resources are available to be employed in order to support teachers, learners or researchers in different phases of the teaching/learning process, namely: design, enactment, and evaluation. Such a landscape is full of promising outcomes, but at the same time its complexity generates many obstacles that impede taking full advantage of the potential benefits. Finding a route through to effective uptake of methods and tools has proved particularly resilient to solution in the case of technology-supported innovative pedagogies, such as Computer Supported Collaborative Learning (CSCL) (Dillenbourg, Jarvela, & Fischer, 2009).

Several approaches to enable a more effective and efficient uptake of CSCL have been proposed that reflect broader movements in the TEL or e-learning field. The research field appears fragmented so that we can find similar proposals related to: formal and informal visual design languages (Botturi & Stubbs, 2008); pedagogies, tools and learning design (Conole, Dyke, Oliver, & Seale, 2004, Conole, 2009a); CSCL scripting (Weinberger, Collar, Dimitriadis, Mäkitalo-Siegl, & Fischer, 2009); and, pedagogical design patterns for CSCL (Hernández, Asensio, Dimitriadis, & Villasclaras, 2010). Each of these initiatives aims to leverage informed design, use and reuse of teaching/learning activities, based on sound pedagogical strategies, techniques validated in practice, or quality resources (tools and contents). Even though different terminologies are used, all share a common basis in providing what we will term here *Mediating Artefacts (MA)*, - theories, techniques, visual representations, pedagogical patterns, etc. - to stakeholders, so that they can employ them during the whole lifecycle of the teaching/learning activities within a certain context (see Conole, 2008 for an explanation of our use of the term Mediating Artefacts).

We can think of the Collaborative Learning Flow Patterns (CLFP) (Hernández, Asensio, & Dimitriadis, 2005) as an illustrating example of such Mediating Artefacts. These patterns represent well-established techniques for collaborative learning that regulate the flow of learning activities, well established and used CSCL patterns include "*jigsaw*", "*pyramid*" and "*think-pair-share*" – each provides a different, structured learning design for fostering collaboration. Patterns such as the Collaborative Learning Flow Patterns (CLFP) have been successfully implemented in the Collage[1] authoring tool within a pattern-supported design process for new CSCL scripts. From a cultural historical activity theory, the term Learning Design in this case is used to describe the research field that is developing tool and resources to support the design of learning activities (Cross & Conole, 2008). Patterns are an important sub-set of Mediating Artefacts, which give a structured description that is well understood by educational practitioners and serve as an "interface" for practitioners when they are faced with the task of generating effective learning designs or scripts that scaffold the learning process. The usefulness of such patterns is even more distinctive when the final product of the educational practitioners is a Unit of Learning (UoL) computationally represented in a standard Educational Modeling Language, such as IMS-LD (IMS, 2003). Teachers as the main stakeholders and orchestrators of the learning activities need guidance that is closer to their own mindset and practical restrictions and not on those imposed by a technical specification. Thus, the *Collage* tool, which acts as a further MA that builds on the

CLFPMA, has been developed, used and validated in many practical situations (Hernández et al., 2006). Such a tool supports the design process for CSCL scripts, taking advantage of the patterns that reflect recurrent solutions to recurrent problems, through textual and visual descriptions of tensions, solutions and examples. Thus, an educational practitioner generates potentially effective CSCL designs that may additionally use adequate tools and resources (Vega, Bote, Asensio, Gómez, Dimitriadis, & Jorrín, 2010).

The revisiting of the issue of providing effective MA for CSCL design has been prompted by a significant new problem and opportunity that is offered by the widespread availability of Open Educational Resources (OER). The term OER was coined in 2002 at a UNESCO-hosted forum as:

The open provision of educational resources, enabled by information and communication technologies, for consultation, use and adaptation by a community of users for non-commercial purposes. (D'Antoni, 2008, p. 7)

Such learning material is freely available and will often be based on well-tested and effective learning material. However they will typically have been designed for specific contexts and offered on the assumption that they will be used for individual learning. It is therefore especially challenging to analyze how they can be repurposed for new innovative uses, as in the case of CSCL.

Despite significant investment in the development of high quality OER repositories and a vibrant international community committed to the OER movement (D'Antoni, 2008), evidence from evaluation studies on repurposing of OER indicates that uptake of OER for alternative teaching situations does not occur frequently (McAndrew et al., 2009, Hellman, 2009). Furthermore those who will actually adapt and repurpose them are a much smaller group than those who are willing to take and use existing ones. The reasons for this lack of repurposing are complex and mirror many of the challenges identified more generally through learning design research (See for example Lockyer, Bennett, Agostinho, & Harper, 2008).

In this chapter we consider related aspects of using design to encourage practitioners to engage with reuse of OER for CSCL. Two particular approaches are considered; first to make the inherent designs in OER more explicit; and, second, to see the designs themselves in the form of pedagogic patterns as potential Mediating Artefacts to support and guide the deconstruction and repurposing process. There is a third important component that is only briefly considered here which is the need to provide an appropriate social-technical infrastructure to encourage and facilitate the sharing of experiences and designs. The latter component is addressed in greater detail in reports on other aspects of our work (See Conole and Culver (2009) for a detailed discussion on the use of social networking to foster debate and Conole and McAndrew (2010) for an articulation of our vision for the OLnet initiative which is developing a socio-technical infrastructure to support users and researchers of OER). To this end in this chapter we describe how we are amalgamating our research work to date in the domains of pedagogical patterns and learning designs specifically for this purpose. We outline a framework for OER design and associated Mediating Artefacts. We report on the analysis of evaluation data drawn from a series of workshops, which test out this framework and conclude with an outline of planned further research activities.

The work builds on two strands of research. The OU Learning Design Initiative (http://ouldi.open.ac.uk) has developed a methodology for learning design that consists of tools, methods and approaches aimed at helping practitioners make more informed and pedagogically effective design decisions when creating learning activities or resources. The work is based on an empirical evidence base of data about the design process and consists of three main strands: representing pedagogy, guiding the design process and facilitating sharing and discussion around learning and teaching ideas. A key aspect of the work, of direct relevance to the work reported here is the work on representation (Cross & Conole. 2008). We have developed a number of visual representations that can be used to articulate designs. In addition we have produced a visualization tool, CompendiumLD, which can be used to guide the creation of visual designs (Conole, Brasher, Cross, Weller, Clark, & White, 2008). The CSCL research group at the University of Valladolid has developed and trialed a CSCL collaborative pedagogical pattern language. This consists of a set of collaborative patterns, derived from good practice (Hernández et al., 2010) examples of which were introduced in illustrating *CLFP* and *Collage* earlier in this section.

In the work described here we combine the visualization work and the collaborative patterns with the intention of using them as a basis for deconstructing and repurposing OER. Thus, we expect to provide support to practitioners in designing and enacting effective CSCL activities that build on the enormous potential of OER, bringing closer two significant research and practice communities.

In the next section we outline how the concept of a Mediating Artefact can provide a link from a theoretical position to a practical one. This then led into a series of workshops that refined our understanding and position. One of these workshops is presented in detail where we address our two key conjectures:

1. That making designs more explicit will help understanding of OER.
2. Providing a set of patterns describing collaborative use will enable rethinking of OER from an individual learning context to a collaborative case.

In the concluding section we will revisit these aspects but we may anticipate part of the associated discussion and findings. The associated study using the workshop data allowed us to make a significant progress towards validating the proposed framework. Taking into account the holistic nature of the framework, one can argue that all types of MA may be used to facilitate the design and repurposing process. It is worth flagging up at this stage that the evidence is stronger for the second aspect that is the use of patterns to inspire rethinking, rather than the first, where designs are used to aid understanding. This has led to some revision of our own plans as the costs in developing an additional layer of design description are relatively high and may not deliver as many benefits as hoped, while the use of existing patterns to inspire is relatively low cost and may well offer greater benefit. However, the costs of producing valid pedagogical patterns ready to be used by practitioners should also be considered, and therefore a balanced approach should be followed.

A MEDIATING ARTEFACTS FRAMEWORK FOR OER REPURPOSING

The overall approach adopted is socio-cultural in nature (See Daniels, Wertsch, & Cole for a recent edited collection, 2007), focusing on identification and utilization of a range of Mediating Artefacts to enable design and repurposing of OERs. The Mediating Artefacts are drawn from our two underpinning research areas – learning design and pedagogical patterns and are related to an existing OER effectiveness framework developed in previous work (Conole & McAndrew, 2010) to help ground this perspective. The framework is briefly described here, before discussing the data captured in the workshops. The framework has some proposed hypotheses that needed to be both tested and refined in applying the framework:

- Every OER has an inherent design; in order to deconstruct and repurpose the OER it is valuable to make this design explicit.
- Practitioners have a range of potential Mediating Artefacts which they can utilize when they are repurposing OER.
- Mediating Artefacts may help both with the articulation and representation of the design process, as well as guiding the process itself.

Figure 1 illustrates the central part of our framework. Our hypothesis is that firstly, clearer articulation of the design of an OER will lead to greater repurposing and secondly that different Mediating Artefacts can be used to facilitate the design and repurposing of OER. The diagram shows that when a designer (which could be a "teacher" or a "student" designing their own learning) creates an OER they can use a range of Mediating Artefacts to support this process. In our work we have articulated four main types of Mediating Artefacts of importance, which are the central focus of our framework:

- *Learning design visualizations:* We have articulated a range of representations around the design process (from an individual learning activity or resource to whole curriculum level). Of particular relevance for the work described here is our "task-orientated swim line" representation. In addition we have developed a tool for visualizing designs – CompendiumLD (http://compendiumld.open.ac.uk).
- *Learning design methods:* We see methods as schema to help guide design thinking. We have developed a number including a pedagogy profile method (which helps map student tasks across a course), a 3-D "tools in use" pedagogy framework and a "pedagogy-principles" matrix. More on this work can be found in an Ariadne article (Conole, 2008) and a blog posting on course representations (Conole, 2009b).
- *Pedagogical patterns:* A rich set of pedagogical patterns has now been developed through international research in the field, representing the articulation of good practice across different types of pedagogy; we focus in particular on the CSCL pedagogical patterns language.
- *Web 2.0 sharing and discussing:* We have developed a social networking site for finding, sharing and discussing learning and teaching ideas, Cloudworks[2]. We see this as being used both as a mechanism for finding ideas, other designs and schema, as well as a place for sharing and discussing the design and repurposing of OER. The site contains links to learning object and OER repositories, learning design and

Figure 1. Mediating Artefacts in the design process

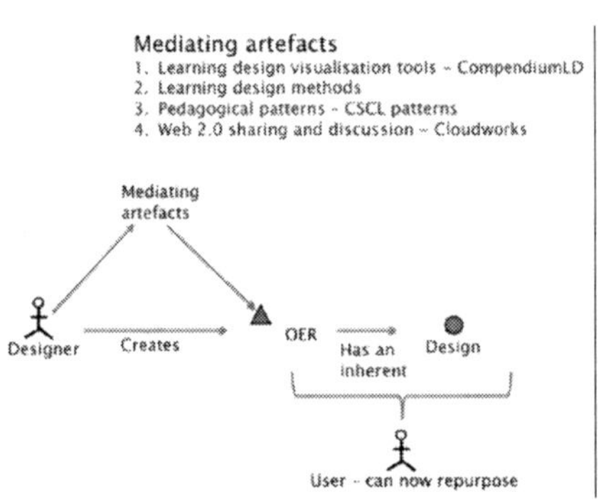

Figure 2. Design, use and repurposing of an OER

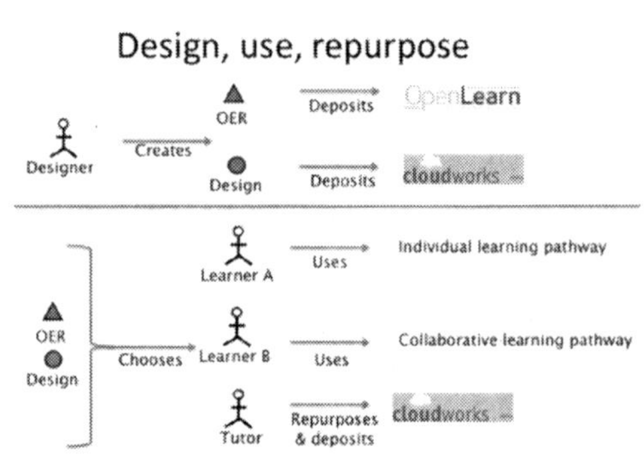

pedagogical patterns sites, as well as more generic examples of learning and teaching. The core 'objects' in Cloudworks is a 'cloud', which is a learning and teaching idea or design. 'Clouds' can be discussed and cumulatively improved or added to.

Figure 2 builds on Figure 1 and provides a walk through of how these Mediating Artefacts can be used, for both design and repurposing. In this example the design includes a decision point that enables the user to choose either a simple individual learning pathway or a collaborative learning pathway based on established CSCL pedagogical patterns. The first row replicates Figure 1, but indicates that the OER produced is deposited in a repository (in this case OpenLearn), whilst the design is deposited in a possibly separate environment that encourages comment and social sharing (in this case Cloudworks). The second half of the diagram illustrates how this OER and its design can then be repurposed in three different ways. In the first example the OER is used "as is" in an individual learning pathway. In the second example a learner capitalizes on the embedded collaborative pedagogical pattern in the design and hence adopts a collaborative learning pathway. In the third example a tutor repurposes the OER to provide both a new OER and associated design.

Finally Figure 3 shows the complete OER effectiveness framework. The central panel represents the "design in action", where the first of our four types of MA is used (Type 1 MA - visualization using CompendiumLD). The left hand side shows how the designer draws on existing resources from OER repositories, Pedagogical Patterns, Design Methods and Web 2.0 sharing sites to get inspiration and ideas and to help guide the design process (Types 2-4 MA). Finally, the right hand side shows how the generated OER and its design can then be re-deposited back into the system for future use.

Figure 3. The OER effectiveness framework

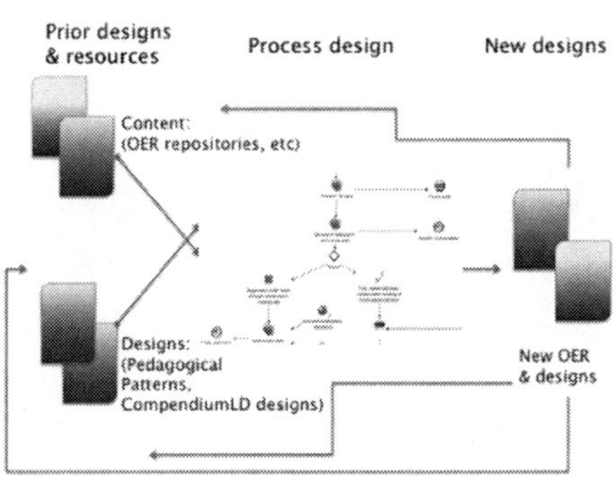

The framework is a proposed description for an actual process but is based on existing analysis of behavior within teams developing content at The Open University. However a key issue to be addressed is whether the framework is actually valid in the context of OER, and if so whether the elements of the framework need to be given different priorities as they are mapped to an implementation.

TESTING THE FRAMEWORK THROUGH WORKSHOPS

In order to test our approach a number of workshops were held between May – June 2009. The first was a workshop at the EDEN conference in Gdansk, the second was an in-house staff development workshop for the OU's Business School and the third was a workshop as part of the OLnet initiative. The format and timing of the workshops varied but all shared the same essence in terms of using visual representations and collaborative patterns. In this chapter we will focus in particular on the OLnet workshop, but where appropriate data from the EDEN and Business School workshops will be included.

Workshop Outline

The workshop was structured in order to provide an opportunity to test our hypotheses outlined earlier in terms of both the role of clearer design descriptions and pedagogic patterns. Sixteen participants attended the all-day workshop; all were interested in technology-enhanced learning, but the degree of knowledge and experience of involvement in OER research varied. Ten of its participants belonged to the Open University, most could be considered as experts in educational technology, although their expertise was related to different aspects of the workshop, i.e. OER, LD, Patterns or CSCL, while only a couple of them were directly related to the Olnet initiative. It should be noted that due to the specific authentic characteristics of the workshop and its participants, it is not likely that we may reproduce it in a new situation, although triangulating data from similar workshops may contribute in strengthening the findings or simply shed new light in the issues highlighted in this paper. The workshop consisted of the following main sections:

- Introduction
- Think-pair-share activity (a CSCL pattern in itself): representing a resource/OER
- Using a visual design representation to understand a resource/OER
- Representing an OER as a visual design
- Using the CSCL collaborative pedagogical patterns to make the OER more collaborative
- Evaluation and reflection

The workshop was video recorded and subsequently transcribed. In addition all participants completed an evaluation exercise at the end of the workshop where they were asked questions around the content and process of the workshop, what they liked and how the workshop could be improved.

Discussion

Analysis of the data revealed a number of themes that are discussed here. Part of our approach is predicated on the notion that OER have inherent designs and that if we can make those designs more explicit this will aid repurposing. A number of themes emerged with respect to this, which are discussed in this section. In the following sections participants are represented as P1, P2, etc. while the workshop facilitators are indicated as F1, F2, etc. In the following section references to CSCL patterns are indicated in italics.

Articulating the Design of a Resource

Firstly, issues around definitions. Participants did not appear to have a shared understanding of what an OER was. Definitions ranged from the notion of an OER as something you create for educational purposes and make freely available for others to use and adapt through to defining them simply as freely available resources. The first exercise (to think of a resource and represent its design) demonstrated that participants had difficulty articulating their design. This finding aligns well with previous research showing a lack of uptake and use of OER. They used a variety of mechanisms to represent the design – from narrative accounts or bullet lists through to some form of visual representation. The exercise raised the question of 'what do we mean by design?' and 'how can we best represent it?' Non-linear or more complex designs were not surprisingly also more complex to represent and share – for example OER where there was a number of different potential learning paths or where there was an element of choice. In addition, there is an issue as to whether a sequence of content or activities is represented. Different personal preferences emerged in terms of how participants chose to represent their designs. These preferences can be liked to the participants' prior knowledge and experience of design, but are also related to individuals' preferred methods of understanding.

"**P1**: No, I tend to think textual…really considering it in ways"

Textual representations can also vary in what they emphasise about the design – some may be description, others more metaphorical and others still more operational – for example a bullet list articulating steps in a learning sequence. A common approach adopted by the participants was to have a temporal sequence. Another strategy was to focus mainly on the content and associated resources. Participants started from different perspectives; some began by considering the learning objectives, whilst others started with the content or activities.

P2: "My resource is a design by itself. So, it is the design of an activity, it is the representation of that, a few bullet points and then a graphical representation. .... So the resource basically represents arrows pointing into a sequence of the activities."

It was interesting to see the extent to which each of the representations was easily sharable with others. More often than not a dialogic engagement was necessary to help make meaning of the design and to clarify misunderstandings. The exercise and subsequent discussion enabled us to tease out both the main facets of design and participants' different perspectives and approaches. In addition to articulating objectives, content and tasks, some of the participants evidenced a subtler level of design – associated with the inherent principles of the design

P3: "My resource is task-driven, so that is the principle and also it integrates many pedagogies into the content, so, and also it is question based."

In terms of principles we explored a little whether or not they had articulated a principle around individuality/collaboration. A range of characteristics was identified as being associated with the design – the objectives, generic characteristics, sequence of tasks undertaken, individual or collaborative focus. These characteristics map well to the components inherent in any learning activity (see Conole, 2008 for a description of a Learning Activity taxonomy). Within this range of characteristics, participants recognised that it was important to focus in terms of clarifying what information was essential to communicate so that the activity could be subsequently taken up and adapted by others.

F1: "Just try to think again of what elements you wrote down and what elements you used when you tried to explain it to your neighbour and try to think whether they were mainly based on objectives, mainly based on the characteristics of the activities, of a temporal sequence or …"

A number of conclusions can be drawn from this first exercise:

- There are many different ways of representing and understanding an activity.
- The *"think-pair-share"* pedagogical pattern proved effective in terms of getting equity of discussion across a group and promoting participation, collaboration and critical thinking.
- Adaptation of OER to meet different needs and how this can be articulated in the design was raised as an issue, in particular adaptation to meet the needs of different students and their approaches to learning.
- One of the participants raised the issue about the conditions of effectiveness, in other words to what extent can we say that a pedagogical pattern (even if it has been derived from a distillation of extensive good practice) will actual work in a particular context, i.e. to what extent can generic patterns be effective in specific contexts?

P4: "I think this is very interesting also to hear about, if you say this is a pattern then to think of the conditions of the effectiveness, in what conditions, even in the physical context, in…what are these conditions or how can we improve these conditions so that these patterns become effective. Also for what kind of problems it is…"

A cloud was set up in Cloudworks to capture the plenary discussions around the *"think-pair-share"* activity (see http://cloudworks.ac.uk/index.php/cloud/view/1800.html). The cloud includes a visual representation of the activity, which is discussed more in the next section. An example of one of the participant's designs is available online (See http://niallw.wordpress.com/2009/06/30/olnet-workshop/). The representations were also discussed in Cloudworks (http://cloudworks.ac.uk/index.php/cloud/view/1811.html).

Task Swim-Line Representation

Participants were introduced to the task swim-line representation for learning activities. Figure 4 shows a swim-line presentation of the *"think-pair-share"* activity produced in CompendiumLD. The diagram shows two swim-lines – one for a participant and one for the workshop facilitator. For each role there is a line of the tasks that person undertakes, three tasks in the case of the participant and two for the facilitator. Times associated with each task are indicated to the left of each task icon and are aggregated in the top right hand corner. Outputs from the pair discussion and the plenary summary are also shown.

In a swim-line representation, the central focus is the sequence of tasks the student undertakes, alongside are connections to any tools and resources associated with each task. Additional lines can be added for other roles involved in an activity, the most common being a line indicating what the tutor is doing at each stage. Participants were given a detailed swim-line representation of a task on a master-level course in Online and Distance Education and were asked to consider whether this representation enabled them to get a good overview of the task and for them to consider to what extent the learning outcomes had been achieved (see the associated Cloud for this on Cloudworks http://cloudworks.ac.uk/cloud/view/1801).

Figure 4. The swim-line presentation of the think-pair-share activity

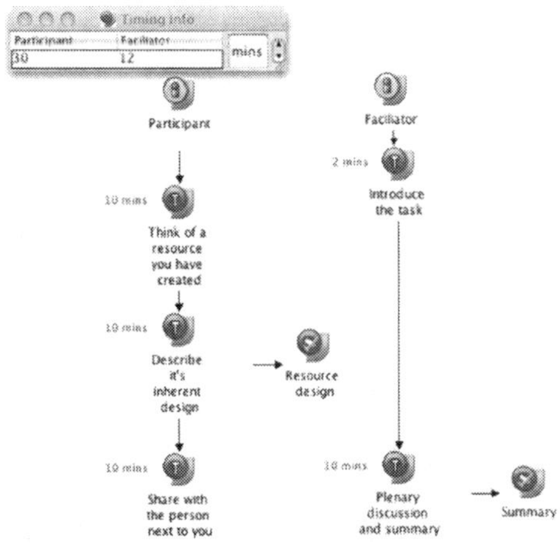

Participants were positive about the idea of representing designs visually and could see that such representations had a number of advantages compared to more textual representations. They stated that visualization provides a means of getting a quick overview of the design. However a number of participants also wanted to have an indication of the time allocation for each task. This is in fact possible with CompendiumLD but wasn't included in the particular representation they looked at. Moreover, they cautioned that there was still a time investment in terms of making sense of the design and that this should not be underestimated in terms of acting as a potential barrier to using such representations.

P5: "I think it is a really good way of representing courses but it takes you a little while to see how to use."

There were also issues in terms of what is presented in the visualization, for whom, and for what purpose. This relates to the earlier discussion about what characteristics or components of a design as most important and most needed in terms of capturing the essence of the design.

P6: "It represented the course quite well at one level in terms of what the designer intended once we worked out (missing comment) but when you look down the support for the learner you've got (missing comment), but there was no space for what the learner is actually doing and how they are interacting."

F2: "That you can represent courses in a whole lot of different ways and the point we are trying to get across is an understanding of how you can interpret those and the value and limitations of those representations. There isn't one perfect representation for all, but they do have different purposes, so that is exactly the point we are trying to get across."

Some of the more subtle intentions of the design were missing for some of the participants, which raised the question of how and to what extent could inherent pedagogy be represented?

P4: "This is a kind of representation which engages on the physical level, you may have other people, like pedagogical level, I don't know, what I thought was missing about this, is that it would be good to understand how each of these activities contributes to what way, to what extent to the learning outcome…"

One of the participants suggested that it would be valuable to have multiple views of the same design each view representing a different aspect.

P7: "So probably having different layers of visualization of the same structure could help filter the relevant information if you are looking at the learning objectives, or if you are looking at interactions, something like that, so, other thing that we were thinking about it probably what is missing is a legend of the different items, because we understood that there is a mixing of 2 layers, one is devoted to the designer, for example, all the questions in blue are annotations for the designers while for example it is very clear that the sequence for students is talking to the student verbally, it is talking to him, so probably having the legends saying ok, question mark annotation for the designer and the red bits are feedbacks we had from one evaluation and then filtering visually this information according to the task you are following."

Another argued that visualization potentially has additional power, if a semantic dimension is included.

P7: "A semantic of visualizations, really we understood that some of the connection are more related to cognitive activities of the design where as others are tactical activities of the use (missing comment) and cause and some other connection are like database connections with the resources and what they are looking, so probably having different semantic of the connections and representations."

A related software tool to CompendiumLD, Cohere (http://cohere.open.ac.uk/), enables the visualization and semantic linking of ideas and concepts, but as yet we have not explored its use in depth in a learning design context. Participants could see the value in Pedagogical Patterns acting as guidance in the design decision making process, particularly if they could be layered alongside the evolving design.

P4: "This could also help you to create a more effective design about how well you look at the patterns you are using the implicit ones, make it explicit and ask yourself 'well, wouldn't it be better if we use this or that pattern', so rather than just having notes with arrows you want to look at the course regularity where you are actually using patterns and then you can have collaborative level of (missing comment), but you can also have different pedagogical…"

Nonetheless participants felt there was still a lot of interpretation needed on the part of the reader of the design.

P8: "When I look through that, I have some difficulty in thinking how much unpacking needs to take place with the learning design… that a lot of that knowledge is in there, a lot of the steps are in there, but they are not a part of the task sequence, not part of a learning sequence."

Paper-based or digital designs have difficult values and purposes; similarly a design representation can be seen as both a static, final *product* and as an interactive ongoing representation of the *process* of design. For example, with respect to the value of CompendiumLD, participants stated that they found it easy to understand and easy to create designs with.

P9: "The good thing about the CompendiumLD, at least the paper version, I have seeing the software one, it provides you with an easy to follow structure, you have a straightforward layout."

P9: "…I mean for me to read and produce these kinds of maps is fairly easy."

Finally, one participant argued that there may be issues for non-IT users in terms of interpreting and using visual designs and in particular specialized software such as CompendiumLD (although this has not been our experience from evaluation of visualization workshops we have run):

P9: "I don't know if it would be that easy for somebody not really IT-related. In computer science we have been trained to think in that way."

OER Reconstruction

The workshop discussions illustrated that participants had a lot of difficulty making sense of the OER in its raw state, often feeling that they needed more information.

P5: "For me, if I was trying to re-use that I would want some more specificity where these tasks hit the learning objectives, more specific in order to represent and inform the design."

We argue that this is because repurposing OER involves additional levels of complexity to designing a learning activity from scratch; namely that the OER first needs to be understood, deconstructed and then redesigned. Participants began to see the value of thinking using the swim-line representation as a means of helping guide them through these levels of complexity.

P10: "When you start to think sequentially you actually identify points that need to be described."

Often activities have inherent generic patterns but because there is so much specific detail within the design (do this, do that, use this tool or resource, etc.) these generic patterns are difficult to abstract. Related to this issue of course is the fact that there are different levels and degrees of granularity associated with a design. And designs may be created with different audiences in mind, foregrounding different aspects of the design (the activities, semantics or the pedagogy). A design intended for another teacher may be very different to a design explicitly for use with students for example. All of these factors influence the nature of the design and the level of detail. There is a trade off between providing a simple representation or a more detailed, complex one. An alternative to including more details in the design itself is to link to a more detailed critique of the resource as a dialogic discussion around the OER and its design. This is the intention of the notion of a "cloud" as anything to do with learning and teaching (from a description of a teaching practice, to a full detailed design) in our social networking site (Cloudworks) for sharing learning and teaching ideas and designs.

F1: "So hopefully, one of the things that one might expect is that if somebody has the resource and also has the diagram and especially some type of diagram that presents some patterns, patterns in the sense of the repeated ways of the activities, then probably you go through the essence… I mean something of added value because you see the resource and also you see the design, do you get something more than just seeing the design? Than just seeing the resource?"

Participants found it much more difficult to create a representation of the design of a resource when it was not a resource that they themselves had created. This is because analyzing a resource as a visual design is a complex process involving different aspects of interpretation and representation. Articulation of the inherent pedagogical pattern might help to alleviate that cognitive load and allow the user to make more informed choices about how to repurpose the resource. Quotes from participants show the strategies they used to deconstruct and interpret the OER:

P7: "We started following the only structure we had, so the bullets, so ok, we look at the bullets but then we realize that because we are looking at activity one it has a sequence, so our representation is completely flat, so what are we going to do? A list of steps drawn by a line? if you want to create a representation of OERs which is not yours and for which you are not the author, you probably need to go through a very long process of understanding the resource very well, reading it and then creatively starting to see in which way you want to represent it and in this sense having another persons framework adds limitations"

Other issues emerged in terms of interpretation of existing designs; two issues in particular - a lack of time to engage with the detailed rich narrative, and a lack of motivation. In terms of motivation this was because in a sense this was a fake exercise – the resources participants were looking at were not related to their own discipline or real teaching context. In contrast a similar activity in a workshop with OU Business school staff engaged in designing a new course worked much better, because in that case the OER chosen was directly related to their real-life design needs. There is an interesting tension, in that there is an assumption that OER will save time because you are repurposing something someone else has produced, whereas it is questionable to what extent this is true:

P10: "The question 'I don't have time to read through this resource' is a key question, because isn't that partly what OER is all about and if there is a sense that when having OER there is time vacant for setting up what is going to be a benefit to somebody, should have the time to read the resource to know if it is any good, so the question is 'what kind of representation would not only give us a surface level description of the resource but would also tell us in what ways it is any good'. It seems to me that at the moment this workshop is about that 'design is implicitly good', i.e. a good design will implicitly mean a good resource."

Another aspect of importance that participants mentioned was identifying the quality and provenance of the resource; i.e. designs need to do more that display the sequence of activities, users need some indication of how effective and fit for purpose it is. There are two ways in which this can be included. Firstly, in the design representation itself, however the more detail that is included in the design the more complex it is. Secondly, an alternative is to have a wrap-around dialogue about the resource and its design, in a tool such as Cloudworks.

The data revealed that deconstruction and subsequent reconstruction of OER is complex, indeed it is possible to identify four layers that need to be considered to make most effective repurposing of an OER:

1. Visual representation of the design – how can the implicit OER design be made more explicit and hence shareable?
2. Opinion of goodness – how appropriate is the OER for different contexts?
3. Transferability through pedagogical pattern – how can generic patterns be applied to specific contexts?
4. Layer of discussion, critique and contextualisation – how can sites like Cloudworks act as a supporting structure to foster debate between those using the same OER?

The following quote from one of the facilitators summarizing the discussions encapsulates the general consensus from the workshop that articulation of designs is useful, but multi-faceted and complex:

F1: " That there is not one single representation because it depends on the intention and on the ability, how it is represented."

Value of Patterns

Participants could see the value of using pedagogical patterns as a means of encapsulating and sharing good practice. They grasped the concept of patterns and could see how they applied in an OER context.

F1: "These chunks of interactions that are repeated and probably were in the mind of the original designers, that you analyze what is going on. So, the point over here is that probably if you see all these representations, this could at least allow you to go through the original resource in an easier way."

In terms of incorporating collaborative dimensions to the patterns, participants stated that they first identified where there was a problem with the existing OER that adding collaborative dimension would help with. In choosing which patterns to consider they took account of the fact that groups are not homogeneous.

P11: "People work at different speeds with different levels of understanding and the patterns we looked for were the ones that enabled sharing the tasks and we chose 2 that seemed to be appropriate and compatible because we had limited amounts of time and wanted to have compatibility, so one was *jigsaw* and the other *enriching the learning process* ..."

For one group a key criterion in choosing a pattern was that it would address this issue of different types of learners. They also realized that incorporation of collaborative activities would result in an increase of time on the activity and that this needed to be taken into account. Inclusion of patterns also increased the complexity of the OER and raised new logistical issues. In the end this group chose *jigsaw* and *enriching the learning process*:

P11: "Within activity 1 we realized that in order to do this we had to expand the time to allow for the collaboration within the group. Then we had a logistical problem because if you had two patterns the one after the other there wasn't enough time. Thus, we chose that within the large group, the faster group – subgroup – should be able to deal quite quickly with the activities occupying the main group, and then go ahead and read."

Participants seemed to value the description of the scripts and the guidance they offered in terms of making design decisions

P11: "That the prescription that is in here (showing CSCL script) is really helpful."

Another group started by incorporating the *brainstorming* pattern; they focused in on the part of the OER around knowledge development, and then they used the *brainstorming* pattern as a trigger to repurpose the OER:

P4: "In the brainstorming session people will come up with the concepts etc and in the later session we have an assessment, group self-assessment where we can actually discuss and then we select the methods and we try to set-up a role-playing game where we have a social work situation as an opening game, then we pick on the distinction between counties and then we have different concepts and then we pick the group assessment, so a completely out of the blue extension..."

Another group identified a problem the learners might work on and used a combination of the *pyramid*, *brainstorming* and *jigsaw* pattern. The patterns use a different type of visual representation from the task swim-line discussed earlier, and the quote below where the participant refers to the pyramid pattern as a "triangle" evidences how much of an indirect influence the visual representation has had. This group's use of three patterns in combination also demonstrates the power of being able to combine and adapt patterns in different ways. Other pedagogical patterns workshops we have run have revealed similar patterns of behavior.

P6: "The main pattern is the triangle one [i.e. the *pyramid* pattern] and so that gives different levels, so then we go to *brainstorming* with this particular case, so it is a particular type of family with a child who needs particular care and so we talk through and identify the issues as a group, then they would break-out and we thought we would use the *jigsaw* pattern breaking them into couples or groups of threes and research these issues they had identified which were things like legal issues, availability issues, the care, the special needs costs, that sort of thing. Having done that we would come back again and recombine and in a larger group discuss the more in depth issues."

The purpose of this part of the workshop was to focus on enhancing the OER with collaborative elements; this enabled us to provide a limited set of patterns. This has clear advantages but also some disadvantages; inevitably some participants wanted to include alternative pedagogical approaches, for example to encourage reflection or support a problem-based learning approach. There is a tricky balance between a succinct manageable set and meeting all potential needs and interests

P10: "The problems for me as far as the script is concerned is that it is not a problem solving activity it is a collaboration around people becoming more collective and more aware, so I wasn't able to find anything that directly expressed that in here."

P12: "'This is great, this is great, this is great…' for students, but sometimes this is difficult too because if you have 10 patterns combined…"

The following quote is a good example showing explicitly how one of the groups worked through the choice and combination of patterns:

P12: "So we chose the *jigsaw* one, then we assumed how would someone give this to the whole class, so you might have 100 students, we need some kind of structuring because the information is too big, so we decided to put a *pyramid* because it allowed us to meet a couple of experts then we form bigger groups plus we have some kind of… and then we also, in the first phase of the *jigsaw* we thought that it would be a good idea applying a pattern of guiding questions for that phase of the *jigsaw*, so we say 'read that, think of your previous experience and try to match it' the same way you did, I mean, lets put 3-4 questions just to guide the classroom and the last phase of the *jigsaw* apply to 'Enriched discussion' to refine these conversations."

Others approached it from a different angle – looking more generally at how people might collaborate.

P13: "We didn't look at the specific story, we want to see if we could answer the question 'How people collaborate best?' 'What is the best possible pattern combination if there is one?' for people to collaborate and for everyone to engage in the process because if you have big groups or small groups where there is an expert."

Some felt that working solely from the visual representation of the design was limiting, that working with the patterns offered more flexibility.

P13: "The patterns allow you more freedom in mixing different patterns depending on what you want to achieve"

But digging deeper the visual and pattern representations seem to have different uses as different stages of the design process:

P7: "So I would say that we used the Compendium just to explore the content of the text, decide on what (is) the problem we need to focus on and then the last phase was really supported by all the learning patterns."

Analysis of this limited set of data together with direct feedback and comments reinforce the view that design descriptions offer a more limited range of benefits than the patterns, at least within the workshop. In terms of acting as Mediating Artefacts both had acted to provide channels of communication and shared reference points, however while the designs had encouraged reflection on past practice, the patterns had facilitated a more forward looking view. However, as stated above, all types of Mediating Artefacts were useful in a certain point of the process, and therefore further evidence is necessary in order to assess the relative value of each type of artefacts. In the final section we reflect on what this means for our own view of working with OER and how we might need to review and adjust the overall framework.

REFLECTION AND CONCLUSION

The workshop explored both visual learning design representations and the use of patterns with the same participant group. In each case benefits have been identified but what was notable was that the rationale for the learning designs in this context was less obvious to the participants. They could see the value in working with author-provided designs but questioned whether any other designs that were derived by examination of existing open content would be as valuable. Describing design was seen as a difficult and unfamiliar task:

- having multiple solutions;
- many options for what to include;
- being hard to interpret in a consistent way;
- only able to capture partial details in the example representations; and,
- needing additional information for clarification.

In contrast the use of the pedagogic patterns in the context of the workshop to reinterpret individual OER for a collaborative situation received a much more positive reception:

- few patterns are needed to get started and gain benefit;
- the patterns apply in many different situations;
- they encouraged thinking at different levels; and,
- encouraged a fresh view of resources.

Combining both design representations and existing patterns in a single workshop has allowed us to compare reactions on two key components in our developing framework and has led to a review of the relative weighting that we should put into the two pieces of work. While those in the workshop supported the value of good representation for design, the effort in building any comprehensive collection of such representations is high. A previous attempt to incorporate such designs into the workflow of building an OER repository (McAndrew & Goodyear, 2007) had only resulted in a small proportion having designs. Furthermore those designs were not produced by the original author and hence have reduced value, seen by workshop participants as one option among many. The move to a more social network approach as described in the framework offers the potential to address this flaw, but only if the practical and intellectual cost of producing designs is much lower than appears to be the case.

The data obtained through this set of workshops aligns with previous results with respect to the use of Collaborative Learning Flow Patterns (CLFP) as a means of guiding teachers in the process of designing CSCL scripts (Hernández et al., 2010) or the use of assessment patterns within an integrated process of designing teaching/learning and assessment activities (Villasclaras, Isotani, Hayashi, & Mizoguchi, 2009). The effective visual representations of the patterns, their relation with the organization of the resulting scripts, and their familiarity to the practitioners enable them as powerful Mediating Artefacts towards the generation of effective CSCL scripts. Thus, based on this data, one can consider that patterns (together with the rest of Mediating Artefacts described in this chapter) may enable production of pedagogically informed designs for CSCL that take advantage of the OER enormous potential.

Patterns in this case are distinguished from designs in that they are produced in order to communicate particular approaches rather than describe particular content, i.e. they are not tied to a specific resource. There is a range of initiatives that have also provided openly available sets of patterns, such as the CLFP used in this case. The published work associated with those patterns has tended to focus on the methods of elicitation rather than the use of the patterns. In the case of Open Educational Resources we need to move from making content available to helping people understand how to make good use of that content. The next stage in our work is therefore to further examine the patterns that are available and offer them within an environment that encourages a rethinking of OER as giving a basis for many different learning experiences rather than tied strongly to their original context. We also need to extend this work from considering collaborative approaches to address other patterns such as assessment, reflection, and problem-based learning for example. The workshops have provided us with an opportunity to test our the framework and have demonstrated the value of articulating the stages involved in deconstructing and reconstructing OER, along with identification of a range of Mediating Artefacts to support the design process. The role of patterns in the emerging model is to inspire teachers and learners to take advantage of the openness in content, tools and methods that OER represents. As a next stage we want to explore how to foster dialogic engagement around OER as an alternative to explicit representation with the design itself. We see this as potentially providing inspiration and support as well as acting as a mechanism for peer critiquing and quality evaluation. We are starting to explore how our social networking site for sharing learning and teaching ideas and design – Cloudworks – can be used to facilitate this process.

We plan to build on this work by further refining the combined set of Mediating Artefacts drawn from Learning Design and Pedagogical Patterns. We intend to use these in both real and virtual workshops, using Cloudworks as a facilitating interface. We would like to explore how these ideas might be extended to include other pattern languages.

ACKNOWLEDGMENT

Part of the research work presented in this paper was funded by The William and Flora Hewlett Foundation to the OLnet initiative and the Spanish Ministry of Science and Education (project TIN2008-03023/TSI). Prof. Dimitriadis acknowledges the financial support of the Hewlett Foundation and the University of Valladolid for supporting his visiting fellowship, as well as the contributions of the Gsic/Emic research group at the University of Vallodolid. The authors would like to thank Dr Elpida Makriyannis, Andrew Basher, Dr Tina Wilson and the workshop participants for their invaluable contributions.

REFERENCES

Beetham, H., & Sharpe, R. (2007). *Rethinking pedagogy for a digital age*. London, UK: RoutledgeFalmer.

Botturi, L., & Stubbs, T. (Eds.). (2008). *Handbook of Visual Languages for Instructional Design. Theories and Practices*. Hershey, PA: IGI Global.

Cole, M., & Engeström, Y. (1993). A cultural-historical approach to distributed cognition. In Salomon, G. (Ed.), *Distributed cognitions: Psychological and educational considerations* (pp. 1–46). Cambridge, UK: Cambridge University Press.

Conole, G. (2008). Capturing practice: the role of mediating artefacts in learning design. In L. Lockyer, S. Bennett, S. Agostinho, & B Harper (Eds), *Handbook of Research on Learning Design and Learning Objects: Issues, Applications and Technologies* (187-207). Hershey, PA: IGI Global.

Conole, G. (2009a). Capturing and representing practice. In Tait, A., Vidal, M., Bernath, U., & Szucs, A. (Eds.), *Distance and E-learning in Transition: Learning Innovation, Technology and Social Challenges*. London, UK: John Wiley and Sons.

Conole, G. (2009b). *Course representations*, blog posting, 10th June 2009, Retrieved March 20, 2010, from http://e4innovation.com/?p=328

Conole, G., Brasher, A., Cross, S., Weller, M., Clark, P., & White, J. (2008). Visualising learning design to foster and support good practice and creativity. *Educational Media International*, *54*(3), 177–194. doi:10.1080/09523980802284168

Conole, G., & Culver, J. (2009). The design of Cloudworks: applying social networking to foster the exchange of learning and teaching ideas and design. *Computers & Education*, *54*(3), 679–692. doi:10.1016/j.compedu.2009.09.013

Conole, G., Dyke, M., Oliver, M., & Seale, J. (2004). Mapping pedagogy and tools for effective learning design. *Computers & Education*, *43*(1-2), 17–33. doi:10.1016/j.compedu.2003.12.018

Conole, G., & McAndrew, P. (2010). OLnet: a new approach to supporting the design and use of Open Educational Resources. In M. Ebner & M. Schiefner (Eds), *Looking toward the future of technology enhanced education: ubiquitous learning and the digital nature* (123-144). Hershey, PA: IGI Global.

Cross, S., & Conole, G. (2008). *Learn about Learning Design*, Learn About Series, Open University: Milton Kynes, UK. Retrieved April, 13, 2010, from http://ouldi.open.ac.uk/Learn%20about%20learning%20design.pdf

D'Antoni, S. (2008). *Open Educational Resources. The way forward. Deliberations of an international community of interes*t. UNESCO International Institute or Educational Planning. Retrieved March 20, 2010, from http://learn.creativecommons.org/wp-content/uploads/2008/03/oer-way-forward-final-version.pdf

Daniels, H., Wertsch, J., & Cole, M. (2007). *The Cambridge companion to Vygotsky*. Cambridge, UK: Cambridge University Press.

Dillenbourg, P. Jarvela, S. & Fischer, F. (2009). The evolution of research on Computer-Supported Collaborative Learning. From design to orchestration. In S. Ludvigsen et al. (Eds), *Technology-Enhanced Learning. Principles and Products* (3-19). New York: Springer Verlag.

Hellman, L. (2009). An Evaluation of the Open Education Resources for the Open Schools' Project. *SAIDE Newsletter, 15*(3).

Hernández, D., Asensio, J. I., Dimitriadis, Y., & Villasclaras, E. D. (2010). Pattern languages for generating CSCL scripts: from a conceptual model to the design of a real situation. In P. Goodyear & S. Retalis (Eds.) *E-learning, design patterns and pattern languages* (49-64*)* Sense Publishers.

Hernández, D., Asensio, J. I., & Dimitriadis, Y. A. (2005). Computational Representation of Collaborative Learning Flow Patterns using IMS Learning Design. *Journal of Educational Technology & Society*, *8*(4), 75–89.

Hernández, D., Villasclaras, E. D., Jorrín, I. M., Asensio, J. I., Dimitriadis, Y., & Ruiz, I. (2006). COLLAGE, a Collaborative Learning Design Editor Based on Patterns. *Journal of Educational Technology & Society*, *9*(1), 58–71.

Lockyer, L., Bennett, S., Agostinho, S., & Harper, B. (Eds.). (2008). *Handbook of Research on Learning Design and Learning Objects: Issues, Applications and Technologies*. Hershey, PA: IGI Global.

McAndrew, P., & Goodyear, P. (2007). Representing practitioner experiences through learning design and patterns. In H. Beetham & R. Sharpe (Eds), *Rethinking Pedagogy for a Digital Age* (92-102). London, UK: Routledge.

McAndrew, P., Santos, A., Lane, A., Godwin, S., Okada, A., Wilson, T., et al. (2009). *OpenLearn Research Report 2006-2008*. The Open University, Milton Keynes, England. Retrieved March 20, 2010, from http://oro.open.ac.uk/17513/

Vega, G., Bote, M. L., Asensio, J. I., Gómez, E., Dimitriadis, Y., & Jorrín, I. M. (2010). Semantic search of tools for collaborative learning with the Ontoolsearch system. *Computers & Education*, *54*(4), 835–848. doi:10.1016/j.compedu.2009.09.012

Villasclaras, E. D., Isotani, S., Hayashi, Y., & Mizoguchi, R. (2009). Collaborative Learning: Design from Macro- and Micro-Script Perspectives. In *Proceedings of AIED 2009 Frontiers in Artificial Intelligence and Applications* 200 (1), (pp.231-238).

Weinberger, A., Collar, I., Dimitriadis, Y., Mäkitalo-Siegl, K., & Fischer, F. (2009). Computer-supported collaboration scripts: Theory and practice of scripting CSCL. Perspectives of educational psychology and computer science. In S. Ludvigsen et al. (Eds), *Technology-Enhanced Learning. Principles and Products* (155-174). New York, NY: Springer Verlag.

KEY TERMS AND DEFINITIONS

Collaborative Learning Flow Patterns: Pedagogical design patterns that focus more on the learning flows within collaborative learning situations.

CSCL Scripts: They correspond to an approach of setting up and facilitating effective collaborative learning supported by computers through instructional support or scaffold.

Design Patterns: They capture reusable knowledge about a contextualized problem and its associated, broadly accepted, solution. Patterns are decoupled when they are applied, but they work together with other interconnected patterns to generate emergent contextualized wholes (pattern languages).

Learning Design: Learning Design is a methodology to help practitioners make more effective decisions about how they design learning activities and courses. It consists of a set of tools and resources, which include visual representations for making the design process more explicit, step by step guidance on the design process and tools for support the sharing and discussion of good practice.

Pedagogical Patterns: A more concrete category of design patterns that capture and communicate good practices in learning and teaching processes.

Think-Pair-Share: A pedagogical pattern according to which each learner thinks individually on a question, then two learners pair and discuss their ideas about the question, and finally the whole classroom shares the ideas and eventually votes for the best or most appropriate ideas.

ENDNOTES

1 Collage, described later in this paragraph, is a standalone tool, predecessor of Webcollage, which is an IMS-LD script authoring tool. It's aimed at teachers who would like to create their own collaboration script with embedded assessment. Webcollage (http://sourceforge.net/projects/webcollage/) is currently in a beta version undergoing an extensive review by experts and educational practitioners.

2 Cloudworks is a social networking site for sharing and discussing learning and teaching ideas and designs (http://cloudworks.ac.uk). The core objects in the site are 'clouds'. Clouds can be anything to do with learning and teaching. They might be a short description of a teaching innovation, or information about how a particular tool can be used to support learning. Alternatively they might be information about useful learning and teaching resources. Clouds can be grouped into collections of clouds, called 'Cloudscapes'.

Chapter 13
Teaching Routines to Enhance Collaboration Using Classroom Network Technology

Angela Haydel DeBarger
SRI International, USA

William R. Penuel
SRI International, USA

Christopher J. Harris
SRI International, USA

Patricia Schank
SRI International, USA

ABSTRACT

This chapter presents an argument for the use of teaching routines (pedagogical patterns) to engage students in collaborative learning activities using the Group Scribbles classroom network technology. Teaching routines are a resource for structuring student opportunities to learn within lessons. They address known challenges associated with making the most of classroom network technology by scaffolding teacher enactment, enabling contingent teaching, and providing an anchor for expanding practice. In this chapter, the authors articulate the theoretical and empirical basis for using teaching routines to support diagnostic interactive formative assessment of student learning. The authors describe the goals and features of routines, types of collaboration instantiated in the routines, technological aspects of Group Scribbles, teachers' perceived utility of the routines, and anticipated implementation challenges of the routines within lessons designed for middle school Earth science.

DOI: 10.4018/978-1-61692-898-8.ch013

INTRODUCTION

Classroom network technologies enable unique forms of participation in classrooms in which elements of online learning are integrated fully into face-to-face instruction. This class of technologies includes student response systems ("clickers"), networked graphing calculators, and tools that enable participatory simulations. With these technologies, students can work online in private and group spaces while simultaneously participating in classroom activities. These technologies have been the focus of much research in recent years (see, Penuel, Roschelle, & Abrahamson, 2005, for a review), though explicit attention to how teachers can use them well has not been widely studied.

To make the most of classroom network technologies, teachers need support for the design and enactment of classroom teaching strategies to use in conjunction with them. Our candidate for the form that support should take is what we call a teaching routine. Teaching routines are *recurring patterned sequences of interaction that teachers and students jointly enact to organize opportunities for student learning in classrooms.* Routines are familiar features of classrooms, and remarkably stable and recognizable across large timescales and distances; they form part of the very "grammar of schooling" (Tyack & Cuban, 1995). Many routines are enacted principally through classroom discourse, as when teachers pose students a question whose answer is known to the students, students respond, and the teacher evaluates the response (Mehan, 1979). Classroom formats for organizing student participation in class, such as recitation, small group discussion, and whole-class discussion are ubiquitous and differ little in structure from subject to subject (Nystrand, Wu, & Gamoran, 2003).

This chapter provides an overview of the challenges to using classroom network technology that routines are intended to address, presents examples of routines developed for a new classroom network technology called *Group Scribbles*, shows how routines have been embedded in lessons designed for middle school Earth teachers, and describes professional development for teachers in using routines. The chapter also presents evidence about how teachers perceive the potential of routines and challenges they anticipate in using them.

BACKGROUND

Technology can transform how teachers organize learning opportunities for students in the classroom. Technology readily facilitates re-use of learning processes (Koper, 2003; Schroeder & Spannagel, 2005; Zumbach, Muhlenbrock, Jansen, Reimann, & Hoppe, 2002), by providing a record of interaction that can be used as a guide for enacting processes again so that they can become routine sequences of interaction. In addition, with the aid of certain forms of classroom network technology, learners can participate anonymously, in ways that may facilitate their willingness to ask for help when they do not understand something (Davis, 2003). With this technology, students can engage in participatory simulations and acts of collective representation that help them master difficult subject matter, from complex adaptive systems in biology to functions in algebra (Hegedus & Kaput, 2004; Stroup, Ares, & Hurford, 2005; Wilensky & Stroup, 2000).

Collaborative Scripts and Design Patterns

The introduction of technology either to change the medium of learning (e.g., from face-to-face to online learning) or to augment face-to-face interaction may necessitate the development of new teaching routines and transformation of existing routines to make the most of new affordances of technology (Penuel, 2008; Roschelle, Knudsen, & Hegedus, in press). Designers of educational technologies have been aware of the need, potential, and limitations of designing sequences of interactions to better facilitate learning for some time. For example, recognizing that on their own, students may not collaborate effectively to learn together, designers have developed collaborative scripts that prescribe how students should form groups, interact, and approach problem solving (e.g., Hoppe & Ploetzner, 1999). Such scripts may facilitate collaboration, but they also have the potential to overly constrain learners' efforts to collaborate to learn in certain situations (Dillenbourg, 2002).

In an effort to help designers of collaborative, classroom network technologies ensure that technology supports a wide, rather than limited, number of ways learners can collaborate, other teams have sought to articulate sets of collaborative design patterns. The notion of a design pattern comes from the field of architecture, where the term refers to common features of well-designed spaces (Alexander, Ishikawa, & Silverstein, 1977). DiGiano and colleagues (2003) developed a set of collaborative design patterns to guide the design of software for emerging classroom network technology, such as networked graphing calculators. Their design patterns articulate different sequences of collaborative activity that could be used to organize learning opportunities across different subject areas. Their intent was to enable designers to think broadly about collaboration, not on the one hand to build in features that "over script" while at the same time supporting the kind of structuring of interaction that research suggests is optimal for individual and group learning.

A limitation of these earlier approaches is that they provide little guidance to *teachers* for how they are to make the most of classroom network technologies. The need for such guidance arises from reviews of research that suggest that unless teachers are able to use the technology to promote discussion and reflection on student thinking, the technology alone is unlikely to improve teaching and learning (Judson & Sawada, 2002). In fact, many teachers do not use classroom network technologies in ways that promote discussion and reflection; not surprisingly, these teachers choose to use technologies less often than those who employ the technology in more powerful ways (Penuel, Boscardin, Masyn, & Crawford, 2007). Below, we review specific challenges teachers face in using these technologies, for which we have designed teaching routines as a tool to address.

Specific Challenges to Teaching with Classroom Network Technologies

One way that the potential of classroom network technologies becomes limited is in how they are used to engage students in thinking about content. One of the most common routines, the I-R-E (initiation-response-evaluation) sequence in which teachers pose a question to students, students answer, and the teacher evaluates the response, offers little room for dialogue among students (Mehan, 1979; Wells, 1993). In science classrooms, the use of this sequence also limits opportunities for students to articulate complex concepts and arguments that are the hallmark of scientific reasoning (Lemke, 1990). Studies of K-12 teachers' use of classroom network technologies indicate many teachers use I-R-E sequences with the technology, without much classroom discussion (e.g., Penuel et al., 2007). These teachers see less benefit from using the technology, and our conjecture is that they see less benefit because using classroom network technologies in this way does not take sufficient advantage of the shared display as a focal point for attention, discussion, and reflection.

Another challenge is to motivate students to participate in and learn from activities. Particularly in scientific investigations, it can be difficult to help students connect what they are doing to the scientific question (Petrosino, 1998). Students' conceptual development may depend on teachers' providing explanations of phenomena and on learning from text (Klahr & Nigam, 2004), but students may not be motivated to learn from these sources. Classroom network technologies have the potential to help teachers track student progress and also keep students motivated and on task by responding to check-in or reflection questions, but teachers may not be aware of how to incorporate these kinds of procedures with the technologies.

One of the greatest challenges of teaching may be the need for teachers to make multiple decisions about what to do next during a single lesson based on their diagnoses of individuals' and classes' changing understanding of content (Hinds, 2002; Solomon & Morocco, 1999). On the fly, teachers must decide whether to provide feedback to all students or particular students. If feedback is appropriate, teachers need to determine when it should be provided and what form it should take (e.g., written, verbal). Not only are aggregating and interpreting data challenging for teachers who typically have limited training in analysis of assessment data and face multiple demands on their time, but support materials packaged with classroom network technologies and curricula rarely provide this type of "what if" guidance about what to do when students are having difficulty mastering a concept.

TEACHING ROUTINES AS A TOOL FOR HELPING TEACHERS MAKE THE MOST OF CLASSROOM NETWORK TECHNOLOGIES

Teachers need tools beyond curriculum and infrastructure to overcome these known challenges. Teaching routines are designed to help teachers make the most of classroom network technology to improve student learning in the classroom. Depending on their role in the classroom, the grain-size of a teaching routine may vary from a small part of an instructional session (e.g., checking in about progress on a task) to spanning several days or weeks (e.g., an inquiry cycle beginning with identifying research questions, then testing hypotheses in investigations, analyzing results, drawing conclusions, and reflecting on what was learned).

Enhance Classroom Communication

A primary goal for teaching routines is to enhance student opportunities to communicate with the teacher and with peers about their thinking. Classroom network technology makes it possible for teachers to pose questions to *all* students and thus to learn about the class's state of knowledge. In addition, response system technology allows the cycle of question-and-answer to take place in a very short time, thereby providing students and teachers with rapid feedback without slowing the pace of teaching (Roschelle, Penuel, & Abrahamson, 2004). To make the most of network technologies, routines facilitate the design of classroom activities to create multiple opportunities for students to participate, both by contributing responses to student questions and by discussing their thinking with peers and the class. Routines enhance classroom communication by providing guidance about how to facilitate classroom conversations, structuring interactions among peers and small groups, and focusing discussions on epistemological ways of thinking within a domain.

Drawing upon the underlying components of the Peer Instruction model for guiding teaching with student response systems, as well as those of a similar method developed by the Physics Education Research Group at the University of Massachusetts (Dufresne & Gerace, 2004), routines provide useful scaffolds for teachers in orchestrating discussions. Researchers have observed that discussion based on the distribution of student responses encourages student thinking about alternative ways of addressing a concept or problem (Dufresne, Gerace, Leonard, Mestre, & Wenk, 1996) and aids in developing deeper student understanding of the meaning of concepts (Judson & Sawada, 2002). Explanation to a peer has the potential to transform students' misconceptions (Judson & Sawada, 2002). Response systems facilitate discussion by providing an anchor (aggregate responses on a shared display) and a set of artifacts to which students can refer in the process of building knowledge (Truong, Griswold, Ratto, & Star, 2002).

Routines encourage *dialogic,* as opposed to *monologic,* forms of communication (Bakhtin, 1981; Holquist, 1990). Dialogic communication occurs whenever teachers' and students' utterances anticipate and respond to one another, and where the course of a conversation cannot easily be predicted ahead of time. By contrast, monologic communication "speaks with one voice," often the teacher's, and the speaker is not necessarily concerned with learning about the audience's interests, concerns, or questions but rather with compelling them to be, do, or act in a particular way. When students have more opportunity to engage in genuine classroom dialogue rather than recitation, they learn more (Nystrand & Gamoran, 1991). Analyses of learning in science classrooms also highlight the potential of classroom conversations in which students shape the flow and direction of discussion. For example, van Zee and Minstrell (1997) demonstrate a model for orchestrating discussion in which the main goal is to elicit what students think, rather than to evaluate them, and in which subgoals of conversations emerge through particular conversational moves and are not dictated ahead of time by the teacher. These kinds of discussions facilitate students' development of scientific explanations, as well as reflection and revision of ideas about subject matter (diSessa & Minstrell, 1998). Teaching routines may be useful in improving dialogic communication in the classroom, since at present, teachers do not use them widely and many find them more difficult to orchestrate than monologic forms of classroom communication.

While routines are not content- or domain-specific they are structured around important epistemological ways of thinking in a domain. In the case of science, these ways of thinking include designing questions, relating processes, and data creation. Because routines are designed to be applied in multiple instances within a curriculum, specific questions are not identified within a routine, but the steps of a routine are intended to inspire the design of diagnostic questions that will allow teachers to elicit deeper student reasoning.

Diagnostic questioning is consistent with a growing body of cognitive science research that suggests it is necessary to engage rather than ignore problematic student ideas in order to promote conceptual change in science (diSessa & Minstrell, 1998; National Research Council, 1999; Posner, Strike, Hewson, & Gerzog, 1982; Smith, diSessa, & Roschelle, 1993-1994). The diagnostic approach, in its emphasis on eliciting student thinking, stands in contrast with the typical approach of science curricula and with the view of some advocates (e.g., Muthukrishna, Carnine, Grossen, & Miller, 1999) that focus solely on teaching correct concepts to students. To stimulate discussion, researchers have suggested that questions that yield divergent student responses are more effective than those that are easy or lead all students to a single answer (Beatty, Gerace, Leonard, & Dufresne, 2006). The timing of questions further shapes the nature of information an instructor gains about student understanding. Questions posed after a lecture or explanation can be used to check understanding (Dufresne, et al., 1996). Together, these findings suggest it matters not just *what* questions to ask but also *when* to ask them. Teaching routines explicitly address the kinds of questions that are appropriate for diagnosing student understanding as well as when they should be posed to students. As a result, teachers who use routines should be better equipped to address problematic student ideas within and across lessons.

Motivate Students to Participate Productively

A critical role for routines is to create an appetite for learning concepts by tackling a challenge, reflecting on it, and realizing that additional learning is needed (Daniel L. Schwartz & Bransford, 1998). To accomplish this task, routines need to help foster a classroom environment that supports students' developing goals for learning. The emphasis on grades and high-stakes performances that is typical in classroom and standardized assessments creates the opposite kind of environment, namely one in which students orient toward displaying competence and avoiding situations that would show them to be confused or lacking in skill (Maehr & Midgley, 1991; Wigfield, Eccles, & Rodriguez, 1998). By contrast, when teachers provide feedback that is task-focused and that gives specific guidance about how students can improve, assessment can actually help motivate students to learn and create a classroom environment that encourages students to adopt goals for content and skill mastery (Black & Harrison, 2001; Butler, 1987; Butler & Nisan, 1986).

An example of a routine that has as its primary goal motivating learning through feedback is a writing conference (Harris, 1986), in which a student presents a sample of original writing to a teacher or peer, gets feedback, and then revises their paper. The conference begins with an initial effort by the student—planning and producing a draft of his or her own creative or expository writing. Typically, it is the student who selects the topic and organizes the text; students rarely have more than a broad assignment from the teacher to constrain their creativity or imagination. The conference with the teacher or peer is an event where students get feedback, not to make a final judgment on their performance, but to motivate them to make changes to the text to make it clearer, more compelling, more engaging. Students are likely to be motivated to revise their writing on the basis of the conference, to the extent that they are motivated by a desire to write for an external audience, a desire that can be enhanced by the very act of the writing conference.

Improve Teachers' Ability to Use Feedback to Engage in Contingent Teaching

Classroom network technology can play an integral role in improving feedback, by making it easy for teachers to involve all students in assessment and making visible the range of student ideas at any point in a student's learning trajectory (Roschelle, et al., 2004). Classroom network technologies are systems of technology in which individual devices for students and teachers are connected to a local, or classroom-based network; a mechanism to display contributions of students to the system is usually part of the technology (Penuel, in press). Research on this technology suggests its potential for dramatically increasing participation of students, facilitated by the ability to pose questions to all students simultaneously, aggregate results, and present them for all to see and discuss (Penuel, et al., 2005).

Routines of various kinds facilitate teachers' becoming efficient in making instructional decisions on the fly (Calderhead, 1981). Routines can recommend alternative sequences of activities for teachers to follow, depending on how their students are learning from particular curriculum activities. If, furthermore, as a consequence of following a routine in which students have been given the opportunity to learn and are still having difficulty with a concept or skill, routines provide a basis for revising plans for future lessons. Routines can provide such information when they elicit the range of student ideas about a concept (van Zee & Minstrell, 1997), enable active student participation in assessment activities (Black & Wiliam, 1998; Dufresne, et al., 1996), and foster divergent thinking about particular problems (Beatty, et al., 2006; Stroup, et al., 2005).

TEACHING ROUTINES FOR GROUP SCRIBBLES

A central focus of our work has entailed developing routines that leverage Group Scribbles to support teaching and learning of important science content and practices. Group Scribbles (groupscribbles.sri.com) is a general-use collaborative application developed by SRI International. It offers instructors and students a powerful metaphor for thinking about and realizing collaborative learning activities. The metaphor is based on common physical artifacts from the classroom: adhesive notes, bulletin boards, whiteboards, stickers, pens and markers. Participants can scribble contributions on sheets similar to adhesive notes and jointly manage the movement of these electronic notes within and between public and private paces. Because Group Scribbles encourages decentralized control and individual initiative within a collective framework, students are highly involved in both contributing and responding to content.

Group Scribbles allows for open-ended questions that require students to construct an answer *interactively* using a range of representations, including text, sketches, and images. Group Scribbles displays can be continuously manipulated as the discussion proceeds to support emergent collaborative activity. In addition, Group Scribbles supports simple creation of individual and group workspaces to support flexible classroom configurations and highly parallel interactions. Figure 1 displays an image of a Group Scribbles board with student responses.

A classroom activity can take place entirely within the Group Scribbles environment and the software allows *in situ* assessments of student thinking. This potentially affords the teacher much richer and finer-grained diagnosis of student understanding that is situated within the particu-

Figure 1. Screenshot of group scribbles boards

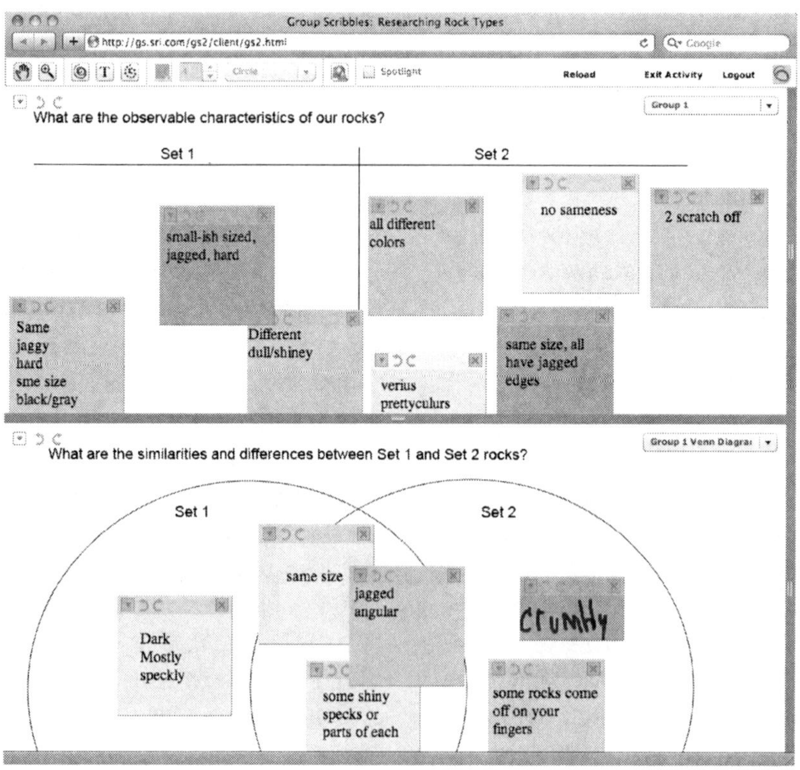

lar learning occasion. The open-ended structure provides the opportunity for a more contextualized understanding of potentially problematic student ideas and allows teachers to take new and more innovative instruction paths based on their professional interpretation. Teachers using Group Scribbles are able to assess and respond to actual student images and language in an improvisational fashion. They can use multiple attributes of student work as basis for further discussion—either to illustrate a specific misunderstanding or to reframe and re-present knowledge. With this increased flexibility in types of student responses that may be collected, there is the additional challenge of unpacking how students' responses reflect their underlying conceptualizations of the content.

Although Group Scribbles does not require teaching routines, the flexibility of this software provides an excellent occasion for their use. The teaching routines that we have developed help to scaffold for teachers sequences of instructional moves that promote discussion and reflection on student thinking and take advantage of the affordances of Group Scribbles. An outcome of our design process was a collection of seven teaching routines that provide a frame for teachers to enact different sequences of movement across public and private workspaces and between computer-mediated and face to face communication to make student thinking transparent. Each teaching routine describes a sequence of instructional moves for creating a particular kind of interactive formative assessment opportunity.

Our seven teaching routines support seven types of interactive formative assessments with Group Scribbles: concept mapping, data creating and sharing, question posing and categorizing, interpreting images, designing tests, and predicting. Each teaching routine follows a design principle aligned to how people learn (National Research Council, 1999). Table 1 outlines the seven teaching routines used in Group Scribbles along with their respective design principles and a brief description of how each routine enhances classroom communication, motivates student participation, and supports contingent teaching practices by improving teachers' ability to adjust instruction. Many of these routines include individual, small group, and whole class work or discussion; all require some student construction of knowledge. To facilitate formative interactions among the teacher and students, a teaching routine can encompass part of an instructional session or an entire instructional session. Some of the routines are particularly well suited for formatively assessing students' inquiry skills (e.g., *Group Data Creation and Comparison*).

Each teaching routine was designed to serve as a template from which an instructional designer, such as a teacher or curriculum developer, can create more specified interactive assessment opportunities. For example, the teaching routine *Group Data Creation and Comparison* (shown in Figure 2) identifies the key steps for enacting the routine to support students in collaborative collecting, organizing, sharing, and comparing of data. Because the teaching routine is generic in design and not linked to specific science content or lessons, it can be used as a foundation for creating assessment opportunities with Group Scribbles within or across lessons and units of instruction encompassing the same or different content. In this way, teaching routines encourage a level of consistency in assessment practice that enables both teachers and students to gain familiarity and comfort with enacting formative assessment over time.

Interactive Formative Assessments Based on Teaching Routines

The final step in our process was to use the teaching routines to develop content-specific *interactive formative assessments* (IFAs) within lessons of a middle school Earth Systems science curriculum. An IFA is a technology-supported formative assessment designed to promote student learning through the teacher's use of diagnostic question-

Table 1. Teaching routines for group scribbles (GS)

Routine	Design Principle	Instantiation	Goals
Concept Mapping	Construction of causal or other links among concepts helps students grasp important relationships among ideas and enrich their knowledge networks.	Students create concept maps in GS and iteratively revise and refine them with their peers.	*Communication*: Students discuss, debate, and refine their thinking with peers and teacher about how ideas relate to one another. *Participation*: Comparing and contrasting ideas encourages students to reflect upon, clarify and refine their own ideas. *Contingent Teaching*: The teacher gains insight into students' thinking and how students connect ideas.
Design a Test	Designing a scientific experiment, test, model, or procedure helps students learn how to investigate hypotheses.	Students develop an experimental design including independent and dependent variables on a GS board. They invite peer comment, review, and feedback on their designs prior to conducting their experiments/tests.	*Communication*: Students critique and provide feedback on each other's test design. *Participation*: Students use their refined procedures to test their ideas. *Contingent Teaching*: The teacher has an opportunity to assess students' understanding of test design and implementation.
Group Data Creation and Comparison	Organizing and comparing data helps students understand key data to be collected and appropriate representational forms that can be used to display data.	Students work in small groups to organize and represent data using GS. They discuss similarities and differences among the groups' data.	*Communication*: Students present data for peer review and discuss different ways to organize and represent data. *Participation*: Students' own contributions, including data, are a centerpiece of classroom work. *Contingent Teaching*: The teacher obtains feedback on students' abilities in organizing, representing and interpreting data.
Model-based Reasoning: Constructing a Model	Constructing models helps students understand causal relations.	Students construct models (e.g., images, maps, drawings, and pictures) in GS to describe phenomena and their underlying processes. They note the occurrence of processes or events and discuss why these processes/events occur in similar or different locations on the model.	*Communication*: Students share and discuss their models. *Participation*: Students create their own models to represent processes. *Contingent Teaching*: The teacher has an opportunity to assess students' understanding of how two or more processes are related.

continued on following page

Table 1. Continued

Model-based Reasoning: Interpreting and Using a Model	Interpreting and using models helps students understand causal relations.	Students interpret or explain a visual model posted in GS to explore phenomena and their underlying processes. They note the occurrence of processes or events and make predictions about these processes/ events using the model.	*Communication*: Students discuss components of models and how models represent phenomena. *Participation*: Students explore and compare features of models. *Contingent Teaching*: The teacher has an opportunity to assess students' understanding of how two or more processes are related.
Predict with Reasons	Making a prediction (stated outcome) supported with reasons based on conjecture or partial evidence helps students develop reasoning skills and understand the underlying scientific significance of an investigation.	Students describe a likely outcome/prediction for a test, observation, or model using GS. They discuss underlying reasoning for the prediction, and revisit the prediction after an experiment, test, or event is completed.	*Communication*: Students discuss, compare, and refine their thinking about likely outcomes of an experiment, test, or event. *Participation*: Students have a personal investment in conducting an experiment, test, or event. *Contingent Teaching*: Pressing students to base predictions on reasoning provides insight into how well students grasp the significance of investigations.
Question Posing and Categorizing	Developing and refining questions helps students identify questions that can be tested in investigations.	Students use GS to collaboratively generate and share research questions. They discuss similarities and difference among their questions.	*Communication*: Students collaborate with each other to generate and refine research questions. *Participation*: Students are invited to generate questions that will guide their own research. *Contingent Teaching*: Student-generated questions provide feedback to the teacher on students' grasp of the type of questions that are researchable.

ing and contingent teaching techniques. An IFA is a unique form of formative assessment because classroom network technology, in this case Group Scribbles, supports even greater collaboration and interaction among the teachers and students than are typically possible in classrooms. The adaptive assessment and instructional sequences in IFAs support the practices of eliciting student ideas and using feedback in formative ways to inform decisions about what to do next during instruction. All IFAs developed for this project adhere to four key principles, elaborated below.

IFAs build from existing curriculum materials. We have chosen to build assessments using a

Figure 2. Group data creation and comparison routine

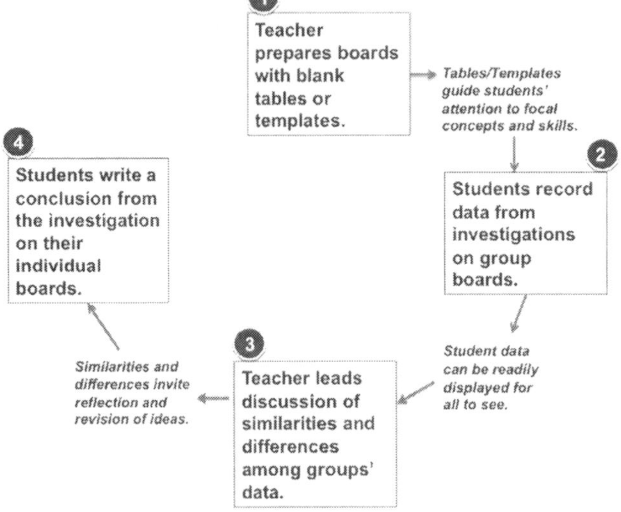

particular middle-school Earth science curriculum, *Investigating Earth Systems*, for a number of reasons. First, these materials are already widely adopted, and focused additions to the curriculum have a good chance at being incorporated into future editions of the curriculum. If that happens, the scalability of our materials is greatly enhanced. Second, these materials have been evaluated in an efficacy trial; when coupled with professional development that prepares teachers to adapt these materials to their local standards, the curriculum can be effective in increasing student learning in Earth science (Gallagher & Penuel, 2009). Third, the curriculum provides a useful anchor point for constraining development of both activities and assessments. Our aim is not to develop summative assessments but rather assessments that can be used to adjust instruction. Embedding them into materials teachers use to plan instruction provides the kind of guidance teachers can use to make the most of assessment information.

IFAs incorporate routines. When assessments incorporate routines, they can serve as models for teacher adaptation and lesson creation. Incorporating the routines into assessments will make visible the versatility of routines as resources for development and will also provide concrete illustrations that reflect our best thinking about how assessments can be designed with the technologies.

IFAs incorporate learning processes consistent with research on how students learn from participating in assessment activities in science. Key processes for learning from assessment in science activities are feedback and student reflection. Feedback helps students understand what they know and also to know how to improve (Black & Harrison, 2001; National Research Council, 2001). Network technology provides another source of feedback that may be important to learning: feedback on what others know and are having difficulty learning (Penuel, et al., 2005). Good classroom assessments also have students reflect on and revise their ideas (Black & Wiliam, 1998; National Research Council, 1999, 2001). Network technology supports reflection indirectly, by providing a focus (a shared display) for reflection, but to be effective, teachers must facilitate discussion of ideas to make reflection an integral part of a networked classrooms. The assessments will provide examples of how to foster reflection

Figure 3. Model-based reasoning: Constructing a model routine

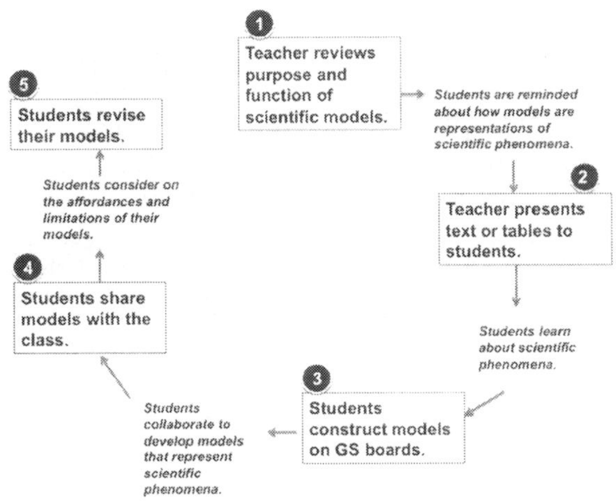

by providing more concrete guidance than do the teaching routines about questions to pose and about how to orchestrate classroom discussions.

IFAs integrate diverse sources of expertise. Developing assessments that incorporate network technology, employ routines, and assess Earth science content and skills requires a diverse set of expertise. Software engineers are needed to clarify the current and possible capabilities of the technology and to support classroom implementation. Learning scientists are needed to develop lesson plans using routines that reflect what we know about how people learn. Assessment and subject matter experts are needed to develop diagnostic questions and see to it that the connections encouraged in the IFAs reflect both accurate and significant content. Teachers' perspectives are needed to address questions about what is feasible to implement in real classrooms with students at particular grade levels.

In our work, each IFA has the same components as a teaching routine but is tailored to a lesson and its learning goals. Because IFAs are embedded within lessons and directly align with the target content of lessons, they can only be used with Group Scribbles in specified lesson contexts. For example, the *Model-based Reasoning: Constructing a Model* routine (Figure 3) was used to design an IFA within an Earth Systems lesson on tectonic plate boundaries (Table 2). In this way, a teaching routine becomes a resource for designing IFAs within lessons. As illustrated in Table 2, each step in the routine becomes instantiated within the *Ring of Fire* IFA.

In the Ring of Fire IFA, students explore an area in and around the Pacific Ocean, called the *Ring of Fire*, where large numbers of earthquakes and volcanic eruptions occur. This is due to the movement of the tectonic plates that exist in the area. The use of Group Scribbles as an interactive formative assessment space enables the teacher to "make thinking visible" by creating a public display of students' contributions to a map of the Ring of Fire. In this IFA, students use the tools in Group Scribbles to show and label the locations of volcanoes, earthquakes and plates in the Ring of Fire. The Ring of Fire IFA assumes that students have had some prior exposure to content on developing and revising models, the structure of Earth's interior, convection, and plate motion. This IFA is situated within an investigation in which students begin to explore relationships among events we observe on Earth's surface (e.g., earthquakes and volcanoes) and plate tectonics.

To enact this IFA, the teacher needs access to the Group Scribbles server, a teacher computer

Table 2. Instantiation of model-based reasoning: Constructing a model routine in ring of fire interactive formative assessment (IFA)

Steps in *Constructing a Model* Routine	Steps in *Ring of Fire* IFA
STEP 1. Teacher reviews purpose and function of models. The teacher prompts students about the features of models: (1) Models represent things that cannot be seen easily; (2) Model creation involves cycles of refinement as new evidence is gathered; and (3) Models are not perfect representations of phenomena.	Students are reminded that maps can be used to represent the location of Earth's landforms and that scientists use maps to understand the relationships among geologic phenomena that occur on Earth.
STEP 2. Teacher presents text or tables to students. The teacher can refer students to a textbook or web site or the text can be written in Group Scribbles (GS). Tables might be data tables from which students have to infer patterns that are created by some underlying phenomenon.	Students conduct research on their assigned topic (volcanoes, earthquakes, or plate boundaries).
STEP 3. Students construct models on GS boards. Students work in groups to construct a visual model representing scientific phenomena. Students might use evidence to create an appropriate model of changes in Earth's surface, create an accurate map of Earth's landforms, or create a reasonable model of dynamic Earth processes.	The teacher creates 3 GS boards [(1) Volcanoes, (2) Earthquakes, (3) plate boundaries] and uploads a background image of the map of the North Pacific Ocean and surrounding land masses. In their groups, students collaborate to find volcanoes, earthquakes or plate boundaries on the map. • Group 1 marks major volcanoes (using the red triangle stamp tool) and labels their locations by name and country using scribble notes. • Group 2 marks major earthquakes (using the blue circle stamp tool) and labels their locations and year of occurrence using scribble notes. • Group 3 draws major plate boundaries (using orange lines) and labels the plates they separate using scribble notes.
STEP 4: Students share models with the class. Each student group presents their model, and the teacher facilitates a discussion so that students can consider the affordances and limitations of their models. Questions posed by the teacher may include: • What about the Earth does this model present? • Why did this group place [Landform X] on this place in the map? *Continue until all groups have explained their reasoning.* • What's missing from this model that's important to the [change, landforms, process] we're discussing today? • How could this group improve their model?	The teacher can project each group's board or display multiple group boards at the same time. The teacher may ask the following questions: • Based on the various maps, what patterns do you see? **(Key idea: Earthquakes and volcanoes tend to follow the plate boundaries around the Pacific Ocean)** • Using what you have learned in this unit's investigation as a guide, what is a *model* that could explain the patterns you see? **(Key idea: The co-occurrence of earthquakes and volcanoes in this region is explained by convergent plate boundaries, in which ocean crust subducts under continental crust and produces magma)**
STEP 5: Students revise their models.	In their groups, students scribble on their boards a model for how volcanoes, earthquakes and plate boundaries are related..

with web browser, a projector connected to the teacher's computer, and student computers with web browser and Group Scribbles. The teacher has teams of students conduct research on different aspects of the Ring of Fire (volcanoes, earthquakes, or plate boundaries). Teams use the internet and classroom text materials to research information regarding their assigned feature of the Ring of Fire. Each team creates a Group Scribbles board to showcase their learning. To facilitate discussion, the teacher can arrange the display to display multiple boards simultaneously. Examples of questions to promote discussion along with target responses are also included in the IFA, as shown in Table 2.

Considerations in the Design and Implementation of Teaching Routines

Teaching routines can be a powerful resource in supporting instructional planning and decision making during instruction. However, there are some important considerations to take into account in the design of teaching routines.

Designing Teaching Routines

The identification of which process should be represented in a teaching routine is of critical importance, particularly because routines are intended to be used repeatedly by teachers and students. Well-designed routines will reflect processes that are essential to student learning in the domain and will articulate steps for how students can engage in the process through collaboration. In the domain of science, inquiry skills such as designing an experiment or creating and using models are examples of important processes that should be considered as the basis for teaching routines. Although developing an infinite number of routines representing different processes may be possible, it is not ideal. Rather, it is preferable to develop a smaller set of routines that are focused on critical processes and that can be used repeatedly in classes to engage students in appropriate ways of learning in a domain.

When considering the steps that should be represented in a teaching routine, we caution against over-specification. To enhance the applicability and use of routines with different content, steps are best written at a general level that provide guidance to the teacher about what to do next but also allow some flexibility in how they can be implemented. In addition, when routines overly constrain student interactions they potentially reduce authentic cognitive and social engagement and student motivation that naturally occur as a result of collaboration (Dillenbourg, 2002).

Designers of teaching routines must also attend to how classroom network technologies can be used to support student engagement in the steps of a routine. Particularly when teaching routines require collaboration, it is important that the technologies assist students in the types of communication and ways of thinking intended by the routine. When the technology is a poor fit, it may become a distraction for students and teachers. When the technology enhances students' ability to communicate and collaborate, greater learning gains should be possible (Krajcik, 2001).

Implementing Teaching Routines

Implementing a teaching routine requires moving from the generic steps in the routine to an instantiation of a routine in a lesson or assessment, which involves tailoring the routine to incorporate specific content. Care needs to be taken that the steps in the routine are adequately addressed, the content of the lesson is appropriate for the routine, and routines are appropriate for supporting students in achieving the desired learning objectives.

Using Teaching Routines to Design IFAs as a Professional Development Opportunity

In so far as teaching routines offer strategies to address complex interactions in the classroom, we view them as having great potential for professional development for teachers. We have conducted several workshops and teleconferences with teachers on teaching routines. A key feature of the professional development was to involve teachers as co-designers of IFAs with learning scientist researchers, assessment developers, and Earth scientists (Penuel, Roschelle, & Shechtman, 2007). The teachers involved in the design of these teaching routines were from the middle- and high-school in large urban school districts that include diverse student populations in terms of ethnicity and socio-economic status.

The co-design process with teachers first involved the unpacking of the IFAs drafted by the project team. Through this process the relationships among the teaching routines and the components of the IFAs were made explicit. To complete drafts of new teaching routines and IFAs, small groups worked collaboratively. Each group was assigned a range of expertise: a learning expert, an Earth science content expert, a teacher, a technology specialist, and a researcher. Not only did this activity result in the creation of IFAs for others to use; the act of design also was intended to be a form of professional development for participating teachers. By providing teachers with access to diverse expertise, we hoped to extend the range of what teachers could imagine was possible with the technology and the curriculum.

A key reason that we created teaching routines was to enable teachers to use them to design lessons on their own, as the need arises. The project's vetted IFAs are likely to be only one source of inspiration for teachers in doing so. By reviewing and unpacking routines embedded in IFAs, our intent is to provide teachers with the tools they will need to make the most of Group Scribbles technology. We have planned a series of professional development sessions (workshops and teleconferences) to identify ways that teaching routines can be incorporated effectively into classroom activities and to obtain feedback on the teaching routines and IFAs. Routines, as a structure, are abstract. To master their use and application, teachers will need examples of concrete instantiations of each routine before they will be ready to design their own routine-based activities.

To date, co-design teachers have reported that most teaching routines clearly articulate how the steps in the routines achieve the goals of enhancing communication, student participation and contingent teaching. In addition, teachers believe that the routines will help students learn high-level skills such as interpreting images, monitoring their understanding, designing experiments, and communicating specific information clearly. Several teachers predicted challenges related to classroom management, such as: (1) figuring out the "right amount of time" to allow students to answer questions, (2) keeping students on task during group work, (3) building in time for discussion and revision to each group's ideas, and (4) managing responses from multiple groups/individuals. As is common in design efforts, we anticipated that multiple cycles of testing and refinement of teaching routines and IFAs would be necessary.

FUTURE RESEARCH DIRECTIONS

Future research studies are planned to investigate further how often and reliably teachers integrate teaching routines in their instruction, how students of different backgrounds and attitudes perceive the IFAs and Group Scribbles technology, and how implementation varies for teachers with different levels of content knowledge and prior experience with using technology in their classrooms. These data on implementation will inform planning for revisions to the intervention in three ways. First, data will be used to identify additional technology support and training needs if teachers report that they experience significant difficulties that affect more than one to two students when they use Group Scribbles. Second, the data will be used to focus efforts to identify phases of instruction where teachers find it easier to use the teaching routines. Third, data from teaching routines and IFAs that were not successfully enacted will be analyzed to determine whether they need to be revised or eliminated, or whether additional training should be provided to teachers.

CONCLUSION

Teaching routines are designed to address some of the biggest barriers to using online classroom network technologies to collect and aggregate student data and make instructional decisions on the basis of those data. Teaching routines used in conjunction with classroom network technologies, such as Group Scribbles, have the potential to advance knowledge and understanding about classroom practices that build from research on student learning, assessment, cognitive science, and teacher learning to address major challenges to effective use of classroom network technologies. When instantiated as an IFA sequence in the classroom, teaching routines are intended to increase student opportunities to communicate with the teacher and with peers about their thinking, to motivate students to participate and learn from lectures, investigations, and readings, and to encourage student feedback to inform the teacher about how to adjust instruction.

One of the most important contributions of this approach is that teaching routines make explicit good teaching practices with classroom network technology. In the past, teaching has been described as a profession where practice is "privatized," that is, where instructional decisions are largely left to individual teachers to make and where opportunities to observe colleagues teach are limited (Little, 1990; Lortie, 1975). Both accountability systems and efforts to promote opportunities for teachers to learn from one another, however, aim to expand the horizon of visible practice and bring teachers' practice into closer alignment to improve student learning (Little, 2002; 2003; O'Day, 2002).

The process of making practice visible to peers is aided when teachers can develop a common language for describing their practice (Grossman & McDonald, 2008). In our work, that common language will be provided by teaching routines, and we expect it will serve not only as a resource for teachers to use to enable their own collaborative learning but also as a "boundary object" for anchoring discussions where researchers and teachers are both present and discussing how to improve a particular activity.

As specifications of sequences of an IFA, teaching routines can also serve as a resource for instructional design. In developing curriculum or in planning instruction, individuals and teams benefit from models for how to structure resources and opportunities for student learning (Gallagher & Penuel, 2009). To the extent that these resources instantiate principles of how people learn, these routines also make it more likely that the lessons developed will promote student learning. For example, teaching routines that embed into their designs what have been called "quasi-repetitive activity cycles" have been shown to familiarize students with the process of learning from reflection (Schwartz, Lin, Brophy, & Bransford, 1999; Vye, et al., 1998). The first time students encounter demands for reflection, they may not know how to learn from collaborative reflection; by repeating cycles of learning and reflection, though, students gain experience in learning from revising their own ideas in conversation with others.

ACKNOWLEDGMENT

This material is based on work supported by the National Science Foundation under grant DRL-0822314 (Developing Contingent Pedagogies: Integrating Technology-Enhanced Feedback into a Middle School Science Curriculum to Improve Conceptual Teaching and Learning). Any opinions, findings, and conclusions or recommendations expressed in this material are those of the authors and do not necessarily reflect the views of the National Science Foundation.

REFERENCES

Alexander, C. N., Ishikawa, S., & Silverstein, M. (1977). *A pattern language: Towns, buildings, construction*. New York: Oxford University Press.

Bakhtin, M. M. (1981). *The dialogic imagination: Four essays* (Emerson, C., & Holquist, M., Trans.). Austin, TX: University of Texas Press.

Beatty, I. D., Gerace, W. J., Leonard, W. J., & Dufresne, R. J. (2006). Designing effective questions for classroom response system teaching. *American Journal of Physics*, *74*(1), 31–39. doi:10.1119/1.2121753

Black, P., & Harrison, C. (2001). Feedback in questioning and marking: The science teacher's role in formative assessment. *The School Science Review*, *82*(301), 55–61.

Black, P., & Wiliam, D. (1998). Assessment and classroom learning. *Assessment in Education*, *5*(1), 7–74. doi:10.1080/0969595980050102

Butler, R. (1987). Task-involving and ego-involving properties of evaluation: Effects of different feedback conditions on motivational perceptions, interest, and performance. *Journal of Educational Psychology*, *79*(4), 474–482. doi:10.1037/0022-0663.79.4.474

Butler, R., & Nisan, M. (1986). Effects of no feedback, task-related comments, and grades on intrinsic motivation and performance. *Journal of Educational Psychology*, *78*(3), 210–216. doi:10.1037/0022-0663.78.3.210

Calderhead, J. (1981). A psychological approach to research on teachers' classroom decision making. *British Educational Research Journal*, *7*(1), 51–57. doi:10.1080/0141192810070105

Davis, S. (2003). Observations in classrooms using a network of handheld devices. *Journal of Computer Assisted Learning*, *19*(3), 298–307. doi:10.1046/j.0266-4909.2003.00031.x

DiGiano, C., Yarnall, L., Patton, C., Roschelle, J., Tatar, D., & Manley, M. (2003). Conceptual tools for planning for the wireless classroom. *Journal of Computer Assisted Learning*, *19*(3), 284–297. doi:10.1046/j.0266-4909.2003.00030.x

Dillenbourg, P. (2002). Over-scripting CSCL: The risks of blending collaborative learning with instructional design. In P. A. Kirschner (Ed.), *Three worlds of CSCL: Can we support CSCL?* (pp. 61-91). Heerlen, Nederland: Open University of the Netherlands.

diSessa, A. A., & Minstrell, J. (1998). Cultivating conceptual change with benchmark lessons. In Greeno, J. G., & Goldman, S. V. (Eds.), *Thinking practices in mathematics and science learning* (pp. 155–187). Mahwah, NJ: Lawrence Erlbaum Associates.

Dufresne, R. J., & Gerace, W. J. (2004). Assessing-To-Learn: Formative assessment in physics instruction. *The Physics Teacher*, *42*(7), 428–433. doi:10.1119/1.1804662

Dufresne, R. J., Gerace, W. J., Leonard, W. J., Mestre, J. P., & Wenk, L. (1996). Classtalk: A classroom communication system for active learning. *Journal of Computing in Higher Education*, *7*(2), 3–47. doi:10.1007/BF02948592

Gallagher, L. P., & Penuel, W. R. (2009, April). *Preparing teachers to design instruction in middle school Earth science: Impacts of three professional development programs on student learning.* Paper presented at the Annual Meeting of the American Educational Research Association, San Diego, CA.

Grossman, P., & McDonald, M. (2008). Back to the future: Directions for research in teaching and teacher education. *American Educational Research Journal*, *45*(1), 184–205. doi:10.3102/0002831207312906

Harris, M. (1986). *Teaching one-to-one: The writing conference*. Urbana, IL: National Council of Teachers of English.

Hegedus, S. J., & Kaput, J. (2004, September). *An introduction to the profound potential of connected algebra activities: Issues of representation, engagement and pedagogy.* Paper presented at the 28th Conference of the International Group for the Psychology of Mathematics Education, Bergen, Norway.

Hinds, M. (2002). *Teaching as a clinical profession: A new challenge for education*. New York: Carnegie Corporation of New York.

Holquist, M. (1990). *Dialogism*. London: Routledge. doi:10.4324/9780203330340

Hoppe, U. H., & Ploetzner, R. (1999). Can analytic models support learning in groups? In Dillenbourg, P. (Ed.), *Collaborative learning: Cognitive and computational approaches* (pp. 147–168). Oxford, UK: Elsevier.

Judson, E., & Sawada, D. (2002). Learning from past and present: Electronic response systems in college lecture halls. *Journal of Computers in Mathematics and Science Teaching, 21*(2), 167–181.

Klahr, D., & Nigam, M. (2004). The equivalence of learning paths in early science instruction: Effects of direct instruction and discovery learning. *Psychological Science, 15*(10), 661–667. doi:10.1111/j.0956-7976.2004.00737.x

Koper, R. (2003). Combining reusable learning resources and services with pedagogical purposeful units of learning. In Littlejohn, A. (Ed.), *Reusing online resources: A sustainable approach to e-learning* (pp. 46–59). London: Routledge.

Krajcik, J. S. (2001). Supporting science learning in context: Project-based learning. In Tinker, R. F., & Krajcik, J. S. (Eds.), *Portable technologies* (pp. 7–28). New York: Plenum Publishers.

Lemke, J. L. (1990). *Talking science: Language, learning, and values*. Norwood, New Jersey: Ablex.

Little, J. W. (1990). The persistence of privacy: Autonomy and initiative in teachers' professional relations. *Teachers College Record, 91*(4), 508–536.

Little, J. W. (2002). Locating learning in teachers' communities of practice: Opening up problems of analysis in records of everyday work. *Teaching and Teacher Education, 18*(8), 917–946. doi:10.1016/S0742-051X(02)00052-5

Little, J. W. (2003). Inside teacher community: Representations of classroom practice. *Teachers College Record, 105*(6), 913–945. doi:10.1111/1467-9620.00273

Lortie, D. (1975). *Schoolteacher: A sociological study*. Chicago: University of Chicago Press.

Maehr, M. L., & Midgley, C. (1991). Enhancing student motivation: A school-wide approach. *Educational Psychologist, 26*(3-4), 399–427. doi:10.1207/s15326985ep2603&4_9

Mehan, H. (1979). *Learning lessons: Social organization in the classroom*. Cambridge, MA: Harvard University Press.

Muthukrishna, N., Carnine, D., Grossen, B., & Miller, S. (1999). Children's alternative frameworks: Should they be directly addressed in science instruction? *Journal of Research in Science Teaching, 30*(3), 233–248. doi:10.1002/tea.3660300303

National Research Council. (1999). *How people learn: Brain, mind, experience*. Washington, D.C: National Academy Press.

National Research Council. (2001). *Classroom assessment and the National Science Education Standards*. Washington, D.C: National Academy Press.

Nystrand, M., & Gamoran, A. (1991). Instructional discourse, student engagement, and literature achievement. *Research in the Teaching of English, 25*(3), 261–290.

Nystrand, M., Wu, L. L., & Gamoran, A. (2003). Questions in time: Investigating the structure and dynamics of unfolding classroom discourse. *Discourse Processes, 32*(5), 135–198. doi:10.1207/S15326950DP3502_3

O'Day, J. A. (2002). Complexity, accountability, and school improvement. *Harvard Educational Review, 72*(3), 293–329.

Penuel, W. R. (2008). Making the most of one-to-one computing in networked classrooms. In Voogt, J., & Knezek, G. (Eds.), *International handbook of information technology in primary and secondary education* (pp. 925–931). Dordrecht, The Netherlands: Springer. doi:10.1007/978-0-387-73315-9_59

Penuel, W. R. (in press). Classroom uses of technology to manage instruction *International Encyclopedia of Education*. Oxford, UK: Elsevier.

Penuel, W. R., Boscardin, C. K., Masyn, K., & Crawford, V. M. (2007). Teaching with student response systems in elementary and secondary education settings: A survey study. *Educational Technology Research and Development, 55*(4), 315–346. doi:10.1007/s11423-006-9023-4

Penuel, W. R., Roschelle, J., & Abrahamson, A. L. (2005). Research on classroom networks for whole-class activities. Proceedings of *the IEEE International Workshop on Wireless and Mobile Technologies in Education* (pp. 222-229). Los Alamitos, CA: IEEE.

Penuel, W. R., Roschelle, J., & Shechtman, N. (2007). The WHIRL co-design process: Participant experiences. *Research and Practice in Technology Enhanced Learning, 2*(1), 51–74. doi:10.1142/S1793206807000300

Petrosino, A. J. (1998). *The use of reflection and revision in hands-on experimental activities by at risk children.*, Unpublished dissertation. Vanderbilt University, Nashville, TN.

Posner, G., Strike, J., Hewson, P., & Gerzog, W. (1982). Accommodation of a scientific conception: Toward a theory of conceptual change. *Science Education, 66*(2), 221–227. doi:10.1002/sce.3730660207

Roschelle, J., Knudsen, J., & Hegedus, S. J. (in press). From new technological infrastructures to curricular activity systems: Advanced designs for teaching and learning. In Jacobson, M. J., & Reimann, P. (Eds.), *Designs for learning environments of the future: International perspectives from the learning sciences*. New York: Springer.

Roschelle, J., Penuel, W. R., & Abrahamson, A. L. (2004). The networked classroom. *Educational Leadership, 61*(5), 50–54.

Schroeder, U., & Spannagel, C. (2005). The role of interaction records in active learning processes: Proceedings of *the IADIS Virtual Multi Conference on Computer Science and Information Systems (MCCSIS)* (pp. 99-104). Algarve, Portugal: International Association for Development of the Information Society.

Schwartz, D. L., & Bransford, J. D. (1998). A time for telling. *Cognition and Instruction, 16*(4), 475–522. doi:10.1207/s1532690xci1604_4

Schwartz, D. L., Lin, X., Brophy, S., & Bransford, J. D. (1999). Toward the development of flexibly adaptive instructional designs. In Reigeluth, C. (Ed.), *Instructional design theories and models: A new paradigm of instructional theory* (*Vol. II*, pp. 183–214). Mahwah, NJ: Earlbaum.

Smith, J. P. III, diSessa, A. A., & Roschelle, J. (1993-1994). Misconceptions reconceived: A constructivist analysis of knowledge in transition. *Journal of the Learning Sciences, 3*(2), 115–163. doi:10.1207/s15327809jls0302_1

Solomon, M. Z., & Morocco, C. (1999). The diagnostic teacher. In Solomon, M. Z. (Ed.), *The diagnostic teacher: Constructing new approaches to professional development* (pp. 231–246). New York: Teachers College Press.

Stroup, W., Ares, N., & Hurford, A. (2005). A dialectic analysis of generativity: Issues of network supported design in mathematics and science. *Journal of Mathematical Thinking and Learning, 7*(3), 181–206. doi:10.1207/s15327833mtl0703_1

Truong, T. M., Griswold, W. G., Ratto, M., & Star, L. (2002). *The ActiveClass project: experiments in encouraging classroom participation*. San Diego, CA: University of California.

Tyack, D., & Cuban, L. (1995). *Tinkering toward utopia: A century of public school reform*. Cambridge, MA: Harvard University Press.

van Zee, E. H., & Minstrell, J. (1997). Using questioning to guide student thinking. *Journal of the Learning Sciences*, *6*(2), 227–269. doi:10.1207/s15327809jls0602_3

Vye, N., Schwartz, D., Bransford, J., Barron, B. J. S., Zech, L., & Cognition and Technology Group at Vanderbilt (1998). SMART environments that support monitoring, reflection, and revision. In D. Hacker, J. Dunlosky & A. C. Graesser (Eds.), *Metacognition in educational theory and practice*. Mahwah, NJ: Erlbaum.

Wells, G. (1993). Reevaluating the IRF sequence: A proposal for the articulation of theories of activity and discourse for the analysis of teaching and learning in the classroom. *Linguistics and Education*, *5*(1), 1–37. doi:10.1016/S0898-5898(05)80001-4

Wigfield, A., Eccles, J. S., & Rodriguez, D. (1998). The development of children's motivation in school contexts. *Review of Research in Education*, *23*(1), 73–118. doi:10.3102/0091732X023001073

Wilensky, U., & Stroup, W. M. (2000, June). *Networked gridlock: Students enacting complex dynamic phenomena with the HubNet architecture.* Paper presented at the The Fourth Annual International Conference of the Learning Sciences, Ann Arbor, MI.

Zumbach, J., Muhlenbrock, M., Jansen, M., Reimann, P., & Hoppe, U. H. (2002). Multidimensional tracking in virtual learning teams: An exploratory study. In Stahl, G. (Ed.), *Computer support for collaborative learning: Foundations for a CSCL community* (pp. 650–651). Mahwah, NJ: Erlbaum.

ADDITIONAL READING

Black, P. (2003). The importance of everyday assessment. In Atkin, J. M., & Coffee, J. (Eds.), *Everyday assessment in the science classroom* (pp. 1–12). Arlington, VA: NSTA Press.

Blumenfeld, P. C., Marx, R. W., & Harris, C. J. (2006). Learning environments. In Damon, W., Lerner, R. M., Renninger, K. A., & Sigel, I. E. (Eds.), *Handbook of child psychology: Child psychology in practice* (6th ed., *Vol. 4*, pp. 297–342). Hoboken, NJ: Wiley.

Borko, H. (2004). Professional development and teacher learning: mapping the terrain. *Educational Researcher*, *33*(8), 3–15. doi:10.3102/0013189X033008003

Brecht, J., DiGiano, C., Patton, C., Tatar, D., Chaudhury, R., Roschelle, J., & Davis, K. (2006). Coordinating networked learning activities with a general-purpose interface. *Proceedings of mLearn 2006, the 5th World Conference on Mobile Learning*. Banff, Alberta, Canada.

Minstrell, J. (2001). Facets of students' thinking: Designing to cross the gap from research to standards-based practice. In Crowley, K., Schunn, C. D., & Okada, T. (Eds.), *Designing for science: Implications for professional, instructional, and everyday science*. Mahwah, NJ: Lawrence Erlbaum Associates.

Minstrell, J., & Kraus, P. (2005). Guided inquiry in the science classroom. In National Research Council (Ed.), *How students learn: History, mathematics, and science in the classroom* (pp. 475-514). Washington, D.C: National Academies Press.

Minstrell, J., & van Zee, E. (2003). Using questioning to assess and foster student thinking. In Atkin, J. M., & Coffee, J. (Eds.), *Everyday assessment in the science classroom* (pp. 61–74). Arlington, VA: NSTA Press.

Moraveji, N., Inkpen, K., Cutrell, E., & Balakrishnan, R. (2009). A mischief of mice: Examining children's performance in single display groupware systems with 1 to 32 mice. *Proceedings of the 27th international conference on Human factors in computing systems (CHI '09),* 2157-2166. New York: ACM.

National Research Council. (2007). *Taking science to school: Learning and teaching science in grades K-8*. Washington, D.C: National Academies Press.

Patton, C., Tatar, D., & Dimitriadis, Y. (2008). Trace theory, coordination games and GroupScribbles. In J. Voogt & G. Knezek (Eds.), *International Handbook of Information Technology in Primary and Secondary Education*, chapter on *Emerging Technologies*, 921-934. New York: Springer.

Pellegrino, J. W., Chudowsky, N., & Glaser, R. (2001). *Knowing what students know: The science and design of educational assessment*. Washington, D.C: National Academy Press.

Penuel, W. R., Lynn, E., & Berger, L. (2006). Classroom assessment with handheld computers. In van 't Hooft, M., & Swan, K. (Eds.), *Ubiquitous computing in education: Invisible technology, visible impact* (pp. 103–125). Mahwah, NJ: Erlbaum.

Roschelle, J., Tatar, D., Chaudhury, S. R., Dimitriadis, Y., Patton, C., & DiGiano, C. (2007). Ink, improvisation, and interactive engagement: Learning with tablets. *Computer*, *40*(9), 38–44. doi:10.1109/MC.2007.321

Sawyer, R. K. (Ed.). (2006). *The Cambridge handbook of the learning sciences*. New York: Cambridge University Press.

Shepard, L. (2000). The role of assessment in a learning culture. *Educational Researcher*, *29*(7), 4–14.

KEY TERMS AND DEFINITIONS

Classroom Network Technology: Technology that enables teachers and students to share questions, ideas, data, or responses via a local classroom network.

Co-Design: Collaborative process in which researchers, teachers, and software developers design an educational innovation.

Contingent Teaching: Adjusting instruction on the basis of particular patterns of student behavior.

Diagnostic Question: Question designed to elicit student preconceptions and relate student responses to known goal or problematic understandings related to the domain.

Formative Classroom Assessment: A process that provides feedback to teachers and students about students' understanding and thus can be used to help teachers adjust their instruction to better address students' learning needs.

Interactive Formative Assessment (IFA): A technology-supported formative assessment designed to promote student learning through the teacher's use of diagnostic questioning and contingent teaching techniques.

Peer Instruction: An instructional approach in which a question is posed to students and students first develop their own response then work in small groups to reach consensus on a response.

Teaching Routine: A recurring, patterned sequence of interaction teachers and students jointly enact to organize opportunities for student learning in classrooms.

Chapter 14
Assessing the Performance of Learners Engaged in Computer-Supported Collaborative Problem-Solving Activities

Symeon Retalis
University of Piraeus, Greece

Ourania Petropoulou
University of Piraeus, Greece

Georgia Lazakidou
University of Piraeus, Greece

ABSTRACT

Teachers often utilise a Computer-Supported Collaborative Learning (CSCL) strategy to teach a concept, a method, a problem, and so forth. Following guidelines from a script (based on a CSCL strategy), they must ultimately assess their students' performance during their engagement in various learning activities; however, content and process assessments differ from script to script. Thus, a teacher faces a serious problem during content and process assessment. Here, the authors present a holistic framework for performance assessment and specify indexes for it. The authors aim to facilitate the teacher/evaluator's work by equipping him or her with easy-to-apply tools and techniques for in-depth analysis of interactions. Finally, they describe our application of the proposed framework in an exploratory case study of a problem-solving activity in which a complex collaborative strategy is applied.

INTRODUCTION

Complex collaborative learning strategies (such as Pyramid, Jigsaw, Think Pair Share, Think Aloud Pair Problem Solving) have been widely used in instructional practice. Teachers who use the dynamics and qualities of various collaborative strategies design and develop respective collaborative learning scripts. Scripts describe the way learners should collaborate, i.e., the sequence of tasks, the distribution of roles, the deliverables, etc. Learners who participate in such collaborative learning

DOI: 10.4018/978-1-61692-898-8.ch014

scripts become involved in a grid of interaction patterns, i.e., learner-learner, learner-teacher, and learner-resources interactions (Moore, 1989).

It is well known that assessment plays a very important role in the instructional process since it gives learners an opportunity to receive substantive feedback on their understanding and competency (Kodri, 2003). Feedback gives learners an opportunity to understand what they have done and to compare their performance to self-set goals as well as to group-set goals. Assessing group and individual performance in collaborative learning scripts is not an easy task (Marcos, Martinez, & Dimitriadis, 2005; Petropoulou, Lazakidou, Retalis, & Vrasidas, 2007). A teacher should have good insights into students' learning behaviour when evaluating their performance in collaborative tasks in order to correlate student's behaviour while executing collaborative tasks with the grades given on assessment of their deliverables (Barros & Verdejo, 2000; Poole, 2000; Martínez, Dimitriadis, & De La Fuente, 2003; Saltz, Hiltz, & Turoff, 2004; Ho & Swan, 2007).

For this reason teachers usually develop frameworks for assessing learners' performance that take various aspects of collaborative learning sessions into consideration. These frameworks are used for product assessment as well as for performance assessment. Product assessment focuses on the grading of the actual learners' deliverables to evaluate whether a skill has been applied or some concept has been learned. Performance assessment is based more on the process used by learners than on the final product. It relies on the judgment of the teacher who observes the learners' behaviour as they perform a predetermined set of tasks. Thus a framework should be developed that can be used with a computer-supported collaborative learning script and enable the teacher to analyse, with a list of specific criteria, the level of quality of a product and of performance.

Currently, few reusable assessment frameworks exist for computer-supported collaborative learning (CSCL) scripts based on well-known collaborative learning strategies. Reusable assessment frameworks have become a necessity since they can facilitate teachers' burdensome mission of learner assessment (Voyiatzaki, Margaritis, & Avouris, 2006; Daradoumis, Martínez, & Xhafa, 2006). A teacher needs guidance and support in analysing, measuring, and correlating the complex data that can be gathered during collaborative learning activities so they can be used to effectively and efficiently assess students' individual and group performance (Chan & van Aalst, 2006; Daradoumis et al., 2006; Zinn & Scheuer, 2006; Swan, Shen, & Hiltz, 2006).

Fortunately, several recent studies have focused on analysis of participation and interaction of students and teachers in CSCL settings (Persico, Pozzi, & Sarti, 2009). In these studies, various indicators have been proposed for the analysis of interaction among students. These indicators can be used to assess the performance of individuals and groups. Thus, assessment frameworks with associated assessment rubrics that make use of these indicators should be proposed.

Our chapter aims to identify those indicators that can be used/reused to build a conceptual framework with the associated rubrics for teachers to use to assess students' productivity and performance when engaged in CSCL tasks. The expected benefits of reusability of indicators are the following:

a. The teacher will be better able to monitor the collaborative learning process and determine the degree of success of each designed collaborative learning task, thus providing learners with appropriate feedback.
b. Students will be able to easily find out for themselves the aspects of their collaborative and individual learning behaviour that need strengthening.

An exemplar case for the reuse of indicators and assessment rubrics will be shown. This case concerns a complex collaborative problem-solving script that follows the principles of the e-ARMA collaborative strategy.

The rest of the chapter is structured as follows: Section 2 contains a brief state-of-the-art literature review of interaction analysis (IA) indicators and associated tools and techniques that have been applied in CSCL settings. Section 3 gives an overview of our proposed framework for the assessment of collaborative learning tasks by reusing the existing indicators. The way in which this framework has been applied to the e-ARMA stepwise collaborative learning strategy that tries to augment learners' problem-solving and self-regulation skills will be also shown. In the e-ARMA case, selected analysis tools and techniques such as ColAT (Avouris, Komis, Margaritis, & Fiotakis, 2004) and social network analysis (SNA) (Wasserman & Faust, 1997) have been used to measure some of the proposed interaction analysis indicators. The evaluation findings are presented. Conclusions and future research directions are also discussed at the end of the chapter.

INTERACTION ANALYSIS INDICATORS, TOOLS, AND TECHNIQUES IN CSCL

Interaction Analysis has been the focus of many recent research studies attempting to develop assessment frameworks and methods within complex CSCL environments. These studies revolve around two main axes: (1) evaluation of the collaborative process and of the product of collaboration with the aim of supporting the collaborative action and the tracking of those factors that affect the learning product (Barros, & Verdejo, 2000; Martínez, Dimitriadis, & De La Fuente, 2003; Soller, Jermann, Muehlenbrock, & Martinez, 2004; Spada, Meier, Rummel, & Hauser, 2005; Law, 2005; Puntambekar, 2006; Pozzi, Manca, Persico, & Sarti, 2007; Collazos, et al., 2007), (2) the evaluation of performance of learners who engage in computer-supported collaborative learning scripts (Daradoumis et al., 2006). Many more studies and research proposals exist for the first axis than for the second, which is a hot research topic nowadays (Hernánez-Leo et al., 2008).

Various analysis and reporting tools have also been developed to support the first axis of researchers' interest (Barros, & Verdejo, 2000; Avouris, Dimitracopoulou, Komis, & Fidas, 2002; Reffay, & Chanier, 2003; Bratitsis & Dimitracopoulou, 2005; De Laat, Lally, Lipponen, & Simons, 2005; Dimitracopoulou et al., 2006; Retalis, Papasalouros, Psaromiligkos, Siskos, & Kargidis, 2006; Dimitracopoulou, 2007; Saltz, Hiltz, Turoff, & Passerini, 2007). These kinds of tools gather data from participants' actions and messages exchanged in a collaborative learning environment and analyses them according to various defined indicators (e.g., division of labour, total number of messages/actions per learner/group, ratio of writing/reading messages to learner/group, social network density, learner's degree of centrality, social network centralisation degree, percentage of read learning material per learner/group).

Concerning the second axis of research trends, the main focus of this chapter, Daradoumis et al.'s (2006) study is the most in-depth study in the field of individual and group performance evaluation within a CSCL process. In that study an assessment framework is proposed, comprising of four parameters: task performance, group functioning, social support, and help services. Student/group learning outcomes, the student's contributing behaviour during task realisation, and self-evaluation performance belong to the "task performance" parameter. "Group functioning" concerns the active participation, role playing, well-balanced contributions, and interaction patterns that facilitate the group's proper functioning and processing. The "social support" parameter refers to members' commitment to collaboration, joint learning, and accomplishment of common goals, level of peer involvement, and their influential role in the involvement of others. Finally, the "help services" parameter includes the timely, qualitative, relevant, comprehensible, and readily applied kind of help provided to students.

Equally important and complementary is Zinn and Scheuer's (2006) research that seeks to identify those aspects of evaluation that give meaning to the assessment process from the perspective of teachers. In their research, a number of indicators (such as volume of collaboration messages exchanged, navigational patterns, historical usage data of learning resources) were studied. It was found that teachers want to have access to information related to student performance (e.g., success rate per type of exercise, mastery level for a concept, skill, or method, amount of time spent per activity type rather than information such as navigational style, past activity patterns, and ratio of social activities to all activities that seems less interesting and meaningful to them during the assessment task.

More recently, Persico, Pozzi, and Sarti (2009) attempted to construct a sound, general-purpose model to monitor and evaluate collaborative learning processes that take advantage of information and communication technologies and are typically conducted from a distance. The model takes into consideration four dimensions: participative, social, cognitive, and teaching. This study highlights the workload and the time needed to analyse those dimensions during a collaborative learning activity as well as the need for a teacher/evaluator to be familiar with this type of evaluation process. The researchers emphasise the need for semi-automatic tools that can support this process.

All the valuable studies described above have many aspects in common, including assessment rubrics, techniques, and interaction analysis indicators; nevertheless, simply mentioning a plethora of interaction analysis indicators is not sufficient for teachers to assess individual and group performance. Teachers need guidance in methodically applying these indicators in their own cases. This is why the reusability of indicators as well as the existence of assessment frameworks that give guidance to teachers on their application when assessing CSCL tasks is needed (see Figure 1). The present chapter attempts to meet this need by proposing commonly used reusable interaction analysis indicators that can easily be applied in collaborative learning scripts. It also shows how to apply these indicators by giving an example of their application in a CSCL script based on the e-ARMA CSCL strategy.

Figure 1. Assessment requirements during implementation of a collaborative learning script

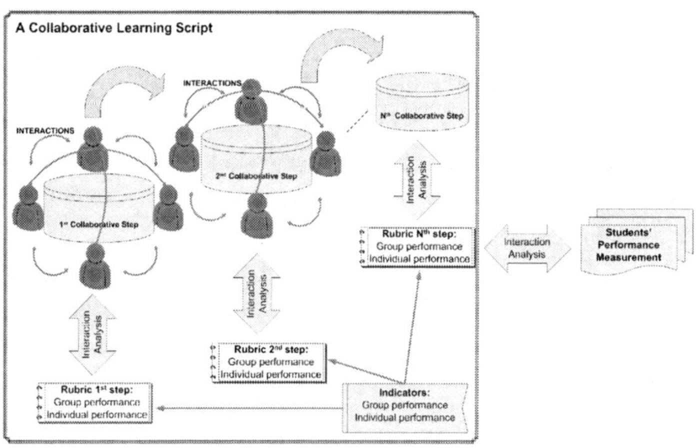

PROPOSED STUDENT ASSESSMENT FRAMEWORK IN A CSCL ENVIRONMENT

The development of a well-structured performance assessment framework should include distinctive indicators for every phase of a collaborative strategy. Our proposed framework comprises two axes that measure student performance in a CSCL environment: (a) the quality of learning products and (b) the quality of the collaboration related to the volume and quality of interactions in a CSCL environment.

Axes of the Proposed Assessment Framework

The first axis concerns all deliverables of individual or group action (e.g., learners' assignments). Both quantitative and qualitative aspects of the quality of learning products should be accounted for.

Indicators for quantitative analysis of quality of learning products

- Grading of learner's ongoing and final learning products (e.g., final reports, tests, exercises, quizzes)
- Group's overall performance in specific tasks (e.g., group's average score)
- Mastery level of each concept/skill/method/competency (e.g., individual scores that prove knowledge growth [novice, advanced, expert], individual score versus class mean of success/failure)
- Number of steps performed in a multi-step exercise (e.g., number of correct, wrong, or incomplete steps)
- Learner's most significant contributions to the task (e.g., first draft of a deliverable, creation of elements in a concept map, all expressed in numbers or percentages)
- Ratio of correct to incorrect steps per session correlated with task difficulty

Indicators for qualitative analysis of quality of learning products

- Quality of the content of learner's proposed final solution (such as single/alternative solution presented)
- List of most frequently diagnosed mistakes and misconceptions

The second axis refers to the necessity for specifying the effects of particular categories of interactions within a CSCL environment (Dillenbourg, 1999) for the accomplishment of learning products. These interactions refer to the grid of interactions developed between peers (learner-learner), learner-tutor (L-T), and learner-content (L-C). This grid strongly affects learning products. The three types of interaction play a key role in CSCL.

Thus, we not only measure what students deliver in a CSCL environment but also how they produced their deliverables. We propose that this entire spectrum of interactions should be captured and analysed accordingly. Specifically, in terms of learner-learner interactions (L-L) we propose evaluation of the following elements:

Descriptives of Participation Behaviour

- Total number of actions (e.g., counts of mouse clicks or contributions)
- Total number of messages learners exchanged with each other (per week/per day)
- Total number of notes (per week/per day)
- Time frequency and sequence of individual and group actions
- Learner behaviour compared with that of other group members
- Who reads/writes whose notes (active/passive participation)

The Level of Communication Behaviour

- Direction of information flow (different kinds of communication among participants)
- Total number of follow-up postings
- Total number of thread initiations

Type and Quality of Collaboration

- Number and nature of contributions to the task (per learner)
- Content of learners' contributions, in terms of the following:
    - Division of labour among participants
    - Role playing (equal contribution/ leading role within a group, number of social nets)
    - Mutual engagement of participants in a coordinated effort to solve a problem
    - Development of trust, social cohesiveness, sense of belonging
    - Ratio of social activities to overall activities
    - Number of relationships established among a group of learners
    - Members' motivational and emotional support to their peers
    - Number of help requests by learner

Concerning learner-tutor interactions (L-T), the following indicators can be used:

Intervention

- Time and reason for tutor's intervention (Netiquette, provision of feedback, instructions, opinions, summary of learners' comments, discourse facilitation, encouragement, acknowledgment or reinforcement of a learner's contribution, diagnosis of misconceptions)
- Type of intervention (actions, messages) during an online activity
- Recipient(s) of tutor's intervention
- Tutor's participation patterns
- Total number of notes posted (per week/ per day)

Help Services

- Timely help
- Relevance of help to learner's needs
- Conception of tutor's help by learners
- Application of tutor's help by learners

Learner-content interactions (L-C) are illustrated mainly by the learner's navigational behaviour and include the following indicators:

Total Usage and Activity Times

- Amount of time a learner spends with the system (per session)
- Number of sessions
- History of past usage

Activity Types

- Average time spent on each activity
- Distribution of activity types
- History of past activity patterns

Course Coverage

- Percentage of available material read
- Percentage of available exercises tackled
- History of past percentages

Learning Content Usage

- Amount of time spent per concept/skill/ method/competency
- Number of learning activities per concept/ skill/method/competency
- Sequential learning paths per session (e.g., theory, example, exercise)
- History of past learning content

- Learners' preferences for concept/skill/method/competency
    - List of accessed and (potentially) read course material
    - List of most frequently looked-up terms
    - Learner classification
    - History of past learner classification

APPLYING THE REUSABLE INDICATORS IN A CSCL SCRIPT

e-ARMA Computer Supported Collaborative Learning Strategy

The e-ARMA strategy fosters the development of self-regulative skills in mathematics problem solving (Lazakidou, Retalis, Paraskeva, & Kargidis, 2007). E-ARMA comprises four phases, as shown in Figure 2.

Specifically, in the first phase (the observation phase) a problem-solving steps model is observed. In our case we used Sternberg's (2003) model of six steps: problem identification, definition of problem, construction of a strategy, organisation of information, allocation of resources, monitoring and evaluating of problem solving. The second phase (the collaboration phase) includes two subphases: learners first work in groups of four and then collaborate in pairs. The third phase (the semi-guidance phase) refers to specific guidance given to learners on implementing the problem-solving model on their own. The last phase (the individual phase) concerns individual problem-solving activity when no support is provided to learners. Except for the first phase, these phases require learners' active engagement and action while they are exposed to multiple social models; thus multiple interactive relationships occur. During collaboration in the four subphases of the scripts, each step of Sternberg's model is taken by a different member of the group in turn. While learners work in pairs there are two active roles: observer and problem solver. The observer takes

Figure 2. Four phases of e-ARMA strategy development

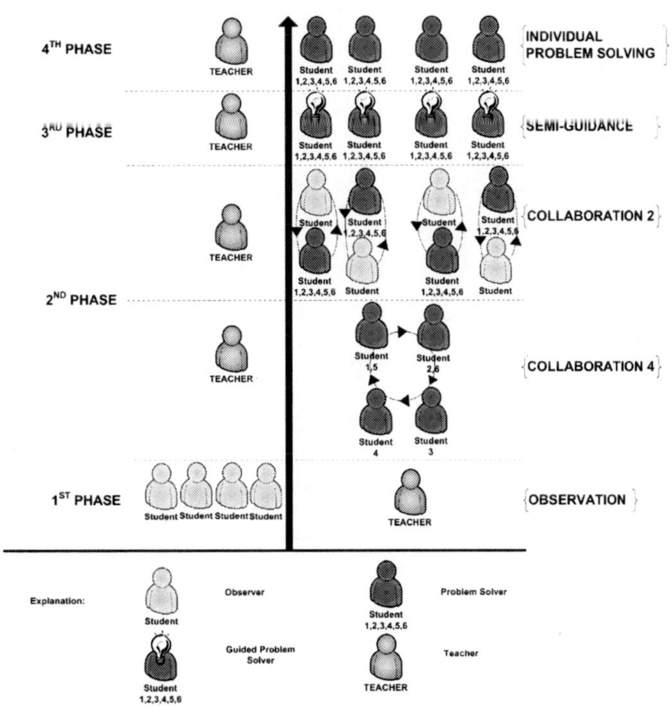

responsibility for facilitating the implementation of steps whenever the problem solver is in difficulty. The roles alternate between members.

The role of the teacher in such a complex CSCL script becomes demanding as he or she is required to monitor and assess the learning progress of each student during the four separate phases of the script.

Implementation of a script like the one described above is achieved through the use of shared-space synchronous collaborative tools like Synergo (Avouris et al., 2004), CoolModes, Belvedere, and others. Luckily, these tools, especially Synergo, offer the possibility of recording the tasks undertaken by students so the teacher can study and analyse them.

Based on these axes of the proposed assessment framework, interaction analysis indicators can be reused and adjusted to the requirements of the e-ARMA collaborative learning strategy. Table 1 lists the indicators per axis and specifies the related interaction analysis indicators. For the purposes of this case study we show how six specified indicators can be reused.

Quality of Collaboration includes the "division of labour" indicator, which concerns the assessment of each student's individual performance while he/she collaborates either with the other three members of his/her group (collaboration of four) or with a peer (collaboration in pairs). Division of labour can be calculated with the formula $Y + Z/3$ for the activity in collaboration of four (where Y represents the individual's performance and Z, the other members' performance). The formula is transformed to $Y + Z$ for the activity of collaboration in pairs. Performance of individual role playing is important since in most CSCL scripts the execution of various tasks per role is vital to the student's acquisition of knowledge and skills. Moreover, a teacher needs to know whether the rules of collaboration were implemented as predefined and whether divergent paths were recorded. For example, during the collaboration in pairs the role of solver requires the student to execute a number of problem-solving steps before he/she reaches a solution, while the role of observer requires intervening whenever a problem-solving path diverges from what is ex-

Table 1. Proposed indicators for learners' assessment in a CSCL environment

	Quality of Collaboration	**Quality of Learning Products**
1st Phase		
Observation	*Learners are not assessed*	
2nd Phase		
Collaboration of 4	- Division of labour - Number of communication actions -Nature of contributions	- Ratio of correct to number of steps done - Mastery level for each method - Amount of time spent per activity type
Collaboration in pairs	- Division of labour	- Ratio of correct to number of steps done - Mastery level for each method - Amount of time spent per activity type
3rd Phase		
Semi-guidance		- Ratio of correct to number of steps done - Mastery level for each method - Amount of time spent per activity type
4th Phase		
Individual activity		- Ratio of correct to number of steps done - Mastery level for each method - Amount of time spent per activity type

pected by raising an objection, asking for explanations, clarification, etc. All these interventions can be assessed according to a rubric of self-regulated strategies (Lazakidou et al., 2007). In addition, a teacher needs to know how many, in which direction ("Number of communication actions"), and what type of messages were exchanged during the collaboration phase ("Nature of contributions"). There is a simple way to calculate this indicator: if a student sends and receives messages he/she receives 3 points; if he/she only sends messages, 2 points; but if he/she only receives messages, 1 point. The messages are also annotated and analysed based on their content. Thus, the quality of messages is assessed according to a rubric for self-regulated strategies.

To assess the quality of learning products, the collaborative problem-solving process must be analysed. The teacher here tries to determine the correct actions (i.e., the correct problem-solving steps) performed by each student in the CSCL environment. The indicator called "Ratio of correct steps to the overall number of steps done" can be used. This indicator shows the relationship between the correct execution of Y number of steps and the overall number of steps done (Z). For example, if a student (solver) executes all problem-solving steps while collaborating in pairs, but only five correct, he/she receives 15 points (5*6/2). In collaboration with four, all problem solvers receive the same points. For example, if a group has completed four to six problem-solving steps correctly, each member receives 64 points (4*6/6). In addition, the final product is assessed ("Mastery level for each method") as well as the duration of each activity type ("Amount of time spent per activity type"). The grading of mastery level for each method scales while the script progresses. The issue of time spent per activity type is critical to a learning script that aims at fostering self-regulatory skills. As students are constantly called to solve more and more problems of approximately the same difficulty, the requirement for more rapid and accurate performance becomes greater and students are awarded more points. In this exemplar case, we have defined the maximum duration for the collaboration of four as 25 minutes (1 point), for collaboration in pairs, 20 minutes (2 points), for semi-guided activity, 15 minutes (3 points), and for individual activity, 10 minutes (5 points).

Proposed IA Techniques and Tools

To assess student performance based on the proposed reused indicators, the teacher needs to analyse students' messages, their specific problem-solving tasks, and the learning products they have recorded in the log files of a synchronous collaborative learning environment. To our knowledge, there is no single tool that can support this assessment task. A teacher usually uses several interaction analysis tools. The same applies for the exemplar case of the e-ARMA strategy (Figure 3).

More specifically, the quality of collaboration can be assessed with the ColAT: Collaborative Analysis Tool (Avouris et al., 2004). The quality of learning products cannot be automatically assessed. The teacher usually assesses student performance at each step of the CSCL process by analysing the video playback of the collaboration process (again with the aid of the ColAT tool). In addition, ColAT can show the exact duration of each problem-solving activity while the technique of observation can contribute to the assessment of the accuracy of the final problem solution. As shown in Figure 3, the role of the teacher is essential in multidimensional assessment of the CSCL process.

EVALUATION OF THE FRAMEWORK IN THE E-ARMA CSCL SCRIPT

To investigate the applicability of the proposed assessment framework, we applied it in two consecutive learning rounds aimed at the development of self-regulatory problem-solving skills using the

Figure 3. Proposed techniques and tools for purposes of IA

Individual Activity	Mastery level for each method Ratio of correct to number of steps done	Time spent per activity type	
Semi-Guid.	Mastery level for each method Ratio of correct to number	Time spent per activity type	
Coll. 2	Mastery level for each method Ratio of correct to number of steps done	Time spent per activity type Division of labor Nature of contributions	
Coll. 4	Mastery level for each method Ratio of correct to number of steps done	Time spent per activity type Division of labor Nature of contributions	Communication actions

Synergo synchronous CSCL tool. In this chapter, we show the analysis of the data gathered from the interactions of four 5th-grade students. They participated for two teaching hours (1 hour per learning round) after getting accustomed to the e-ARMA CSCL phases and the Synergo tool. Figure 4 shows the assessment of students' performance according to the aforementioned framework and the indicators per phase of the e-ARMA strategy (the students' assessment during the semi-guidance step was not included since it did not add much to overall understanding of the assessment process). According to the students' profiles, Z and K were poor solvers in mathematics, X was a solver at an intermediate level, and Y was a good problem solver. Except for Z, the students had great interest in science courses.

As shown in Figure 4, it is feasible to apply the proposed assessment to assess the final product as well as the grid of interactions in the CSCL environment. Thus, the teacher can acquire a clear picture of students' individual and group behavior.

It is obvious that during the second learning round students improved their performance, as expected. Moreover, it would be interesting to attempt to correlate knowledge level (problem-solving capacity) and learners' interest with their performance in each indicator. For example, students who are poor solvers (e.g., Z) can get more points in the axis of quality of collaboration than other learners if they perform well, allowing the teacher to motivate them to actively participate.

Thus, it is shown that assessment of learners per phase of collaborative strategy can be applied with satisfying results; yet, this method of assessment may enhance new correlations between total results and separate indicators. This can be very helpful for the teacher who struggles to evaluate learning processes and plan/design subsequent learning activities. It can also be very helpful for students to more easily understand how the teacher assesses their performance.

Although the proposed performance assessment framework is evidently applicable, as shown above, we tried to evaluate its quality based on the following criteria: (a) validity, (b) reliability, and (c) objectivity of an assessment task. These criteria were proposed by Johnson, Penny, and Gordon (2009) and Wiggins (1990) for measuring the quality of performance assessment framework. Validity of an assessment task refers to the accurate assessment of defined goals. Reliability refers to the consistency of the produced results, and objectivity refers to the limitation of graders'

Figure 4. Results of the group of four learners

			1st Learning Round				2nd Learning Round			
			X	Y	Z	K	X	Y	Z	K
1st Phase – Observation										
2nd Phase – Collaboration of 4										
Indicators (max.22)	Quality of Collaborat. (max 14)	Div.of lab. (max 2)	1.3	1.3	0.7	0.7	2	2	2	2
		Num. com. acts. (max 9)	6	6	0	4	1	8	3	3
		Mastery of skill (max 3)	2	3	0	1	0	1	1	0
	Subtotal		**9.3**	**10.3**	**0.7**	**5.7**	**3**	**11**	**6**	**5**
	Quality of Learning Products (max 8)	Correct/total actions (max 6)	5	5	5	5	6	6	6	6
		Mastery of method (max 1)	0	0	0	0	1	1	1	1
		Duration (max 1)	1	1	1	1	1	1	1	1
	Subtotal		**6**	**6**	**6**	**6**	**8**	**8**	**8**	**8**
2nd Phase – Collaboration of 2										
			1st Learning Round				2nd Learning Round			
			X	Y	Z	K	X	Y	Z	K
	Quality of Collaboration (max 6)	Division of labour (max 6)	5	5	3		6	5	3.5	5.5
	Subtotal		**5**	**5**	**3**	**5**	**6**	**5**	**3.5**	**5.5**
Indicators (max.22)	Quality of Learning Products (max 16)	Correct/Total steps (max 12)	8	6.7	5		10	12	6.7	6.7
		Mastery of Method (max 2)	1.5	2	0		0.7	2	0	1.5
		Duration (max 2)	2	2	2		2	2	2	2
	Subtotal		**11.5**	**10.7**	**7**	**10.2**	**12.7**	**16**	**8.7**	**10.2**
4th Phase – Individual Activity										
			1st Learning Round				2nd Learning Round			
			X	Y	Z	K	X	Y	Z	K
Indicators (max. 34)	Quality of Learning Products (max 34)	Correct/Total Steps (max 24)	10	20	20	16	24	24	16	20
		Subtotal	**10**	**20**	**20**	**16**	**24**	**24**	**16**	**20**
		Mastery of Method (max 5)	4	5	4	2,5	5	5	4	5
		Duration (max 5)	3	1	3	3	3	5	3	3
		Subtotal	**7**	**6**	**7**	**42.9**	**8**	**10**	**7**	**8**
Total (max 78)			**48.8**	**58**	**43.7**	**69.9**	**61.7**	**74**	**49.2**	**56.7**

over-subjectivity that can cause unfair results for students. Thus, we interviewed a teacher responsible for a learning script to get her opinion on the quality of the proposed performance assessment framework as well as her suggestions for it. All her answers were positive, and she emphasised that in the proposed framework her role has not been overlooked while securing a certain degree of objectivity. She mentioned that the framework helped her better identify the process from the product assessment tasks. She said that the framework is quite open and could contain other indicators if needed (e.g., hits or visits to the files uploaded for students to read). She also mentioned that this assessment task is not trivial and needs better support from tools that should be interoperable.

Of course, to determine the quality of the proposed performance assessment framework we need to test its reliability, validity, and objectivity in a larger sample, and this is a priority.

CONCLUSION AND FUTURE RESEARCH DIRECTIONS

The present chapter proposed assessment of computer-supported collaborative learning activities by proposing two basic axes of measured student performance and related interaction analysis indicators. It is evident that techniques and tools should be available that will allow teachers and evaluators to collect, analyse, and interpret the vast amount of data that can be gathered during a CSCL session in an efficient and effective way. This is consistent with Tennyson and Schott's (1997) proposal for involvement by future teachers in the process of formative evaluation. Our proposal concerns the specification of interaction analysis indicators that aim to facilitate teachers' work by equipping them with easy-to-apply tools and techniques for an in-depth analysis of student behaviour and performance in a CSCL environment. A teacher can select from a set of available indicators the ones that most closely fit the requirements of the applied collaborative learning strategy as well as the appropriate tools and techniques that will facilitate measurement of student performance. In this chapter, an example of the reuse of some indicators has been given. Although this exemplar case study reveals that a teacher can assess student performance more accurately, the assessment process is time consuming. Interaction analysis tools must be developed that will not only analyse the data gathered during the CSCL session but also report the findings in a teacher-friendly format, that is, in the form of rubrics and graphs. This is an open research problem that researchers should attempt to solve by designing interoperable tools such as DEGREE (Barros & Verdejo, 2000), COLEMON (Fesakis, Petrou, & Dimitracopoulou, 2004), ColAT (Avouris et al., 2004), iPET (Saltz et al., 2007), and AnalyticsTool (Petropoulou et al., 2008).

ACKNOWLEDGMENT

This work has been partially supported by the EU IST FP7 idSpace project: "Tooling of and training for collaborative, distributed product innovation" -2008-216199 as well as the eLAT project: "eLearning Analytics Tool: Analyzing Student Behavior in Online Learning Management Systems" partially funded by the Cyprus Research Promotion Foundation.

REFERENCES

Avouris, N., Dimitracopoulou, A., Komis, V., & Fidas, C. (2002). OCAF: An object-oriented model of analysis of collaborative problem solving. In Stahl, G. (Ed.), *CSCL 2002* (pp. 92–101). Hillsdale, NJ: Lawrence Erlbaum Associates, Inc.

Avouris, N., Komis, V., Margaritis, M., & Fiotakis, G. (2004). An environment for studying collaborative learning activities. *Journal of International Forum of Educational Technology and Society*, *7*(2), 34–41.

Barros, M., & Verdejo, M. (2000). Analysing learner interaction processes in order to improve collaboration. The DEGREE approach. *International Journal of Artificial Intelligence in Education*, *11*(3), 221–241.

Bratitsis, T., & Dimitrakopoulou, A. (2005). Data recording and usage interaction analysis in asynchronous discussions: The DIAS system. In *Proceedings of the 12th International Conference on Artificial Intelligence in Education AIED*, In C. Choquet, V. Luengo, A. Merceron (Eds.), *Proceedings of the Workshop on Usage Analysis in Learning Systems*, The Netherlands, Amsterdam.

Chan, C., & van Aalst, J. (2006). Learning, assessment and collaboration in computer-supported environments. In. P. Dillenbourg (Series Ed), J.W. Strijbos, P.A. Kirschner & R.L. Martens (Vol Eds). *Computer-supported collaborative learning: Vo 13. What we Know about CSCL and implementing it in higher education* (pp. 87-112). Boston: Kluwer Academic/Spinger Verlag.

Collazos, C.A., Guerrero, L.A., Pino, J.A., Renzi, S., & Klobas, J., Ortega, et al. (2007). Evaluating Collaborative Learning Processes using System-based Measurement. *Journal of Educational Technology & Society, 10*(3), 257–274.

Daradoumis, T., Martínez, A., & Xhafa, F. (2006). A layered framework for evaluating on-line collaborative learning interactions. *International Journal of Man-Machine Studies, 64*(7), 622–635.

De Laat, M., Lally, V., Lipponen, L., & Simons, P. R. J. (2005). *Patterns of interaction in a networked learning community: Squaring the circle.* Retrieved October, 2008, from http://eprints.soton.ac.uk/17267/

Dimitracopoulou, A. (2007). Computer based Interaction Analysis supporting self-regulation: Achievements and prospects of an emerging research field. In Kinshuk et al. (Eds.), *Proceedings of CELDA 2007. Cognition and Exploratory Learning in Digital Age. IADIS International Congress.*

Dimitracopoulou, A., Vosniadou, S., Gregoriadou, M., Avouris, N., & Kollias, V. Gogoulou, et al., (2006). The field of computer based interaction analysis for the support of participants regulation in social technology based learning environments: State of the art and perspectives. In D. Psillos, & V. Dagdidelis (Eds.), *Proceedings of the 5th Hellenic Congress with International Participation: Information and Communication Technologies in Education* (pp. 997-1000). Thessaloniki, Greece: HICTE.

Fesakis, G., Petrou, A., & Dimitracopoulou, A. (2004). Collaboration activity function: An interaction analysis instrument for computer supported collaborative learning activities. In *Proceedings of the 4th IEEE International Conference on Advanced Learning Technologies (ICALT 2004*).

Hernánez-Leo, D., Santos, P., Villasclaras-Fernández, E. D., Navarrete, T., Asensio-Pérez, J. I., Blat, J., & Dimitriadis, Y. (2008). Educational Patterns as a Guide to Create Units of Learning and Assessment. In *Proceedings of the 2008 Eighth IEEE international Conference on Advanced Learning Technologies* (pp.1055-1056). Santaber, Cantabria, Spain. Washington, DC: IEEE Computer & Society.

Ho, C. H., & Swan, K. (2007). Evaluating online conversation in an asynchronous learning environment: An application of Grice's cooperative principle. *The Internet and Higher Education, 10*(1), 3–14. doi:10.1016/j.iheduc.2006.11.002

Johnson, R. L., Penny, J. A., & Gordon, B. (2009). *Assessing Performance: Designing, Scoring, and Validating Performance Tasks*. New York: The Guilford Press.

Kodri, F. (2003). Performance assessment in the classrooms. *Ingenious, 1*(1), 21–30.

Law, N. (2005). Assessing learning outcomes in CSCL settings. In *Proceedings of the 2005 conference on Computer supported collaborative learning: the next 10 years!* (pp. 373-377). The International Society of the Learning Sciences (ISLS).

Lazakidou, G., Retalis, S., Paraskeva, F., & Kargidis, T. (2007, September 21st-22nd). Computer-supported collaborative scenarios for evolving self-regulatory skills in math education. In [Nicosia, Cyprus.]. *Proceedings of the International Council of Educational Media Annual Conference, 2007*, 111–123.

Marcos, A., Martinez, A., & Dimitriadis, Y. (2005). Towards adaptable interaction analysis in CSCL. In *Proceedings of the 12th International Conference on Artificial Intelligence. Workshop on Representing and Analyzing Collaborative Interactions, AIED 2005*, Amsterdam: IOS Press. Retrieved January 15, 2010, from http://gsic.tel.uva.es/uploaded_files/31306_AIED_workshop6_short_paper_jamarcos.doc

Martínez, A., Dimitriadis, Y., & De La Fuente, P. (2003). Contributions to analysis of interactions for formative evaluation in CSCL. In M. Llamas, M.J. Fernandez, & L.E. Anido (Eds), *Computers and education: Towards of lifelong learning society* (pp. 227-238). Amserdam: Kluwer Academic.

Moore, G. (1989). Three types of interaction. *American Journal of Distance Education, 3*(2), 1–6. doi:10.1080/08923648909526659

Persico, D., Pozzi, F., & Sarti, L. (2009), A model for monitoring and evaluating CSCL. In (Eds.) Juan, A.A., Daradoumis, T., Xhafa, F., Caballe, S., Faulin, J., *Monitoring and Assessment in Online Collaborative Environments: Emergent Computational Technologies for E-learning Support*. Hershey, PA: IGI Global.

Petropoulou, O., Lazakidou, G., Retalis, S., & Vrasidas, C. (2007). Analysing interaction behaviour in network supported collaborative learning environments: A holistic approach. *International Journal of Knowledge and Learning, 3*(4&5), 450–464. doi:10.1504/IJKL.2007.016705

Petropoulou, O., Retalis, S., Siassiakos, K., Karamouzis, S., & Kargidis, T. (2008). Helping educators analyse interactions within networked learning communities: A framework and the AnalyticsTool system. In *Proceedings of the 6th International Conference on Networked Learning* Halkidiki, Greece.

Poole, D. M. (2000). Student participation in a discussion-oriented online course: A case study. *Journal of Research on Computing in Education, 33*(2), 162–177.

Pozzi, F., Manca, S., Persico, D., & Sarti, L. (2007). A general framework for tracking and analysing learning processes in computer-supported collaborative learning environments. *Innovations in Education and Teaching International, 44*(2), 169–179. doi:10.1080/14703290701240929

Puntambekar, S. (2006). Analysing collaborative interactions: divergence, shared understanding and construction of knowledge. *Computers & Education, 47*(3), 332–351. doi:10.1016/j.compedu.2004.10.012

Reffay, C., & Chanier, T. (2003). How social network analysis can help to measure cohesion in collaborative distance-learning. In. B. Wason, S. Ludvigson, & U. Hoppe (Eds), *Proceedings of the international conference on computer support for collaborative learning: Designing for change in networked learning.* (pp. 343-352). Dordrecht: Kluwer Academic Publishers.

Retalis, S., Papasalouros, A., Psaromiligkos, Y., Siskos, S., & Kargidis, T. (2006). Towards networked learning analytics – a concept and a tool. *The 5th International Conference on Networked Learning.* Retrieved April 9, 2010, from http://www.networkedlearningconference.org.uk/past/nlc2006/abstracts/pdfs/P41%20Retalis.pdf

Saltz, J. S., Hiltz, S. R., & Turoff, M. (2004). Student social graphs: Visualizing a student's online social network. *The 2004 ACM conference on Computer supported cooperative work* (pp. 596-599). New York: Association for Computng Machinery (ACM).

Saltz, J. S., Hiltz, S. R., Turoff, M., & Passerini, K. (2007). Increasing participation in distance learning courses. *IEEE Internet Computing, 11*(3), 36–44. doi:10.1109/MIC.2007.64

Soller, A., Jermann, P., Muehlenbrock, M., & Martinez, A. (2004). Designing computational models of collaborative learning interaction: Introduction to the workshop proceedings. In *Proceedings of the 2nd International Workshop on Designing Computational Models of Collaborative Learning Interaction, ITS 2004. Lecture Notes in Computer Science vol.3220* (pp.5-12). Berlin, Heidelberg: Springer-Verlag

Spada, H., Meier, A., Rummel, N., & Hauser, S. (2005). A new method to assess the quality of collaborative process in CSCL. [Taiwan.]. *The CSCL, 2005*, 622–631.

Sternberg, R. J. (2003). *Cognitive Psychology* (3rd ed.). Belmont, CA: Thomson Wadsworth.

Swan, K., Shen, J., & Hiltz, S. R. (2006). Assessment and collaboration in online learning. *Journal of Asynchronous Learning Networks, 10*(1), 45–62.

Tennyson, R. D., & Schott, F. (1997). Instructional design theory, research, and models. In Tennyson, R. D., Schott, F., Seel, N. M., & Dijkstra, S. (Eds.), *Instructional design: International perspective* (pp. 1–18). Mahwah, NJ: Lawrence Erlbaum Associates.

Voyiatzaki, E., Margaritis, M., & Avouris, N. (2006). Collaborative interaction analysis. The teachers' perspective. In Kinshuk et al. (Eds) *The Sixth IEEE International Conference on Advanced Learning Technologies (ICALT'06)*, (345-349). Los Alamitos, CA: IEEE Computer Society

Wasserman, S., & Faust, K. (1997). *Social network analysis: Methods and applications*. Cambridge, MA: Cambridge University Press.

Wiggins, G. (1990). The case for authentic assessment. *Practical Assessment, Research & Evaluation, 2*(2). Retrieved January 2, 2010, from http://PAREonline.net/getvn.asp?v=2&n=2

Zinn, C., & Scheuer, O. (2006). Getting to know your learner in distance learning contexts. Innovative Approaches Innovative Approaches for Learning an d Knowledge Sharing, *1st European Conference on Technology Enhanced Learning (EC-TEL 2006), Lecture Notes in Computer Science vol.4227* (437-451). Berlin, Heidelberg: Springer-Verlag.

ADDITIONAL READING

Lazakidou, G., Paraskeva, F., & Retalis, S. (2007). The transitory phase to the attainment of self-regulatory skill in mathematical problem-solving. *International Education Journal, 8*(1), 71–81.

Petropoulou, O., Lazakidou, G., Retalis, S., & Vrasidas, C. (2008). Evaluating the learning effectiveness of collaborative problem solving in computer-mediated settings. In Lytras, M., Tennyson, R., & dePablos, P. O. (Eds.), *Knowledge Networks: the Social Software Perspective*. Hershey, PA: IGI Global.

Petropoulou, O., Vasilikopoulou, M., & Retalis, S. (2009). Enriched Assessment Rubrics: A new medium for enabling teachers easily assess students' performance when participating to complex interactive learning scenarios. *Operational Research: An International Journal.* Berlin, Heidelberg: Springer Verlag. Retrieved April 9, 2010, from http://www.springerlink.com/content/22t43hh637q26617/fulltext.pdf

KEY TERMS AND DEFINITIONS

Assessment: A method for analyzing and describing student learning outcomes or program achievement of objectives.

Educational Assessment: Educational assessment is the process of measure learners' progress and achievement of learning outcomes (knowledge, skills, attitudes and beliefs) and reporting, usually in measurable terms, those outcomes to students, parents, and administrators.

Evaluation: A value judgment about the results of assessment data. For example, evaluation of student learning requires that educators compare student performance to a standard to determine how the student measures up. Depending on the result, decisions are made regarding whether and how to improve student performance.

Interaction Analysis Indicators: Interaction analysis indicators measure learners' collaborativity and the spectrum of their interactions in collaborative learning settings.

Learning Strategy: A Learning strategy is a stepwise approach for achieving learning objectives and determine pre-instructional activities, information presentation, learners' roles and activities, testing, and follow-through.

Performance Assessment: A method for assessing how well students use their knowledge and skills in order to do something.

Rubric: A rubric is an authentic assessment tool, i.e. a qualitative scoring guide that seeks to evaluate a student's performance at learning tasks based on the sum of a full range of criteria rather than a single numerical score.

Chapter 15
Implementing Computer-Interpretable CSCL Scripts with Embedded Assessment:
A Pattern Based Design Approach

Eloy David Villasclaras-Fernández
University of Valladolid, Spain

Juan Ignacio Asensio-Pérez
University of Valladolid, Spain

Davinia Hernández-Leo
University Pompeu Fabra, Spain

Yannis Dimitriadis
University of Valladolid, Spain

Luis de la Fuente-Valentín
Carlos III University of Madrid, Spain

Alejandra Martínez Monés
University of Valladolid, Spain

ABSTRACT

This chapter presents a proposal for a pattern-based approach for Computer Supported Collaborative Learning (CSCL) scripts that aims to integrate learning and assessment activities. After a general presentation of the approach, the chapter will focus on a case study which covers the whole life-cycle of a CSCL script with embedded assessment activities. The case, which took place in the context of a computer-mediated learning environment, includes the design, instantiation, enactment and evaluation of the script. Focusing on the relevance of the assessment activities which are integrated in the script, the case study illustrates the complexity of formalizing computer-interpretable CSCL scripts with embedded assessment. The usage of design patterns is proposed as a means of providing support and hiding the

DOI: 10.4018/978-1-61692-898-8.ch015

complexity of creating and enacting such scripts. The case study shows the feasibility of this approach, and provides information about the requirements of CSCL script authoring tools to employ assessment and learning design patterns to support non-expert designers in those tasks.

INTRODUCTION

Scripting in Computer Supported Collaborative Learning (CSCL) has been researched for several years as a way of improving the chances of achieving learning. In spite of the potential benefits of collaboration in learning scenarios, relying on the students to organize their own collaboration processes may result in low quality collaboration. In order to tackle the risks of free collaboration, macro-scripts have been proposed (Dillenbourg, 2002). This type of script describes the pedagogical method used to organize a session of collaborative learning (Dillenbourg & Tchounikine, 2007). A macro-script guides participants (students and teachers) along a learning session by defining the sequence of activities that need to be completed, the roles that the participants may assume, and the tasks assigned to each role. In addition, the script may be completed by external resources, which can be used by the participants to carry out the activities, as well as the description of the learning outcomes expected from the script (Kollar, Fischer, & Hesse, 2006). CSCL scripts may also describe how to form groups, and the distribution of resources among the participants (Kobbe, 2006).

In the CSCL field, technology can play different roles (Suthers, 2005). In this chapter we will look into computer support in the form of guidance for participants in a learning scenario according to CSCL scripts. Learning Management Systems (LMSs) have been used to manage automatically the enactment of the activities planned in the script. In other words, scripts, adequately represented, can be processed by LMSs in order to guide students and teachers along the sequence of activities, providing adequate instructions of the tasks to be done, providing the allocated resources (e.g., documents or collaboration software tools), or handling groups automatically (Bote-Lorenzo, Gómez-Sánchez, Vega-Gorgojo, Dimitriadis, Asensio-Pérez, & Jorrín-Abellán, 2008; Cid, Fuente-Valentín, Gutiérrez, Pardo, & Kloos, 2007). For this purpose, computer-interpretable Educational Modeling Languages (EMLs) have been proposed, such as PoEML (Caeiro, 2008), IMS-LD (IMS, 2003), etc. These EMLs allow the definition of the components that compose a script, such as activities, activity sequencing, definition of roles/groups, resources, etc. With these components, a script formalized in a EML can be interpreted by a software system to guide the participants along the script: indicating the groups that each participants belongs to, the activities they have to carry out, and the resources available for that purpose.

The task of designing collaboration scripts offers the chance of thinking carefully what learning activities are most suitable in order to achieve the expected learning objectives before actually going to the classroom. With a similar rationale, defining the assessment plan to be applied along the learning activities can pursue the same objective: assessment can be used not only to grade students, but to create adequate conditions to promote the learning objectives (Dochy & McDowell, 1997; Shepard, 2000). Actually, the role of assessment in enhancing learning has been thoroughly discussed; assessment can be used to improve collaborative learning, for instance by delivering feedback to students, who can then adapt their work or interaction processes to the feedback (Black & Wiliam, 1998). On the other hand, it has been argued that the teacher should employ assessment results continuously in order to introduce corrections in the learning process as necessary (Stiggins, 2002). Giving feedback, monitoring the students, or understanding what changes need to be introduced in the script (to correct problems detected through the assessment process) are some potential usages of the assessment results. Therefore, the assessment plan can be part of the pedagogical method, taking place not only at the end but throughout the learning process. Additionally, assessment not only needs to be considered for its potential benefits, but also for its effect on students and the learning processes. For instance, assessment serves as a guide to students about the most important elements of a course; this will affect the effort they put into different activities or tasks, as students tend to dedicate more attention to those with a greater weight in their grades (Macdonald, 2003). In addition, assessment needs to be defined taking into account that students will adapt their efforts and strategies to it (Chan & van Aalst, 2004). This is especially important in collaborative learning: first, assessment can be used to make students value the collaborative learning parts of a course (in other words, inadequate assessments may fail to make students value collaborative work) (Boud, Cohen, & Sampson, 1999). In addition, collaborative work may require different assessment techniques, perhaps different from 'traditional' assessments such as tests and questionnaires. In order to assess appropriately collaborative work and the potential learning benefits expected from it, it has been argued that new assessment techniques are necessary (Shepard, 2000).

The importance of designing effective collaboration scripts motivates the efforts carried out within the CSCL research community to support designers in this task, for instance the CoSSICLE project (CoSSICLE, 2005) or the work of Hernández-Leo et al. (2006). This is especially relevant in the case of non-expert designers, such as teachers without wide knowledge about collaborative learning or technical specifications. The usage of these EMLs to model scripts has been regarded as demanding a high level of expertise (Griffiths, Blat, Garcia, Vogten, & Kwong, 2005). Supporting this type of designers in the conception and design of assessment plans for collaborative learning scripts, taking into account the aforementioned interrelationship between assessment and learning, is the main goal of the work presented here. For this purpose, the usage of design patterns is investigated.

From their conception as a tool for designers in the field of architecture, design patterns have been applied to different domains. The practice of teaching and learning has also been the focus of pattern developers in their search for general solutions to common problems that arise over and over. Also in the field of Technology Enhanced Learning (TEL), design patterns have been proposed to tackle a wide range of problems (E-LEN, 2004; Goodyear et al., 2004; PPP, 2005; TELL, 2005). In this chapter we are interested in the application of pedagogical patterns for CSCL, which describe good practices in setting collaborative learning situations. Pedagogical patterns again cover a wide range of problems, such as motivating students, or choosing the right materials for a learning session (PPP, 2005). This chapter continues the research conducted by Hernández-Leo (2007) in the application of pedagogical patterns to support designers. While originally Collaborative Learning Flow Patterns (CLFPs) had been proposed, the application of these patterns in combination with assessment design patterns is the focus of the work presented here.

Several works have focused on the proposal of patterns for the design of assessment, such as (Delozanne, Le Calvez, Merceron, & Labat, 2007) and (Mislevy et al., 2003). These works illustrate that the design of assessment can also be tackled by the application of design patterns. This chapter is interested in the technology requirements around the whole life-cycle of CSCL scripts with embedded assessment. Specifically, this paper focuses on scripts formalized with IMS-LD. Formal models have been proposed for assessment as well, such as (Almond, Steinberg, & Mislevy, 2002; Joosten-ten Brinke et al., 2007; Miao, Tattersall, Schoonenboom, Stevanov, & Aleksieva-Petrova, 2007); with the objective of establishing a standard specification for the description of assessments (which could be shared among institutions and practitioners), IMS Question and Test Interoperability (IMS-QTI) (IMS, 2006) was proposed. While this specification has the advantage that can be integrated easily with IMS-LD scripts, its ability to describe different assessment techniques has been questioned. IMS-QTI is capable of modeling tests, which can be composed by a wide range of item types; however, other assessment techniques, such as 360° feedback, peer assessment, self assessment, on-the-job assessment, or portfolio assessment, cannot be modeled with that specification (Griffiths et al., 2005).

These issues (the challenge of designing scripts, the relevance of assessment, the complexity of EMLs, and the need for new assessment techniques) motivate the application of design patterns for assessment to support non-expert designers, with a focus on the generation of computer-interpretable CSCL scripts with embedded assessment. Assessment design patterns are intended to help designers in the management of complex assessment techniques. Additionally, integrating assessment patterns in authoring software tools is expected to facilitate the development of the whole life-cycle of CSCL scripts formalized with IMS-LD. This approach is explained in detail in the following section, and is further illustrated in this chapter through a case study, developed around an authentic learning scenario. After this, the next section describes the case study, the design and enactment of a CSCL script with embedded assessment, as well as the results from the study. Finally, the conclusions are discussed.

DESIGN OF CSCL SCRIPTS WITH EMBEDDED ASSESSMENT

As indicated before, the usage of design patterns to facilitate the design of collaborative learning activities is an approach that has been developed by several works in the literature. Among these, we will highlight the development of Collaborative Learning Flow Patterns (CLFPs) to propose different structures of collaborative learning activities that have been validated in the practice. Examples of CLFPs are the JIGSAW (explained in more detail in the following section), PYRAMID, or THINK PAIR SHARE (see Hernández-Leo, 2007).

Each CLFP presents a collaborative technique with different potential learning benefits. The PYRAMID, for instance, is characterized by students forming groups that become bigger as the session progresses. In this way, students are encouraged first to discuss a problem in a small group, but later different groups merge forcing the students to compare potentially different answers and to agree on a common solution to the given problem. THINK PAIR SHARE, on the other hand, is intended to make all the students participate (thus preventing students from hiding). In a THINK PAIR SHARE, students have first to ponder individually a question given by the teacher. Before the teacher asks the students their answers, however, they are allowed a few minutes to discuss with a partner (the PAIR part of the activity). In this way, students are more willing to share their answers, since they had time to compare and discuss, and the 'shame' of a wrong answer is shared with another student.

Such patterns have been integrated in an authoring tool, *Collage* (Hernández-Leo et al., 2006) (see Figure 1), which enables the designers to browse, select and particularize one or several design patterns to create a script for a specific scenario. *Collage* is aimed at non-expert designers. On the one hand, the usage of CLFPs gives information to designers, potentially without experience on collaborative learning, about a series of learning techniques: the learning benefits they

Figure 1. User interface of Collage. In the figure, a script composed by a JIGSAW *(in the left) and a* PEER REVIEW *(in the right).*

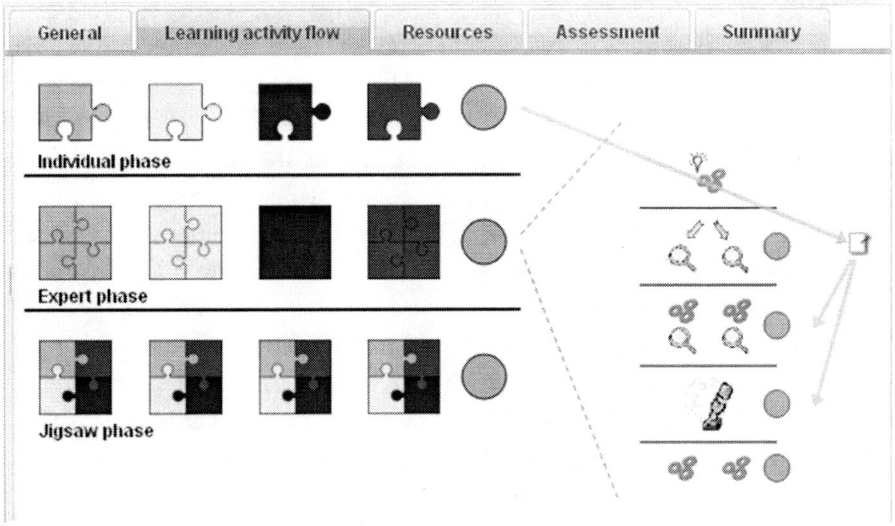

are expected to promote, their complexity, and the type of learning activity that they are intended for. With this information, non-expert designers can choose and adapt these techniques to their own practice, rather than creating new collaborative learning activities from scratch.

On the other hand, since the patterns are integrated in *Collage*, this software authoring tool can handle automatically the formalization of scripts with IMS-LD. In this way, CLFPs facilitate the task of creating computer-interpretable scripts. CLFPs help closing the gap between designing the pedagogical method of a script and formalizing it with an EML. Furthermore, CLFPs have been used for further tasks related to the life-cycle of CSCL scripts. As shown in Figure 2, this life-cycle would include the design phase, in which the script is produced; the instantiation phase, in which an instance of the script is set up to be enacted in a specific learning scenario; the enactment phase, in which the participants carry out the activities as prescribed by the script; finally, the adequacy of the script to the expected learning objectives could be analyzed in the evaluation phase, in order to re-design the script accordingly (Villasclaras-Fernández, Hernández-Gon-

Figure 2. Life-cycle of a CSCL script

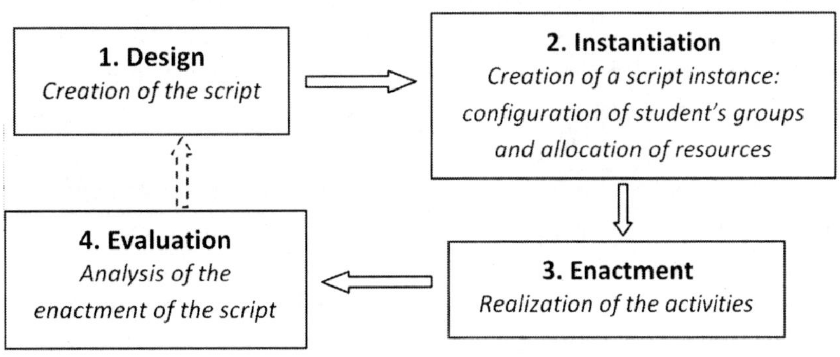

zalo, Hernández-Leo, Asensio-Pérez, & Dimitriadis, 2009). The requirements and challenges of the instantiation and enactment phases depend on the characteristics of the design. With respect to this, CLFPs have also been used in a complementary software tool, *InstanceCollage* (Villasclaras-Fernández, Hernández-Gonzalo et al., 2009). *InstanceCollage* uses a similar graphical interface to facilitate the task of creating and populate the needed number of groups for a specific scenario (with a concrete number of students). Both in *Collage* and *InstanceCollage*, the complexity of the IMS-LD specification is hidden from the designers, and the structure of the collaboration scripts are represented in a graphical way (see Figure 1). The usage of CLFPs in both tools illustrates that pedagogical design patterns can play a role in several phases of the life-cycle of CSCL scripts.

Among the aspects of collaborative learning design that *Collage* does not provide explicit support for, we can point out the configuration of assessment activities embedded in the script. As discussed in the previous section, assessment can be seen as an integral part of a learning session. Therefore, a collaboration script can describe assessment activities that are expected to complement the learning activities, for instance by promoting the expected learning benefits, or simply to indicate the users of the script (in the case the script is shared among teachers) how to evaluate the learning activities described in the script. However, there is another reason to include an assessment plan in the script: embedding assessment activities in a CSCL script would enable the automatic delivery or support for this type of activities, potentially using the same technological infrastructure (e.g., an LMS). Thus, technological issues are also related to the description of assessment activities as well.

The rest of this section describes the approach taken in the case study presented below to tackle the design, by non-expert designers, of CSCL scripts that contain assessment activities. In this approach, there are two elements that are offered to designers to describe assessment: design patterns for assessment techniques, such as PEER REVIEW, ROLE DETECTION (Villasclaras-Fernández, Hernández-Leo, Asensio-Pérez, & Dimitriadis, 2009), INDIVIDUAL TEST, etc.; and a conceptual model of the features that define how the assessment plan is integrated within the learning activities that compose the script (assessment integration model) (Villasclaras-Fernández, Hernández-Leo, Asensio-Pérez, Dimitriadis, & Martínez-Monés, 2009).

The assessment design patterns proposed in this approach cover several aspects of the configuration of assessment. These include patterns of different type assessment tasks, such as TEST, ROLE DETECTION or REPORT REVIEW; the organization of roles related to assessment (for instance, RANDOM MEMBER ASSESSMENT or SELF ASSESSMENT refer to the assignation of assessment-specific roles to students); the sequencing of activities involved in or related to the assessment process; the organization of the exchange of documents (for instance, Peer review describes the document flow between 'authors' and 'reviewers'); and, finally, the purpose of the assessment (PEER REVIEW is intended to provide feedback to the students, while SHARED GRADES proposes a specific way of using assessment results to grade students in groups).

Designers can thus browse the patterns in order to examine well-known assessment techniques. However, since the objective is to design assessment within CSCL scripts, the approach presented here is based on the combination of assessment design patterns and CLFPs. Each type of pattern tackles the design of a specific aspect of a design: the configuration of the assessment plan and the structure of the learning activities, respectively. In order to define the role of assessment within the script, the assessment integration model proposes the following features:

- The most basic information that needs to be configured is the 'location' of the assessment activities (in which an assessor performed the assessment of student's work, performance, collaboration, etc.). This location is defined by integrating the assessment activity within the activity sequence of the script. In addition, by assigning the assessment activity to a concrete role of the script, the assessor is defined, whether it is the teacher or the students.

- Besides the location, it is necessary to specify the assessed activity, which represents the students' work that is to be assessed.
- Finally, the description of the assessment is completed by specifying how the assessment results are used along the script. More specifically, three different assessment purposes have been codified in *Collage*: to grade students (summative assessment), to provide feedback to students (indicating also in which activity the students will have access to the feedback), and to support instructional decisions (in other words, to introduce changes in the script in case the assessment results indicate it is necessary).

The goal of *Collage* is twofold. On the one hand to provide support to designers through an intuitive and user-friendly interface. Considering that the configuration of CSCL scripts is a complex task, the graphical representation must enable the user to understand clearly the structure of the script, the assessment plan, and the relationship between this and the learning activities. On the other hand, the authoring tool should manage automatically the production of a computer-interpretable representation of the CSCL script. *Collage* is intended to use the information about the integration between assessment and learning activities to automatically configure the script according to the learning activities and the assessment plan created by the designer.

Next section will illustrate how the patterns and the assessment integration model support the whole life-cycle of a CSCL script with embedded assessment.

CASE STUDY

The approach presented in the previous section has been put to practice in a case study developed at the University of Valladolid. The context of the case was a doctorate course on Distributed Processing Architectures. Five students attended the course, which was organized as a series of face-to-face sessions as well as distance work between sessions. The case study covered only three of these sessions, spanning a period six weeks.

This course is interesting with respect to the approach presented here since a collaborative learning strategy was employed to organize students' work. The teachers also regularly used technology support during the lessons: a *Wiki* system was employed to host the schedule of the course, resources posted by the teachers; the students could edit the *Wiki* pages to present their contributions to the planned learning activities. The case study presented here covers only those sessions and distance work corresponding to the application of a CSCL script. The script, formalized into IMS-LD, was enacted through the.*LRN* LMS, which includes an IMS-LD player (Cid et al., 2007).

The script was developed following the approach presented in the previous section. The case study covered the design, the instantiation of the script (in the IMS-LS player included in.*LRN*) and the enactment; in this experience, the evaluation phase was carried out only with research purposes, as reported in this chapter: the script was only used in one cycle, and was not re-designed. The teachers of the course had previous experience in collaborative learning, but nevertheless they applied design patterns (CLFPs and assessment design patterns) in the creation of the script; besides this, their knowledge of IMS-LD and the specific features of the chosen

IMS-LD player were limited. Therefore, this case study is interesting with respect to the central topic of this chapter since it represents an example of the application of pedagogical design patterns to one iteration of the whole life-cycle (although the evaluation phase was not used to improve the script) of a collaboration script: design patterns were applied in the design phase, during which the script was produced, but the case study allows us to analyze how the patters served to implement an IMS-LD script that can actually be enacted in an authentic learning scenario.

The rest of this section presents the research objectives of the case study, the characteristics of the proposed script, the technological issues around its life-cycle, and finally the results of the case study.

Research Objectives

The main objective of this case study is to analyze the integration of assessment activities within CSCL scripts, considering the motivation for doing so discussed in the previous sections. This case study adopts two restrictions or challenges that increase the complexity of achieving this integration.

The first of these challenges arises from the fact that the script is intended to be enacted through an LMS; current EMLs lack specific vocabulary to describe assessment activities. While there are proposals to tackle this issue, they are in an early stage of development and could not be used to enact the script. In spite of this, one goal of this case study was to illustrate the possibility of enacting a complex IMS-LD collaboration script. This script contains not only learning activities, whose enactment has been previously studied (Hernández-Leo et al., 2007), but also an assessment plan that introduced several technical requirements, as described later. Therefore, the first issue is the possibility of enacting scripts that contain complex assessment plans embedded in CSCL scripts, with current technology.

The second challenge is the fact that the teachers are not expert designers. This issue is related to understanding how the formalization of CSCL scripts with embedded assessment can be automated in software tools, for instance *Collage*. Therefore, the second issue of this case study was whether the integration assessment model captures relevant information about assessment activities. In this way the case study is intended to present a real scenario for which the assessment integration model (i.e., the information that links the assessment plan and the learning activities) captures relevant information.

These issues are seen under the point of view of the pattern-based approach, since the usage of patterns determines to a great extent the design process followed to create the script, the formalization into EMLs such as IMS-LD, and the features of the produced scripts. Therefore, this case study serves to illustrate how the application of a combination of assessment and learning patterns can help non-expert designers in the creation and application of a CSCL script with embedded assessment.

Design of the Script

The collaboration learning activities and assessment were planned following the proposal described in the previous section. Therefore, pedagogical design patterns were chosen and combined by the designers in order to create the pedagogical method of the script. The designers in this case were the two teachers involved in the course.

The context of the course determined the suitability of different design patterns, both for collaborative learning activities and assessment activities. The fact that the course involved studying two different topics (grid services and peer-to-peer distributed systems) indicated that the JIGSAW CLFP would be a potentially effective collaborative learning technique to encourage interaction between students. Since the number of students was low, organizing students in two different groups (matching the number of topics) was straightforward, facilitating the configuration of the JIGSAW. The time schedule of the course was also relevant. Since there were long spans of time between face-to-face sessions, it was possible to organize activities, both for teachers and students between these sessions, complementing the work carried out in the classroom.

A JIGSAW (Aronson, Blaney, Stephan, Sikes, & Snapp, 1978) can be used to organize students solve a problem that can be divided into several subproblems; in this case, understanding each architecture for distributed systems accounted for one subproblem. According to the JIGSAW, students would start working individually (first phase, or *Individual Phase*), on either one of the two topics, thus becoming an expert. The individual phase was conceived as distance work. Later, during a face-to-face session the "experts" would join in *Expert Groups* (second phase, or *Expert Phase*), during which they continue working on their assigned topics. In the next face-to-face session (three weeks later), *Jigsaw Groups* would be formed, with an "expert" from each topic. Their task in this third phase (*Jigsaw Phase*) requires the different expertise developed in previous phases. Therefore, the JIGSAW was used to organize the structure of the whole experience, defining the grouping of students (including the change from *Expert Groups* to *Jigsaw Groups*) and the types of activities and goals of each session. However, more detailed instructions are necessary to guide the participants along the activities; these include activity descriptions in natural texts as well as the selection of resources to be provided to students in each activity. Additionally, while during the individual phase the students are simply asked to read some material and complete a concept map, the *Expert* and *Jigsaw Phases* were more complex; these two phases followed the following structure:

Each collaborative learning phase begins with a face-to-face activity, in which the students work in groups in the classroom. Their task involves reviewing their previous work and completing a document: a report and a conceptual map.

After the face-to-face session, the teachers review and assess the documents created by the students. The teachers can write a review of the document (intended to be delivered to the authors); additionally, the teachers have the chance of assigning complementary activities to the students (independently for each group) if necessary.

If complementary activities have been set, the students must complete them before the following phase.

This structure, also depicted in Figure 3, is based on the application of a simple assessment design pattern: REPORT REVIEW. This pattern simply proposes an activity for the teachers in which then must review a document created by the students.

The combination of the JIGSAW and the REPORT REVIEW pattern determines to some extent the pedagogical method of the script. The method is completed by the concrete instructions given in each activity (both for teachers and students). Additionally, the pedagogical method is completed by the definition of the relationships (as proposed by the assessment integration model) between the assessment pattern applied in this case and the rest of activities involved in the case:

- Identifying the assessed activities. The teachers must assess the learning activity in which they write a report and create a concept map. Therefore, these documents will be accessible to the teachers for review. Additionally, the assessment will be independent for each group (there are two *Expert Groups* in the *Expert Phase* and two *Jigsaw Groups* in the *Jigsaw Phase*).
- Identifying the students' activities in which the feedback written by the teachers will be handed out to the corresponding students. The first purpose for carrying out the assessment is to provide students with feedback: reviews of the students' documents. This means that the review will be

Figure 3. Structure of the script

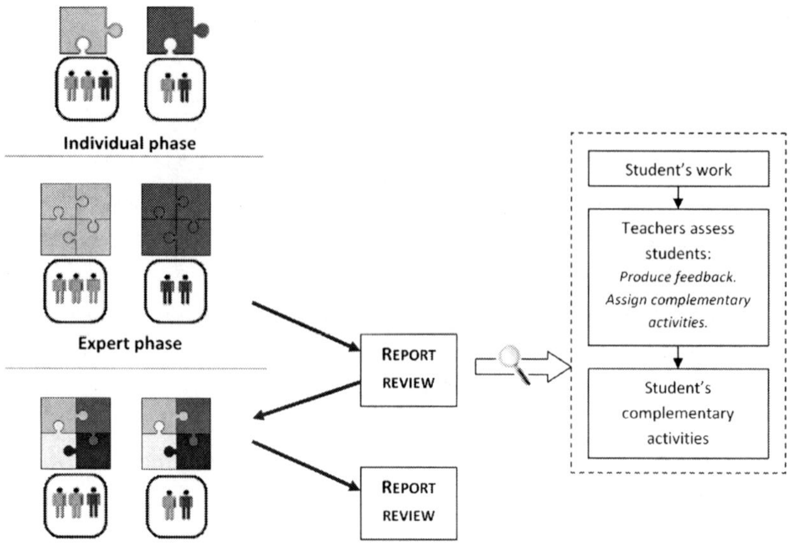

delivered to the students in a later activity, which is also defined in the script.

- Identifying the activities in which the teacher uses the assessment results to introduce changes in the script. The second purpose of the assessment is to monitor the learning process and introduce changes in the script if necessary. In this case, the teachers decided that they would like to have complementary activities (initially empty and hidden) for the students, so that if necessary they are able to activate them and configure them (including instructions and resources for the students).

This information (selection of patterns; adding activity descriptions and resources; and configuring the aforementioned relationships between assessment and learning activities) enable the teacher to configure in a relatively simple manner the pedagogical method of the script. In this case study, the composition of the pedagogical method was carried out in a meeting, in which these elements were decided and put to paper. After this step was completed, the teachers did not have to intervene in the rest of the design process, which involved producing an IMS-LD script that could be enacted in the.*LRN* player as described in the following section.

While several case studies have analyzed the design and enactment of CSCL scripts created from design patterns (CLFPs), this case is interesting since assessment activities were described explicitly, with the objective of having assessment-specific support from the LMS during the enactment of the script. Assessment in this case study is integrated in such a way as to reinforce the pedagogical method of the JIGSAW. Especially in the change between the *Expert* and *Jigsaw Phase*, the previously described assessment structure was intended to increase the chances that the objectives of the *Expert Phase* are met: all students should have the required knowledge in order to move onto the *Jigsaw Phase*, in which their partners will have to rely on each other's expertise.

Implementation, Instantiation of the Script

After the pedagogical design has been defined, the second step involved the creation of a computer-interpretable representation of the script, formalized with IMS-LD. The formalization of the script was done without intervention of the teachers involved in the case study. In spite of this, it is expected that the definition of the pedagogical method, as described before, would be sufficient for a software authoring tool to complete this task automatically.

The creation of the sequence of learning activities, definition of groups, and assignation of activities to different roles was entirely defined by the chosen CLFP (JIGSAW). These patterns have been shown previously to be useful to support the creation of IMS-LD scripts to comply with their pedagogical method (Hernández-Leo et al., 2006). Hernández-Leo, Asensio-Pérez, and Dimitriadis (2005) discuss the creation of IMS-LD scripts from patterns, and show the output of Collage as a computer-interpretable script. The innovative aspect of this case study was the integration of assessment activities in the script. This integration required the usage of complex features of IMS-LD. With respect to the configuration of learning activities, the integration of assessment presented two difficulties: first the definition of the IMS-LD script depended on the number of groups and students that participated in the course (which is defined in the instantiation phase). Second, the configuration of the IMS-LD script depended on the specific IMS-LD player to be used. In this case the *.LRN* IMS-LD player was employed, which enabled specific features of IMS-LD, and presented a specific interface to those features.

Therefore, the completion of the design and the instantiation of the script for a specific player and a concrete number of participants had to be realised at the same time. In order to integrate the assessment in the script, the following configuration was implemented through IMS-LD:

The document flow had to be organized to facilitate the completion of assessment, including the access to feedback. Therefore, the script had to indicate that the reports created by each group were to be accessible by the teachers in each assessment activity. Later, the feedback created by the teachers should be delivered automatically to the corresponding groups. In this case, the configuration of the script depended on the number of groups: the document flow needed to be configured in advance for each group (two groups in each assessment activity) independently.

In order to enable the activation of complementary activities, the script had to include hidden activities from the start. Additionally, these activities had to be linked with resources (pages of the *Wiki* system) capable of containing the feedback written by the teachers. These components were created in advance (before the script was enacted) due to the limitations of the IMS-LD player, which did not allow the creation of new activities on the fly. Additionally, the number of groups also determined the number activities and resources that were created.

Especially relevant during this step of the formalization of the script was the creation of instructions for the teachers as to how to complete the assessment activities. While the teachers themselves had planned the assessment activities, the instructions for them were necessary due to the complexity in using the system to complete some of the tasks related to the assessment plan. The teachers' tasks were part of the script (support-activities in IMS-LD). The description of these activities explained the teachers how to access the students' documents, how to write the feedback for them and how to activate and configure the additional activities if necessary. These instructions were, therefore, dependant on the specific technological support used in the case study: the *.LRN* player and the *Wiki* webpage to host documents.

Therefore, the formalization of the script depended on two issues: the number of groups and the specific IMS-LD player. The dependence of the specific features of the player increases the complexity of configuring flexibility in the script, as the teacher would need to be aware of the operation of the player. This further justifies the need to hide this function from the designers. In the case study, however, this was not a problem, and the final result was a IMS-LD compliant script which could be enacted for the number of participants involved in the case study (5 students and 2 teachers).

Results

This section describes the results of the case study. The main sources of data are the questionnaires filled in by the students and the teachers at the end of the experience, the observations of the design task involving the teachers, the observations of the development of the face-to-face sessions, and the notification from students of events (through email) that occurred during the distance activities. With respect to the questionnaires, only four students filled in the questionnaires. Logs generated by the computer systems (the LMS and the *Wiki* system) were also available.

Before focusing on the set research objectives, we are first interested in the effects of deploying the script in the course. When asked their opinion on the necessity and usefulness of the LMS to manage the learning activities, the students were divided in their perceptions on this issue. Two students indicated that using the LMS had been useful for the face-to-face sessions and very useful for distance activities; they noted that "*[the LMS] is very useful because it reinforces the learning process, taking into account that the teacher cannot give all the information*" or that it simply is "*useful as a reminder of the task set up by the teacher at the beginning of the sessions*". On the other hand, the other two students indicated that the LMS had not been useful. These two students agree that "*the scheme of the learning activities was not very complex and the group was small*", and also that the system "*introduces another point of complexity*". However, these two students agree that the LMS facilitates following the sequence of activities, which was the original goal behind setting up the system. In any case, according to the students the usage of the LMS did not introduce additional workload: two students indicate that the workload is equal to that of other activities of the course, and the other two stated that the workload was actually less.

With respect to the perception of the students about the effectiveness of the script to improve their learning, the students indicated that the learning activities had been "*useful*" (3 students) or "*very useful*" (1 student). They highlighted the importance of "*... the obligation of being able to understand what you propose, in order to explain the rest*" (part of the JIGSAW pedagogical method), and that "*feedback in real-time promotes the reinforcement of those points that were unclear*". Therefore, the students found the script useful in order to study the topics of the course, in spite of the opinion that the script was too simple to require the use of an LMS (instead of only the *Wiki* system, as they did regularly in the course). Actually, the script was designed in such a way that the students' tasks were relatively simple with respect to the use of the LMS. The system was expected to manage different groups independently, and this functionality worked as expected. On the other hand, the teachers' activities included more complex functionality, such as the possibility of introducing changes in the script.

The first research objective set for this case study was whether it is possible to enact the script with currently available technology. The observations taken during the face-to-face sessions and the logs confirm that it was possible to carry out all the activities as planned during the design of the pedagogical method. However, some problems arose during enactment:

- At one point, the students were unable to access the activities they were expected to carry out. This was due to the fact that the teachers had not indicated in the LMS that the previous phase had been completed. Since the teachers were in charge of managing the completion of each phase of the script, this prevented the students to continue with their work.

- The teachers needed to ask the staff responsible for the management of the LMS how they should write the feedback for the students so that it would be visible. This revealed that the instructions for the teachers to complete the assessment (including giving feedback and adapting the script if necessary) were not sufficient.

Both problems were solved with the intervention of the staff responsible for managing the LMS. However, the problems indicated that the formalization of the script actually did not satisfy completely the expected goal: that the script, though not formalized by the teachers, would be able to guide the participants in the realization of the activities.

With respect to the second issue, that is, the description of the assessment plan embedded in the script, we are interested in the perception of the students about the impact of the assessment in the learning process. All students indicated that the feedback was "*useful*", and the access to it (which was particularized for each group) was "*easy*" or "*very easy*". However, one student pointed out that "*I missed some further comment, that is, I understand the comments, revise my proposal, and... that's all?*" Similarly, the students were asked about the additional activities (for those cases when they had to complete them). With respect to this, two students indicated that the additional activities had been useful, since "*... [they] have motivated debate and interchange for a better understanding of the concepts of the course*". However, one of these students noted that another iteration would have been useful in order to rehearse the concepts and to share the points of view of all the students. The other two students, on the other hand, had troubles finding the additional activities, so they didn't value this aspect of the script.

The teachers commented on this second issue that the feedback had been "*useful*" and that the possibility to introduce changes in the script was "*very useful, since there are things that cannot be anticipated or are overlooked during the design*". The case study illustrated thus the possibility of describing an assessment plan, including the way that the assessment results are to be used, and the possibility of enacting this assessment plan in a real scenario. More importantly, they noted that the formalized script implemented correctly the planned pedagogical method. The usage of the assessment pattern Report review, in spite of its simplicity, serves to determine a set of features of the script that would be difficult to manage by the designers (the document flow and the assignation of assessment-related roles).

This second issue must also be seen from a technical point of view. The description of the assessment plan during the design phase with the teachers was sufficient to create the script in several aspects. For instance, the script described adequately the organization of the assessment activities; this is achieved using the components of the IMS-LD specification. In addition, the delivery of feedback is also defined sufficiently in the script; however, when, to what students/groups and in which activities the feedback is delivered is not defined in IMS-LD, but as additional information. Eventually, this additional information can be implemented in an IMS-LD compliant script, by using properties; however, this implementation is complex and has to be handled specifically for the purpose of managing the task of moving a document between groups and/or activities.

However, the configuration of the changes of the script is more complex. The particular way in which the teachers could modify the script after each assessment activity could not be modeled using the integration assessment model, so the description in natural language of the expected functionality was necessary. This means that, with respect to this point, an authoring tool would not have had enough information to complete the formalization of the script. In the case study, the script was thus modified manually after the design phase. While this was possible, the main problem is that the implementation of the functionality for the teacher to introduce changes in the script was not IMS-LD compliant: activity description could be modified by the teacher through the *Wiki* system (external to the IMS-LD script), and the activation of needed activities was done using specific functionality of the.*LRN* player, which may be different from that offered in other IMS-LD players. This meant that the script was eventually particularized for the technological context: the usage of a *Wiki* and the.*LRN* player determined the final implementation of the script, rendering it incompatible with other technological settings.

CONCLUSION

This chapter focuses on one approach to the problem of designing CSCL scripts with embedded assessment. The usage of design patterns appears as a promising solution to support non-expert designers in the creation of CSCL scripts in which the assessment plan is explicit. Through a case study, this chapter shows how non-expert designers can propose a script using a small number of elements: two patterns (Jigsaw and Report review), the description of activities for the students and the needed resources, and some assessment-specific information concerning the role of assessment along the script.

The implementation and formalization of the script indicates that it is possible to use IMS-LD and current players in order to support not only learning activities, but also assessment-related functionalities (document flow, in order to have access to documents to review or to deliver feedback) and the possibility of introducing changes in the script, thus enabling the assessment function of correcting the identified problems of the script. The usage of patterns and a formal model to describe this information is intended to enable the development of software tools that can perform the formalization of the script automatically. However, the description of the changes to be introduced in the script was done only partially in a way understandable by software authoring tools. This means that the integration assessment model described in this paper is not sufficient to cover all the information needed by such authoring tools. One possible way of tackling this limitation would be the combination of another type of pattern: patterns for flexibility (Demetriadis, Magnisalis, & Karakostas, 2009); in this way, the exact way in which changes in the script can be introduced would be described by these patterns. Thus, these patterns could indicate the authoring tool how to prepare the script to be adaptable according to assessment results.

Another issue that arose in this case study was the interrelationship between the design and the instantiation phase, which could not be separated. While this does not prevent the usage of software tools to manage automatically the formalization and instantiation of CSCL scripts with embedded assessment, this issue increases the difficulty of sharing and reusing IMS-LD scripts among practitioners or in different scenarios. The complexity of some of the features required by the integration of assessment means that in the current version of IMS-LD the design will not be completely independent from the instantiation phase.

In spite of these problems, the lessons learnt in this case study will be used to continue the development of Collage. Having different patterns (CLFPs, assessment design patterns and potentially other types of patterns as well) enables designers to reuse well-known learning strategies in order to compose a complete CSCL script. Assessment design patterns use assessment-specific vocabulary, and are supported by documentation about the usage and potential benefits and problems of each assessment technique. Thus, they can be understood by non-expert designers, who can integrate these techniques into their own practice, while having software authoring tools handle the complexity of formal specifications.

REFERENCES

Almond, R. G., Steinberg, L. S., & Mislevy, R. J. (2002). Enhancing the design and delivery of assessment systems: A four-process architecture. *Journal of Technology, Learning, and Assessment*, *1*(5), 1–64.

Aronson, E., Blaney, N., Stephan, C., Sikes, J., & Snapp, M. (1978). *The jigsaw classroom*. Thousand Oaks, CA: Sage Publications.

Black, P., & Wiliam, D. (1998). Assessment and classroom learning. *Assessment in Education: Principles. Policy & Practice*, *5*(1), 7–74.

Bote-Lorenzo, M. L., Gómez-Sánchez, E., Vega-Gorgojo, G., Dimitriadis, Y., Asensio-Pérez, J. I., & Jorrín-Abellán, I. M. (2008). Gridcole: a tailorable grid service based system that supports scripted collaborative learning. *Computers & Education*, *51*(1), 155–172. doi:10.1016/j.compedu.2007.05.004

Boud, D., Cohen, R., & Sampson, J. (1999). Peer learning and assessment. *Assessment & Evaluation in Higher Education*, *24*(4), 413–426. doi:10.1080/0260293990240405

Caeiro, M. (2008). PoEML: a separation-of-concerns proposal to instructional design. In Botturi, L., & Stubbs, T. (Eds.), *Handbook of Visual Languages for Instructional Design: Theories and Practices* (pp. 185–209). Hershey, PA: IGI Global.

Chan, C. K. K., & van Aalst, J. (2004). Learning, assessment and collaboration in computer supported environments. In P. Dillenbourg (Series Ed.), J. W. Strijbos, P. A. Kirschner, and R. L. Martens (Vol. Eds.), *Computer-supported collaborative learning: Vol 3. What we know about CSCL and implementing it in higher education* (pp. 87–112). Boston: Kluwer Academic Publishers.

CoSSICLE. (2005). *Computer-Supported Scripting of Interaction in Collaborative Learning Environments Kaleidoscope-NoE ERT website*. Retrieved 13 April, 2010, from http://www.iwm-kmrc.de/cossicle/

del Cid, J. E., de la Fuente-Valentín, L., & Gutiérrez, S. Pardo, & A., Kloos, C. D. (2007). Implementation of a Learning Design Run-Time Environment for the. LRN Learning Management System. *Journal of Interactive Media in Education,* Burgos D. (Ed) *Adaptation and IMS Learning Design. Special Issue 2007/07*

Delozanne, E., Le Calvez, F., Merceron, A., & Labat, J. (2007). A Structured Set of Design Patterns for Learners' Assessment. *Journal of Interactive Learning Research*, *18*(2), 309–333.

Demetriadis, S., Magnisalis, I., & Karakostas, A. (2009). Adaptive Patterns in Systems for Collaborative Learning and the Role of the Learning Design Specification. In *Proceedings of the Scripted vs. Free CS Collaboration: Alternatives and Paths for Adaptable and Flexible CS Scripted Collaboration Workshop, CSCL09* (pp. 44-48). The International Society of the Learning Sciences (ISLS).

Dillenbourg, P. (2002). Over-Scripting CSCL: The Risks of the provision of service instances is a critical feature: Blending Collaborative Learning with Instructional Design. In Kirschner, P. A. (Ed.), *Inaugural Address, Three Worlds of CSCL. Can We Support CSCL?* (pp. 61–91). Heerlen, The Netherlands: Open Universiteit Nederland.

Dillenbourg, P., & Tchounikine, P. (2007). Flexibility in macro-scripts for computer supported collaborative learning. *Journal of Computer Assisted Learning*, *23*(1), 1–13. doi:10.1111/j.1365-2729.2007.00191.x

Dochy, F., & McDowell, L. (1997). Assessment as a tool for learning. *Studies in Educational Evaluation*, *23*(4), 279–298. doi:10.1016/S0191-491X(97)86211-6

E-LEN. (2004). *E-LEN Project Website*. Retrieved 13 April, 2010, from http://www2.tisip.no/E-LEN/

Goodyear, P., Avgeriou, P., Baggetun, R., Bartoluzzi, S., Retalis, S., Ronteltap, F., & Rusman, E. (2004). Towards a pattern language for networked learning. In Banks, S., Goodyear, P., Hodgson, V., Jones, C., Lally, V., McConnell, D., & Steeples, C. (Eds.), *Proceedings of Networked learning 2004* (pp. 449–455). Lancaster, UK: LancasterUniversity.

Griffiths, D., Blat, J., Garcia, R., Vogten, H., & Kwong, K.-L. (2005). Learning Design Tools. In Koper, R., & Tattersall, C. (Eds.), *Learning Design - A Handbook on Modelling and Delivering Networked Education and Training* (pp. 109–136). Berlin: Springer.

Hernández-Leo, D. (2007). *A pattern-based design process for the creation of CSCL macro-scripts computationally represented with IMS LD*. Unpublished doctoral dissertation. University of Valladolid, Spain.

Hernández-Leo, D., Asensio-Pérez, J. I., & Dimitriadis, Y. (2005). Computational Representation of Collaborative Learning Flow Patterns Using IMS Learning Desing. *Journal of Educational Technology & Society*, *8*(4), 75–89.

Hernández-Leo, D., Bote-Lorenzo, M. L., Asensio-Pérez, J. I., Gómez-Sánchez, E., Villasclaras-Fernández, E. D., Jorrín-Abellán, I. M., & Dimitriadis, Y. (2007). Free- and Open Source Software for a Course on Network Management: Authoring and Enactment of Scripts based on Collaborative Learning Strategies. *IEEE Transactions on Education*, *50*(4), 292–301. doi:10.1109/TE.2007.904589

Hernández-Leo, D., Villasclaras-Fernández, E. D., Asensio-Pérez, J. I., Dimitriadis, Y., Jorrín-Abellán, I. M., Ruiz-Requies, I., & Rubia-Avi, B. (2006). Collage: A collaborative learning design editor based on patterns. Special Issue on *Learning Design*. *Journal of Educational Technology & Society*, *9*(1), 58–71.

IMS Global Learning Consortium. (2003). *IMS Learning Design specification*. Retrieved 13 April, 2010, from http://www.imsglobal.org/learningdesign/

IMS Global Learning Consortium. (2006). *IMS Question & Test Interoperability specification*. Retrieved April 2010 from http://www.imsglobal.org/question/

Joosten-ten Brinke, D., van Bruggen, J., Hermans, H., Burgers, J., Giesbers, B., Koper, R., & Latour, I. (2007). Modeling assessment for re-use of traditional and new types of ssessment. *Computers in Human Behavior*, *23*(6), 2721–2741. doi:10.1016/j.chb.2006.08.009

Kobbe, L. (2006). *Framework on multiple goal dimensions for computer-supported scripts, Kaleidoscope, D21.2.1*. Final.

Kollar, I., Fischer, F., & Hesse, F. W. (2006). Computer-supported collaboration scripts - a conceptual analysis. *Educational Psychology Review*, *18*(2), 159–185. doi:10.1007/s10648-006-9007-2

Macdonald, J. (2003). Assessing online collaborative learning: Process and product. *Computers & Education*, *40*(4), 377–391. doi:10.1016/S0360-1315(02)00168-9

Miao, Y., Tattersall, C., Schoonenboom, J., Stevanov, K., & Aleksieva-Petrova, A. (2007). Using open technical e-learning standards and service-orientation to support new forms of e-assessment. In Griffiths, D., Koper, R. and Liber O. (Eds.), *Proceedings of the second TENCompetence Open Workshop on Service Oriented Approaches and Lifelong Competence Development Infrastructures* (pp. 183-190). Bolton, UK: The Institute for Educational Cybernetics.

Mislevy, R., Hamel, L., Fried, R., Gaffney, T., & Haertel, G. Hafter, et al. (2003). *Design patterns for assessing science inquiry (PADI Technical Report 1)*. Menlo Park, CA: SRI International

PPP. (2005). The pedagogical patterns project. Retrieved 30 September, 2009, from http://www.pedagogicalpatterns.org/

Shepard, L. A. (2000). The role of assessment in a learning culture. *Educational Researcher*, *29*(7), 4–14.

Stiggins, R. J. (2002). Assessment Crisis: The Absence of Assessment FOR Learning. *Phi Delta Kappan*, *83*(10), 758–765.

Suthers, D. (2005). Technology affordances for intersubjective learning: A thematic agenda for CSCL.In *Proceedings of the International conference of Computer Support for Collaborative Learning (CSCL 2005). The Next 10 years!* (662 – 671). The International Society of the Learning Sciences (ISLS).

TELL. (2005). *Design patterns for teachers and educational (system) designers*. Retrieved 13 April, 2010, from http://cosy.ted.unipi.gr/images/stories/design-patterns/TELL_pattern_book.pdf

Villasclaras-Fernández, E. D., Hernández-Gonzalo, J. A., Hernández-Leo, D., Asensio-Pérez, J. I., & Dimitriadis, Y. (2009). InstanceCollage: a tool for the particularization of collaborative IMS-LD scripts. *Journal of Educational Technology & Society*, *12*(3), 56–70.

Villasclaras-Fernández, E. D., Hernández-Leo, D., Asensio-Pérez, J. I., & Dimitriadis, Y. (2009). Incorporating assessment in a pattern-based design process for CSCL scripts, *Computers in Human Behavior. Special Issue on Design Patterns for Augmenting E-Learning Experiences*, *25*(5), 1028–1039.

Villasclaras-Fernández, E. D., Hernández-Leo, D., Asensio-Pérez, J. I., Dimitriadis, Y., & Martínez-Monés, A. (2009). Towards embedding assessment in CSCL scripts through selection and assembly of learning and assessment patterns. In *Proceedings of the 9th international conference on Computer supported collaborative learning*, vol.1. (pp. 507-511). The International Society of the Learning Sciences (ISLS).

KEY TERMS AND DEFINITIONS

Embedded Assessment: In this chapter, assessment refers to those activities intended to gather information about the students' knowledge, skills, abilities and/or work. Moreover, assessment is considered as part of CSCL scripts, and therefore assessment activities are integrated or embedded within such scripts.

Pedagogical Design Pattern: The documentation of a solution to a problem that arises frequently in the preparation of learning activities. Pedagogical Design Patterns offer solutions that have been validated in the experience, and that can be reused in a wide range of scenarios.

Collaborative Learning Flow Pattern (CLFP): A type of pedagogical pattern, which proposes a specific solution to the configuration of the structure of CSCL macro-scripts. CLFPs typically propose a role/group structure and a sequence of phases and activities, intended to achieve certain types of learning objectives.

Assessment Pattern: A type of Pedagogical Pattern, which proposes a specific solution to the configuration of one or several aspects of an assessment. The assessment patterns mentioned in this chapter tackle aspects such as the distribution of assessment-related roles, the configuration of assessment activities, assessment resources, the integration of the assessment results in a pedagogical method, etc.

Chapter 16
The Support of Virtual 3D Worlds for Enhancing Collaboration in Learning Settings

Christian Gütl
Graz University of Technology, Austria & Curtin University of Technology, Australia

ABSTRACT

Collaborative learning activities apply different approaches in-class or out-of-class, which range from classroom discussions to group-based assignments and can involve students more actively as well as stimulate social and interpersonal skills. Information and communication technology can support collaboration, however, a great number of pre-existing technologies and implementations have limitations in terms of the interpersonal communication perspective, limited shared activity awareness, and a lack of a sense of co-location. Virtual 3D worlds offer an opportunity to either mitigate or even overcome these issues. This book chapter focuses on how virtual 3D worlds can foster the collaboration both between instructors and students as well as between student peers in diverse learning settings. Literature review findings are complemented by the results of practical experiences on two case studies of collaborative learning in virtual 3D worlds: one on small group learning and one on physics education. Overall findings suggest that such learning environment's advantages are a promising alternative to meet more easily and spontaneously; and that an integrated platform with a set of tools and a variety of communication channels provides real life world phenomena as well as different ones. On the negative side, there are usability issues in relation to the technical limitations of 3D world platforms and applications, which reduce the potential for learning in such collaborative virtual environments.

DOI: 10.4018/978-1-61692-898-8.ch016

INTRODUCTION

In the beginning of the 21st century, our knowledge-driven and globalized society demands more than ever to adapt continuously skills and knowledge but also soft skills become increasingly important, such as the ability to communicate and collaborate in a multidisciplinary and intercultural group. Thus, modern instructional design, learning goals and processes as well as appropriate learning environments must support this situation properly. Not surprisingly, new educational strategies have been developed, which emphasize self-directed learning, collaborative learning, experiential-based learning, active participating and content creation (Bransford, Brown, & Cocking, 2000; Rogers, Liddle, Chan, Doxey, & Isom, 2007). By narrowing down to collaboration in the learning process, activities apply different approaches in-class or out-of-class, which range from classroom discussions to group-based assignments. Such learning settings can involve students more actively as well as stimulate social and interpersonal skills. (Smith & MacGregor, 1992; Dillenbourg, Baker, Blaye, & O'Malley, 1996; Stacey, 1999)

Information and communication technology can support collaborative learning and enable participation of students who are geographically dispersed. A great variety of technologies and applications have been invented and implemented over the last decades which are described elsewhere, such as in (Craig, 2007; Jacobson, Kim, Miao, Shen, & Chavez, 2010; Redfern & Naughton, 2002; Safran, Helic, & Gütl, 2007; Stacey, 1999). A remarkable emerging trend is envisioned to make a convergence between the real and virtual world using enhanced forms of communication and intelligent information access. Along these lines, combining a set of technology trends, such as Semantic Web, Social Web, Media Centric Web, Pervasive & Ubiquitous Web, 3D Web, may further enhance and stimulate collaborative learning activities (Silva, Rahman, & El Saddik, 2008).

One of the promising and powerful technologies in the context of communication and collaboration for online learning communities are virtual 3D worlds, which have become increasingly popular within the last few years. Although virtual reality and immersive worlds have been active research fields for many years, technology was not ready for complex application scenarios until recently. Since then, *massively multiplayer online games (MMOG)* such as 'World of Warcraft' or *massively multiplayer online worlds (MMOW)* such as 'Second Life' have not only attracted a myriad of virtual inhabitants but have also resulted in real money turnovers. It is estimated that 80 percent of active internet users will have some sort of online presence in virtual worlds by end of 2011. New business opportunities, however, are opposed by the fact that some 90 percent of commercial virtual world projects fail partly because they focus on technology rather than on the users' needs. In order to avoid the same pitfalls of past e-learning solutions by just applying new technology to traditional learning approaches, multidisciplinary research efforts are required to develop new collaborative learning for virtual 3D world settings. (Gartner, 2007; Gartner, 2008; Gütl, 2008; Kumar et al., 2008; Jacobson et al. & Chavez, 2010; Kappe & Gütl, 2009; Redfern & Naughton, 2002)

This book chapter focuses on the nature of collaboration both between instructors and students as well as between student peers and how virtual 3D worlds can foster the collaboration process in diverse learning settings. First a theoretical overview of collaborative learning and how technologies - specifically virtual 3D worlds - can support such learning settings are provides. Based on these theoretical findings, two case studies of collaborative learning in virtual 3D worlds are discussed: one on small group learning and one on physics experiments.

BACKGROUND

Collaborative Learning and Technological Support

Collaborative learning can be seen as an abstract concept involving joined intellectual effort by the learning community built of students and teachers in a wide range of settings. The learning group mutually searches for understanding or meaning, explores solutions or creates some sort of product. In such learning settings not only role and behaviors of students change significantly, but also teachers change their role towards experts who coach students. (Dillenbourg et al., 1996; So & Brush, 2006; Bernard, Rojo de Rubalcava, & St-Pierre, 2000; Smith & MacGregor, 1992)

A great variety of studies following different research paradigms has been undertaken which focuses on effects, conditions and interactions of collaborative learning activities. Results have shown that, compared to individualistic instructional approaches, collaborative learning activities can be more effective in terms of student achievements, attitude of learning experiences and motivational aspects. There are, however, also challenges and issues. For example, designing and implementing collaborative learning activities can be time consuming, and relationships between teachers and students can be confusing and disorientating. Furthermore, low achievers progressively become passive when they collaborate with high achievers. Typical tasks in collaborative learning are skill & knowledge acquisition, joined planning, categorization as well as promoting and negotiating differences in perspectives and solutions. (Alavi & Dufner, 2005; Dillenbourg et al., 1996; Smith & MacGregor, 1992; So & Brush, 2006)

Although e-learning has been an active field of researchers and practitioners since decades, few success stories have been reported. Among other issues, projects have mainly focused on fancy technology instead of considering properly users' requirements; also they have purely transformed established learning situations into new media. (Gütl, 2008) Studies with particular focus on distance education (DE) have shown problems of high average dropout rates and low level of quality learning. Reasons put forward for these problems include (a) a feeling of isolation, (b) procrastination, (c) lack of multiple communication channels, and (d) difficulties related to self-regulation. (Bernard et al., 2000) Pre-packaged multimedia educational products and most of the web-based educational resources did not sufficiently support social interaction. Collaborative online learning can improve or even overcome these problems. (Redfern & Naughton, 2002)

The above mentioned theories and findings have contributed to increase the interest in collaborative learning and led to a great variety of information and communication based tools which have been developed over the last decades. Focusing on *computer-supported collaborative learning* (CSCL), some early preliminary work (such as the "Virtual Classroom") started already in the 1980s, but significant community building and increasing activities on this topic have not started before the late 1980s. Since that time, a myriad of collaborative learning tools have been developed. These tools can be classified into synchronous collaboration support (such as application sharing and video conferencing) and into asynchronous collaboration support (such as collaborative writing and discussion forums). (Koschmann, 2001; Stahl, Koschmann, & Suthers, 2006).

Effected by the high complexity of influential factors on collaborative learning and the great variety of technological support and concrete design of tools, evaluation and research findings on collaborative tools in practical learning settings show a blurred picture including both successful and unsuccessful implementations. (Alavi & Dufner, 2005; Stahl, Koschmann, & Suthers, 2006) Despite the great potential of collaborative learning tools, a great number of pre-existing technologies and implementations have several deficiencies in their use in relation to the interpersonal communication perspective. These deficiencies implicate limited transmission of interpersonal and social information; more concrete they restrict the social presence, diminish social context cues and restrict numbers of communication channels (in particular nonverbal communication). Usage of videoconferencing or the integration of audio-video-based presence of the learning community may overcome the problem at least partly. Still there is the problem of limited shared activity awareness and there is indeed not the feeling of co-location. (Redfern & Naughton, 2002) To mitigate or even overcome these problems, collaborative virtual environments, such as virtual 3D worlds and distributed virtual reality systems, can be viewed as a promising and powerful alternative for collaborative learning.

Collaborative Virtual Environments

According to Blascovich, Loomis, Beall, Swinth, Hoyt and Bailenson (2002), *virtual environments* (VE) can be viewed as *"synthetic sensory information that leads to perceptions of environments and their contents as if they were not synthetic."* Typical computers generate the multimodal information streams of such a virtual environment and enable real-time interaction between users and the VE (Bailenson, Yee, Blascovich, Beall, Lundblad, & Jin, 2008). In order to narrow down to *collaborative virtual environments (CVE)* a very generic definition was given by Snowdon, Churchill and Munro (2001): *"A CVE is a computer-based, distributed, virtual space or set of places. In such places, people can meet and interact with others, with agents or with virtual objects. CVEs might vary in their representational richness from 3D graphical spaces, 2.5D and 2D environments, to text-based environments. Access to CVEs is by no means limited to desktop devices, but might well include mobile or wearable devices, public kiosks, etc."* (Snowdon, Churchill, & Munro, 2001). To be consistent with the general definition of virtual environment, the representational richness has to be extended also by other senses such as sound and touch, which might also be supported by literature review in Bailenson et al. (2008). Following this generic and open definition of CVE, different types of application in the context of collaborative learning can be identified which will be discussed in the remainder of this section.

Firstly, *online games,* which have been available for more than a decade, enable players to interact in the game environment. Such online games have been developed from small group games (such as *Quake*) to massive multiplayer online games (such as *World of Warcraft*) designed to scale for a very large number of users simultaneously. Representations in game worlds have increasingly become realistic and some of them provide interesting interaction patterns and collaboration features in world. Such online worlds not only provide a sense of presence but some also enable users to develop knowledge and skills, such as domain and strategic knowledge as well as speed of processing, decision-making and social skills. Even learning communities can evolve which organize and maintain knowledge out of world to master in world tasks and missions. Additionally, a variety of educational online games have become available which not only can help to increase motivation and fostering of collaboration but also enhance knowledge acquisition and metacognitive skills. (Jacobson et al., 2010; Kumar et al., 2008; Lim, Nonis, & Hedberg, 2006; Schrader & McCreery, 2008)

Secondly, *immersive virtual reality* (IVR) can be viewed as *"complex technologies that replaced real-world sensory information with synthetic stimuli such as 3D visual imagery, spatialized sound, and force or tactile feedback."* (Bowman & McMahan, 2007) Early research on multisensory virtual experience goes back at least to the 1950s, and since the 1980s it became a research topic of great interest and a great variety of technologies as well as applications have been developed. The goal of IVRs is that users experience a computer-generated artificial environment or world as if it were real. Four main technologies - modeling & management system for virtual world artifacts, appropriate graphical rendering system, visual/aural/haptic interfaces, and tracking system of user position and orientation – enable immersive perception and therefore a feeling of presence. One class of virtual reality applications is designed for single user access which can be used in learning settings such as simulation, virtual experiments as well as exploration of structures and phenomena. The other class of application involves more than one user leading to *immersive multi-user virtual environments* (IMUVE) which consequently not only enables to perceive the feeling of presence but also supports collaboration activities. Users are often represented by an animated human-like character or avatar and may include animations of body movements, facial expressions, hand gestures and lip-synchronization. Such multimodal communication streams can positively effect social presence. (Bailenson et al. 2008; Bowman & McMahan, 2007; Brooks, 1999; Bryson, 1996; Carlson, 2009; Leung & Chen, 2001; Roussos, Johnson, Leigh, Vasilakis, Barnes, & Moher, 1997; Streuber & Chatziastros, 2007)

Thirdly, *virtual worlds* can be viewed as a closely related concept of immersive multi-user virtual environments. Unlike IMUVE virtual worlds are not only characterized by immersion, feeling of presence and social interaction but they are also a persistent online environment, where a large population of users can interact over time. The notion of virtual worlds has a long history in religions and literature, however, one of the very early computer-based implementation was MUD (Multi User Dungeon) in 1978 which allowed users to interact in a text-based virtual environment. Since the mid 1980s two-dimensional (2D) and three-dimensional (3D) virtual worlds have been developed. More recently, interests of researchers, industry and practitioners have resulted in virtual worlds like *Second Life*, *Open Sim*, Sony *Home* and Sun *Wonderland* (since 2010 cuntinued as community project *Open Wonderland*). These new types of virtual worlds, *massively multiplayer online worlds* (MMOW) or *Virtual 3D Worlds* (V3DW) build on 3D models and enhanced 3D graphic and audible world presentation but human-"online world"-interaction is mainly restricted to 2D computer screens, stereo sound, keyboard and mouse. Such settings are viewed as not entirely immersive but technologies for the consumer market (such as 3D monitors and projectors) and appropriate interfaces accessing virtual worlds will soon overcome these restrictions. (Jacobson et al., 2010; Kappe & Gütl, 2009; Schrank, 2009; Schroeder, 2008; Sivan, 2008)

In general, such virtual 3D worlds help to recreate real world scenarios or to create complete new ones either with real world physical phenomena or different ones. V3DWs are composed by static or interactive objects and avatars as the digital representatives of the users acting and interacting in the world. Such worlds may provide experiences to understand concepts, explore and learn as well as to socialize or purely have fun. (Bailenson et al. 2008; Chroittaro & Ranon, 2007; Jacobson et al., 2010; Schrank, 2009) Some of the platforms even allow their users to build collaboratively their own objects or worlds. Furthermore, 3D worlds provide different verbal (voice and text chat both public and private) but also nonverbal (locomotion, gaze and gesture) communication channels (Johnson & Rickel, 2000), which also impact the social presence of self and others (Blascovich et al., 2002). Consequently, this technology raises a great interest in application domains such as gaming, e-commerce, engineering, design, architecture, medicine, education, and training (Bouras & Tsiatsos, 2006; Rose, Attree, Brooks, Parslow, Penn, & Ambihaipahan, 2000; Bray & Konsynski, 2007).

Based on the information outlined so far it is obvious that virtual 3D worlds can be applied in a wide range of applications for learning and training purposes. The authors Chittaro and Ranon (2007) define several contexts for the usage of such worlds according to the specific objectives of the learning settings:

- Formal education (in classroom settings or laboratory settings) in a controlled, supervised environment
- Informal education either guided or unguided in museums, zoos, and the like
- Distance learning including self-instruction and learning settings where teachers, tutors and students are involved
- Vocational training to acquire skills and knowledge for tasks and roles in business
- Special needs education for people with physical and cognitive disabilities

Focusing further on collaborative learning aspects, advantages of virtual 3D worlds in this context include:

- *Multiple communication channels* both verbal and non-verbal communication can increase the social awareness and improve the knowledge transfer and understanding (De Lucia, Francese, Passero, & Tortora, 2008; So & Brush, 2006)
- *Presence* (feeling to be part of the virtual environment) can effect suspension of disbelief and increase motivation and productivity (Bouras & Tsiatsos, 2006)
- *Awareness* of other avatars, the environment and activities impact the dynamic of group communication (Bouras & Tsiatsos, 2006)
- *Reducing barriers* between students, tutors and instructors (Kemp & Livingstone, 2006)
- *Belonging to a community* which creates a virtual social space and can positively impact learning outcome (De Lucia, Francese, Passero, & Tortora, 2008)
- *Facilitating collaboration* on 3D artefacts or other content which becomes increasingly important in modern working and learning processes (Kemp & Livingstone, 2006)

Over the last few years a great variety of collaborative learning environments based on 3D worlds have been researched, developed and evaluated; see for example Coffman and Klinger (2007), Bailenson et al. (2008), Jacobson et al. (2010), Lee (2009), Monahan, McArdlea and Bertolotto (2008), Sivan (2008), and Prasolova-Førland (2008). The remainder of this book chapter focuses on the application of virtual 3D worlds as collaborative learning tool in two case studies: one on small group learning and the other one on physics experiments.

CASE STUDY I: GROUP LEARNING SUPPORT IN GEOGRAPHICAL DISPERSED ENVIRONMENTS

Motivation and Requirements

This case study reports on the preliminary results of a research endeavor which aims at providing alternative ways to university students in geographically dispersed learning environments to work together in small groups. The remainder of this section is based on Gütl, Chang, Kopeinik and Williams, (2009), and Chang, Gütl, Kopeinik and Williams, (2009).

This research initiative was originally motivated by a very specific situation in Australia's higher education sector which emerged within the last few years. According to government reports, the rapidly developing economy will require more well-qualified employees at graduated level. To increase the rate of higher qualified people universities need to attract a broader demographic of students including people located in regional or remote areas and those who are in workforce. Already 12% of students who enrolled in higher educational programs in Australia are located in regional or remote areas of their universities and the above mentioned situation will cause a dramatic increase in the future. There is also a similar situation on the teachers' side. Consequently institutions are looking for innovative technologies and approaches to support distance education. The *School of Information Systems* at *Curtin University of Technology* in Western Australia is in particular interested in alternative ways to engage in collaborative learning activities for students in geographically dispersed environments.

In response to this need for a collaborative learning environment a research project using a virtual 3D world technology was developed to take advantage of features such as participant's awareness of other participants (avatars) and their activities, multiple communication channels, perceptions of being within the environment, and enablement of social interaction. Requirements on an abstract level can be organized in three aspects: *organizational aspects* include strategies to (1) complement existing learning environment with the possibility of providing alternative activities for remote learning, (2) easy to access and use by students and teachers, and (3) consideration of network policy and firewall restrictions. The *pedagogical aspects* include the enabling of (1) collaborative learning in small groups, (2) tutoring and teacher consultation, (3) support learning tasks with appropriate toolsets and (4) scaffold inter-group and intra-group discussion. Lastly, the *technological aspects* to consider include (1) access from within and outside the campus, (2) easy to install and operate system, and (3) minimum hardware requirements for the client (both students and teachers).

Overview of the Learning Environment

Guided by the requirements outlined in the previous section, it has been decided to develop the collaborative learning environment within the virtual 3D world Second Life (SL), see also Linden Labs (2009). In order to foster group learning we aimed at the following goals: (1) make the environment a pleasant place to spend time, (2) enable and facilitate communication between students and teachers, and (3) provide useful tools for collaborative work; see also (Chang, Gütl, Kopeinik, & Williams, 2009).

Based on the above mentioned goals, a form of room metaphor is the basic principle of the design for the collaborative learning space. As depicted in Figure 1, the prototype implementation has four equally equipped buildings for collaborative group learning activities as well as a teacher

Figure 1. A bird's eye view of the collaborative learning environment including four separated group learning rooms (1), the teacher's office (2), and the recreation area (3)

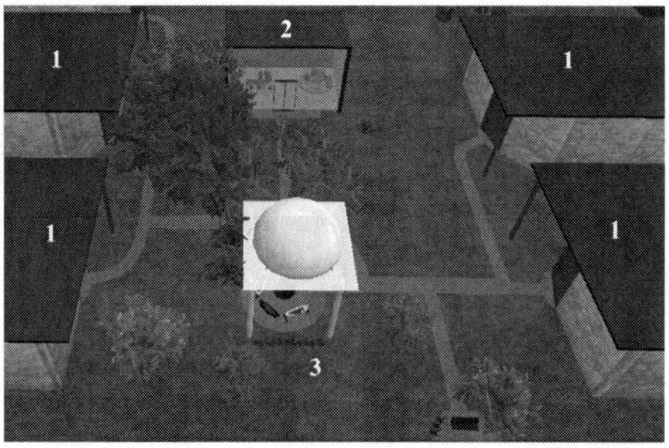

room for meetings and a recreation area for social interaction. Each of the areas will be discussed in the remainder of this section.

The collaborative *group learning areas* are placed around the social interaction space, each of which is meant to be used by one of the learning groups. In order to indicate and provide privacy, the areas are designed as closed bungalows with an entrance door which can only be opened by students of the learning group, but others can also be invited to visit the learning room. Each of the group learning rooms is equipped to facilitate communication, discussion and collaborative learning activities (see also Figure 2). Each of the rooms provides the following tools: (a) an *appointment setter tool* which allows students and teachers to coordinate their meetings for both schedule and agenda items. (b) A *Slide presenter board* offers a platform to create and share presentations and sequences of pictures. (c) The *Brain storming board* is a tool intended to develop and express ideas collaboratively. (d) The *Whiteboard tools* can be used for uploading and annotating pictures as well as developing mind maps. (e) The *Media Board* enables the learner group to display Web pages and work collaboratively on documents using Google Docs service. In order to secure communication and content, appropriate access rights have been implemented for each of the above mentioned tools.

The *teacher's room* (see also Figure 4) provides a place for teachers to meet with students for consultation hours and formal or informal meetings. To this end, the room was designed in two different zones to accommodate both formal and casual settings for meetings. At this phase of the implementation no collaboration support tools have been implemented in this area. The *recreation area* (see also Figure 3) provides a social area for students to relax, meet, and discuss ideas with others. In order to initiate discussion a sequence of subject relevant news or statements are highlighted on a notice board.

In order to improve and further enhance the collaborative learning environment, a preliminary qualitative study focusing on both the students' and teachers' evaluation has been administered.

Study Setup

The subjects in the learning scenario are students enrolled in the course "Business Problem Analysis" offered at the School of Information Systems at Curtin University of Technology, Western Australia, in semester one, 2009. In this course, student performance is measured with three assessment items. One of these assessment items (collaboratively elaborating problems on a given topic and creating a document) was alternatively offered as traditional face-to-face group work and

Figure 2. Group learning room providing a meeting space and tools for collaborative learning activities

Figure 3. Recreation space supporting social interaction and intergroup communication

alternatively as an activity in the developed collaborative learning environment; both options were designed for the same group size of 3 participants.

The research method was organized as follows: (1) in the introductory lecture not only the course outline was presented but also the collaborative learning environment, the option to complete one of the assessment items online including an overview of the learning activity, and basics about the study have been introduced. (2) All subjects were requested to complete a pre-survey which focused on demographic information as well as on general information about learning preferences and familiarity with computers and e-learning platforms. (3) Each of the subjects had to take the decision by middle of the term whether to complete the assignment in the traditional way or by using the Second Life virtual learning environment. (4) Each of the subjects who had decided to use the learning environment was also asked to complete a post questionnaire which focused on their experience of the virtual learning environment. It is reported that this research involving humans was reviewed and approved by the responsible ethics authority at the university.

Evaluation Results and Discussion

Of 20 students enrolled in the course 16 completed the pre-questionnaire. Demographic data and IT

Figure 4. Teacher's room supporting virtual consultation hours and virtual meetings

experience of the 16 subjects can be summarized as follows: (a) *gender*: 50% male and 50% female; (b) *age group*: 87.5% between 18 - 24, 12.5% between 25 - 30; (c) *nationality*: 18.75% Australian, 81.25% Non-Australian; (d) *level of computer experience*: 81.25% highly experienced 18.75% little experienced, (e) *level of e-learning experience*: 100% are experienced.

By focusing on questions regarding familiarity of virtual 3D worlds, the study revealed that 11 students (68.75% of subjects) regularly play computer games and 7 (43.75%) use virtual 3D environment. Only one student used Second Life but 9 (56.25%) were interested to use it. Subjects' perception to use Second Life as learning environment was quite good, 62.5% found it useful, 18.75 equally not useful or did not know. Interestingly, only two students (12.5%) would have had problems meeting the system requirements to run Second Life on their computers. Despite the quite good attitude and the interest, only 6 students (37.5%) finally decided to volunteer in the online experiment. Reasons for not taking advantage of using the online version included increased workload to get familiarized with the new virtual environment and concerns about instability (e.g. downtime, access and maneuvering). Another important aspect was that students were familiar with face-to-face collaboration and how to deal with negotiating and collaboration but they mentioned anxiety due to the inexperience with collaboration in the online learning environment.

Interestingly, 5 of the 6 students (83.3%) who selected the online option were female. Compared with the findings of Griffiths and Hunt (1995) who suggested that males are easier to motivate to play online games and more likely to occupy themselves in such games than females, this is one of the surprising findings. It is also worth mentioning that the 6 students who volunteered spent less time on computer games than the other subjects. The 6 volunteering students were split into groups of three. All subjects have successfully contributed and finished the assessment task, the post-questionnaire and answered some questions in an unstructured interview.

Starting with the aspect of getting prepared to use the collaborative learning environment, results have shown that subjects had no difficulties setting up Second Life and on average they spent 2.25 hours to get themselves familiar with the environment. However, a few subject had some problems during the collaboration phase to operate appropriately in the learning environment and to take advantages of the tools offered in the environment. To overcome these issues in future it is recommended not only to give a short introduction at the beginning of the course but also to give a training session before the groups start to work on the assignment.

Subjects' perception of using SL as learning environment is quite positive as for each of the following statement 5 out of 6 (83.3%) agreed that (a) it offers flexibility in respect of time, (b) it saves traveling time, (c) it supports collaborative tasks, and (d) it enables social interaction. Subjects also found the SL learning environment encouraging and conductive for learning. They have also indicated that it is more convenient to meet in SL which can be supported by the following statements: "easier to work around group members with other commitments", "time saving regarding traveling time", "flexible to meet group members even during the night".

One of the limitations of the second part of the study was the small sample size, although it was a decision that was deliberately made to allow students to take their own decision either to select to the face-to-face setting or use the newly developed environment. Nevertheless, the results reveal the perception of the group of students which also enables us to improve and further enhance the collaborative learning environments.

On the negative side, in particular poor interface usability of SL distracted the students. They found in particular that SL was not intuitive to operate and that there was no built-in function to enable collaborative working on documents and sharing them in the SL world. The provided functions based on the media board and 'Google Docs' services were appreciated but subjects were still required to edit the content 'out of world'. Students also emphasized serious problems using the built-in voice communication and rated the text chat as more convenient; one group even indicated the use of Skype as communication channel. From the learning point of view, subjects responded that they were under a lot of pressure trying to complete the assignment being not very familiar with the learning environment. Also students found it time consuming to use the virtual learning environment and did not like the virtual consultation hours. The inability to express emotions with the avatars was also encountered as a part of the subject's frustrations. They also emphasized limitations of the provided tools to express their thoughts and sketch their ideas appropriately. Almost all of the students indicated that improvements in terms of usability and functionality are required for the whiteboard, the media board and the brain storming board.

Despite these responses, students reported using SL also helped them to plan and organize their works and such an integrated environment supported them to work together effectively. These arguments are illustrated with the following statements: "it helped organize the group", "it is easier to put documents together because they are online and everyone can contribute", "meeting can be on the minute through chat", "environment provides media to leave messages or ideas for other group members".

The lecturer who was not familiar with SL before the experiment responded similarly to the students that it took some time to get familiarized with the system; and to set up a learning environment in SL required a lot of planning, effort and time. On the positive side the lecturer mentioned that such environments enable students to work remotely. On the negative side the lecturer emphasized that it was not really known to whom one is acting because of the quasi-anonymity of the avatars. It was also suggested that names or numbers for all the buildings of the environment and some signposts would improve orientation 'in world'. Furthermore, it was also recommended that an extensive and thorough training for all staff participants and students before the starting date would be beneficial.

From the development point of view, the dedicated programming language in SL, Linden Script Language (LSL), is simple to use and a variety of online tutorials and preexisting tools as well as interactive objects are available. No problems were encountered during the creation of 3D contents in particular using the built-in editor. However, if applying external tools, it is time consuming to integrate and resize the models. Some of the main issues we encountered during the design and implementation of the environment caused by the restrictions of SL's functionality are: (a) avatars can look into closed buildings or rooms, (b) management of group and user rights is time consuming, and providing a set of tools becomes complex in terms of rights management, and (c) media cannot be scrolled. From the organizational viewpoint, the learning environment in SL is hosted outside the university which may effect issues such as sustainability, privacy but also costs for uploading images. More detailed evaluation results can be found elsewhere in Gütl, Chang, Kopeinik and Williams (2009).

This first case study has shown that a virtual learning environment in Second Life can support collaborative learning activities in small groups through awareness and multimodal communication streams as well as having tools integrated in a single environment. The virtual learning environment supports students and teachers to meet more spontaneously even if they are geographically dispersed. Although the learning environment makes use of the benefits of virtual 3D worlds, technical restrictions, usability issues of world and learning tools as well as efforts for participants to familiarize with the environment provide room for further research and development activities.

CASE STUDY II: COLLABORATIVE VIRTUAL ENVIRONMENT FOR PHYSICS EXPERIMENTS

Motivation and Requirements

The second case study gives an overview of the preliminary results of research activities enabling students and instructors who are geographically dispersed to administer collaboratively physics experiments and experience phenomena. The remainder of this section is based on Scheucher, Bailey, Gütl, and Harward (2009), and Scheucher, Belcher, Bailey, dos Santos and Gütl (2009).

This research project has been motivated by a situation in university physics education where although pedagogical concepts and technological learning support have developed, a main pedagogical problem still remains which effects physics education from secondary school up to university level. Students have great difficulties to relate phenomena observed in lab or in real world to physics theory and formula. Although there are various tools (such as simulations, virtual and remote experiments) available for classroom presentations or students' individual usage, collaborative activities in such learning tasks can help to bring students to higher achievement levels.

In order to develop a collaborative learning environment supporting physics education of complex theories and phenomena, it was decided to build on a virtual 3D world as a potential tool. The aim of this tool is not to recreate face-to-face classroom settings but to design and develop a learning space to complement and expand classroom activities. One of the high-level requirements was to provide an enhanced collaborative learning environment which enables hands-on experiences not possible in traditional classroom settings. These include (1) facilitating 3D visualizations to simulate formal mathematical models, (2) making unseen phenomena seen and more understandable, (3) providing controllable computer-generated analogs of real-world objects and processes, (4) enabling students and instructors to interact collaboratively with experiments, (5) experiencing immersion and awareness, and (6) scaffolding social interaction.

Overview of the Learning Environment

For a first prototype implementation it has been decided to take the "Force on a Dipole" experiment which is part of TEALSim (Technology Enabled Active Learning Project (TEAL) Simulation System) (TEAL, 2009). TEALSim has been developed for Studio Physics at Massachusetts Institute of Technology (MIT). The experiment "Force on a Dipole" (see also Figure 5) is one of the remote experiments which have been effectively integrated in the TEAL curriculum. The experiment has originally enabled students to interact remotely with the laboratory setup, change parameters like current and frequency, observe the movements of the small magnet suspended vertically by a spring retrieving a video stream, and synchronously watch a 3D simulation making the magnetic fields visible. Although the effective integration of such types of experiments in the curricula, they are designed and developed for student's individual use and not to give benefit to collaborative learning approaches. To overcome this problem, the virtual experiment has been implemented into a collaborative virtual environment.

Carefully reviewing existing virtual 3D worlds, requirements and the technology of the pre-existing version of the experiment have led to build the collaborative learning environment based on Sun Wonderland V 0.4. Project Wonderland (WL) which is entirely written in Java and is a toolkit for creating collaborative virtual environments; see also (Scheucher, Bailey, Gütl, & Harward, 2009). WL supports modeling and rendering 3D

Figure 5. Remote experiment "Force on a Dipole" located at CECI, MIT

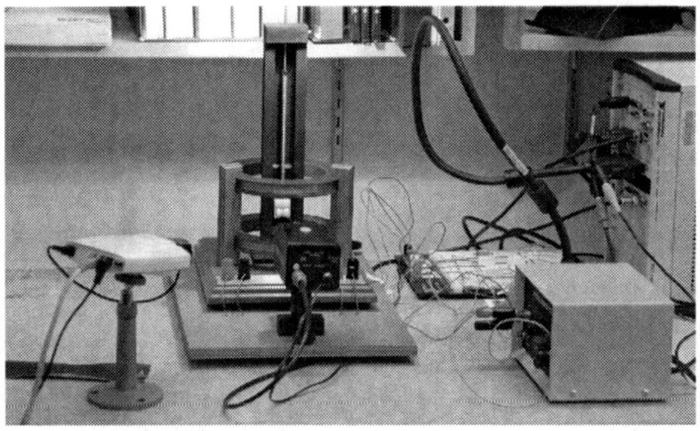

worlds where users can interact with each other's avatars and objects 'in world'. WL also provides a set of tools for communication and collaboration, such as text and voice chat, shared whiteboards, HTML and PDF viewer, streaming video and shared virtual desktops. The WL platform also allows developing and integrating other applications by means of WL cell architecture and interfaces which have also been used to integrate the "Force on Dipole" experiment (see Figure 6).

The experiment is remotely controlled 'in world' by a panel wall depicted on the left-hand side of Figure 6. Each of the students' avatars can take control and adjust settings such as current and frequency. Graphic plots show actual values (retrieved and continuously updated form experiment's place) over time of signal generator, coil current and magnet position. On the right-hand side of Figure 6 there is a video wall placed in world which shows an online video stream of the remote experiment. The 3D simulation of the experiment is located in the middle of Figure 6. It is worth pointing out that both the remote experiment and the simulation are synchronized and enabled participants to perceive different views including the magnetic field.

The collaborative learning environment was designed to enable students to work collaboratively on the experiment but also for instructors to guide the learning task and scaffold understanding. The learning group could make use of multiple communication channels: voice and text chat as well as avatar's non-verbal communication. Furthermore, the learning group could also make use of the other collaboration tools provided by the WL system.

Figure 6. "Force on a Dipole" experiment in collaborative virtual environment Wonderland

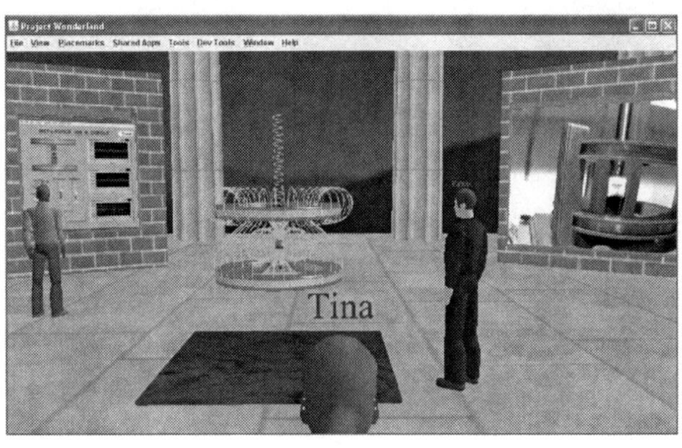

Study Setup

The subjects of the experiment both female and male were recruited from MIT undergraduate students who have already completed the "Electricity and Magnetism Course" and have therefore not only prior knowledge about the topic but have also worked with TEALSim experiments. For the experiment three subjects each were formed and the same teacher who gave the above mentioned course also took the role of the teacher in the virtual world. In order to have controlled experiment conditions, each group was placed in a computer lab like environment and each subject had his or her own working space with a laptop. An instructor guided the subjects through the study and observed them. The teacher was placed separately in a closed room with no direct contact to the student groups.

It is important to emphasize that this research involving humans has been reviewed and was approved for clearance by the responsible ethic authority of the university. The research method was organized as follows: (1) read document describing important information about the survey procedure (10 minutes), (2) introduction of the virtual environment and the 'Force on a Dipole' experiment (20 minutes), (3) Web-based pre-questionnaire collecting demographic information as well as interest in and usage of 3D applications (15 minutes), (4) online physics experiment in developed collaborative learning environment (35 minutes), (5) post-questionnaire getting information on subject's perception of use, benefits and limitations of the learning environment (15 minutes).

The class scenario in the virtual world was organized as follows: after login into the virtual world subjects get 5 minutes time to learn how to navigate and communicate 'in world' and get familiar with the virtual learning space and its collaboration features. After this phase the teacher took over and started with the learning task. He gave the student group an introduction on the experiment setup in virtual world and explained in detail the simulation's visualization, the control panel and how to adjust the settings. Having finished this introductory phase, the teacher worked with each of the students but has also integrated the other students on the experiment activities. More precisely he guided one student after the other through different variants of the experiment and discussed with the student group any phenomena related questions. All subjects of the group got involved by different activities and had the chance to follow the communication also from other peers. Thus they got different viewpoints and learned from their peers' engagement with the teacher as a collaborative learning process. The setting also enabled the students to share their knowledge and opinions during the experiment activities and reflect on phenomena.

Evaluation Results and Discussion

For this preliminary study 6 students aged between 18 and 24 years were recruited. In terms of the subjects' preferences for learning behavior, they liked to learn individually as well as in groups of 2 or more. In case of individual learning at subjects' places, 66.7% indicated that they preferred to ask peers if problems occurred in understanding the learning content. As a means of communication with peers, 83.3% named peer-to-peer as a preferred media. Surprisingly, perceptions of usefulness of Web-based application for communicating with peers for learning purposes was rated low with 66.67% answered negatively and only 33.3% affirmatively. Also interesting are the results on their interest in 3D games: 25% of subjects played several times per month, 25% hardly ever and 50% never. In terms of familiarity and attitude of electromagnetism and 3D simulations, all of the subjects reported positive experience with 3D simulations in physics education, knowledge about TEAL simulations and 66.67% have already used the original version of the "Force on a Dipole" experiment.

During the online activities in class the instructor was able to observe that subjects really enjoyed the environment. They were curious and interested in details of the experiment in virtual world. For example they moved around to watch the dynamic of simulated and visualized fields, they even took the opportunity to fly around getting other perspectives of the physical phenomena. Subjects also were interested to watch closely the video wall to see the remote experiment. They also liked the whiteboard tool to interact and start communicating

The results of the post-questionnaire demonstrated positive feedback in terms of learning experiences and understanding. All participants had the feeling of being together with other students in virtual world and stressed that it was a pleasant experience to communicate with others like in the real world. During the experiment they felt like working together in a laboratory place. Subjects liked to have voice chat as well as text chat, and prefer these chat features in combination with nonverbal avatar communication and awareness more than just video conferencing. Overall they liked the learning environment which enabled them to learn at home, to communicate or even collaborate with their peers, and to talk to and get guidance from the teacher. The overall positive perception of the virtual learning environment may also be backed by the fact that the attitude on the estimated usefulness of 3D virtual worlds has changed from pre-questionnaire to post-questionnaire to the better for all addressed activities, namely to meet new people, to get together with friends, for collaborative meetings, and for collaborative learning purposes.

In order to focus on some interesting details, 50% of subjects had some reservations against working in groups within virtual learning environments. Subjects had the feeling that such virtual learning environments could not replace working together in real world, however, if face-to-face settings were not possible they also indicated that virtual learning environments could offer great opportunities. On some other aspects subjects emphasized positive and negative responses as the following selection illustrates: (a) distance *Collaboration:* "It allows for a great experience when distance is a problem." "While I don't think there will ever be a perfect substitute for real-life interaction, I think this is still a vast improvement over phone calls, video chats, and simple interactive whiteboards." (b) *3D learning space:* "All information is in one place: graphs, video, simulations", "It's much quicker and more interactive than a traditional experiment.", "I enjoyed how each user had control, and that it was not dominated by one user, like some real-life labs." (c) *Learning process and small group interactions:* "Easier to ask for clarification of miscommunications or misunderstandings, being able to see the same data at the same time and have it explained." (d) *Real vs. virtual presence:* "Hands on is really fun, and students will miss out that part of the experiment", "Sometimes it's hard to know what everyone is doing/looking at unless they tell you or their avatar is clearly looking at one thing"

Finally, from the usability viewpoint we were aware of some design issues which also turned out as a result of the experiment. One problem which was emphasized by the students and the teacher as well addressed the placements of the components of the experiment in virtual world which were located in a too wide-spread area. It was suggested to arrange the components in a more compact way to see all of them at same time without moving around. Another issue was that students could not communicate non-verbally in a sufficient natural way. More details of the study can be found elsewhere in Scheucher, Belcher, Bailey, dos Santos and Gütl (2009).

This case study has shown that a virtual 3D world is seen at least as an alternative way to access and performs physics experiments in small groups. The feeling of immersion and the possibility to experience unseen phenomena by 3D simulations combined with real lab settings in a collaborative environment attracted students' attention and kept them motivated. The restriction of the early version of Wonderland on expressiveness of avatars in communication patterns and usability issues on the experiment components in virtual world requires further research and development activities.

LESSONS LEARNED AND PRACTICAL IMPLICATIONS

Starting with general implications from literature review, many e-learning projects failed because of insufficient pedagogical design, inappropriate usage of technologies and a lack of supportive project management. In order to be successful, the learning environment and its technological support need to be carefully planned and all main stakeholders have to be involved in the design process. Fancy features and new technologies must not end up in themselves but should be carefully selected to be in line with the pedagogical objectives and learners' needs.

In order to narrow down to Virtual 3D Worlds (V3DW) as a subclass of collaborative virtual environments, educators and developers can make use of the following advantages in the design of learning environments and settings: multiple communication channels both verbal and non-verbal, reducing barriers between users, feeling of immersion and presence in the environment, awareness of co-learners and objects as well as their (inter-)activities, facilitating collaborative activities on objects and tools, re-creating "real-world" or creating "artificial-world" scenarios, and supporting community building.

Various V3DW are available for educational implementations which can be classified in different dimensions to support the selection process: (1) closed software vs. open source, (2) V3DW as a service vs. local installation, (3) freedom to create and change objects and environments vs. pre-defined learning settings. Also security and privacy issues as well as requirement in terms of ICT-infrastructure (such as internet access policy, client and server application policy, and performance issues) and development environment (programming language, development tools, and availability of libraries, modules and tools) need to be considered.

Second Life provides the virtual environment as a service and charges for a place (comparable to a Web space) or an island (comparable to server hosting) to create learning applications but also for media uploads. 'In world' applications are easy to create and a wide range of (learning) tools and applications is available but there are also limitations in terms of integrating external applications and media types; for example collaborative writing is not supported. Sun Wonderland or Open Wonderland is entirely written in Java, released as open source software and can be easily extended by a convenient and flexible module approach. Also the platform enables programmers and even users to integrate external applications easily. However, the learning curve of development is much steeper and the hosting of the server application must be organized. Both platforms have usability issues (such as limited nonverbal avatar communication and voice chat) and performance issues (such as a limited number of concurrent avatars as well as media or applications in an area).

Despite the above mentioned limitations, both teachers and learners had a positive attitude on V3DW as a tool for collaborative education in geographically dispersed settings. In particular they like the feeling of being together in the environment and aware of each other, to share activities, and to socialize. They also report on the benefit to meet easily at anytime from any place and having all necessary tools together in one environment. On the negative side are concerns on the reliability of the application and the effort to familiarize with the platform. Thus it is recommended to provide lectures on the platform and learning environment, practical training in computer labs and technical support.

To learn about students' preferences and behaviors, in both outlined case studies students were given flexibility in terms of performing the learning process and a limited selection of tools to use. However, for further use cases and detailed experiment recommendations in literature (Coffman & Klinger, 2007; Lee, 2009; Jacobson et al., 2010) will be followed by designing the learning process by well-constructed context-depended activities fostering collaborative learning and appropriate assessment methods. Also pedagogical objectives and learners' preferences require a flexible virtual learning environment in terms of the usage of different collaborative learning tools and learning settings.

SUMMARY AND FUTURE WORK

Our knowledge-driven and globalized society has led to different modern educational strategies including collaborative learning. Such activities apply different approaches in-class or out-of-class which range from classroom discussions to group-based assignments. Collaborative learning can involve students more actively as well as stimulate social and interpersonal skills. Despite the great potential of collaborative learning tools, a great number of pre-existing technologies and implementations have several deficiencies within their use from the interpersonal communication perspective, face limited shared activity awareness and in addition there is also a lack of feeling of co-location. *Virtual 3D worlds* can mitigate or even overcome these problems. Such virtual worlds are characterized by immersion, feeling of presence and social interaction but also to be a persistent online environment, where a large population of users can interact over time. Two case studies have shown that virtual 3D worlds can be used to develop and implement collaborative virtual learning environments for small groups. Learner groups appreciate such environments as an interesting alternative to meet more easily and spontaneously in particular in case they are geographically dispersed. They also like to have such an integrated platform with a set of tools and a variety of communication channels. Virtual 3D worlds also provide promising ways to experience real life world phenomena or different ones in a secure environment and to make invisible phenomena visible. Although collaborative learning environments based on virtual 3D worlds such as Second Life and Open Wonderland have a great potential to make use of immersion as well as the feeling of presence and social interaction, technical restriction and usability issues of 3D world and applications built on top of them reduce significantly the potential of current collaborative virtual learning environments.

On a short term view, we will improve the two learning environments according to the preliminary findings and further administer quantitative and qualitative user studies. On a mid-term perspective, we are interested to provide a solution for a flexible collaborative virtual learning environment which can be configured or even adapted according to needs of the learner group, pedagogic and didactic objectives. This also includes our vision on a highly interactive environment which allows learner groups to experience a great variety of real world phenomena and which also allows hands-on experiments. On a long term view, we are convinced that research and learning communities will approach the notion of not only having a convergence of real and virtual worlds but also to make use of intelligent information access and a 'web' of interlinked virtual worlds where users can easily jump around. Consequently we predict *e-learning 3.0* as virtual learning environment which will not only allow people to learn *anytime* and *everywhere* but also to experience *anything* (real world phenomena or others such as macro world and micro world) *anyhow* (various ways of access such as full immersion or 2,5D on mobile devices) supported by a community of real agents (such as learners, teachers, experts) and virtual agents (such as pedagogical intelligent agents and virtual student peers).

ACKNOWLEDGMENT

Development and survey of the first case study are part of research resulting of visiting academic activities of Simone Kopeinik and Christian Gütl in the School of Information Systems at Curtin University of Technology. The visits were supported and sponsored by School of Information Systems and Curtin Business School, Curtin University of Technology, Perth, Australia and the IICM at Graz University of Technology, Austria. The great work of Simone Kopeinik and the support of Vanessa Chang and Robert Williams as well as the participating students at Curtin University are particularly acknowledged.

Development and survey of the second case study are part of research resulting of visiting academic activities of Tina Scheucher and Christian Gütl in the Center for Educational Computing Initiatives at the MIT. The visits were supported and sponsored by the Center for Educational Computing Initiatives, MIT, USA and the IICM at Graz University of Technology, Austria. The great work of Tina Scheucher and the support of V. Judson Harward, John Belcher and Philip H. Bailey as well as the participating students at the MIT are particularly acknowledged.

REFERENCES

Alavi, M., & Dufner, D. (2005). Technology-mediated collaborative learning: A research perspective. In Hiltz, S. R., & Goldman, R. (Eds.), *Learning together online: Research on asynchronous learning networks* (pp. 191–213). Mahwah, NJ: Lawrence Erlbaum.

Bailenson, J. N., Yee, N., Blascovich, J., Beall, A. C., Lundblad, N., & Jin, M. (2008). The Use of Immersive Virtual Reality in the Learning Sciences: Digital Transformations of Teachers, Students, and Social Context. *Journal of the Learning Sciences*, *17*(1), 102–141. doi:10.1080/10508400701793141

Bernard, R. M., Rojo de Rubalcava, B., & St-Pierre, D. (2000). Collaborative online distance learning: Issues for future practice and research. *Distance Education*, *21*(2), 260–277. doi:10.1080/0158791000210205

Blascovich, J., Loomis, J., Beall, A. C., Swinth, K. R., Hoyt, C. L., & Bailenson, J. N. (2002). TARGET ARTICLE: Immersive Virtual Environment Technology as a Methodological Tool for Social Psychology. *Journal Psychological Inquiry*, *13*(2), 103–124. doi:10.1207/S15327965PLI1302_01

Bouras, C., & Tsiatsos, T. (2006). Educational virtual environments: design rationale and architecture. *Multimedia Tools and Applications*, *29*(2), 153–173. doi:10.1007/s11042-006-0005-7

Bowman, D. A., & McMahan, R. P. (2007). Virtual Reality: How Much Immersion Is Enough? *Computer*, *40*(7), 36–43..doi:10.1109/MC.2007.257

Bransford, J.D., Brown, A.L., & Cocking; R.R. (Eds.) (2000). *How People Learn: Brain, Mind, Experience, and School.* Expanded Edition. Washington D.C: National Academies Press.

Bray, D. A., & Konsynski, B. R. (2007). Virtual worlds: multi-disciplinary research opportunities. SIGMIS. *Database*, *38*(4), 17–25.

Brooks, F. (1999). What's Real About Virtual Reality? *IEEE Computer Graphics and Applications*, *16*(6), 16–27. doi:10.1109/38.799723

Bryson, S. (1996). Virtual reality in scientific visualization. *Communications of the ACM*, *39*(5), 62–71. doi:10.1145/229459.229467

Carlson, W. (2009). *A Critical History of Computer Graphics and Animation – Section 17 - Virtual Reality*. last retrieved September 14, 2009, from http://design.osu.edu/carlson/history/lesson17.html

Chang, V., Gütl, C., Kopeinik, S., & Williams, R. (2009). Evaluation of Collaborative Learning Settings in 3D Virtual Worlds. *International. Journal of Emerging Technologies in Learning (iJET), 4* 6-17. Special Issue: ICL2009, Chittaro, L., & Ranon, R. (2007). Web3D technologies in learning, education and training: Motivations, issues, opportunities. *Computers & Education, 49*(1), 3–18.

Coffman, T., & Klinger, B., M. (2007). Utilizing Virtual Worlds in Education: The Implications of Practice. *International Journal of Social Sciences, 2*(1), 29–33.

Craig, E. M. (2007). Changing paradigms: managed learning environments and Web 2.0. *Campus-Wide Information Systems, 24*(3), 152–161. doi:10.1108/10650740710762185

De Lucia, A., Francese, R., Passero, I., & Genoveffa Tortora, G. (2008). Development and evaluation of a virtual campus on Second Life: The case of SecondDMI. *Computer & Education, 52*(1), 220-233. etrieved April 2, 2010, from http://www.sciencedirect.com/science/article/B6VCJ-4TGGCKR-1/2/b7a76e15ede1c82b93c1c081cd5eb1ba

Dillenbourg, P., Baker, M., Blaye, A., & O'Malley, C. (1996). The evolution of research on collaborative learning. In Spada, E., & Reiman, P. (Eds.), *Learning in Humans and Machine: Towards an interdisciplinary learning science* (pp. 189–211). Oxford, UK: Elsevier.

Gartner (2007). Gartner Says 80 Percent of Active Internet Users Will Have A "Second Life" in the Virtual World by the End of 2011. *Press Release, Gartner Research Inc.,* April 24th, 2007. Retrieved September 9, 2009, from http://www.gartner.com/it/page.jsp?id=503861

Gartner (2008). Gartner Research Inc. Gartner Says 90 Percent of Corporate Virtual World Projects Fail within 18 Months. *Press Release, Gartner Research Inc.,* Mai 15th, 2008. Retrieved September 9, 2009, from http://www.gartner.com/it/page.jsp?id=670507

Griffiths, M. D., & Hunt, N. J. A. (1995). Computer Game Playing in Adolescence: Prevalence and Demographic Indicators. *Journal of Community & Applied Social Psychology, 5*(3), 189–193. doi:10.1002/casp.2450050307

Gütl, C. (2008). *Enhanced Computer-based Support for Personalized Learning Activities.* Post Doctoral Lecture Thesis. Graz University of Technology, Austria. Retrieved September 10, 2009, from http://www.iicm.tugraz.at/guetl/publications/2008/Guetl%202008%20-%20Habil%20final.pdf

Gütl, C., Chang, V., Kopeinik, S., & Williams, R. (2009). 3D Virtual Worlds as a Tool for Collaborative Learning Settings in Geographically Dispersed Environments. In M.E. Auer (Ed.), *ICL 2009* (310-323). Vienna, Austria: International Association of Online Engineering.

Jacobson, M. J., Kim, B., Miao, C., Shen, Z., & Chavez, M. (2010). Design Perspectives for Learning in Virtual Worlds. In Jacobson, M. J., & Reimann, P. (Eds.). *Designs for learning environments of the future: International perspectives from the learning sciences* (111-142). Berlin, Heidelberg: Springer.

Johnson, W. L., & Rickel, J. W. (2000). Animated Pedagogical Agents: Face-to-Face Interaction in Interactive Learning Environment. *International Journal of Artificial Intelligence in Education, 11*(1), 47–78.

Kappe, F., & Gütl, C. (2009). Enhancements of the realXtend framework to build a Virtual Conference Room for Knowledge Transfer and Learning Purposes. In [Chesapeake, VA: AACE]. *Proceedings of EDMEDIA, 2009*, 4113–4120.

Kemp, J., & Livingstone, D. (2006). Putting a Second Life 'Metaverse' Skin on Learning Management Systems. In *Proceedings of the Second Life Education Workshop, Part of the Second Life Community Convention* (13-18). Paisley, UK: The University of Paisley.

Koschmann, T. (2001). Revisiting the paradigms of instructional technology. In G. Kennedy, M. Keppell, C. McNaught & T. Petrovic (Eds.), Meeting at the Crossroads. *Proceedings of the 18th Annual Conference of the Australian Society for Computers in Learning in Tertiary Education.* (pp. 15-22). Melbourne, Australia: Biomedical Multimedia Unit, The University of Melbourne.

Kumar, S., Chhugani, J., Changkyu Kim, C., Kim, D., Nguyen, A., & Dubey, P. (2008). Second Life and the New Generation of Virtual Worlds. *Computer, 41*(9), 46–53. doi:10.1109/MC.2008.398

Lee, M.J.W. (2009). How can 3D virtual worlds be used to support collaborative learning? An analysis of cases from the literature. *Journal of e-Learning and Knowledge Society, 5*(1), 149–158

Leung, W. H., & Chen, T. (2001). Creating a Mulituser 3D Virtual Environment. *IEEE Signal Processing Magazine, 18*(May), 9–16. doi:10.1109/79.924884

Lim, C. P., Nonis, D., & Hedberg, J. (2006). Gaming in a 3D multiuser virtual environment: engaging students in Science lessons. *British Journal of Educational Technology, 37*(2), 211–231. doi:10.1111/j.1467-8535.2006.00531.x

Linden Labs. (2009). Second Life – What is Second Life? *Linden Lab, San Francisco, USA.* Retrieved 22 August, 2009, from http://secondlife.com/whatis/

Monahan, T., McArdlea, G., & Bertolotto, M. (2008). Virtual reality for collaborative e-learning. *Computers & Education, 50*(4), 1339–1353. doi:10.1016/j.compedu.2006.12.008

Prasolova-Førland, E. (2008). Corresponding Author Contact InformationAnalyzing place metaphors in 3D educational collaborative virtual environments. *Computers in Human Behavior, 24*(2), 185–204. doi:10.1016/j.chb.2007.01.009

Redfern, S., & Naughton, N. (2002). Collaborative Virtual Environments to Support Communication and Community in Internet-Based Distance Education. *Journal of Information Technology Education, 1*(3), 201–211.

Rogers, P. C., Liddle, S. W., Chan, P., Doxey, A., & Isom, A. (2007) A Web 2.0 Learning Platform: Harnessing Collective Intelligence, *Turkish Online Journal of Distance Education* 8(3). Retrieved April, 13, from http://tojde.anadolu.edu.tr/tojde27/pdf/article_1.pdf

Rose, F. D., Attree, E. A., Brooks, B. M., Parslow, D. M., Penn, P. R., & Ambihaipahan, N. (2000). Training in virtual environments: transfer to real world tasks and equivalence to real task training. *Ergonomics, 43*(4), 494–511. doi:10.1080/001401300184378

Roussos, M., Johnson, A. E., Leigh, J., Vasilakis, C. A., Barnes, C. R., & Moher, T. G. (1997). NICE: Combining Constructionism, Narrative, and Collaboration. *Computer Graphics, 31*(3), 62–63. doi:10.1145/262171.262264

Safran, C., Helic, D., & Gütl, C. (2007). E-Learning practices and Web 2.0. In Auer, M. (Ed.), *Proc. of Interactive Computer Aided Learning (ICL 2007), Sep. 2007.* Villach, Austria.

Scheucher, B., Bailey, P. H., Gütl, C., & Harward, V. J. (2009). Collaborative Virtual 3D Environment for Internet-accessible Physics Experiments. *International Journal of Online Engineering* (republished), *5* (1) Special issue Rev. 2009, 65-71.

Scheucher, B., Belcher, J. W., Bailey, P. H., dos Santos, F. R., & Gütl, C. (2009). Evaluations Results of a 3D Virtual Environment for Internet-accessible Physics Experiments. In Auer, M. (Ed.), *Proc. of Interactive Computer Aided Learning (ICL 2009), Sep. 2009*. Villach, Austria.

Schrader, P. G., & McCreery, M. (2008). The acquisition of skill and expertise in massively multiplayer online games. *Educational Technology Research and Development, 56*(5-6), 557–574. doi:10.1007/s11423-007-9055-4

Schrank, D. (2009). *A Trustful Payment System for Virtual Worlds - Design and Implementation of a Payment System for Virtual Worlds*. Master Thesis, Graz University of Technology, Austria. Retrieved April 5, 2010, from http://www.iicm.tugraz.at/home/cguetl/projects/PaymentSystemForVirtualWorlds/Schrank_Thesis.pdf

Schroeder, R. (2008). Defining Virtual Worlds and Virtual Environments. *Journal of Virtual Worlds Research, Vol.1* (1). Retrieved April, 2, 2010, from http://journals.tdl.org/jvwr/article/download/294/248

Silva, J. M., Mahfujur Rahman, A. S., & El Saddik, A. (2008). Web 3.0: a vision for bridging the gap between real and virtual. In *Proceedings of the 1st ACM international workshop on Communicability design and evaluation in cultural and ecological multimedia systems* (9-14). New York: ACM.

Sivan, Y. (2008). 3D3C Real Virtual Worlds Defined: The Immense Potential of Merging 3D, Community, Creation, and Commerce. *Journal of Virtual Worlds, 1* (1). Retrieved September 15, 2009, from http://journals.tdl.org/jvwr/article/viewArticle/278

Smith, B. L., & MacGregor, J. T. (1992). What is collaborative learning? In Goodsell, A. S., Maher, M. R., and Tinto, V. (Eds.), *Collaborative Learning: A Sourcebook for Higher Education* (9-22). University Park, PA: National Center on Post-secondary Teaching, Learning, and Assessment.

Snowdon, D., Churchill, E. F., & Munro, A. J. (2001). Snowdon, D., Churchill, E.F. & Munro, A.J. Collaborative Virtual Environments: Digital Spaces and Places for CSCW: An Introduction. In Churchill, E. F., Snowdon, D., & Munro, A. J. (Eds.), *Collaborative Virtual Environments: Digital Places and Spaces for Interaction* (pp. 77–98). London: Springer Verlag.

So, H. J., & Brush, T. (2006). Student perceptions of cooperative learning in a distance learning environment: Relationships with social presence and satisfaction. *Annual Meeting of the American Educational Research Association (AERA),* April 2006, San Francisco, California.

Stacey, E. (1999). Collaborative Learning in an Online Environment. *Journal of Distance Education, 14*(2), 14–33.

Stahl, G., Koschmann, T., & Suthers, D. (2006). Computer-supported collaborative learning: An historical perspective. In Sawyer, R. K. (Ed.), *Cambridge handbook of the learning sciences* (pp. 409–426). Cambridge, UK: Cambridge University Press.

Streuber, S., & Chatziastros, A. (2007). Human Interaction in Multi-User Virtual Reality. *Proceedings of the 10th International Conference on Humans and Computers (HC 2007)* (pp.1-6) Aizu, Japan: University of Aizu, TEAL (2009). Technology Enabled Active Learning (TEAL), Visualizing Electricity and Magnetism at MIT. *MIT*. Retrieved September, 20, 2009, from http://web.mit.edu/8.02t/www/802TEAL3D/teal_tour.htm

KEY TERMS AND DEFINITIONS

Collaborative Learning: Is an abstract concept involving joined intellectual effort by a group of in a wide range of settings.

Collaborative Virtual Environment: Is a virtual space where peoples' avatars can interact with other avatars, non-personal character avatars and intelligent objects in a representational richness including senses such as visual, sound and touch.

Computer-Supported Collaborative Learning: Joined intellectual effort by a learning community is supported by means of computer programs and media.

Immersive Virtual Reality: Technology that replaces real world sensory information with synthetic stimuli such as 3D visual and sound impressions, and force or tactile feedback.

Virtual Environments: Aims on the perception of syntactic sensory information as if they were not synthetic.

Virtual World: Can be characterized by immersion, feeling of presence and social interaction in a persistent online environment, where a large population of users can interact over time.

Chapter 17
From Active Reading to Active Dialogue:
An Investigation of Annotation-Enhanced Online Discussion Forums

Cindy Xin
Simon Fraser University, Canada

Geoffrey Glass
Simon Fraser University, Canada

Andrew Feenberg
Simon Fraser University, Canada

Eva Bures
Bishops University, Canada

Phil Abrami
Concordia University, Canada

ABSTRACT

Our research aims to improve online discussion forums. The authors identify typical problems in online discussion that create difficulties for learners and describe a pedagogical approach emphasizing the importance of moderating in dealing with these problems. The usual design of discussion forums in learning management systems is not helpful but can be improved by specific add-ons. The authors describe a software add-on to the Moodle discussion forum called Marginalia that was designed to implement our preferred pedagogy. They focus on annotation, aiding the retrieval of archived material, helping participants build upon one another's ideas, and encouraging participants to write "weaving" messages that connect ideas and summarize the discourse. Preliminary studies of this software found a number of uses, some of them unexpected. The chapter concludes with an analysis of two trial classes employing Marginalia.

DOI: 10.4018/978-1-61692-898-8.ch017

INTRODUCTION

Human interaction through text based discussion forums is widely employed in online education today. Over the past two decades, many researchers have written about the pedagogical potential of forums for reflection, critical thinking, and collaborative learning. But a number of recent studies have found that there is a lack of deep engagement, and that students do not view forums as a space for critical discourse (Fahy, 2005; Friesen, 2009; Gao & Wong, 2008; Garrison, Anderson, & Archer, 2001Lee & Jeong, 2009; Osman & Duffy, 2009; Rourke & Kanuka, 2007; Shea & Bidjerano, 2009).

Why is this the case? Are forums essentially useless, or can they be improved to promote active and critical engagement? In our previous research we have argued that leadership or moderating is one of the key factors determining the quality of learning in online forums (Feenberg, 1989; Feenberg & Xin; 2003; Xin & Feenberg, 2007). This claim is supported by a number of studies (Celentin, 2007; Meyer, 2003; Garrison, 2001; Luebeck & Bice, 2005). We proposed a set of moderating functions that are fulfilled primarily by the teacher but that can be more or less distributed among the members of the class. These functions bear both social and intellectual content. They include many activities we associate with leadership of discussion in a face-to-face context, such as recognizing participants' contributions and summarizing discussion at key points. The effective performance of these functions initiates, sustains, and advances dialogue online as well as in the classroom. Unfortunately the technical environment in typical web forums does not facilitate moderating. The lack of adequate moderating may explain the failure of many forums to add much value to online courses. Widely used forums, such as those in popular course management systems like WebCT, Blackboard, and Moodle, are little different from those used in the early days of web-based course management systems. Indeed, apart from cosmetic changes, most current forum interfaces are quite similar to the original newsgroup programs from which they descend. Some pedagogically advanced systems have been developed, such as Knowledge Forum (Bereiter & Scardamalia, 2003; Scardamalia, 2004), and TextWeaver (Xin & Feenberg, 2002), but thus far they have not succeeded in entering the mainstream. Knowledge Forum, for example, is based on the theory of "knowledge building" through "scaffolding" user contributions with tags that signify their function in the discourse. It has a rather complex interface and requires a difficult apprenticeship. As a result, it has not achieved widespread adoption despite being well regarded by many educational technologists. Our TextWeaver software was a user-friendly education specific program designed to support a pedagogy emphasizing moderating. In theory such a pedagogy should lead to more and better interaction and intelligent reuse of the forum posts. But TextWeaver was conceived as an application program just before such programs were supplanted by learning management systems running on the web. It too failed to reach a wide audience. In an attempt to address both the pedagogical limitations of existing forums and the problem of adoption, we have developed Marginalia as a web based descendent of TextWeaver (Marginalia, 2010; Xin & Glass, 2005). Marginalia is an open source extension to Moodle that adds annotation and several other features useful for enhancing online discussion. Annotation has gained a certain popularity on the Web as a technique to make interactions more effective. A number of studies have found it helpful for online learning and collaboration (Bateman, Brooks, Mccalla & Brusilovsky, 2007; Carusi, 2003; Farzan & Brusilovsky, 2008; Huang, Huang & Hsieh, 2008; Kaplan & Chisik, 2005; Lee & Calandra, 2004; Nokelainen, Miettinen, Kurhila, Floréen & Tirri, 2005; Wolfe, 2008). By leveraging the popularity of Moodle, we are able to introduce many people to our software and the pedagogy it supports. In any case, the availability of many Moodle sites will enable us to make a thorough test of the hypothesis that annotation and effective moderating can improve educational forums. This paper begins with a discussion of the theoretical grounding of our Marginalia software. This is followed by a discussion of the problems we have identified in existing online forums. We then present its design and explain how Marginalia attempts to address the problems we have identified. Next we share our initial observations on Marginalia's trial use in online classrooms. The paper ends with a summary and a discussion of future research directions.

THE DYNAMICS OF ONLINE DISCUSSION

Online web forums generate a "rolling present," an extended period in which relevance is determined by previous comments. This enables participants to check the appropriateness of their own contributions. But this unique temporal experience has a serious flaw from the standpoint of educational work: the rolling present seems to authorize forgetfulness of the virtual past. Forum design tends to hinder easy movement between the current activity in the discussion and older material, between what is read and what is written, between a given piece of text and other text to which it refers.

This is not simply a matter of static relationships between pieces of text or ideas, but traces the movement and activity of participants. These relationships are essential to a cumulative discussion in which knowledge is gradually gained and deepened. The movement of knowledge acquisition in the forum is cyclical, but it is not repetitive; it is recursive, a spiral rather than a circle. Each time we write or recall, we propel ourselves and the discussion forward. In our earlier research we developed a model of engaged collaborative discourse that describes this cyclical phenomenon (Xin & Feenberg, 2007).

Our model identifies two basic processes in online educational contexts, "intellectual engagement" and "communication." Intellectual engagement is the focus of the collaborative activities. The teacher or a student introduces a theme of discussion and the participants contribute ideas and comment on each other's contributions. In a well-designed course, intellectual engagement is structured by a purposeful agenda related to a disciplinary tradition. If successful, it leads to conceptual change for individuals and gradual convergence for the group. Convergence need not mean agreement but may also take the form of mutual understanding around explicitly developed themes of discussion. We call intellectual engagement, so understood, the foreground process.

This foreground process is constantly supported by the background communication process. "Communication" signifies all the actions and interactions that maintain the flow of messages. Communication has familiar social and psychological aspects that are always involved in human interaction, but we focus also on a cognitive aspect that is particularly significant for the intellectual engagement in which education online consists. This cognitive aspect is the sharing of meanings and assumptions, without which discussion collapses into misunderstanding and confusion. Studies in conversation analysis call this the development of a tacit "common ground" underlying the explicit surface phenomena of the discussion. When interlocutors indicate mutual understanding, for example by tacit signs such as nodding, they implicitly enlarge the common ground of meanings and assumptions on the basis of which their remarks are constructed. Participants in educational forums also test their understanding of the new concepts and theories under discussion in each message they write. The explicit theme of discussion serves as a basis of the test which remains in the background as an implicit question addressed to the group. But unlike in everyday conversation, confirmation online must take an explicit written form since no non-verbal cues are available. When a message is well received, its author can be confident of having mastered the concepts deployed in writing it. The background and foreground processes feed each other, creating the circular motion that advances the discussion as a whole. These two processes are in fact combined in every message in the seamless flow of online talk.

The imbrication of intellectual and communication processes is typical of human communication in general. It is rare that communicative acts have a single well-defined function. Normally, when we speak or write, we do several things at the same time. The resulting complexity of communication is so familiar it is easily overlooked. When we ask if it is time to eat, we may be taken to mean that we are hungry. When we reply to a remark by nodding or saying "yes," we implicitly urge our interlocutor to continue. When we use a certain slang expression we signify our membership in the group that uses that expression. And so on. Though this observation is obvious, its consequences are often overlooked in the course of research, for example, in studies that identify specific utterances with single functions.

The multiplicity of functions and meanings attached to communicative acts proves to be particularly important for understanding online leadership. Most observers agree that online discussions in educational contexts do not flow seamlessly all by themselves. Without maintenance and cultivation, they often stumble (Berge, 1995; Anderson, Rourke, Garrison, & Archer, 2001). As a consequence the participants either do not engage at all or do not engage critically. A good discussion requires strong but not overbearing leadership through complex interventions combining substantive contributions to the discourse with facilitation of the communication process. In online education leadership is usually exercised by the teacher, but leadership functions are often performed by students as well. In fact, we argue that discussions tend to be more successful when this responsibility is shared among the participants.

We summarize leadership activities in ten moderating functions under three categories (Feenberg, 1989; Xin & Feenberg, 2007):

Contextualizing functions: These functions provide a shared framework of rules, roles and expectations for the group and include such performances as stating the theme of the discussion and establishing a communication model (opening discussions), suggesting rules of procedure for the discussion (setting the norms), managing the forum overtime (setting the agenda), and referring to online and offline materials (referring).

Monitoring functions. These functions help participants know if they have successfully obeyed the groups' norms and fulfilled the expectations laid down for them. They include such activities as referring explicitly to participants' comments to acknowledge their contributions (recognition), soliciting comments from individuals or the group (prompting), and assessing or providing feedback on participant accomplishment (assessing).

Meta functions. These functions have to do with the management of process and content and include such activities as repairing communication links (meta comments), summarizing the results of intellectual engagements (weaving), and assigning specific roles to participants (delegating).

Moderating functions mediate between the two basic processes of intellectual engagement and communication so that the discussion as a whole is maintained and advanced. In all these activities the two-sidedness of moderating – social and intellectual – is the key to online pedagogy. Here are some examples:

- The course agenda, implemented in periodic topic raisers, gives a loose academic structure to a discussion that might otherwise lack focus and wander off into multiple monologues or trivialities. Without an agenda participants may become discouraged and fail to see the relevance of the discussion to the course.

Table 1. Summary of moderating functions

Contextualizing functions
1. ***Opening Discussions***. The moderator must provide an opening comment that states the theme of the discussion and establishes a communication model. The moderator may periodically contribute "topic raisers" or "prompts" that open further discussions within the framework of the forum's general theme.
2. ***Setting the norms***. The moderator suggests rules of procedure for the discussion. Some norms are modeled by the form and style of the moderator's opening comments. Others are explicitly formulated in comments that set the stage for the discussion.
3. ***Setting the agenda***. The moderator manages the forum over time and selects a flow of themes and topics of discussion. The moderator generally shares part or all of the agenda with participants at the outset.
4. ***Referring***. The conference may be contextualized by referring to materials available on the Internet, for example, by hyperlinking, or offline materials such as textbooks.
Monitoring functions
5. ***Recognition***. The moderator refers explicitly to participants' comments to assure them that their contribution is valued and welcome, or to correct misapprehensions about the context of the discussion.
6. ***Prompting***. The moderator addresses requests for comments to individuals or the group. Prompting includes asking questions and may formalized as assignments or tasks. It may be carried out by private messages or through public requests in the forum.
7. ***Assessing***. Participant accomplishment may be assessed by tests, review sessions, or other formal procedures.
Meta functions
8. ***Meta-commenting***. Meta-comments include remarks directed at such things as the context, norms or agenda of the forum; or at solving problems such as lack of clarity, irrelevance, and information overload. Meta-comments play an important role in maintaining the conditions of successful communication.
9. ***Weaving***. The moderator summarizes the state of the discussion and finds threads of unity in the comments of participants. Weaving recognizes the authors of the comments it weaves together, and often implicitly prompts them to continue along lines that advance the conference agenda.
10. ***Delegating***. Certain moderating functions such as weaving can be assigned to individual participants to perform for a shorter or longer period.

- Gaining active participation does not go without saying but requires attention from the teacher. In the absence of tacit signs such as looks and nods explicit recognition of contributions is essential to assuring participants that they are on the right track. When students use new concepts in ways that show a lack of understanding, the teacher's recognition can take the form of interventions that help to build a correct and shared understanding.
- Perhaps the most important moderating function from a pedagogical standpoint is summarizing the discussion. In face-to-face settings, the fast pace of discussion and problems of time sharing constitute major obstacles to mutual understanding. We cherish those rare individuals who can sum up what has been said so far and point out the similarities and differences between the various ideas that have been brought up. Such interventions put participants in touch with each other's ideas, recognize their contributions, shape a consensus, and prepare the stage for the next round of discussion. In online discussion forums, this summarizing activity is called "weaving" (Feenberg, 1989; Kaye, 1992; Scardamalia & Breiter, 1991; Sorensen, E. & Takle, 2001). Students can be assigned to write weaving comments as a challenge to their ability to engage with the ideas of others. This is a valuable way to fulfill the dialogic potential of online education but it is made technically difficult by a number

of problems with online forums we outline in the next section.

PROBLEMS OF EXISTING FORUMS

Participants in online discussions encounter a number of problems, some due to technical limitations, others related to the asynchronous nature of the medium. Many of these problems might be ameliorated with better technical design.

1. *Reading and Writing.* Reading and writing are not independent tasks. Critical engagement with a text (so-called "active reading") requires the reader to formulate her reactions by taking notes on posts and writing replies. But writing a note or reply involves alternating writing with reading, shifting back and forth between the two modes. If this is difficult, reflections are likely to be lost before they can be recorded. In a busy forum many participants may simply choose not to write at all as their memory of the posts that interest them fades amidst the task of reading a large amount of new material.
2. *Visual Disconnection.* Related posts are often not displayed together. In many cases, they are not visible at the same time, or if they are, they are reduced to subject lines which seldom reflect the contents of the message. In many cases, participants reply to a post simply because it is convenient, not because what they want to say bears directly on what they are replying to. This problem of disconnection weakens attribution and pulls attention away from significant posts. It also makes use of the archive difficult since its "threads" may be false leads to relevant content.
3. *Short Attention Span.* People tend to focus on the most recent posts, leaving older posts and ideas behind (Hewitt, 2003). This applies equally to writing and to reading. The visual disconnection mentioned above contributes to this, as does the nonlinear nature of a discussion that breaks into multiple threads. This can derail the discussion, or it can lead to repetition: rather than advancing the discussion, posts are likely to unknowingly repeat ideas that have already been discussed.
4. *Under-used Archive.* One of the key advantages of online discussion over face-to-face conversation is the presence of an archive. Older posts can be revisited and consulted at any time. However, archives are hard to reference and are relatively unstructured; despite their promise they are under-used. This amplifies the problem of the short attention span since not only do posts fall out of memory quickly, but it is difficult to go back and find them later. The contents of many forums could be valuable resources, but end up being lost to view even before the discussion is finished, or never found at all by interested people who were not participants in the discussion but have access to its transcript.
5. *Communication Anxiety.* Phatic expressions such as "Hey, how's it going?" "Yes, go on" "See you later" are common in face-to-face conversation, and are essential for keeping a conversation going. Non-verbal signs such as looks and facial expressions supply additional tacit cues to assure interlocutors that their remarks are heard or to signal that the communication is threatened and needs repair. The paucity of phatic expressions and the absence of non-verbal signs online amplifies communication anxiety and results in people hesitating to participate. Lurking and low levels of activity are the bane of online forums (Feenberg, 1989). Many standard forums supply emoticons in an attempt to compensate, but this is a feeble solution to a major problem.
6. *Quoting.* Quoting is a common and important part of written dialogue. It recognizes the

contributions of others, indicates the lineage of ideas, and promotes interaction. However, many current forums do not provide easy ways for people to quote each other's remarks. Copying and pasting passages of text from previous posts is cumbersome and time consuming, especially when those texts are difficult to recall and locate. This can lead to lower interactivity, and ultimately affect idea development.

7. *Tagging*. Turoff (1991) notes that effective discussion software should allow individuals to classify their contributions into meaningful categories that reflect their relevance and significance according to the nature of the topic, the objective of the discussion, and the characteristics of the group. While this suggests a rather formalized scheme, such as is discussed in relation to learning objects, a more modest and more easily implemented practice of classification would be helpful. We will call such classifications "tags." Individualized tagging of forum content enables participants to find for later use items of interest identified in the course of reading. It facilitates recall and supports more targeted searching (Marlow, Naaman, Boyd & Davis, 2006). Standard forums do not provide such capability.
8. *Weaving*. Given the fact that the record of a web based discussion is available for retrieval and study, this activity is much easier than in face-to-face settings. However, it still requires considerable effort. As a result, weaving messages are rare. We argue that the compound problems of reading and writing, visual disconnection, quoting, and tagging contribute to this rarity. Forums can and should be improved to make weaving easier.

MARGINALIA

Many add-ons have been proposed to overcome the limitations of existing discussion forums. Calvani and his collaborators identify the following essential elements of an improved forum design for the Moodle Learning Management System (Calvani, Fini, Pettenati, & Sarti, 2006). They write from the standpoint of Computer Supported Collaborative Learning (CSCL):

1. basic CSCL functions; more specifically some functions of a traditional discussion forum, with the objective of selecting some essential functions and make them particularly ergonomic and effective;
2. some management functions; such as rules to activate specific actions, features for interactions tracking and evaluation of contribution coherence, with the objective of avoiding potential risks (dispersiveness, overload, respect of due dates, etc.) through more structured dialogic activities;
3. some functions to support reflection and metacognition, to help the community in the definition of its own path to effective knowledge construction (Calvani, et al., 2006).

A number of add-ons have been developed for the Moodle web forum which reflect the first of these desiderata by extending the capability of the system for synchronous conferencing (Conroy, 2008; Jonnavithula, 2008; Key To School, 2010). This capability is enhanced by various programs that enable forum users to deliver visually interesting presentations online. We have developed Marginalia as an extension to the Moodle discussion forum with other aspects of the first and especially the third points in mind. The design is based on the pedagogical approach outlined above and aims specifically to support the moderating functions and improved access to the forum archive. The following is a discussion of Marginalia's design and features.

To overcome the limitations of existing discussion forums and to facilitate the exercise of the moderating functions, we have developed Marginalia as an extension to the Moodle discussion forum. The following is a discussion of its design and features.

Creating and editing annotations. The software's core feature is annotation: the capability to highlight passages of text in forum posts and write short notes in the margin next to them, just as the reader of a book might underline passages and scribble notes in the margin. Using the technique of annotating text mitigates many of the problems with web forums discussed above, and opens up their full potential in education.

In Marginalia an annotation can be edited after creation. Figure 1 illustrates annotated forum posts.

Annotations allow users to read and write simultaneously and to collect what they find to be the most interesting or important ideas in a discussion for future reference. Marginal notes are not intended to substitute for forum posts; rather they are snapshots of a reader's immediate (and often incomplete) thoughts. Being able to see the marginal notes alongside the posts creates the visual connection between the reader's reactions and the context, a link that is typically missing in standard forums. In addition to this primary function of annotations, they recognize the writer of the comment to which they have been attached.

Public vs. private annotations. When a user creates an annotation, she may choose to make it private or public. If it is private, only she can view it. If it is public, it is available for others to read. By default, all annotations are public. We made this design choice hoping that people would share. Indeed, they did, and to our surprise, they used the margin as a second channel of communication, as will be detailed in the results section of this paper.

Summary of annotations. To facilitate retrieval and make use of archived materials, annotations are also collected together on a separate summary page, where they are displayed alongside the highlighted excerpt to which they refer. The summary can be searched and filtered. For example, a user might choose to search the summary for annotations containing a particular phrase, or view only

Figure 1. Marginalia annotations in Moodle forum

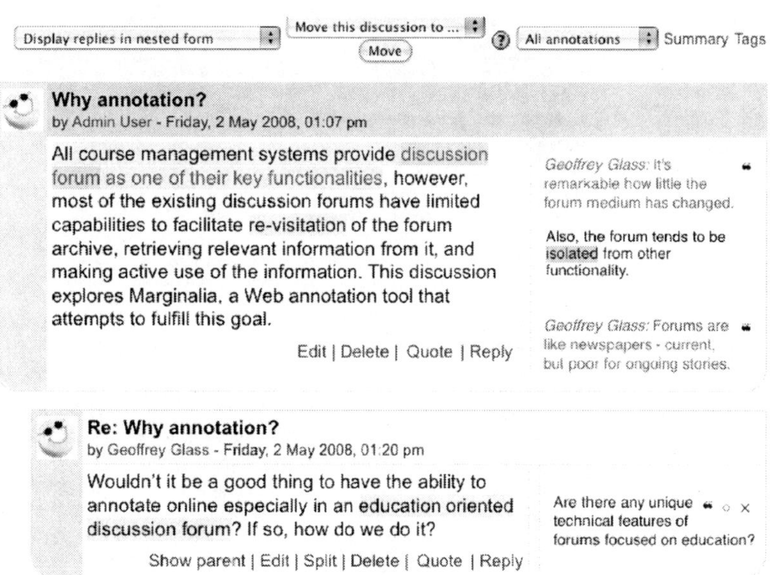

annotations by a particular user. The summary page is shown in Figure 2.

The summary page, along with the quoting feature described next, are designed to support the writing of weaving messages. The writer can use his or her own annotations and tags to identify passages on which to comment in a weaving message.

Quoting. We implemented a special quoting feature to make it easier to quote other discussion posts and encourage recognition. To use this feature, a participant highlights a passage of text and then simply click on the quote button. The highlighted text is automatically pasted into the reply window with a hyperlink to its original post. This can be done repeatedly to include multiple quotes in a single reply, as in a weaving comment. A quote button beside margin notes allows them to be quoted in the same fashion. This is particularly useful for writing comments that develop a reaction first expressed in the margin.

Tagging. Marginalia makes it easy to establish and use a fixed vocabulary for marginal notes. Marginalia detects when the same note is used more than once and offers to auto-complete subsequent uses. The note is then called a "tag." Standard schemas like this can be pedagogically valuable. For example, a teacher can create a set of pre-defined tags for students to apply when reading each other's posts; this can be used to drive various types of further engagement, such as main points to be summarized, new areas of discussion, questions to be followed up, and so on. In another application, a language or writing teacher can tag errors in order to summarize problems of usage with reference to students' contributions. Alternatively, tagging can be used for content analysis, or to simplify future retrieval of annotations about a particular topic.

In summary, Marginalia is intended to make it easier to read, recall, and write forum posts, to help participants perform the moderating functions, to acknowledge each other's contributions, question

Figure 2. Marginalia summary page

Find [ ] (Go) (?)

Showing annotations by anyone in discussion "Why annotation?":

Discussion: Why annotation?

Re: Why annotation? by Geoffrey Glass	we come to conceptualize of public opinion is in two forms: the local, common sense and the positivist public opinion poll	how has non-local technology changed the significance and influence of these forms?	❝ geof
	Habermas describes this sense of opinion as "a basically suspicious repute among the multitude" (p. 89)	quote	❝ geof
Re: Why annotation? by Cindy Xin	their ability to facilitate re-visitation is still limited	I would really like to see clean integration of forums with wikis, so that it would be easy to push text to the archive.	❝ ○ x Me
	asynchronous discussion	A benefit of online education.	❝ ○ x Me
	value-added ways	Ideas must remain in motion, always changing.	❝ ○ x Me
Weaving by Geoffrey Glass	Making notes while reading creates an archive	Can be a social activity.	❝ ○ x Me
	"weaving" comments	one purpose of Marginalia	❝ geof
↑source & author	*↑highlighted text*	*↑margin note*	*↑user*

Subscribe to updates to this page (only recent public annotations will be included).

and solicit further comments, strengthen communication links, and help teachers provide feedback on students' posts. Marginalia is expected to be especially useful for gathering the ideas and references for writing effective weaving comments.

METHODOLOGY

Research Questions

Our main research questions are:

1. How is Marginalia used and how do our users perceive its usefulness?
2. What kind of conversations or social interactions, if any, does Marginalia support?
3. In what ways, if any, does Marginalia support revisitation, reflection, and idea development?

Participants and Procedures

Participants were from two mixed-mode classes: an upper undergraduate class in philosophy and a graduate class in e-learning. The undergraduate philosophy class met face-to-face on a weekly basis. Ten students and one instructor (total 8 male, 3 female) participated in the two-week online discussion in the last two weeks of the semester during which the research was implemented. All students were regular full-time undergraduates. The online discussion topic was the public sphere. The students were told at the outset that one of them would be asked to write a weaving message at the end of the discussion. Indeed, one male student was asked and he wrote a weaving message.

The graduate e-learning class met face-to-face on a bi-weekly basis. The two-week online discussion took place in the middle of the semester (sixth and seventh weeks). Six people (1 male, 5 female) participated in the research. A guest instructor, who is the first author of this article, led the two-week discussion on online interaction. The course instructor took a participant role like the four regular students who were part-time working adults. Table 2 provides a summary.

Both classes received a demonstration of the Marginalia software before they started their online discussion. All participants had participated in online discussion before. A questionnaire was emailed to all the participants (n=17). Nine responded.

The two classes varied significantly in terms of their content of discussion, number of participants, and mix of gender. Both used the software over a period of two weeks.

Methods

No experimental design was used at this initial stage of our research, as we mainly wanted to observe how teachers and students used the tool. Both quantitative and qualitative methods were used for analysis of the results. Basic descriptive statistics of posts and annotations provided a measure of activity volume and its similarity and variance between classes. Content analysis applied to both forum posts and annotations allowed us to look into the nature and quality of users' writing and to trace the lineage of idea development. A coding scheme based on the moderating functions achieved an inter-rater reliability of 0.71 (Fleiss kappa) with three raters. The unit of analysis is

Table 2. Summary of the online discussions of the two classes

Class	Time of offering	Topic of discussion	Forum duration	# of Participants
Philosophy	Fall 2007	The public sphere	2 wks	11 (8 M, 3 F)
e-Learning	Spring 2009	Online interaction	2 wks	6 (1 M, 5 F)

the message. A message can perform multiple functions and therefore may be assigned to multiple categories. We also used keyword analysis to identify topics of discussion and their associated posts and marginal notes. Combined with the analysis of the use of moderating functions, this allowed us to see how topics were raised and developed. It also showed the interaction between participants, the building of common ground, and the dynamic movement between the two processes of communication and intellectual engagement. A survey of user experiences and perceptions helped us to explore further details about usage, such as the use of private notes, and to verify the interpretations of the online transcripts.

OBSERVATIONS FROM INITIAL TRIAL CLASSES

Basic Usage

We did a basic usage count of the level of activity in the two classes. All the analyses in this section include the data from both the students and the instructors. The 11 participants of the philosophy class made 25 discussion posts. Five of the participants used Marginalia, creating 84 annotations – 16.8 per user (standard deviation 14.7). The 7 participants of the e-learning class made 45 posts. All but two used Marginalia, creating a total of 178 annotations – 29.7 per user (standard deviation 16.7). Table 3 summarizes the usage of the two classes.

The above table shows that the e-learning class had much higher levels of activity than the philosophy class in terms of both the total and average number of posts created and the total and average number of marginal notes created. This difference may be due to the fact that the e-learning class met less frequently than the philosophy class and relied more heavily on online discussion. The e-learning class was also more interested in the tool given the focus of the course and topic of the discussion. The different timing of these two two-week online discussions (one at the end of the semester and the other right in the middle) may also have contributed to the difference in levels of activities. It should be noted in any case that many of the posts in the philosophy class were lengthy and well argued. However given the very different nature of the two classes and the absence of controls, it is impossible to tell for sure what factors caused the variances in the data.

Despite the differences, one thing does stand out: users created many more annotations than forum posts. Also, the student asked to write a weaving message at the end of a week's discussion in the philosophy class made 2.5 times number of annotations (33) as the next most prolific student (who made 13), and 11 times as many as the least prolific (who made 3).

Still more revealing was an examination of how the annotations were used, and the survey responses of the participants.

All together we received 9 survey responses out of 17 participants. Seven out of the nine respondents had used Marginalia and two did not, though the latter reported that they tried the software and would have made use of it if there were more time for discussion. One student from

Table 3. Activity and usage level of the two classes

Class	Forum duration	# of Participants	# of Posts	Avg # of post per participant	# (%) of Marginalia (M) Users	# of Annotations	Avg # of Notes per M user
Philosophy	2 wks	11	25	2.3	5 (45%)	84	16.8
e-Learning	2 wks	6	45	7.5	6 (100%)	178	29.7

the philosophy class said s/he wished the tool had been used for the whole semester.

Highlighting and annotation were by far the most used features, followed by the summary page. Two instructors and one student used tagging. Two students from the philosophy class reported that they would have used the tagging feature had the online forum lasted longer than two weeks. As a newly-developed feature, quoting was introduced only at the end of the last class (e-Learning). Only two people used the feature. In our previous research on the use of quoting in TextWeaver, we found it was one of the most popular features.

The following comments by students and teachers provide more detail about usage. They are not grounds for making claims about the effectiveness of Marginalia; rather they are here to illustrate the kind of testimonies we have received from our users.

Active Reading

At the level of the individual forum participant, marginalia provides a way to easily record thoughts while reading. Based on our own study of the users' annotations, we observed that they were created to

- clarify in one's own mind what is happening in a post and record such thoughts;
- paraphrase or restate the highlighted text in the reader's own words;
- summarize what was said in the highlighted text;
- make connections to other readings, thoughts, or personal experience;
- label texts under keywords or tags

Users commented,

"I used the highlight function to mark up other people's texts for personal referencing when the time came to write my own response."

"I used the highlights and annotations as a sort of index for the whole discussion."

"I used highlighting and annotation in the same way I'd use them when reading a physical text. It reminded me of what I found significant and allowed me to summarize entire discussions with ease."

"I made a few notes relating to my readings for the term paper"

The immediacy of the margin - always available directly beside the text being read - makes it easy to write quick notes. One user remarked, "This technology is like thought graffiti. Captures instant ideas in a flexible manner. [It] was the immediacy and the personalization of the annotations. They can be 'of the moment'- as is graffiti - sort of 'writing on the wall' but with some thought behind it - pedagogical thought."

These comments tell us that Marginalia has blurred the line between reading and writing, making it easier for readers to quickly and reflectively engage with a post. This is evident simply from the number of highlights and marginal notes made by the users. In particular, one user said, "I'm also finding that I'm writing to express my thoughts on others' text entries as a way of engaging myself with the text - that I interact with the text, makes me more connected to the message and therefore hopefully more engaged as a learner."

Past and Present

Marginalia allows users to do more than just add notes to the posts: it allows users to interact with the texts through various types of sorting and filtering. Six out of eight survey respondents (not counting the Marginalia non-user) reported that they referred back to their annotations when writing new posts. For example, they commented,

"I used summary page to scan my own annotations."

"I used the annotations as a memory aid, so that I could write a summary of the discussion."

"I liked being able to go back [to the annotations] and reread for clarification or to pick up on something I had missed earlier."

"I found myself constantly going back over things to review."

The experience of reviewing the written record of a forum discussion is completely different from that of a participant in the action. The latter is situated in a "rolling present", while the former is witnessing the surviving evidence of a conversation. The use of annotation creates a second-order temporality bridging the past and the present. As one user put it, "I like the fact that you can reignite your points by using Marginalia - i.e. you can go back and highlight a key point and essentially 'say it again' in the margins with perhaps a more directed question."

Of course all discussions do this to some degree. With no reference to the past there would be no thread of conversation, no connection between isolated statements or posts. The discussion would suffer from a narrow attention span, likely repeating itself or going off on a tangent. Marginalia extends and refines the cyclical process of taking elements of the past and incorporating them into the present with new ideas and material. Its features support continuity with change over a longer time span, enriching and deepening the discussion.

From Private to Public

We anticipated that most users would use the forum margin as they might use the margin in a book: to make notes for future personal reference, as described above. However, only one user reported private use. She said she made a couple of private notes, once because she disagreed with something in a post but did not want to contest it or "open a can of worms', once for use in a paper that had nothing to do with the class discussion.

All other notes were public. Had we chosen a different default, presumably the results would have been different. Defaulting to private might change the character of usage significantly but not necessarily for the better. It was because their notes were public that participants were able to use the margin as a second channel of communication.

Chit-Chat

Margin notes were often more conversational than the more careful writing in forum posts. Initially, when we found students carrying out conversations in the margin, we thought this would create further confusion in an already multi-threaded discussion. Besides which, the margin is small and not designed for discussion. Regardless, participants persisted in talking to each other in the margin. In a number of cases someone would highlight a passage of text and make a note in the margin. Then someone else would reply with a second note on the same passage. Further responses often followed. Perhaps the model for this unexpected usage was text messaging, Twitter or the "Wall" in Facebook, interfaces with which we were less familiar than the students.

We worried that the margin would clog up. We observed users splitting text across multiple margin notes to circumvent Marginalia's 250-character-per-note limit. Yet when all the notes in the margin reached a certain length, seldom much exceeding the length of the post, users stopped adding more. Any further discussion was folded back into the main flow of the forum.

As we watched participants engage in the margin, we realized we had been wrong: these conversations had a positive impact. They promoted more dialogue. Short notes provided an easy way for reluctant participants to overcome communication anxiety and get involved. A good portion of the notes were simple statements of agreement or support, such as "I agree" or "Thanks."

One user pointed out that marginal notes sometimes resemble the non-verbal cues in face-to-face conversations. Because they are shared, and because it is so easy for many users to make a short comment, they contribute to the sense that the whole group is present and participating. Such brief responses reassure participants and build common ground but are relatively rare in conventional forums where an entire post might feel wasted on a single word.

Here are some comments from users that confirm these observations.

"I am beginning to think of 'thought graffiti,' or annotations as being rather like the non-verbal communication you get during a face-to-face discussion. Instead of nods, to agree with what you are saying, or frowns and a tilting of the head to express confusion, or a little remark that indicates that person is listening and comprehending what you are saying, this discussion has annotations. They add a group feeling to the discussion because now we can read not only what one person is writing (or listen to what one person is saying), we can also read the rest of the groups' immediate responses (or smiles, or nods, or frowns) and hear their interjections into the conversation."

Another user pointed out the use of the technology to call for responses to what she had written: "I am passionately interested in this tool. As a user of discussion forums, I've had many post[s] fail to get a response. Some of these times I've taken it personally, as I posted something that is important to me and when it isn't picked up by someone, I find it sometimes disheartening... This technology allows me to go back to my post, add another layer of clarification/or expansion which might perhaps then evoke a response."

Annotation can reduce the community anxiety participants often feel when they receive no response. A response to a post – any response – is generally interpreted as a success while silence means failure (Feenberg, 1989). Additionally, the sender of a message needs to know not only that it was received, but how it was received. Writing online can be uncomfortable without the nods of the head, smiles, glances, and tacit signs which in everyday conversation often take the place of words.

One user commented: "[T]here is more motivation to post when it is fuelled by something dynamic and interactive, something conversational and social—Marginalia, for example... There's a certain joy in the pursuit of responding to graffiti. It hearkens back to the human need for call-and-response."

This use of the margin as a form of lightweight conversation (often less serious than what was carried out in posts) lubricated the discussion. It thus fulfilled important social functions in online conversation. Even when they had nothing substantive to say, these notes helped to involve people in the cycle of reading and writing by which the discourse proceeded and developed.

Recursion

While chit-chat and "nods on the side" were significant uses of Marginalia, they were not the only uses. Often the margin played an important role in deepening substantive discussion in the forum.

In the e-learning class, students used Marginalia extensively as a conversation tool, responding to the authors of posts and to the authors of other marginal notes. These responses were either comments or questions, often triggering a stream of conversation in the margin.

We observed that many times when a new message was posted, comments about it quickly appeared in the margin. These mini-conversations branched off from the main discussion, forming a background in which participants could clarify points, repair communication breakdowns, or chat socially. Sometimes these conversations introduced new ideas. When this happened, the ideas introduced in the margin were often brought to the main discussion area where they were elaborated in more detail.

Thus the social nature of the activity in the margin contributed to the recursive development of the discussion. Ideas and attention shifted between the foreground forum posts and the background conversation in the margin. The two spaces fed each other, driving the overall discussion forward. At the individual level understanding was enhanced, while the group enlarged their common ground and established mutual understanding and convergence of ideas.

Moderating

We observed that Marginalia helped people to perform the moderating functions. Each public annotation recognizes the post author unless the author made the annotation herself. Many notes also performed functions such as prompting, referring, and meta commenting. Short weaving notes that linked multiple ideas together also appeared in the margin.

The performance of moderating functions via marginal notes varied between the two classes. The e-learning class had significantly higher level of performance (79% of the total notes) compared to the philosophy classes (20%). The overall level of interaction in the e-learning class was also noticeably higher. Although it is difficult to pin point the cause of the difference, in both classes Marginalia helped people to perform the moderating functions in various ways. Many notes performed one or more functions. These marginal notes questioned each other, provided materials and context for discussion, clarified misunderstanding or confusion, and repaired communication breakdowns. Table 4 provides a summary.

Note:

1. Since by definition, each highlight or marginal note is a form of recognition to the post author, instead of counting them all, we counted only the replies in the marginal notes. A reply is defined as an explicit response to a question or comment in a post, or an explicit response to a marginal note.
2. A note can perform multiple functions and therefore can be assigned multiple times. In calculating the total, a note counts and only counts once when it performed one or more functions.

Summary of Observations

Based on our initial observations of these two online classroom trials, we conclude that the annotation technique is used to

- index and recall,
- think and reflect,
- explain and clarify, and
- share and communicate.

Further study will be necessary to support our initial conclusion that using Marginalia improves the exercise of the moderating functions through both forum posts and marginal notes, and encourages forum participants to be more engaged with the text and with each other.

FUTURE RESEARCH AND DEVELOPMENT

So far our strategy of keeping our software open source and making it a plug-in to the popular Moodle system has proven successful. A num-

Table 4. Use of prompting, recognition, referring, meta-commenting, and weaving via marginal notes of the three classes

Class	# of Users	# of Anno-tations	# of prompt-ing	# of reply [1]	# of referr-ing	# of meta comment-ing	# of weaving	Total [2]
Philosophy	5	84	12 (14.3%)	0 (0%)	4 (4.8%)	1 (1.2%)	0 (0%)	17 (20.2%)
e-learning	6	178	25 (14.0%)	139 (78.1%)	20 (11.2%)	27 (15.2%)	4 (2.2%)	140 (78.7%)

ber of institutions in Canada have been testing Marginalia. These include Simon Fraser University, Bishops University, University of Victoria, Kwantlen Polytechnic University, Thompson Rivers University, and Capilano University. We have received an overwhelming amount of positive feedback. This typically includes comments on the ease of use and elegant interface of the program. One of the biggest advantages for teacher is the ability to easily provide in-context feedback to their students. One teacher emailed us, "Using Marginalia in my Moodle Forums has changed my teaching fundamentally. Correcting/commenting my students translations – I'm teaching Latin and Greek – has become very convenient for me and clear for my students." Students appreciate the ability to quickly interact with others and make brief low-stake comments. In addition to this feedback, we also received many valuable suggestions for improvement. For example, some users have requested that teachers be able to share annotations privately with individual students. Many users have suggested that Marginalia extend its features to the Moodle Assignment tool.

As the software is being used in more online classrooms, we need to continue observing usage patterns, verifying our initial findings, and studying the use of the tool in connection with other channels of communication (e.g., face-to-face, email, online chat) in blended or completely online learning environments. We also want to examine whether certain user behavior patterns emerge. For example, would the conversational gravity shift from the main discussion area to the margin for some users? Would previously reluctant group members participate more because of the availability of Marginalia?

We plan to conduct controlled experiments to investigate the social and pedagogical effects of Marginalia. Does Marginalia indeed enhance online interaction, and under what conditions? Does it increase the level of critical engagement, and under what conditions?

A number of faculty members from various disciplines such as English, communication, business, nursing, computer science and social science have expressed interest in using Marginalia in their classes. We are keen to see how Marginalia is used with the different pedagogies appropriate to literary criticism, case history analysis, contract negotiation, programming, etc.

Both tagging and quoting features are relatively new. We need to continue observing how users make use of them and what effect they have on interaction and learning if any.

New developments are always on the horizon. As more and more people use Marginalia in more and more diverse contexts, we hope to refine the software and perhaps to inspire others to design similar program for other platforms. This is a cyclical process that will continue as the idea of online annotation gains in popularity.

CONCLUSION

Online discussion forums are intended to add human contact between teachers and students to online education. This goal is widely shared by educational theorists and teachers skeptical of automated learning. But problems with online forums are commonplace and some recent research has cast doubt on their educational value. This article examines the sources of these problems and introduces a solution based on software features supporting appropriate pedagogical strategies. The Marginalia software described here is a pedagogy driven design that is easy to install and use. The pedagogy it supports emphasizes the role of leadership—"moderating"—in organizing successful education forums. Moderating functions are identified and explained briefly on the basis of earlier work by the authors. Good moderating contributes to learning by encouraging participation and interaction while delivering an academic agenda.

Annotation, a key feature of the software, is seen as a technique that can be used in many ways to promote interaction and learning. It facilitates access to and re-use of forum materials and makes it easier for teachers and students to recognize and comment on each others' efforts. Annotation changes the way time is experienced in forums by prolonging the domain of relevance.

Tests on Marginalia in trial classes are analyzed here in view of understanding usages and improving the software. The software was employed in expected ways with some success by students and teachers in these classes, but students innovated unanticipated usages as well. Future work on the software will have to take into account what was learned in these first trial classes.

REFERENCES

Anderson, T., L. Rourke, Garrison, D. R, Archer, W. (2001). Assessing teaching presence in a computer conferencing environment. *Journal of Asynchronous Learning Networks, 5(2)*.64-74

Bateman, S., Brooks, C., Mccalla, G., & Brusilovsky, P. (2007). Applying collaborative tagging to e-learning. In *Proceedings of the Workshop on Tagging and Metadata for Social Information Organization, 16th International World Wide Web Conference (WWW'07)* (pp.548-556), ACM, New York.

Bereiter, C., & Scardamalia, M. (2003). Learning to work creatively with knowledge. In E. De Corte, L. Verschaffel, N. Entwistle, & J. van Merriënboer (Eds.), *Unravelling basic components and dimensions of powerful learning environments*. EARLI Advances in Learning and Instruction Series; Retrieved January 9, 2010, from http://ikit.org/fulltext/inresslearning.pdf

Berge, Z. L. (1995). Facilitating computer conferencing: Recommendations from the field. *Educational Technology, 15*(1), 22–30.

Calvani, A., Fini, A. Pettenati, M. C., & Sarti, L. (2006). Remarks on CSCL theories applied to open source solutions for the design of collaborative learning environments. *Journal of e-Learning and Knowledge Society, 2(1)*, 21-74.

Carusi, A. (2003). Taking philosophical dialogue online. *Discourse: Learning and Teaching in Philosophical and Religious Studies, 3*(1), 95–156.

Celentin, P. (2007). Online training: Analysis of interaction and knowledge building patterns among foreign language teachers. *Journal of Distance Education, 21*(3), 39–58.

Conroy, J. (2008, February 01). Moodle gets WiZiQ - A free virtual classroom add-on. *CMS Wire*. Retrieved January 9, 2010, from http://www.cmswire.com/cms/web-cms/moodle-gets-wiziq-a-free-virtual-classroom-addon-002260.php

Fahy, P. J. (2005). Two methods of assessing critical thinking in computer-mediated communications (CMC) transcripts. *International Journal of Instructional Technology and Distance Learning, 2*(3).

Farzan, R., & Brusilovsky, P. (2008). AnnotatEed: A social navigation and annotation service for web-based educational resources. *New Review of Hypermedia and Multimedia, 14*(1), 3–32. doi:10.1080/13614560802357172

Feenberg, A. (1989). The written world. In Mason, R., & Kaye, A. (Eds.), *Mindweave: Communication, computers, and distance education* (pp. 22–39). Oxford, UK: Pergamon Press.

Feenberg, A., & Xin, M. C. (2003). Facilitation. In A. DiStefano, K. E. Rudestarn, & R. Silverman (Eds.), *Encyclopedia of Distributed Learning*, London: Sage Publications.pp. 163-166. Retrieved September 18, 2009, from http://www.textweaver.org/facilitation.htm

Friesen, N. (2009). Genre and CSCL: The Form and Rhetoric of the Online Posting. *International Journal of Computer-Supported Collaborative Learning*, *2*(4), 171–185. doi:10.1007/s11412-009-9060-1

Gao, F., & Wong, D. (2008). Student engagement in distance learning environments: A comparison of threaded discussion forums and text-focused wikis. *First Monday*, 13 (1). Retrieved September 18, 2009, from http://www.uic.edu/htbin/cgiwrap/bin/ojs/index.php/fm/article/view/2018/1921

Garrison, D. R., Anderson, T., & Archer, W. (2000). Critical thinking in a text-based environment: Computer conferencing in higher education. *The Internet and Higher Education*, *11*(2), 1–14.

Garrison, D. R., Anderson, T., & Archer, W. (2001). Critical thinking and computer conferencing: A model and tool to assess cognitive presence. *American Journal of Distance Education*, *15*(1), 7–23. doi:10.1080/08923640109527071

Hewitt, J. (2003). How habitual online practices affect the development of asynchronous discussion threads. *Journal of Educational Computing Research*, *28*(1), 31–45. doi:10.2190/PMG8-A05J-CUH1-DK14

Huang, Y.-M., Huang, T.-C., & Hsieh, M.-Y. (2008). Using Annotation Services in a Ubiquitous Jigsaw Cooperative Learning Environment. *Journal of Educational Technology & Society*, *11*(2), 3–15.

Jonnavithula, L. (2008). *Improving the interfaces of online discussion forums to enhance learning support*. Unpublished master thesis, Massey University, Palmerston North, New Zealand. Retrieved January 9, 2010, from http://muir.massey.ac.nz/bitstream/10179/968/1/02whole.pdf

Kaplan, N., & Chisik, Y. (2005). Reading alone together: creating sociable digital library books. *ACM IDC05: Interaction Design and Children* (88-94). New York:ACM Press.

Kaye, A. R. (1992): Learning Together Apart. In Kaye, A. R. (ed.)*: Collaborative Learning Through Computer Conferencing. NATO ASI Series, vol. 90, the Najaden Papers* (1-24). Berlin, Heidelberg: Springer-Verlag.

Key To School. *Moodle Add-ons*. Retrieved January 9, 2010, from http://www.keytoschool.com/moodle/add-ons

Lee, J. K., & Calandra, B. (2004). Can embedded annotations help high school students perform problem solving tasks using a Web-based historical document? *Journal of Research on Technology in Education*, *36*(4), 65–84.

Lee, J. M., & Jeong, A. (2009). The effects of argument mapping on critical thinking process in computer-supported collaborative argumentation. Paper presented at the *American Educational Research Association Annual Conference,* San Diego, USA, April 13-17.

Luebeck, J. L., & Bice, L. R. (2005). Online discussion as a mechanism of conceptual change among mathematics and science teachers. *Journal of Distance Education*, *20*(2), 21–39.

Marginalia (2010). *An open source Web annotation tool.* Retrieved April 2, 2010, from http://www.geof.net/code/annotation

Marlow, C., & Naaman, M. boyd, d., & Davis, M. (2006). Tagging Paper, Taxonomy, Flickr, Academic Article, to Read. *Hypertext '06* (31-40). New York: ACM Press.

Meyer, K. A. (2003). Face-to-face versus threaded discussions: The role of time and higher-order thinking. *Journal of Asynchronous Learning Networks*, *7*(3), 55–65.

Nokelainen, P., Miettinen, M., Kurhila, J., Floréen, P., & Tirri, H. (2005). A shared document-based annotation tool to support learner-centred collaborative learning. *British Journal of Educational Technology*, *36*(5), 757–770. doi:10.1111/j.1467-8535.2005.00474.x

Osman, G., & Duffy, T. (2009). Scaffolding critical discourse in online problem-based scenarios: The role of articulation and evaluative feedback. Paper presented at the *American Educational Research Association Annual Conference,* San Diego, USA, April 13-17.

Rourke, L., & Kanuka, H. (2007). Barriers to online critical discourse. *International Journal of Computer-Supported Collaborative Learning, 2*(1), 105–126. doi:10.1007/s11412-007-9007-3

Scardamalia, M. (2004). *CSILE/Knowledge Forum. In education and Technology: An encyclopedia* (pp. 183–192). Santa Barbara, CA: ABC-CLIO.

Scardamalia, M., & Bereiter, C. (1991). Higher levels of agency for children in knowledge building: a challenge for the design of new knowledge media. *Journal of the Learning Sciences, 1*(1), 37–68. doi:10.1207/s15327809jls0101_3

Shea, P., & Bidjerano, T. (2009). Community of inquiry as a theoretical framework to foster "Epistemic engagement" in online education. Paper presented at the *American Educational Research Association Annual Conference,* San Diego, USA, April 13-17.

Sorensen, E., & Takle, E. (2001) Collaborative knowledge building in web-based learning: assessing the quality of dialogue. In *Proceedings of the World Conference on Educational Multimedia, Hypermedia and Telecommunications* (pp.772–1777). Chesapeake, VA Association for the Advancement of Computers in Education (AACE).

Turoff, M. (1991). Computer-mediated communication requirements for group support. *Journal of Organizational Computing, 1*(1), 85–113. doi:10.1080/10919399109540151

Wofle, J. (2008). Annotations and the collaborative digital library: Effects of an aligned annotation interface on student argumentation and reading strategies. *International Journal of Computer-Supported Collaborative Learning, 3*(2), 141–164. doi:10.1007/s11412-008-9040-x

Xin, M. C., & Feenberg, A. (2002). Designing for Pedagogical Effectiveness: TextWeaver. In *Proceedings of the 35th Annual Hawaii International Conference on System Sciences.* Los Alamitos, CA: IEEE Computer Society Press.

Xin, M. C. & Feenberg, A. (2007). Pedagogy in cyberspace: The dynamics of online discourse. *E-Learning*, 4(4), 415-423. Also published in *Journal of Distance Education, 21(2),* 1-25.

Xin, M. C., & Glass, G. (2005). Enhancing Online Discussion through Web Annotation. In G. Richards (Ed.), *Proceedings of the World Conference on E-Learning in Corporate, Government, Healthcare, and Higher Education* (pp.3212-3217). Chesapeake, VA: AACE.

KEY TERM AND DEFINITION

Moderating Functions: Are a set of communicative functions exercised by teachers and students to manage the process of online discussion.

Chapter 18
Modeling, Enacting, Sharing and Reusing Online Collaborative Pedagogy with CeLS

Miky Ronen
Holon Institute of Technology (HIT), Israel

Dan Kohen-Vacs
Holon Institute of Technology (HIT), Israel

ABSTRACT

This chapter presents the potential and challenges of a new approach for the design of a platform aimed to foster and support the use of collaborative techniques in actual educational settings. CeLS is a web-based environment aimed to provide teachers of all subject domains and levels with a flexible tool for creating, enacting and sharing CSCL activities. CeLS special feature is the controllable data flow: the ability to selectively reuse learners' artifacts from previous stages according to various Social Settings in order to support design and enactment of rich multi-stage scripts. CeLS offers content free templates and a searchable repository of sample activities previously implemented with students. Teachers can explore these resources and adapt them to suit their needs, or create new scripts from basic building blocks. During the last four years the system was piloted by teachers from 13 Colleges and Universities and by school teachers. The chapter presents CeLS approach focusing on its unique features, examples of activities implemented with students and some insights on teachers as developers of online collaborative activities and as active contributors to the development of the environment.

BACKGROUND

One of the declared advantages of technology for teaching and learning is its potential to support collaborative learning. The actual realization of this potential depends on the tools and facilities available to teachers. The first generation of e-learning systems regarded learning as an individual process mainly based on content resources. As a result, the corresponding standards developed for Learning Management Systems (LMS) focused on the organization of the resources. Additional tools for conducting free communication with the teacher and between peers (discussion group

DOI: 10.4018/978-1-61692-898-8.ch018

boards, chats, groupware) were provided, but these elements were not integrated with the other parts of the LMS.

Collaborative activities have existed and were successfully implemented by teachers well before the era of e-learning. These activities are not just free discussions or creating group products, but instructional strategies that comprise of *well-defined structures* (scripts), consisting of *distinct stages* that are *interconnected and based on each other* in various ways. Scripting is used to promote learning by structuring and regulating the interaction so that learners are compelled to follow a specific pre defined sequence of activities that would have a better chance to foster the cognitive process appropriate to the learning task (Dansereau, 1988; King, 2007; Kobbe et al. 2007). According to Dillenbourg (2002) the definition of a script requires five attributes: the task that students have to perform, the composition of the group, the way that the task is distributed within and among groups, the mode of interaction and the timing of the phase, while in computer supported collaborative learning (CSCL), the script is reified in the interface of the learning environment. Dillenbourg and Jermann (2007) regard CSCL scripts as part of an *integrated learning* approach: since CSCL should not be considered as an exclusive pedagogical approach, scripts may contain face to face and other activities (not performed in front of the computer) as well as individual elements, while the whole activity is orchestrated and controlled by the teacher.

The cognitive, computational and educational perspectives of scripting computer supported collaborative learning are elaborated in a recently published book (Fischer, Kollar, Mandl, & Haake, 2007).

Dillenbourg and Jermann (2007) identified seven aspects of added value brought up by the use of technology for collaboration scripts: *Connecting* participants enabling remote activity, *Sharing* spaces for collaborative actions, *Management* facilitating logistics aspects, *Reification* of the script in a dedicated interface, *Scaffolding* as part of the activity environment, *Traceability* of actions for teacher analysis and students' reflection and *Adaptability* of the script according to dynamical data and events.

New specifications for Instructional Management Systems based on the concept of Leaning Design (IMS-LD) have emerged only recently (Hummel, Manderveld, Tattersall, & Koper, 2004). The IMS-LD engine (CoperCore) and editor (RELOAD) specify a template that enables creation of synchronized and personalized and collaborative workflow through a course. New management systems were developed according to these specifications, such as COWS (Peter & Vantroys, 2005) and Gridcole (Bote-Lorenzo, et al., 2004). An advanced approach for creation, customization and reuse of collaborative sequences of a learning activity flow is addressed by LAMS (Dalziel, 2003).

The limitations of the IMS-LD specifications for the design of environments that would enable the *enactment* of CSCL scripts are presented and discussed by Miao, Harrer, Hoeksema, and Hoppe (2007). These limitations are related to the insufficient support to the modeling of groups, artifacts, dynamic features, complicated control flow and varied forms of social interaction. More specifically, when the different environments and tools used to facilitate the actions involved in a pedagogical scenario are not integrated, it is difficult to *follow and to support the flow of information* in order to relate to prior actions and to *reuse products* created by the participants in previous phases. The data flow problem of IMS-LD in collaborative learning is further described and addressed by Palomino-Ramírez, Bote-Lorenzo, Asensio-Pérez, and Dimitriadis (2008).

One way to cope with these challenges is to create dedicated environments that support specific types of scripts representing meaningful pedagogical methods (macro-scripts) (Dillenbourg & Jermann, 2007; Dillenbourg & Hong, 2008; Tchounikine, 2008). The author in such environment has some control of the script's characteristics and can adjust some of its parameters. This approach allows detailed exploration of the impact and efficacy of specific scripts but does not provide a solution for modeling and enacting a large variety of scripts. Besides the general drawbacks of computer mediated communication versus face to face and the risk of "over scripting" (Dillenbourg, 2002), the major problem of using CSCL scripts is the loss of *flexibility* resulting from technological constraints and from the teacher's inability to modify the script in real time (Dillenbourg & Jermann, 2007).

Since pedagogical scripts and teachers' needs may be endlessly varied, a *generic* approach and system supporting complicated control flow and relating actions to various social structures is required, in order to allow *maximal flexibility* for the instructional design.

INTRODUCTION

This chapter presents CeLS (Collaborative e-Learning Structures), an approach for the design a web-based environment aimed to provide teachers with a practical and flexible tool for creating and conducting *online structured collaborative activities* in the actual educational setting. We shall first present CeLS approach and the general architecture for modeling collaboration scripts, focusing on the unique features. The design and enactment of scripts with CeLS will be demonstrated by two examples: competition and jigsaw. We shall then present two of the system's building blocks and their potential for script modeling. The following section will address the implementation of CeLS in actual educational settings: teachers as CSCL scripts developers and as active contributors to the system development. We shall conclude with a summary addressing the potential and challenges of CeLS approach for CSCL research and practice.

CELS APPROACH TO MODELING COLLABORATION SCRIPTS

CeLS is a web-based approach designed to enable teachers to design, enact, share and reuse collaboration scripts and incorporate them in the existing instructional setting for any subject and level, from elementary school to higher education (Ronen, Kohen-Vacs, & Raz-Fogel, 2006). Our major concerns were: usability, flexibility and sharing between teachers. The design was primarily aimed at asynchronous activities that can be performed with large classes. In this section we shall present CeLS approach and its general architecture for modeling collaboration scripts.

A CSCL script designed in CeLS may include any number of stages (Figure 1). A stage comprises of a combination of basic building blocks, while each building block generates a certain type of interface in the student's environment. The unique feature in the CeLS approach is its ability to control the data flow in order to *reuse* learners' inputs and products from previous stages and to relate *actions* on these products to different social requirements.

There are five types of building blocks that can be used to create a script (Figure 1):

(1) **Presentation** objects create passive presentations of information (text, links, media). This information can be provided by the teacher or consist of learners' *products* from previous stages. A product can be an organized collection of items contributed by individual participants (identified or anonymous) or a single item that results from a collaborative action of a group (for instance a shared document).

(2) **Input** objects create interfaces that allow participants to submit *new data* to the system as individual or as group artifacts. Inputs may include: text, hyperlinks, media, attached files, voting on various scales, replies to questionnaires or rubrics and shared documents.

(3) **Interaction** objects create interfaces that allow participants to *interact with individual or group products* submitted in previous stages, in various ways: by commenting, grading, ranking, and categorizing via text or graphic manipulations.
(4) **Communication** objects create interfaces that allow participants to *freely* communicate with each other and with the teacher, by a synchronous discussion board.
(5) **Operational** objects do not affect the student's interface. They provide the ability to group participants according to different criteria based on their inputs and actions. This facility enables the design and implementation of adaptation patterns (Ronen & Kohen, 2009) and we will further detail later.

Each object has particular properties that can be adjusted by the author (teacher) in order to adapt the resulting interface and its function to the specific needs of the activity. Some properties are generic, for instance, if the completion of an object is mandatory or not, and others are particular to the object or to its type, for instance, maximum and minimum text length and imposing the use of a certain vocabulary for a Text Input object.

The building blocks are merely interface entities and do not carry any pedagogical meaning. It is only their combination as stages forming a script that creates such meaning, or not. This architecture offers maximal flexibility for the creation of scripts and for their adaptation to teachers' needs and pedagogical creativity.

Social Structures and Social Settings

In CeLS approach the social aspects are the key for controlling the data flow within a script. As shown in Figure 1, each building block can be assigned with particular Social Settings that determine what information would be presented or which artifacts would be offered for interaction to each participant. The Social Settings may use pre-defined Social Structures that represent the characteristics of students' grouping. These entities will be described in details in the following sections.

Figure 1. CeLS approach to the design of collaboration scripts

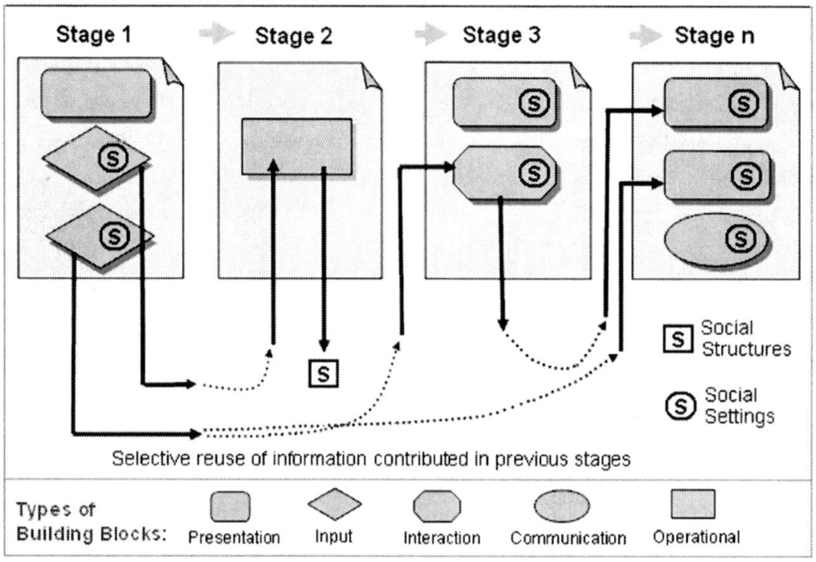

Social Structures

Each activity in CeLS has to be assigned to a master group. A master group can consist of one class or be a merged community of classes, enabling a teacher to run collaborative activities with students from the same or different institutions.

A master group can be structured to include families of groups, representing subjects assigned to the groups and roles played by groups' members. A family of groups has specific properties such as maximum number of members and their generic or particular names. For instance: a "project" family that would include groups of four students each playing a specific role.

The Social Structure of a master group may consist of many simultaneous definitions of different families of groups with different sizes, used by the same or different teachers for various pedagogical purposes.

Social Settings

The Social Settings attributed to a script building block determine *what* will be presented and *to whom*. This definition automatically controls the data flow defined by the script three levels: individual, group (and role) and master group (class or community).

The Social Settings options (Figure 2) include:

- **Master group:** Display or react to all, some (random) or specific items contributed by individual members. These items are presented anonymously or not, according to teacher's definition.
- **Group product:** Display or react to all, some (random) or specific group artifacts.

The Random option offered for these settings distributes the items uniformly between the participants so that each item would have similar chances to be presented and reacted upon. As will be shown later, this option is extremely useful for conducting activities in realistic settings that may involve many individual contributions or a large number of group products.

- **Within own group/role:** An action performed only between the members of the same group/role. This action could be performed online such as creating a shared document or be a single input of a group artifact that results from a face to face activity.

Figure 2. Defining the Social Settings of an object - What will be presented and to whom. In this example each learner in the master group will be presented (or react to) three of the 'Project' group products, presented anonymously (not including the product of her own group).

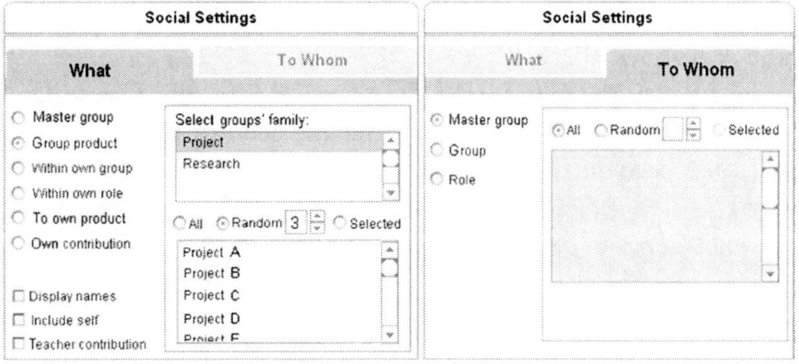

- **To own product:** Each participant will be presented with the peer reactions to her individual or group artifact.
- **Own contribution:** Each participant will be presented with her own contribution to a previous stage.

Figure 2 shows the Social Settings options that are currently available. The options offered to the script author would be automatically adapted to the type of the specific building block so that only the relevant ones will be presented when editing a script (see Figures 3b and 5b). The use of the Social Settings for the design of scripts will be demonstrated in the examples presented in the next sections.

Since the functionality of a script is determined by attributing social properties to the script's building blocks, different participants may encounter different information, perform actions on different data items, or perform different actions, during the same activity stage. As a result, the process represented by the script is not identical for all participants.

It is important to note that the Social Settings are an *integral part of the activity definition* and are kept intact when the activity is duplicated for reuse with a different group of students. The Social Structures are organizational definitions and *do not have to be populated* (assigned with members) in order to create or to edit an activity.

Students can be assigned to groups and roles just before the enactment, in one of the following ways:

- *Automatically*: Whenever suitable pedagogically (grouping can be arbitrary) the system may automatically assign students to groups and roles according to the defined group size.
- *Self registration*: Whenever possible and suitable pedagogically, it is advisable to allow students to express their preferences in order to feel in control. A specific (Input) building block is dedicated for creating an interface that allows students to self register to groups and to roles in the group. Since self grouping of the students may be related to personal issues ("love David", "can't stand Rachel") rather than to the content and learning, the teacher could decide whether to show the identity of the members that have been already registered to each group, or not to.
- *Manually*: Manual teacher control is always available. She can view the identity of the students enrolled to each group and make changes if necessary.

The Student Interface

The student interface is created dynamically according to the student's identity, enabling learners to access activities to which they are enrolled. The interface is kept as simple as possible and specifically adapted to the activity stage so that students can focus on the task at hand. The necessary information (instructions materials and scaffolding) is an integral part of the activity stage. Previous peer products are gathered in one place, within Presentation or Interaction objects, in an organized manner, preventing the need to open and scan many messages. As described earlier, different students may encounter different information and interact with different peer products, according to the script definition.

EXAMPLES

The CeLS flexible architecture enables creation and enactment of an endless variety of online collaborative activities, representing various pedagogical approaches. We shall present two common examples that demonstrate the use of CeLS for designing and enacting CSCL scripts.

Competition and Peer Product Assessment

Figure 3 presents the general structure of a simple 'Competition' activity. In such activity the participants are challenged to produce an artifact according to certain criteria, then to act as judges that evaluate peers' artifacts.

A competition activity consists of three main stages (Figure 3).

Stage 1. Artifacts submission

A. Presentation of the activity, materials and instructions.

B. Artifacts submission. This building block used to enable submission is defined according to the type of the artifact (text, media, attached file) and its specific required properties, for instance: text 100-200 words, JPG image not exceeding 300kB, or a link to a certain domain name. The artifacts submitted can be individual or group products, as defined by the Social Settings of the object.

Stage 2. Assessment

C. Presentation of the stage detailing the evaluation criteria for the judges.

D. Assessments' submission. The building block used to create an interface presenting the artifacts and enabling the judges to submit their assessments is adapted to the pedagogical needs of the activity. In case of an overall evaluation it can be a single or a multiple selection option (select the best artifact/s), or a "Grade and Comments" option (provide a grade on a given scale). If a more detailed evaluation is required, then the interface would be a questionnaire or a rubric, addressing various criteria. The teacher can control the number of artifacts that will be presented to each participant for evaluation. If the activity is performed in a large class and involves many artifacts, or if the artifacts are complex and their assessment requires considerable effort, it would be advisable to restrict the load and present each judge with a limited number of artifacts. This action is performed using the "Random X" option in the Social Settings of the building block, for example, present to each participant 6 of the individual artifacts (Figure 3b). In a competition activity the artifacts are presented anonymously to the peers.

Stage 3. Results and reflection

E. Introduction

F. Presentation of the artifacts, the overall results and the details (the specific grades and

Figure 3. (a) The general structure of a competition activity. (b) An example of the Social Settings of the Interaction building block D.

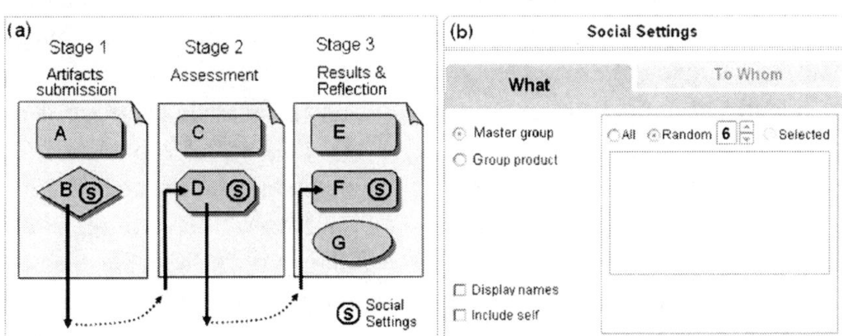

comments to each artifact). The author can show the evaluation details for all artifacts (presented anonymously) or to use the "To own product" in the Social Settings (Figure 2), presenting each participant only with the details for his product.

G. Reflecting on the activity using a free group discussion.

While artifacts and assessments are presented anonymously to the peers, the teacher can always view students' identity for all contributions and, if necessary, she can also edit or delete contributions.

The script shown in Figure 3 represents the basic structure of a 'Competition' activity. This structure can be changed and adapted by adding building blocks and stages, for instance, stage 2 can be preceded by a formative evaluation phase, during which one or more peers comment on each artifact and provide suggestions for improvements, then the amended artifacts would be submitted to the competition.

Many competition and peer product assessment activities were created and enacted by teachers in various subject domains and levels. The types of artifacts submitted were text (including specific vocabulary), links, images, video, and files of various types.

In order to demonstrate the "look and feel" of the author and student interfaces we present a simple example involving images only. Figure 4 shows the author and student interfaces of a competition activity performed in a course on Usability for undergraduate students. This specific activity was related to the annual international event of the World Usability Day (http://www.worldusabilityday.org/). Groups of 2-3 students were challenged to identify usability issues around the campus and take photos, using their mobile phones. Then each group submitted their best example to a class competition (Figure 4a). In the next stage each student was presented with the photos submitted by the other groups, asked to select his favorite and to explain his selection (Figure 4b). After collecting all votes, the results were presented and discussed (Figure 4c, the textual parts are not shown in the figure). This example demonstrates the mechanism of selectively using information submitted: the second element in the author interface of stage 2 (Figure 4b) is a single selection (Interaction) that refers to an Input item (Submit photo) from the previous stage, while the second (Presentation) item in stage 3 (The results) refers to the data collected in Stage 2 (Figure 4c).

Jigsaw

Figure 5 presents the structure of a jigsaw activity. In order to create an activity that involves groups and roles in the groups, the teacher has to define first the Social Structures that would be used by the activity. For example: each group consists of four students playing roles of: architect, interior designer, engineer and salesman. As explained before, the groups and roles do need to be 'populated' in order to design the script.

In this jigsaw variant the first stage of the activity is dedicated to self registration of students to groups and to role selection in each group (Stage 1 – B). The teacher can decide whether to show students the identity of the other enrolled members, or not. This action 'populates' the Social Structures defined by the script. In the second stage students are provided with shared document editing spaces dedicated to each role (Stage 2-E, Figure 5b), while each student will communicate and cooperate with the holders of the same role from the other groups. In the next stage, the roles' artifacts created in the previous stage are presented to all (Stage 3-G) and each group would cooperate towards producing their group artifact using a group shared space (Stage 3-H). This actual cooperation does not have to be performed online and the group product does not necessarily have to be a document. It could result in any artifact of an electronic format such as image, a PowerPoint presentation, a website or video, while the building block H is defined

Figure 4. Author and student interfaces in a competition activity

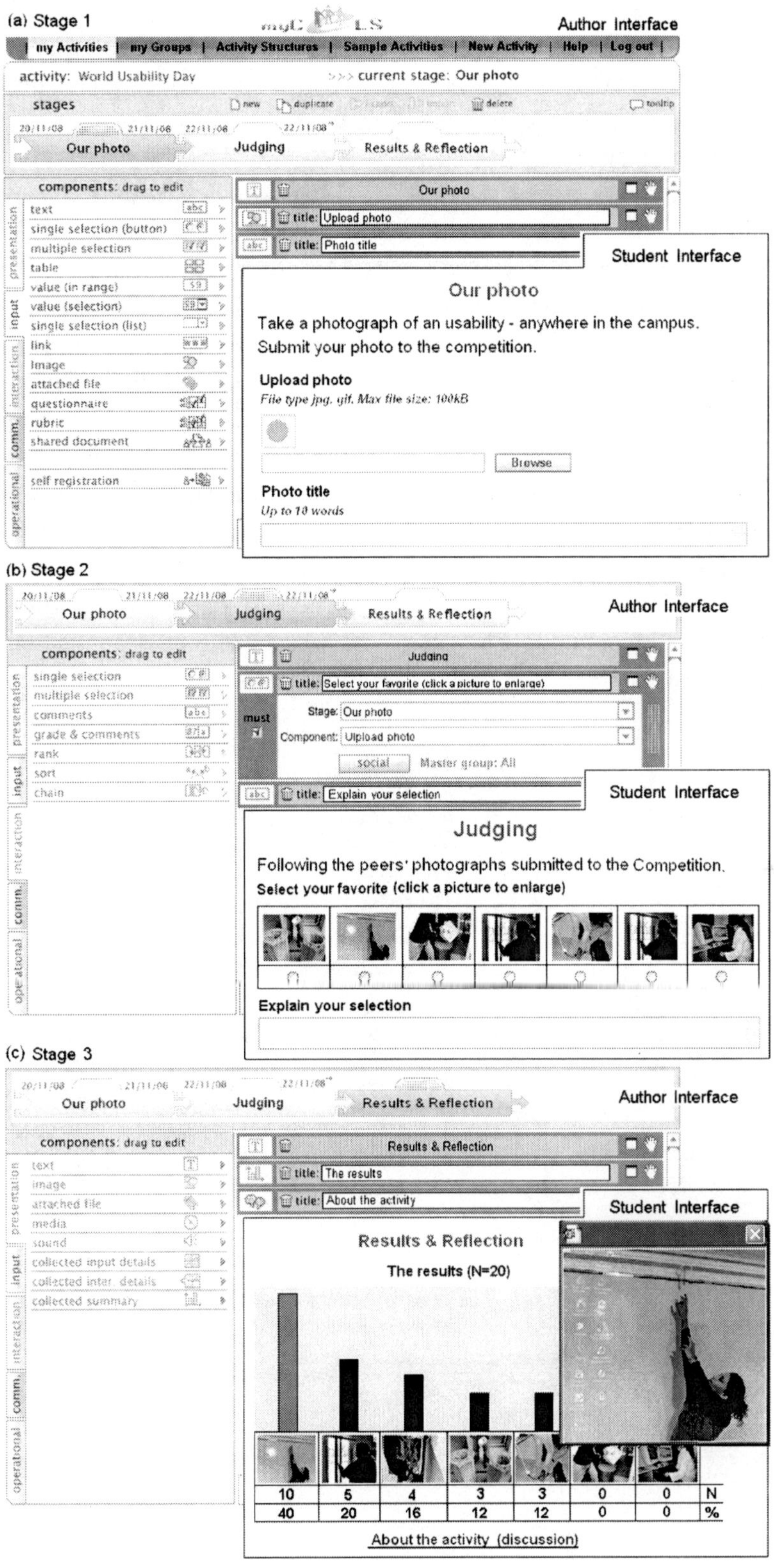

according to the artifact's required format. This jigsaw example also includes a peer product evaluation activity (Stage 4). Each student would be presented with the artifacts of the other groups (some or all) and would be asked to provide feedback on these artifacts (Stage 4-J). Feedback can be provided in various ways, as one overall comment or scaffolded by interfaces that refer to different criteria (such as a rubric).

The last stage summarizes the activity and includes the presentation of all artifacts, peers comments to all or own artifacts (Stage 5-L) and a reflection as a free discussion (Stage 5-M).

BUILDING BLOCKS OF SPECIAL INTEREST

CeLS offers a large collection of building blocks that can be used to create a stage (see author interface Figure 4). Detailing all these elements and their specific properties is beyond the scope of this chapter. However, two of the building blocks may be of special interest and will be detailed in the following sections.

The CeLS Shared Document Editing

Collaborative activities may include parts in which participants cooperate online to create a text based artifact (as in the jigsaw example). Such actions can be supported by existing facilities (like Google Docs) and incorporated in a CeLS script, while the external facility is addressed by a link that will regarded by CeLS as a group product. The key issue in CeLS architecture is the ability to follow the flow of information and to relate actions to participants and to Social Structures. Even if CeLS environment enables connectivity to external user account data-bases it is not always

Figure 5. (a) The general structure of a jigsaw activity. (b) An example of the Social Settings of the Interaction object E: an environment shared by participants playing the same role in all groups.

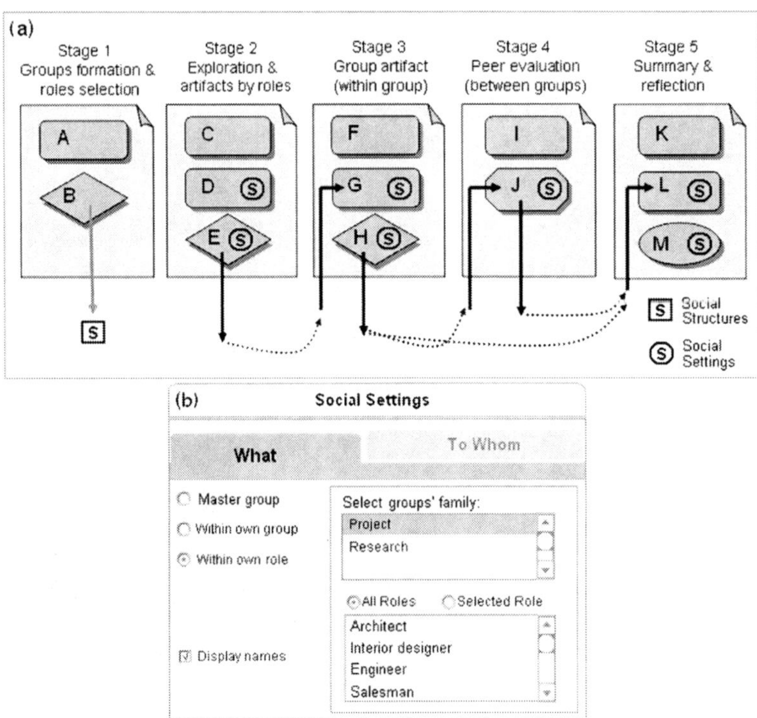

possible to access and to control the user accountability in an external application. Therefore, in addition to using external facilities there was a need to design and integrate a dedicated interface for shared editing that could be directly controlled by the Social Settings. The first natural choice was a wiki-like interface (Cunningham, 1998). Wikis are becoming extensively used for creating and conducting collaborative educational activities (Duffy & Bruns, 2006; Pearce, 2009) and even as a substitution of course websites (Guzdial, Rick, & Kehoe, 2001).

Thomas, King, Minocha, and Taylor (2008) explored students' use of wikis and summarize the limitations and drawbacks of these environments for conducting collaborative activities in academic courses. Among these are the incompatibility with usual documents style and the difficulty to follow changes and understand who contributed what during the activity. Even if the technology enables it, tracking changes in an active wiki environment is very difficult. Tracking by marking all specific changes becomes irrelevant if students download the content, edit it with Word then paste their whole corrected version.

In CeLS approach the shared editing space is not a stand alone element but one of many other interfaces that may coexist in an activity stage. Therefore, the shared editing space does not necessarily have to include a free communication facility, which already exists in CeLS and can be offered simultaneously.

One of our special needs was to be able to use the resulting artifact as a resource in the following stages and to present it as a document. As a result of all these considerations, the CeLS shared editing environment has the following characteristics:

- A simple web editing interface that does not require use of HTML syntax (Figure 6a). The content can be directly copied and pasted from Word documents.
- There is no tracking of specific changes within the document, but instead, it is the *student's responsibility* to summarize the changes he has made in his version. This action is mandatory (Figure 6a) for saving a new version of the document.
- All versions are saved and related to their editors' identity (Figure 6b).

Figure 6. Shared document in CeLS: (a) The editing interface (b) Versions of the document

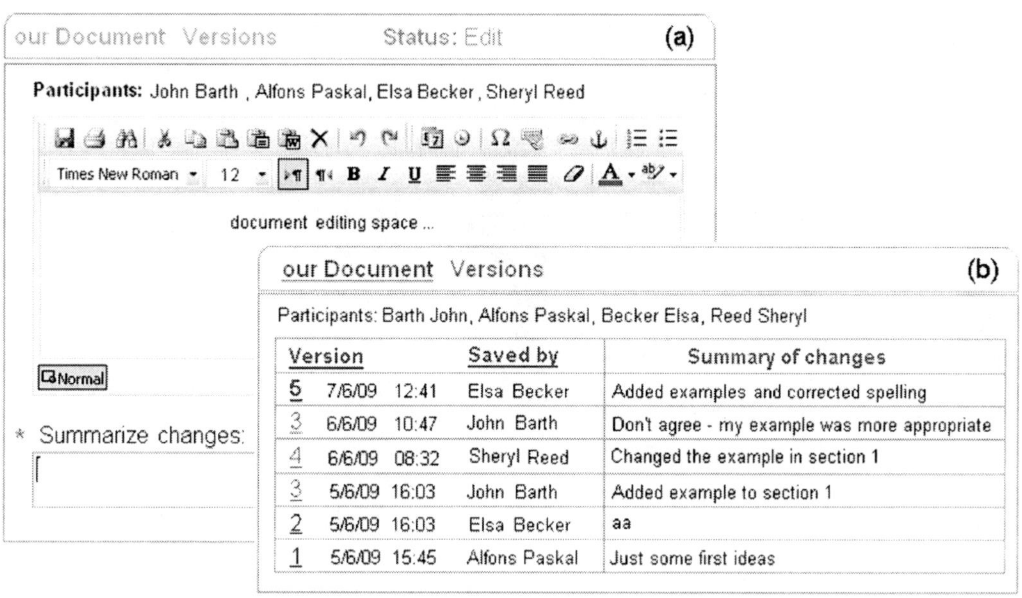

- Any old version can be "defined as last", reversing changes that were previously made.
- A document can be locked (for a certain period of time) to prevent simultaneous editing of the same version.

Figure 6 shows the editing interface (a) and an example of the versions list (b). In this example the student John reversed the order to version 3, after version 4 was created by Sheryl. This action canceled the changes made in version 4, then, version 5 would be based on version 3. When students first use this shared document editing, the mandatory "Summarize changes" seems to some as an unnecessary burden and they insert meaningless text, just to fulfill the technical requirement and to be able to submit their inputs (as in Version 2 Figure 6b). Since meaningless text in the description of versions may hold back the group, students realize it and usually apply self regulation, asking peers to make the effort to provide the appropriate information.

Grouping by Inputs

The idea of adaptation according to students' inputs was inspired by Dillenbourg's ArgueGraph script (Dillenbourg, 2002). In this script, the replies to given questions are used to form dyads of students with different original opinions. Then each dyad is asked to reach a common understanding and provide one single answer. Such group formation mechanism is the basis for the application of the SWISH (Split Where Interaction Should Happen) approach (Dillenbourg & Jermann, 2007).

The CeLS basic architecture, using Social Settings of actions related to Social Structures, enabled us to generalize the 'group by input' approach to any group size and number of dimension and to make it available for use in any script created and enacted with the system. A special (Operational) 'group by input' building block (Figure 7a) is dedicated to the definition and creation of Social Structures by previous inputs. These inputs are students' replies to a collection of questions that can address cognitive aspects diagnosing knowledge, understanding and possible misconceptions, refer to affective aspects identifying attitudes, personal views and preferences, or to both.

Figure 7a shows a simple example of forming groups of students by their replies to one question: the 'similar' and the 'different' options would create homogenous or heterogeneous groups of certain size in the aspect/s defined. The 'identical' option would group together the participants with identical replies to the questions presented.

Figure 7. (a) The "group by input" building block (b) Applying by the social settings

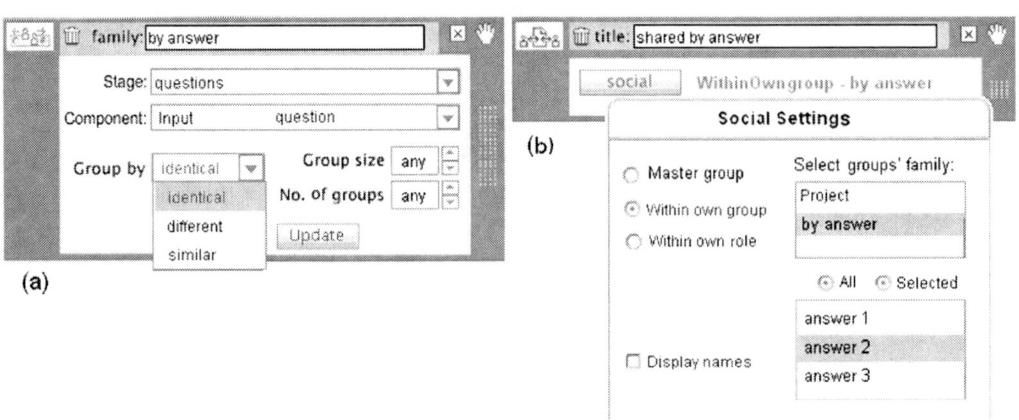

The script adaptation according to students' inputs is performed by attributing the relevant Social Settings to a building block, for instance; presenting different information and resources, different tasks or even different ways of collaboration. An example of a simple adaptation according to the replies to a three items question is presented in Figure 7b: a shared document interface and relevant instructions are provided *only* to the students who responded "answer2", while, in the same stage, the other students (who replied answer1 or answer3) may be presented with a different activity.

As all other building blocks, the grouping by input action is an *integral part of a script*, and will be duplicated along with the activity for reuse with another class. When the script is enacted with students it would define the relevant Social Structures and performs automatic group creation according to the inputs and the criteria defined by the script. In a real setting, groups that are formed automatically may be unbalanced or void. Therefore, manual teacher control should always be applied in order to ensure an effective flow of the activity, or sometimes even abandon the idea and introduce 'on the fly' changes in the script.

Sharing and Reusing Activities

CeLS scripts are not pre-programmed entities but are created by a run-time engine that manages dynamic activity metadata and properties. An Activity is tagged by three types of metadata:

- *Descriptive metadata provided by the author:* author identity, activity name, instructional goals and specific remarks and recommendations.
- *Runtime created metadata*: This metadata is *automatically produced* when the activity is defined or edited, for instance: the number and order of stages and their contents, the relevant Social Structures and the Social Settings.
- *Informational metadata produced by the system*: This data is extracted from the actual implementation of the activity with students, reflecting its 'history and evolution': how many times it was used, where and by whom, in which subject matter domain, how many students had participated, and how the activity was changed.

This metadata is used to support and facilitate sharing and reusing of the pedagogical resources. Teachers can search for existing activities according to their instructional goals, content domain, target population, group size, and other characteristics included in the metadata. The teacher can view the activity's history and even contact the authors for personal advice.

Figure 8 offers a glance at the Sample Activities option. The teacher can view the activities as they were implemented with students, including students' contributions to all stages. When viewed in the Sample Activities all contributions are presented anonymously to protect students' privacy. If a teacher decides to adopt the pedagogical approach and to duplicate the activity, a copy of the activity script will be created in her personal activities list. Then she can change any element of the script to suit the content and her pedagogical needs. As described in the previous section, the Social aspects are an integral part of the script definition. Therefore, if the duplicated activity uses any Social Settings based on specific Social Structures (groups and roles), these Structures will be added to the master group assigned with the duplicated activity. For instance if the teacher duplicates a Jigsaw script using "project" groups of 4 with specific roles (as in Figure 5) and assigns this activity to her class (master group), that had no previous definitions of groups, the relevant definitions would be automatically added to the existing master group. In order to enact the script the teacher has to 'populate' these groups, manually, automatically or by students' self registration.

Activities become visible in the Sample Activities repository only after they have been enacted and approved by their author (teacher). Since the system metadata includes all the information on the source and the creator of each activity, credit is always given to the original author. Even in the Web2 era, sharing still seems to be an issue and some of the teachers are suspicious about others being able to "copy" and use their activities.

IMPLEMENTATION

CeLS is not a comprehensive LMS. It is used in conjunction with the institution's LMS (e.g., Moodle) or as a standalone environment. It is specifically designed to encourage and support teachers to consider and to apply collaborative online pedagogy, by providing facilities that are not available in LMS.

CeLS is piloted in Israel by teachers in 13 universities and colleges, in schools (Primary to High schools) and in teacher courses, in a variety of subjects including: social science, languages, science, technology, education, medical professions, informatics, arts (Abrahamov & Ronen, 2008). Teachers have created and enacted many variants of scripts representing strategies such as: analyzing a common database, competition, conflict resolving, peer products evaluation (Kali & Ronen, 2008), e-games and various combinations of the above.

Teachers as CSCL Scripts Developers

The typical training process begins with a workshop conducted with groups of 10-20 teachers.

Figure 8. Sample activities: sharing and reusing pedagogical resources

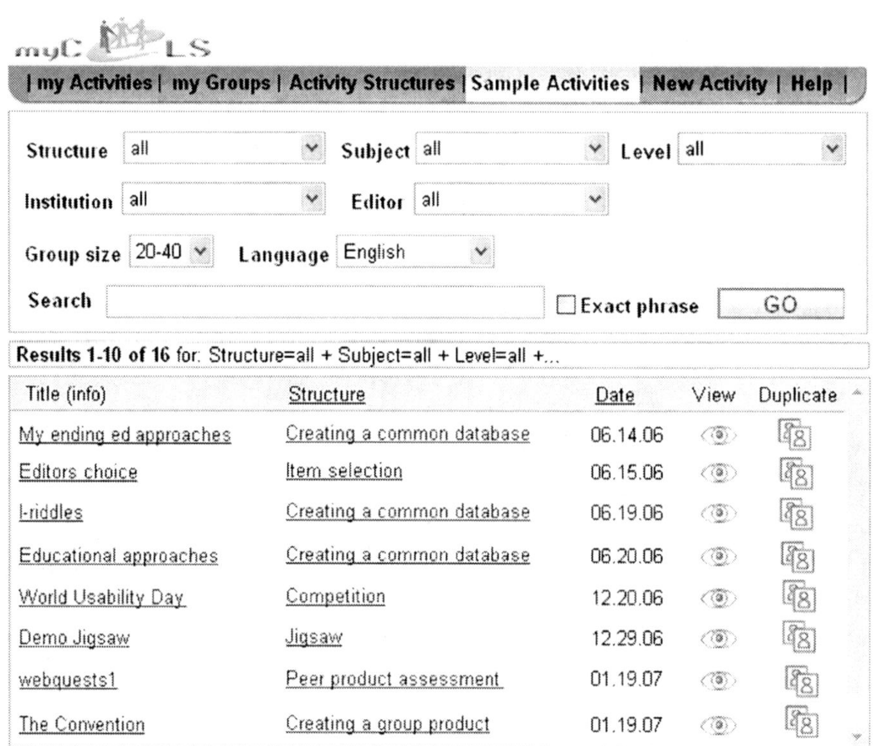

The workshop consists of three parts (Ronen, Kohen-Vacs, & Harrer, 2009):

(a) *Introduction and experiencing as students:* Teachers self register as students and perform several activities, including a competition and an activity that involves creating and evaluating a group artifact. The content of the specific activities are tailored to the group characteristics (school or University teachers).
(b) *Basic Authoring*: Systems' approach for script modeling is presented. The authoring of the activities experienced in the previous phase is revealed and explained. Examples of other types of activities are presented and discussed.
(c) *Teachers' ideas and suggestions*: Teachers are challenged to propose ideas for scripts that they would like to perform with their students. Whenever possible teachers' ideas are immediately implemented and demonstrated. This activity reveals participants views about collaborative online activities, which is not always favorable, and their understanding of the script modeling approach. Implementing the concepts of Social Structures and Social Settings is certainly a challenge since it is different from any other online approach they are familiar with.

Teachers who express interest to try the system receive an authoring code. From this point on they are provided with personal pedagogical and technical support (via electronic communication). Advanced workshops are conducted for groups of teachers at the institution level.

As beginners, most teachers prefer to start "safely" duplicating an existing example from the Sample Activities repository and adapting it to their specific content, with slight variations. These examples are usually similar to the ones they have experienced as students during the first training phase, such as the 'competition' (presented in the previous section). This may be the main reason of the popularity of the 'competition' which was adapted and implemented in numerous activities for a variety of subject domains from elementary school to graduate courses.

As teachers became familiar with the system's approach and potential for creating scripts and gained confidence they departed from the specific examples and designed their own new activities, using the basic building blocks. Most teachers adopted or created one or two scripts, adapted them to suit their courses and reused them each semester, while introducing changes and improvements based on their experiences with students.

Some of the teachers that used CeLS with students did not actually exploit the system's potential for peer collaboration and interaction; instead, they tended to create activities that resemble their common practices when using LMS. These activities usually consisted of one stage: collecting students' inputs and sometimes offering a space for discussion.

A group of users that can be clearly identified are the leading innovators. These daring and creative teachers constantly looked for new ideas that they can apply with the system and tried them with their students. These teachers also provided a major contribution to the system's development, as described in the next section.

Teachers as Active Contributors to the Development of the Environment

The system development is a dynamic and continuous process actively involving users. Many of the CeLS options originated from teachers' requests and suggestions, after they have familiarized with the environment and used it with their students. Following three examples:

- An Education teacher designed a multi-stage activity planned for several weeks. At the beginning of the activity each student was asked to express his attitudes on a specific issue then several stages of class debate took place, during which the participants presented and organized the considerations. One of the instructional goals was to make students realize the changes of their own personal views after being exposed to the variety of peers' ideas. The teacher was concerned that students may not remember their own original attitudes, expressed in the early stage. As a result, we have added the 'Own contribution' option that enables the script designer to present each participant with his own contribution to a specific input in a prior stage. This option was later used by teachers for other similar activities involving reflection on attitude changes, or just as a reminder of an early (own) content contribution in a later stage.

- In an undergraduate Informatics course the teacher challenged her students to create riddles similar to the ones presented in the Informatics Olympiad. She planned to use these artifacts in the next stages to conduct a competition activity. After reviewing the submitted artifacts, she realized that only some of the riddles were suitable for her purpose, while others were too easy or not properly phrased. Unfortunately, at this point she could not complete the activity as planned in CeLS and had to download the selected artifacts and continue the activity in class. This experience resulted in the addition of the 'Selected' option to the Social Settings (Figure 2), enabling the teacher to decide which of the submitted artifacts to use in a following action in the next stage. This option cannot be defined in advance; it is applicable only during runtime, after artifacts are submitted and the teacher can view them before presenting them to peers.
- One of the facilities provided to the teacher is viewing all contributions at all times, regardless of what she has decided to present to students in a current stage. This facility is necessary in order to enable the teacher to effectively orchestrate the activity flow, especially in cases that use a "post before view" approach (Duffy, Dueber, & Hawley, 1998). In the first versions teachers could only view, but not interfere with these contributions. System's use in actual settings revealed numerous cases in which automatic and uncontrolled reuse of a student's original contribution would hinder and disturb the activity flow, for instance, providing students in the next stages irrelevant or improper texts. As a result, the option of editing or deleting students' contributions was added, in order to enhance teachers' control whenever necessary.

POTENTIAL AND CHALLENGES

New practical potential offered by technology poses new challenges. In this section we shall refer to: potential for CSCL research, system's development - technological and pedagogical aspects and sharing scripts as pedagogical resources.

CeLS as a Tool for Empirical Research in CSCL

Instructional Design of CSCL Activities

CeLS is only an environment and tool for designing, conducting and sharing collaborative activities. At this point we neither restrict, nor imposed, any specific instructional designs. An activity that may seem non-collaborative may still be pedagogically valid and effective in various ways. Dealing with aspects of students' learning, that do or do not occur via the use of CeLS is beyond the scope of this chapter. In any case, the pedagogical efficacy is a related to the instructional design rather than to the tool used for enactment.

The flexibility offered by CeLS for designing and enacting collaboration scripts offers new potential for empirical testing of integrative pedagogical strategies that may involve actions in all social planes (individual, small group, class and community) and combine collaborative activities performed online with other types of collaboration (face to face, in front of the computer). Therefore, CeLS provides a tool for conducting research on the pedagogical efficacy of specific activities and exploring different variants of scripts in various domains and settings (e.g., Kali & Ronen, 2008).

Professional Development of Teachers

What has not been studied much yet is how teachers adopt the use of scripts, how their own role and conceptions of learning fit with the ones represented by scripting (Hakkinen & Makitalo, 2007), or how teachers conceptions may change as a result becoming script developers and users.

The availability of a working environment that enables teachers to incorporate practices in their daily work offers new opportunities for exploring these issues on a large scale.

CeLS Development: Pedagogical and Technological Aspects

The CeLS environment is far from being complete. It does not support all the complex needs of modeling the endless possible variations of structured collaborative activities. In fact, many of the script ideas suggested by creative users would require additional development. Technologically speaking, the modular architecture enables us to continuously add building blocks and to refine and enhance the systems by providing more complex options for Social Structures and sophisticated Social Settings.

The main challenge is balancing between usability and complexity. Every new feature added may enrich the pedagogical potential but, at the same time, also alienate teachers and prevent them from even considering using the environment in their daily practice.

The major critique on developing a stand alone approach and environment is related to the limited connectivity and interoperability with other e-learning systems. Our first concern was indeed pragmatic, aiming to address the challenge of providing teachers and researchers with a flexible and working environment. Nevertheless, the CeLS environment could be interfaced with external systems. A first exemplary integration was achieved between the CeLS platform and MoCoLADe, a visual authoring environment that simulates and models scripts defined in the IMS/LD format (Harrer, Kohen-Vacs, Roth, Malzah, Hoppe, & Ronen, 2009). Efforts in this direction will continue along with the platform development.

Sharing and Reusing Scripts as Pedagogical Resources

A major challenge presented by a flexible system like CeLS is how to support effective sharing and reusing of a vast collection of scripts that are continuously created. A large number of available resources may be confusing or even overwhelming. The limited prototype tested with a small number of teachers resulted in more than a hundred variants of several basic structures. Sharing and reusing scripts as pedagogical resources is very different from sharing content materials. Our pilot study revealed that the characteristics that may interest teachers are not necessarily the subject domain or the age group it was used for, but aspects related to the specific instructional design offered by an activity. Tagging activities with particular 'nick names' names is evidently ineffective.

Since the emergence of LD the representation and reusability of the learning process (not only content) became an issue of concern (Griffiths & Blat, 2005; Hernández-Leo, Asensio-Pérez, Dimitriadis, Bote-Lorenzo, Jorrín-Abellán, & Villasclaras-Fernández, 2005). Hernández-Leo, Harrer, Dodero, Asensio-Pérez, and Burgos

(2007) proposed a *create-by-reuse framework* that elucidates different approaches for the creation of Units of Learning via the reuse of learning design solutions at different levels of granularity and completeness.

One of the results of the Kaleiodoscope project offers a dedicated "Framework for the Specification of Collaboration Scripts" (Kobbe, 2005). This framework would enable the description and the formalization of collaboration activities by addressing the "script components" and the "script mechanism". The implementation of this framework is demonstrated in Dillenbourg & Jermann, (2007) for SWISH model activities. The proposed hierarchy classifies scripts by categories representing major instructional strategies (*schema*), such as conflict and jigsaw, then uses different types of sub-categories (*classes*), representing content free didactic approach. The more specific levels are *instances* of the scripts applied in specific content domains and *sessions* are script instances including student-specific data.

As a stating point, CeLS activities are classified by major schemata (such as conflict, jigsaw and competition) while some of the detailed characteristics (instances and sessions), such as the subject domain expressed in the activity metadata, can be used to retrieve an existing resource.

A rough classification is not satisfactory for a large collection that can be created with a flexible system, since each script can be implemented in different ways with many variants. Furthermore, an Activity Structure may include combinations of several instructional strategies. An a-priori detailed classification may be useful for anticipated activities but it does not offer a solution for new structures that are developed by users and continuously added to the system repository.

The classification should be *clear* and *usable to teachers* and must refer to the concepts the practitioners are familiar with (Kobbe, 2005) and to their practical needs. These needs are not necessarily related in the teachers' minds to learning theories or even with instructional strategies, but may possibly refer to other superficial characteristics. A typical example was a physics teacher looking for activities dealing with *visual representations* (images), while this approach eventually led her to find, then effectively adopt and adapt an activity created for an art course. Another challenge lies in following and making sense of the variations of a structure, since even a small detail in the design of the script can make the difference (Kali & Ronen, 2005).

SUMMARY AND CONCLUSION

One of the crucial questions in CSCL is how to facilitate the teachers' design and use of collaboration scripts (Hakkinen & Makitalo, 2007). We have presented an approach and tool that addresses some of the endlessly varied and complex needs of running structured collaborative activities in real educational settings. CeLS is not a comprehensive LMS. It is currently used in conjunction with available LMS or as a standalone environment. It does not provide solutions for all types of online collaborative activities nor is it meant to replace groupware or collaborative environments designed for learning in specific subject domains. Rather it is designed to encourage and support teachers to incorporate online collaborative activities into their daily practice by providing them with a flexible tool and many examples that they can *explore*, *adopt* and *adapt*. Teachers can also express their pedagogical creativity and design new scripts from basic building blocks. The early adopters are teachers, at all levels and subject matter domains, who are already trying to use the available technology for conducting collaborative activities in their courses. CeLS has enabled them to design and implement pedagogical activities that were very difficult or impossible to handle before.

CeLS provides a tool for conducting empirical research on the pedagogical efficacy of specific collaborative activities and for exploring how teachers adopt the use of scripts. The findings will present new directions for improving the design of the future versions and a deeper insight into the potential and challenges of using technology for conducting online scripted collaborative learning.

REFERENCES

Abrahamov, S., & Ronen, M. (2008). Double blending: online theory with on-campus practice in photography instruction. *Innovations in Education and Training International*, *45*(1), 3–14.

Bote-Lorenzo, M., Vaquero-Gonzalez, L., Vega-Gorgojo, G., Dimitriadis, Y., Asensio-Perez, J., Gomez-Sanchez, E., et al. (2004). A tailorable collaborative learning system that combines OGSA grid services and IMS-LD scripting. In *Proceedings of the Tenth International Workshop on Groupware: Design, Implementation and Use* (pp. 305-321). Berlin, Germany: Springer-Verlag.

Cunningham, W. (1998). *The wiki wiki web*. Retrieved September 13, 2009, from http://c2.com/cgi/wiki?WikiWikiWeb

Dalziel, J. (2003). Implementing Learning Design: The Learning Activity Management System (LAMS). In Crisp G., Thiele, D., Scholten, I., Barker, S., & Baron, J. (Eds.), *Proceedings of the 20th Annual Conference of the Australasian Society for Computers in Learning* (pp. 593-596), Adelaide, Australia: ASCILITE

Dansereau, D. (1988). Cooperative learning strategies. In Weinstein, C. E., Goetz, E. T., & Alexander, P. A. (Eds.), *Learning and study strategies: Issues in assessment, instruction, and evaluation* (pp. 103–120). New York: Academic Press.

Dillenbourg, P. (2002). Over-scripting CSCL: The risks of blending collaborative learning with instructional design. In Kirschner P. (Ed.), *Three worlds of CSCL: Can we support CSCL?* (pp. 61-91). Heerlen: Open University of the Netherlands.

Dillenbourg, P., & Hong, F. (2008). The mechanics of CSCL macro scripts. *International Journal of Computer-Supported Collaborative Learning*, *3*(1), 3–23. doi:10.1007/s11412-007-9033-1

Dillenbourg, P., & Jermann, P. (2007). Designing Integrative Scripts. In Fischer, F., Kollar, I. Mandl, H., & Haake, J.M. (Eds.), *Scripting Computer-Supported Collaborative Learning: Cognitive, Computational and Educational Perspectives, Computer-Supported Collaborative Learning Series, Vol. 6*, (pp. 275-302). New York: Springer.

Duffy, P., & Bruns, A. (2006). The Use of Blogs, Wikis and RSS in Education: A Conversation of Possibilities. In [Brisbane, Australia: QUT.]. *Proceedings of the Online Learning and Teaching Conference, 2006*, 31–38.

Duffy, T. M., Dueber, B., & Hawley, C. L. (1998). Critical Thinking in a Distributed Environment: A Pedagogical Base for the Design of Conferencing Systems. In Bonk, C. J. & King K. S. (Eds.), *Electronic Collaborators: Learner-centered Technologies for Literacy, Apprenticeship and Discourse* (p. 73). Mahawah, NJ: LEA associates.

Fischer, F. Kollar, I., Mandl, H., & Haake, J.M. (Eds.) (2007). *Scripting CSCL: Cognitive, Computational and Educational Perspectives, CSCL Series, Vol. 6*. New York: Springer.

Griffiths, D., & Blat, J. (2005). The Role of Teachers in Editing and Authoring Units of Learning Using IMS Learning Design. *Advanced Technology for Learning*, *2*(4), 243–251.

Guzdial, M., Rick, J., & Kehoe, C. (2001). Beyond Adoption to Invention: Teacher-Created Collaborative Activities in Higher Education. *Journal of the Learning Sciences*, *10*(3), 265–279. doi:10.1207/S15327809JLS1003_2

Hakkinen, P., & Makitalo-Siegl, K. (2007) Educational perspectives on scripting CSCL. In Fischer, F., Kollar, I. Mandl, H., & Haake, J.M. (Eds.), *Scripting Computer-Supported Collaborative Learning: Cognitive, Computational and Educational Perspectives, Computer-Supported Collaborative Learning Series, Vol. 6* (pp. 263-274). New York: Springer.

Harrer, A., Kohen-Vacs, D., Roth, B., Malzah, N., Hoppe, U., & Ronen, M. (2009). Design and enactment of collaboration scripts – An integrative approach with graphical notations and learning platforms. In *Proceedings of the CSCL 2009 Conference* (pp.198-200). International Society of the Learning Sciences (ISLS).

Hernández-Leo, D., Asensio-Pérez, J., Dimitriadis, Y., Bote-Lorenzo, M., Jorrín-Abellán, I., & Villasclaras-Fernández, E. (2005). Reusing IMS-LD Formalized Best Practices in Collaborative Learning. *Advanced Technology for Learning*, *2*(4), 223–232. doi:10.2316/Journal.208.2005.4.208-0865

Hernández-Leo, D., Harrer, A., Dodero, J., Asensio-Pérez, J., & Burgos, D. (2007). Framework for the Conceptualization of Approaches to "Create-by-Reuse" of Learning Design Solutions. *Journal of Universal Computer Science*, *13*(7), 991–1001.

Hummel, H., Manderveld, J., Tattersall, C., & Koper, R. (2004). Educational modeling language and learning design: new opportunities for instructional reusability and personalized learning. *International Journal of Learning Technology*, *1*(1), 111–126. doi:10.1504/IJLT.2004.003685

Kali, Y., & Ronen, M. (2005). Design principles for online peer-evaluation: Fostering objectivity. In Koschmann, T., Suthers, D., & Chan, T. (Eds.), *CSCL 2005* (pp. 247–251). Mahwah, NJ: Lawrence Erlbaum Associates.

Kali, Y., & Ronen, M. (2008). Assessing the assessors: Added value in web-based multi-cycle peer assessment in higher education. *Research and Practice in Technology Enhanced Learning*, *3*(1), 3–32. doi:10.1142/S1793206808000434

King, A. (2007). Scripting collaborative learning process: a cognitive perspective. In Fischer, F., Kollar, I. Mandl, H., & Haake, J.M. (Eds.), *Scripting Computer-Supported Collaborative Learning: Cognitive, Computational and Educational Perspectives*, Computer-Supported Collaborative Learning Series, Vol. 6, (pp. 13-37). New York: Springer.

Kobbe, L. (2005). *Framework on multiple goal dimensions for computer-supported scripts*, Kaleidoscope project. Retrieved September 10, 2009 from: http://hal.archives-ouvertes.fr/docs/00/19/02/97/PDF/Lars-Kobbe-2005.pdf

Kobbe, L., Weinberger, A., Dillenbourg, P., Harrer, A., Hämäläinen, R., & Häkkinen, P. (2007). Specifying computer-supported collaboration scripts. *International Journal of Computer-Supported Collaborative Learning*, *2*(2-3), 211–224. doi:10.1007/s11412-007-9014-4

Miao, Y., & Harrer, A. Hoeksema, K. & Hoppe, U. (2007). Modeling CSCL scripts - a reflection of learning design approaches. In Fischer, F. Kollar, I., Mandl, H., & Haake, J.M. (Eds.), *Scripting CSCL: Cognitive, Computational and Educational Perspectives*, CSCL Series, Vol. 6, (pp. 117-136). New York: Springer.

Palomino-Ramírez, L., Bote-Lorenzo, M. L., Asensio-Pérez, J. I., & Dimitriadis, Y. (2008). LeadFlow4LD: Learning and Data Flow Composition-based Solution for Learning Design in CSCL. In Briggs, R.O. et al. (Eds.), *Proceedings of 14th International Workshop, CRIWG 2008. Groupware: Design, Implementation, and Use*. Lecture Notes in Computer Science. Vol. 5411. (266-280). New York: Springer.

Pearce, J. (2009). Using wiki in education. *The science of spectroscopy*. Retrieved September 10, 2009, from: http://www.scienceofspectroscopy.info/edit/index.php?title=Using_wiki_in_education

Peter, Y., & Vantroys, T. (2005). Platform Support for Pedagogical Scenarios. *Journal of Educational Technology & Society*, *8*(3), 122–137.

Ronen, M., & Kohen-Vacs, D. (2009). Designing and applying adaptation patterns embedded in the scripts. *Proceedings of the International Workshop on Adaptive Systems for Collaborative Learning, INCoS 2009* (306-310). New York: IEEE Computer Society Press.

Ronen, M., Kohen-Vacs, D., & Harrer, A. (2009). Modelling, creating and enacting online collaborative scripts. In Dimitracopoulou, A., Claire O'Malley, C., Daniel Suthers, D. & Reimann P. (Eds.), *Computer Supported Collaborative Learning Practices: CSCL2009 Community Events Proceedings* (p. 218). International Society of the Learning Sciences (ISLS).

Ronen, M., Kohen-Vacs, D., & Raz-Fogel, N. (2006). Adopt & Adapt: Structuring, Sharing and Reusing Asynchronous Collaborative Pedagogy. In Barab, S., Hay, K., & Hickey., D. (Eds.), *Proceedings of the 7th international conference on Learning sciences* (pp. 599-606). International Society of the Learning Sciences (ISLS).

Tchounikine, P. (2008). Operationalizing macro-scripts in CSCL technological settings. *International Journal of Computer-Supported Collaborative Learning*, *3*(2), 193–233. doi:10.1007/s11412-008-9039-3

Thomas, P., King, D., Minocha, S., & Taylor, J. (2008). Wikis supporting authentic, collaborative activities: lessons from distance education. In Whitton, N. & McPherson, M. (Eds.), *Proceedings of the 15th Association for Learning Technology Conference (ALT-C 2008)* (pp.74-83). Leeds, UK: University of Leeds.

KEY TERMS AND DEFINITIONS

Activity: An online script implemented in the CeLS system.

Building Block: The basic element used to create the interface that represents an activity stage.

Group Product: One of the possible definitions of the Social Settings. Refers to the electronic artefact resulting from an action performed by students from the same group or students sharing the same role. The action could be performed online using a shared space, or face to face. The product can be a text, image, link, file of any kind, or a reply to a questionnaire or rubric.

Master Group: The group to which an activity is assigned, typically a class.

Social Settings: A property that can be assigned to each of the building blocks that defines what information will be presented to whom or which artifacts would be offered for interaction. In case of group actions the Social Settings use the definitions of groups and roles specified in the Social Structures.

Social Structures: Defines the characteristics of students' grouping in a master group. May include simultaneous definitions of different families of groups with different sizes and roles attributed to group members.

Stage: A part of an activity that is performed simultaneously by all (or some) of the members of the master group. A stage is limited in time, assigned with starting and ending date and time. Different students may encounter different information or perform different actions in the same stage, according to the script's design.

Compilation of References

Abrahamov, S., & Ronen, M. (2008). Double blending: online theory with on-campus practice in photography instruction. *Innovations in Education and Training International, 45*(1), 3–14.

Acker, S. R., & Levitt, S. R. (1987). Designing videoconference facilities for improved eye contact. *Journal of Broadcasting & Electronic Media, 31*(2), 181–191.

Ackerman, R., & Goldsmith, M. (2008). Learning directly from screen? Oh-no, I must print it! Metacognitive analysis of digitally presented text learning. In Eshet, Y., Caspi, A., & Geri, N. (Eds.), *Learning in the technological era* (*Vol. 3*, pp. 1–7). Raanana, Israel: Open University of Israel.

Ackerman, R. (2009). The Subjective Feelings of Comprehension and Remembering Accompanying Text Learning On-Screen. In Y. Eshet-Alkalai, A. Caspi, S. Eden, N. Geri, & Y. Yair (Eds.), *Proceedings of the Chais conference on instructional technologies research 2009. Vol. 4 Learning in the technological era*, (pp. 1-7) Raanana, Israel: The Open University of Israel.

Adams, J. (2008). Understanding the factors limiting the acceptability on online courses and degrees. *International Journal on E-Learning*, 7(4), 573–587.

Agostinho, S., Lefoe, G., & Hedberg, J. (1997). *Online collaboration for effective learning: A case study of a postgraduate university course.* Retrieved September 14, 2009, from http://ausweb.scu.edu.au/proceedings/agostinho/paper.html

Akkoyunlu, B., & Yilmaz Soylu, M. (2006). A study on student's views on blended learning environment. *Turkish Online Journal of Distance Education,* 7(3), art.3.

Alavi, M., & Dufner, D. (2005). Technology-mediated collaborative learning: A research perspective. In Hiltz, S. R., & Goldman, R. (Eds.), *Learning together online: Research on asynchronous learning networks* (pp. 191–213). Mahwah, NJ: Lawrence Erlbaum.

Alexander, C. N., Ishikawa, S., & Silverstein, M. (1977). *A pattern language: Towns, buildings, construction.* New York: Oxford University Press.

Ally, M. (2004). Foundations of educational theory for online learning. In Anderson, T., & Elloumi, F. (Eds.), *Theory and practice of online learning* (pp. 3–31). Athabasca, AB: Athabasca University.

Almond, R. G., Steinberg, L. S., & Mislevy, R. J. (2002). Enhancing the design and delivery of assessment systems: A four-process architecture. *Journal of Technology, Learning, and Assessment, 1*(5), 1–64.

Alvarez, S. (2005). Blended learning solutions. In B. Hoffman (Ed.), *Encyclopedia of Educational Technology*. Retrieved March 20, 2010, from http://edweb.sdsu.edu/eet/

Alvarez-Torres, M. (2001). *On 'chatting' in the foreign language classroom.* Clearing House Item 00098655, 74(6), 313–316.

Anderson, R. C., & Pearson, P. D. (1984). A schema-theoretic view of basic processes in reading comprehension. In Pearson, P. D. (Ed.), *Handbook of reading research* (pp. 255–291). New York: Longman.

Anderson, T. (2004). Teaching in an online learning context. In T. Anderson & F. Elloumi, (Eds.). *Theory and practice of online learning*. Retrieved April 9, 2010, from http://www.cde.athabascau.ca/online_book/

Anderson, T., L. Rourke, Garrison, D. R, Archer, W. (2001). Assessing teaching presence in a computer conferencing environment. *Journal of Asynchronous Learning Networks, 5*(2).64-74

Andriessen, J., Baker, M., & Suthers, D. (2003). Argumentation, computer support, and the educational context of confronting cognition. In Andriessen, J., Baker, M., & Suthers, D. (Eds.), *Arguing to learn: Confronting cognitions in computer-supported collaborative learning environments* (pp. 1–25). Dordrecht, The Netherlands: Kluwer.

Araque, F., Roldan, C., & Salguero, R. (2009). Factors influencing university drop out rates. *Computers & Education, 53*(3), 563–574. doi:10.1016/j.compedu.2009.03.013

Aronson, E., Blaney, N., Stephan, C., Sikes, J., & Snapp, M. (1978). *The jigsaw classroom*. Beverly Hills, CA: Sage.

Aronson, E., & Patnoe, S. (1997). *The jigsaw classroom: Building cooperation in the classroom* (2nd ed.). New York: Longman.

Aronson, E., Blaney, N., Stephan, C., Sikes, J., & Snapp, M. (1978). *The jigsaw classroom*. Thousand Oaks, CA: Sage Publications.

Avouris, N., Komis, V., Margaritis, M., & Fiotakis, G. (2004). An environment for studying collaborative learning activities. *Journal of International Forum of Educational Technology and Society, 7*(2), 34–41.

Avouris, N., Dimitracopoulou, A., Komis, V., & Fidas, C. (2002). OCAF: An object-oriented model of analysis of collaborative problem solving. In Stahl, G. (Ed.), *CSCL 2002* (pp. 92–101). Hillsdale, NJ: Lawrence Erlbaum Associates, Inc.

Babiuk, G. (2005). A Full Bag of "Tech Tools" enhances the reflective process in Teacher Education. In C. Crawford et al. (Eds.), *Proceedings of the Society for Information Technology and Teacher Education International Conference 2005* (pp. 1873-1877). Chesapeake, VA: AACE.

Bailenson, J. N., Yee, N., Blascovich, J., Beall, A. C., Lundblad, N., & Jin, M. (2008). The Use of Immersive Virtual Reality in the Learning Sciences: Digital Transformations of Teachers, Students, and Social Context. *Journal of the Learning Sciences, 17*(1), 102–141. doi:10.1080/10508400701793141

Baker, M., & Lund, K. (1997). Prompting reflective interactions in a CSCL environment. *Journal of Computer Assisted Learning, 13*(3), 175–193. doi:10.1046/j.1365-2729.1997.00019.x

Baker, M., Hansen, T., Joiner, R., & Traum, D. (1999). The role of grounding in collaborative learning tasks. In Dillenbourg, P. (Ed.), *Collaborative Learning: Computational and Cognitive Approaches* (pp. 31–63). Oxford, UK: Elsevier Science.

Bakhtin, M. (1981). *The Dialogic Imagination*. Austin, TX: University of Texas Press.

Bakhtin, M. M. (1981). *The dialogic imagination: Four essays* (Emerson, C., & Holquist, M., Trans.). Austin, TX: University of Texas Press.

Barnes, L., Christensen, R., & Hansen, A. (1994). *Teaching and the case method*. Boston, MA: Harvard Business School Press.

Barros, M., & Verdejo, M. (2000). Analysing learner interaction processes in order to improve collaboration. The DEGREE approach. *International Journal of Artificial Intelligence in Education, 11*(3), 221–241.

Barrows, H. S. (1985). *How to design a problem-based curriculum for the preclinical years*. New York: Springer.

Barrows, H. S. (1988). *The tutorial process*. Springfield, Ill: Southern Illinois Press.

Barrows, H. S. (2002). Is it truly possible to have such a thing as dPBL? *Distance Education, 23*(1), 119–122. doi:10.1080/01587910220124026

Barrows, H. S., & Tamblyn, R. M. (1980). *Problem-based learning: An approach to medical education*. New York: Springer.

Bartlett, F. C. (1932). *Remembering: An experimental and social study*. Cambridge, UK: Cambridge University Press.

Bateman, S., Brooks, C., Mccalla, G., & Brusilovsky, P. (2007). Applying collaborative tagging to e-learning. In *Proceedings of the Workshop on Tagging and Metadata for Social Information Organization, 16th International World Wide Web Conference (WWW'07)* (pp.548-556), ACM, New York.

Beatty, I. D., Gerace, W. J., Leonard, W. J., & Dufresne, R. J. (2006). Designing effective questions for classroom response system teaching. *American Journal of Physics*, *74*(1), 31–39. doi:10.1119/1.2121753

Beetham, H., & Sharpe, R. (2007). *Rethinking pedagogy for a digital age*. London, UK: RoutledgeFalmer.

Benbunan-Fich, R., & Hiltz, S. R. (1999). Educational applications of CMCS: Solving case studies through asynchronous learning networks. *Journal of Computer Mediated Communication Studies, 4* (3) March 1999. Retrieved July 15, 2009, from http://jcmc.indiana.edu/vol4/issue3/benbunan-fich.html

Bentley, R., Appelt, W., Busbach, U., Hinrichs, E., Kerr, D., & Sikkel, S. (1997). Basic Support for Cooperative Work on the World Wide Web. *International Journal of Human-Computer Studies*, *46*(6), 827–846. doi:10.1006/ijhc.1996.0108

Bereiter, C. (2002). *Education and mind in the knowledge age*. Mahwah, NJ: Erlbaum.

Bereiter, C., Scardamalia, M., Alexander, P. A., & Winne, P. H. (2006). Education for the Knowledge Age: Design-Centered Models of Teaching and Instruction. In Alexander, P. A., & Winne, P. H. (Eds.), *Handbook of educational psychology* (pp. 695–713). Mahwah, NJ: Lawrence Erlbaum Associates.

Bereiter, C., & Scardamalia, M. (1992). Cognition and curriculum. In Jackson, P. (Ed.), *Handbook of research on curriculum* (pp. 517–542). New York: Macmillan.

Bereiter, C., & Scardamalia, M. (2003). Learning to work creatively with knowledge. In E. De Corte, L. Verschaffel, N. Entwistle, & J. van Merriënboer (Eds.), *Unravelling basic components and dimensions of powerful learning environments*. EARLI Advances in Learning and Instruction Series; Retrieved January 9, 2010, from http://ikit.org/fulltext/inresslearning.pdf

Berge, Z. L. (1995). Facilitating computer conferencing: Recommendations from the field. *Educational Technology*, *15*(1), 22–30.

Bergin, J., Eckstein, J., & Manns, M. L., & Wallingford, E., (2001). Patterns for Gaining Different Perspectives. *A Part of the Pedagogical Patterns Project Pattern Language Version 0.6.* Retrieved March 20, 2010, from http://pedagogicalpatterns.org/current/gaindiffperspective.pdf

Bernard, R. M., Rojo de Rubalcava, B., & St-Pierre, D. (2000). Collaborative online distance learning: Issues for future practice and research. *Distance Education*, *21*(2), 260–277. doi:10.1080/0158791000210205

Berthoff, A. E. (1981). *The making of meaning*. Portsmouth, NH: Heinemann Boynton/Cook Publishers.

Bird, L. (2007). The 3 C's Design Model for Networked E-Learning: A tool for Novice Designers. *Innovations in Education and Teaching International*, *26*(3), 153–168. doi:10.1080/14703290701251231

Bishop, J. (2007). Increasing participation in online communities: A framework for human-computer interaction. *Computers in Human Behavior*, *23*(4), 1881–1893. doi:10.1016/j.chb.2005.11.004

Björck, U. (2002). Distributed problem-based learning in social economy – key issues in students' mastery of a structured method of education. *Distance Education*, *23*(1), 85–103. doi:10.1080/01587910220123991

Black, P., & Harrison, C. (2001). Feedback in questioning and marking: The science teacher's role in formative assessment. *The School Science Review*, *82*(301), 55–61.

Black, P., & Wiliam, D. (1998). Assessment and classroom learning. *Assessment in Education*, *5*(1), 7–74. doi:10.1080/0969595980050102

Blascovich, J., Loomis, J., Beall, A. C., Swinth, K. R., Hoyt, C. L., & Bailenson, J. N. (2002). TARGET ARTICLE: Immersive Virtual Environment Technology as a Methodological Tool for Social Psychology. *Journal Psychological Inquiry*, *13*(2), 103–124. doi:10.1207/S15327965PLI1302_01

Blumenfeld, P. C., Marx, R. W., Soloway, E., & Krajcik, J. (1996). Learning with Peers: From small group cooperation to collaborative communities. *Educational Researcher*, *25*(8), 37–40.

Blythe, S. (2001). Designing online courses: user-centered practices. *Computers and Composition*, *18*(4), 329–346. doi:10.1016/S8755-4615(01)00066-4

Bonk, C. J., & Graham, C. R. (Eds.). (2006). *The Handbook of Blended Learning: Global Perspectives, Local Designs*. San Francisco, CA: Pfeiffer.

Bonk, C., Olson, T., Wisher, R., & Orvis, K. (2002). Learning from focus groups: An examination of blended learning. *Journal of Distance Education*, *17*(3), 97–118.

Booker, Q. E., & Rebman, C. M. Jr. (2005). E-student retention: factors affecting customer loyalty for online program success. *Issues in Information Systems*, *6*(1), 183–189.

Bos, N., Sadat, N., & Shami, S. (2006). Adapting a Face-to-Face *Role-Playing* Simulation for Online Play. *Educational Technology Research and Development*, *54*(5), 493–522. doi:10.1007/s11423-006-0130-z

Bote-Lorenzo, M. L., Gómez-Sánchez, E., Vega-Gorgojo, G., Dimitriadis, Y., Asensio-Pérez, J. I., & Jorrín-Abellán, I. M. (2008). Gridcole: a tailorable grid service based system that supports scripted collaborative learning. *Computers & Education*, *51*(1), 155–172. doi:10.1016/j.compedu.2007.05.004

Bote-Lorenzo, M., Vaquero-Gonzalez, L., Vega-Gorgojo, G., Dimitriadis, Y., Asensio-Perez, J., Gomez-Sanchez, E., et al. (2004). A tailorable collaborative learning system that combines OGSA grid services and IMS-LD scripting. In *Proceedings of the Tenth International Workshop on Groupware: Design, Implementation and Use* (pp. 305-321). Berlin, Germany: Springer-Verlag.

Botturi, L., & Stubbs, T. (Eds.). (2008). *Handbook of Visual Languages for Instructional Design. Theories and Practices*. Hershey, PA: IGI Global.

Boud, D., & Feletti, G. (1997). *The challenge of problem-based learning*. London, UK: Kogan Page.

Boud, D., Cohen, R., & Sampson, J. (1999). Peer learning and assessment. *Assessment & Evaluation in Higher Education*, *24*(4), 413–426. doi:10.1080/0260293990240405

Bouras, C., Giannaka, E., & Tsiatsos, T. (2008). Exploiting Virtual Environments to Support Collaborative E-Learning Communities. *International Journal of Web-Based Learning and Teaching Technologies*, *3*(2), 122.

Bouras, C., & Tsiatsos, T. (2006). Educational virtual environments: design rationale and architecture. *Multimedia Tools and Applications*, *29*(2), 153–173. doi:10.1007/s11042-006-0005-7

Bowman, D. A., & McMahan, R. P. (2007). Virtual Reality: How Much Immersion Is Enough? *Computer*, *40*(7), 36–43..doi:10.1109/MC.2007.257

Bozarth, J., Chapman, D. D., & LaMonica, L. (2004). Preparing for Distance Learning: Designing an Online Student Orientation Course. *Journal of Educational Technology & Society*, *7*(1), 87–106.

Bransford, J.D., Brown, A.L., & Cocking; R.R. (Eds.) (2000*). How People Learn: Brain, Mind, Experience, and School.* Expanded Edition. Washington D.C: National Academies Press.

Bratitsis, T., & Dimitrakopoulou, A. (2005). Data recording and usage interaction analysis in asynchronous discussions: The DIAS system. In *Proceedings of the 12th International Conference on Artificial Intelligence in Education AIED,* In C. Choquet, V. Luengo, A. Merceron (Eds.), *Proceedings of the Workshop on Usage Analysis in Learning Systems*, The Netherlands, Amsterdam.

Bray, D. A., & Konsynski, B. R. (2007). Virtual worlds: multi-disciplinary research opportunities. SIGMIS. *Database*, *38*(4), 17–25.

Brewer, W. F., & Nakamura, G. V. (1984). The nature and functions of schemas. Center for the Study of Reading, Technical Report Bo. 325. In Wyer, R. S., & Krull, T. K. (Eds.), *Handbook of social cognition* (*Vol. 1*, pp. 119–160). Mahwah, NJ: Lawrence Erlbaum.

Brookfield, S. (1987). *Developing critical thinkers: challenging adults to explore alternative ways of thinking and acting*. San Francisco, CA: Jossey- Bass.

Brookfield, S. (1995). *Becoming a critically reflective teacher*. San Francisco, CA: Jossey Bass.

Brookfield, S., & Preskill, S. (2005). *Discussion as a way of teaching*. San Francisco, CA: Jossey Bass.

Brooks, L. W., & Dansereau, D. F. (1983). Effects of structural schema training and text organization on expository prose processing. *Journal of Educational Psychology*, *75*(6), 811–820. doi:10.1037/0022-0663.75.6.811

Brooks, L. W., & Dansereau, D. F. (1983). Effects of structural schema training and text organization on expository prose processing. *Journal of Educational Psychology*, *75*(6), 811–820. doi:10.1037/0022-0663.75.6.811

Brooks, F. (1999). What's Real About Virtual Reality? *IEEE Computer Graphics and Applications*, *16*(6), 16–27. doi:10.1109/38.799723

Brown, A. L., & Campione, J. C. (1990). Communities of learning and thinking: Or a context by any other name. [Basel,CH: Karger.]. *Contributions to Human Development*, *21*, 108–125.

Brown, R. E. (2001). The process of community-building in distance learning classes. *Journal of Asynchronous Learning Networks*, *5*(2), 18–35.

Brown, S., & McIntyre, D. (1995). *Making sense of teaching*. Buckingham, UK: Open University Press.

Browne, E. (2003). Conversations in cyberspace: A study of online learning. *Open Learning*, *18*(3), 245–259. doi:10.1080/0268051032000131017

Brufee, K. A. (1999). *Collaborative Learning: Higher Education Interdependence, the authority of knowledge*. Baltimore, MD: The John Hopkins University.

Bruhn, J. (2000). *Förderung des kooperativen Lernens über Computernetze. Prozess und Lernerfolg beim dyadischen Lernen mit Desktop-Videokonferenzen*. Frankfurt am Main, Germany: Peter Lang.

Bruner, J. (1996). *The Culture of Education*. Cambridge, MA: Harvard University Press.

Bryson, S. (1996). Virtual reality in scientific visualization. *Communications of the ACM*, *39*(5), 62–71. doi:10.1145/229459.229467

Bump, J. (1990). Radical changes in classroom discussion using network computers. *Computers and the Humanities*, *24*(1-2), 49–65. doi:10.1007/BF00115028

Butera, F., & Buchs, C. (2005). Reasoning together: From focusing to decentering. In Girotto, V., & Johnson-Laird, P. N. (Eds.), *The shape of reason* (pp. 193–203). Hove, UK: Psychology Press.

Butler, R. (1987). Task-involving and ego-involving properties of evaluation: Effects of different feedback conditions on motivational perceptions, interest, and performance. *Journal of Educational Psychology*, *79*(4), 474–482. doi:10.1037/0022-0663.79.4.474

Butler, R., & Nisan, M. (1986). Effects of no feedback, task-related comments, and grades on intrinsic motivation and performance. *Journal of Educational Psychology*, *78*(3), 210–216. doi:10.1037/0022-0663.78.3.210

Caeiro, M. (2008). PoEML: a separation-of-concerns proposal to instructional design. In Botturi, L., & Stubbs, T. (Eds.), *Handbook of Visual Languages for Instructional Design: Theories and Practices* (pp. 185–209). Hershey, PA: IGI Global.

Calderhead, J. (1981). A psychological approach to research on teachers' classroom decision making. *British Educational Research Journal*, *7*(1), 51–57. doi:10.1080/0141192810070105

Calvani, A., Fini, A. Pettenati, M. C., & Sarti, L. (2006). Remarks on CSCL theories applied to open source solutions for the design of collaborative learning environments. *Journal of e-Learning and Knowledge Society, 2(1),* 21-74.

Cameron, T., Barrows, H. S., & Crooks, S. M. (1999). Distributed Problem-Based Learning at Southern Illinois University School of Medicine. In C. Hoadley & J. Roschelle (Eds.). *Computer Support for Collaborative Learning. Designing New Media for a New Millenium: Collaborative Technology for Learning, Education, and Training* (86-94), Palo Alto,CA: Stanford University.

Cañas, A. J., Hill, G., Carff, R., Suri, N., Lott, J., Eskridge, T., et al. (2004). CmapTools: A Knowledge Modeling and Sharing Environment. In A.J. Cañas, J.D. Novak, and F.M. González, (Eds.), *Proceedings of Concept Maps: Theory, Methodology, Technology, The First International Conference on Concept Mapping* (125-133). Pamplona, Spain: Universidad Pública de Navarra.

Carlson, W. (2009). *A Critical History of Computer Graphics and Animation – Section 17 - Virtual Reality.* last retrieved September 14, 2009, from http://design.osu.edu/carlson/history/lesson17.html

Carr, S. (2000). As distance education comes of age, the challenge is keeping the students. *The Chronicle of Higher Education, 46*, A39–A41.

Carter, K. (1990). Teachers' knowledge and learning to teach. In Houston, W. R. (Ed.), *Handbook of research on teacher education* (pp. 291–310). New York, NY: Macmillan.

Carusi, A. (2003). Taking philosophical dialogue online. *Discourse: Learning and Teaching in Philosophical and Religious Studies, 3*(1), 95–156.

Caspi, A., & Blau, I. (2008). Social presence in online discussion groups: testing three conceptions and their relations to perceived learning. *Social Psychology of Education, 11*(3), 323–346. doi:10.1007/s11218-008-9054-2

Castelli, S., Vanin, L., & Brambilla, M. (2006). Il modello di orientamento "a stanze". Analisi dei bisogni e formazione universitaria a distanza. *Tecnologie Didattiche, 39*, 57–66.

Cavanaugh, J. (2005) Teaching Online – A Time Comparison. *Online Journal of Distance Learning Administration.* Retrieved March 20, 2010 from http://www.westga.edu/~distance/ojdla/spring81/cavanaugh81.htm

Celentin, P. (2007). Online training: Analysis of interaction and knowledge building patterns among foreign language teachers. *Journal of Distance Education, 21*(3), 39–58.

Chan, C. K. K., & van Aalst, J. (2004). Learning, assessment and collaboration in computer supported environments. In P. Dillenbourg (Series Ed.), J. W. Strijbos, P. A. Kirschner, and R. L. Martens (Vol. Eds.), *Computer-supported collaborative learning: Vol 3. What we know about CSCL and implementing it in higher education* (pp. 87–112). Boston: Kluwer Academic Publishers.

Chan, C., & van Aalst, J. (2006). Learning, assessment and collaboration in computer-supported environments. In. P. Dillenbourg (Series Ed), J.W. Strijbos, P.A. Kirschner & R.L. Martens (Vol Eds). *Computer-supported collaborative learning: Vo l3. What we Know about CSCL and implementing it in higher education* (pp. 87-112). Boston: Kluwer Academic/Spinger Verlag.

Chang, V., Gütl, C., Kopeinik, S., & Williams, R. (2009). Evaluation of Collaborative Learning Settings in 3D Virtual Worlds. *International. Journal of Emerging Technologies in Learning (iJET), 4* 6-17. Special Issue: ICL2009, Chittaro, L., & Ranon, R. (2007). Web3D technologies in learning, education and training: Motivations, issues, opportunities. *Computers & Education, 49*(1), 3–18.

Chun, D. (1994). Using computer networking to facilitate the acquisition of interactive competence. *System, 22*(1), 17–31. doi:10.1016/0346-251X(94)90037-X

Clark, H. H., & Brennan, S. E. (1991). Grounding in communication. In Resnick, L. B. (Ed.), *Perspectives on socially shared cognition* (pp. 127–149). Washington, DC: American Psychological Association. doi:10.1037/10096-006

Clark, H. H., & Brennan, S. E. (1991). Grounding in communication. In Resnick, L. B., Levine, J. M., & Teasley, S. D. (Eds.), *Perspectives on socially shared cognition* (pp. 127–149). Washington, DC: American Psychological Association. doi:10.1037/10096-006

Clark, H. H., & Carlson, T. B. (1982). Speech acts and hearer's beliefs. In Smith, N. V. (Ed.), *Mutual knowledge* (pp. 1–36). New York, NY: Academic Press.

Clift, R. T., Mullen, L., Levin, J., & Larson, A. (2001). Technologies in context: Implications for teacher education. *Teaching and Teacher Education, 17*(1), 33–50. doi:10.1016/S0742-051X(00)00037-8

Coffman, T., & Klinger, B., M. (2007). Utilizing Virtual Worlds in Education: The Implications of Practice. *International Journal of Social Sciences, 2*(1), 29–33.

Cohen, E. G. (1994). Restructuring the classroom: Conditions for productive small groups. *Review of Educational Research, 64*(1), 1–35.

Cohen, E. G., & Lotan, R. A. (1995). Producing equal-status interaction in the heterogeneous classroom. *American Educational Research Journal, 32*(1), 99–120.

Cole, M., & Engeström, Y. (1993). A cultural-historical approach to distributed cognition. In Salomon, G. (Ed.), *Distributed cognitions: Psychological and educational considerations* (pp. 1–46). Cambridge, UK: Cambridge University Press.

Cole, M., & Engeström, Y. (1993). A cultural-historical approach to distributed cognition. In Salomon, G. (Ed.), *Distributed cognitions: Psychological and educational considerations* (pp. 1–46). Cambridge, UK: Cambridge University Press.

Colgan, C. (2005). Computer blogs: Boon or bane? *Education Digest: Essential Readings Condensed for Quick Review, 71*(4), 57–63.

Collazos, C.A., Guerrero, L.A., Pino, J.A., Renzi, S., & Klobas, J., Ortega, et al. (2007). Evaluating Collaborative Learning Processes using System-based Measurement. *Journal of Educational Technology & Society, 10*(3), 257–274.

Conole, G., Brasher, A., Cross, S., Weller, M., Clark, P., & White, J. (2008). Visualising learning design to foster and support good practice and creativity. *Educational Media International, 54*(3), 177–194. doi:10.1080/09523980802284168

Conole, G., & Culver, J. (2009). The design of Cloudworks: applying social networking to foster the exchange of learning and teaching ideas and design. *Computers & Education, 54*(3), 679–692. doi:10.1016/j.compedu.2009.09.013

Conole, G., Dyke, M., Oliver, M., & Seale, J. (2004). Mapping pedagogy and tools for effective learning design. *Computers & Education, 43*(1-2), 17–33. doi:10.1016/j.compedu.2003.12.018

Conole, G., Brasher, A., Cross, S., Weller, M., Clark, P., & White, J. (2008). Visualising learning design to foster and support good practice and creativity. *Educational Media International, 54*(3), 177–194. doi:10.1080/09523980802284168

Conole, G., & Culver, J. (2009). The design of Cloudworks: applying social networking to foster the exchange of learning and teaching ideas and design. *Computers & Education, 54*(3), 679–692. doi:10.1016/j.compedu.2009.09.013

Conole, G. (2009a). Capturing and representing practice. In Tait, A., Vidal, M., Bernath, U., & Szucs, A. (Eds.), *Distance and E-learning in Transition: Learning Innovation, Technology and Social Challenges*. London, UK: John Wiley and Sons.

Conole, G. (2008). Capturing practice: the role of mediating artefacts in learning design. In L. Lockyer, S. Bennett, S. Agostinho, & B Harper (Eds), *Handbook of Research on Learning Design and Learning Objects: Issues, Applications and Technologies* (187-207). Hershey, PA: IGI Global.

Conole, G. (2009b). *Course representations*, blog posting, 10th June 2009, Retrieved March 20, 2010, from http://e4innovation.com/?p=328

Conole, G. (2010), Learning Design – making practice explicit, Keynote and paper, ConnectEd Conference, 2nd International Conference on Design Education, 28th June 2010, Sydney, http://oro.open.ac.uk/21864/.

Conole, G., & McAndrew, P. (2010). OLnet: a new approach to supporting the design and use of Open Educational Resources. In M. Ebner & M. Schiefner (Eds), *Looking toward the future of technology enhanced education: ubiquitous learning and the digital nature* (123-144). Hershey, PA: IGI Global.

Conrad, D. (2005). Building and Maintaining Community in Cohort-Based Online Learning. *Journal of Distance Education, 20*(1), 1–20.

Conrad, D. (2002). Deep in the hearts of learners: Insights into the nature of online community. *Journal of Distance Education*, *17*(1), 1–19.

Conroy, J. (2008, February 01). Moodle gets WiZiQ - A free virtual classroom add-on. *CMS Wire*. Retrieved January 9, 2010, from http://www.cmswire.com/cms/web-cms/moodle-gets-wiziq-a-free-virtual-classroom-addon-002260.php

CoSSICLE. (2005). *Computer-Supported Scripting of Interaction in Collaborative Learning Environments Kaleidoscope-NoE ERT website*. Retrieved 13 April, 2010, from http://www.iwm-kmrc.de/cossicle/

Cox, R., & Brna, P. (1995). Supporting the use of external representations in problem solving: The need for flexible learning environments. *Journal of Artificial Intelligence in Education*, *6*(2-3), 239–302.

Craig, E. M. (2007). Changing paradigms: managed learning environments and Web 2.0. *Campus-Wide Information Systems*, *24*(3), 152–161. doi:10.1108/10650740710762185

Cress, U. (2008). The need for considering multi-level analysis in CSCL research. An appeal for the use of more advanced statistical methods. *International Journal of Computer-Supported Collaborative Learning*, *3*(1), 69–84. doi:10.1007/s11412-007-9032-2

Cross, S., & Conole, G. (2008). *Learn about Learning Design*, Learn About Series, Open University: Milton Kynes, UK. Retrieved April, 13, 2010, from http://ouldi.open.ac.uk/Learn%20about%20 learning%20design.pdf

Cross, S., & Conole, G. (2008). *Learn about Learning Design*, Learn About Series, Open University: Milton Kynes, UK. Retrieved April, 13, 2010, from http://ouldi.open.ac.uk/Learn%20about%20learning%20design.pdf

Cucchiara, S., Spadaro, P. F., & Ligorio, M. B. (2008). Identità e comunità in contesti collaborativi: un'esperienza blended universitaria [Identity and community in collaborative contexts: a blended university experience]. *Qwerty*, *1*, 23–48.

Cunningham, W. (1998). *The wiki wiki web*. Retrieved September 13, 2009, from http://c2.com/cgi/wiki?WikiWikiWeb

Curriculum, Technology, & Education Reform (CTER) (2009). *CTER online master of education program, Uuniversity of Illinois at Urbana-Champaign*, retrieved March 20, 2010 from http://wik.ed.uiuc.edu/index.php/Role_playing

Curtis, D. D., & Lawson, M. J. (2001). Exploring collaborative online learning. *Journal of Asynchronous Learning Networks*, *5*(1), 21–34.

D'Antoni, S. (2008). *Open Educational Resources. The way forward. Deliberations of an international community of interest*. UNESCO International Institute or Educational Planning. Retrieved March 20, 2010, from http://learn.creativecommons.org/wp-content/uploads/2008/03/oer-way-forward-final-version.pdf

Dalziel, J. (2003). Implementing Learning Design: The Learning Activity Management System (LAMS). In Crisp G., Thiele, D., Scholten, I., Barker, S., & Baron, J. (Eds.), *Proceedings of the 20th Annual Conference of the Australasian Society for Computers in Learning* (pp. 593-596), Adelaide, Australia: ASCILITE

Danchak, M. M. (2002) Bringing Affective Behavior to e-Learning. *The Technology Source.* Retrieved March 20, 2010, from http://technologysource.org/article/bringing_affective_behavior_to_elearning/

Daniels, H., Wertsch, J., & Cole, M. (2007). *The Cambridge companion to Vygotsky*. Cambridge, UK: Cambridge University Press.

Daniels, H., Wertsch, J., & Cole, M. (2007). *The Cambridge companion to Vygotsky*. Cambridge, UK: Cambridge University Press.

Dansereau, D. F. (1988). Cooperative learning strategies. In Weinstein, C. E., Goetz, E. T., & Alexander, P. A. (Eds.), *Learning and study strategies: Issues in assessment, instruction, and evaluation* (pp. 103–120). New York: Academic Press.

Dansereau, D. (1988). Cooperative learning strategies. In Weinstein, C. E., Goetz, E. T., & Alexander, P. A. (Eds.), *Learning and study strategies: Issues in assessment, instruction, and evaluation* (pp. 103–120). New York: Academic Press.

Daradoumis, T., Martínez, A., & Xhafa, F. (2006). A Layered Framework for Evaluating Online Collaborative Learning Interactions. *International Journal of Human-Computer Studies. Special Issue on ". Theoretical and Empirical Advances in Groupware Research, 64*(7), 622–635.

Daradoumis, T., Martínez, A., & Xhafa, F. (2006). A layered framework for evaluating on-line collaborative learning interactions. *International Journal of Man-Machine Studies, 64*(7), 622–635.

Daradoumis, T., & Xhafa, F. (2005). Problems and Opportunities of Learning together in a Virtual Learning Environment. In Roberts, T. S. (Ed.), *Computer-Supported Collaborative Learning in Higher Education* (pp. 218–233). Hershey, PA: Idea Group Press.

David, J. (2008). What research says about project-based learning. *Educational Leadership, 65*(5), 80–82.

Davis, S. (2003). Observations in classrooms using a network of handheld devices. *Journal of Computer Assisted Learning, 19*(3), 298–307. doi:10.1046/j.0266-4909.2003.00031.x

Dawson, S. (2006). A study of the relationship between student communication interaction and sense of community. *The Internet and Higher Education, 9*(3), 153–162. doi:10.1016/j.ihcduc.2006.06.007

de Bono, E. (1994). *Parallel thinking: from Socratic thinking to de Bono thinking*. Middlesex, UK: Viking.

De Corte, E. (2003). Designing learning environments that foster the productive use of acquired knowledge and skills. In De Corte, E., Verschaffel, L., Entwistle, N., & Merrienboer, J. J. G. v. (Eds.), *Powerful learning environments: Unravelling basic components and dimensions* (pp. 21–33). Amsterdam, The Netherlands: Pergamon.

De Corte, E. (1996). Learning theory and instructional science. In Reimann, P., & Spada, E. (Eds.), *Learning in humans and machines* (pp. 97–109). Oxford, UK: Elsevier.

De Corte, E. (2003). Designing learning environments. In Verschaffel, L., Entwistle, N., & Merrienboer, J. J. G. v. (Eds.), *Powerful learning environments: Unravelling basic components and dimensions* (pp. 21–33). Amsterdam, The Netherlands: Pergamon.

De Jong, T., & Ferguson-Hessler, M. G. M. (1996). Types and qualities of knowledge. *Educational Psychologist, 31*(2), 105–113. doi:10.1207/s15326985ep3102_2

De Laat, M., Lally, V., Lipponen, L., & Simons, P. R. J. (2005). *Patterns of interaction in a networked learning community: Squaring the circle.* Retrieved October, 2008, from http://eprints.soton.ac.uk/17267/

De Lucia, A., Francese, R., Passero, I., & Genoveffa Tortora, G. (2008). Development and evaluation of a virtual campus on Second Life: The case of SecondDMI. *Computer & Education, 52*(1), 220-233. etrieved April 2, 2010, from http://www.sciencedirect.com/science/article/B6VCJ-4TGGCKR-1/2/b7a76e15ede1c82b93c1c081cd5eb1ba

De Simone, C., Lou, Y., & Schmid, R. F. (2001). Meaningful and interactive distance learning supported by the use of metaphor and synthesizing activities. *Journal of Distance Education, 16*(1), 85–101.

del Cid, J. E., de la Fuente-Valentín, L., & Gutiérrez, S. Pardo, & A., Kloos, C. D. (2007). Implementation of a Learning Design Run-Time Environment for the. LRN Learning Management System. *Journal of Interactive Media in Education,* Burgos D. (Ed) *Adaptation and IMS Learning Design. Special Issue 2007/07*

Delfino, M., & Manca, S. (2007). The expression of social presence through the use of figurative language in a web-based learning environment. *Computers in Human Behavior, 23*(5), 2190–2211. doi:10.1016/j.chb.2006.03.001

Delfino, M., & Persico, D. (2007). Online or face-to-face? Experimenting with different techniques in teacher training. *Journal of Computer Assisted Learning, 23*(5), 351–365. doi:10.1111/j.1365-2729.2007.00220.x

Delozanne, E., Le Calvez, F., Merceron, A., & Labat, J. (2007). A Structured Set of Design Patterns for Learners'Assessment. *Journal of Interactive Learning Research*, *18*(2), 309–333.

Demetriadis, S., Magnisalis, I., & Karakostas, A. (2009). Adaptive Patterns in Systems for Collaborative Learning and the Role of the Learning Design Specification. In *Proceedings of the Scripted vs. Free CS Collaboration: Alternatives and Paths for Adaptable and Flexible CS Scripted Collaboration Workshop, CSCL09* (pp. 44-48). The International Society of the Learning Sciences (ISLS).

Dennen, V. P. (2000). Task structuring for online problem based learning: A case study. *Journal of Educational Technology & Society*, *3*(3), 329–336.

Dennis, A. R. (1996). Information exchange and use in small group decision making. *Small Group Research*, *27*(4), 532–550. doi:10.1177/1046496496274003

Dennis, A. R., & Valacich, J. S. (1999). Rethinking media richness: towards a theory of media synchronicity. In *Proceedings of the 32nd Annual Hawaii International Conference on Systems Sciences* (pp.1-10). Los Alamitos, CA: IEEE Press

DeWert, M. H., Babinski, L. M., & Jones, B. D. (2003). Safe passages: Providing online support to beginning teachers. *Journal of Teacher Education*, *54*(4), 311–320. doi:10.1177/0022487103255008

Dickey, M. D. (2003). Teaching in 3D: Pedagogical affordances and constraints of 3D virtual worlds for synchronous distance learning. *Distance Education*, *24*(1), 105–122. doi:10.1080/01587910303047

Dickey, M. D. (2005). Three-dimensional virtual worlds and distance learning: two case studies of Active Worlds as a medium for distance education. *British Journal of Educational Technology*, *36*(3), 439–451. doi:10.1111/j.1467-8535.2005.00477.x

DiGiano, C., Yarnall, L., Patton, C., Roschelle, J., Tatar, D., & Manley, M. (2003). Conceptual tools for planning for the wireless classroom. *Journal of Computer Assisted Learning*, *19*(3), 284–297. doi:10.1046/j.0266-4909.2003.00030.x

Dillenbourg, P., & Traum, D. (2006). Sharing solutions: Persistence and grounding in multimodal collaborative problem solving. *Journal of the Learning Sciences*, *15*(1), 121–151. doi:10.1207/s15327809jls1501_9

Dillenbourg, P. (Ed.). (1999). *Collaborative Learning. Cognitive and Computational Approaches. Advances in Learning and Instruction Series*. New York: Elsevier Science Inc.

Dillenbourg, P., & Tchounikine, P. (2007). Flexibility in macro-scripts for computer supported collaborative learning. *Journal of Computer Assisted Learning*, *23*(1), 1–13. doi:10.1111/j.1365-2729.2007.00191.x

Dillenbourg, P., & Hong, F. (2008). The mechanics of CSCL macro scripts. *International Journal of Computer-Supported Collaborative Learning*, *3*(1), 3–23. doi:10.1007/s11412-007-9033-1

Dillenbourg, P. (1999). What do you mean by 'collaborative learning. In Dillenbourg, P. (Ed.), *Collaborative learning: Cognitive and computational approaches* (pp. 1–19). Oxford, UK: Elsevier.

Dillenbourg, P., & Jermann, P. (2007). Designing integrative scripts. In Fischer, F., Kollar, I., Mandl, H., & Haake, J. M. (Eds.), *Scripting computer-supported collaborative learning. Cognitive, computational and educational perspectives*. Dordrecht, The Netherlands: Springer. doi:10.1007/978-0-387-36949-5_16

Dillenbourg, P. (2002). Over-Scripting CSCL: The Risks of the provision of service instances is a critical feature: Blending Collaborative Learning with Instructional Design. In Kirschner, P. A. (Ed.), *Inaugural Address, Three Worlds of CSCL. Can We Support CSCL?* (pp. 61–91). Heerlen, The Netherlands: Open Universiteit Nederland.

Dillenbourg, P., Baker, M., Blaye, A., & O'Malley, C. (1996). The evolution of research on collaborative learning. In Spada, E., & Reiman, P. (Eds.), *Learning in Humans and Machine: Towards an interdisciplinary learning science* (pp. 189–211). Oxford, UK: Elsevier.

Dillenbourg, P. (2002). Over-scripting CSCL: The risks of blending collaborative learning with instructional design. In P. A. Kirschner (Ed), *Three worlds of CSCL. Can we support CSCL?* (pp. 61-91). Heerlen, Nederland: Open Universiteit Nederland.

Dillenbourg, P. (2002). Over-scripting CSCL: The risks of blending collaborative learning with instructional design. In P. A. Kirschner (Ed.), *Three worlds of CSCL: Can we support CSCL?* (pp. 61-91). Heerlen, Nederland: Open University of the Netherlands.

Dillenbourg, P. Jarvela, S. & Fischer, F. (2009). The evolution of research on Computer-Supported Collaborative Learning. From design to orchestration. In S. Ludvigsen et al. (Eds), *Technology-Enhanced Learning. Principles and Products* (3-19). New York: Springer Verlag.

Dillenbourg, P., & Jermann, P. (2007). Designing Integrative Scripts. In Fischer, F., Kollar, I. Mandl, H., & Haake, J.M. (Eds.), *Scripting Computer-Supported Collaborative Learning: Cognitive, Computational and Educational Perspectives, Computer-Supported Collaborative Learning Series, Vol. 6*, (pp. 275-302). New York: Springer.

Dimitracopoulou, A. (2007). Computer based Interaction Analysis supporting self-regulation: Achievements and prospects of an emerging research field. In Kinshuk et al. (Eds.), *Proceedings of CELDA 2007. Cognition and Exploratory Learning in Digital Age. IADIS International Congress.*

Dimitracopoulou, A., Vosniadou, S., Gregoriadou, M., Avouris, N., & Kollias, V. Gogoulou, et al., (2006). The field of computer based interaction analysis for the support of participants regulation in social technology based learning environments: State of the art and perspectives. In D. Psillos, & V. Dagdidelis (Eds.), *Proceedings of the 5th Hellenic Congress with International Participation: Information and Communication Technologies in Education* (pp. 997-1000). Thessaloniki, Greece: HICTE.

diSessa, A., & Minstrell, J. (1998). Cultivating conceptual change with benchmark lessons. In Greeno, J., & Goldman, S. (Eds.), *Thinking practices in mathematics and science learning* (pp. 155–188). Hillsdale, NJ: Lawrence Erlbaum.

diSessa, A. A., & Minstrell, J. (1998). Cultivating conceptual change with benchmark lessons. In Greeno, J. G., & Goldman, S. V. (Eds.), *Thinking practices in mathematics and science learning* (pp. 155–187). Mahwah, NJ: Lawrence Erlbaum Associates.

Dobson, M. (1999). Information enforcement and learning with interactive graphical systems. *Learning and Instruction, 9*(4), 365–390. doi:10.1016/S0959-4752(98)00052-8

Dobson, M., & McCracken, J. (1997). Problem based learning: A means to evaluate multimedia courseware in science & technology in society. In T. Muldner & T. C. Reeves (Eds.), *Educational Multimedia/Hypermedia and Telecommunications.* Charlottesville, VA: Association for the Advancement of Computing in Education (AACE).

Dochy, F., & McDowell, L. (1997). Assessment as a tool for learning. *Studies in Educational Evaluation, 23*(4), 279–298. doi:10.1016/S0191-491X(97)86211-6

Doise, W., & Mugny, G. (1984). *Social Processes in Children's Learning.* Cambridge, UK: University Press.

Duch, B. J., Groh, S. E., & Allen, D. E. (2001). *The Power of Problem-Based Learning.* Sterling, VA: Stylus Publishing, LLC.

Duffy, P., & Bruns, A. (2006). The Use of Blogs, Wikis and RSS in Education: A Conversation of Possibilities. In [Brisbane, Australia: QUT.]. *Proceedings of the Online Learning and Teaching Conference, 2006*, 31–38.

Duffy, T. M., Dueber, B., & Hawley, C. L. (1998). Critical Thinking in a Distributed Environment: A Pedagogical Base for the Design of Conferencing Systems. In Bonk, C. J. & King K. S. (Eds.), *Electronic Collaborators: Learner-centered Technologies for Literacy, Apprenticeship and Discourse* (p. 73). Mahawah, NJ: LEA associates.

Dufresne, R. J., & Gerace, W. J. (2004). Assessing-To-Learn: Formative assessment in physics instruction. *The Physics Teacher, 42*(7), 428–433. doi:10.1119/1.1804662

Dufresne, R. J., Gerace, W. J., Leonard, W. J., Mestre, J. P., & Wenk, L. (1996). Classtalk: A classroom communication system for active learning. *Journal of Computing in Higher Education, 7*(2), 3–47. doi:10.1007/BF02948592

Dunlap, J. (2005). Workload Reduction in Online Courses: Getting Some Shuteye. *Performance Improvement*, *44*(5), 18–26. doi:10.1002/pfi.4140440507

Dweck, C. S., & Elliot, E. S. (1983). Achievement motivation. In Mussen, P., & Hetherington, E. M. (Eds.), *Handbook of child psychology* (pp. 643–691). New York: Wiley.

Eastmond, D. V. (1994). Adult distance study through computer conferencing. *Distance Education*, *15*(1), 128–152. doi:10.1080/0158791940150109

Eckloff, M. (2006). Using sociodrama to improve communication and understanding. *et Cetera. 63,* (3), *259-270..*

Edwards, M. A., & Fintan, C. (2001). Supporting the Collaborative Learning of Practical Skills with Computer-mediated Communications Technology. *Journal of Educational Technology & Society*, *4*(1), 80–92.

E-LEN. (2004). *E-LEN Project Website*. Retrieved 13 April, 2010, from http://www2.tisip.no/E-LEN/

Elliot, A. J., & McGregor, H. (2001). A 2x2 achievement goal framework. *Journal of Personality and Social Psychology*, *80*(3), 501–519. doi:10.1037/0022-3514.80.3.501

Ellis, C. A., Gibbs, S. J., & Rein, G. L. (1991). Groupware: Some issues and experiences. *Communications of the ACM*, *34*(1), 35–58. doi:10.1145/99977.99987

Ellis, R. A., Goodyear, P., Prosser, M., & O'Hara, A. (2006). How and what university students learn through online and face-to-face discussion: Conceptions, intentions, and approaches. *Journal of Computer Assisted Learning*, *22*, 244–256. doi:10.1111/j.1365-2729.2006.00173.x

Eraut, M. (1994). *Developing professional knowledge and competence*. London, UK: Falmer Press.

Ertl, B., Fischer, F., & Mandl, H. (2006). Conceptual and socio-cognitive support for collaborative learning in videoconferencing environments. *Computers & Education*, *47*(3), 298–315. doi:10.1016/j.compedu.2004.11.001

Ertl, B., Reiserer, M., & Mandl, H. (2002). Kooperatives Lernen in Videokonferenzen. *Unterrichtswissenschaft*, *30*(4), 339–356.

Ertl, B., Fischer, F., & Mandl, H. (2006). Conceptual and socio-cognitive support for collaborative learning in videoconferencing environments. *Computers & Education*, *47*(3), 298–315. doi:10.1016/j.compedu.2004.11.001

Ertl, B., Kopp, B., & Mandl, H. (2006). Fostering collaborative knowledge construction in case-based learning in videoconferencing. *Journal of Educational Computing Research*, *35*(4), 377–397. doi:10.2190/A0LP-482N-0063-J480

Ertl, B., Kopp, B., & Mandl, H. (2008). Supporting learning using external representations. *Computers & Education*, *51*(4), 1599–1608. doi:10.1016/j.compedu.2008.03.001

Ertl, B., Kopp, B., & Mandl, H. (2007). Supporting collaborative learning in videoconferencing using collaboration scripts and content schemes. In Fischer, F., Kollar, I., Mandl, H., & Haake, J. M. (Eds.), *Scripting computer-supported communication of knowledge – cognitive, computational and educational perspectives* (pp. 213–236). Berlin Heidelberg, Germany: Springer.

Ertl, B., Kopp, B., & Mandl, H. (2005). Effects of an individual's prior knowledge on collaborative knowledge construction and individual learning outcomes in videoconferencing. In Koschmann, T., Chan, T.-W., & Suthers, D. D. (Eds.), *Computer supported collaborative learning 2005: the next 10 years!* (pp. 145–154). Mahwah, NJ: Lawrence Erlbaum Associates.

Ertl, B. (2003). *Kooperatives Lernen in Videokonferenzen. Förderung von individuellem und gemeinsamem Lernerfolg durch external repräsentierte Strukturangebote [Cooperative learning in videoconferencing. Support of individual and cooperative learning outcomes by representational aids].* [Dissertation, Ludwig-Maximilians-Universität München]. Retrieved April 8, 2010 from http://edoc.ub.uni-muenchen.de/archive/ 00001227/01/ Ertl_Bernhard_M.pdf

Ethell, R. G., & McMeniman, M. M. (2000). Unlocking the knowledge in action of an expert practitioner. *Journal of Teacher Education*, *51*, 87–101. doi:10.1177/002248710005100203

Fahy, P. J. (2005). Two methods of assessing critical thinking in computer-mediated communications (CMC) transcripts. *International Journal of Instructional Technology and Distance Learning*, *2*(3).

Fannon, K. (2005). *'Needle-stick'- A Role-Play Simulation: Transformative Learning in Complex Dynamic Social Systems*. Retrieved March 20, 2010, from http://www.avetra.org.au/downloads/Vol2_1%20-%202003%20-%20Fannon.pdf

Farzan, R., & Brusilovsky, P. (2008). AnnotatEed: A social navigation and annotation service for web-based educational resources. *New Review of Hypermedia and Multimedia*, *14*(1), 3–32. doi:10.1080/13614560802357172

Feenberg, A. (1989). The written world. In Mason, R., & Kaye, A. (Eds.), *Mindweave: Communication, computers, and distance education* (pp. 22–39). Oxford, UK: Pergamon Press.

Feenberg, A., & Xin, M. C. (2003). Facilitation. In A. DiStefano, K. E. Rudestarn, & R. Silverman (Eds.), *Encyclopedia of Distributed Learning*,London: Sage Publications.pp. 163-166. Retrieved September 18, 2009, from http://www.textweaver.org/facilitation.htm

Fenstermacher, G. D. (1994). The knower and the known: The nature of knowledge in research on teaching. In Darling-Hammond, L. (Ed.), *Review of Research on Teaching* (*Vol. 20*, pp. 3–56). Washington, DC: American Educational Research Association.

Fesakis, G., Petrou, A., & Dimitracopoulou, A. (2004). Collaboration activity function: An interaction analysis instrument for computer supported collaborative learning activities. In *Proceedings of the 4th IEEE International Conference on Advanced Learning Technologies (ICALT 2004)*.

Fichter, D. (2005). Intranets, wikis, blikes, and collaborative working. *Online*, *29*(5), 47–50.

Finn, K. E., Sellen, A. J., & Wilbur, S. B. (Eds.). (1997). *Video-mediated communication*. Mahwah, NJ: Lawrence Erlbaum.

Finnegan, C. (2006). Technology: Revolutionizing or Transforming College? *Innovative Higher Education*, *31*(3), 143–145. doi:10.1007/s10755-006-9015-7

Fischer, F., Bruhn, J., Gräsel, C., & Mandl, H. (2000). Kooperatives Lernen mit Videokonferenzen: Gemeinsame Wissenskonstruktion und individueller Lernerfolg. *Kognitionswissenschaft*, *9*(1), 5–16. doi:10.1007/s001970000028

Fischer, F., Bruhn, J., Gräsel, C., & Mandl, H. (2002). Fostering collaborative knowledge construction with visualization tools. *Learning and Instruction*, *12*(2), 213–232. doi:10.1016/S0959-4752(01)00005-6

Fischer, F., Kollar, I., Mandl, H., & Haake, J. M. (2007). *Scripting computer-supported communication of knowledge–Cognitive, computational, and educational perspectives*. New York: Springer.

Fischer, F., Bruhn, J., Gräsel, C., & Mandl, H. (2000). Kooperatives Lernen mit Videokonferenzen: Gemeinsame Wissenskonstruktion und individueller Lernerfolg. *Kognitionswissenschaft*, *9*(1), 5–16. doi:10.1007/s001970000028

Fischer, F., Bruhn, J., Gräsel, C., & Mandl, H. (2002). Fostering collaborative knowledge construction with visualization tools. *Learning and Instruction*, *12*(2), 213–232. doi:10.1016/S0959-4752(01)00005-6

Fischer, F., Bruhn, J., Gräsel, C., & Mandl, H. (2000). Kooperatives Lernen mit Videokonferenzen: Gemeinsame Wissenskonstruktion und individueller Lernerfolg [Cooperative learning with video-conferencing systems: Collaborative knowledge construction and individual learning outcomes]. *Kognitionswissenschaft*, *9*(1), 5–16. doi:10.1007/s001970000028

Fischer, F., & Mandl, H. (2005). Knowledge convergence in computer-supported collaborative learning - the role of external representation tools. *Journal of the Learning Sciences*, *14*(3), 405–441. doi:10.1207/s15327809jls1403_3

Fischer, F. Kollar, I., Mandl, H., & Haake, J.M. (Eds.) (2007). *Scripting CSCL: Cognitive, Computational and Educational Perspectives, CSCL Series, Vol. 6*. New York: Springer.

Fisher, B. (2009). *Role play as a teaching method in multi-stakeholder natural resource* 2006, Lao PDR. Retrieved March 20, 2010, from http://www.mekong.es.usyd.edu.au/projects/mli/initiatives_partners/role-play_manual_ubu.pdf

Folger, J. P., Poole, M. S., & Stutman, R. K. (2005). *Working Through Conflict: Strategies for Relationships, Groups, and Organizations* (5th ed.). Boston: Pearson/Allyn and Bacon.

Fowler, C., & Mayes, J. (2000). Learning Relationships from Theory to design. In Squires, D., Conole, G., & Jacobs, G. (Eds.), *The Changing Face of Learning Technology* (pp. 39–50). Cardiff, UK: University of Wales Press.

Francescato, D., Mebane, M., Porcelli, R., Attanasio, C., & Pulino, M. (2007). Developing professional skills and social capital through computer-supported collaborative learning in university contexts. *International Journal of Human-Computer Studies*, *65*, 140–152. doi:10.1016/j.ijhcs.2006.09.002

Frieden, S. (1999). Support Services for Distance Education. *Journal of Educational Technology & Society*, *2*(3), 48–54.

Friedman, L. B., & McCullough, J. (1992). Computer conferencing as a support mechanism for teacher-researches in rural high school. In Waggoner, M. D. (Ed.), *Empowerment networks: Computer conferencing in education* (pp. 139–156). Englwood Cliffs, NJ: Prentice Hall.

Friend, M. (2000). Myths and misunderstandings about professional collaboration. *Remedial and Special Education*, *21*(3), 130–132, 160. doi:10.1177/074193250002100301

Friend, M. & Cook, (2009). *Interactions: Collaboration skills for school professionals*. (6th ed.). Toronto, ON: Pearson Education.

Friesen, N. (2009). Genre and CSCL: The Form and Rhetoric of the Online Posting. *International Journal of Computer-Supported Collaborative Learning*, *2*(4), 171–185. doi:10.1007/s11412-009-9060-1

Fullan, M. (1993). *Change forces: Probing the depths of educational reform*. London, UK: Falmer Press.

Gallagher, L. P., & Penuel, W. R. (2009, April). *Preparing teachers to design instruction in middle school Earth science: Impacts of three professional development programs on student learning.* Paper presented at the Annual Meeting of the American Educational Research Association, San Diego, CA.

Gambrell, L. (2004). Shifts in Conversations: Teacher-led, Peer-Led, and Computer-Mediated Discussions. *The Reading Teacher*, *58*(2), 212–216. doi:10.1598/RT.58.2.9

Gao, H., Baylor, A. L., & Shen, E. (2005). Designer Support for Online Collaboration and Knowledge Construction. *Journal of Educational Technology & Society*, *8*(1), 69–79.

Gao, F., & Wong, D. (2008). Student engagement in distance learning environments: A comparison of threaded discussion forums and text-focused wikis. *First Monday*, 13 (1). Retrieved September 18, 2009, from http://www.uic.edu/htbin/cgiwrap/bin/ojs/index.php/fm/article/view/2018/1921

Garrison, D. R., & Anderson, T. (2003). *E-learning in the 21st century: A framework for research and practice*. London, UK: RoutledgeFalmer. doi:10.4324/9780203166093

Garrison, D. R., Anderson, T., & Archer, W. (1999). Critical inquiry in a text-based environment: Computer conferencing in higher education. *The Internet and Higher Education*, *2*(2/3), 87–105. doi:10.1016/S1096-7516(00)00016-6

Garrison, D. R., & Cleveland-Innes, M. (2005). Facilitating Cognitive Presence in Online Learning: Interaction is not Enough. *American Journal of Distance Education*, *19*(3), 133–148. doi:10.1207/s15389286ajde1903_2

Garrison, D. R., Anderson, T., & Archer, W. (2001). Critical thinking, cognitive presence, and computer conferencing in distance education. *American Journal of Distance Education, 15*(1), 7–23. doi:10.1080/08923640109527071

Garrison, D. R., & Anderson, T. (2003). [st *century: A framework for research and practice.* London, UK: Routledge Falmer.]. *E-learning*, •••, 21.

Garrison, D. R., Anderson, T., & Archer, W. (2000). Critical inquiry in a text-based environment: Computer conferencing in higher education. *The Internet and Higher Education, 2*(2–3), 87–105.

Garrison, D. R., Anderson, T., & Archer, W. (2001). Critical thinking, cognitive presence, and computer conferencing in distance education. *American Journal of Distance Education, 15*(1), 7–23. doi:10.1080/08923640109527071

Garrison, D. R., Anderson, T., & Archer, W. (2000). Critical thinking in a text-based environment: Computer conferencing in higher education. *The Internet and Higher Education, 11*(2), 1–14.

Garrison, D. R., Anderson, T., & Archer, W. (2001). Critical thinking and computer conferencing: A model and tool to assess cognitive presence. *American Journal of Distance Education, 15*(1), 7–23. doi:10.1080/08923640109527071

Gartner (2007). Gartner Says 80 Percent of Active Internet Users Will Have A "Second Life" in the Virtual World by the End of 2011. *Press Release, Gartner Research Inc.*, April 24th, 2007. Retrieved September 9, 2009, from http://www.gartner.com/it/page.jsp?id=503861

Gartner (2008). Gartner Research Inc. Gartner Says 90 Percent of Corporate Virtual World Projects Fail within 18 Months. *Press Release, Gartner Research Inc.*, Mai 15th, 2008. Retrieved September 9, 2009, from http://www.gartner.com/it/page.jsp?id=670507

Gehring, G. (1994). A degree program offered entirely online: Does it work? In D. Foster and D. Jolly (Eds.), *Proceedings of the Third International Symposium on Telecommunication in Education* (pp. 104-106), November 10-13, Albuquerque, New Mexico.

Gideonse, H. D. (1999). What is a case? What distinguishes case instruction? In Sudzina, M. (Ed.), *Case study applications for teacher education* (pp. 1–7). Boston: Allyn & Bacon.

Gijbels, D., Dochy, F., van den Bossche, P., & Segers, M. (2005). Effects of problem-based learning: A meta-analysis from the angle of the assessment. *Review of Educational Research, 75*(1), 27–61. doi:10.3102/00346543075001027

Cognition and Technology Group at Vanderbilt. (2000). Adventures in anchored instruction: Lessons from beyond the ivory tower. In Glaser, R. (Ed.), *Advances in instructional psychology: Educational design and cognitive science* (pp. 35–99). Mahwah, NJ: Erlbaum.

Glaser, J., Raghavan, K., & Baxter, G. P. (1992). *Cognitive theory as the basis for design of innovative assessment: Design characteristics of science assessments* (No. CSE Tech. Rep. No. 349). Los Angeles, CA: University of California, National Center for Research on Evaluation, Standards, and Student Testing.

Glasser, R., & Bassok, M. (1989). Learning theory and the study of instruction. *Annual Review of Psychology, 40*, 631–666. doi:10.1146/annurev.ps.40.020189.003215

Golberg, M. (1997). CALOS: First results from an experiment in computer-aided learning for operating systems. In *Proceedings of the ACM's 28th SIGCSE Technical Symposium on Computer Science Education. SIGCSE, 29*(1), 48-52.

Gonzalez, M. G., Burke, M. J., Santuzzi, A. M., & Bradley, J. C. (2003). The impact of group process variables on the effectiveness of distance collaboration groups. *Computers in Human Behavior, 19*, 629–648. doi:10.1016/S0747-5632(02)00084-5

Goodwin, C., & Heritage, J. (1990). Conversation analysis. *Annual Review of Anthropology, 19*, 283–307. doi:10.1146/annurev.an.19.100190.001435

Goodyear, P., Avgeriou, P., Baggetun, R., Bartoluzzi, S., Retalis, S., Ronteltap, F., & Rusman, E. (2004). Towards a pattern language for networked learning. In Banks, S., Goodyear, P., Hodgson, V., Jones, C., Lally, V., McConnell, D., & Steeples, C. (Eds.), *Proceedings of Networked learning 2004* (pp. 449–455). Lancaster, UK: LancasterUniversity.

Grabinger, R. S., & Dunlap, J. C. (2002). Problem-based learning as an example of active learning and student engagement. *Lecture Notes in Computer Science Vol. 2457, Advances in Information Systems* (375-384). London, UK: Springer Verlag.

Graddol, D. (1989). Some CMC discourse properties and their educational significance. In Mason, R., & Kaye, A. (Eds.), *Mindweave: Communication, computers and distance education* (pp. 236–241). New York: Pergamon Press.

Graffam, B. (2007). Active learning in medical education: Strategies for beginning implementation. *Medical Teacher*, *29*(1), 38–42. doi:10.1080/01421590601176398

Graham, C. R. (2006). Blended learning systems: definition, current trends and future directions. In Bonk, C. J., & Graham, C. R. (Eds.), *Handbook of blended learning: Global perspectives, local designs* (pp. 3–21). CA: Pfeiffer.

Griffiths, M. D., & Hunt, N. J. A. (1995). Computer Game Playing in Adolescence: Prevalence and Demographic Indicators. *Journal of Community & Applied Social Psychology*, *5*(3), 189–193. doi:10.1002/casp.2450050307

Griffiths, D., & Blat, J. (2005). The Role of Teachers in Editing and Authoring Units of Learning Using IMS Learning Design. *Advanced Technology for Learning*, *2*(4), 243–251.

Griffiths, D., Blat, J., Garcia, R., Vogten, H., & Kwong, K.-L. (2005). Learning Design Tools. In Koper, R., & Tattersall, C. (Eds.), *Learning Design - A Handbook on Modelling and Delivering Networked Education and Training* (pp. 109–136). Berlin: Springer.

Grossman, P., & McDonald, M. (2008). Back to the future: Directions for research in teaching and teacher education. *American Educational Research Journal*, *45*(1), 184–205. doi:10.3102/0002831207312906

Grossman, P., Wineburg, S., & Woolworth, S. (2001). Toward a theory of teacher community. *Teachers College Record, 103*(6), 942-1012, Retrieved September 3, 2009, from http://www.tcrecord.org/Content.asp?ContentId=10833

Guglielmino, L. M., & Guglielmino, P. J. (2003). Identifying Learners. Who are ready for E-Learning and supporting their success. In G. M. Piskurich (Ed.), *Preparing Learners for E-Learning* (pp. 19-33). San Francisco, CA: Pfeiffer (John Wiley & Sons, Inc.).

Gunawardena, D. N., & Zittle, F. (1997). Social presence as predictor of satisfaction within a computer mediated conferencing environment. *American Journal of Distance Education*, *11*(3), 8–25. doi:10.1080/08923649709526970

Gütl, C. (2008). *Enhanced Computer-based Support for Personalized Learning Activities*. Post Doctoral Lecture Thesis. Graz University of Technology, Austria. Retrieved September 10, 2009, from http://www.iicm.tugraz.at/guetl/publications/2008/Guetl%202008%20-%20Habil%20final.pdf

Gütl, C., Chang, V., Kopeinik, S., & Williams, R. (2009). 3D Virtual Worlds as a Tool for Collaborative Learning Settings in Geographically Dispersed Environments. In M.E. Auer (Ed.), *ICL 2009* (310-323). Vienna, Austria: International Association of Online Engineering.

Guzdial, M., & Turns, J. (2000). Effective discussion through a computer-mediated anchored forum. *Journal of the Learning Sciences*, *9*(4), 437–469. doi:10.1207/S15327809JLS0904_3

Guzdial, M., & Turns, J. (2000). Effective discussion through a computer-mediated anchored forum. *Journal of the Learning Sciences*, *9*(4), 437–469. doi:10.1207/S15327809JLS0904_3

Guzdial, M., Rick, J., & Kehoe, C. (2001). Beyond Adoption to Invention: Teacher-Created Collaborative Activities in Higher Education. *Journal of the Learning Sciences*, *10*(3), 265–279. doi:10.1207/S15327809JLS1003_2

Haake, J. M., & Pfister, H. R. (2007). Flexible scripting in net-based learning groups. In Fischer, F., Mandl, H., Haake, J. M., & Kollar, I. (Eds.), *Scripting computer-supported communication of knowledge - Cognitive, computational, and educational perspectives*. Berlin, Heidelberg: Springer.

Hakkarainen, K., Lipponen, L., & Järvela, S. (2002). Epistemology of inquiry and computer-supported collaborative learning. In Koshmann, T. D. (Eds.), *CSCL 2: Carrying Forward the Conversation* (pp. 129–156). Mahwah, N.J.: Laurence Erlbaum Associates.

Hakkinen, P., & Makitalo-Siegl, K. (2007) Educational perspectives on scripting CSCL. In Fischer, F., Kollar, I. Mandl, H., & Haake, J.M. (Eds.), *Scripting Computer-Supported Collaborative Learning: Cognitive, Computational and Educational Perspectives, Computer-Supported Collaborative Learning Series, Vol. 6* (pp. 263-274). New York: Springer.

Hansford, D., & Wylie, A. (2001). *Evaluating online collaborative learning: A case study in increasing student participation*. Retrieved July 21, 2009, from http://scs.une.edu.au/CF/Papers/pdf/Hansford.pdf

Hara, N., Bonk, C. J., & Angeli, C. (2000). Content analysis of online discussion in an applied educational psychology course. *Instructional Science*, *28*(2), 115–152. doi:10.1023/A:1003764722829

Hara, N., & Kling, R. (2000). Students' distress with a Web-based distance education course: an ethnographic study of participants' experiences. *Information Communication and Society*, *3*(4), 557–579. doi:10.1080/13691180010002297

Hara, N., & Kling, R. (2001). Student distress in web-based distance education. *EDUCAUSE Quarterly*, *24*(3), 68–69.

Harackiewicz, J. M., Barron, K. E., Pintrich, P. R., & Elliot, A. J., Thrash, Tm. M. (2002). Revision of achievement goal theory: Necessary and Illuminating. *Journal of Educational Psychology*, *94*(3), 638–645. doi:10.1037/0022-0663.94.3.638

Harasim, L. (1986). Educational applications of computer conferencing. *Journal of Distance Education*, *1*(1), 59–70.

Harasim, L., Hiltz, S. R., Teles, L., & Turoff, M. (1998). *Learning networks: A field guide to teaching and learning online*. Cambridge, MA: MIT Press.

Harasim, L. (Ed.). (1990). *Online education: Perspectives on a new medium*. New York, NY: Praeger-Greenwood.

Harasim, L. (1989). Online education: A new domain. In Mason, R., & Kaye, T. (Eds.), *Mindweave: Computers, communications and distance education* (pp. 50–62). Oxford, UK: Pergamon Press.

Härder, J. (2003). *Wissenskommunikation mit Desktop-Videokonferenzsystemen: Strukturierungsangebote für den Wissensaustausch und gemeinsame Inferenzen.* Unpublished dissertation, Albert-Ludwigs-Universität, Freiburg, Germany.

Harrer, A., Kohen-Vacs, D., Roth, B., Malzah, N., Hoppe, U., & Ronen, M. (2009). Design and enactment of collaboration scripts – An integrative approach with graphical notations and learning platforms. In *Proceedings of the CSCL 2009 Conference* (pp.198-200). International Society of the Learning Sciences (ISLS).

Harris, M. (1986). *Teaching one-to-one: The writing conference*. Urbana, IL: National Council of Teachers of English.

Hatano, G., & Inagaki, K. (1991). Sharing cognition through collective comprehension activity. In Resnick, L. B., Levine, J. M., & Teasley, S. D. (Eds.), *Perspectives on socially shared cognition* (pp. 331–348). Washington, DC: American Psychological Association. doi:10.1037/10096-014

Hazari, S., North, A., & Moreland, D. (2009). Investigating pedagogical value of wiki technology. *Journal of Information Systems Education*, *20*(2), 187–198.

Headley, S. (2005). Five Role I Play in Online Courses. *Journal of Online Education, 2* (1). Retrieved March 20, 2010, from http://www.innovateonline.info/index.php?view=article&id=78

Hegedus, S. J., & Kaput, J. (2004, September). *An introduction to the profound potential of connected algebra activities: Issues of representation, engagement and pedagogy.* Paper presented at the 28th Conference of the International Group for the Psychology of Mathematics Education, Bergen, Norway.

Heider, F. (1958). *The psychology of interpersonal relations.* New York, NY: Wiley. doi:10.1037/10628-000

Helling, K. (2006). *Einfluss von Wissensschema und Ressourcenverteilung auf die Erstellung einer gemeinsamen externalen Repräsentation und den kooperativen Lernerfolg in Videokonferenzen. Aspekte der Bearbeitung und Koordination.* Unpublished Magister Thesis, Ludwig-Maximilians-Universität München.

Hellman, L. (2009). An Evaluation of the Open Education Resources for the Open Schools' Project. *SAIDE Newsletter, 15*(3).

Henri, F. (1992). Computer conferencing and content analysis. In Kaye, A. R. (Ed.), *Collaborative Learning Through Computer Conferencing: The Najaden Papers* (pp. 115–136). New York: Springer.

Hermans, H. (2004). Mediated identity in the emerging digital age: A dialogical perspective. *Identity: An international Journal of theory and research, 4*(4), 297-405.

Hernández, D., Asensio, J. I., & Dimitriadis, Y. A. (2005). Computational Representation of Collaborative Learning Flow Patterns using IMS Learning Design. *Journal of Educational Technology & Society, 8*(4), 75–89.

Hernández, D., Villasclaras, E. D., Jorrín, I. M., Asensio, J. I., Dimitriadis, Y., & Ruiz, I. (2006). COLLAGE, a Collaborative Learning Design Editor Based on Patterns. *Journal of Educational Technology & Society, 9*(1), 58–71.

Hernández, D., Asensio, J. I., & Dimitriadis, Y. A. (2005). Computational Representation of Collaborative Learning Flow Patterns using IMS Learning Design. *Journal of Educational Technology & Society, 8*(4), 75–89.

Hernández, D., Villasclaras, E. D., Jorrín, I. M., Asensio, J. I., Dimitriadis, Y., & Ruiz, I. (2006). COLLAGE, a Collaborative Learning Design Editor Based on Patterns. *Journal of Educational Technology & Society, 9*(1), 58–71.

Hernández, D., Asensio, J. I., Dimitriadis, Y., & Villasclaras, E. D. (2010). Pattern languages for generating CSCL scripts: from a conceptual model to the design of a real situation. In P. Goodyear & S. Retalis (Eds.) *E-learning, design patterns and pattern languages* (49-64) Sense Publishers.

Hernández-Leo, D., Asensio-Pérez, J. I., & Dimitriadis, Y. (2005). Computational Representation of Collaborative Learning Flow Patterns Using IMS Learning Desing. *Journal of Educational Technology & Society, 8*(4), 75–89.

Hernández-Leo, D., Bote-Lorenzo, M. L., Asensio-Pérez, J. I., Gómez-Sánchez, E., Villasclaras-Fernández, E. D., Jorrín-Abellán, I. M., & Dimitriadis, Y. (2007). Free- and Open Source Software for a Course on Network Management: Authoring and Enactment of Scripts based on Collaborative Learning Strategies. *IEEE Transactions on Education, 50*(4), 292–301. doi:10.1109/TE.2007.904589

Hernández-Leo, D., Villasclaras-Fernández, E. D., Asensio-Pérez, J. I., Dimitriadis, Y., Jorrín-Abellán, I. M., Ruiz-Requies, I., & Rubia-Avi, B. (2006). Collage: A collaborative learning design editor based on patterns. Special Issue on *Learning Design. Journal of Educational Technology & Society, 9*(1), 58–71.

Hernández-Leo, D., Harrer, A., Dodero, J., Asensio-Pérez, J., & Burgos, D. (2007). Framework for the Conceptualization of Approaches to "Create-by-Reuse" of Learning Design Solutions. *Journal of Universal Computer Science, 13*(7), 991–1001.

Hernández-Leo, D. (2007). *A pattern-based design process for the creation of CSCL macro-scripts computationally represented with IMS LD.* Unpublished doctoral dissertation. University of Valladolid, Spain.

Hernánez-Leo, D., Santos, P., Villasclaras-Fernández, E. D., Navarrete, T., Asensio-Pérez, J. I., Blat, J., & Dimitriadis, Y. (2008). Educational Patterns as a Guide to Create Units of Learning and Assessment. In *Proceedings of the 2008 Eighth IEEE international Conference on Advanced Learning Technologies* (pp.1055-1056). Santaber, Cantabria, Spain. Washington, DC: IEEE Computer & Society.

Herring, S. C. (2004). Computer-mediated discourse analysis. An approach to researching online behavior. In Barab, S. A., Kling, R., & Gray, J. H. (Eds.), *Designing for virtual communities in the service of learning* (pp. 338–376). Cambridge, MA: Cambridge University Press.

Hertz-Lazarowitz, R., Kirkus, V. B., & Miller, N. (1992). Implications of current research on cooperative interaction for classroom application. In Hertz-Lazarowitz, R. (Ed.), *Interaction in cooperative groups: The theoretical anatomy of group learning* (pp. 253–280). New York: Cambridge University Press.

Hewitt, J. (2001). Beyond threaded discourse. *International Journal of Educational Telecommunications*, *7*(3), 207–221.

Hewitt, J. (2003). How habitual online practices affect the development of asynchronous discussion threads. *Journal of Educational Computing Research*, *28*(1), 31–45. doi:10.2190/PMG8-A05J-CUH1-DK14

Hewitt, J. (2003). How habitual online practices affect the development of asynchronous discussion threads. *Journal of Educational Computing Research*, *28*(1), 31–45. doi:10.2190/PMG8-A05J-CUH1-DK14

Hiltz, S. R. (1994). *The virtual classroom: learning without limits via computer networks*. Norwood, NJ: Ablex Publishing Corporation.

Hiltz, S. R., & Wellman, B. (1997). Asynchronous learning networks as a virtual classroom. *Communications of the ACM*, *40*(9), 44–49. doi:10.1145/260750.260764

Hiltz, S. R., & Benbunan-Fich, R. (1997). Supporting collaborative learning in asynchronous learning networks. Invited keynote address for the *Symposium on Virtual Learning Environments and the role of the Teacher.* Milton Keynes, England April 28th, 1997. Retrieved July 12, 2009, from http://web.njit.edu/~hiltz/CPProject/unesco.htm

Hinds, M. (2002). *Teaching as a clinical profession: A new challenge for education*. New York: Carnegie Corporation of New York.

Hinsz, V. B., Tindale, R. S., & Vollrath, D. A. (1997). The emerging conceptualization of groups as information processors. *Psychological Bulletin*, *121*(1), 43–64. doi:10.1037/0033-2909.121.1.43

Ho, C. H., & Swan, K. (2007). Evaluating online conversation in an asynchronous learning environment: An application of Grice's cooperative principle. *The Internet and Higher Education*, *10*(1), 3–14. doi:10.1016/j.iheduc.2006.11.002

Hollingshead, A. B. (1996). Information suppression and status persistence in group decision making. The effects of communication media. *Human Communication Research*, *23*(2), 193–219. doi:10.1111/j.1468-2958.1996.tb00392.x

Holquist, M. (1990). *Dialogism*. London: Routledge. doi:10.4324/9780203330340

Hoppe, U. H., & Ploetzner, R. (1999). Can analytic models support learning in groups? In Dillenbourg, P. (Ed.), *Collaborative learning: Cognitive and computational approaches* (pp. 147–168). Oxford, UK: Elsevier.

Hou, H., Chang, K., & Sung, Y. (2007). An analysis of peer assessment online discussions within a course that uses project-based learning. *Interactive Learning Environments*, *15*(3), 237–251. doi:10.1080/10494820701206974

Hron, A., Hesse, F.-W., Reinhard, P., & Picard, E. (1997). Strukturierte Kooperation beim computerunterstützten kollaborativen Lernen. *Unterrichtswissenschaft*, *25*(1), 56–69.

Hron, A., Hesse, F. W., Cress, U., & Giovis, C. (2000). Implicit and explicit dialogue structuring in virtual learning groups. *The British Journal of Educational Psychology*, *70*(1), 53–64. doi:10.1348/000709900157967

Hsu, Y. C., & Shiue, Y. M. (2005). The effect of self-directed learning readiness on achievement comparing face-to-face and two-way distance learning instruction. *International Journal of Instructional Media*, *32*(2), 143–155.

Huang, Y.-M., Huang, T.-C., & Hsieh, M.-Y. (2008). Using Annotation Services in a Ubiquitous Jigsaw Cooperative Learning Environment. *Journal of Educational Technology & Society*, *11*(2), 3–15.

Hull, D. M., & Saxon, T. F. (2009). Negotiating of meaning and co-construction of knowledge: An experimental analysis of asynchronous online learning. *Computers & Education*, *52*(3), 624–639. doi:10.1016/j.compedu.2008.11.005

Human-Vogel, S., & Bouwer, C. (2005). Creating a complex learning environment for mediation of knowledge construction in diverse educational settings. *South African Journal of Education*, *25*(4), 229–238.

Hummel, H., Manderveld, J., Tattersall, C., & Koper, R. (2004). Educational modeling language and learning design: new opportunities for instructional reusability and personalized learning. *International Journal of Learning Technology*, *1*(1), 111–126. doi:10.1504/IJLT.2004.003685

Hunt, J. (2009). Attitude is Everything. *Diverse Issues in Higher Education*, *26*(3), 19–25.

Hutchinson, N. L. (1999). *Teaching exceptional children and adolescents: A Canadian casebook*. Scarborough, ON: Prentice Hall Allyn & Bacon Canada.

Hyllegard, D., Deng, H., & Hunter, C. (2008). Why do students leave online courses? Attrition in community colleges distance learning courses. *International Journal of Instructional Media*, *35*(4), 429–243.

IMS Global Learning Consortium. (2003). *IMS Learning Design specification*. Retrieved 13 April, 2010, from http://www.imsglobal.org/learningdesign/

IMS Global Learning Consortium. (2006). *IMS Question & Test Interoperability specification*. Retrieved April 2010 from http://www.imsglobal.org/question/

Jacobson, M. J., Kim, B., Miao, C., Shen, Z., & Chavez, M. (2010). Design Perspectives for Learning in Virtual Worlds. In Jacobson, M. J., & Reimann, P. (Eds.). *Designs for learning environments of the future: International perspectives from the learning sciences* (111-142). Berlin, Heidelberg: Springer.

Jeong, H., & Chi, M. T. H. (2007). Knowledge convergence and collaborative learning. *Instructional Science*, *35*(4), 287–315. doi:10.1007/s11251-006-9008-z

Jeong, H., & Chi, M. T. H. (1999, April). *Constructing shared knowledge during collaboration and learning*. Paper presented at the AERA Annual Meeting, Montreal, Canada.

Johnson, R. D., Hornikb, S., & Salas, E. (2008). An empirical examination of factors contributing to the creation of successful e-learning environments. *International Journal of Human-Computer Studies*, *66*(5), 356–369. doi:10.1016/j.ijhcs.2007.11.003

Johnson, D., Johnson, R., & Holubec, E. (1998). *Cooperation in the classroom*. Boston, MA: Allyn & Bacon.

Johnson, R. L., Penny, J. A., & Gordon, B. (2009). *Assessing Performance: Designing, Scoring, and Validating Performance Tasks*. New York: The Guilford Press.

Johnson, W. L., & Rickel, J. W. (2000). Animated Pedagogical Agents: Face-to-Face Interaction in Interactive Learning Environment. *International Journal of Artificial Intelligence in Education*, *11*(1), 47–78.

Jonassen, D. H. (2000). Toward a design theory of problem solving. *Educational Technology Research and Development*, *48*(4), 63–85. doi:10.1007/BF02300500

Jonassen, D., Davidson, M., Collins, C., Campbell, J., & Haag, B. B. (1995). Constructivism and computer-mediated communication in distance education. *American Journal of Distance Education*, *9*(2), 7–26. doi:10.1080/08923649509526885

Jonassen, D. (2003). Using cognitive tools to represent problems. *Journal of Research on Technology in Education, 35*(3), 362–379.

Jonassen, D. (2006). On the role of concepts in learning and instructional design. *Educational Technology Research and Development, 54*(2), 177–196. doi:10.1007/s11423-006-8253-9

Jonassen, D., Howland, J., Marra, R. M., & Crismond, D. (2008). *Meaningful learning with technology* (3rd ed.). Upper Saddle River, NJ: Pearson/Merrill Prentice Hall.

Jonassen, D. H. (1996). *Computers in the classroom: Mindtools for critical thinking*. Columbus, OH: Merrill/Prentice-Hall.

Jonassen, D., Carr, C., & Yueh, H. (1998). Computers as mindtools for engaging learners in critical thinking. *TechTrends, 43* (2), 24--32. Retrieved June 12, 2009, from http://www.siue.edu/education/techready/5_Software_Tutorials/5_AncillaryPages/Mindtools.pdf

Jonnavithula, L. (2008). *Improving the interfaces of online discussion forums to enhance learning support*. Unpublished master thesis, Massey University, Palmerston North, New Zealand. Retrieved January 9, 2010, from http://muir.massey.ac.nz/bitstream/10179/968/1/02whole.pdf

Joosten-ten Brinke, D., van Bruggen, J., Hermans, H., Burgers, J., Giesbers, B., Koper, R., & Latour, I. (2007). Modeling assessment for re-use of traditional and new types of ssessment. *Computers in Human Behavior, 23*(6), 2721–2741. doi:10.1016/j.chb.2006.08.009

Judson, E., & Sawada, D. (2002). Learning from past and present: Electronic response systems in college lecture halls. *Journal of Computers in Mathematics and Science Teaching, 21*(2), 167–181.

Jun, J. (2005). Understanding E-dropout. *International Journal on E-Learning, 4*(2), 229–240.

Kagan, S. (1992). *Cooperative learning* (7th ed.). San Juan Capistrano, CA: Resources for Teachers, Inc.

Kagan, S. (1994). *Cooperative learning*. San Clemente, CA: Kagan Publishing.

Kagan, S. (1985). Co-op Co-op: A flexible cooperative learning technique. In R. Slavin, S. Sharan, S. Kagan, R., Hertz-Lazarowitz, C. Webb and R. Schmuck (Eds.), *Learning to cooperate cooperating to learn*, (pp.437-452). New York: Plenum Press.

Kain, D. (2006). Choose Colleagues Before Friends for Teaching Teams. *Education Digest*, •••, 53–57.

Kali, Y., & Ronen, M. (2008). Assessing the assessors: Added value in web-based multi-cycle peer assessment in higher education. *Research and Practice in Technology Enhanced Learning, 3*(1), 3–32. doi:10.1142/S1793206808000434

Kali, Y., & Ronen, M. (2005). Design principles for online peer-evaluation: Fostering objectivity. In Koschmann, T., Suthers, D., & Chan, T. (Eds.), *CSCL 2005* (pp. 247–251). Mahwah, NJ: Lawrence Erlbaum Associates.

Kanuka, H., Rourke, L., & Laflamme, E. (2007). The Influence of Instructional Methods on the Quality of Online Discussion. *British Journal of Educational Technology, 38*(2), 260–271. doi:10.1111/j.1467-8535.2006.00620.x

Kanuka, H., Rourke, L., & Laflamme, E. (2007). The influence of instructional methods on the quality of online discussion. *British Journal of Educational Technology, 38*(2), 260–271. doi:10.1111/j.1467-8535.2006.00620.x

Kaplan, N., & Chisik, Y. (2005). Reading alone together: creating sociable digital library books. *ACM IDC05: Interaction Design and Children* (88-94). New York:ACM Press.

Kappe, F., & Gütl, C. (2009). Enhancements of the realXtend framework to build a Virtual Conference Room for Knowledge Transfer and Learning Purposes. In [Chesapeake, VA: AACE]. *Proceedings of EDMEDIA, 2009*, 4113–4120.

Kassop, M. (2003) Ten Ways Online Education Matches, or Surpasses, Face-to-Face Learning. *The Technology Source,* Retrieved March 20, 2010 from: http://technologysource.org/article/ten_ways_online_education_matches_or_surpasses_facetoface_learning/

Kaye, A. R. (1992): Learning Together Apart. In Kaye, A. R. (ed.)*: Collaborative Learning Through Computer Conferencing. NATO ASI Series, vol. 90, the Najaden Papers* (1-24). Berlin, Heidelberg: Springer-Verlag.

Kelley, H. H. (1973). The processes of causal attribution. *The American Psychologist*, *28*, 107–128. doi:10.1037/h0034225

Kemp, J., & Livingstone, D. (2006). Putting a Second Life 'Metaverse' Skin on Learning Management Systems. In *Proceedings of the Second Life Education Workshop, Part of the Second Life Community Convention* (13-18). Paisley, UK:The University of Paisley.

Kerr, N. L., & Bruun, S. (1983). The dispensability of member effort and group motivation losses: Free rider effects. *Personality and Social Psychology Bulletin*, *44*(1), 78–94. doi:10.1037/0022-3514.44.1.78

Key To School. *Moodle Add-ons*. Retrieved January 9, 2010, from http://www.keytoschool.com/moodle/add-ons

Kiesler, S., & Sproull, L. (1987). *Computing and change on campus*. New York: Cambridge University Press.

Kim, A. J. (2000). *Community Building on the Web: Secret Strategies for Successful Online Communities*. Berkeley, CA: Peachpit Press.

King, A. (2007). Scripting collaborative learning processes: a cognitive perspective. In Fischer, F., Kollar, I., Mandl, H., & Haake, J. M. (Eds.), *Scripting computer-supported communication of knowledge – cognitive, computational and educational perspectives* (pp. 13–37). Berlin Heidelberg, Germany: Springer.

Kirschner, P., Strijbos, J., Kreijns, K., & Beers, P. J. (2004). Designing electronic collaborative learning environments. *Educational Technology Research and Development*, *52*(3), 47–66. doi:10.1007/BF02504675

Klahr, D., & Nigam, M. (2004). The equivalence of learning paths in early science instruction: Effects of direct instruction and discovery learning. *Psychological Science*, *15*(10), 661–667. doi:10.1111/j.0956-7976.2004.00737.x

Klobas, J. E., & Haddow, G. (2000). Evaluating the impact of computer-supported international collaborative teamwork in business education. *International Journal of Educational Technology*, *2*(1).

Kobbe, L. (2006). *Framework on multiple goal dimensions for computer-supported scripts, Kaleidoscope, D21.2.1*. Final.

Kobbe, L., Weinberger, A., Dillenbourg, P., Harrer, A., Hämäläinen, R., & Häkkinen, P. (2007). Specifying computer-supported collaboration scripts. *International Journal of Computer-Supported Collaborative Learning*, *2*(2-3), 211–224. doi:10.1007/s11412-007-9014-4

Kobbe, L. (2005). *Framework on multiple goal dimensions for computer-supported scripts,* Kaleidoscope project. Retrieved September 10, 2009 from: http://hal.archives-ouvertes.fr/docs/00/19/02/97/PDF/Lars-Kobbe-2005.pdf

Kodri, F. (2003). Performance assessment in the classrooms. *Ingenious*, *1*(1), 21–30.

Kollar, I., Fischer, F., & Hesse, F. W. (2006). Collaboration scripts - A conceptual analysis. *Educational Psychology Review*, *18*(2), 159–185. doi:10.1007/s10648-006-9007-2

Kollar, I., Fischer, F., & Hesse, F. W. (2006). Computer-supported collaboration scripts - a conceptual analysis. *Educational Psychology Review*, *18*(2), 159–185. doi:10.1007/s10648-006-9007-2

Kolodner, J. L. (2007). The roles of scripts in promoting collaborative discourse in learning by design. In Fischer, F., Kollar, I., Mandl, H., & Haake, J. M. (Eds.), *Scripting computer-supported communication of knowledge – cognitive, computational and educational perspectives* (pp. 237–262). Berlin Heidelberg, Germany: Springer.

Konstanidis, A., Tsiatsos, T., & Pomportsis, A. (2009). Collaborative virtual learning environments: Design and evaluation. *Multimedia Tools and Applications*, *44*, 279–304. doi:10.1007/s11042-009-0289-5

Koper, R., & Tattersall, C. (Eds.). (2005). *Learning Design: A handbook on modeling and delivering networked education and training*. Berlin, Germany: Springer.

Koper, R. (2003). Combining reusable learning resources and services with pedagogical purposeful units of learning. In Littlejohn, A. (Ed.), *Reusing online resources: A sustainable approach to e-learning* (pp. 46–59). London: Routledge.

Kopp, B., Ertl, B., & Mandl, H. (2006). Wissensschema und Skript - Förderung der Anwendung von Theoriewissen auf die Aufgabenbearbeitung in Videokonferenzen. *Zeitschrift für Entwicklungspsychologie und Pädagogische Psychologie*, *38*(3), 132–138. doi:10.1026/0049-8637.38.3.132

Kopp, B., & Mandl, H. (2006). Gemeinsame Wissenskonstruktion. In Bierhoff, H.-W., & Frey, D. (Eds.), *Handbuch der Sozialpsychologie und Kommunikationspsychologie* (pp. 504–509). Göttingen, Germany: Hogrefe.

Kopp, B., & Mandl, H. (2007). Fostering Argumentation with Script and Content Scheme in Videoconferencing. In: C. Chinn, G. Erkens, & S. Puntambekar (Eds.), *Proceedings of Mice, Minds and Society – The Computer Supported Collaborative Learning Conference, 8* (pp. 382-392), New Jersey: International Society of the Learning Sciences.

Kopp, B., & Mandl, H. (2008). *Collaborative online learning: A heterogeneous phenomenon.* Paper presented at the Conference on Knowledge Construction in E-Learning Context. (pp.23-29). Aachen University: Sun SITE Central Europe, RWTH. Retrieved April, 13, 2010, from http://ftp.informatik.rwth-aachen.de/ Publications/CEUR-WS/Vol-398/S1_KoppEtAl.pdf

Kopp, B., Schnurer, K., & Mandl, H. (2009). Collaborative learning in virtual seminars: Analyzing learning processes and learning outcomes. In C. O'Malley, D. Suthers, P. Reimann & A. Dimitracopoulou (Eds.), *Proceedings of Computer Supported Collaborative Learning Practices – CSCL 2009 Conference*. (pp.151-160). New Jersey: International Society of the Learning Sciences.

Kordaki, M., Siempos, H., & Daradoumis, T. (2009). Collaborative learning design within open source e-learning systems: lessons learned from an empirical study. In Magoulas, G. (Ed.), *Submitted as a chapter in: E-Infrastructures and Technologies for Lifelong Learning: Next Generation Environments*. Hershey, PA: IGI Global.

Koschmann, T. (1996). Paradigm shifts and instructional technology. In Koschmann, T. (Ed.), *CSCL: Theory and practice of an emerging paradigm* (pp. 1–23). Mahwah, NJ: LEA.

Koschmann, T. (2001). Revisiting the paradigms of instructional technology. In G. Kennedy, M. Keppell, C. McNaught & T. Petrovic (Eds.), Meeting at the Crossroads. *Proceedings of the 18th Annual Conference of the Australian Society for Computers in Learning in Tertiary Education.* (pp. 15-22). Melbourne, Australia: Biomedical Multimedia Unit, The University of Melbourne.

Kotovsky, K., Hayes, J. R., & Simon, H. A. (1985). Why are some problems hard? Evidence from Tower of Hanoi. *Cognitive Psychology*, *17*(2), 248–294. doi:10.1016/0010-0285(85)90009-X

Kotovsky, K., & Fallside, D. (1989). Representation and transfer in problem solving. In Klahr, D., & Kotovsky, K. (Eds.), *Complex information processing: The impact of Herbert A. Simon* (pp. 69–108). Hillsdale, NJ: Lawrence Erlbaum.

Kozma, R. (1999). Students collaborating with computer models and physical experiments. In C. Hoadley & J. Roschelle (Eds.), *CSCL '99*. (314-322). Mahwah, NJ: Lawrence Erlbaum Associates

Krajcik, J. S. (2001). Supporting science learning in context: Project-based learning. In Tinker, R. F., & Krajcik, J. S. (Eds.), *Portable technologies* (pp. 7–28). New York: Plenum Publishers.

Krauss, R. M., & Fussell, S. R. (1990). Mutual knowledge and communicative effectiveness. In Galegher, J., Kraut, R. E., & Egido, C. (Eds.), *Intellectual teamwork: Social and technological foundations of cooperative work* (pp. 111–145). Hillsdale, NJ: Lawrence Erlbaum Associates.

Kreber, C. (2001). Learning experientially through case studies: A conceptual analysis. *Teaching in Higher Education*, *6*(2), 217–228. doi:10.1080/13562510120045203

Kreijins, K., Kirschner, P. A., & Jochems, W. (2003). Identifying the pitfalls for social interaction in computer-supported collaborative learning environments: a review of research. *Computers in Human Behavior, 19*(3), 335–353. doi:10.1016/S0747-5632(02)00057-2

Kuh, G. D., & Hu, S. (2001). The effects of student-faculty interaction in the 1990s. *The Review of Higher Education, 24*(3), 309–332. doi:10.1353/rhe.2001.0005

Kuhn, D., Weinstock, M., & Flaton, R. (1994). Historical reasoning as theory-evidence coordination. In Carretero, M., & Voss, J. F. (Eds.), *Cognitive and Instructional Processes in History and the Social Sciences* (pp. 377–401). Hillsdale, NJ: Lawrence Erlbaum Associates.

Kukolja Taradi, S., Taradi, M., Radic, K., & Pokrajac, N. (2005). Blending problem-based learning with Web technology positively impacts student learning outcomes in acid-base physiology. *Advances in Physiology Education, 29*, 35–39. doi:10.1152/advan.00026.2004

Kumar, S., Chhugani, J., Changkyu Kim, C., Kim, D., Nguyen, A., & Dubey, P. (2008). Second Life and the New Generation of Virtual Worlds. *Computer, 41*(9), 46–53. doi:10.1109/MC.2008.398

Kurtz, G., & Amichai-Hamburger, Y. (2008). *Psychosocial well-being and attitudes toward e-learning.* Paper presented at the 3rd Chais Conference, Raanana, Israel.

Lambert, J., & Cuper, Y. (2008). Technology, transfer, and teaching: The impact of a single technology course on preservice teachers' computer attitudes and ability. *Journal of Technology and Teacher Education, 16*(4), 395–410.

Lambiotte, J. G., Skaggs, L. P., & Dansereau, D. F. (1993). Learning from lectures: effects of knowledge maps and cooperative review strategies. *Applied Cognitive Psychology, 7*(6), 483–497. doi:10.1002/acp.2350070604

Larkin, J. H. (1989). Display-based problem solving. In Klahr, D., & Kotovsky, K. (Eds.), *Complex information processing: The impact of Herbert A. Simon* (pp. 319–341). Hillsdale, NJ: Lawrence Erlbaum.

Larson, J. R. Jr, Christensen, C., Franz, T. M., & Abbott, A. S. (1998). Diagnosing groups: The pooling, management, and impact of shared and unshared case information in team-based medical decision making. *Journal of Personality and Social Psychology, 75*(1), 93–108. doi:10.1037/0022-3514.75.1.93

Latané, B., Williams, K., & Harkins, S. (1979). Many hands make light the work: The causes and consequences of social loafing. *Journal of Personality and Social Psychology, 37*(6), 822–832. doi:10.1037/0022-3514.37.6.822

Lave, J., & Wenger, E. (1991). *Situated learning: Legitimate peripheral participation.* New York: Cambridge University Press.

Lave, J., & Wenger, E. (1991). *Situated learning: Legitimate peripheral participation.* Cambridge, MA: Cambridge University Press.

Law, N. (2005). Assessing learning outcomes in CSCL settings. In *Proceedings of the 2005 conference on Computer supported collaborative learning: the next 10 years!* (pp. 373-377). The International Society of the Learning Sciences (ISLS).

Lazakidou, G., Retalis, S., Paraskeva, F., & Kargidis, T. (2007, September 21st-22nd). Computer-supported collaborative scenarios for evolving self-regulatory skills in math education. In [Nicosia, Cyprus.]. *Proceedings of the International Council of Educational Media Annual Conference, 2007*, 111–123.

Lazonder, A. W., Biemans, H. J. A., & Wopereis, I. G. J. H. (2000). Differences between Novice and Experienced Users in Searching Information on The World Wide Web. *Journal of the American Society for Information Science American Society for Information Science, 51*(6), 576–581. doi:10.1002/(SICI)1097-4571(2000)51:6<576::AID-ASI9>3.0.CO;2-7

Lebaron, J., & Miller, D. (2005). The Potential of Jigsaw Role Playing to Promote the Social Construction of Knowledge in an Online Graduate Education Course. *Teachers College Record, 107*(8), 1652–1675. doi:10.1111/j.1467-9620.2005.00537.x

Lee, J. (2001). Instructional Support for Distance Education and Faculty Motivation, Commitment, Satisfaction. *British Journal of Educational Technology*, *32*(2), 153–160. doi:10.1111/1467-8535.00186

Lee, J. K., & Calandra, B. (2004). Can embedded annotations help high school students perform problem solving tasks using a Web-based historical document? *Journal of Research on Technology in Education*, *36*(4), 65–84.

Lee, J. M., & Jeong, A. (2009). The effects of argument mapping on critical thinking process in computer-supported collaborative argumentation. Paper presented at the *American Educational Research Association Annual Conference,* San Diego, USA, April 13-17.

Lee, M.J.W. (2009). How can 3D virtual worlds be used to support collaborative learning? An analysis of cases from the literature. *Journal of e-Learning and Knowledge Society*, *5*(1), 149–158

Lemke, J. L. (1990). *Talking science: Language, learning, and values*. Norwood, New Jersey: Ablex.

Leung, W. H., & Chen, T. (2001). Creating a Mulituser 3D Virtual Environment. *IEEE Signal Processing Magazine*, *18*(May), 9–16. doi:10.1109/79.924884

Light, P., & Light, V. (1999). Analysing asynchronous learning interactions: Computer-mediated communication in a conventional undergraduate setting. In Littleton, K., & Light, P. (Eds.), *Learning with computers: Analysing productive interaction* (pp. 162–178). New York, NY: Routledge.

Ligorio, M. B., & Annese, A. (in press). Blended activity design approach: A method for innovating e-learning communities in higher education. In Blachnio, A., Przepiorka, A., & Rowinski, T. (Eds.), *Internet in Psychology Research*. Warsaw: Cardinal Stefan Wyszynski University Press.

Ligorio, M. B., Annese, S., Spadaro, P. F., & Traetta, M. (2008). Building intersubjectivity and identity in on-line communities. In B. M. Varisco (Ed.), *Psychological, pedagogical and sociological models for learning and assessment in virtual communities of practice* (pp. 57-91). Milano, IT: Polimetrica.

Lim, J., Kim, M., Chen, S., & Ryder, C. (2008). An empirical investigation of student achievement and satisfaction in different learning environments. *Journal of Instructional Psychology*, *35*(2), 113–119.

Lim, C. P., Nonis, D., & Hedberg, J. (2006). Gaming in a 3D multiuser virtual environment: engaging students in Science lessons. *British Journal of Educational Technology*, *37*(2), 211–231. doi:10.1111/j.1467-8535.2006.00531.x

Linden Labs. (2009). Second Life – What is Second Life? *Linden Lab, San Francisco, USA.* Retrieved 22 August, 2009, from http://secondlife.com/whatis/

Little, J. W. (1990). The persistence of privacy: Autonomy and initiative in teachers' professional relations. *Teachers College Record*, *91*(4), 508–536.

Little, J. W. (2002). Locating learning in teachers' communities of practice: Opening up problems of analysis in records of everyday work. *Teaching and Teacher Education*, *18*(8), 917–946. doi:10.1016/S0742-051X(02)00052-5

Little, J. W. (2003). Inside teacher community: Representations of classroom practice. *Teachers College Record*, *105*(6), 913–945. doi:10.1111/1467-9620.00273

Littlejohn, A., & Pegler, C. (2006). *Preparing for Blended E-Learning: Understanding Blended and Online Learning*. London, UK: Routledge.

Livingston, C., & Borko, H. (1989). Expert- novice differences in teaching: A cognitive analysis and implications for teacher education. *Journal of Teacher Education*, *41*(1), 36–41. doi:10.1177/002248718904000407

Lloyd, G., & Wilson, M. (2001). Offering Prospective Teachers Tools to Connect Theory and Practice: Hypermedia in Mathematics Teacher Education. [Norfolk, VA: AACE.]. *Journal of Technology and Teacher Education*, *9*(4), 497–518.

Lobry de Bruyn, L. A. (2004). Monitoring online communication: can the development of convergence and social presence indicate an interactive learning environment? *Distance Education*, *25*(1), 67–81. doi:10.1080/0158791042000212468

Lobry de Bruyn, L. (2002). *Description of Problem Based Learning in Natural Resource Management.* Retrieved March 21, 2007, from http://www.learningdesigns.uow.edu.au/exemplars/info/LD28/index.html.

Lobry de Bruyn, L. A., & Prior, J. C. (2001). Changing student learning focus in natural resource management education – Problems (and some solutions) with using problem-based learning. In L. Richardson, & J. Lidstone (Eds), *Proceedings of the Joint International Conference Flexible learning for a flexible society. ASET/HERDSA 2000* (pp. 441-451). Toowoomba, Queensland Australia: ASET/HERDSA.

Lockyer, L., Bennett, S., Agostinho, S., & Harper, B. (Eds.). (2008). *Handbook of Research on Learning Design and Learning Objects: Issues, Applications and Technologies*. Hershey, PA: IGI Global.

Lockyer, L., Bennett, S., Agostinho, S., & Harper, B. (Eds.). (2008). *Handbook of Research on Learning Design and Learning Objects: Issues, Applications and Technologies*. Hershey, PA: IGI Global.

Lortie, D. (1975). *Schoolteacher: A sociological study*. Chicago: University of Chicago Press.

Lou, Y., Abrami, P. C., Spence, J. C., Poulsen, C., Chambers, B., & d'Apollonia, S. (1996). Within-Class Grouping: A Meta-Analysis. *Review of Educational Research, 66*(4), 423–458.

Luebeck, J. L., & Bice, L. R. (2005). Online discussion as a mechanism of conceptual change among mathematics and science teachers. *Journal of Distance Education, 20*(2), 21–39.

Lykourentzou, I., Giannoukos, I., Nikolopoulos, V., Mpardis, G., & Loumos, V. (2009). Dropout prediction in e-learning courses through the combination of machine learning techniques. *Computers & Education, 53*(3), 950–965. doi:10.1016/j.compedu.2009.05.010

Lyman, F. (1981). The responsive classroom discussion. In Anderson, A. S. (Ed.), *Mainstreaming Digest*. College Park, MD: University of Maryland College of Education.

Macdonald, J. (2003). Assessing online collaborative learning: Process and product. *Computers & Education, 40*(4), 377–391. doi:10.1016/S0360-1315(02)00168-9

MacKnight, C. B. (2000). Teaching critical thinking through online discussion. *EDUCAUSE Quarterly, 23*(4), 38–41.

Maddux, C. (2004). Developing *Online Courses:* Ten Myths. *Rural Special Education Quarterly, 23*(2), 27–33.

Maehr, M. L., & Midgley, C. (1991). Enhancing student motivation: A school-wide approach. *Educational Psychologist, 26*(3-4), 399–427. doi:10.1207/s15326985ep2603&4_9

Mäkitalo, K., Weinberger, A., Häkkinen, P., Järvelä, S., & Fischer, F. (2005). Epistemic cooperation scripts in online learning environments: Fostering learning by reducing uncertainty in discourse? *Computers in Human Behavior, 21*, 603–622. doi:10.1016/j.chb.2004.10.033

Manca, S., & Delfino, M. (2007). Learners' representation of their affective domain through figurative language in a web-based learning environment. *Distance Education, 28*(1), 25–43. doi:10.1080/01587910701305293

Marcos, A., Martinez, A., & Dimitriadis, Y. (2005). Towards adaptable interaction analysis in CSCL. In *Proceedings of the 12th International Conference on Artificial Intelligence, Workshop on Representing and Analyzing Collaborative Interactions, AIED 2005*, Amsterdam: IOS Press. Retrieved January 15, 2010, from http://gsic.tel.uva.es/uploaded_files/31306_AIED_workshop6_short_paper_jamarcos.doc

Marginalia (2010). *An open source Web annotation tool.* Retrieved April 2, 2010, from http://www.geof.net/code/annotation

Markus, H., & Nurius, P. (1986). Possible selves. *The American Psychologist, 41*(9), 954–969. doi:10.1037/0003-066X.41.9.954

Marlow, C., & Naaman, M. boyd, d., & Davis, M. (2006). Tagging Paper, Taxonomy, Flickr, Academic Article, to Read. *Hypertext '06* (31-40). New York: ACM Press.

Martin, D. C., & Blanc, R. (1984). Improving Reading Comprehension through Reciprocal Questioning. Techniques. *Life Long Learning*, *7*(4), 29–31.

Martínez, A., Dimitriadis, Y., & De La Fuente, P. (2003). Contributions to analysis of interactions for formative evaluation in CSCL. In M. Llamas, M.J. Fernandez, & L.E. Anido (Eds), *Computers and education: Towards of lifelong learning society* (pp. 227-238). Amserdam: Kluwer Academic.

Masiello, I., Ramberg, R., & Lonka, K. (2005). Attitudes to the application of a web-based learning system in a Microbiology course. *Computers & Education*, *45*(2), 171–185. doi:10.1016/j.compedu.2004.07.001

Mason, R., & Kaye, A. (Eds.). (1989). *Mindweave: Communication, computers and distance education*. New York: Pergamon Press.

Mason, R., & Lockwood, F. (1994). *Using communications media in open and flexible learning*. London: Kogan Page.

Mason, R., & Kaye, A. (1990). Towards a new paradigm for distance education. In Harasim, L. (Ed.), *Online education: Perspectives on a new environment* (pp. 15–38). New York: Praeger.

Mason, R. (1991). Moderating educational computer conferencing. *DEOSNEWS,* 1(19). Retrieved April 9, 2010, from http://www.emoderators.com/papers/mason.html

Matters, G. (2005, June). *Designing Assessment Tasks for Deep Thinking.* Paper presented at the Twelfth Annual Conference of the Curriculum Corporation, Brisbane, Australia. Retrieved March 20, 2010, from http://cmslive.curriculum.edu.au/verve/_resources/Matters_edited.pdf

McAndrew, P., & Goodyear, P. (2007). Representing practitioner experiences through learning design and patterns. In H. Beetham & R. Sharpe (Eds), *Rethinking Pedagogy for a Digital Age* (92-102). London, UK: Routledge.

McAndrew, P., Santos, A., Lane, A., Godwin, S., Okada, A., Wilson, T., et al. (2009). *OpenLearn Research Report 2006-2008.* The Open University, Milton Keynes, England. Retrieved March 20, 2010, from http://oro.open.ac.uk/17513/

McAndrew, P., Santos, A., Lane, A., Godwin, S., Okada, A., Wilson, T., et al. (2009). *OpenLearn Research Report 2006-2008.* The Open University, Milton Keynes, England. Retrieved March 20, 2010, from http://oro.open.ac.uk/17513/

McCollum, K. (1997). A professor divides his class in two to test value of online instruction. *The Chronicle of Higher Education*, *43*(24), A23.

McDonald, J. (2003). Assessing online collaborative learning: Process and product. *Computers & Education*, *40*(4), 377–391. doi:10.1016/S0360-1315(02)00168-9

McGrath, J., & Hollingshead, A. (1994). *Groups Interacting With Technology*. Thousand Oaks, CA: Sage.

McGrath, J. E. (1991). Time, Interaction and Performance (TIP). A Theory of Groups. *Small Group Research*, *22*, 147–174. doi:10.1177/1046496491222001

McGrath, J. E. (1990). Time matters in groups. In Galegher, J., Kraut, R. E., & Egido, C. (Eds.), *Intellectual teamwork: Social and technological foundations of cooperative work* (pp. 23–61). Hillsdale, NJ: Lawrence Erlbaum Associates.

McLean, R. S. (1999). Meta-communication widgets for knowledge building in distance education. In C. Hoadley, & J. Roschelle (Eds.), Proceedings of the *Computer Support for Collaborative Learning (CSCL) Conference* (383-390), Mahwah, NJ: Lawrence Erlbaum Associates.

McLoughlin, D., & Mynard, J. (2009). An analysis of higher order thinking in online discussions. *Innovations in Education and Teaching International*, *46*(2), 147–160. doi:10.1080/14703290902843778

Mehan, H. (1979). *Learning lessons: Social organization in the classroom*. Cambridge, MA: Harvard University Press.

Meyer, K. A. (2003). Face-to-face versus threaded discussions: The role of time and higher-order thinking. *Journal of Asynchronous Learning Networks*, *7*(3), 55–65.

Mezirow, J. (1991). *Transformative dimensions of adult learning*. San Francisco, CA: Jossey- Bass.

Miao, Y., & Harrer, A. Hoeksema, K. & Hoppe, U. (2007). Modeling CSCL scripts - a reflection of learning design approaches. In Fischer, F. Kollar, I., Mandl, H., & Haake, J.M. (Eds.), *Scripting CSCL: Cognitive, Computational and Educational Perspectives*, CSCL Series, Vol. 6, (pp. 117-136). New York: Springer.

Miao, Y., Tattersall, C., Schoonenboom, J., Stevanov, K., & Aleksieva-Petrova, A. (2007). Using open technical e-learning standards and service-orientation to support new forms of e-assessment. In Griffiths, D., Koper, R. and Liber O. (Eds.), *Proceedings of the second TENCompetence Open Workshop on Service Oriented Approaches and Lifelong Competence Development Infrastructures* (pp. 183-190). Bolton, UK: The Institute for Educational Cybernetics.

Millis, B. J., & Cottell, P. G. (1998). *Cooperative Learning for Higher Education Faculty. ACE, Series on Higher Education.* Phoenix, AZ: Oryx Press.

Mislevy, R., Hamel, L., Fried, R., Gaffney, T., & Haertel, G. Hafter, et al. (2003). *Design patterns for assessing science inquiry (PADI Technical Report 1).* Menlo Park, CA: SRI International

Monahan, T., McArdlea, G., & Bertolotto, M. (2008). Virtual reality for collaborative e-learning. *Computers & Education, 50*(4), 1339–1353. doi:10.1016/j.compedu.2006.12.008

Moore, G. (1989). Three types of interaction. *American Journal of Distance Education, 3*(2), 1–6. doi:10.1080/08923648909526659

Moore, M. (1993). Three types of interaction. In Harry, K., John, M., & Keegan, D. (Eds.), *Distance education: new perspectives*. London, UK: Routledge.

Moreland, R. L. (2000). Transactive memory: learning who knows what in work groups and organizations. In Thompson, L., Messik, D., & Levine, J. (Eds.), *Shared Cognition in Organizations: The Management of Knowledge* (pp. 3–31). Hillsdale, NJ: Lawrence Erlbaum.

Moscovici, S. (1980). Toward a theory of conversion behavior. In L. Berkowitz /Ed.) [New York: Academic Press]. *Advances in Experimental Social Psychology, 13*, 209–239. doi:10.1016/S0065-2601(08)60133-1

Moskaliuk, J., Kimmerle, J., & Cress, U. (2008). Learning and knowledge building with Wikis: The impact of incongruity between people's knowledge and a Wiki's information. In G. Kanselaar, V. Jonker, P.A. Kirschner, & F.J. Prins (Eds.), *International perspectives in the learning sciences: Cre8ing a learning world*, (Vol. 2 pp. 99-106). *Proceedings of the 8th International Conference for the Learning Sciences – ICLS 2008*. Utrecht, The Netherlands: International Society of the Learning Sciences, Inc.

Muirhead, B. (2001). Enhancing social interaction in computer-mediated distance education. *Ed at a Distance Journal, 15*(4). Retrieved April 8, 2010, from http://ifets.ieee.org/discussions/discuss_sept2000.html

Murphy, K. L., Mahoney, S. E., Chen, C., Mendoza-Diaz, N. V., & Yang, X. (2005). A Constructivist Model of Mentoring, Coaching, and Facilitating Online Discussions. *Distance Education, 26*(3), 341–367. doi:10.1080/01587910500291454

Murray, B. (2000). Reinventing Class Discussion Online. *Monitor on Psychology, 31*(4). Retrieved March 20, 2010, from http://www.apa.org/monitor/apr00/reinventing.html

Muthukrishna, N., Carnine, D., Grossen, B., & Miller, S. (1999). Children's alternative frameworks: Should they be directly addressed in science instruction? *Journal of Research in Science Teaching, 30*(3), 233–248. doi:10.1002/tea.3660300303

Naidu, S., Barrett, J., & Olson, P. (2000). Improving instructional effectiveness with computer-mediated communication. In Squires, D., Conole, D., & Jacobs, G. (Eds.), *The Changing Face of Learning Technology*. Cardiff, UK: University of Wales Press.

National Research Council. (1999). *How people learn: Brain, mind, experience*. Washington, D.C: National Academy Press.

National Research Council. (2001). *Classroom assessment and the National Science Education Standards.* Washington, D.C: National Academy Press.

NCES - National Center for Education Statistics - U.S. Department of Education. (2008). *Distance Education at Degree-Granting Postsecondary Institutions: 2006-07.* Retrieved September 1, 2009, from http://nces.ed.gov/pubsearch/pubsinfo.asp?pubid=2009044

Nel, L., & Wilkinson, A. (2006). Enhancing Collaborative Learning in a Blended Learning Environment: Applying a Process Planning Model Export. *Systemic Practice and Action Research, 19*(6), 553–576. doi:10.1007/s11213-006-9043-3

Nelson, D., & Blenkin, C. (2007). The Power of Online Role-Play Simulations: Technology in Nursing Education. *International Journal of Nursing Education Scholarship, 4*(1). Retrieved March 20, 2010, from http://www.bepress.com/ijnes/vol4/iss1/art1

Nemeth, C. J. (1986). Differential contributions of majority and minority influence. *Psychological Review, 93*(11), 23–32. doi:10.1037/0033-295X.93.1.23

Noël, S., & Robert, J.-M. (2004). Empirical study on collaborative writing: what do co-authors do, use, and like? *Computer Supported Cooperative Work, 13*(1), 63–89. doi:10.1023/B:COSU.0000014876.96003.be

Nokelainen, P., Miettinen, M., Kurhila, J., Floréen, P., & Tirri, H. (2005). A shared document-based annotation tool to support learner-centred collaborative learning. *British Journal of Educational Technology, 36*(5), 757–770. doi:10.1111/j.1467-8535.2005.00474.x

Nonnecke, B., & Preece, J. (2003). Silent participants: Getting to know lurkers better. In Leug, C., & Fisher, D. (Eds.), *From usenet to CoWebs: Interacting with social information spaces* (pp. 110–132). Amsterdam, The Netherlands: Springer-Verlag.

Notar, C., Wilson, K., & Montgomery, M. (2005). A distance learning model for teaching higher order thinking. *College Student Journal, 39*(1), 17.

Novak, J. D. (1977). *A theory of education.* Ithaca, NY: Cornell University Press.

Novak, J. D., & Gowin, D. B. (1984). *Learning how to learn.* New York and Cambridge, UK: Cambridge University Press.

Nystrand, M., & Gamoran, A. (1991). Instructional discourse, student engagement, and literature achievement. *Research in the Teaching of English, 25*(3), 261–290.

Nystrand, M., Wu, L. L., & Gamoran, A. (2003). Questions in time: Investigating the structure and dynamics of unfolding classroom discourse. *Discourse Processes, 32*(5), 135–198. doi:10.1207/S15326950DP3502_3

O'Reilly, T. (2005). *What is Web 2.0?* Retrieved December 20, 2009, from http://oreilly.com/web2/archive/what-is-web-20.html

O'Connaill, B., Whittaker, S., & Wilbur, S. (1993). Conversations over video conferences: An evaluation of the spoken aspects of video-mediated communication. *Human-Computer Interaction, 8*(4), 389–428. doi:10.1207/s15327051hci0804_4

O'Day, J. A. (2002). Complexity, accountability, and school improvement. *Harvard Educational Review, 72*(3), 293–329.

O'Donnell, A. M., & Dansereau, D. F. (2000). Interactive effects of prior knowledge and material format on cooperative teaching. *Journal of Experimental Education, 68*(2), 101–118. doi:10.1080/00220970009598497

O'Donnell, A. M., & King, A. (Eds.). (1999). *Cognitive perspectives on peer learning.* Mahwah, NJ: Lawrence Erlbaum.

Offir, B., Lev, Y., & Bezalel, R. (2008). Surface and deep learning processes in distance education: Synchronous versus asynchronous systems. *Computers & Education, 51*(3), 1172–1182. doi:10.1016/j.compedu.2007.10.009

Orrill, C. H. (2002). Supporting online PBL: Design considerations for supporting distributed problem solving. *Distance Education, 23*(1), 41–57. doi:10.1080/01587910220123973

Osborn, A. F. (1963). *Applied imagination: Principles and procedures of creative problem solving* (Third Revised Edition). New York: Charles Scribner's Sons.

Osman, G., & Duffy, T. (2009). Scaffolding critical discourse in online problem-based scenarios: The role of articulation and evaluative feedback. Paper presented at the *American Educational Research Association Annual Conference,* San Diego, USA, April 13-17.

Paechter, M. (2003). *Wissenskommunikation, Kooperation und Lernen in virtuellen Gruppen. Lengerich.* Germany: Pabst Publisher.

Palincsar, A. S., & Brown, A. L. (1984). Reciprocal teaching of comprehension-fostering and comprehension-monitoring activities. *Cognition and Instruction, 1*(2), 117–175. doi:10.1207/s1532690xci0102_1

Palloff, R. M., & Pratt, K. (1999). *Building learning communities in cyberspace: Effective strategies for the online classroom.* San Francisco, CA: Jossey-Bass.

Palloff, R. M., & Pratt, K. (2005). *Collaborating online: Learning together in community.* San Francisco, CA: John Wiley & Sons, Inc.

Palloff, R., & Pratt, K. (2004). *Collaborating Online: Learning Together in Community.* New York: Jossey-Bass.

Palloff, M. R., & Pratt, K. (2004). Learning together in Community: Collaboration Online. *Proceedings of the 20th Annual Conference on Distance Teaching and Learning.* Retrieved April 8, 2010, from http://www.uwex.edu/disted/conference/Resource_library/proceedings/04_1127.pdf

Palomino-Ramírez, L., Bote-Lorenzo, M. L., Asensio-Pérez, J. I., & Dimitriadis, Y. (2008). LeadFlow4LD: Learning and Data Flow Composition-based Solution for Learning Design in CSCL. In Briggs, R.O. et al. (Eds.), *Proceedings of 14th International Workshop, CRIWG 2008. Groupware: Design, Implementation, and Use.* Lecture Notes in Computer Science. Vol. 5411. (266-280). New York: Springer.

Pan, S. L., & Scarbrough, H. (1999). Knowledge management in Practice: An Exploratory Case Study. *Technology Analysis and Strategic Management, 11*(3), 359–374. doi:10.1080/095373299107401

Panitz, T. (1997). Faculty and Student Resistance to Co-operative Learning. *Cooperative Learning and College Teaching, 7(*2).

Paulsen, M. F. (1995). *The Online Report on Pedagogical Techniques for Computer-mediated Communication.* Retrieved July 3, 2009, from http://www.nettskolen.com/forskning/19/cmcped.html

Pearce, J. (2009). Using wiki in education. *The science of spectroscopy.* Retrieved September 10, 2009, from: http://www.scienceofspectroscopy.info/edit/index.php?title=Using_wiki_in_education

Penuel, W. R., Boscardin, C. K., Masyn, K., & Crawford, V. M. (2007). Teaching with student response systems in elementary and secondary education settings: A survey study. *Educational Technology Research and Development, 55*(4), 315–346. doi:10.1007/s11423-006-9023-4

Penuel, W. R., Roschelle, J., & Shechtman, N. (2007). The WHIRL co-design process: Participant experiences. *Research and Practice in Technology Enhanced Learning, 2*(1), 51–74. doi:10.1142/S1793206807000300

Penuel, W. R. (2008). Making the most of one-to-one computing in networked classrooms. In Voogt, J., & Knezek, G. (Eds.), *International handbook of information technology in primary and secondary education* (pp. 925–931). Dordrecht, The Netherlands: Springer. doi:10.1007/978-0-387-73315-9_59

Penuel, W. R. (in press). Classroom uses of technology to manage instruction *International Encyclopedia of Education.* Oxford, UK: Elsevier.

Penuel, W. R., Roschelle, J., & Abrahamson, A. L. (2005). Research on classroom networks for whole-class activities. Proceedings of *the IEEE International Workshop on Wireless and Mobile Technologies in Education* (pp. 222-229). Los Alamitos, CA: IEEE.

Perrine, R. M., & Spain, J. W. (2008). Impact of a Pre-Semester College Orientation Program: Hidden Benefits? *Journal of College Student Retention: Research. Theory into Practice*, *10*(2), 155–169.

Persico, D., Pozzi, F., & Sarti, L. (2009). Design Patterns for Monitoring and Evaluating CSCL Processes. *Computers in Human Behavior*, *25*(5), 1020–1027. doi:10.1016/j.chb.2009.01.003

Persico, D., Pozzi, F., & Sarti, L. (2009), A model for monitoring and evaluating CSCL. In (Eds.) Juan, A.A., Daradoumis, T., Xhafa, F., Caballe, S., Faulin, J., *Monitoring and Assessment in Online Collaborative Environments: Emergent Computational Technologies for E-learning Support*. Hershey, PA: IGI Global.

Peter, Y., & Vantroys, T. (2005). Platform Support for Pedagogical Scenarios. *Journal of Educational Technology & Society*, *8*(3), 122–137.

Petropoulou, O., Lazakidou, G., Retalis, S., & Vrasidas, C. (2007). Analysing interaction behaviour in network supported collaborative learning environments: A holistic approach. *International Journal of Knowledge and Learning*, *3*(4&5), 450–464. doi:10.1504/IJKL.2007.016705

Petropoulou, O., Retalis, S., Siassiakos, K., Karamouzis, S., & Kargidis, T. (2008). Helping educators analyse interactions within networked learning communities: A framework and the AnalyticsTool system. In *Proceedings of the 6th International Conference on Networked Learning* Halkidiki, Greece.

Petrosino, A. J. (1998). *The use of reflection and revision in hands-on experimental activities by at risk children.*, Unpublished dissertation. Vanderbilt University, Nashville, TN.

Pettenger, M., & Young, N. (2008). Investigating the Impact of Role Play Simulations on Student Learning: An Assessment Model. In *Conference Papers - ISA's 49th, International Studies Association, 2008, Annual Convention, Bridging Multiple Divides.* Hilton San Francisco, San Francisco, CA, USA. Retrieved April 13, from http://www.allacademic.com/meta/p250818_index.html

Pfister, H.-R., Wessner, M., Holmer, T., & Steinmetz, R. (1999). Negotiating about shared knowledge in a cooperative learning environment. In C. Hoadley, & J. Roschelle (Eds.), *Computer Support for Collaborative Learning* (pp. 454-457). *Proceedings of the CSCL '99 Conference*. Palo Alto, CA: Stanford University.

Piechura-Couture, K., Tichenor, M., Touchton, D., Maciasaac, E., & Heins, H. D. (2006). Co-teaching: A model for education reform. *Principal Leadership*, *6*(9), 39–43.

Pipek, V., & Wulf, W. (1999). A groupware's life. In Bødker, S., Kyng, M. and Schmidt, K. (eds.). *Proceedings of the 6th European Conference on Computer-Supported Cooperative Work*. (199-218), Dordrecht, The Netherlands: Kluwer Academic Publishers.

Piskurich, G. M. (Ed.). (2003). *Preparing Learners for E-Learning*. San Francisco, CA: Pfeiffer (John Wiley & Sons, Inc.).

Piskurich, G. M., & Piskurich, J. F. (2003). Utilizing a classroom approach to prepare learners for E-Learning. In G. M. Piskurich (Ed.), *Preparing Learners for E-Learning* (pp. 45-72). San Francisco, CA: Pfeiffer (John Wiley & Sons, Inc.).

Poole, D. M. (2000). Student participation in a discussion-oriented online course: A case study. *Journal of Research on Computing in Education*, *33*(2), 162–177.

Posner, G., Strike, J., Hewson, P., & Gerzog, W. (1982). Accommodation of a scientific conception: Toward a theory of conceptual change. *Science Education*, *66*(2), 221–227. doi:10.1002/sce.3730660207

Pozzi, F. (2009). Using collaborative techniques in virtual learning communities. *EC-TEL2009 -. Lecture Notes in Computer Science*, *5794*, 670–675. doi:10.1007/978-3-642-04636-0_66

Pozzi, F., Manca, S., Persico, D., & Sarti, L. (2007). A general framework for tracking and analysing learning processes in computer-supported collaborative learning environments. *Innovations in Education and Teaching International*, *44*(2), 169–179. doi:10.1080/14703290701240929

PPP. (2005). The pedagogical patterns project. Retrieved 30 September, 2009, from http://www.pedagogicalpatterns.org/

Prasolova-Førland, E. (2008). Corresponding Author Contact InformationAnalyzing place metaphors in 3D educational collaborative virtual environments. *Computers in Human Behavior*, *24*(2), 185–204. doi:10.1016/j.chb.2007.01.009

Prensky, M. (2001, October). "*Digital Natives, Digital Immigrants*" Retrieved September 10, 2009, from http://www.marcprensky.com/writing

Pressley, M., & McCormick, C. B. (1995). *Advanced educational psychology for educators, researchers, and policymakers*. New York, NY: Harper Collins.

Puntambekar, S. (2006). Analysing collaborative interactions: divergence, shared understanding and construction of knowledge. *Computers & Education*, *47*(3), 332–351. doi:10.1016/j.compedu.2004.10.012

Quiamzade, A., & Mugny, G. (2001). Social influence dynamics in aptitude tasks. *Social Psychology of Education*, *4*, 311–334. doi:10.1023/A:1011388821962

Raleigh, D. (2000). Keys to Facilitating Successful Online Discussions. *Teaching with Technology Today, 7* (4). Retrieved March 20, 2010, from http://www.uwsa.edu/ttt/raleigh.htm

Redding, T. R. (2003). Preparing Your Learners for My E-Learning. An E-Learning Vendor's Point of View. In G. M. Piskurich (Ed.), *Preparing Learners for E-Learning* (pp. 155-168). San Francisco, CA: Pfeiffer (John Wiley & Sons, Inc.).

Redfern, S., & Naughton, N. (2002). Collaborative Virtual Environments to Support Communication and Community in Internet-Based Distance Education. *Journal of Information Technology Education*, *1*(3), 201–211.

Reeves, D. (2009). Three challenges of Web 2.0. *Educational Leadership*, *66*(6), 87–89.

Reffay, C., & Chanier, T. (2003). How social network analysis can help to measure cohesion in collaborative distance-learning. In. B. Wason, S. Ludvigson, & U. Hoppe (Eds), *Proceedings of the international conference on computer support for collaborative learning: Designing for change in networked learning.* (pp. 343-352). Dordrecht: Kluwer Academic Publishers.

Reichelt, M. (2000). Case studies in L2 teacher education. *ELT Journal*, *54*(4), 346–353. doi:10.1093/elt/54.4.346

Reiserer, M., Ertl, B., & Mandl, H. (2002). Fostering collaborative knowledge construction in desktop videoconferencing. Effects of content schemes and cooperation scripts in peer-teaching settings. In Stahl, G. (Ed.), *Computer support for collaborative learning: Foundations for a CSCL community – CSCL 2002* (pp. 379–388). Hillsdale, NJ: Lawrence Erlbaum.

Reiserer, M. (2002). *Peer-Teaching in Videokonferenzen. Effekte niedrig- und hochstrukturierter Kooperationsskripte auf Lernprozess und Lernerfolg.* Unpublished Dissertation, Ludwig-Maximilians-Universität München, München, Germany.

Renkl, A., Mandl, H., & Gruber, H. (1996). Inert knowledge: Analyzes and remedies. *Educational Psychologist*, *31*(2), 115–121. doi:10.1207/s15326985ep3102_3

Retalis, S., Papasalouros, A., Psaromiligkos, Y., Siskos, S., & Kargidis, T. (2006). Towards networked learning analytics – a concept and a tool. *The 5th International Conference on Networked Learning.* Retrieved April 9, 2010, from http://www.networkedlearningconference.org.uk/past/nlc2006/abstracts/pdfs/P41%20Retalis.pdf

Rheingold, H. (2006, November 1), *"Social Bookmarking, Tagging, Music/Photo/Video Sharing"* Message posted. Retrieved April 9, 2010, from https://www.socialtext.net/medialiteracy/index.cgi?social_bookmarking_tagging_music_photo_video_sharing

Rice, R. (1994). Network analysis and computer-mediated communication systems. In Galaskiewka, S. W. J. (Ed.), *Advances in social network analysis* (pp. 167–203). Newbury Park, CA: Sage.

Richardson, J. C., & Swan, K. (2003). Examining Social Presence in Online Courses in Relation to Students' Perceived Learning and Satisfaction. *Journal of Asynchronous Learning Networks*, *7*(1), 68–88.

Roberts, T. S. (2005). Computer-supported collaborative learning in higher education: An introduction. In: Roberts, T. S. (ed). *Computer-supported collaborative learning in higher education* (1–18). Hershey, PA: Idea Group Publishing.

Rogers, P. C., Liddle, S. W., Chan, P., Doxey, A., & Isom, A. (2007) A Web 2.0 Learning Platform: Harnessing Collective Intelligence, *Turkish Online Journal of Distance Education* 8(3). Retrieved April, 13, from http://tojde.anadolu.edu.tr/tojde27/pdf/article_1.pdf

Ronen, M., & Kohen-Vacs, D. (2009). Designing and applying adaptation patterns embedded in the scripts. *Proceedings of the International Workshop on Adaptive Systems for Collaborative Learning, INCoS 2009* (306-310). New York: IEEE Computer Society Press.

Ronen, M., Kohen-Vacs, D., & Harrer, A. (2009). Modelling, creating and enacting online collaborative scripts. In Dimitracopoulou, A., Claire O'Malley, C., Daniel Suthers, D. & Reimann P. (Eds.), *Computer Supported Collaborative Learning Practices: CSCL2009 Community Events Proceedings* (p. 218). International Society of the Learning Sciences (ISLS).

Ronen, M., Kohen-Vacs, D., & Raz-Fogel, N. (2006). Adopt & Adapt: Structuring, Sharing and Reusing Asynchronous Collaborative Pedagogy. In Barab, S., Hay, K., & Hickey., D. (Eds.), *Proceedings of the 7th international conference on Learning sciences* (pp. 599-606). International Society of the Learning Sciences (ISLS).

Roschelle, J., Penuel, W. R., & Abrahamson, A. L. (2004). The networked classroom. *Educational Leadership*, *61*(5), 50–54.

Roschelle, J., Knudsen, J., & Hegedus, S. J. (in press). From new technological infrastructures to curricular activity systems: Advanced designs for teaching and learning. In Jacobson, M. J., & Reimann, P. (Eds.), *Designs for learning environments of the future: International perspectives from the learning sciences*. New York: Springer.

Roschelle, J. (1996). Learning by collaborating: Convergent conceptual change. In Koschmann, T. (Ed.), *CSCL: Theory and practice of an emerging paradigm* (pp. 209–248). Mahwah, NJ: Lawrence Erlbaum.

Roschelle, J., & Teasley, S. D. (1995). The construction of shared knowledge in collaborative problem solving. In O'Malley, C. (Ed.), *Computer Supported Collaborative Learning* (pp. 69–97). Berlin, Heidelberg: Springer.

Rose, F. D., Attree, E. A., Brooks, B. M., Parslow, D. M., Penn, P. R., & Ambihaipahan, N. (2000). Training in virtual environments: transfer to real world tasks and equivalence to real task training. *Ergonomics*, *43*(4), 494–511. doi:10.1080/001401300184378

Roth, W. M. (2009). *Dialogism: A Bakhtinian Perspective on Science and Learning*. Rotterdam: Sense Publisher.

Rourke, L., Anderson, T., Garrison, D. R., & Archer, W. (2001). Assessing social presence in asynchronous text-based computer conferencing. *Journal of Distance Education*, *14*(3), 51–70.

Rourke, L., Anderson, T., Garrison, D. R., & Archer, W. (1999). Assessing social presence in asynchronous text-based computer conferencing. *Canadian Journal of Distance Education*, *14*(2), 50–71.

Rourke, L., & Kanuka, H. (2007). Barriers to online critical discourse. *International Journal of Computer-Supported Collaborative Learning*, *2*(1), 105–126. doi:10.1007/s11412-007-9007-3

Rourke, L., Anderson, T., Garrison, D. R., & Archer, W. (2001). Methodological issues in the content analysis of computer transcripts. *International Journal of Artificial Intelligence in Education*, *12*(1), 8–22.

Roussos, M., Johnson, A. E., Leigh, J., Vasilakis, C. A., Barnes, C. R., & Moher, T. G. (1997). NICE: Combining Constructionism, Narrative, and Collaboration. *Computer Graphics*, *31*(3), 62–63. doi:10.1145/262171.262264

Rovai, A. (2007). Facilitating online discussions effectively. *The Internet and Higher Education*, *10*(1), 77–88. doi:10.1016/j.iheduc.2006.10.001

Rovai, A. P. (2002). Building sense of community at a distance. *International Review of Research in Open and Distance Learning*, *3*(1), 1–16.

Rovai, A. P. (2003). Strategies for grading online discussions: Effects on discussions and classroom community in Internet-based university courses. *Journal of Computing in Higher Education*, *15*(1), 89–107. doi:10.1007/BF02940854

Rovai, A. P. (2004). A constructivist approach to online college learning. *The Internet and Higher Education*, *7*(2), 79–93. doi:10.1016/j.iheduc.2003.10.002

Rovai, A. P., & Jordan, H. M. (2004). Blended learning and sense of community: A comparative analysis with traditional and fully online courses. *International Review of Research in Open and Distance Learning*, *5*(2).

Rovai, A. P. (2002). Sense of community, perceived cognitive learning, and persistence in asynchronous learning networks. *The Internet and Higher Education*, *5*(4), 319–332. doi:10.1016/S1096-7516(02)00130-6

Rovai, A. P. (2007). Facilitating online discussions effectively. *The Internet and Higher Education*, *10*(1), 77–88. doi:10.1016/j.iheduc.2006.10.001

Rummel, N., Ertl, B., Härder, J., & Spada, H. (2003). Supporting collaborative learning and problem-solving in desktop-videoconferencing settings. *International Journal of Educational Policy, Research, and Practice*, *4*(1), 83–115.

Rummel, N., & Spada, H. (2005). Learning to collaborate: An instructional approach to promoting collaborative problem solving in computer-mediated settings. *Journal of the Learning Sciences*, *14*(2), 201–241. doi:10.1207/s15327809jls1402_2

Rummel, N., & Spada, H. (2005). Learning to collaborate: An instructional approach to promoting collaborative problem solving in computer-mediated settings. *Journal of the Learning Sciences*, *14*(2), 201–241. doi:10.1207/s15327809jls1402_2

Rummel, N., & Spada, H. (2007). Can people learn computer-mediated collaboration by following a script? In Fischer, F., Kollar, I., Mandl, H., & Haake, J. M. (Eds.), *Scripting Computer-Supported Collaborative Learning* (pp. 39–55). New York: Springer. doi:10.1007/978-0-387-36949-5_3

Rummel, N., & Spada, H. (2007). Can people learn computer-mediated collaboration by following a script? In Fischer, F., Kollar, I., Mandl, H., & Haake, J. (Eds.), *Scripting computer-supported collaborative learning: Cognitive, computational and educational perspectives* (pp. 39–55). New York: Springer. doi:10.1007/978-0-387-36949-5_3

Ryan, R. M., & Deci, E. L. (2000). Intrinsic and extrinsic motivation: classic definitions and new directions. *Contemporary Educational Psychology*, *25*(1), 54–67. doi:10.1006/ceps.1999.1020

Safran, C., Helic, D., & Gütl, C. (2007). E-Learning practices and Web 2.0. In Auer, M. (Ed.), *Proc. of Interactive Computer Aided Learning (ICL 2007), Sep. 2007*. Villach, Austria.

Salas, A. (2006). The Rosy Future of Distance Ed. *The Hispanic Outlook in Higher Education,* 33-38.

Salomon, G., & Globerson, T. (1989). When teams do not function the way they ought to. *International Journal of Educational Research*, *13*(1), 89–99. doi:10.1016/0883-0355(89)90018-9

Salomon, G., & Perkins, D. N. (1998). Individual and social aspects of learning. *Review of Research in Education*, *23*(1), 1–24. doi:10.3102/0091732X023001001

Salomon, G., & Globerson, T. (1989). When teams do not function the way they ought to. *The Journal of Educational Research*, *13*(1), 89–100. doi:10.1016/0883-0355(89)90018-9

Salomon, G. (1992). Effects with and of computers and the study of computer-based learning environments. In De Corte, E., Linn, M. C., Mandl, H., & Verschaffel, L. (Eds.), *Computer-based learning environments and problem solving* (pp. 249–263). Berlin Heidelberg, Germany: Springer.

Saltz, J. S., Hiltz, S. R., Turoff, M., & Passerini, K. (2007). Increasing participation in distance learning courses. *IEEE Internet Computing, 11*(3), 36–44. doi:10.1109/MIC.2007.64

Saltz, J. S., Hiltz, S. R., & Turoff, M. (2004). Student social graphs: Visualizing a student's online social network. *The 2004 ACM conference on Computer supported cooperative work* (pp. 596-599). New York: Association for Computng Machinery (ACM).

Scardamalia, M., & Bereiter, C. (1994). Computer Support for Knowledge-Building Communities. *Journal of the Learning Sciences, 3*(3), 256–283. doi:10.1207/s15327809jls0303_3

Scardamalia, M., & Bereiter, C. (2003). Knowledge building. In *Encyclopedia of education* (2nd ed., pp. 1370–1373). New York, NY: Macmillan Reference.

Scardamalia, M. (2004). *CSILE/Knowledge Forum. In education and Technology: An encyclopedia* (pp. 183–192). Santa Barbara, CA: ABC-CLIO.

Scardamalia, M., & Bereiter, C. (1991). Higher levels of agency for children in knowledge building: a challenge for the design of new knowledge media. *Journal of the Learning Sciences, 1*(1), 37–68. doi:10.1207/s15327809jls0101_3

Scardamalia, M., & Bereiter, C. (2007). Fostering communities of learners and knowledge building: An interrupted dialogue. In Campione, J. C., Metz, K. E., & Palincsar, A. S. (Eds.), *Children's learning in the laboratory and in the classroom: Essays in honor of Ann Brown* (pp. 197–212). Mahwah, NJ: Erlbaum.

Scardamalia, M., & Bereiter, C. (2006). Knowledge building: Theory, pedagogy, and technology. In Sawyer, K. (Ed.), *Cambridge handbook of the learning sciences* (pp. 97–118). New York: Cambridge University Press.

Scardamalia, M. (2002). Collective cognitive responsibility for the advancement of knowledge. In B. Smith (Ed.) *Liberal education in a knowledge society*, 67-98. Chicago, ILL: Open Court.

Schank, R. C., & Abelson, R. P. (1977). *Scripts, plans, goals and understanding*. Hillsdale, NJ: Lawrence Erlbaum.

Scheucher, B., Belcher, J. W., Bailey, P. H., dos Santos, F. R., & Gütl, C. (2009). Evaluations Results of a 3D Virtual Environment for Internet-accessible Physics Experiments. In Auer, M. (Ed.), *Proc. of Interactive Computer Aided Learning (ICL 2009), Sep. 2009*. Villach, Austria.

Scheucher, B., Bailey, P. H., Gütl, C., & Harward, V. J. (2009). Collaborative Virtual 3D Environment for Internet-accessible Physics Experiments. *International Journal of Online Engineering* (republished), *5* (1) Special issue Rev. 2009, 65-71.

Schrader, P. G., & McCreery, M. (2008). The acquisition of skill and expertise in massively multiplayer online games. *Educational Technology Research and Development, 56*(5-6), 557–574. doi:10.1007/s11423-007-9055-4

Schrank, D. (2009). *A Trustful Payment System for Virtual Worlds - Design and Implementation of a Payment System for Virtual Worlds*. Master Thesis, Graz University of Technology, Austria. Retrieved April 5, 2010, from http://www.iicm.tugraz.at/home/cguetl/projects/PaymentSystemForVirtualWorlds/Schrank_Thesis.pdf

Schroeder, R. (2008). Defining Virtual Worlds and Virtual Environments. *Journal of Virtual Worlds Research, Vol. 1* (1). Retrieved April, 2, 2010, from http://journals.tdl.org/jvwr/article/download/294/248

Schroeder, U., & Spannagel, C. (2005). The role of interaction records in active learning processes: Proceedings of *the IADIS Virtual Multi Conference on Computer Science and Information Systems (MCCSIS)* (pp. 99-104). Algarve, Portugal: International Association for Development of the Information Society.

Schwartz, D. L., & Bransford, J. D. (1998). A time for telling. *Cognition and Instruction, 16*(4), 475–522. doi:10.1207/s1532690xci1604_4

Schwartz, D. L., Lin, X., Brophy, S., & Bransford, J. D. (1999). Toward the development of flexibly adaptive instructional designs. In Reigeluth, C. (Ed.), *Instructional design theories and models: A new paradigm of instructional theory* (*Vol. II*, pp. 183–214). Mahwah, NJ: Earlbaum.

Schwarz, B. B., Neuman, Y., & Biezuner, S. (2000). Two wrongs may make a right: If they argue together! *Cognition and Instruction*, *18*(4), 461–494. doi:10.1207/S1532690XCI1804_2

Shafer, I. (2008). *Team Teaching: Education for the Future. Dept of education and training / new south wales.* Retrieved March 20, 2010, from http://www.usao.edu/~facshaferi/teamteaching.htm.

Shapiro, E., & Dempsey, C. (2008). Conflict Resolution in Team Teaching a Case Study in Interdisciplinary Teaching. *College Teaching*, *56*(3), 157–162. doi:10.3200/CTCH.56.3.157-162

Sharan, S., & Hertz-Lazarowitz, R. (1980). A group-investigation method of cooperative learning in the classroom. In Sharan, P. Hare, C. Webb & R. Hertz-Lazarowitz (Eds.), *Cooperation in education*. Provo, Utah: Brigham Young University Press.

Shea, P., & Bidjerano, T. (2009). Community of inquiry as a theoretical framework to foster "Epistemic engagement" in online education. Paper presented at the *American Educational Research Association Annual Conference,* San Diego, USA, April 13-17.

Shemla, A., & Nachmias, R. (2007). Current State of Web-Supported Courses at Tel-Aviv University. *International Journal on E-Learning*, *6*(2), 235–246.

Shepard, L. A. (2000). The role of assessment in a learning culture. *Educational Researcher*, *29*(7), 4–14.

Shepperd, J. A. (1993). Productivity loss in performance groups: A motivation analysis. *Psychological Bulletin*, *113*(1), 67–81. doi:10.1037/0033-2909.113.1.67

Shibley, I. (2006). Interdisciplinary Team Teaching: Negotiating Pedagogical Differences. *College Teaching*, *54*(3), 271–275. doi:10.3200/CTCH.54.3.271-274

Sikora, A. C., & Carroll, C. D. (2002). *Postsecondary education descriptive analysis reports (NCES 2003-154). US Department of Education, National Center for Education Statistics*. Washington, DC: US Government Printing Office.

Silva, J. M., Mahfujur Rahman, A. S., & El Saddik, A. (2008). Web 3.0: a vision for bridging the gap between real and virtual. In *Proceedings of the 1st ACM international workshop on Communicability design and evaluation in cultural and ecological multimedia systems* (9-14). New York: ACM.

Silverman, R., Welty, W. M., & Lyon, S. (1996). *Case studies for teacher problem solving* (2nd ed.). New York: McGraw-Hill.

Sivan, Y. (2008). 3D3C Real Virtual Worlds Defined: The Immense Potential of Merging 3D, Community, Creation, and Commerce. *Journal of Virtual Worlds, 1* (1). Retrieved September 15, 2009, from http://journals.tdl.org/jvwr/article/viewArticle/278

Slavin, R. E. (1978). Student teams and achievement divisions. *Journal of Research and Development in Education*, *12*, 39–49.

Smith, J. P. III, diSessa, A. A., & Roschelle, J. (1993-1994). Misconceptions reconceived: A constructivist analysis of knowledge in transition. *Journal of the Learning Sciences*, *3*(2), 115–163. doi:10.1207/s15327809jls0302_1

Smith, B. L., & MacGregor, J. T. (1992). What is collaborative learning? In Goodsell, A. S., Maher, M. R., and Tinto, V. (Eds.), *Collaborative Learning: A Sourcebook for Higher Education* (9-22). University Park, PA: National Center on Postsecondary Teaching, Learning, and Assessment.

Snowdon, D., Churchill, E. F., & Munro, A. J. (2001). Snowdon, D., Churchill, E.F. & Munro, A.J. Collaborative Virtual Environments: Digital Spaces and Places for CSCW: An Introduction. In Churchill, E. F., Snowdon, D., & Munro, A. J. (Eds.), *Collaborative Virtual Environments: Digital Places and Spaces for Interaction* (pp. 77–98). London: Springer Verlag.

So, H.-J., & Brush, T. A. (2008). Student perceptions of collaborative learning, social presence and satisfaction in a blended learning environment: Relationships and critical factors. *Computers & Education, 51*(1), 318–336. doi:10.1016/j.compedu.2007.05.009

So, H. J., & Brush, T. (2006). Student perceptions of cooperative learning in a distance learning environment: Relationships with social presence and satisfaction. *Annual Meeting of the American Educational Research Association (AERA),* April 2006, San Francisco, California.

Sodian, B., Zaitchik, D., & Carey, S. (1991). Young children's differentiation of hypothetical beliefs from evidence. *Child Development, 62*(4), 753–766. doi:10.2307/1131175

Sogunro, O. (2004). Efficacy of role-playing pedagogy in training leaders: some reflections. *Journal of Management Development, 23*(3/4), 335–339.

Soller, A., Jermann, P., Muehlenbrock, M., & Martinez, A. (2004). Designing computational models of collaborative learning interaction: Introduction to the workshop proceedings. In *Proceedings of the 2nd International Workshop on Designing Computational Models of Collaborative Learning Interaction, ITS 2004. Lecture Notes in Computer Science vol.3220* (pp.5-12). Berlin, Heidelberg: Springer-Verlag

Solomon, M. Z., & Morocco, C. (1999). The diagnostic teacher. In Solomon, M. Z. (Ed.), *The diagnostic teacher: Constructing new approaches to professional development* (pp. 231–246). New York: Teachers College Press.

Song, L., Hannafin, M., & Hill, J. (2007). Reconciling Beliefs and Practices in Teaching and Learning. *Educational Technology Research and Development, 55*(1), 27–51. doi:10.1007/s11423-006-9013-6

Sorensen, E., & Takle, E. (2001) Collaborative knowledge building in web-based learning: assessing the quality of dialogue. In *Proceedings of the World Conference on Educational Multimedia, Hypermedia and Telecommunications* (pp.772–1777). Chesapeake, VA Association for the Advancement of Computers in Education (AACE).

Spada, H., Meier, A., Rummel, N., & Hauser, S. (2005). A new method to assess the quality of collaborative process in CSCL. [Taiwan.]. *The CSCL, 2005*, 622–631.

Spadaro, P. F., Sansone, N., & Ligorio, M. B. (2009). Role-taking for Knowledge Building in a Blended Learning course. *Journal of e-Learning and Knowledge Society, 5*(3), 11-21.

Spitzer, D. R. (2002). Don't Forget the High-Touch with the High-Tech in Distance Learning. In Rossett, A. (Ed.), *The ASTD E-Learning Handbook* (pp. 164–174). New York: McGraw-Hill.

Springfield, E. (2005). How to create an online course. *University of Michigan School of Nursing*. Retrieved April 8, 2010, from http://www.nursing.umich.edu/facultyresources/bestPractices/ edTechText.doc

Stacey, E. (2002). Social presence online: Networking learners at a distance. *Education and Information Technologies, 7*(4), 287–294. doi:10.1023/A:1020901202588

Stacey, E. (1999). Collaborative Learning in an Online Environment. *Journal of Distance Education, 14*(2), 14–33.

Stagg, C., Peterson, S., & Slotta, J. (2009). Saying Yes to Online Learning: A First – Time Experience Teaching an Online Graduate Course in Literacy Education. *Literacy Research and Instruction, 48*(2), 120–137. doi:10.1080/19388070802226303

Stahl, G., Koschmann, T., & Suthers, D. (2006). Computer-supported collaborative learning: An historical perspective. In Sawyer, R. K. (Ed.), *Cambridge handbook of the learning sciences* (pp. 409–426). Cambridge, UK: Cambridge University Press.

Stasser, G., & Titus, W. (1985). Pooling of unshared information in group decision making: Biased information sampling during discussion. *Journal of Personality and Social Psychology, 48*(6), 1467–1478. doi:10.1037/0022-3514.48.6.1467

Stasser, G., & Titus, W. (1985). Pooling of unshared information in group decision making: Biased information sampling during discussion. *Journal of Personality and Social Psychology*, *48*(6), 1467–1478. doi:10.1037/0022-3514.48.6.1467

Stegmann, K. (2008). *Argumentative Knowledge Construction. Analysing and Facilitating Discursive Processes, Cognitive Processes, and Knowledge Acquisition During Collaborative Argumentation in Online Discussions*. Dissertation, Ludwig-Maximilians-University.

Stegmann, K., Weinberger, A., Fischer, F., & Mandl, H. (2004). Scripting argumentative knowledge construction in computer-supported learning environments. In *Proceedings of the EARLI SIG 2004*. (pp.320-330). Retrieved April, 13, 2010, from http://www.iwm-kmrc.de/workshops /SIM2004/?go=prog

Sternberg, R. J., & Horvath, J. A. (1995). A prototype view of expert teaching. *Educational Researcher*, *24*(6), 9–17.

Sternberg, R. J. (2003). *Cognitive Psychology* (3rd ed.). Belmont, CA: Thomson Wadsworth.

Stewart, D. (2008). Classroom management in the online environment. *Journal of Online Learning and Teaching*, *4*(3), 371–375.

Stiggins, R. J. (2002). Assessment Crisis: The Absence of Assessment FOR Learning. *Phi Delta Kappan*, *83*(10), 758–765.

Streuber, S., & Chatziastros, A. (2007). Human Interaction in Multi-User Virtual Reality. *Proceedings of the 10th International Conference on Humans and Computers (HC 2007)* (pp.1-6) Aizu, Japan: University of Aizu, TEAL (2009). Technology Enabled Active Learning (TEAL), Visualizing Electricity and Magnetism at MIT. *MIT*. Retrieved September, 20, 2009, from http://web.mit.edu/8.02t/www/802TEAL3D/teal_tour.htm

Strijbos, J., Martens, R. L., Jochems, W. M. G., & Broers, N. J. (2007). The effect of functional roles on perceived group efficiency during computer-supported collaborative learning: A matter of triangulation. *Computers in Human Behavior*, *23*(1), 353–380. doi:10.1016/j.chb.2004.10.016

Stroup, W., Ares, N., & Hurford, A. (2005). A dialectic analysis of generativity: Issues of network supported design in mathematics and science. *Journal of Mathematical Thinking and Learning*, *7*(3), 181–206. doi:10.1207/s15327833mtl0703_1

Sudzina, M. (1999). *Case study applications for teacher education*. Boston, MA: Allyn & Bacon.

Sugrue, B. (1995). A theory-based framework for assessing domain-specific problem solving ability. *Educational Measurement: Issues and Practice*, *14*(3), 29–36. doi:10.1111/j.1745-3992.1995.tb00865.x

Sullivan, N., & Pratt, E. (1996). A comparative study of two ESL writing environments: A computer-assisted classroom and a traditional oral classroom. *System*, *29*(4), 491–501. doi:10.1016/S0346-251X(96)00044-9

Sutherland, L., Marcus, G., & Jessup, A. (2005). From face-to-face to blended learning: issues and challenges in redesigning a professional course. In Brew, A., & Asmar, C. (Eds.), *Higher Education in a changing world, Research and Development in Higher Education* (*Vol. 28*, pp. 551–558). Sydney, Australia: HERDSA.

Suthers, D. (2001). Towards a systematic study of representational guidance for collaborative learning discourse. *Journal of Universal Computer Science*, *7*(3), 254–277.

Suthers, D. D., & Hundhausen, C. D. (2003). An experimental study of the effects of representational guidance on collaborative learning processes. *Journal of the Learning Sciences*, *12*(2), 183–218. doi:10.1207/S15327809JLS1202_2

Suthers, D. D. (2001). Towards a systematic study of representational guidance for collaborative learning discourse. *Journal of Universal Computer Science*, *7*(3), 254–277.

Suthers, D. (2005). Technology affordances for intersubjective learning: A thematic agenda for CSCL.In *Proceedings of the International conference of Computer Support for Collaborative Learning (CSCL 2005). The Next 10 years!* (662 – 671). The International Society of the Learning Sciences (ISLS).

Suthers, D. D., & Hundhausen, C. D. (2001). Learning by constructing collaborative representations: An empirical comparison of three alternatives. In P. Dillenbourg, A. Eurelings & K. Hakkarainen (Eds.), *Proceedings of the First European Conference on Computer-Supported Collaborative Learning (euroCSCL)* (pp. 577-584). Maastricht, The Netherlands: McLuhan Institute.

Swan, K., & Shih, L. F. (2005). On the nature and development of social presence in online course discussions. *Journal of Asynchronous Learning Networks*, *9*(3), 115–136.

Swan, K., Shen, J., & Hiltz, S. R. (2006). Assessment and collaboration in online learning. *Journal of Asynchronous Learning Networks*, *10*(1), 45–62.

Swan, K. (2003). Developing social presence in online course discussions. In Naidu, S. (Ed.), *Learning and teaching with technology: Principles and practices* (pp. 147–164). London, UK: Kogan Page.

Tannenbaum, J. E. (1996). *Practical ideas on alternative assessment for ESL students.* Washington, DC. (ERIC Clearinghouse on Languages and Linguistics, ED395500).

Taylor, V. (2005). Online group projects: Preparing the instructors to prepare the students. InRoberts, T. S. (ed). *Computer-supported collaborative learning in higher education* (19–50). Hershey, PA: Idea Group Publishing.

Tchounikine, P. (2008). Operationalizing macro-scripts in CSCL technological settings. *International Journal of Computer-Supported Collaborative Learning*, *3*(2), 193–233. doi:10.1007/s11412-008-9039-3

TELL. (2005). *Design patterns for teachers and educational (system) designers*. Retrieved 13 April, 2010, from http://cosy.ted.unipi.gr/images/stories/design-patterns/TELL_pattern_book.pdf

Tennyson, R. D., & Schott, F. (1997). Instructional design theory, research, and models. In Tennyson, R. D., Schott, F., Seel, N. M., & Dijkstra, S. (Eds.), *Instructional design: International perspective* (pp. 1–18). Mahwah, NJ: Lawrence Erlbaum Associates.

Thalemann, S., & Strube, G. (2004). Shared knowledge in collaborative problem solving: Acquisition and effects. In K. Forbus, D. Gentner, & T. Regier (Eds.), *Proceedings of the 26th Annual Conference of the Cognitive Science Society* (pp. 1333-1338). Mahwah, NJ: Erlbaum. Retrieved April 6, 2010, from http://www.cogsci.northwestern.edu/cogsci2004/papers/paper317.pdf

Thomas, R. (2000). Evaluating the Effectiveness of the Internet for the Delivery of an MBA programme. *Innovations in Education and Training International*, *37*(2), 97–102.

Thomas, P., King, D., Minocha, S., & Taylor, J. (2008). Wikis supporting authentic, collaborative activities: lessons from distance education. In Whitton, N. & McPherson, M. (Eds.), *Proceedings of the 15th Association for Learning Technology Conference (ALT-C 2008)* (pp.74-83). Leeds, UK: University of Leeds.

Tomasetto, C., Mucchi-Faina, A., Alparone, F. R., & Pagliaro, S. (2009). Differential effects of majority and minority influence on argumentation strategies. *Social Influence*, *4*(1), 33–45. doi:10.1080/15534510802257510

Trekles Milligan, A., & Buckenmeyer, J. A. (2008). Assessing students for online learning. *International Journal on E-Learning*, *7*(3), 449–461.

Truong, T. M., Griswold, W. G., Ratto, M., & Star, L. (2002). *The ActiveClass project: experiments in encouraging classroom participation.* San Diego, CA: University of California.

Turoff, M. (1991). Computer-mediated communication requirements for group support. *Journal of Organizational Computing*, *1*(1), 85–113. doi:10.1080/10919399109540151

Tutty, J. I., & Klein, J. D. (2008). Computer-mediated instruction: A comparison of online and face-to-face instruction. *Educational Technology Research and Development*, *56*(2), 101–124. doi:10.1007/s11423-007-9050-9

Tyack, D., & Cuban, L. (1995). *Tinkering toward utopia: A century of public school reform.* Cambridge, MA: Harvard University Press.

U.S. Department of Education. (2009). *Evaluation of evidence-based practices in online learning: A meta-analysis and review of online learning studies.* Washington, DC: Office of Planning, Evaluation, and Policy Development. Retrieved September 3, 2009, from http://www.ed.gov/about/offices/list/opepd/ppss/reports.html.

University of Florida – Center for Instructional Technology and training (2007). *Role Play*. Retrieved March 20, 2010, from http://www.citt.ufl.edu/toolbox/toolbox_rolePlay.php

Van Boxtel, C., van der Linden, J., Roelofs, E., & Erkens, G. (2002). Collaborative concept mapping: Provoking and supporting meaningful discourse. *Theory into Practice*, *41*(1), 40–46. doi:10.1207/s15430421tip4101_7

Van Eemeren, F. H., Grootendorst, R., & Henkemans, F. S. (1996). *Fundamentals of argumentation theory - A handbook of historical backgrounds and contemporary developments*. Mahawah, NJ: Lawrence Erlbaum.

Van Eijl, P., & Pilot, A. (2003). Using a virtual learning environment in collaborative learning: Criteria for success. *Educational Technology*, *43*(2), 54–56.

Van Horn, R. (2007). Web applications and google. *Phi Delta Kappan*, *88*(10), 727–792.

van Zee, E. H., & Minstrell, J. (1997). Using questioning to guide student thinking. *Journal of the Learning Sciences*, *6*(2), 227–269. doi:10.1207/s15327809jls0602_3

Vanin, L., Castelli, S., Pepe, A., & Addimando, L. (2008). Orienting, preparing and supporting. An academic guidance model to orient distance student. In Cartelli, A., & Palma, M. (Eds.), *Encyclopedia of ICT* (pp. 1–9). Hershey, PA: Idea Group Inc.

Vanin, L., & Castelli, S. (2010). Informarsi, informare, formare. Il caso Nettuno in Bicocca. *Giornale Italiano di Psicologia dell'Orientamento, 11*(1), 48-61.

Vanin, L., Castelli, S., & Brambilla, M. (2007). Il profilo formativo allargato: un ruolo strategico nella formazione a distanza. In P. G. Rossi (Ed.), *Progettare e-Learning: processi, materiali, connettività, interoperabilità e strategie* (pp. 504-515). Macerata: EUM.

Veerman, A., & Veldhuis-Diermanse, E. (2001). Collaborative learning through computer-mediated communication in academic education. In P.Dillenbourg, A. Eurelings, & K. Hakkarainen(Eds.), *Proceedings of the 1st European conference on computer-supported collaborative learning. European perspectives on computer-supported collaborative learning* (pp.625-632). Maastricht, the Netherlands: University of Maastricht Press.

Vega, G., Bote, M. L., Asensio, J. I., Gómez, E., Dimitriadis, Y., & Jorrín, I. M. (2010). Semantic search of tools for collaborative learning with the Ontoolsearch system. *Computers & Education*, *54*(4), 835–848. doi:10.1016/j.compedu.2009.09.012

Villasclaras, E. D., Isotani, S., Hayashi, Y., & Mizoguchi, R. (2009). Collaborative Learning: Design from Macro- and Micro-Script Perspectives. In *Proceedings of AIED 2009 Frontiers in Artificial Intelligence and Applications* 200 (1), (pp.231-238).

Villasclaras-Fernández, E. D., Hernández-Leo, D., Asensio-Pérez, J. I., Dimitriadis, Y., & Martínez-Monés, A. (2009). Towards embedding assessment in CSCL scripts through selection and assembly of learning and assessment patterns. In *Proceedings of the 9th international conference on Computer supported collaborative learning*, vol.1. (pp. 507-511). The International Society of the Learning Sciences (ISLS).

Villasclaras-Fernández, E. D., Hernández-Gonzalo, J. A., Hernández-Leo, D., Asensio-Pérez, J. I., & Dimitriadis, Y. (2009). InstanceCollage: a tool for the particularization of collaborative IMS-LD scripts. *Journal of Educational Technology & Society*, *12*(3), 56–70.

Villasclaras-Fernández, E. D., Hernández-Leo, D., Asensio-Pérez, J. I., & Dimitriadis, Y. (2009). Incorporating assessment in a pattern-based design process for CSCL scripts, *Computers in Human Behavior. Special Issue on Design Patterns for Augmenting E-Learning Experiences*, *25*(5), 1028–1039.

Vogler, K., & Long, E. (2003). Team Teaching Two Sections of the Same Undergraduate Course: a Case Study. *College Teaching*, *51*(4), 122–127. doi:10.1080/87567550309596426

Vonderwell, S., & Zachariah, S. (2005). Factors influencing participation in online learning. *Journal of Research on Technology in Education*, *38*(2), 213–230.

Voyiatzaki, E., Margaritis, M., & Avouris, N. (2006). Collaborative interaction analysis: The teachers' perspective. In Kinshuk et al. (Eds) *The Sixth IEEE International Conference on Advanced Learning Technologies (ICALT '06)*, (345-349). Los Alamitos, CA: IEEE Computer Society

Vye, N., Schwartz, D., Bransford, J., Barron, B. J. S., Zech, L., & Cognition and Technology Group at Vanderbilt (1998). SMART environments that support monitoring, reflection, and revision. In D. Hacker, J. Dunlosky & A. C. Graesser (Eds.), *Metacognition in educational theory and practice*. Mahwah, NJ: Erlbaum.

Waltonen-Moore, S., Stuart, D., Newton, E., Oswald, R., & Varonis, E. (2006). From Virtual Strangers to a Cohesive Online Learning Community: The Evolution of Online Group Development in a Professional Development Course. *Journal of Technology and Teacher Education*, *14*(2), 287–312.

Wan, Z., Wang, Y., & Haggerty, N. (2008). Why people benefit from e-learning differently: The effects of psychological processes on e-learning outcomes. *Information & Management*, *45*(8), 513–521. doi:10.1016/j.im.2008.08.003

Wang, M., Laffey, J., & Poole, M. J. (2001). The construction of shared knowledge in an internet-based shared environment for expeditions (iExpeditions). *International Journal of Educational Technology*, *2*, 1-16. Retrieved April 6, 2010, from http://www.ed.uiuc.edu/ijet/v2n2 / v2n2feature.html

Warschauer, M., Turbee, L., & Roberts, B. (1996). Computer learning networks and student empowerment. *System*, *24*(1), 1–14. doi:10.1016/0346-251X(95)00049-P

Wasserman, S., & Faust, K. (1997). *Social network analysis: Methods and applications*. Cambridge, MA: Cambridge University Press.

Webb, N. (1989). Peer interactions and learning in small groups. *International Journal of Educational Research*, *13*(1), 21–31. doi:10.1016/0883-0355(89)90014-1

Webb, N. (1992). Testing a theoretical model of student interactions and learning in small groups. In Hert-Lazarowitz, R., & Miller, N. (Eds.), *Interaction in co-operative groups: the theoretical anatomy of group learning* (pp. 102–119). London, UK: Cambridge University Press.

WebKF (Web Knowledge Forum). (2000). *Information and demo at the World Wide Web*. Retrieved January 4, 2010, from http://www.knowledgeforum.com

Wegner, D. M., Giuliano, T., & Hertel, P. T. (1985). Cognitive interdependence in close relationships. In Ickes, W. J. (Ed.), *Compatible and incompatible relationships* (pp. 253–276). New York: Springer.

Weinberger, A. (2003). *Scripts for computer-supported collaborative learning*. München, Germany: Unpublished Inaugural-Dissertation, Ludwig-Maximilians-Universität.

Weinberger, A., Ertl, B., Fischer, F., & Mandl, H. (2005). Epistemic and social scripts in computer-supported collaborative learning. *Instructional Science*, *33*(1), 1–30. doi:10.1007/s11251-004-2322-4

Weinberger, A., Stegmann, K., & Fischer, F. (2007). Knowledge convergence in collaborative learning: Concepts and assessment. *Learning and Instruction*, *17*(4), 416–426. doi:10.1016/j.learninstruc.2007.03.007

Weinberger, A., Reiserer, M., Ertl, B., Fischer, F., & Mandl, H. (2003). Facilitating collaborative knowledge construction in computer-mediated learning with structuring tools. In Bromme, R., Hesse, F., & Spada, H. (Eds.), *Barriers and biases in net based communication. Norwell: Kluwer.*

Weinberger, A., Stegmann, K., Fischer, F., & Mandl, H. (2007). Scripting argumentative knowledge construction in computer-supported learning environments. In Fischer, F., Kollar, I., Mandl, H., & Haake, J. M. (Eds.), *Scripting Computer-Supported Collaborative Learning* (pp. 191–211). New York: Springer. doi:10.1007/978-0-387-36949-5_12

Weinberger, A. (2003). *Scripts for computer-supported collaborative learning.* Dissertation, Ludwig-Maximilians-University Munich, Germany. Retrieved April, 13, 2010 from http://hal.archives-ouvertes.fr/docs/00/19/01/71/PDF/Weinberger_2003.pdf

Weinberger, A., Collar, I., Dimitriadis, Y., Mäkitalo-Siegl, K., & Fischer, F. (2009). Computer-supported collaboration scripts: Theory and practice of scripting CSCL. Perspectives of educational psychology and computer science. In S. Ludvigsen et al. (Eds), *Technology-Enhanced Learning. Principles and Products* (155-174). New York, NY: Springer Verlag.

Weinberger, A., Reiserer, M., Ertl, B., Fischer, F., & Mandl, H. (2003). *Faciliating collaborative knowledge construction in computer-mediated learning with structuring tools.* Retrieved 08.09.2009, from http://epub.ub.uni-muenchen.de /archive/00000266/

Weisband, S. (2002). Maintaining awareness in distributed team collaboration: Implications for leadership and performance. In Hinds, P., & Kiesler, S. (Eds.), *Distributed work* (pp. 311–333). Cambridge, MA: MIT Press.

Wells, G. (1993). Reevaluating the IRF sequence: A proposal for the articulation of theories of activity and discourse for the analysis of teaching and learning in the classroom. *Linguistics and Education, 5*(1), 1–37. doi:10.1016/S0898-5898(05)80001-4

Wenger, E. (1998). *Communities of Practice. Learning, Meaning and Identity.* Cambridge, UK: Cambridge University Press.

Wenger, E. (1998). *Communities of practice. Learning, meaning, and identity.* Cambridge, MA: Cambridge University Press.

Wenger, E. (2006). *Communities of practice: A brief introduction.* Retrieved August 15, 2009, from http://www.ewenger.com/theory/

Wheeler, S., Kelly, P., & Gale, K. (2005). The influence of online problem-based learning on teachers' professional practice and identity. *ALT-J Research In Learning Technology, 13*(2), 125–137.

Wigfield, A., Eccles, J. S., & Rodriguez, D. (1998). The development of children's motivation in school contexts. *Review of Research in Education, 23*(1), 73–118. doi:10.3102/0091732X023001073

Wiggins, G. (1990). The case for authentic assessment. *Practical Assessment, Research & Evaluation, 2*(2). Retrieved January 2, 2010, from http://PAREonline.net/getvn.asp?v=2&n=2

Wilensky, U., & Stroup, W. M. (2000, June). *Networked gridlock: Students enacting complex dynamic phenomena with the HubNet architecture.* Paper presented at the The Fourth Annual International Conference of the Learning Sciences, Ann Arbor, MI.

Williams, A., Tanner, D., & Jessop, T. (2007). The creation of virtual communities in a primary initial teacher training programme. *Journal of Education for Teaching, 33*(1), 71–82. doi:10.1080/02607470601098336

Williams, J., & Chinn, S. (2009). Using Web 2.0 to support the active learning experience. *Journal of Information Systems Education, 20*(2), 165–174.

Williams, J., & Jacobs, J. (2004). Exploring the use of blogs as learning spaces in the higher education sector. *Australasian Journal of Educational Technology, 20*(2), 232–237.

Winter, E., & McGhie-Richmond, D. (2005). Using computer conferencing and case studies to enable collaboration between experienced and novice teachers. *Journal of Computer Assisted Learning, 21*, 118–129. doi:10.1111/j.1365-2729.2005.00119.x

Wittenbaum, G. M., Hubbell, A. P., & Zuckerman, C. (1999). Mutual enhancement: Toward an understanding of the collective preference for shared information. *Journal of Personality and Social Psychology*, *77*(5), 967–978. doi:10.1037/0022-3514.77.5.967

Wittenbaum, G. M., & Stasser, G. (1996). Management of information in small groups. In Nye, J. L., & Brower, A. M. (Eds.), *What's social about social cognition? Research on socially shared cognition in small groups* (pp. 3–28). Thousand Oaks, CA: Sage Publications.

Wofle, J. (2008). Annotations and the collaborative digital library: Effects of an aligned annotation interface on student argumentation and reading strategies. *International Journal of Computer-Supported Collaborative Learning*, *3*(2), 141–164. doi:10.1007/s11412-008-9040-x

Wu, D., & Hiltz, S. (2003). *Online Discussions and Perceived Learning.* Paper presented at the Ninth Americas Conference on Information Systems. Retrieved March 20, 2010, from http://citeseerx.ist.psu.edu/viewdoc/download?doi=10.1.1.98.8584&rep=rep1&type=pdf

Xin, M. C. & Feenberg, A. (2007). Pedagogy in cyberspace: The dynamics of online discourse. *E-Learning*, 4(4), 415-423. Also published in *Journal of Distance Education, 21(2),* 1-25.

Xin, M. C., & Feenberg, A. (2002). Designing for Pedagogical Effectiveness: TextWeaver. In *Proceedings of the 35th Annual Hawaii International Conference on System Sciences*. Los Alamitos, CA: IEEE Computer Society Press.

Xin, M. C., & Glass, G. (2005). Enhancing Online Discussion through Web Annotation. In G. Richards (Ed.), *Proceedings of the World Conference on E-Learning in Corporate, Government, Healthcare, and Higher Education* (pp.3212-3217). Chesapeake, VA: AACE.

Yang, Y., Ting, C., Newby, T., & Bill, R. (2005). Using Socratic Questioning to Promote Critical Thinking Skills Through Asynchronous Discussion Forums in Distance Learning Environments. *American Journal of Distance Education*, *19*(3), 163–181. doi:10.1207/s15389286ajde1903_4

Yates, S. J. (1997). Gender, identity and CMC. *Journal of Computer Assisted Learning*, *13*(4), 281–290. doi:10.1046/j.1365-2729.1997.00031.x

Yip, W. (2002). Student's perceptions of the technological supports for problem-based learning. *Education and Information Technologies*, *7*(4), 303–312. doi:10.1023/A:1020957320335

Yli-Luoma, P. V. J., & Naeve, A. (2006). Towards a semantic e-learning theory by using a modelling approach. *British Journal of Educational Technology*, *37*(3), 445–459. doi:10.1111/j.1467-8535.2006.00615.x

Zhang, J., & Norman, D. A. (1994). Representations in distributed cognitive tasks. *Cognitive Science*, *18*(1), 87–122. doi:10.1207/s15516709cog1801_3

Zhang, J. (1997). The nature of external representations in problem solving. *Cognitive Science*, *21*(2), 179–217. doi:10.1207/s15516709cog2102_3

Zhang, J., & Norman, D. A. (1994). Representations in distributed cognitive tasks. *Cognitive Science*, *18*(1), 87–122. doi:10.1207/s15516709cog1801_3

Zinn, C., & Scheuer, O. (2006). Getting to know your learner in distance learning contexts. Innovative Approaches Innovative Approaches for Learning an d Knowledge Sharing, *1st European Conference on Technology Enhanced Learning (EC-TEL 2006), Lecture Notes in Computer Science vol.4227* (437-451). Berlin, Heidelberg: Springer-Verlag.

Zumbach, J., Muhlenbrock, M., Jansen, M., Reimann, P., & Hoppe, U. H. (2002). Multi-dimensional tracking in virtual learning teams: An exploratory study. In Stahl, G. (Ed.), *Computer support for collaborative learning: Foundations for a CSCL community* (pp. 650–651). Mahwah, NJ: Erlbaum.

About the Contributors

Francesca Pozzi is researcher at the Institute for Educational Technology of the Italian National Research Council (CNR). She holds a PhD in Languages, Cultures and ICT from the University of Genoa. Her major research interests include the design and implementation of online courses in CSCL contexts, the design of strategies and techniques for fostering online collaboration, and issues in monitoring and evaluating the learning process in CSCL.

Donatella Persico is senior researcher at the Institute for Educational Technology of the Italian National Research Council (CNR). She has been active in the field of educational technology, theory and applications, since 1981. Her major interests include instructional design, e-learning, self-regulated learning and teacher training. She is author of educational material and scientific publications of various kinds, including books, educational software, multimedia material and research papers concerning various aspects of educational technology. She is co-editor of the Italian Journal Tecnologie Didattiche and has been in charge of several national and international projects.

* * *

Philip C. Abrami is Professor, Research Chair, and Director of the Centre for the Study of Learning and Performance (CSLP), Concordia University. His research interests include educational technology, social psychology of education and research synthesis.

Juan Ignacio Asensio Pérez received the MS and the PhD degrees in telecommunications engineering from University of Valladolid, in 1995 and 2000, respectively. He is currently an Associate Professor at the Department of Signal Theory, Communications and Telematics Engineering, University of Valladolid. His research interests include distributed systems and, particularly, distributed CSCL applications and integrated systems and network management.

Barbara Biglan is an Associate Professor of Education for Chatham University and teaches at both the graduate and undergraduate levels. She has both teaching and administrative experience in grades k -12 and has been involved in implementation of technology in the classroom environment for a number of years. During her tenure at Chatham has been involved in the development of online courses for the Education Department. She has presented research related to technology and education at numerous national and international conferences.

Eva Bures has been an assistant professor at Bishop's University's School of Education since 2004. She is also a faculty member of the Centre for the Study of Learning and Performance. She earned a BA in French Literature at Reed College, and her PhD in educational technology at Concordia University. Her main interest is how to support innovative learning and assessment processes through computer-mediated communication ('talking via computers'), especially in small groups. She focuses on how to improve the quality of online dialogue. She is also interested in how feedback from teachers and peers on e-portfolios can support learning processes.

Gráinne Conole is Professor of E-Learning in the Institute of Educational Technology at the Open University in the UK. Her research interests include the use, integration and evaluation of Information and Communication Technologies and e-learning and the impact of technologies on organisational change. She heads up a new research strand of activity within IET, 'Learning in an Open World". Two of her current areas of interest are how learning design can help in creating more engaging learning activities and on Open Educational Resources research. Updates on current research and reflections on e-learning research generally can be found on her blog www.e4innovation.com. She has extensive research, development and project management experience across the educational and technical domains; funding sources have included the EU, HEFCE, ESRC, JISC and commercial sponsors. She serves on and chairs a number of national and international advisory boards, steering groups, committees and international conference programmes. She has published and presented over 300 conference proceedings, workshops and articles, including over 100 publications on a range of topics, including the use and evaluation of learning technologies. She is co-editor of the RoutledgeFalmer book 'Contemporary perspectives on e-learning research'.

Ulrike Cress is head of the Knowledge Construction Lab at the Knowledge Media Research Center in Tuebingen, Germany. She is doing research on learning with new media in formal settings as well as in informal and web-settings. She is interested in computer-supported learning, in knowledge management, and the development and implementation of media-based learning scenarios. In particular she works on the social and cognitive processes of people constructing new knowledge.

Thanasis Daradoumis holds a PhD in Computer Science (Polytechnic University of Catalonia-Spain), a Masters in Computer Science (University of Illinois), and a Bachelors in Mathematics (University of Thessaloniki-Greece). Currently he is assistant professor at the Department of Cultural Informatics, University of the Aegean, Greece and collaborating professor at the department of Computer Sciences, Multimedia and Telecommunications, Open University of Catalonia, Spain. His research focuses on e-learning, Web-based instruction and evaluation, distributed and adaptive learning, CSCL, CSCW, interaction analysis, and grid technologies. He is co-director of the DPCS (Distributed Parallel and Collaborative Systems) Research Laboratory [http://dpcs.uoc.es/]. He has written over 100 papers.

Luis de la Fuente Valentín received the Telecommunication Engineer degree from University of Valladolid, in 2005, and the MS from the Carlos III University, Madrid, Spain, in 2007. He is currently studying towards a PhD degree in telecommunications engineering at the Carlos III University, where he is a teaching assistant. His research interests include computer supported learning, especially the work on technical educative specifications such as IMS Learning Design.

Yannis A. Dimitriadis received the engineering degree from the National Technical University of Athens, Greece (1981), the M.S. from the University of Virginia (1983) and two PhD degrees from the University of Valladolid (1992 and 1995), both in telecommunications engineering. He is Professor of Telematics Engineering and director of GSIC/EMIC, a multidisciplinary research group focusing on Computer Supported Collaborative Learning since 1997. His general research interests include Computer Supported Collaborative Learning and distributed systems, while he currently works on an effective telematic support to educational practitioners, so that they may flexibly design and deploy learning designs, through the use of good educational practices and the integration of existing third-party services.

Bernhard Ertl is senior researcher at the Universität der Bundeswehr München. He has realized several research projects in the context of gender in computer and science teaching including projects with national and EU funding, e.g. SESTEM (Supporting Equality in Science Technology and Mathematics related choices of careers), PREDIL (Promoting Equality in Digital Literacy) and "Comparative study on gender differences in technology enhanced and computer science learning: Promoting equity". A further focus of research is on issues like video-mediated learning, Internet collaboration and online-courses with a particular focus on the support of collaborative knowledge construction by the methods of scripts and structured communication interfaces. Bernhard Ertl earned his Diploma in computer science from the Ludwig Maximilian University Munich in 1998 and his Doctorate in education 2003. From 1999 to 2006, he was researcher at the Department Psychology of Ludwig Maximilian University of Munich and worked with Professor Heinz Mandl in DFG-funded research projects focusing on collaborative learning, e.g. "Collaborative Learning in Graphics-enhanced Tele-learning Environments" and "Collaborative Knowledge Construction in Desktop Videoconferencing".

Andrew Feenberg is Canada Research Chair in Philosophy of Technology in the School of Communication of Simon Fraser University. He is the author of Transforming Technology, Questioning Technology, Alternative Modernity, Heidegger and Marcuse, and Reason and Experience, co-author of When Poetry Ruled the Streets, and co-editor of Technology and the Politics of Knowledge, Modernity and Technology, and The Essential Marcuse. He has taught at Duke University, San Diego State University, the University of Paris, and the University of Tokyo.

Geoffrey Glass is a PhD student studying communication at Simon Fraser University, where he is investigating the online commons. He designed and implemented Marginalia.

Katia Gonzalez-Acquaro EdD received her Doctorate in Education from Teachers College, Columbia University. She is an Assistant Professor of Education at Wagner College in New York. Her research interests are related to curriculum design and implementation, inclusive practices and discourse, online learning, and the use of collaborative groupings and Web 2.0 tools in teaching and learning.

Christian Guetl is Assistant Professor and Key Researcher at the IICM at Graz University of Technology, Austria, and Adjunct Research Professor at the School of Information Systems, Curtin University of Technology, Perth, Western Australia. He holds a doctoral degree in computer science. His active research is in Information Retrieval and Visualization, Adaptive Systems, Virtual Worlds for educational purpose, and Kowledge & Skill Assessment and Feedback and he is involved in national and international research projects on these topics. He is also involved in the organization of conferences and workshops, such as the IEEE EDUCON, IEEE DEST, ViWo and CAF.

Christopher Harris is a researcher in science education at the Center for Technology in Learning at SRI International. His research interests include the design and study of science learning environments that capitalize on innovative technologies and make learning accessible for students of diverse backgrounds and abilities. At SRI, his research often involves practical work in K-12 classrooms and informal science contexts for the purpose of informing both research and practice. His recent publications have addressed science education policy, science assessment, design-based research of learning environments, inquiry-based teaching, and authenticity in science education.

Angela Haydel DeBarger is a senior research scientist at the Center for Technology in Learning at SRI International. Her research interests include the design and analysis of technology-supported assessments for formative purposes, the application of principles of Evidence-Centered Design (ECD) and Universal Design for Learning (UDL) to classroom and state assessments, and the investigation of how formative assessments can support students' cognitive and motivational engagement. Her recent publications have addressed teachers' data-informed decision making practices, formative assessment approaches in chemistry teaching and learning, and the use of ECD and UDL principles in assessment design.

Kathrin Helling MA is research associate at the Universität der Bundeswehr München and University of Innsbruck, Department of Education. She has experience as researcher and project manager in several national projects and European projects in the frame of the Lifelong Learning Programme. A focus of her research is on gender aspects in the context of computer-supported mathematics, science and informatics teaching and related career choices of women. At the Institute for Future Studies in Innsbruck she worked on the development of computer-based learning scenarios and curricula for specific target groups (e.g. people of the age group 50+, learners with low educational achievement). She also trained trainers in using learning management systems and educational technologies. Kathrin Helling has worked in a DFG-funded research project at the Ludwig Maximilian University of Munich. The focus of this research was on supporting collaborative learning processes in video conferencing by the methods of scripts and structuring the communication of learners. She has gained her magister diploma in education science in 2006 at the Ludwig Maximilian University Munich.

Davinia Hernández Leo received the MS (2003) and the PhD degrees in telecommunications engineering (2007) from University of Valladolid. She is currently a lecturer at the Department of Information and Communications Technologies of Pompeu Fabra University and member of the GTI research group. Her main research interests are Educational Telematics, Computer Supported Collaborative Learning, techniques for the design of educational situations, and learning technology standards and specifications.

Aemilian Hron is a senior researcher at the Knowledge Media Research Center in Tübingen, Germany. He is doing research on cooperative knowledge acquisition and knowledge exchange with new media. Moreover, he is working on issues of using digital media in school education.

Dan Kohen is a faculty member of the Instructional Systems Technologies Department, HIT, the coordinator of department's technological activities, and the development manager of the CeLS project. He got his MSc in Professional Communications form Clark University, US. His PhD thesis (in progress) at the Technion focuses on the architecture and representation of web-based collaboration scripts.

Birgitta Kopp Dr. phil, is member of the Institute of Empirical Pedagogic and Pedagogical Psychology at the Ludwig-Maximilians-University of Munich since 2001. She did her PhD in 2005 on "Effects of schema-based support on argumentation and performance in collaborative learning in videoconferencing". She worked in several projects which were funded by the German Research Foundation, the Federal Ministry of Education and Research and the European Commission. Furthermore, research in companies is also part of her work. In all these projects, her research focus includes collaborative learning, learning with new media, blended learning, support methods, design of virtual learning environments, evaluations.

Maria Kordaki holds a PhD in Educational Technology, a Masters in Education, a diploma in civil engineering and a Bachelor in Mathematics, University of Patras, Greece. Currently she is assistant professor at the Department of Cultural Informatics, University of the Aegean, Greece. She also served as collaborative professor in the Hellenic Open University, the Dept of Computer Engineering and Informatics and the department of Mathematics, University of Patras, Greece. Her research focuses on social and constructivist learning theories in the design and evaluation of educational software and technology supported learning. She has published over 120 scientific papers and 9 books.

Georgia Lazakidou completed her PhD research on September 2008 in E-learning from the University of Piraeus. She is a research assistant at the University of Piraeus, Greece and member of the CosyLab research group participating in various European funded research and development projects. Her publication list contains more than 30 items and her research interests concern the instructional design, computer supported collaborative learning in primary education, and elearning design patterns.

M. Beatrice Ligorio is Associated Professor at the University of Bari (IT). She graduated in Psychology at the University of Rome and, in 1999, she received her PhD in Psychology of Communication at the University of Bari. She has been a NATO fellow to collaborate at the Community of Learners model (A. Brown, University of Berkeley, CA). She collaborated to many European, international, and national projects. She published many articles on international journals and recently she edited two books in Italian about educational technology. She is the president of the Collaborative Knolwedge Building Group (www.ckbg.org) and the editor of the journal Qwerty. Her main research interests are on educational technology, models of community, cultural psychology, socio-constructivism, dialogical approach, digital identity, blended learning, m-learning.

Lisa Lobry de Bruyn holds a Bachelor of Science (1st Class Honours) and a PhD from the University of Western Australia, and more recently a Certificate in Higher Education from University of New England, both located in Australia. She is a senior lecturer, and has been involved in teaching many areas of natural resources at tertiary level in University of New England, Australia since 1993. Her innovative teaching methods have been recognised and showcased in four Australian University Teaching Committee grants. She is the author or co-author of over 75 refereed journal, book chapters and conference papers encompassing a wide range of interests including soil agroecology, soil condition monitoring, ethnopedology, natural resource management and scholarship in teaching and learning, with an emphasis on problem-based learning and active learning strategies that are student centred. Lisa is committed to engaging with students in the process of learning and for them to realise their full potential and to approach life's challenges with confidence and inquisitiveness.

Ron Lombard has been an Assistant Professor of Education for Chatham College since 2000, after 30 years as both a classroom teacher and administrator. He serves as an instructor and advisor at both graduate and undergraduate levels and during his tenure at Chatham has been involved in the development of online courses for the Education Department. He has presented research related to technology and education at numerous conferences and published chapters on the same topic for numerous texts.

F. Feldia Loperfido is a PhD student in Educational Psychology at the University of Bari. In 2008 she graduated in Psychology at University of Bari. Her main research interests are about communicational processes in blended contexts. She studies the relevance of Bakhtin for the educational approach, to find the dialogic and polyphonic dynamics in learning processes.

Stefania Manca is a researcher at the Institute for Educational Technology of the Italian National Research Council (CNR). Her main interests are the analysis of social and cognitive processes in Computer Supported Collaborative Learning environments and the analysis of specific linguistic features used to express and construct the social dimension in asynchronous-based learning environments.

Heinz Mandl Dr. phil., Dipl.-Psych., Professor of Education and Educational Psychology at the Ludwig-Maximilians-University of Munich, Dean of the Faculty of Psychology and Education (1995-2000). President of the European Association for Research on Learning and Instruction (1989 –1991). Oevre Award for Outstanding Contributions to the Science of Learning & Instruction (EARLI, 2003). Main research areas are knowledge management, acquisition and use of knowledge, learning with new media, net-based knowledge communication, design of virtual learning environments. Co-Editor of several journals and book series. Co-Initiator of several research programmes of Deutsche Forschungsgemeinschaft (DFG). Applied research and development projects in knowledge management and e-learning.

Alejandra Martínez Monés received the MS and PhD degrees in computer science from the University of Valladolid, in 1997 and 2003, respectively. She is currently an Associate Professor at the University of Valladolid. Her research activity focuses on the technological support to the evaluation of Computer Supported Collaborative Learning settings.

Patrick McAndrew is director of the Open Learning network (OLnet) and of Research and Evaluation for OpenLearn, open content initiative, for a two year period 2006-2008 and Senior Lecturer in the Institute of Educational Technology (IET). As Associate Director (Learning & Teaching) he is a member of the executive team for IET. From 2002 to 2005 he was Head of the Centre for Information Technology in Education. Active areas include: researching and evaluating learner and provider issues in the use of open content and free educational resources, projects based in the IET UserLab addressing issues in the development of learning models around learning objects and learning design, evaluation focused on the gathering of formative data from students and the evolution of course materials, the use of knowledge management as a way to support the sharing of information and development of a Knowledge Network, the reuse of materials and software for learning and the design of web-based courses.

Donna McGhie-Richmond is an Assistant Professor in Educational Psychology and Leadership Studies at the University of Victoria. An experienced teacher educator, she holds a Ph.D. in Special Education from the Ontario Institute for Studies in Education / University of Toronto (OISE/UT). Dr. McGhie-Richmond's research examines the relationship among teacher knowledge, beliefs, and practices and student learning outcomes in inclusive classrooms. She has expertise in assistive and computer technologies. As an early adopter of online learning technologies Dr. McGhie-Richmond is particularly interested in the transformative role of technology on instruction and learning.

Sieglinde Neudert is a research assistant at the Knowledge Media Research Center in Tübingen, Germany. She is doing research on the evaluation of e-learning platforms and online-tutorials, and she is engaged in instructional design of new media. Moreover, she develops and manages online-surveys, and carries out statistical data analysis in research projects.

William Penuel is Director of Evaluation Research for the Center for Technology at SRI International. His expertise is in the areas of technology-supported classroom-based assessment, program evaluation, and science and technology education policy. His research projects examine the effects of networked handheld computers on science and mathematics learning, the relationship between professional development activities and curriculum implementation in science, and the effects of intra-organizational dynamics on reform implementation. His recent publications have addressed preparing teachers to design instruction for deep understanding and investigating the effects of state policies and professional development on science curriculum implementation.

Ourania Petropoulou is a PhD candidate in the University of Piraeus. Her research interests concern the interaction analysis in computer supported collaborative learning environments, and instructional design. She is member of the CoSyLab research group at the University of Piraeus, Greece and works as a public servant in the Biomedical Engineering Laboratory, School of Electrical and Computer Engineering, National Technical University of Athens (NTUA) from September 1998 until now.

Stephen Preskill is currently Professor and Chair of the Education Department at Wagner College in Staten Island, New York. He has over 30 years of experience at all levels of education and is the co-author of three books. His latest volume, Learning as a way of leading: Lessons from the struggle for social justice, was published in 2009. In 1984, he earned his PhD from the University of Illinois at Urbana-Champagne in Educational Policy Studies. His teaching and research interests center on leadership and teaching narratives, dialogue in education, school renewal through democratic practice, and education as the practice of nonviolence.

Symeon Retalis is an Associate professor at the Department of Digital Systems, University of Piraeus. Also, he is the director of the Cosy Learning Lab which performs research and development in the fields of elearning material and systems development, and usability engineering. He has participated in various European R&D projects and serves in the editorial boards of international journals. His publication list contains more than 80 items.

Miky Ronen is the chair of the Instructional Systems Technologies Department at the Holon Institute of Technology (HIT). Graduated from the Tel-Aviv University (Physics) in 1979 and got her PhD (Science Education) from the Weizmann Institute of Science in 1986. Her research focuses on the instructional design of interactive learning environments, the incorporation of technology in the teaching and learning process and the professional development of teachers with respect to the use of technology enhanced methods.

Nadia Sansone is a junior research assistant in Psychology at the University of Bari, Italy. Her research work is focused on blended university courses, with a main interest on virtual role-play. Her expertise is about tutoring online. She has been acting as e-tutor for several blended university courses. She participated to a few Italian projects about dialogical approach and educational technology. She also published a few articles about Computer Supported Collaborative Learning and online tutorship on national journals. Her main research interests are virtual environments and digital identity, blended learning, and socio-constructivism.

Patricia Schank is a cognitive and computer scientist at SRI's Center for Technology in Learning, where she works with multidisciplinary teams to design, develop, and test innovative learning technology. At SRI, she has led the development of technology to support collaborative learning and online communities, software and curriculum to help students and teachers visualize nanoscale phenomena, and simulation-based assessments to measure science learning. Her recent publications have addressed participatory design, Computer-Supported Collaborative Learning, and analysis of online educator networks.

Paola Francesca Spadaro is research assistant at University of Bari, Italy. In 2003 she graduated in Psychology at Sapienza University (Rome) and in 2007 she obtained a PhD in Educational Psychology at University of Bari. She obtained regional and international research fellowships to study in depth research methodologies, teaching methods, and theoretical advance in the field of the psychological processes involved in using educational technologies. She collaborated to local and national research projects regarding the study of psychological processes involved in technological innovation in various contexts: SME, professional and university learning. Her research interests are the building of identity and intersubjectivity in digital contexts.

Luca Vanin works for the Department of Psychology, at the University of Milan Bicocca (Milan, Italy). His research fields are online guidance system to prepare students, e-learning, online interaction analysis, community design and management, and web communication. He is a member of CKBG (Collaborative Knowledge Building Group).

Eloy David Villasclaras Fernández received the MS degree in telecommunication engineering from the University of Valladolid, Spain, in 2005. He is currently studying towards a PhD degree in telecommunications engineering at the University of Valladolid, where he is a teaching assistant. His research interests include Computer Supported Collaborative Learning and, particularly, the work on the life-cycle of CSCL scripts with embedded assessment.

Eileen C. Winter is the Director of Academic Programmes and Research Director at the Institute of Child Education and Psychology in Ireland. A chartered psychologist and teacher, she holds a PhD from Queen's University, Belfast. Dr. Winter is a longstanding and experienced teacher educator having taught psychology and special needs in Canada and Ireland. Her research interests cover a number of key special needs areas particularly policy and practice, ethics, the role of children in special needs research, special needs in pre-service teacher education and in continuing professional development for teachers and associated professionals.

Cindy Xin is a Program Director at the Learning and Instructional Development Centre of Simon Fraser University. She is currently a member of a team that develops open source technologies for improving online discussion forums. Her research interests include CSCL, educational technology, and discourse analysis.

Index

D

E

F

G

H

I

J

K

CPSIA information can be obtained at www.ICGtesting.com
263785BV00008B/147-174/P

9 781616 928988